A HISTORY
of ROME

A HISTORY *of* ROME

Second Edition

MARCEL LE GLAY
Late Emeritus Professor at the Sorbonne, Paris IV

JEAN-LOUIS VOISIN
Senior Lecturer at the University of Bourgogne

YANN LE BOHEC
Professor at the University of Lyon III

With new material by
DAVID CHERRY
Associate Professor of History at Montana State University

Translated by
ANTONIA NEVILL

Copyright © Presses Universitaires de France 1991, 1994
English translations copyright © Blackwell Publishers Ltd 1996, 2001
Additional material for the second edition copyright © David Cherry 2001

First edition published as *Histoire Romaine* by Presses Universitaires de France 1991
Second edition 1994

First published in English by Blackwell Publishers Ltd 1996
Reprinted 1997 (three times)
Second edition published by Blackwell Publishers Ltd 2001

10 9 8 7 6 5 4 3 2 1

Blackwell Publishers Inc.
350 Main Street
Malden, Massachusetts 02148
USA

Blackwell Publishers Ltd
108 Cowley Road
Oxford OX4 1JF
UK

Library of Congress Cataloging-in-Publication Data is available for this book.

ISBN   0 631 21858 0
        0 631 21859 9 (pbk)

British Library Cataloguing in Publication Data

A CIP catalogue record for this book is available from the British Library.

Typeset in 10 on 13 pt Galliard
by Best-set Typesetter Ltd., Hong Kong

Printed and bound in Great Britain by Biddles Ltd, Guildford and King's Lynn

This book is printed on acid-free paper

CONTENTS

PLATES

FIGURES

GENEALOGICAL TABLES

PREFACE TO THE
SECOND EDITION

The enthusiastic response that greeted this book's publication (in English) in 1996 has made it both possible and desirable to expand and to update it. This second edition incorporates a number of improvements, many of them suggested by readers, including a more extensive treatment of the causes of the First Carthaginian War, and of Hannibal's purposes on the eve of the Second. Coverage of the period of the late Republic has been expanded to include Pompey's arrangements in Syria and Palestine 64–63 BC, the story of Caesar's conquest of Gaul, and a more detailed examination of the political developments of 63–44 BC that forever changed the shape of the Roman world – the so-called conspiracy of Catiline, the purposes and behavior of the First Triumvirate, the causes and course of the civil war between Caesar and Pompey.

To remedy what was probably the most obvious inadequacy of the first edition, a new section entitled "Private Life: Women and Family" has been added to chapter 6. It examines, among other things, the structure and demography of the Roman family, and the so-called "emancipation" of women in the late Republic, including changes in the rules that governed marriage and divorce.

New, also, is the "Guide to Greek and Roman Writers," which is intended to provide readers with both a broad overview of the nature of the surviving literature and an introduction to the characteristics of individual authors and their works. The "Guide to Further Reading" has been brought up to date. And two maps have been added, one of the city of Rome in the early third century BC (chapter 4), the other showing Roman conquests in the period 148–30 BC (chapter 5).

David Cherry, 2000

PREFACE TO THE
FIRST EDITION

No work of this kind, intended for students, has existed until now. There has been a growing need for a book that will clearly and effortlessly give them the basic knowledge they need in order to flesh out the analytical criticisms of texts and documents they have to produce, and to derive the maximum benefit from the specialized courses available to them.

In order to meet this double target in a volume of reasonable size and handy format, we have emphasized events, but without neglecting ideas. We have chosen to present a chronological and factual narrative, but not at the expense of civilization, institutions, and economic and social problems, which all have their place.

We have not pursued originality at all costs. We sometimes give our personal points of view, but we avoid argument. Nor have we set out to write a textbook as the term is usually understood. We were thinking rather of a volume of *initiation* into the history of Rome. Hence our use of sources to persuade readers that nothing can compare with reading the documents. Here too, of course, as in the exposition of events, choices have constantly been made – often quite drastically. A glossary supplies definitions of words not explained in the text, and of some Latin terms that can be translated only approximately.

We have added an extensive guide to further reading, and the text contains a large number of maps (which does not mean that there is no need to refer to good atlases). The history of mankind cannot be understood without constant reference to the realities of geography.

Rome cannot be isolated from Greece. Their contacts were numerous well before the Roman political grip on the Greek-speaking world and the Hellenistic cultural grip on Rome. The Empire was a Roman universe (*imperium Romanum*), but it was composed of two civilizations, the Latin West and the Graeco-Latin East, which separated in late antiquity to center around Rome and Constantinople.

We are jointly responsible for the book as a whole, with part I edited by M. Le Glay, part II by J.-L. Voisin, and part III by Y. Le Bohec.

It will be good if students become familiar with this enthralling history of a small town which became the capital of the greatest and most enduring empire history has known. If they find in it matter for reflection, that will be even better.

The authors

ABBREVIATIONS

Most Romans had two or more names – the first name or *praenomen* and the name of the *gens* (clan), the *nomen*. There could also be a third name or *cognomen*. The commonest *praenomina* are generally abbreviated: A. = Aulus; C. = Gaius; Cn. = Gnaeus; D. = Decimus; L. = Lucius; M. = Marcus; M' = Manius; P. = Publius; Q. = Quintus; Ser. = Servius; Sex. = Sextus; Sp. = Spurius; T. = Titus; Ti. = Tiberius.

INTRODUCTION
Rome and the Mediterranean

The site, development, and entire history of Rome were to a large extent influenced by geography. Of the three great Mediterranean peninsulas, the Italian was the most favored: its central position between the Greek and Iberian peninsulas, together with the fact that, while it has the smaller land mass, and extends farther into the sea, it is solidly attached to the European continent by the rich Po valley, made it the fruitful meeting-ground for trading and cultural movements between the eastern and western Mediterranean, and similarly between peoples from the north and those living around the sea.

The eastern half of the Mediterranean was for thousands of years at the heart of brilliant civilizations, and sometimes great empires, contending for mastery of the seas and trade routes: in the south, the Egyptian Empire of the Pharaohs; in the east, the Phoenician cities dominating the coastal areas; in the north, the Mycenaeans, who inherited the civilization of Crete. Between 1500 and 1000 BC, the Mycenaeans reached the coasts of Sicily, southern Italy, Etruria, and the Adriatic (hence in Homer's *Odyssey* the sometimes very precise descriptions of Italian shores). And as early as the eleventh century BC, those able traders, the Phoenicians, must in their turn have penetrated the western Mediterranean. At all events, in the eighth century they established trading settlements in Sicily, Sardinia, and North Africa (Utica, Carthage), and on the Iberian peninsula (Cadiz). On the site of Rome itself a colony of people from Tyre managed to install itself as early as the eighth or seventh century in the area that became the Forum Boarium (livestock market). The Greeks followed and rivaled the Phoenicians, and not only in Sicily and southern Italy; their colonizing movements also reached southern Gaul (Marseille was founded around 600 BC by Phocaeans from Asia Minor), and then the Iberian peninsula.

The western half of the Mediterranean was fringed by peoples of great diversity, generally living in tribes or racial groups, with a mainly agricultural economy, and a culture and religion reflecting their daily preoccupations and their activities as warriors.

In the coastal regions of the Maghreb (present-day Algeria, Morocco, and Tunisia), the settled, wheat-eating Berber peoples (Libyans, Numidians, Moors) did not live as completely on the "fringes of history" as has been thought; they could have had contact with Sicily to the east and the Iberian peninsula to the west, and in any case certainly had contact with the Phoenicians: Punic civilization (or that of the Phoenicians of the west) was imposed in eastern Tunisia by wealthy Carthage, and elsewhere in the form of trading settlements scattered along the coastline, as far as the borders of Cyrenaica to the east, and to the west at least as far as the south of present-day Morocco.

The Iberian peninsula, where the fertile coastal plains are in striking contrast with the highlands of the interior, was occupied by peoples with widely different civilizations. Iberians, Celtiberians, and the Celtic populations of the northwest grouped around their *castros* or hill forts, had scarcely anything in common apart from their devotion to their war leaders and their religious nature. As early as the eighth century BC, the large mining centers were active, notably in the Guadalquivir valley (kingdom of Tartessus). These were what attracted the Phoenicians, followed by the Greeks.

In southern Gaul, the Ligurian and Celto-Ligurian peoples of the east, and the Iberians and Celtiberians of the west, who were sometimes grouped in confederations, and often led by an aristocracy of chiefs acknowledged by the collective whole, were brought into contact with the Greek world as early as the seventh century BC by Rhodian traders and by the Phocaean colonists from Marseille, who subsequently spread as far as Ampurias (*emporion* = trading post) in the west, and Nice (Nikaia) and Antibes (Antipolis) in the east. Trading relations were also formed with the Greeks of Magna Graecia (the Greek cities in southern Italy) and with the Etruscans.

The hinterland or continental mainland must not be overlooked, because of the great migrations of peoples which on more than one occasion brutally interrupted the history of the Italian peninsula and transformed its population. In the immediately pre-Christian millennia, the movements of peoples that affected territories later influenced by Rome and its culture are particularly:

- In the south, the activities of the peoples of the sea and desert.
- In the north, Indo-European, and notably Celtic, invasions.

The "peoples of the sea" have already been mentioned in connection with the Phoenicians and the Greeks. Leaving aside the legendary traditions which sometimes obscure history, there is textual and archaeological evidence of the settlement, as early as the Bronze Age, of the Ibero-Ligurians, and in Sicily of the Sicani and Siculi (perhaps one and the same race of conquerors). It is possible that the Siculi were the original population of Italy.

As for the desert peoples, from around 1500 BC they were the "Equidians," horse-breeders and waggon-drivers who, having become excellent horsemen (the Gaetuli and Garamantes), were the ancestors of the Tuaregs. Their presence in the Sahara and their activities as warriors and traders had a great influence on the history of the Maghreb, which was often governed by the relations between nomads and settled tribes.

In the north, in the second millennium BC, it was Indo-European invasions that brought to the Mediterranean countries peoples who practiced cremation, and used horses and waggons. It is difficult to reconstruct and date their movements. There are records of the existence of vast fields of cinerary urns in Silesia and Pannonia (present-day Hungary) from around 1300–1200 BC. After the year 1000 this civilization of urn-fields gradually dwindled until the eighth century BC. At that point the Hallstatt civilization (named after an archaeological site at Hallstatt in Styria) triumphed in the first Iron Age. In Italy, the Latins were probably the first of the Indo-European peoples to arrive in the peninsula. Only a part of them settled in Latium, while others went off to Sicily. When they adopted a settled way of life, they practiced body burial. Early in the fifth century BC, when the Hallstatt culture was in its final stages, there appeared a new civilization, known as that of La Tène (after the name of a Swiss archaeological site); it corresponded with the second Iron Age. This was the era of the Lady of Vix (an ancient skeleton discovered at the site) and the formation of a Gaulish "nationality," characterized by original art forms, highly developed craftsmanship, and its own religion, which mingled deified animal and natural forces and anthropomorphic divinities, its rites and myths preserved through the oral teachings of the Druids.

The arrival of the Indo-Europeans was one of the major events in the history of the West. It had profound repercussions on the peopling of Italy.

PART I

From the Origins to the Empire

THE ORIGINS OF THE "ROMAN MIRACLE"

The Roman achievement, sometimes referred to as the "Roman miracle," consisted of this: a small town in Latium began by dominating other Latin townships, then established its authority over the Italian peninsula before going on to impose itself on the Mediterranean world and beyond for at least eight centuries. Of all the questions raised by Rome's historic destiny, the question of its origins immediately comes to the fore. It is all the more interesting, but also all the more difficult, because of the numerous legends that surround it (for instance, Roma, daughter of Telephus, himself the son of Herakles/Hercules, who would make Rome an Etruscan town; or Romos, son of Ulysses, who would make it Greek). The origin of the Latin town is not in fact mentioned in any dependable historical document.

SOURCES

First come the literary sources that pass on the traditions. They were gathered together chiefly by Cicero (106–43 BC), Virgil (70–19 BC), Livy (59 BC–AD 17 or 64 BC–AD 12), and Dionysius of Halicarnassus (*fl.* during the reign of Augustus), who were thus all far removed from the events, and, moreover, prepared to embellish what they received, in order to serve the cause of the Roman "nation." Their sources were scanty: there were no written documents before about 600 BC; the burning of Rome by the Gauls in 390 BC destroyed many of those relating to the earlier period; and the early authors were in any case simple annalists. Among these early authors was Fabius Pictor, who lived at the time of Hannibal, at the end of the third century BC, and who was the first to turn Roman history into a literary topic. He himself had used legends and Greek writings that allowed him to go back as far as 420/400 BC. Beyond that there are no literary documents. We have to turn to archaeological data.

The results of excavations allow tradition to be compared with fact, and to be supplemented when it falls short. Traces of prehistoric Italy are not lacking. Tools and tombs take us back to the Palaeolithic era. The domestication of animals, the beginnings of agriculture and mining, and the first constructed dwellings, palafittes built on the water's edge, date from Neolithic and Chalcolithic times. The Bronze Age, marked by the great Indo-European invasions, saw the appearance of terramares, sites known chiefly in northern Italy, where terraces of black earth (*terra mar(n)a* = marl-earth) on piles mark the locations of villages of farmers' huts, sometimes surrounded by an earth levee coupled with a trench, with cemeteries for cremation burials nearby. Farther south, along the Apennines, semi-nomadic shepherds lived in caves, or in villages of huts, and practiced body burial. These representatives of the "Apenninic" civilization used a distinctive type of pottery, fragments of which have been found at the Forum Boarium, on the site of the future Rome. The Iron Age witnessed a new transformation because of fresh invasions. These introduced three new types of tombs into Italy: pit tombs for cinerary urns, trench tombs for body burials, and burial chambers surmounted by circular tumuli.

Archaeology thus illuminates the peopling of Italy. In Latium, material that has emerged from the burial sites of the Latin villages discovered on the slopes of the Alban Hills reveals a civilization that cradled the future Rome. Important evidence going back to its earliest times has been found on the site of the Forum Boarium, on the Palatine and Esquiline hills of Rome, and in the area where the Forum was later built.

With the second part of the seventh century BC, which saw the Latins adopt consonantal writing – the alphabet originally appeared during the second millennium – inscriptional data become available. The earliest item is the gold fibula from the Bernardini tomb at Praeneste (Palestrina), bearing the first "Latin" inscription that we possess, though its authenticity is disputed. Next comes the Vase of Duenos, found between the Quirinal and the Viminal: composed of three little receptacles joined together, it bears an important but somewhat inscrutable text. Then comes the quadrangular *cippus*, or monumental pillar, made of tuff, that was found under the black stone (*lapis niger*) of the Forum: the boustrophedon inscription (written alternately from right to left and left to right) of the sixth–fifth century BC engraved on this has also been given widely varying explanations.

Of course, from the fourth century on, literary, archaeological, and inscriptional sources become more numerous and reliable. From the third century on, there are also numismatic or coin sources. In the late Republic, coinage was not only an instrument of trade; it also served, by means of iconography and wording, as propaganda for the politicians engaged in issuing or financing it.

1 / ITALY BEFORE ROME

*I*N THE MIDDLE OF THE EIGHTH CENTURY BC, THE TIME ASSIGNED BY TRADITION TO THE FOUNDING OF ROME, ITALY WAS A PATCHWORK OF PEOPLES, SOME LONG SETTLED, OTHERS STILL ON THE MOVE. AMONG THESE PEOPLES, TWO BECAME ESTABLISHED WHO RAPIDLY CAME TO DOMINATE THE NORTH AND SOUTH OF THE PENINSULA: THE ETRUSCANS AND THE GREEKS, BOTH, VERY EARLY ON, EXERCISING A PROFOUND INFLUENCE ON THE BUDDING TOWNSHIP THAT WAS TO BECOME ROME. WITH THE PHOENICIANS WHO SET UP THEIR TRADING POSTS AND THE GREEKS THEIR COLONIES, THE EAST GAINED PREDOMINANCE IN THE WESTERN HALF OF THE MEDITERRANEAN BASIN.

THE PEOPLES OF PRIMITIVE ITALY

Of the pre-Indo-European, Mediterranean inhabitants of Italy, composed of aboriginals and of immigrants from overseas, several elements survived, such as the Ligures, primitive mountain-dwellers, settled north of Etruria on the shores of the Gulf of Genoa and in the Maritime Alps. Likewise the Sicani, Sicilian aboriginals, according to tradition, who had been pushed back to the south-western part of the island (around Gela and Agrigentum) by the Siculi, who had come from the Italian peninsula in the thirteenth or eleventh century BC (unless these two peoples were related, if not identical). In the view of most modern authors, the Siculi have a fundamentally Mediterranean background: their matriarchal customs, traces of which remain in the rites of sacred prostitution practiced later in the sanctuary of Aphrodite on Mount Eryx, were foreign to the customs of Indo-European populations. They seem to have been closely related to the Oenotri, the Chones, the Morgates, and the Itali (originally only the tip of Bruttium was called Italy), names given by the Greeks – who regarded them all as Pelasgi (prehistoric inhabitants of Greece) – to the indigenous populations of the south of the peninsula. Here we may recognize the all-Pelasgic doctrine inspired by Dionysius of Halicarnassus, a Greek who aimed to prove that the Italians were Greek in origin, an obviously incorrect generalization.

A pre-Indo-European substratum therefore existed, but it was not homogeneous, although linguists have claimed to find traces of a linguistic community. Some historians hold that these peoples, the Pelasgi, Ligures, Siculi, Oenotri, etc., who according to the legend recounted by Virgil were at the origin of primitive Rome, all boil down to a single unity, one founded on the mythological relationships whose beginnings lie in Arcadia. According to Virgil, Rome was even an Arcadian foundation. Of course, this is legend, but "a fable is a historical fact, and one of the most valuable because it reveals to us the soul of dead peoples" (J. Bayet). The Arcadians certainly played an effective role in the colonization of southern Italy, whence the Arcadian legends reached Latium.

Following the Indo-European invasions which, in the second millennium, submerged the greater part of Europe, Iran and India, new transalpine peoples came to settle in Italy, often overlaying older, indigenous strata. Thus we find:

- The Veneti in the region of the Po delta. Of Illyrian origin, according to Herodotus, they maintained close relations with the coastal regions of the western Adriatic. The inscriptions of Este, Magre (near Vicenza), and Padua bear witness to the use of an archaic Indo-European language.
- Later, in the sixth–fifth centuries by infiltration, and then in the fourth in a massive flood, came the Celtic populations: Insubres, Cenomani, Boii, Lingones, and Senones. They became so dominant in the Po valley that it came to be called Cisalpine Gaul. Their authority and culture spread as far as Etruscan Felsina (Bologna), whose historic role as the gateway to the main passage from the Po valley to Tuscany was then established.
- The Umbri, who for a time were dominant in central Italy, occupied the hinterland of the Adriatic coast as far as the upper Tiber. Their Osco-Umbrian language is known notably from the famous text of the Eugubine Tablets, seven bronze plaques which give the rituals and tutelary divinities of the town of Iguvium (Gubbio) on the River Metaurus.
- On the same coast, they were followed by the Piceni, who settled in the region of Ancona.
- Farther south, the Sabines and Samnites adjoined the Latini on the east and south-east. These populations, known as "Sabelli," were joined by the Marsi on the borders of Lake Fucinus, the Volsci in the Pontine plain, and the Campani in the Naples region, where they encountered the Osci and the Ausoni, who had settled there before them. The name Osci (farmers) derives from *Ops*, which means productive activity and is found in *opus*, indicating work and especially work on the land.
- Still farther south, on the Adriatic coast, were to be found the Frentani, the Apuli, including the Messapian-speaking Daunians and Peucetians, and lastly,

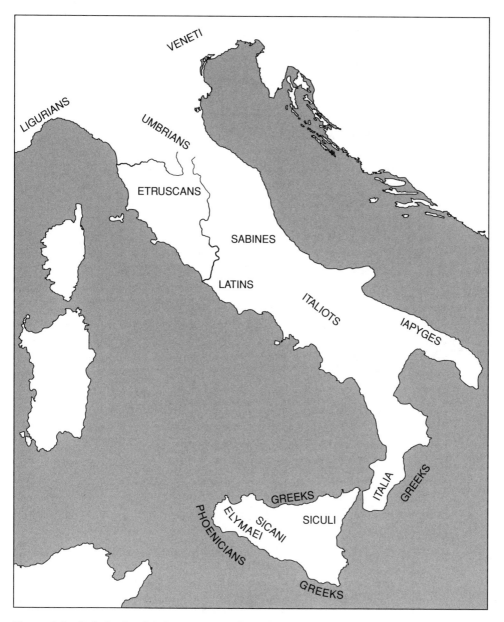

Figure 1.1 Italy in the eighth century BC: the Italic peoples

around Tarentum, the Iapygians or Messapians, whose Illyrian origin, attributed to them by the early authors, is confirmed by a study of the names of both places and peoples.

■ On the other side of the "boot," the Lucani and Bruttii overlay the indigenous strata represented by the Oenotri, Chones, Morgates, and Itali.

■ In the midst of all these peoples, the Latini occupied only the plain of central Italy between the Tiber and the Alban Hills. It is a plain dotted with hills capable of providing refuge and defense, giving onto the Tyrrhenian sea by way of a coast that is scarcely hospitable, it is true, and linked to the hinterland by a navigable river, the Tiber, that played an essential role in the choice of Rome's site. In proto-historic Italy, the Latins were probably the oldest and certainly the most important of the Indo-European peoples who had migrated to the peninsula. Recent excavations of the burial sites of Lavinium, Antium, and Villa Cavaletti have revealed for the period between 1000 and 875 BC hut-shaped cinerary urns, the same as have been excavated from the pit tombs on the site of the Roman Forum. There, as in Rome, the rite of body burial only gradually replaced that of cremation. From among the small towns of Latium, archaeology also gives us findings that confirm the primacy of Alba over Rome, a primacy already attested by literary sources.

■ Northward, beyond the Tiber, as far as the Arno and the Apennines, stretched the land of the Etrusci. The origin of this people remains an enigma and, to say the least, much argued about. Did they come from the north or the east? (The land of Urartu, present-day Armenia, has been suggested, for the same cauldrons with griffons' heads are found there as in Etruria.) Or were they aboriginals subjected to various cultural influences? Each theory has arguments and objections for and against. Perhaps it must be allowed that they were not a new people, but rather a new civilization which developed in an indigenous setting.

One thing is certain: by the early seventh century, those whom the Greeks called Tyrrhenoi and the Latins Etrusci or Tusci had become strongly established in Etruria, and, contrary to what was long believed, as early as that time their sphere of influence extended beyond the River Silarus (Sele) as far as the Salerno region. They soon colonized Campania – at Volturnum (Capua) and Pompeii, Etruscan inscriptions furnish the proof. And toward the north they extended their influence, if not their dominion, as far as the Po valley, where traces of their culture abound. There, as in their own area, they created towns: Felsina (Bologna) and Melpum (Milan) are two instances.

The Cultures of Primitive Italy

The cultures of primitive Italy were less varied than the peoples themselves. It would be erroneous to make a firm distinction, using the evidence of funerary rites, even between, on the one hand, the cultures of the aboriginal peoples, or at least the ones belonging to the Mediterranean substratum, and on the other, those of the peoples of Indo-European origin. For the separation can no longer be maintained between those who exclusively practiced body burial (the first) and those who used only cremation (the second). At the most one may speak of dominant customs; a mixture of customs came into effect very early on. Among one and the same people cremation and inhumation were practiced sometimes in the same period and sometimes in successive periods. Funerary rites, therefore, do not always constitute a criterion for belonging to a specific ethnic group.

There was also a relative uniformity in ways of life. Except in the Apennines, where very primitive mountain-dwellers lived (from the Abruzzi came the strange colossal statue of the masked warrior of Capestrano), pastoral and agri-cultural ways of life went on side by side, together with survivals of hunting and fishing. The result of both land and climate – one sixth of Italian soil is mountainous and grassland – livestock breeding and the practice of transhu-mance occupied an essential place in rural activity: either they predominated or, as in Tuscany and central Italy, they complemented agriculture. There in the spring the flocks gave place to crops. From Latium the flocks moved annually toward rich Umbria. From that came trade between the two regions, and with trade, conflict. Hence also the importance of the Tiber in their relations. All this economic activity nevertheless remained at a very primitive level.

On the other hand, there was a wide variety of languages, even if some of them show affinities. For the most part they belonged to the Indo-European family, one of them at least of a very archaic branch. Indo-European was indeed an enduring cultural element. Latin, for example, preserved Indo-European words designating the most ancient forms of religious, constitutional, and family life expressed in Indo-European: e.g. *rex, flamen, credo, pater, mater.*

Closely akin to Latin is Faliscan. Venetan is known by inscriptions on votive stelae from Este; Umbrian by the Gubbio Tablets; and its relative, Oscan, was used by all the peoples of the south-west. The Sabines, Marsi, Volsci, and Piceni similarly had their own dialects.

Outside these Indo-European languages, but penetrated by elements bor-rowed from them, was Ligurian. There was also Messapian or Iapygian, which has affinities with Illyrian. And there was also, of course, Etruscan, to which we shall return. For among this mix of cultures in the Italy of the eighth century

BC, there was one that stood out clearly from the rest by virtue of its progress and its brilliance.

ETRUSCAN CULTURE

This highly original civilization was characterized by three principal features. First and foremost it was an urban civilization. In an Italy of villages, Etruria alone had towns. These were ritually founded and were endowed with enclosing walls, gates, and temples built in stone, features that would be passed on to Roman town development. It was a federation of twelve city-states with magistrates who, in the event of grave danger, would make themselves subject to a dictator (*macstrna* = *mastarna*). This later happened in Rome, at the end of the reign of the first of the Tarquins, with the coming to power of Mastarna (= Servius Tullius). A state structure, of course, implies political and social institutions. Governed first by kings (*lucumons*) surrounded by *fasces*, symbols of their authority, and adorned with well-known insignia (the gold crown and scepter surmounted by an eagle), the Etruscan peoples replaced them in the fifth century with annual magistrates or *zilath* (in Latin, *praetores*). Again, there was a similar political change in Rome from monarchy to republic in the early fifth century. Etruscan society was patrician and almost feudal: a class of nobles formed the oligarchy of the *principes* (men of note who held power in the cities), until the rural plebeians forced their way in. Below was an immense servile class (though slaves could be emancipated and, once freed, could join the followers of the great men).

Moreover, in a primitive rural Italy, the Etruscan civilization was materially and technically developed. Thanks to an advanced knowledge of hydraulics, the Etruscans practiced drainage and irrigation. Furthermore, skilled craftsmen, who were not unaware of Greek techniques, constructed for them shafts and tunnels to exploit the deposits of tin, copper, and iron which abounded in Etruria. These and the iron on the island of Elba were made use of for commercial purposes. Among their most remarkable products were arms, tools, and domestic furnishings in bronze and iron (chiefly mirrors and small chests), and pottery (notably impasto and *bucchero nero*).

Their culture, both national and eclectic, assured the Etruscans of an unchallenged primacy in three fields, the best known and most enigmatic of which was religion. The Etruscan religion was a revealed religion, a religion of books (not of "the" Book, like the Bible of the Hebrews). The sacred books of the prophets, of whom the chief was Tages, laid down the Etruscan religion once and for all by setting out the rules concerning ritual and prescribing the life of states and of men (*libri rituales*), the manner of interpreting thunder and lightning (*libri fulgurales*), and the art and method of observing the entrails of sacrificial victims (*libri haruspicinales*), and by providing the knowledge necessary

Plate 1.1 Etruscan tomb painting: Ceres, the goddess of grain, with armed attendants. 6th century BC.

to conduct a man into the next world (*libri acheruntici*), the whole thing forming a science, the *disciplina Etrusca*. It was thus a highly ritualistic religion: the famous bronze liver of Piacenza, an image of the sky marked out in compartments bearing the names of the gods, was used as a reference in hepatoscopy for examining the livers of animals offered to the gods. It was also a highly developed religion. Under a Triad (Tinia = Jupiter, Uni = Juno, Menrva = Minerva), venerated in tripartite temples (as the temple of Jupiter Capitolinus in Rome was to be), a pantheon was formed similar to that of the Greeks:

Plate 1.2 Etruscan terracotta sarcophagus: husband and wife reclining on a couch. Cerveteri, 6th century BC.

Voltumna/Vertumnus, "the first of the gods of Etruria," according to Varro, Turan = Aphrodite, Fufluns = Dionysos, Turms = Hermes, Sethlans = Hephaistos, Hercle = Herakles, Maris = Ares, Nethuns = Neptune, etc.

In their conception of the next world, the Etruscans were, it seems, influenced by both the Middle East and Greece. Their Paradise was a place of coolness, music, and banquets; their Hell a place of melancholy and grief, of suffering and tortures for the wicked, a place where two monstrous spirits reigned, half-man half-beast, Charun (the Greek Charon) and Tuchulcha (see the Tarquinian tomb of Orcus, or Hades). However, the evil funerary divinities could be appeased by the blood of combatants (a rite some historians consider to be the origin of gladiatorial fights). Hence the scenes of funerary combat to be seen on the frescos of Etruscan tombs (notably those of Francesco of Vulci's tomb).

Etruscan art was no less developed or national than Etruscan religion. It too was very much influenced by Hellenism, which it introduced into central Italy. That influence appears particularly in:

- Sculpture in-the-round (e.g. the Apollo of Veii) and bas-reliefs, statuettes, tripods, and candelabra in bronze, and the painted terracotta decoration covering the temples. Starting in the fourth century, the decorating of sarcophagi and cinerary urns with mythological reliefs became the general practice.
- Painting, known particularly through the frescos in tombs, notably at Tarquinii; it has been said that Etruscan painting is a "reflection of the great archaic painting, lost in Greece."
- Pottery: alongside the Greek vases, mainly Attic, revealed in their thousands by the necropoleis, a not inelegant native pottery (notably in *bucchero*) took its place. Greek vases were not only imported, but also made locally, for example the famous seventh-century water vases of Caere.

Etruscan architecture was no less splendid than Etruscan art. Rome was informed by it in three areas: town planning (checkerboard layout and enclosing walls in freestone, in immense polygonal bond, or rectangular bond, known as *opus quadratum*); the construction of temples (rectangular in plan, with a tripartite cella on a podium, and architectural decoration in polychrome terracotta); and the arrangement of tombs (either a funeral chamber topped by a tumulus and decorated with frescos, or a tomb made of rock, decorated and filled with precious objects). The great princely tombs of the seventh century (Regolini-Galassi at Caere, Bernardini and Barberini at Praeneste) are distinguished by the richness of their furnishings (gold, ivory, vases).

The Etruscan language, which bears, naturally enough, the traces of borrowings from Greek and Italic dialects, is no longer considered to be an Indo-European tongue – affinities are sought with Basque, Caucasian, and (chiefly) pre-Hellenic dialects. It is known to us through some 10,000 inscriptions, unfortunately for the most part very short, late-period epitaphs, allowing no great progress to be made in our knowledge of the language. The latest discovery (the Pyrgi inscriptions, bilingual in Etrusco-Punic) proved disappointing in this respect.

The Etruscan alphabet, disseminated throughout Italy, became the model by which Italy became literate.

THE EAST'S GRIP ON THE WEST

While the Etruscans settled north of the Tiber and rapidly extended their power as far as the Po valley in the north and Campania in the south, two other peoples

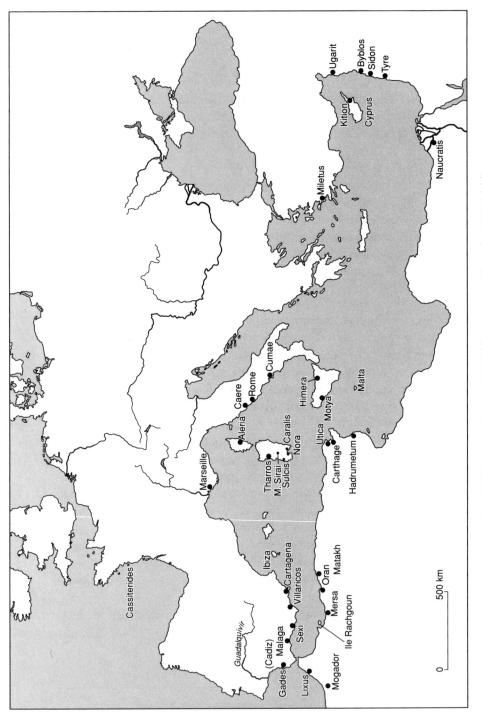

Figure 1.2 Phoenician expansion (from J. Heurgon, *Rome et la Méditerranée occidentale*, PUF, 1980)

Ugarit
Byblos
Sidon
Tyre
Kition
Cyprus
Naucratis
Miletus
Cumae
Rome
Caere
Aleria
Himera
Malta
Motya
Utica
Caralis
Nora
Carthage
Hadrumetum
Tharros
M. Sirai
Sulcis
Marseille
Ibiza
Cartagena
Villaricos
Oran
Matakh
Mersa
Ile Rachgoun
Cassiterides
Guadalquivir
(Cadiz)
Malaga
Sexi
Gades
Lixus
Mogador

0   500 km

were gaining a foothold in Italy: the Phoenicians and the Greeks. Their settlements bear witness to the vitality of the East and the strength of its expansion in the western Mediterranean.

PHOENICIAN SETTLEMENT AND CULTURE

At least as early as the eleventh century BC, Phoenician navigators from Tyre and Sidon had reconnoitered the African and Iberian coasts. The great princely tombs of Etruria disclose costly objects (in silver and ivory) imported from Phoenicia, or objects manufactured on the spot based on Phoenician models and ranges of images borrowed from the Middle East, revealing a period of eastern influence on Etruscan civilization in the eighth–seventh centuries. And the presence of Phoenician traders is attested not only in Sicily (at Motya), Sardinia (at Sulcis and Nora), and Malta as well, but in the eighth–seventh centuries in Rome itself, where a colony of Tyrians, as has been seen, was able to settle in the area of the Forum Boarium. The founding of the Ara Maxima Herculis, the earliest altar to Hercules in Italy, has been linked with the presence of Tyrian merchants. The features that have encouraged the making of this link are its location, in the Forum Boarium; the fact that its ritual, by its requirement of a tithe offered to the god here as in eastern markets, as well as its religious prohibitions (targeting women, dogs, pigs, and flies, all banned from the sacred precinct), recalls the ritual connected with the sanctuary of the Tyrian Baal-Melqart; the similarity established between the oldest representation of Hercules known in Italy (the god brandishing his club in his right hand) and that attributed to Melqart; the attachment of two families, the Potitii and the Pinarii, to the sanctuary, where they were the favored serving priests right up to the nationalization of the cult in 312 BC, the former having "Canaanite" characteristics (recognized by some, denied by others); and lastly the appearance of the clothing worn by the participants, long "feminine" tunics. Although the link has still not been demonstrated with certainty, there are many indications of its probability, in Rome as, a little later, in Pozzuoli in Campania.

THE GREEKS IN ITALY AND SICILY

Far better known than the coming of the Phoenicians, affirmed by writings and well supported by archaeology, the arrival of the Greeks in the West, and chiefly in southern Italy and Sicily, constituted one of the major events in the history of the Mediterranean in the first millennium BC.

As in the Aegean and on the borders of the Black Sea, Greek colonization began in the Tyrrhenian Sea during the eighth century. Cumae appears to have been both the northernmost and the oldest of the Greek colonial foundations in Italy (ca. 770), followed by Ischia (ca. 740). Other settlements, first of

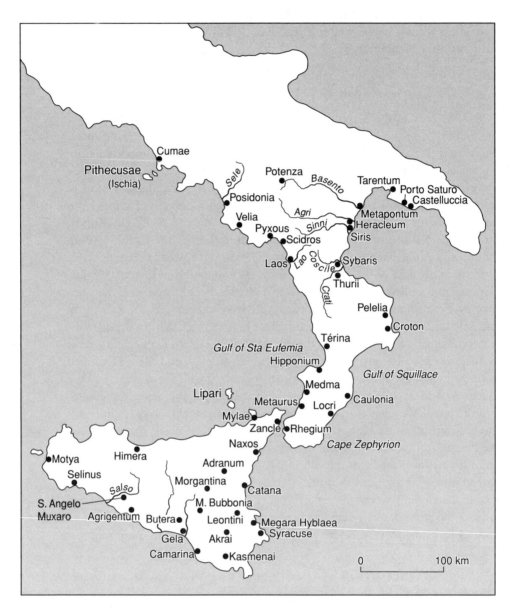

Figure 1.3 Greek colonization (from J. Heurgon, *Rome et la Méditerranée occidentale*, PUF, 1980)

Chalcidian origin, next Megarean, Corinthian, Achaean, and Lacedaemonian, and then Rhodian, Cretan, and Ionian (from Asia Minor), were established, on the one side between Cumae and Rhegium (Reggio di Calabria), and on the other (the instep of the "boot") as far as Tarentum and beyond, as well as along the whole perimeter of Sicily (Trinacria). The density of settlement was such that in the second century BC Polybius used the term "Magna Graecia" (Great Greece) to define that Hellenized south of Italy, a name transmitted by Cicero, who spoke of "the old Italian Greece, that used to be called Great." In fact the name must go back to the sixth century.

In Sicily

After Cumae, the Chalcidians founded Naxos, Leontini, and Catana, and then, in order to dominate the straits, Zancle and (on the mainland) Rhegium; the Megareans established their settlements at Megara Hyblaea (ca. 750) and later at Selinus (ca. 650); the Corinthians installed themselves at Syracuse (ca. 733); and the Rhodians and Cretans at Gela and Acragas (Agrigentum).

In southern Italy

It was mainly the Achaeans, the Laconians, and the Locrians who settled at Sybaris (ca. 750), Croton, Metapontum, Siris, Tarentum (ca. 706), and Locri (ca. 673).

At first brutally repressed by the invaders, the indigenous populations, who in some places simply coexisted and in others actively cooperated with the settlers, were all more or less affected by the phenomenon known today as acculturation. Archaeologists and historians study it through monuments, sculptures, paintings, and especially pottery, emphasizing now the work's originality, now its fidelity to Greek models.

The Greek influence did not affect only the coastal areas and, to a lesser degree, the hinterland, where the Chalcidians, for instance, must have introduced the culture of the olive tree into central Italy. It also touched Rome. It has been remarked that the traditional date of Rome's founding (754/753 BC) matched to within a few years the date given for the settlement of the Achaeans in Sybaris (750), and that the end of the royal epoch in Rome coincided, still according to tradition, with the fall of Sybaris (510 BC). Was that chance?

What is certain is that the Greeks of Magna Graecia, Sicily, and even the Greek mainland traded with Rome as early as the seventh century: the findings of proto-Corinthian, and then Corinthian pottery itself, in excavations on the Palatine, and in the Forum in particular, prove it. Certain too is the fact that, like the Etruscans, the Greeks were to have a profound influence on budding Roman culture. On its law and institutions and art, it goes without saying. But also on its religion. The discovery at Lavinium of a dedication in Greek to the Dioscuri has shown that at the end of the sixth century or beginning of the fifth, Tarentum or Locri, centers of the fervent worship of Castor and Pollux, had contacts in Latium, very close to Rome. But above all, Pythagoras stands out as an enduring spiritual influence. He emigrated from Samos to Croton in about 530 and died at Metapontum. He was regarded by Herodotus as the wisest and most learned of men, and his doctrine inspired the model government of Archytas at Tarentum in the first half of the fourth century, "the first and finest example of a philosopher in power." His influence spread throughout Italy and thus to Rome. As J. Carcopino remarked, "when there was an Italic consciousness, it was Pythagoreanized." With fine disregard for chronology, it was said in Rome that Numa Pompilius, the second king of Rome, had been his disciple. At all events, Pythagoreanism, and later neo-Pythagoreanism, left their mark on Roman thinking, even in the era of the emperor Claudius (AD 41–54), if one can date to this reign the curious subterranean edifice discovered in Rome, known as the Pythagorean basilica of the Porta Maggiore.

Just as Roman art owes much to that of Greece, either by direct contact and influence or through the channel of Magna Graecia, so the literature of Rome also inherited a great deal: the first epic and tragic poets came from Tarentum and Apulia (Livius Andronicus, Ennius, Pacuvius) or from Capua (Naevius); and Roman comedy was invented by Epicharmus, a Sicilian.

Rome was thus born in an Italy whose peoples had complex origins, and amid populations that were very mixed, but dominated by two advanced civilizations, Etruscan and Greek.

2 / THE FORMATION
OF ROME
From Romulus to the Tarquins

*I*T IS STILL VERY DIFFICULT TO SAY ANYTHING DEFINITE ABOUT THE ORIGINS OF
ROME, FOR THEY ARE CLOUDED WITH LEGEND. AGAINST THAT BACKGROUND,
ARCHAEOLOGICAL DISCOVERIES NEVERTHELESS PROVIDE SOME CHRONOLOGICAL
LANDMARKS. EVEN IF WE CANNOT BE CERTAIN ABOUT THE NAMES OF THE FIRST
KINGS, IT SEEMS CLEAR THAT THE LATIN AND SABINE KINGS WERE SUPPLANTED AT
THE BEGINNING OF THE SIXTH CENTURY BC BY ETRUSCAN KINGS, WHO WERE
RESPONSIBLE FOR THE URBAN ORGANIZATION OF WHAT HAD HITHERTO BEEN MERELY
GROUPS OF VILLAGES.

LATIN AND SABINE KINGS

The legends recounted by early Greek and Latin authors recording "events"
that took place in the area of Rome well before the "founding" of the city,
placed by tradition in 754/753 BC, are of interest to historians, even if they are
more mythical than actual. Greek authors write of an Arcadian, Evander, who
about sixty years before the Trojan War settled on the left bank of the Tiber,
where, welcomed by Faunus, king of the aborigines, he installed himself on the
Palatine and subsequently received Herakles on the Forum Boarium. They also
bring in Aeneas, who, after the fall of Troy (variously dated 1193 and 1184
BC), also took refuge in Latium. The Latin writers, notably Fabius Pictor, the
first annalist (ca. 200 BC), tell the story of Romulus and Remus, the twins reared
by a she-wolf, who founded the city on a hill. These legends were gradually
interwoven and embellished, before being given their final literary setting by
Livy and Virgil. They focus on two people: Aeneas and Romulus.

Aeneas, son of Anchises and Venus, is said to have founded Lavinium. His
son, Ascanius, whom the Romans called Iulus to consecrate him as the ancestor of the Julii, is said to have founded Alba Longa. Romulus, his descendant
(some regard him as the grandson of Aeneas), is said in his turn to have founded
Rome. He and his brother Remus, twin sons of the god Mars and an Alban
Vestal, are said to have come from Alba to the banks of the Tiber, and to have
founded the city between 754 and 748 (according to the authors), on April
21, the date held to be its *dies natalis* or day of birth.

Plate 2.1   She-wolf with Romulus and Remus. The original figures of the twins were destroyed in the late Republic; new ones were added during the Renaissance.

Against this legendary backdrop, archaeology provides a more concrete approach, with results that sometimes confirm aspects of the legends. In 1907 the foundations of huts were discovered on the Palatine, near the spot where Romans preserved the memory of Romulus' house (*casa Romuli*). Exposed in 1949, these indicated that the huts were rectangular in plan, with rounded corners, and measured about 4.80 by 3.40 m. The bases were hollowed out of the tuff of the hillside to between 0.4 and 0.5 meters in depth. Holes dug around the perimeter marked the spots where the posts supporting the roof had been sunk. The walls would have been of reeds coated with clay. Outside, a channel collected water and drained it away. In the middle was a larger hole, for the central supporting post, around which there are often traces of the hearth. Lastly, on one side, usually to the south, the door cavity survives. Now, in eighth–seventh century tombs excavated near the Forum, terracotta hut-urns serving as ossuaries have been found whose shape exactly corresponds to the general aspect attributed to these "Romulean" dwellings. Furthermore, pottery picked up from the bases of the huts is dated by specialists to as early as the middle of the eighth century, that is, the traditional time of the "founding" of Rome. It disappears from around 575 BC, with the primitive hut, replaced by the different architecture, of permanent and larger construction, of the Etruscan era.

Other hut bases were discovered in another part of the Palatine, under the imperial palace of the Flavians (end of the first century AD) – these apparently belonged to another village, for there was a tomb between the two sites (the dead did not mingle with the living). Others were sited at the location of the future Forum. In 1988 another small nucleus of dwellings was found. And here there was evidence that even the earliest village was protected by an enclosing wall and thus had a real organization of the kind usually attributed only to the era of the Etruscan kings.

Of the 41 eighth–seventh century tombs excavated early in the twentieth century on the site of the Forum, some took the form of circular pits containing cinerary urns, the others rectangular trenches for body burials, the latter being less old (seventh century). The burial ground ceased to be used at the beginning of the sixth century, a date that obviously marks an important moment in the development of Rome.

Other tombs were found on the Quirinal and Esquiline hills. The material contained in them included weapons, helmets, shields, and even a battle chariot, and shows that here we are dealing with a different people, a race of warriors who buried their dead, and against whom the inhabitants of the Palatine and the Velia must have had to protect themselves with outer defensive walls.

Among these inhabited areas, it is the one on the Palatine and its slopes which, dominating the valley of the future Forum on one side, and on the other the corridor separating the hill from the Tiber, where the livestock market (Forum Boarium) was later established, would play the vital historical role. Livy remarked upon it perfectly in his *Roman History* (V.54.4):

It is not without good reason that gods and men chose this place to build our city: these hills with their pure air; this river which brings us produce from the interior and allows sea convoys to come upstream; a sea handy to our needs, but far enough away to guard us from foreign fleets; our situation in the very center of Italy. All these advantages shape this most favored of sites into a city destined for glory.

Livy emphasized these three features: a river, the Tiber; nearby, hills; a crossroads. He points out the importance of the Isola Tiberina, the island that makes the river fordable by shepherds and their migrating flocks, who in the event of danger can take refuge in the nearby hills, notably the Palatine, setting up their dwellings and raising their defenses. This crossing-point of the river, the import and export route, for the road linking Etruria with Magna Graecia, did not achieve its full value until the sixth century.

To the great historical turning-point of the sixth century belong many of the extraordinary archaeological discoveries recently made in Latium at Prattica di

Mare, on the site of Lavinium: 14 monumental altars, a sacred tomb (called the *heróon* of Aeneas), votive inscriptions, including an archaic dedication in Greek to Castor and Pollux, and an abundant range of terracotta statutes and statuettes of a Minerva, everything datable to the sixth or fifth century BC. At that time the Greek influence and the memory of Aeneas were evident in Latium, with Lavinium seemingly an important religious center contributing much to the archaic Roman religion.

What happened on the Palatine and the other hills of Rome in the middle of the eighth century in 754–748? History or legend? It seems very likely that the Palatine was indeed the cradle of Rome. Some said that Romulus was the son of Aeneas, or the son of Latinus, king of Latium, and a Trojan woman called Roma. Others would have him the offspring of the god Mars and a daughter of Aeneas, Lavinia. He was also said to be the grandson of a king of Alba. Plutarch, who recounts all these legends and gives the "life" of Romulus in detail, compares them with those surrounding Theseus, the hero who founded Athens. Now, whereas he portrays Theseus as a true hero who brought about the federation of the inhabitants of Attica around one city, which became Athens, it is plain to see that, outside Rome, his Romulus has neither a mythical nor a historical personality; he is an invented character, born of a later identification of the god Quirinus (as a deified Romulus) and of the need for a founder in the Greek style adapted to the spirit of Rome. It is possible that Romulus was simply a leader of bands of migrants, perhaps from Latium, surviving on stockbreeding and brigandage. Rome's *dies natalis*, April 21, was also, it may be noted, the feast of Pales, the protectress of flocks, when the *Parilia* or *Palilia* was celebrated, her name of the same root as the Palatine's.

Equally legendary is the list of the seven kings of royal Rome: the number seven was imposed because Fabius Pictor accepted, and made others accept, that the royal period had lasted 245 years, or seven generations of 35 years. In the same way, a facile but fallacious pattern was elaborated by stressing a dualism (inspired by the legends):

- The twins, Romulus and Remus, the chosen one and the outcast.
- The association of Romulus, the Latin, and Titus Tatius, king of the Sabines, whose agreement set the seal on the amity of the two peoples.
- The group or succession of Romulus/Numa Pompilius, i.e. the political founder and the religious creator (Numa was regarded as the inventor of the Roman religion).

This dualism was presented as the prefiguration of the republican consular dyarchy, the patrician–plebeian division, and the duality of certain sacerdotal colleges. An alternation of Latin and Sabine kings in the first four kings of

Rome, intended to ensure the unity born of the meeting between Romulus and Tatius, has also been sought.

Brilliant as well as much criticized, G. Dumézil's attempt to explain Rome's earliest times stands out from the rest. In his view, the history of the earlier Roman kings is pure myth. It is the historicized expression of the functional tripartite division to be found at the basis of all the political, social, and religious systems of the Indo-European peoples. According to him, these peoples had in common three hierarchized bodies, imposed by a shared ideological structure: these three bodies represented and secured the three essential functions of religious sovereignty, military power, and productive force. From that came a society composed of those who held politico-religious power (kings, magistrates, priests), their god Jupiter, god of sovereignty; those who ensured military protection, with Mars, god of war; and those with the ability to produce (farmers, shepherds, craftsmen), with Quirinus their god. From that very ancient state of affairs there survived in Rome the college of the three major *flamines* (priests of a single god): of Jupiter, Mars, and Quirinus. As for the kings, they expressed first the doubling of political and religious sovereignty (Romulus and Numa respectively), then warrior power (Tullus Hostilius), and lastly economic prosperity and social concerns (Ancus Marcius).

Among all these suggestions, what can be regarded as certain?

■ First, that the legends about those very early times were formed gradually, built up on elements of Italic folklore, with contributions from Greek historiography and etiological explanations. From that was born a kind of Vulgate of the origins of Rome, but with variations. In 296 BC the fable of the twins suckled by the she-wolf was already established (that is the date of a bronze group representing the scene of the suckling).

■ Next, that Rome was not founded on April 21, 754/753 BC. Its coming to be was a long and complex process of inhabitation: the erection of huts, clustering in groups of villages around the Palatine, the building of a wall protecting the villages of the seven original hills (Palatium, Velia, Fagutal, Germal, Oppius, Caelius, and Cispius), embracing the Palatine, Esquiline, Velia, and Caelian, but not the Capitol, Quirinal, or Viminal. Remains of walls discovered at the foot of the Palatine could date back to this era in the seventh century.

■ Lastly, that the way of life of the first historic occupants of the site of Rome was essentially pastoral. A civilization of shepherds who followed the totemic cult of the wolf and the ancient rite of the *Lupercalia* (see glossary).

The great moment in the history of Rome's earliest times occurred when it came under the rule of the Etruscans in the sixth century, for that was the origin of its birth as a town.

ETRUSCAN ROME

The birth of Rome as both town and organized state was linked with Etruscan settlement in southern central Italy and the accession in Rome of a dynasty from Etruria. Sallust remarked on this change when he bluntly contrasted the Latino-Sabine royal epoch with that of the foreign "arrogant tyranny" that followed (*Catiline* 6).

THE BIRTH OF THE TOWN

As we saw, the Etruscans knew about urban civilization. They had even organized their twelve peoples of Etruria around a federal center, Volsinii, a wealthy and powerful town. There they had been the first to make an attempt at something approaching Italian unity. As early as the sixth century, their imperialism led some of them to the banks of the Tiber, their presence attested at the foot of the Palatine in the *vicus Tuscus* (Etruscan quarter). The beginnings of the new dynasty also date back to the sixth century. According to tradition it was forged by Tarquin the Elder and continued by Servius Tullius and Tarquin the Proud. Even if there is doubt about their names, and though the chronology is uncertain (especially for the final phase of their dominion), an Etruscan presence is evident:

- Numerous *bucchero* vases, collected from the abodes of both the living and the dead, bear witness to steady commercial relations with Etruria.
- Inscriptions in Etruscan accompanying various articles prove that the shepherds' villages of the nascent Rome opened up to new activities, in both craftsmanship and trade, bringing with them a new social formation that took its place alongside the old aristocracy of the Quirites. The rapid development of this led to the Servian classification.
- Archaeological evidence, as well as legend, indicates the complex military activity in the area of Rome of *condottieri* originally from Vulci, Tarquinii, and Veii.

But the main contribution of Etruscan domination was urban: the real "foundation" of Rome can properly be dated to the sixth century. Its entire future was implicit in two essential acts of civilization:

(1) The drainage of marshy areas is one of the most original features of Etruscan activity. Canals were dug in the lower Po valley, the Tuscan Maremma, and doubtless even in the Pontine marshes (Pliny the Elder, *HN* III.120). In Rome itself, the damp valley of the Forum was dried out and then paved (two

Figure 2.1 Rome at the end of the royal era

techniques perfectly mastered in Etruria). Especially spectacular was the construction of the Cloaca Maxima, the huge drain that emptied into the Tiber
downstream from the Pons Aemilianus (the present-day Ponte Rotto). "It is
said," wrote Pliny (*HN* XXXVI.108), "that Tarquin made the tunnel large
enough to allow the passage of a waggon loaded with hay."

A boom in agriculture followed in Latium and Campania, bringing about
profound changes in rural life, with large estates already appearing.

25

Plate 2.2 Cloaca Maxima, at its outlet to the Tiber. Most of what survives dates to the time of Augustus.

(2) The introduction of new techniques in building in stone resulted in vast works of urban development. To start with, in response to a preoccupation with urban defense shared by the towns in Etruria (as well as Greek cities), there was the construction of an enclosing wall. Two successive walls were built (their traces are still to be seen in Rome). The first, dating from the sixth century, was built in blocks of well-shaped and regularly laid *cappellaccio*. Did this tuff from the Roman countryside rapidly disintegrate? Or was the wall partly destroyed during the seizure of Rome by the Gauls in 390 (or 387)? At all events, it was rebuilt in certain places, and in others repaired with less well cut blocks of tuff known as *grotta oscura*, from the territory of Veii (conquered by Rome in 396). According to Livy, this new wall dated from 378. It must therefore have been erected in the nine or twelve years following the sack of Rome.

When the damp valley of the area of the Forum had been dried out, the site was floored with flagstones. The archaic huts and cemeteries were replaced by a public square, signaling the existence of a state (cf. the *agora* in Greek cities).

In the sixth century, at the same time as the laying down of rich votive deposits of statuettes and tiny altars of Etruscan origin and high-quality Greek vases, new temples also made their appearance. These new stone buildings, with their polychrome terracotta ornamentation, not only did honor to the gods but helped to give Rome an air of urban magnificence. Among them was the temple (discovered under the church of Sant'Omobono on the edge of the Forum Boarium) dedicated, according to tradition, to the goddess Fortuna by Servius Tullius, who was especially attached to this cult. At the end of Etruscan domination, the construction of religious buildings increased: in 509 the temple of Jupiter Capitolinus, in 496 the temple of Saturn, north of the Forum, and in 496–493 the temple of Ceres, Liber, and Libera.

All these material transformations were, of course, linked with profound political, social, and spiritual changes – in short, with the birth of a state.

FORMATION OF THE STATE

Even more than in the "foundation" of an *urbs* (the word seems to be Etruscan in origin), the true revolution lies in the organization of a state, with its administrative framework and its social and political institutions.

The essence of that achievement in Rome is attributed to the Servian reforms, of which Livy (I.43) and Dionysius of Halicarnassus (IV.16) have left a very exact picture, so that of the three Etruscan kings Servius Tullius is the best known. According to some, he was a foreigner, a former slave (*servus*), who had become the son-in-law of Tarquin thanks to the latter's wife Tanaquil, a capable woman who subsequently facilitated his rise to power. According to others, notably the Etruscologist Emperor Claudius, he was a *condottiere*, perhaps Etruscan, named Mastarna (= dictator), a friend of the princes of Vulci, and gained mastery of Rome after eliminating the faction of the Tarquins. At all events, it was he who was credited with the organization of Rome into a state.

Administrative framework

Before then, the *populus*, which, as we have seen, had been increased and modified with the arrival of the Etruscans, was divided into tribes and *curiae*. The three ancient tribes of ethnic origin were the *Ramnes* (Latins, or, in Dumézil's view, those who enjoyed political and religious primacy), the *Tities* (Sabines, or farmers), and the *Luceres* (Etruscans – cf. the root *luc-* as in *lucumo* – or warriors). The new, "Servian" system created tribes on a territorial basis. There were four urban tribes, corresponding to the four areas of Rome (the *Palatina*, *Esquilina*, *Collina*, and *Suburana*), and some 10 rural tribes for its territory, the *ager Romanus*, their number increasing in step with conquests, so that by the middle of the third century there were 31 rural tribes. From the time of the Servian reforms on, all citizens were compulsorily attached to a tribe by tribal area, where, according to Dionysius of Halicarnassus (IV.14), they had to be domiciled and pay their taxes. Because of this, the curial system vanished and a new social classification appeared.

Social organization

Originally, when the clan or *gens* system was in force, each of the three tribes was divided into ten *curiae*. There were thus 30 *curiae*, bearing specific names. This highly number-based system is known from the works of Varro, "one who was obsessed by figures" according to historians who reject this arrangement. What is certain is that, with the Servian reforms, which aimed to integrate the newcomers, representatives of a new form of artisanal and commercial economy, into the social structure, the curial organization was replaced by a fresh system, one based on residence and wealth, and involving a *census*, a registration of all free persons living in Roman territory, and of their property. From that arose a social classification and distribution of political rights based on wealth. A distinction was thus made between five classes of citizens: the first comprised those who possessed capital of at least 100,000 *asses* (an *as* was originally a pound weight in uncoined copper, but was gradually reduced in weight); the second, capital of 75,000; the third 50,000; the fourth 25,000; and the fifth 11,000. (This assessment in *asses* does not in fact correspond with the economic data of the period, when wealth was measured in, roughly, acres of land (*jugera*) and head of livestock (*pecunia*, from *pecus* = flock; later the word came to mean money). It would not have been established on these monetary bases until the second century BC.)

So the *census* system, recalling Cleisthenes' tribal reform in Athens (the abolition of four ancient tribes and establishment of ten new ones), won the day. Politically, it found expression in the *comitia centuriata*, to which we shall return. It also expressed itself in the new, "Servian" military organization.

Servian military organization

Livy (I.42.4–5) was careful to note the parallel between civilian and military rights and duties. Each of the five classes of citizens was divided into *centuriae* (groups of 100 men), half of whom had to serve in the regular army (the *juniores* aged between 17 and 45), and the other half in the reserves (the *seniores*, aged between 46 and 60), all equipped and fed at their own expense. That had two consequences: those whose *census* was lower than 11,000 *asses* (these were the *capite censi*, who had, as it were, nothing but their heads) were (largely) exempt from military service; and orphans, slaves, freed slaves, and citizens who had been stripped of their civic rights were also exempt. Military service (*militia*) was both a duty and a right of the classified citizen who retained his civic rights. On the other hand, military rights and duties in this civic army varied according to class, or, in other words, according to financial status:

■ From the first class, 18 *centuriae* of horsemen and 80 *centuriae* of footsoldiers were recruited, armed at their own expense with offensive and defensive weapons.
■ From the three following classes came 20 *centuriae* apiece of more lightly armed footsoldiers, two *centuriae* of engineers, and two of musicians.
■ The fifth class provided 30 *centuriae* of men armed with slings.

As there was also a single, non-combatant *centuria* of *capite censi*, there were thus 193 *centuriae*, in which the first class occupied a pre-eminent position, to be found also in the political organization.

Political organization

As the *centuria* was both a military and a voting unit, it is obvious that the first class, with its 98 *centuriae*, held an absolute majority in centuriate assemblies. The *comitia centuriata* were thus dominated by the wealthier citizens. The Servian organization, therefore, revealed a clearly timocratic character politically as well as militarily. However, two mitigating factors should be noted:

■ The existence of the patrician order, a kind of hereditary nobility which reserved for itself the great priestly offices, as well as much land. It kept the army supplied with officers and lived surrounded by *clientes* (followers, dependants), whom their patron protected in return for a pledge of loyalty

Servian military organization					
Class	Census	Centuriae	Juniores	Seniores	
1	100,000	*equites*	12	6	18
		pedites	40	40	80
2	75,000		10	10	20
3	50,000		10	10	20
4	25,000		10	10	20
5	11,000		15	15	30
				Engineers	2
				Musicians	2
				Capite censi	1

(*fides*). For example, when the *gens* of the Claudii left its original, Sabine territory to settle in Roman territory, it is said to have come with some 5,000 "clients."

■ The Etruscan royal authority, which substantially reduced the political powers of the centuriate assembly. This assembly gathered fully armed at the sound of the trumpet, basically to acclaim royal plans for the state, war, and the distribution of booty.

Even though restricted, the power to make such decisions belonged to the combatant section of the citizens. This emphasis on the military aspect of political life in the royal era is strongly characteristic of the period of Etruscan domination, especially toward the end, under the last king, known as Tarquin the Proud, who, according to ancient sources, achieved power by means of a violent usurpation.

The end of Etruscan domination

His seizing power by force against the will of the *patres*, and his relying on the support of the people, had already made Tarquin resemble a Greek "tyrant." By denying burial to Servius Tullius, notes Livy, he committed the grave offence of sacrilege. His subsequent behavior further accentuated his likeness to such tyrants, a comparison which the ancient authors did not fail to drive home (the Athenian Pisistratids were his contemporaries). Dionysius of Halicarnassus (IV.41) in particular denounced his tyrannical actions:

■ his creation of a personal armed guard, composed of Romans and foreigners, "ensuring his constant security against any traps that might be set for him";
■ his hostility to the aristocracy and withdrawal into himself, his contempt for (or fear of) the public, his way of dealing with matters of state on his own or with a few private advisers, for whom his favors were reserved;
■ his ambition to form personal bonds with other families, even among those foreign to the town;
■ his concern to increase the town's magnificence by a policy of great public works, which allowed him at the same time to obtain the support of the needy lower classes.

According to ancient sources, the rape of the noble Lucretia pushed the aristocracy's hostility too far and brought about the revolution led by L. Junius Brutus, who, in the words of Tacitus (*Ann.* I.1), "established liberty and the consulate."

Whatever Tacitus may say, L. Junius Brutus is a fabricated character having nothing to do with the expulsion of Tarquin. Tarquin's departure, the result of the decline of Etruscan power, an awakening of the Italic peoples, and internal movements in the colonies of Magna Graecia (the destruction of Sybaris occurred at this time), was occasioned by the intervention of Porsenna, king of Clusium, probably in 509–508. Fleeing first to Tusculum, the last king of Rome died in Cumae in 495. The foundation of the Republic, the result of a rising of the aristocracy (patriciate) of Rome against tyrannical foreign domination, is of uncertain date, perhaps 504, or as late as 480–475.

From the account of Tacitus (and before him Cicero had said the same), it is clear that, for the Romans, the Republic and liberty were thenceforward synonymous. The stress would lie on the last phase of the royal epoch, particularly the tyrannical nature and foreign origin of the last king. Thence arose a profound horror of royalty, feeding republican rhetoric, a horror fatal to Caesar, and never forgotten by Augustus.

Its language remaining virtually free from Etruscan contamination, Rome, all in all, retained little of those earliest times and its experience of the Etruscans, except its urban character, which was, of course, no small thing. But it was, perhaps, its religion that owed most to them.

THE RELIGION OF ARCHAIC ROME

This is a difficult and disputed area, because of the late date of the literary sources, the historian having to make careful use of moralizing evocations of a distant past, and the works of systematizing theologians, and inventive mythographers. For example, the Chant of the Salii (priests of Mars), a kind of rhythmic litany recited by the brotherhood of the twelve Salii during the ceremonies of the cult of Mars, is known only through fragments quoted by Horace, Quintilian, and Varro; but it seems to have been an old ritual in archaic language that the priests themselves no longer understood. With rare exceptions, literary texts of religious interest are much later than the ancient epoch. So it is with the oldest and most important liturgical calendar, that of Antium (Anzio), which is datable only to the late second or early first century BC. Nevertheless, it seems to have preserved references to ancient festivals belonging to the pre-Etruscan Italic time, even if their liturgical development took place in the Etruscan era. It is thus a document that reveals something of the religious feelings, beliefs, and rites of the Romans in the seventh–sixth centuries.

Luckily, archaeology has taken us further.

It is now realized that about the end of the seventh century the earliest huts in the southern part of the area of the Forum were destroyed and replaced by an area of beaten earth that was marked by a *cippus* and thus intended for ritual purposes. A tile-covered edifice was then built there, itself replaced around 580 by a larger, decorated construction, identified as the *Regia* (dwelling of the king). Nearby, a contemporary well lay very close to the site of the future temple of Vesta. So we have here traces of a place of public worship (another proof of the formation of a state), replaced by the *Regia*, associated with a sacred area devoted to Vesta, the goddess of fire, whose worship involved an important role for water. Obviously, the person of the king was closely associated with religion.

At the other end of the site of the Forum, toward the north-east, a space (called the Comitium) was cleared for politico-judiciary purposes, and between 625 and 600 a building was constructed (perhaps the first Curia Hostilia). Then around 580 came the establishment of a place of worship, probably the Volcanal, the sanctuary of fire (like the temple of Vesta at the southern end of the Forum), and the setting up of the famous *cippus* discovered under the "black stone," its celebrated inscription containing the word *rex* and ritual instructions. Here again we find signs of public worship and the presence of the king in a religious context.

Lastly, the discovery on the Capitol of a votive deposit datable to the late seventh or early sixth century BC, and linked therefore with a building other than the later temple of Jupiter, indicates yet again the existence at this time of places of public worship in or about Rome.

From all this we may gather that even at this very early date public worship was already organized, that it was officiated at several places in the town, and that the king was "very much present in the domain of the sacred" (J. Scheid). On this point, archaeology confirms the literary sources. That said, is it possible to recognize the components of a religion already established in the seventh–sixth centuries, the earliest period of which we have any knowledge?

BEFORE ETRUSCAN DOMINATION

Pliny the Elder remarks of the earliest Romans that they were "more sensitive to the mystery of the divine presence than to the visual representation of divinity." It is indeed probable that, after the manner of other Mediterranean peoples, they believed in the existence of mysterious higher forces, not necessarily to be called *numina*. It is likely that the Earth (*Tellus, Terra mater*), in which they laid their dead and which provided them with the means of life, was regarded as the generator of all life, giving rise to religious practices of a naturalist and earthy nature, enriched no doubt by Indo-European conceptions of the world. A very early calendar that we know of, which includes a distinction between "profane" days (*dies fasti*), dedicated to action, and "sacred" days (*dies nefasti*), reserved for the gods and intended to ensure the effectiveness of the work or war of the days of action, may date back to those distant times.

As in the Aegean basin, the ancient Romans must also have honored various animals, plants, and other natural objects, seeing them as the incarnations of higher forces or more simply as divine symbols, without in either case any suggestion of totemism or animal, object, or plant gods. The goat personified the god Faunus, and at the time of the *Lupercalia* (February 15) in honor of this god of fertility, the priests of Lupercus would run round the Palatine, stripped to the waist, their lower parts covered with a goatskin. Jupiter Lapis was incorporated in the flint that can kill, or the thunderbolt; Jupiter Terminus, the boundary stone. Sacred woods, such as Furrina on the Janiculum, were devoted to ancient divinities.

The development of this practical, naturalist, Earth-oriented religion followed, of course, the fluctuations of peoples and events, the very history of Rome. Thus glimpses are revealed, less chronologically than specifically, of very complex components: firstly Italic, a mingling of contributions from the conquering Indo-European peoples (notably Latins), with borrowings from the subjected indigenous Mediterranean peoples, and additions from those peoples neighboring on Latium (Umbrians, Osci, Volsci, etc.); next Etruscan, even before the sixth-century conquest; and lastly Greek, either through direct contact or channeled via the Etruscans, who were profoundly Hellenized even in the sixth century.

Italic components

The religion of the pre-urban (pre-Etruscan) era was characterized by the coexistence, sometimes tributary, of two religious currents. The first, indigenous and Mediterranean, was dominated by the telluric deities of fertility: chthonic divinities responsible for fertility and fruitfulness, above all female deities, versions of the Earth Mother, but also male gods. Thus Quirinus appears to have reigned over the traditionally Sabine lower slopes of the towering hill later called the Quirinal. Summanus, god of night lightning, and Terminus, god of boundaries, dominated the Capitol, on whose slopes Veiovis and Saturn, god of fertility, were ensconced. Italy in its entirety was probably consecrated to Saturn (it is said to have been called Saturnia). According to legend, Saturn was dethroned by his son Jupiter – a mythological transposition of the historical fact of the influx of the Indo-European peoples, and their gods. G. Dumézil, basing himself on literary, ritual, and priestly survivals (notably the pre-eminence of the three *flamines* of Jupiter, Mars, and Quirinus), has stressed the enthronement at the head of the world of the gods in pre-Etruscan Rome of a divine trinity matching the functional division of society at that time: Jupiter, god of the luminous sky; Mars, fighting god and god of fighters; and Quirinus, god of peace and prosperity, the protector of production.

Etruscan and Greek components

In Rome itself, when it had become an urban state, the Etruscans seem to have been responsible for the organization of public worship. This was arranged around the expression of three major concerns, fecundity, victory, and death:

- The purpose of the earliest rituals was to ensure the fertility of the land, and the fruitfulness of flocks and families. Thus there were the *Parilia* (or *Palilia*) and the *Lupercalia*, in honor, respectively, of Pales and Faunus, pastoral deities; the *Fordicidia*, when 30 in-calf cows were offered to the Earth; and the December *Saturnalia*, which commenced the "cereal crop cycle."
- Among the warrior rites, in March there were the dances of the Salii, the horse races of the festival of *Equirria*, and the purification ceremonies of the festivals of *Quinquatrus*, for weapons, and *Tubilustrium*, for battle trumpets, while in October the close of activities was marked by fresh purification ceremonies (*Armilustrium, Tigillum sororium, October equus*).
- The month of February was devoted to the dead (*Parentalia, Feralia*), and was also the month of purifications (*Lupercalia, Regifugium*).

Personal religion centered around the worship of the Lares, Penates, and Genius (guardian deity).

As early as the beginning of the sixth century, Roman religion came under Greek influences, though these are difficult to separate from Etruscan contributions. Via Latium came the cults of Minerva and of the Dioscuri, as we have seen; and by way of Sicily, the cult of Ceres. Moreover, with the influence of Pythagoreanism, a spiritualization of thinking and rites was taking place. Rome's religion in the sixth–fifth centuries BC therefore appears to differ considerably (though not in all points) from that of earlier times.

ROMAN RELIGION IN THE SIXTH AND FIFTH CENTURIES

The pantheon

The early trinity of Jupiter, Mars, and Quirinus gave way to Jupiter Maximus Optimus, Juno, and Minerva, the Capitoline Triad, whose cult, first established on the Quirinal, was subsequently transported to the Capitol, which had become Rome's sacred hill. A temple there, the first true temple constructed in Rome, according to the ancients, was inaugurated in 509, built in the Etruscan manner, with a tripartite cella, its sacred statues in polychrome terracotta (the statue of Jupiter created by an artist from Veii), and its architectural decoration of terracotta plaques embellished with painted reliefs. Jupiter, identified with the Etruscan Tinia by way of the Greek Zeus, is worshiped as the chief of the gods: he is supremely good (*Optimus*), in other words, the pledge of abundance (*Ops*), and supremely great (*Maximus*), master of the divine and the human world. Juno, already venerated in central Italy as the chthonic goddess, a form of the Earth-Mother and likened to the Greek Hera, who is identified with the Etruscan Uni (wife of Tinia), becomes Juno Regina, with many attributes but chiefly being the goddess of women. Minerva, identified with the Etruscan Menrva and Greek Athena, is the goddess of intelligence and spiritual activity, reigning over the arts and craftsmen.

Ritual and the organization of the priesthoods

The very simple ritual of the origins was codified in a calendar. In step with the Calends (first day of the month), the Nones (5th or 7th), and the Ides (13th or 15th), 45 annual festivals were arranged by month, classified in cycles: the war cycle from March to October, the cycle of the dead and purifications in February (the last month of the year), and the agricultural and pastoral cycle (the first part more prominent than the second), from April to December.

Plate 2.3   Colossal statue of Minerva, Roman goddess of handicrafts. National Archeological Museum, Rome.

The organization of the celebrations and strict observance of their rites were bound up with the establishment of the priesthoods (attributed by legend to Numa). The priests – religious officials – were individual or collegial, and were organized in hierarchies. At their head and honored above all the rest, came the "king of the sacred" (*rex sacrorum*), the priest of Janus, a patrician appointed for life. Then came the three major *flamines*, the *flamen Dialis* (the priest of Jupiter), the *flamen Martialis* (Mars), and the *flamen Quirinalis* (Quirinus) (a survival of the first divine trinity), and the 12 minor *flamines*, again each attached to a particular cult. The great pontiff (*pontifex maximus*) was in charge of the college of pontiffs, and later became the chief authority of the Roman religion. There were also two functional colleges: that of the Vestals for the worship of Vesta, and that of the augurs, who specialized in observing the heavens and interpreting auspices. Next came the college of the *epulones*, whose duty was to organize and supervise sacred banquets, and the college of the "men in charge of sacrifices," an important body which helped to spread the "Greek ritual" and thus to transform religious feeling. Mention must also be made of the sodalities (fraternities who specialized in piously preserved archaic rites): the Luperci, the 12 Arval Brethren (cult of Dea Dia), the 12 Salii, and the 20 Fetiales, who imparted a sacred character to declarations of war and peace treaties. The Etruscans introduced the *haruspices*, whose speciality was interpreting lightning and the entrails of sacrificial victims.

New gods and temples

As we have seen, new divinities had been brought into Rome: Minerva, the Dioscuri, Ceres. We must add Diana, who had come from Aricia on Lake Nemi (*Diana Nemorensis*); Fortuna of Praeneste, similarly revered in Antium and several towns in Latium; Hercules, the new personification of Melqart and the Greek Herakles; Mercury, patron of trade, who represented the Greek Hermes. Under Graeco-Etruscan influence, old Italic deities were transformed. For example, Liber Pater, god of fruitfulness, who, assimilated to the Etruscan Fufluns and Thracian Dionysus, became Bacchus, god of wine and resurrection. Similarly, Ceres, an expression of the Earth-Mother, was assimilated, under the influence of Sicily and Magna Graecia, to Demeter, the goddess of cereal crops and the mysteries.

From 509 onwards (with the temple of Jupiter Capitolinus), Rome built a great series of temples: to Saturn in 496, Ceres, Liber, and Libera in 496–493, Mercury in 495, and the Dioscuri in 484.

In this way a "national" religion was born, turning Rome into a sacred city, very conscious of its religious superiority. This it would use as a powerful agent of its will.

FESTIVAL CALENDAR
The three principal cycles

THE CYCLE OF PURIFICATIONS AND THE DEAD

(a) 15 February: *Lupercalia*, festival of Faunus, protector god of flocks, purification of the city.

13–21 February: *Parentalia* and *Feralia*, in honor of the family dead.

(b) 16–17 March: Procession of the *Argei*, the Vestals throw wicker effigies into the Tiber (= sacrifice of purification, cf. the Hebrew scapegoat).

(c) 9–11 May: *Lemuria*, to appease the *lemures* (= ghosts, phantoms).

THE CYCLE OF WAR

(a) 1 March: The Salii bring out the shields of Mars, god of war.

14 March: *Equirria*, dedication of the cavalry horses to Mars.

17 March: *Agonium*, sacrifice to Mars.

19 March: *Quinquatrus*, dedication of weapons to Mars, and festival of Minerva.

23 March: *Tubilustrium*: dedication of the trumpets to Mars.

(b) 15 October: *October equus*, sacrifice of a horse to Mars.

19 October: *Armilustrium*, purification of weapons. Originally marked the end of campaigns.

THE AGARIAN CYCLE

(a) 17 March: *Liberalia*, festival of Liber and Libera, god and goddess of generative functions. Assumption of the *toga virilis* (toga of manhood).

15 April: *Fordicidia*, festival of Tellus. Sacrifice of in-calf cows.

19 April: *Cerialia*, festival of Ceres, who ensures germination.

21 April: *Parilia/Palilia*, festival of Pales, protective goddess of flocks.

23 April: *Vinalia*, festival of new wine.

25 April: *Robigalia*, festival of Robigus, who prevents corn from "rust."

29 April: *Floralia*, festival of Flora, who brings crops into flower.

(b) 21 August: *Consualia*, festival of Consus, god of grain stores.

25 August: *Opalia*, festival of Ops, goddess of plenty.

(c) 11 December: *Agonium*, sacrifice of a victim.

15 December: *Consualia*, festival of Consus.

17 December: *Saturnalia*, festival of Saturn, god of fecundity; the Earth at rest is celebrated. Beginning of the liturgical year of the Arval Brethren (cult of Dea Dia, goddess of fecundity).

3 / THE YOUNG REPUBLIC
The Fifth and Fourth Centuries BC

*I*T WAS ROME'S GOOD FORTUNE TO ACHIEVE THAT URBAN SITUATION AND CONDITION OF STATEHOOD THAT PUT IT IN A POSITION TO BENEFIT FROM THE INFLUENCES OF GREEK CIVILIZATION, AND THEN TO EXPERIENCE ITS FIRST EXPANSION JUST WHEN ETRUSCAN POWER BEGAN TO DECLINE AND RIVALRIES BROKE OUT AMONG THE GREEK COLONIES. NEVERTHELESS, THE TWO CENTURIES FOLLOWING THE EXPULSION OF THE TARQUINS REMAIN "OBSCURE CENTURIES" IN ITS HISTORY. ONLY THE OUTSTANDING FEATURES ARE KNOWN. THIS IS DUE NOT ONLY TO THE PAUCITY OF LITERARY AND ARCHAEOLOGICAL SOURCES, BUT ALSO TO THE "NOBLE VANITY" (J. HEURGON) OF THE GENTES WHO WANTED TO REWRITE HISTORY IN ORDER TO ENDOW THEMSELVES WITH GLORIOUS ANCESTORS.
DESPITE THESE DIFFICULTIES, IT IS POSSIBLE TO FOLLOW THE SOMETIMES TUMULTUOUS BIRTH PROCESS OF THE REPUBLIC, MARKED CHIEFLY BY THE INSTITUTION OF THE CONSULSHIP AND THE FIRST BATTLES AGAINST THE PEOPLES OF LATIUM. IT WAS ACCOMPANIED BY PROBLEMS WITHIN THE STATE AS WELL AS IN ITS RELATIONS WITH ITS NEIGHBORS. THUS BETWEEN 450 AND 390 ROME WAS SEEKING A BALANCE IN BOTH AREAS. THIS BALANCE IT FOUND, NOT WITHOUT DIFFICULTY, IN THE ORGANIZATION OF ITS POLITICAL INSTITUTIONS AND, IN SOCIETY, BY THE FORMATION OF A NEW "NOBILITY."

THE BIRTH OF THE REPUBLIC

Around 296 BC, the pontiffs began to keep up to date and display annual records (*Annales*), with the lists of eponymous magistrates (*Fasti consulares*) serving to date them. For the preceding period they drew up lists larded with "pseudo-ancestors" of the great men of their own era. Thus, the history of the Republic's beginnings, recounted somewhat incoherently by Livy, was all the more falsified because it was more glorious for certain influential men to see their name figure in it associated with the advent of "liberty" and the first expansion of the town. Here we may see nevertheless the republican regime, after several decades of uncertainty, gradually taking shape amid social conflict and wars in Latium.

THIRTY YEARS OF UNCERTAINTY

According to annalistic records, the period 509–474 was rich in political and military events of great importance:

- 509: Departure of Tarquin under pressure from L. Junius Brutus. "I shall now retrace the political and military history of a free Rome," says Livy at the beginning of book II of his *Roman History*, "under magistrates elected for a year and under laws whose authority exceeds that of men." In the mind of the ancients, a close bond existed between the departure of the Etruscans, the end of royalty, and the advent of the Republic.
- 508: War against Tarquin, who had raised troops at Veii and Tarquinii. Intervention of Porsenna at Tarquin's request. Having taken Rome, Porsenna was subsequently defeated near Aricia by the Latins in alliance with the Cumaeans.
- 501: Threat of the Latin League against Rome, which chose a dictator aided by a master of cavalry. In 496, the victory of Rome over the Latins at Lake Regillus near Tusculum (gained with the miraculous help of the Dioscuri) brought about an alliance between the Latin League and Rome, placing Rome on an equal footing with the Latins. That alliance allowed the incursions of the Aequi and Volsci to be repulsed.
- Then conflicts in Rome between the plebeians and the patricians began. In 494, the plebeians withdrew to the Sacred Mount. At that time, inviolable tribunes of the *plebs* were appointed (and according to a certainly anachronistic view) agrarian laws were adopted.
- At the end of the period, Rome found itself engaged in difficult wars against its powerful neighbor, Veii. In 476, having defeated the Veians on the Janiculum, Rome took full advantage of its victory. Two years later, in 474, the Etruscans were vanquished at Cumae by the Cumaeans and their Syracusan allies.

Modern critics have attempted to sort out the true from the false in the annalistic records, the share of historical concealments, errors, and connivances on the part of the *gentes*. The change in the regime remained the matter of prime importance: the move from a sacred royalty to a regime in which power was exercised, collegially or not, by magistrates appointed for a fixed period of time. This was not, incidentally, a purely Roman occurrence; the replacement of the *rex* by a single, supreme magistrate or by groups of magistrates (praetors or consuls) was a phenomenon common to numerous towns in Latium, Etruria, and the Osco-Umbrian territory. In Rome, it appears that, on the passing of royalty, power was exercised first by a *praetor maximus*, named M. Horatius – he is said to have dedicated the temple of Jupiter Capitolinus in 509. At the time, *praetor* meant magistrate; and *maximus* implies that there were several. In fact, Rome was doing no more than borrowing the Etruscan institution of the *zilath* (= in Latin, *praetores*). Later, probably in 449, following the Decemvirate, two consuls were substituted for the praetors: this was a specifically Roman innovation. The consular regime, annual and collegial, became the most characteristic institution of the Republic.

These transformations occurred not in an orderly and tranquil setting, but in the midst of wars and internal conflicts, with events as their handmaiden or midwife.

EXTERNAL WARS

Recent archaeological discoveries made in Latium, at Lanuvium, Satricum (40 km south of Rome), and Falerii (Città Castellana), show that there, as in Etruscan country (Veii, Tarquinii), Etrusco-Greek workshops were in operation producing religious statues and architectural ornamental terracottas of high quality right up until 480–475. These symptoms of an "architectural and religious fever" of Etruscan and Greek inspiration prove that the influence in Latium of those two worlds remained predominant in spite of the conflicts.

These conflicts were, of course, connected with questions of frontiers. Rome's territory, the *ager Romanus*, must have extended to around the fifth or sixth *mille* (thousand paces), particularly toward the Alban Hills: each year the festival of the *Ambarvalia* was marked by a sacrifice celebrated in chapels erected at about the fifth *mille* of every Roman road, the most famous chapel being that of the Arvales on the via Campana. North of the Tiber it encompassed the lands dominated by the Romilii and the Fabii families. Toward the Alban Hills, it included the towns of Bovillae and Alba and the lands of the Papirii bordering on Tusculum. Seaward, the infertile *ager Solonius* extended toward the hinterland of Ardea and Aricia. Toward Sabine country, the alliance in about 504 with the Sabine chief Attius Clausus, who had come to Rome to enrol among the patricians, had not resolved anything – protracted wars became a feature of relations with the Sabines. Frontier problems arose with all these neighboring Latin towns (Ardea, Aricia, and above all Tusculum, which seems to have been pre-eminent at the beginning of the fifth century), as well as the Sabines to the north-east (and, indeed, the Etruscans to the north-west).

From all this stemmed a series of very complex wars:

- With the Latins: in 496 the Roman victory at Lake Regillus brought about the conclusion of a treaty of alliance with them (493), setting Rome on an equal footing. This was an important moment for Rome.
- Against the Volsci, with the help of the Latins, who were joined by the Hernici, a people wedged between the Aequi and the Volsci.

■ Against the Sabines, whose incursions had increased. These lasted until 448, and began again 150 years later.

By defending itself staunchly against its powerful neighbors, Rome began to establish its authority in Latium. And it did so in spite of sometimes bitter internal conflicts.

INTERNAL DIFFICULTIES

The expulsion of the Tarquins having been due in part to the action of patrician families hostile to the Etruscan tyrants, with the backing of the people, it used to be thought that the patricians were at first the only ones to exercise the office of magistrate, before gradually yielding their prerogatives to the plebeians. Recent work has shown that, on the contrary, the plebeians entered history as a political force just after that date. Whereas the patriciate, a senatorial nobility formed as early as the seventh century from powerful families who had emerged from the *patres* (forefathers), was a socially coherent body, assured by hereditary title of certain monopolies, notably religious, the plebeians represented an extremely heterogeneous group of all those who did not belong to the elite, in other words those who were neither patricians nor their clients but for the most part small property owners, artisans, and shopkeepers (classes of persons especially numerous in the Aventine quarter, on the banks of the Tiber, the site of the *emporium*, the first port installation). Shortly after the disappearance of the *regnum* (royal rule), these plebeians found themselves in difficulties. Bad harvests and even a shortage of food made themselves felt (hence the appeal to agrarian deities in 496–493); debts, contracted by small property owners after borrowing at already extortionate rates, became a problem; and a slowing down of business occurred, noticeable in the pottery-vessel trade (hence perhaps the appeal to Mercury).

A close and critical scrutiny of the *fasti* reveals the presence of 12 plebeian consuls between the years 509 and 486, including Sp. Cassius, who had imposed the alliance of 493 on the Latin League.

It seems that in fact the period 509–486 was marked by vigorous political agitations. Notably, there was the withdrawal of the plebeians to the Aventine and to the Sacred Mount across the Anio (generally dated 494). It was a dangerous secession for the patricians, who were thus deprived of their manual workers, as well as for the state, threatened with the creation of a rival state that might ally itself with Rome's enemies, since many plebeians were of foreign origin. It is supposed to have been followed by the appointment of the first tribunes of the *plebs*, two at first, then in 471 four, according to Diodorus, who seems to consider these four to be the earliest.

As an examination of the *fasti* also reveals that between 485 and 470 not a single plebeian consul made an appearance, the conclusion has been drawn that a patrician clamp-down took place at that point, corresponding with the accession to power of the mighty family of the Fabii (then engaged in a war against Veii). From 485 up till 461 only one plebeian managed to become consul. One scents a whiff of bitter internal struggles.

It is understandable that these conflicts, coupled with external wars, should have led, in the middle of the fifth century BC, to the advent of the Decemvirate.

THE DECEMVIRS AND THEIR TASK

The creation of the Decemvirate marked a decisive moment in the history of Roman institutions and civilization. In order to obtain a written code of law and a status that together would put an end to the arbitrary nature of the consular power and of the privileges of the patricians, the plebeians engaged in a long struggle. According to tradition, they organized their own people's assembly based on the territorial tribes (four for the town and 21 for the rural areas of that time); and these "meetings of the *plebs*" (*concilia plebis*), called together by the tribunes, began to take decisions. Again according to tradition, in 462 a tribune, Terentilius Harsa, led a campaign to obtain "written laws establishing the *imperium*," in other words, the limits of consular power. In the end, the patricians yielded.

THE COLLEGE OF DECEMVIRS

In 451 and 450, the consular *fasti* interrupt their regular listings and note the advent of a college of ten extraordinary magistrates, elected, invested with consular authority, and charged with the task of "making laws so that liberty shall be equal for all, from the highest to the lowest" (Livy III.31.7; 34.3). The tribunes of the *plebs* had stood down at the same time as the consuls. The Decemvirs thus had full powers to draw up a legal code. As they had not completed their task at the end of their annual term, a second Decemvirate was elected in May 450 and included plebeians. The integrity of the first group of men was matched by the iniquity of the second. In 449, they tried to make their power permanent. Against them, the *plebs* had to resort to a new secession to the Aventine, and a revolution drove them out of office.

The work of the Decemvirs, now recognized as genuine, was of exceptional importance. Ten Tables of law were drawn up in 451; two more in 450. According to Livy (V.34.6), they contained "the source of all private and public law." Legal experts consider that "with the XII Tables, the Republic developed the most important legislative monument conceived by Rome until the compilations of Justinian" (M. Humbert).

The law of the XII Tables

Before the law was drawn up, it seems that embassies were sent to Greece. Moreover, it is extremely probable that it was inspired not only by Solon's Athenian legislation, but also by that of the lawgivers Zaleucus for Locri and Charondas for Thurii, two towns in Magna Graecia.

The law was exhibited in the Forum on twelve bronze tables, and from then on was learnt by heart by all young Romans – that was still so in Cicero's time. It is known only through mutilated fragments, which, however, allow an appreciation of the whole. Its style was judged to be "dazzling in its clarity, restraint, and conciseness; it attained so high a level of culture" that one is led to believe that it followed a Greek model, or to envisage a later composition (perhaps of the fourth–third century) or, in any event, that it was embellished after the fifth century.

Nevertheless, whatever its precise history, it simultaneously established a legal code and the ground for enduring political institutions.

A legal code

The task of the legislators was to ensure that the law would be equal for all citizens. As indicated by their title (*decemviri legibus scribundis*), it was also a matter of replacing customary law by written law. Henceforward were established:

1 The personal rights of citizens. Property ownership and the family were recognized as fundamentals of the social order. The distinction between *proprietas* (ownership, property), known as "Quirite," and *possessio* (exclusive use or enjoyment) being recognized as an irrefutable fact, the law laid down that, after certain customary time limits, *possessio* could become *proprietas*. The law governing the acquisition of property varied according to whether rural land and livestock were involved (*res mancipi*) or other forms of wealth. In the first type of case there had to be a special formality (*mancipatio*) undergone in the presence of witnesses. It is clear that society was essentially rural, a population in the main of farmers and stockbreeders. Similarly, major crimes were defined: theft, attacks on crops, bearing false witness. Guardianship and the order of inheritance were formalized. Within the family, the limits of paternal authority were fixed. The father of the family ruled no longer the *gens*, but only the *familia* (wife and children); his power was reduced; and a certain amount of female emancipation was provided for. The father still had the right to sell, repurchase, and resell his child, up to three times; after that the child was "emancipated."

2 Relations between citizens and the system of justice. State justice was made accessible to all. In any conflict, the injured party had to try to settle matters with the guilty party; if an agreement was impossible, it was permissible to resort to the "talionic law" (an eye for an eye). The dates, times, and places prescribed for a court appearance had to be notified. And procedural time limits were fixed. Resort to the death penalty was rendered more difficult. And religious preoccupations often made an appearance: *sacer esto* (a phrase used as a curse: let him be taboo!) cut the condemned man off from the community and consigned him to the infernal gods. The state of insolvent debtors was improved, but laws concerning debtors who had been sentenced remained harsh.

A constitutionally important feature was that the death sentence could be pronounced only by the sovereign assembly of the people, that is, the *comitia centuriata*. Thus, for common law crimes (murder by sorcery, arson, false witness causing death) and political crimes, consular criminal jurisdiction disappeared. The consuls kept only their coercive, administrative, and policing power – they therefore retained their lictors, who implemented their right of arrest and summons.

3 The status of the citizen. It is to be noted that within the law a distinction was established between the rich (*assidui*) and the poor (*proletarii*) rather than between patricians and plebeians. As regards the latter, the last two Tables prohibited marriage between members of the patriciate and members of the *plebs*. This seems to illustrate a reaction on the part of the nobles in the face of the rise of the *plebs*; the patricians were seen as a kind of caste. This arrangement, which Cicero considered "inhuman," was revoked in 445 by the Canuleian law.

Political institutions

Once it had been drawn up by the Decemvirs, the law of the XII Tables was submitted to the *comitia centuriata*, who voted for it. It was thus the first "voted law" (*lex rogata*). That decisive action guaranteed the legislative function of this people's assembly (*populus* = the whole body of citizens as distinguished from the *plebs*). By their action, the *comitia* created by Servius Tullius entered "the republican constitutional field of play" (M. Humbert).

However, concerning the institutions of state proper, and chiefly the magistracies, it was the Valerian-Horatian laws of 449, the "logical and immediate consequence" of the law of the XII Tables, that made the constitutional rulings.

THE *LEGES VALERIAE-HORATIAE*

The restoration of the Republic in 449 brought two consuls to power, L. Valerius and M. Horatius, who according to tradition got three laws passed by which the Roman constitution became patricio-plebeian.

1 The inviolability of the tribunes was recognized and confirmed: "Anyone who strikes the tribunes of the *plebs* or the aediles [their assistants] will be consigned to Jupiter, and his goods will be sold to the benefit of Ceres, Liber, and Libera." The guilty person was thus accursed.

2 Official authority was recognized for *plebiscita*, that is, decisions of the *concilia plebis*, acknowledged as decisions of the *populus* assembled in *comitia tributa*. Actually, plebiscites gained the force of law (unconditionally) only after 286 (Hortensian law).

3 The renunciation of consular sovereignty. It became illegal in the future to create a new magistracy without appeal to the people.

Virtually from that moment two very important innovations were brought in:

- The introduction of consular collegiality.
- Official acknowledgement of tribunician *intercessio* or veto: if the tribunes were unanimous, they could block a decision of the consuls which they considered contrary to the interests of the *plebs*. Only the dictator, during his short-lived *imperium*, could escape the tribunes' *intercessio*.

The three Valerian-Horatian laws set the official seal on the gains won by the *plebs*, and patrician Rome gave up the sovereignty of the consular *imperium*. It is understandable that Polybius should have dated the second founding of the Roman constitution from this point.

One fundamental matter was still not settled: plebeian access to the consulship, the supreme magistracy. Nothing prohibited it – but nothing permitted it. Basing itself on tradition (the *mos maiorum* or ancestral right), the patriciate firmly intended to preserve its monopoly. The *plebs*, for its part, mobilized to break that monopoly.

In Search of Equilibrium (449–312 BC)

Examination of the *fasti* reveals struggles which, on this matter of plebeians attaining the consulship, set the *plebs* against the patriciate until 367, the date of the Licinio-Sextian compromise.

Patrician resistance and plebeian demands

It is noteworthy that from 449 to 446 only patricians occupied places in the consular colleges. In 445, one plebeian was to be found. Between 444 and 441, once again only patricians were consuls. In 440 and 439, two plebeians crept in. But from 438 to 435 only patricians were appointed.

In the face of plebeian demands, the patricians tried to fob them off. They instituted military tribunes with consular power (that is, armed with the *imperium*), a magistracy which was open to plebeians but which, at the end of the term of office, did not confer the right to the same privileges as the consulship, namely the consular title, a place of honor in the Senate, the purple toga, and the right to have portraits of ancestors (*ius imaginum*). From 444 – though the college of that year was contested: one patrician and two plebeians – to 432, there seem to have been three of them in each college. The number rose to four from 426 to 406 and became six from 405 to 367.

According to some authors, the institution of the military tribunate was in response less to political demands than to military needs: the necessity to wage war on various fronts. And indeed, as we shall see, Rome in this period found itself facing numerous enemies and grappling with increasingly important wars.

ROME AND ITS ENEMIES

From 444 until 290, conflicts – some very serious – followed one another in Latium, with Veii, with Gaulish invaders, and in Campania.

1 In Latium, Rome, which had been placed on an equal footing with the Latin League and was linked with Aricia by a treaty of alliance, was made arbiter in 444 in a conflict between Aricia and Ardea. It took advantage of that to award itself the territory of Corioli, which opened up the Pontine plain.

2 Conflict broke out around 437 with Veii, the southernmost of the Etruscan cities. The cause was the city of Fidenae, which Veii held in order to control the salt route (*Via Salaria*) and the grain trade between Campania and Etruria, and which Rome wanted to acquire. This important site was captured in 435. Subsequently, Rome attacked Veii itself, and won it after a siege lasting ten years (406–396), led by the dictator Camillus (M. Furius Camillus), who proceeded to "evoke" Juno-Uni, the tutelary goddess of the city (i.e. to call upon the goddess to quit the town): Veii was destroyed and its land annexed by Rome.

In 398, Rome had to wage war against Volsinii and Tarquinii. At that time, Volsinii was the religious center of the Etruscan confederation (the *fanum Voltumnae*). Rome had to break off hostilities and make peace in 390, at the time of the first Gaulish invasion.

3 The first half of the fourth century BC was marked by a historical phenomenon of major political and psychological importance for Rome: the second wave of Celtic invasions.

The civilization of the second Iron Age (known as that of La Tène), which had spread through Europe at the end of the fifth century, was national and, led by an enterprising peasantry enticed by the rich valley lands and the sunshine of the southern countries, and by their reputation for wealth, was intent

Plate 3.1 Gallic prisoner with hands bound. Roman bronze statuette, 1st century BC. British Museum.

on conquest. Perhaps driven on as well by other peoples, between 390 and 329 these predatory barbarians undertook three movements in Italy. The first, between 390 and 380, ended in the capture of Rome. Roman tradition has provided an account of the event, as detailed as it is suspect. Led by Brennus, the Gauls are said to have defeated first the Etruscans near Clusium, then the Romans on the banks of the Allia, a tributary of the Tiber, before seizing Rome itself. Installed on the Forum, they were yet unable to take the Capitol, which was defended by Manlius. Sacked and held to ransom, Rome, it is said, was occupied from July 18, 390 until the following February. Livy's account, however, does not match the list of eponymous magistrates, and today the capture of Rome tends to be dated no earlier than 381. In the end the Gauls retreated, themselves threatened by the Veneti and Alpine peoples.

The Gauls descended a second time in around 358–354, and a notable event during this incursion was the capture of Felsina, to which the Boian Celts gave

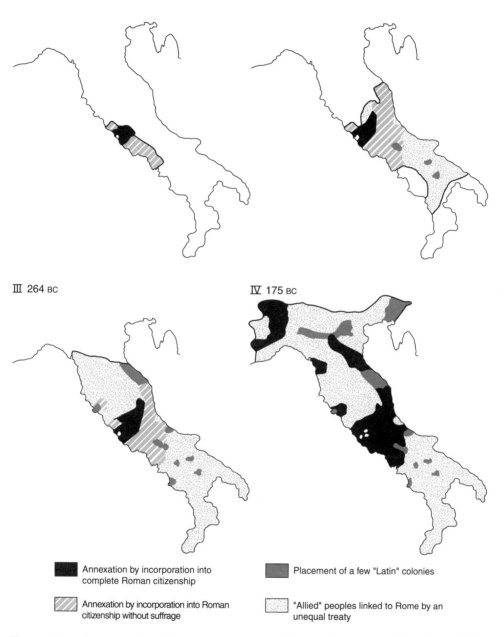

Figure 3.1 The conquest of Italy and organization of territories (from M. Humbert, *Institutions politiques et sociales de l'Antiquité*, Dalloz, 1989)

the name Bononia (Bologna). The invaders ventured into Latium, and some bands as far as Apulia. Confronted by the Romans mobilized by Camillus, they retreated, ravaging Etruria on their way.

A third wave of invaders surged down in around 347–343. Rome was again threatened, but was saved by the dictator L. Furius. In 332–329, one last Gaulish threat hung over Latium, but this time Rome, which had become master of Latium and Campania, imposed a 30-year peace on the Gauls.

If the Gauls' capture of Rome had lamentable historiographical consequences because of the destruction of monuments and archives that it brought about, it also had the effect of strengthening the morale of the Romans, of bringing to the fore amongst them several remarkable men, and of firmly fixing in the Roman mind the memory of the *tumultus Gallicus*, those disorderly hordes of barbarians fighting against all established rules. When Caesar conquered the Gauls, that memory was still vividly present.

4 Between 380 and 291, after succeeding in intimidating Tusculum into accepting a *foedus aequum* (treaty of alliance between equals), which was followed by the submission of those Latin towns that had hitherto been recalcitrant, the pacification of the lands of the Volsci, and the capitulation of Tibur, it was above all in Campania that Rome had to take action.

Master of Latium, Rome found itself a neighbor of the Samnites, who, since the fifth century, had formed a Campanian state whose capital was Capua, which had developed from a simple agricultural center into a large town. In 354, an agreement was sealed between the Romans and the Samnites. Thirteen years later, in 341 (not 343, as tradition would have it), the first of the three Samnite Wars took place:

- First Samnite War: 341.
- Second Samnite War: 327–304.
- Third Samnite War: 298–291.

These were three terrible wars, in which Roman successes were not unbroken and victories far from assured: in 321, two vanquished Roman legions had to pass under the enemy yoke (disaster of the Caudine Forks); in 295, the Battle of Sentinum in northern Umbria was won only after the *devotio* of P. Decius Mus. But once the submission of the Samnites was achieved, these wars resulted in:

- The turning of Capua into a federated municipality (in 334), prior to its annexation between 318 and 312.
- The dissolution of the Latin League and the setting up of Roman colonies in Latium – the port of Ostia was founded about 335.

- The creation of a Roman–Campanian state by agreement between the Roman and Capuan aristocracies, with a shared army and a Roman Senate that welcomed the great Campanian families, notably the Atilii, whose dynamism helped to commit Rome to a maritime policy.
- Entry into direct contact with both the Greek cities of Magna Graecia (Tarentum for example) and the Italic peoples who were in open conflict with those cities. This contact swiftly drew Rome toward the south.
- Contact with Punic Carthage. The Carthaginians had long maintained connections with the Etruscans (see the Pyrgi tablets with bilingual inscriptions), chiefly with the town of Caere, of which Pyrgi was the port. Rome made an alliance with Caere (later a Roman *municipium*, a free town subject to Rome) and in 348 concluded a treaty with Carthage – the first, according to Diodorus Siculus. Livy mentions it, but without saying that it was the first. Polybius, on the other hand, dates the first Roman–Carthaginian treaty to 509 BC. Then it was a question of demarcating the trading and colonization zones of each of the two parties: Rome could not trade in either Sardinia or Africa, except in Carthage, but could do so in Carthaginian Sicily.

It is easy to understand that so many battles and external difficulties in a period of political instability and patrician–plebeian rivalry should have finally led to the compromise found in the Licinio-Sextian plebiscite of 367.

THE LICINIO-SEXTIAN COMPROMISE OF 367 AND ITS CONSEQUENCES

As we have seen, the political situation in Rome had been somewhat confused since 444. After 377 it had been singularly worsened by the activities of two tribunes of the *plebs*, C. Licinius and L. Sextius, who were returned to office ten years running and sowed the seeds of anarchy by boycotting elections and paralyzing the action of the consuls by using their veto. On several occasions, the Senate had to appeal to a dictator to save the situation. Eventually, "a cartel of new men, a midway formation composed of second-order patricians and front-ranking plebeians," was formed (Heurgon). The Senate accepted the famous Licinio-Sextian plebiscite of 367, which settled the following three questions:

- The question of debts, by means of legislation against usury, the institution of a moratorium, and a reduction of current debts.
- The agrarian question, by limiting the extent of possession of lands of the *ager publicus*, that is, lands that had been conquered and annexed and had thus become the property of the Roman people.

■ The question of access to the consulship. This was the main point of the reform. The consulship was re-established. It was now specified that one of the two consuls might be a plebeian. L. Sextius was the first plebeian consul elected as such, and C. Licinius the third (in 364). This decision was a milestone in the history of the Republic's institutions. For the first time, plebeian access to the supreme office was codified.

<h2 style="text-align:center">THE ESTABLISHMENT OF REPUBLICAN PUBLIC OFFICES</h2>

Immediately after this "capitulation," the patricians reacted by imposing new magistracies, reserved for their own members and endowed with powers taken from the consuls. However, during the following decades, the plebeians managed to obtain access to these also.

■ The praetorship for a judiciary magistrate was created in 366. The office was held at first by a single magistrate, who was in charge of civil justice and criminal jurisdiction. He was armed with a civil and military *imperium*, but one inferior to that of the consuls (he was entitled to only six lictors, as opposed to twelve for the consuls). The plebeians gained access to this office in 356.
■ The curule aedileship was introduced, an office entrusted to two magistrates whose duties were to oversee, together with the aediles of the *plebs*, the provisioning of Rome and market regulations. The office was opened to plebeians in 364.
■ In 356, plebeians were similarly eligible for the dictatorship, an office with sovereign, but temporary power, its limit fixed by the accomplishment of a specific task. In 351, it was the turn of the censorship to be opened to plebeians. This office had been created in 443 to carry out a five yearly census of citizens and their assets. Lastly, in 300, the office and dignity of the *pontifex maximus*, last refuge of patrician monopoly, yielded. The *plebs* thus ended up in triumph everywhere. By the close of the fourth century the patrician–plebeian state had been established.

<h2 style="text-align:center">THE ADVENT OF A NEW NOBILITY</h2>

This settlement in Roman society succeeded in giving the Republic the equilibrium, so admired by Polybius, which allowed it to embark on its conquest of the world.

Recent research has in fact emphasized a certain decline of the old patriciate and the appearance of more-open patrician families, such as the Fabii, who no longer disdained to ally themselves with plebeian families (C. Licinius himself seems to have become the son-in-law of a Fabius). At the same time, certain plebeian families began to stand out, acquiring wealth and esteem. Thus a "center party" was formed at the same time as there developed in society a new *nobilitas*, a nobility composed of those, both patrician and plebeian, with an ancestor who had held curule magistracies (aedileship, praetorship, and, above all, consulship).

This new state of affairs naturally brought its own consequences. The Senate was no longer under firm patrician control. The plebeians had a secure place in it. Plebiscites vested with the "authority" of the senators (*auctoritas patrum*) were the equivalent of "laws." And at some time between 318 and 313, the Ovinian plebiscite widened the powers of censors (among whom there had been plebeians since 351) for drawing up the list of senators (the *album senatorium*).

This long history of the *plebs'* political conquests in the fourth century was completed with the great censorship of Appius Claudius Caecus (the Blind) in 312. This highly-colored personage, heir of the Sabine founder of the *gens Claudia*, Attius Clausus, was the first to give his "family" that prominence which rendered it still illustrious under the Empire. A man of vast culture, author of *Sententiae* in Saturnian verse, he made himself famous by two important institutional actions: getting the sons of emancipated slaves admitted to the Senate, and then reorganizing the composition of the "tribes" so as to enable the lower classes (the *humiles*) and freedmen (*liberti*) to be included in them. This open-minded patrician was symbolic of the new nobility then gaining power. But it should also be noted that, by having the Via Appia built from Rome to Capua, he was expressing the expansionist designs of all those among the Romans who were looking toward Magna Graecia and extolling the greatness of Rome.

THE REPUBLIC'S INSTITUTIONS AT THE END OF THE FOURTH CENTURY

After the decemviral reforms and the democratic victories that followed them, the institutions of Rome remained those of an aristocratic republic. A Senate governed, and by its side magistrates ran the state, while the assemblies of the people had their say in the election of magistrates and voting on laws.

THE MAGISTRATES

As Rome lacked a written constitution, magistracies were established as and when they were needed. They were at the same time (in order to avoid a return to personal, tyrannical power) hierarchized, specialized, elective, collegial, and annual.

The only ones to escape election were the "dictator," the "master of cavalry," and the *interrex*. "Dictatorship" was a formal magistracy, but exceptional because of its time limitation (confined to the accomplishment of a precise mission and on no account allowed to last longer than six months) and its removal of collegiality. The dictator, appointed by the consuls on the decision of the Senate, exercised his office only in the civil domain; in military matters he was represented by a "master of cavalry," chosen by himself. With his 24 lictors, the dictator held simultaneously the *imperium* of the two consuls. He thus had sovereign power, though this did not abolish the other magistracies – they were merely subject to his authority for a limited period. And he was not subject to the *intercessio* of the tribunes. Though recourse to the dictatorship was frequent in the fifth and fourth centuries, it became rare in the third, except during the Punic Wars, after which it disappeared until Sulla. The *interrex* was co-opted by patrician senators in the event of the abrupt death or resignation of both consuls. His remit – which lasted only five days – was to have new consuls elected and pass the auspices on to them. Those magistracies which required no election were also exceptions to the rule of annual tenure. So too was the censorship, which lasted eighteen months and was confirmed only every five years.

The ordinary magistrates (censors, consuls, praetors, aediles, tribunes, and quaestors) were thus elected, some (censors and the senior magistrates *cum imperio*, that is, with both civil and military power, jurisdictional and coercive, implying the right to take the auspices: consuls and praetors) by the *comitia centuriata*, the others (minor magistrates: aediles, tribunes, and quaestors) by the *comitia tributa* – thus all by people's assemblies.

ROMAN MAGISTRACIES

- Dictatorship: exceptional and for a limited period. Assistance of a "master of cavalry" for military affairs.
- Censorship: every five years. Duration: 18 months.
- Senior magistracies (with civil and military power): annual and collegial:

  = consulship
  = praetorship

- Minor magistracies (civil power): annual and collegial:

  = aedileship
  = tribunate of the *plebs*
  = quaestorship

The two censors, their office created, as we saw, in 443, were compulsorily former consuls, but had no *imperium* (and therefore no lictors). Their mission was threefold: to take a census of citizens, whom they had to classify, and their possessions, which they had to assess in order to determine the political rights and military duties of each one; to establish the *album senatorium*, with the related right of exclusion for infamy, a power conferred by the Ovinian plebiscite around 318–313; and lastly, to manage the state's patrimony, in particular in the renting out of the *ager publicus* (the collective property of the Roman people, formed from military conquests), the allocation of public lands, the construction and maintenance of public buildings, etc. They were the state's high moral authority.

The two consuls were in some ways the presidents of the Republic. They held the *imperium domi militiaeque*, that is, the *imperium domi*, a sovereign political, judicial, and coercive power within the *pomoerium* (the sacred boundaries of Rome), and the *imperium militiae*, a sovereign military and jurisdictional power in the extra-urban domain.

The praetorship was held by a single praetor, from 366, entrusted with civil jurisdiction (*praetor urbanus*), coupled with another magistrate, after 242, in charge of lawsuits between Roman citizens and foreigners, or between foreigners residing in Rome (*praetor peregrinus*). Others would be created later for provincial administration.

At the time of their creation, in 493, the aediles were at first plebeian. Later, in 366, two curule aedileships were created, patrician to start with and then open to the *plebs*. The aediles had no *imperium*. Their function was to look after the provisioning of Rome, and to care for markets, public order, and the public games.

The four quaestors, dating from the earliest days of the Republic, had chiefly financial powers, in particular concerning the administration of the public treasury (*aerarium*). In the third century, two other quaestors were made responsible for the issuing of currency. Later, others were sent to Sicily and Sardinia.

The tribunes of the *plebs* were magistrates somewhat apart. Compulsorily plebeian originally, they enjoyed a sacrosanct or inviolable person and exercised a major power (only dictators and censors could escape it). Their power of veto could be exercised against any decision by other magistrates, and their power of *auxilium* allowed them to safeguard any citizen who placed himself under their protection. They played an ever-increasing role in the following centuries.

THE PEOPLE'S ASSEMBLIES

The people's assemblies brought together the entire *populus*, i.e. the whole civic community of the *Quirites*. Roman citizenship, whether original (that of the

Plate 3.2 Relief depicting senators.

ingenui) or acquired by emancipation (for *liberti*), consisted of an ensemble of (unevenly distributed) rights and duties. At the end of the fourth century, the whole of the Roman citizen body numbered between 200,000 and 250,000 (adult males), and citizens acted within three assemblies of unequal importance.

The curiate assembly was a relic of the royal epoch, when citizens were grouped in thirty *curiae*. It no longer met, except for formalities – voting on the *lex de imperio*, or law of investiture of magistrates, was the principal one. Early in the Republic the *curiae* were replaced in the proceedings of the assembly by 30 lictors. Thus may be seen how much this institution had deteriorated.

The centuriate assembly was the largest of the people's assemblies. It represented the *populus* divided into five classes and 193 *centuriae*, each of the latter being a voting unit. As we have seen, the first class, with its 98 *centuriae* and the richest citizens, enjoyed an absolute majority. That privilege was further strengthened through a voting practice by virtue of which the *centuria* called upon to cast the first vote (known as a prerogative) was always chosen, randomly, from the 18 equestrian *centuriae* of the first class, the vote of the first most frequently influencing that of the following *centuriae*. When a majority was obtained, voting stopped. In practice, the second class voted only rarely, and the third only in very exceptional circumstances. The *comitia centuriata* elected senior magistrates, military leaders, and censors; and they voted on important laws, such as constitutional laws, formally declared war, etc.

The *comitia tributa* or tribal assembly, reorganized in 312 by Appius Claudius, represented the *populus* divided into "tribes," originally actual tribes but by then tribally denominated groups of individuals, henceforward including the *humiles* (laborers, the proletariat). It elected minor magistrates and voted on plebiscites. It also had judicial competence in matters concerning a public crime for which the penalty did not exceed a fine.

The council of the *plebs* (*concilium plebis*) stood rather apart from the rest. It was an assembly of the *plebs* only, convened by a tribune. From the time when plebiscites gained the force of law, there was a tendency to merge it with the tribal assembly, which was convened, and thus presided over, by a magistrate with *imperium*, and in which plebeians were broadly in the majority.

THE SENATE

The Senate was the paramount assembly of the Republic. Although at the end of the fourth century it did not yet have the fundamental role it played after the Second Punic War, Cicero's words may already be applied to it (*Pro Sestio* 117): "Our ancestors made the Senate the guardian, the defender, the protector of the state; they wanted the magistrates to be the ministers, so to speak, of this imposing Council."

Since the Ovinian law of ca. 318–313, the composition of the Senate had been in the hands of the censors, who, choosing from among "the best," revised the list of its 300 members every five years. In fact, its great stability is noteworthy. Its members (the *seniores* or *patres*) were all former senior magistrates (former censors, consuls, praetors) – later, former curule aediles would enter, and later still, former tribunes. Meeting at the summons of a higher magistrate, who presided over the session, the senators gave their opinion on every matter submitted to them, the first man invited to speak being the *princeps senatus*, the leader or senior man in the Senate, a patrician and former censor. Then other senators could have their turn to speak, in order of their former office. Each member's opinion (*sententia*) having been given, the senators proceeded to vote. The decision, expressing the state's supreme authority (*auctoritas*), was a *senatus consultum* (or decree of the Senate), advice which virtually bound the magistrates.

The authority of the Senate, though still not general, already covered a wide field. Besides the decrees, it expressed itself in the transformation of plebiscites into laws, the supervision of the magistrates' activities, and the supreme control of finances, international affairs, general administration, and justice. In essence, it already guided the policies of Rome. Given that the senators were recruited solely from the nobility, and that the latter, as we have seen, increasingly included people, Italian and soon from outside Italy, who were open to the wider world, one might well wonder what the Senate's role would be in Rome's new politics.

4 / THE GROWTH OF THE REPUBLIC
War and Conquest in the Third Century BC

*O*N THE BRINK OF THE THIRD CENTURY BC, AFTER THE *T*HIRD *S*AMNITE *W*AR, THERE WAS ONLY ONE STATE FROM THE *T*IBER TO *C*UMAE AND FROM THE *T*YRRHENIAN *S*EA TO *L*AKE *F*ICINO. *R*OME AT THAT TIME SEEMED TO BE A CITY THAT HAD MANAGED TO GET THE UPPER HAND OF ITS INTERNAL POLITICAL CONFLICTS. *I*T POSSESSED WELL-BALANCED INSTITUTIONS. *A*LTHOUGH IN THE SOCIAL FIELD NOT EVERYTHING HAD BEEN RESOLVED, ITS TERRITORIAL EXPANSION WAS ALREADY ALLOWING IT AN ECONOMIC DEVELOPMENT THAT WOULD GROW STILL FURTHER, AND A MILITARY STRENGTH CAPABLE OF COPING WITH THE CONQUESTS OPENING UP BEFORE IT. *R*OME FOUND ITSELF INCREASINGLY INVOLVED IN *I*TALIAN AFFAIRS, NOTABLY IN THE SOUTH. *H*ENCE, ITS CONTACTS WITH THE *G*REEK WORLD MULTIPLIED, BRINGING IN THEIR WAKE A *H*ELLENIZATION OF ART AND RELIGION IN THE THROES OF TRANSFORMATION, BUT ALSO AN INCREASINGLY ACTIVE ENGAGEMENT BY THE *R*OMAN *R*EPUBLIC IN *M*EDITERRANEAN AFFAIRS. *O*NLY THERE WOULD *R*OMAN INTERESTS ENCOUNTER AND CLASH WITH THE *C*ARTHAGINIAN INTERESTS WHICH LARGELY DOMINATED IN THE WESTERN BASIN. *F*ROM THAT WOULD ARISE A STRUGGLE BETWEEN *R*OME AND *C*ARTHAGE WHICH, BY ITS DURATION, ITS BITTERNESS, THE MEANS EMPLOYED, AND THE SUCCESSIVE INVOLVEMENT OF NEARLY ALL THE INHABITANTS OF THE *M*EDITERRANEAN SHORES, ASSUMED THE DIMENSIONS OF A DECISIVE CRISIS OF TRANSFORMATION FOR THE *W*EST.

ECONOMY, SOCIETY, ARMY

Naturally, the field, pasture, and grove dominated the Roman economy. As in all ancient civilizations, the rural economy was its life's blood, and this remained a subsistence economy. In view of the richness of Campania's fields and groves, the formation of a Roman–Campanian state was therefore an important event economically as well as politically. While Latium appears to have been given over as much to crop-growing as to pasture, the raising of livestock played an important part, with the seasonal movements of flocks and herds spreading out toward Sabine territory. Medium-sized and small properties seem to have been preponderant at that time. At all events, it was not until the end of the third century that the massive arrival of slaves and the first

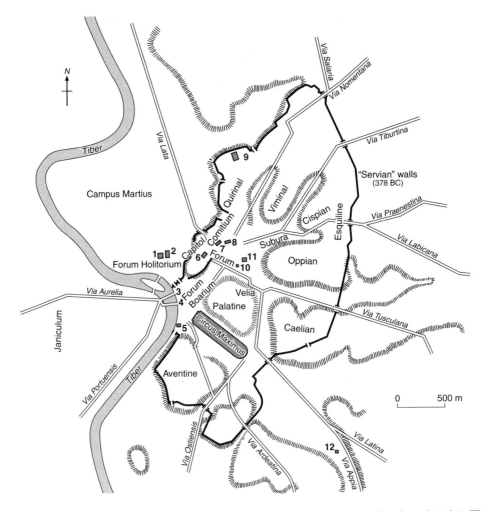

Figure 4.1 The city of Rome in the early third century BC (after F. W. Walbank et al. (eds), *The Cambridge Ancient History*, 2nd edn, CUP, 1989, vol. 7, pt. 2)

1 temple of Apollo (431 BC) 2 temple of Bellona (296 BC) 3 Aemilian bridge 4 Sublician bridge 5 temple of Ceres (493 BC) 6 temple of Saturn (497 BC) 7 Rostra (338 BC) 8 temple of Janus 9 temple of Quirinus (293 BC) 10 temple of Vesta 11 Regia 12 tomb of the Scipios

consequences of foreign wars contributed to the formation of the first large-scale properties.

Nevertheless, as we have seen, as early as the end of the sixth century, the problem had arisen of the debts contracted by small owners committed to excessive borrowing. And in the middle of the fifth the law of the XII Tables had intervened in questions of property to defend the rights of citizens against the "powerful."

On the economic plane, the great event of the first third of the third century was the appearance of Roman coinage, its creation bearing witness both to Rome's economic development and to the new direction of its economy. The origins of the striking of coinage lay in the cities of Asia Minor in the seventh century BC. Rome waited until the beginnings of the war with Pyrrhus, king of Epirus, before it had any money struck. This was a bronze coinage (the *aes grave*). The monetary unit was the *as*, weighing one Roman pound (324 g), this unit being divided into 12 ounces, with further sub-units. The creation of this coinage must have been related to the institution in 289 of the *triumviri monetales*, a college of three young magistrates in charge of issuing the money. Their office was situated on the Capitol, near the temple of Juno, the goddess henceforward called upon to watch over this establishment, as she had watched over Rome and warned it of threatening dangers (cf. the story of the Capitoline geese which raised the alarm at the time of the Gauls' attack; the goose was the symbolic attribute of the goddess). Thus Juno Moneta gave her name to the "monetary" institution. This monetary unit survived until the Second Punic War. Notably, about 235, the prow of a ship figured on the reverse side of the Roman *as*, the symbol of maritime activity and even of domination over the seas.

Another important date in the history of Roman coinage was 269, which saw the minting of silver coinage in Rome. But it was not until the Second Punic War, or, more precisely, about the year 214, that a metrological system was established with equivalence for bronze and silver coinage. The silver denarius, worth 10 bronze *asses*, appeared at that time, replacing the silver quadrigate coin, which had too large a value. Rome thus possessed a light currency, making transactions easier. The requirements of war, intensified by the creation of a fleet, meant that financial difficulties arose very quickly. It proved necessary to revalue the denarius at 16 *asses*. Moreover, monetary manipulations began which affected the metal standard of silver coinage. However, with the denarius, integrated with a coherent and Mediterranean-wide metrological system, Rome was furnished with a currency that was accepted in foreign trade circuits. Moneychangers' shops were set up on the Forum.

From the middle of the fourth century, Roman society, especially Roman high society, underwent important changes, with the formation of a new "nobility," mentioned above, and with the gradual introduction of new men into the ruling classes. There was an Italianization of these classes, acting in favor of Sabines (M' Curius Dentatus), Campanians (the Atilii), Etruscans (the Volumnii and Ogulnii), and Umbrians (the Sempronii). The Furii, Quinctii, and Papirii from Tusculum had already been integrated into Latium. These newcomers brought a fresh dynamism to the ruling classes, in particular the Campanians, who played such an active role in Roman politics in the Mediterranean

THE BIRTH OF ROMAN CURRENCY

- In the beginning, valuation in head of livestock (*pecus*), hence the word *pecunia* = wealth in livestock, then money, fortune, riches.
- Gradual appearance of bronze ingots (*aes rude*), subsequently stamped with a mark, the bull (*aes signatum*).
- 289 BC: appearance of bronze coinage (*aes grave*) with the faces of Janus and Minerva, Creation of the college of three magis-trates responsible for the minting of these coins (the *tres viri monetales*).
- 269 BC: issue in Rome of silver didrachma, depicting Hercules, and the she-wolf suckling the infants Castor and Pollux, then a deified Rome (*Dea Roma*) and Victory holding a palm.
- About 214 BC: issue in Rome of the silver denarius, one denarius = 10 bronze *asses*.

and southern Italy that they could be said to have made the early Punic Wars their own affair.

The Roman army that fought in the service of these policies, and determined no doubt how they should be carried out, had been forged during the wars of the fourth century on the basis of the Servian directions. It thus remained founded on property qualification in the sense that only the five classes of *assidui* were obliged to do service, with, as we have seen, the heavier weapons and the monopoly of the cavalry conferred on wealthy citizens of the first class; the *proletarii* and *capite censi*, with very rare exceptions, were exempt. It was a national army: service (*militia*) was both a right and a duty of the citizen; and unlike the Greek armies, it included no mercenaries. Only at the end of the third century would it take in "allied" contingents, provided by the subject cities and peoples of Italy. It was usually made up of four legions, raised only for the campaign period, that is, during the fine weather from March to October, each of 3,000 heavily armed footsoldiers, 1,200 more lightly armed *velites*, and 300 horsemen. They were distributed equally in two consular armies. Weapons and tactics became established during the course of the wars. Thus it was during the Samnite Wars that the Romans acquired the custom of breaking up the massed body of the legion (perhaps influenced by the tactical arrangement of the Greek phalanx), dividing it into more flexible units, the maniples, composed of two centuries, each containing 60 men. The legionaries were provided with a wooden-handled javelin with a long slender point (*pilum*) and an oblong shield (*scutum*). From Pyrrhus they seem to have borrowed the art of organizing and fortifying their camps (their methodical minds developing this to a point of perfection that would earn the admiration of Polybius), as well as certain principles of maneuver on the field of battle. But their command remained far inferior to that of the professional strategists in the Greek world. Furthermore, at the beginning of the third century, they still had no fleet at their disposal.

Polybius acknowledged that the Roman army was pre-eminent on two counts: the personal worth of the soldiers and their intensive training.

THE CONQUEST OF CENTRAL AND SOUTHERN ITALY

The years 348–338 marked a crucial period in Rome's march toward mastery of the peninsula and a maritime commitment. Its good relations with Caere, at the time Italy's largest city, probably attracted Rome to look toward the open seas. After 291 (end of the Third Samnite War), the new means available to the Roman–Campanian state encouraged it to expand its power.

ROME AND CENTRAL ITALY

The Sabine region was still independent, but because of its geographical position its territory was often crossed by both Roman soldiers and Roman traders. In 290, M' Curius Dentatus, consul at the time, ravaged it as far as the Adriatic. The land was annexed, its towns received prefects to administer them, and the confiscated lands were colonized – thus a Latin colony was established at Hadria (Atri).

Shortly afterwards, the Senonian Gauls attacked Arretium (Arezzo) in Etruria. They were eventually checked, but not until they had neared Volsinii. Pushed back as far as the sea, they lost part of their territory to Rome. A Roman colony was installed at Sena Gallica in 283, and later, in 268, another at Ariminum (Rimini). This brought about the annexation of a large part of the *ager Gallicus* between Ancona and Rimini.

Meanwhile, back in Etruria, the towns were in the throes of internal dissension between democrats and aristocrats, the latter generally supported by Rome. Their territories were gradually lost to Rome and they themselves became "federated" cities (*foederatae*), that is, bound to Rome by a treaty. A Roman colony was settled at Cosa, and in 265 Volsinii was captured and destroyed. It was the end of great Etruria.

Roman territory, which had covered $5,000\,km^2$ after the Latin War, now extended over $27,000\,km^2$.

Rome and Pyrrhus, king of Epirus

In the first quarter of the third century, Rome, though busy in central and north central Italy, found itself engaged in the complex affairs of southern Italy, its introduction coming through the rivalries of Greek colonies there and their problems with the indigenous populations.

In 284, Thurii, the rival of Tarentum, appealed to Rome for help in resisting the Lucani. A Roman consul, dispatched to the site, set up a garrison in the city, a move that inclined Croton, Locri, and Rhegium to join with the Romans, but failed to quieten internal discord – the parties continued to tear one another apart, the pro-Roman aristocrats opposing the anti-Roman democrats.

Two years later, in 282, Tarentum, a Dorian colony with a brilliant past, sent an army to Thurii to drive out Rome's partisans. This caused Rome to intervene in 281 by dispatching an army that ravaged the Tarentine territory. Tarentum made an appeal to Pyrrhus of Epirus.

The ambitions of the king of Epirus did the rest. As we have seen, the Greeks had long been attracted by the West. Among the last projects of Alexander the Great himself had been, so it seems, a planned military operation in the West. In 296, at the age of 23, the young king of Epirus, heir to this tradition or pure adventurer – it is difficult to draw the line – had inherited a very poor, mountainous country, wedged between Illyria, Macedon, Thessalia, and Aetolia. After modernizing his country's pastoral economy and its army, he had stepped up military intervention in Macedon and Thessalia. Having become king of both countries, and thus having doubled his territory and population, he imagined himself to be master of Greece and, like a new Alexander, intended for a great destiny. So, when he had been driven out of Macedon, he was delighted to respond to Tarentum's appeal. His dream at that time was to unite the Greek cities of Magna Graecia, reconcile them with the indigenous peoples of the interior, and thus establish a powerful new kingdom, whence he could set off to reconquer Macedon.

He landed at Tarentum in the spring of 280, with 25,000 men and a number of elephants, these beasts dumbfounding the Romans at their first encounter with them below the walls of Heraclea, where the Epirots gained their initial victory. This success led Pyrrhus into Campania, where he had a failure at Capua. A second victory came at Ausculum, but he again failed to gain advantage from it (hence the expression "Pyrrhic victory"). Negotiations followed between Rome and Pyrrhus, and in 278, concerning the protection of Sicily, between Rome and Carthage. In fact Pyrrhus landed in Sicily. Proclaimed king of Syracuse, then master of Agrigentum, he entered the area of the island controlled by Carthage. His failure at Lilybaeum, the Carthaginian threat, and the rebellion of Sicilians crushed by taxes caused him to re-embark in 275, first for

Plate 4.1   A war-elephant. Roman terracotta plaque.

Italy, and then, driven out by the revolt of the Greek cities, for Epirus, leaving Tarentum with a garrison, which remained there two years. In 272 this "meteoric hero" (J. Heurgon) was killed at the siege of Argos, struck down by a tile thrown by an old woman from the top of her house.

This war was of great importance for Rome on more than one count, but first of all because it made possible new conquests.

THE CAPTURE OF TARENTUM (273–272 BC)

These conquests allowed Rome to complete its grasp on southern Italy. The region of Lucania was the first to yield, and a Roman colony was settled there at Paestum in 273. But naturally it was Tarentum that most aroused the covetousness of the Romans, who sent an army, and the Carthaginians, who sent a fleet. The town's riches and its strategic position justified those ambitions. In 272, Millo, the Epirot head of the garrison, handed the citadel over to the Romans on condition that he and his supporters be given free exit. Tarentum received its "liberty," that is, the status of a free town but with a Roman garrison in its citadel. It had to pay heavy compensation, and the triumph of the two consuls featured a parade of all the statues, paintings, and other marvels seized from the town. Rome had thus subjugated the only city in southern Italy capable of competing with it.

There followed the submission of the whole of southern Italy, Greek and indigenous. It is noteworthy that from this time on, the name "Italia," which had hitherto designated first Calabria and then southern Italy, was extended to cover the entire peninsula.

It is easy to see that the war with Pyrrhus and the capture of Tarentum had an immensely important historical consequence in bringing Rome face to face with Carthage, an army face to face with a navy. The First Punic War was in sight. But before approaching that chapter of Roman and Mediterranean history, it is appropriate to examine another consequence of the direct contacts established with the Greek world: the Hellenization of Rome's art and religion.

THE HELLENIZATION OF ART AND RELIGION

Contrary to what is sometimes said, there had been no Hellenization in Rome in the seventh century BC; the presence of proto-Corinthian and then Corinthian pottery articles in the archaic tombs bears witness only to trading relations. The first Hellenization is datable to the third century. It was the fruit of contacts begun with the Greeks of Magna Graecia, and with the Etruscans, themselves influenced by Greek culture. "Throughout the fourth century, Rome's horizons had remained confined to central Italy" (R. Bianchi-Bandinelli). When those horizons expanded, Rome, and the whole of central Italy, reaped the benefits of the civilization brought into view.

ART

At the end of the fourth century and the beginning of the third, honorific statues, and even equestrian statues, began to make their appearance on the Forum. They were in bronze, or so it would seem, for they have not survived. And there is every reason to think that they came from the Greek cities of southern Italy. It is known that in 275, M' Curius Dentatus, in his triumphal procession celebrating his victory over Pyrrhus and the Samnites, put on show some *deliciae Tarentinae* which included old pictures. It is also known that the capture of Tarentum in 272 was followed by the looting of the town's works of art, for which it was renowned, especially its chased and embossed metalwork. But it is difficult to say what the influence of those works was on Roman

Plate 4.2 An athlete makes a lustration. Roman votive relief, 2nd century BC. Capitoline Museum, Rome.

art of the period. All the more so because Rome in the third century was still largely a town of peasants, with simple, traditional architecture. The temples, to which the greatest care was given, for they were consecrated to the gods, were built either of light materials (which have totally vanished), or in volcanic tuff, with terracotta architectural decoration. However, it should be noted that even in 296 the terracotta quadriga of the temple of Jupiter Capitolinus was replaced by another in bronze, offered by the Ogulnii brothers, who had also had made the famous bronze she-wolf for the Lupercal, the cultic cave on the Palatine. The 2,000 bronze statues seized by the consul M. Fulvius at Volsinii, doubtless looted from the sanctuary of the *fanum Voltumnae*, came to adorn the twin temples of Fortuna and Mater Matuta (the Lady of the Morning) in the Forum Boarium. But, clearly, that was merely decorative addition, foreign to the architecture.

In Italy, and of course in the Hellenized zone above all, the Greek imprint had become ever more noticeable. Thus, at Paestum, the "temple of Peace," probably built in 273 at the time of the settlement of the Latin colony in the Greek city, includes elements borrowed from classical Greek tradition, for instance a Doric frieze with metopes ornamented with a figure. Nevertheless, it was only during the course of the third century that such influences reached central Italy and Rome.

LITERATURE

The second half of the third century witnessed the appearance of what P. Grimal has called "the first generation of Latin literature." It was preceded in the first half of the century by the gradual penetration of Rome by the Greek language, and its direct introduction with the arrival of Greek-speaking prisoners of war reduced to slavery. At the beginning of the third century, Romans had reason to speak Greek: trade relations and religious influences supplied it. After all, was not Greek the language of international relations? In 281, a Roman ambassador sent to Tarentum made a speech in Greek (which, it is true, caused some sniggering). In 272, Livius Andronicus, while still a child, arrived in Rome with other *Graeculi* ("little Greeks"), as they were called, still with a certain scorn. He was the first epic poet to write in Latin, though on Greek subjects. With his translation of the *Odyssey*, he endowed Rome with a national epic by presenting Ulysses as an Italic hero, the mediator between Greece and Italy. Moreover, he created Latin theater. He may have used Greek models in doing so, but it was none the less a great moment in Latin literary history.

GREEK AND EASTERN GODS IN ITALY AND ROME

Seventh century BC: Melqart (Hercules) in Rome on the Forum Boarium(?).

528–509: Introduction of the cult of Apollo from Cumae. The Sibylline Books are purchased from the Sibyl.

Sixth–fifth centuries: Eastern-style Minerva at Lavinium (Latium).

495: Hermes (Mercury) introduced into Rome by Greek traders.

493: Dedication of the temple of Ceres, Liber, and Libera on the Aventine: cult introduced from Sicily. Influence of Etrusco-Greek cult of Dionysus?

484: Dedication of the temple to the Dioscuri (Castores), who were "evoked" from Tusculum on the occasion of the Battle of Lake Regillus.

431: Dedication of Apollo's temple, on the Campus Martius (Field of Mars).

293: After a *pestilentia* (outbreak of contagious disease), introduction of Asklepius/Aesculapius: temple dedicated on the Isola Tiberina in 291.

249: Hades (*Dis Pater*) and Proserpine are honored in the first secular games, known as those of Tarentum (*ludi Tarentini*).

217–216: Vow to the Erycine Venus (Aphrodite of Mount Eryx in Sicily), Graeco-Punic.

212: Sacrifice with Greek rites and annual games in Greek style in honor of Apollo (*ludi Apollinares*).

April 4, 204: Arrival at Ostia and installation on the Palatine of the Black Stone of Pessinus (the baetyl of Cybele, Phrygian Great Mother of the gods). Creation of the *ludi Megalenses*.

April 10, 191: Dedication of the temple of the Great Mother of the gods (Cybele) on the Palatine.

186: Scandal of the Bacchanalia.

181: Dedication of the temple to the Erycine Venus at the Colline gate, fêted by prostitutes.

180: Hygea, or Hygiea (Salus), daughter or consort of Aesculapius, joins him on the Isola Tiberina.

   Destruction of the "Pythagorean books" discovered at the foot of the Janiculum.

175: Expulsion of the Epicurean philosophers from Rome.

146: "Evocation" to Rome of the Carthaginian Tanit.

139: Expulsion of eastern astrologers from Rome.

105: A Serapeum (altar to Serapis) is attested at Pozzuoli in Campania.

Late second century: First Iseum (altar to Isis) attested at Pompeii.

82: Introduction into Rome by Sulla of the Cappadocian cult of Mâ.

59–48: Official destruction of the Isis-Serapis altars on the Capitol.

43: Vow of a temple to Isis.

33: Expulsion from Rome of the Chaldean magi.

RELIGION

The goddesses of Eleusis – Demeter and Kore – who had meanwhile become the Sicilian goddesses bestowing fertility, had been introduced into Rome as early as the beginning of the fifth century BC. Installed on the Aventine, Demeter, under the guise of the Roman Ceres, was adopted by the plebeians as their divine protectress. The temple of Ceres became the religious center of the *plebs*, notably housing the funds of its corporation. Later came Hera of Argos, the goddess with the pomegranate, symbol of fecundity and immortality, who, like Ceres, protected the fruits of the earth. From the Heraion of the Silarus (Sele) she ascended towards Latium as far as Lanuvium, Tibur, and Falerii. Greek influences were also evident in the Hercules installed on the Forum Boarium, who, though not wholly Greek, was not lacking in Greek characteristics.

In the first half of the third century, the Hellenization of Roman religion was advanced in three ways.

1 By the introduction of a new divinity. In 293, following a plague (*pestilentia*, referring here to malaria) and on the indication of the Sibylline Books, an embassy went to Epidaurus to seek the god Asklepius-Aesculapius, to whom a temple was dedicated on the Isola Tiberina in 291. He definitively dethroned the old Latin Apollo, until then venerated as a healing god (*Apollo medicus*). Around 180, his daughter or consort Hygea, likened to the Italic Salus, came to join him.

2 By the introduction of a funeral rite, of apparently Etruscan origin, which had taken root in Magna Graecia, chiefly at Capua: the *munus*, a bloody fight which took place above the tomb of the deceased, who was to be revived by the blood of the combatants. This was the ancestor of the gladiatorial fights (*munus gladiatorium*). In Rome, the first *munus* was organized in 264 on the Forum Boarium – three pairs of men fought.

3 Through the influence of Pythagoreanism and Orphism. The latter was a way of thinking rather than a theological doctrine or religion. It was expressed in collections of sacred verses and oracles attributed to Orpheus, as well as in forms of prayers inscribed on what were known as Orphic tablets. The engraved "Orphic" formulas, such as those found on plates of gold exhumed from tombs at Thurii and Petelia in Magna Graecia, were to help the dead find their way in the Underworld. They were "passports for the next world," distributed in the name of the mythical hero who by love had brought back his Eurydice from the kingdom of Hades-Pluto. It is difficult to say whether these mystical and soteriological influences had touched Roman minds as early as the first half of the third century. However, their presence in Rome then at least marked the beginning of a movement that later profoundly transformed Roman religious

Plate 4.3 Relief depicting victory of a gladiator announced by a trumpeter. The other waits for judgement on his life. 1st century BC.

sensibilities – although less, it should be said, than the repercussions of the Punic Wars.

THE PUNIC WARS

Three wars set Rome against Carthage between 264 and 146 BC:

- the first from 264 to 241
- the second from 218 to 201
- the third from 149 to 146.

71

They represent one of the major events in the history of the Mediterranean basin and the history of Rome.

The First Punic War (264–241 bc)

We know about this first war with Carthage thanks to Polybius (Book I), Livy, Diodorus Siculus (fragments XXII–XXIV), and Dio Cassius (through the Byzantine historian Zonaras), all of them having mined their information from a Greek historian from Agrigentum, Philinos, a contemporary of Hannibal and favorable to the Carthaginians, and from the *Annals* of Fabius Pictor.

Essentially, the conflict arose from the clash of economic interests, linked on the Carthaginian side with the maritime and commercial nature of its might, and on the Roman with a commitment to new policies opening outward to the world.

Carthage, founded at the end of the ninth century BC by Phoenicians from Tyre, had built up for itself in eastern North Africa (present-day Tunisia), along the coasts of that part of Africa, in the south of Spain, and in the islands of the western Mediterranean basin, an extensive trading empire which, in Sicily and then Tarentum, caused it to collide with Roman interests.

Carthage's strength lay, of course, above all in its navy. For its land forces, it resorted largely to mercenaries, and since the war with Pyrrhus had borrowed his use of elephants.

Rome, as we have seen, remained, essentially, a land-based power, its army an army of citizens, beginning to be joined by allied contingents.

Until 273/272, relations between these two powers, the one well established, the other still being formed, were quite correct. Agreements, the first perhaps concluded in 509, and two other, more certain pacts in 348 and 278, had (temporarily) accommodated their interests. In 278, during the war against Pyrrhus, the two states had undertaken not to conclude an agreement with the Epirot unless they did so together, and Carthage, hoping to keep the king on Italian territory, had promised Rome ships and money. Nevertheless, in 273/272 a menacing Carthaginian fleet came and moored facing the port of Tarentum, watching enviously as the Roman army undertook the siege.

The immediate cause of the war, however, and therefore also of Rome's first military intervention outside Italy, was the double-dealing of the Mamertines ("sons of Mars"), a group of former Campanian mercenaries who several years earlier had seized control of the strategically located city of Messana, in northeast Sicily, from which they routinely launched plundering expeditions into Syracusan territory. In 265, the king of Syracuse, Hiero II, responded by attacking the Mamertines, who appealed to Carthage for assistance, and then, fearing that the Carthaginians intended to stay, asked the Roman Senate for both military aid and an alliance. Most of the senators were, according to Polybius, reluctant to agree, not least because they felt that an alliance with the unsavory Mamertines would be undignified. Others warned that if the Romans failed to act, the Carthaginians would rapidly conquer Syracuse and subjugate the whole of Sicily: the Carthaginians, Polybius has them say, would be "dangerous neighbors for them, surrounding them and threatening all parts of Italy." In the end, after debating for what Polybius calls "a long time," the Senate decided not to honor the Mamertines' request. But Appius Claudius Caudex took the issue directly to the popular assembly, which, excited by the prospect of booty – what, according to Polybius, Appius Claudius referred to as "the clear and considerable advantage that each individual might expect" – voted to help them.

The underlying causes of the war, then, would seem to have been these: strategic considerations, according to which a pre-emptive first strike against Carthaginian interests in Sicily might preclude a larger and more dangerous war in Italy (what has sometimes been called "defensive imperialism"); the opportunity for ambitious aristocrats to win military glory; and greed.

A war began that was to last 23 years. Its course was marked by indecisive battles on land and later at sea: in Sicily around Messina and then Agrigentum, and at Mylae (Milazzo, west of Messina), the first Roman naval victory, won by C. Duilius; in Africa, with the astonishing but unsuccessful expedition of C. Atilius Regulus, carried out in 256 against the advice of the Roman elders; and lastly in the Tyrrhenian waters, where, after a serious naval defeat at Drepanum in 249, leading to an immense effort being put into shipbuilding, the Romans won a victory in the Aegates Islands, forcing a peace in 241.

This first Punic War (which the ancients sometimes referred to, more correctly, as the Sicilian war) had important consequences.

First, most of Sicily became a Roman province. The Carthaginians had to quit the entire island, as well as the Lipari islands, lying between Sicily and Italy.

In Carthage, weakened by the defeat and by the payment of a heavy war indemnity, the First Punic War brought in its wake a social revolt, together with the "war of the mercenaries" (from the winter of 241/240 to the beginning of 237), a war from which Rome profited by seizing Sardinia in 238. In 237, to save Carthage and restore its might, the Punic general Hamilcar undertook the conquest of Spain. There he succeeded in setting up a Barcine empire, to which his succes-sor Hasdrubal gave an almost monarchic structure with a capital at Cartagena (New Carthage). In this kingdom, organized after the manner of Hellenistic kingdoms, Hamilcar Barca's son, Hannibal, was unleashed and, starting in 221, began that course which led to the Second Punic War.

Another outcome of the First Punic War was the birth of Rome's naval power, an event of capital importance for the future. Until then Rome had been a city of "landlubbers." But already at the end of the fourth century it had been noticed how much there was to gain by the possession of a fleet: in 311, at a time when it had only the vessels of its allies and maritime colonies at its disposal, Rome had appointed two admirals (*duoviri navales*). Now the necessities of a war fought against the naval might of Carthage compelled the creation of a countervailing naval force. This Rome achieved through a massive and expensive program of shipbuilding. As early as 260, the consuls had at their disposal a squadron of 100 quinqueremes and 20 triremes. It was also a time of Roman technical and strategical inventions, the most remarkable of which was the grapnel, which to some extent transformed naval battles into a war of foot-soldiers on the sea.

This invention was responsible for the first naval success achieved by the Romans, at Mylae in 260. It subsequently inspired them to launch into military and trading expeditions in the Mediterranean. With the acquisition of the two islands of Sicily and Sardinia, Rome gained two important stepping-stones on this path.

THE SECOND PUNIC WAR (218–201 BC)

After twenty-three years of armed peace, war resumed because Hannibal, emerging from the great aristocratic Barcine family, and having inherited their ambitions, became Carthage's military strategist.

Rome, meanwhile, had become master of Italy. After four years of fighting (226–222), it had established itself solidly in Cisalpine Gaul through Cn. Scipio's occupation of Mediolanum (Milan), by building roads, and by the installation in 218 of two Latin colonies beyond the Po, at Cremona and Piacenza.

Meanwhile, too, Hannibal had been preparing for the war some think he eagerly desired. What survives to describe his motives is in fact highly tendentious. Livy preserves a fanciful story, in which Hannibal's father, Hamilcar Barca, instills in his young son a burning hatred for Rome, and makes him promise to avenge Roman treachery. The truth is far less colorful, and a discredit to Rome. Carthaginian military and diplomatic successes in Spain had brought them, by 220, to the region of the city of Saguntum, which was allied to Rome by a treaty of mutual protection, but which was well to the south of the River Ebro, which Rome had declared in 226 to be the northern limit of Carthaginian expansion in Spain. At the urging of Saguntum, the Senate sent an embassy to Hannibal to warn him against attacking the city. Angered by what he no doubt considered to be Roman meddling, Hannibal wrote to Carthage for advice. Soon after (early in 219), he laid siege to Saguntum. It was not until early in the following year, however, after Saguntum had already fallen – the Romans having stood idly by – that the Senate responded, by sending a delegation to Carthage to demand Hannibal's surrender. The Carthaginians opted for war. In May of 218, knowing that he was no match

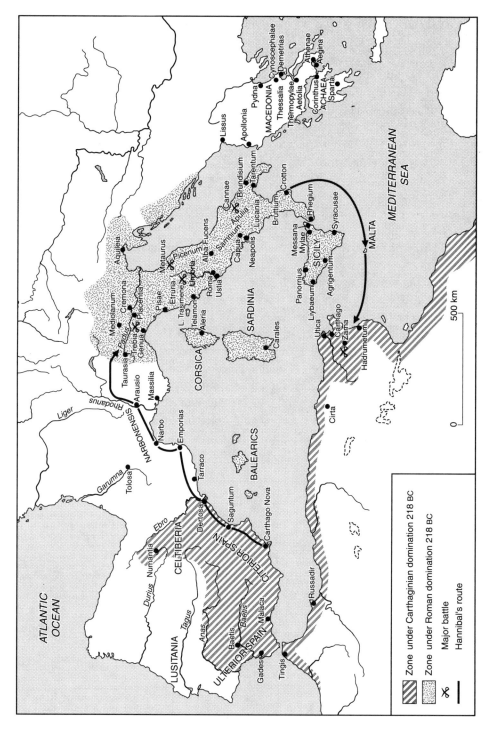

Figure 4.2 The Second Punic War

for Roman naval power, and understanding perhaps that his best chance of success lay in establishing a single front, ideally in Italy, Hannibal set out for the Alps.

It was a dreadful war, lasting seventeen years, and might well be called Hannibal's War, so much was it dominated by the personality and exploits of this great general. Unlike the first war, it was not confined largely to the place where it began – in this case Spain, with the terrible siege of Saguntum – but then raged over Italy, whose sacred soil was profaned for over fifteen years by Carthaginian armies living off the land, and then reached out to Africa, where, repeating Regulus' exploits but with more success, P. Cornelius Scipio succeeded in landing and bringing hostilities to an end, at Zama in 202 – it had touched even the Greek world, where the First Macedonian War was the direct result of the Roman-Punic struggle.

Three phases may be distinguished in the development of hostilities.

Carthaginian operations in Italy, and Rome's difficulties (218–211/210 BC)
Hannibal was banking on a rebellion by the Cisalpine Gauls. And indeed, though at first restrained by the action of the consul P. Scipio, many of them abandoned the cause of Rome after its defeats at the Ticinus and the Trebia. After the further defeat at Lake Trasimene, even part of Picenum followed the victor. On the other hand, Hannibal failed to raise the peoples of central Italy (Marsi, Maruccini, Paeligni); the ravages inflicted by his troops tended rather to set the country against him. That failure spurred him on to enter Campania, where he hoped that Capua would defect to him and where, as master of fertile lands, he counted on setting up a bridgehead with Carthage. His hopes were dashed at first. But the Roman defeat at Cannae in 216 was to have formidable consequences, provoking further serious defections from the Roman cause:

■ In southern Italy, where, besides those among the Bruttians, Lucanians, and Samnites, there was the even more serious defection of Capua and several Campanian towns. Despite the Roman–Campanian state, Capua sided with Hannibal, maneuvering to put Rome in the wrong. A treaty concluded in 215 even planned for the sharing of Italy between Capua and Carthage should the Romans be defeated, and in 214 a project was born for a Carthaginian state in southern Italy. At Tarentum, occupied by a Roman garrison, treachery delivered the gates of the town into the Carthaginians' hands. Metapontum and Thurii followed the example.
■ In Sicily, where the death of the aged Hieron II of Syracuse, one of Rome's allies, allowed Hannibal to proceed with his intrigues there. That caused the

Romans to intervene in Syracuse, which was besieged, in vain, for eight months in 214. A Carthaginian army was able to land and seize Agrigentum. This was the signal for a Sicilian uprising, bringing both the need to keep a Roman army there which would have been very useful on the mainland (the war in Sicily lasted until 209), and the depletion of Rome's grain supplies (Sicily was a major supplier of corn).

■ Lastly in Sardinia, where the natives rebelled after Cannae. Here, Ti. Manlius, thanks to his good knowledge of the country, was able rapidly to overcome the Sardinian rebels, taking prisoner the Carthaginian Hanno, who had come to give them support – in 215 nearly everything seemed settled there.

Rome itself was, however, never in mortal danger. Despite these defections, and the threats that twice hung over the capital, its safety was ensured by the

---

THE SECOND PUNIC WAR

219/218: Siege of Saguntum by Hannibal. Declaration of war by Rome.

218: Hannibal crosses the Pyrenees, then southern Gaul.

217: Roman defeat on the Ticinus.
Roman defeat on the Trebia.
Roman defeat at Lake Trasimene.

216: Roman defeat at Cannae.

216/215: Hannibal at Capua.

215: Agreement between Hannibal and Philip of Macedon.

214: The Romans reoccupy Samnium.

212/211: Siege of Capua and recapture of the town by the Romans.

211: Hannibal marches on Rome, then beats a retreat.

211/210: Roman victories at Syracuse and Agrigentum.

210–206: Scipio's successes in Spain.

209: Recapture of Tarentum by the Romans.

207: Hasdrubal arrives in Italy. He is beaten on the Metaurus.

205: The Decemvirs decide to bring the Black Stone of Pessinus to Rome, so to introduce the cult of Cybele, protectress of the Trojans, "ancestors" of the Romans.

204: Scipio lands in Africa.

202: Scipio's victory at Zama.

201: Peace with Carthage.

unshakeable loyalty of central Italy, the unyielding attitude of the Senate, and the support of the *populus*.

The reconquest of Italy (211–206 BC)

Beginning in 213, Rome's main objective was to reconquer Campania, and punish Capua and the Samnites. Not without difficulty, and in spite of two serious defeats, in that year the consuls managed to surround Capua with a double entrenchment. The siege lasted until 211. Capua's fall was the start of Rome's regaining full control of Italy.

In southern Italy Despite an attempt by Hannibal to break the siege by coming and camping for five days before Rome (before having to withdraw in order to get back to Bruttium), Capua, deserted by the Carthaginians, was finally taken by the Romans. According to Livy, the chief citizens were killed or imprisoned, the populace sold into slavery, and the city's status reduced to that of a rural town.

The years 210–209 were not free from distress for Rome, but there was also a rallying of support: the treasury was empty; but the senators, appealed to by the consul Laevinus, poured their gold and silver into the public coffers. Weariness made itself felt among the allies: in 209, 12 Latin colonies declared themselves exhausted of both men and money, and refused the loans demanded; but 18 others said they were prepared to make any sacrifice.

Roman reaction was also vigorously punitive in the other reconquered areas. Bruttians and Lucanians were debarred from recruitment to the legions and saw their lands confiscated to the advantage of the Roman colonies. Similarly, in Campania, those towns which had allied themselves with Hannibal lost their territories. Thus was formed the *ager Campanus*, some 60,000 ha of the richest lands in Italy placed at the disposal of the Roman Senate.

In 209, Q. Fabius Maximus managed to regain Tarentum, which was sacked, and 30,000 of its inhabitants sold into slavery. The two terrible examples of Capua and Tarentum put an end to all attempts at defection.

End of the war in Sicily This was the work of Claudius Marcellus, who finally seized Syracuse after three years of siege. Looting and pillaging were on an immense scale, but there were few massacres – though poor Archimedes perished, killed while solving a geometry problem. M. Valerius Laevinus also played his part, taking Agrigentum in 209 and after that active in calming things down and restoring Sicily to peace and the production of corn. The year 209 marks the end of Greek Sicily; from then on the island was entirely Roman.

End of the Sardinian revolt The two legions left by Rome had to confront another large uprising, and then pacify the Sardinians, who periodically heard rumors of the arrival of a Carthaginian fleet. Calm was restored between 209 and 207, and the island participated in equipping the expeditionary force of Scipio, who was making ready for his departure for Africa.

The Roman offensive (206–201 BC)

After the successes of 209–207, Rome still experienced some difficult moments, in particular with the arrival in Italy of two other Punic armies. Hasdrubal's, intending to reinforce Hannibal and causing some disturbance in Cisalpine Gaul and Etruria on its way to him, was halted by the Roman victory at the Metaurus and Hasdrubal's death. Mago's, which landed in Liguria in 205 and was well received by some, was beaten in 203, and Mago was then recalled to Carthage following Scipio's landing.

P. Cornelius Scipio's landing in Africa was the great event of the last phase of the war. It was a stroke of genius. Since 210, the young Scipio had been attracting everyone's attention. Dispatched as proconsul to Spain (before he had held any other important office), he had recaptured Cartagena (New Carthage) and, while holding both Saguntum and Cartagena – the two principal maritime bases in the western Mediterranean – had simultaneously put an end to the Barcine empire and made the crossing to Africa possible. Elected consul for 205, after a rough political battle in which supporters and adversaries of an African expedition opposed one another in the Senate, he obtained the province of Sicily, with the right to cross over to the African continent.

He left for Africa in 204 with two legions and their auxiliaries, 35,000 men in all, relying heavily on the help of the Numidian king Massinissa, with whom negotiations had long been going on. He landed near Utica and in the spring of 203 won a brilliant victory over the Punic forces. Carthage recalled first Mago, and then Hannibal, who landed near Hadrumetum (Susa) in the autumn. While attempts at negotiations were proceeding, Scipio made intensive preparations, drilling his troops in a tactic based on that of his opponent. With the decisive assistance of the Numidian cavalry, he won his great victory at Zama (near Ksar Toual Zammel in present-day Tunisia) on October 29, 202.

Peace was achieved only in the spring of 201. Carthage handed over all but ten of its longboats (war vessels) and all its elephants, and pledged itself to pay 10,000 talents over 50 years and not to make war on others without Rome's agreement.

CONSEQUENCES OF THE SECOND PUNIC WAR

As we have seen, the war had important repercussions in Italy. They made themselves felt well beyond 201, if only by the enormous human losses they entailed.

First, Rome had had to provide itself with a powerful military apparatus. Before 218, it had normally maintained between six and eight legions, or between 25,000 and 33,000 men. Between 217 and 203, it mobilized up to 28 legions, i.e. some 120,000 men, added to which were the troops supplied by allies and the men employed in the navy. This unprecedented military effort understandably brought financial difficulties. But Rome took advantage of these to provide itself with a light currency, making its transactions easier.

Next, those testing years brought about a singular strengthening of Roman institutions. The Senate, which had been the soul of the resistance, now enjoyed immense prestige. Its *auctoritas* covered all important decisions and acts in political life. Decimated by the first disasters (80 senators were killed at Cannae), it was brought up to strength by a *lectio senatus* (see glossary). Henceforward, a strict hierarchy was established for recruitment to the Senate: choice was made first, by order of seniority, among former curule magistrates (consuls, praetors), and then among former aediles, tribunes, and quaestors. It thereby became truly an assembly of former magistrates directing the policies of magistrates, gaining further in prestige.

Also, the war had brought to the fore magistrates and generals of great worth, men who, often armed with extraordinary powers, had acquired or displayed personal renown, great ability, and vast ambition. This was notably so in the case of P. Cornelius Scipio *Africanus*, who was the first to bear the title of *imperator* (commander-in-chief, victorious by the grace of the gods). The power of these men, based sometimes on the will of the people more than on that of the Senate, foreshadowed the rise of *imperatores* in the centuries to come.

The First Macedonian War (215–205) was also a repercussion of the Second Punic War. The young king, Philip V, had wanted to profit from Rome's troubles by taking back Illyria, where Rome had established settlements. In 215, he made an agreement with Hannibal, engaging with him to force Rome to give up its Illyrian protectorate. Rome, busy in Italy, responded by making a treaty of alliance with the Aetolians, enemies of the Macedonians in Greece. Eventually, in 205, the Peace of Phoinike was negotiated, by which Rome kept its bridgeheads in Illyria, and apparently consisting in essence of a general pact of non-aggression.

Nevertheless, Rome found itself increasingly involved in Balkan affairs while at the same time it now had important interests in Spain and the western Mediterranean. A new chapter of its history was opening, and in this the Third Punic War would find its place.

5 / CONSEQUENCES OF CONQUEST
The Second Century BC

*A*FTER THE DEATH OF *A*LEXANDER THE *G*REAT *(323* BC*)*, THE MOST IMPORTANT
HISTORICAL PHENOMENON FOR THE FUTURE OF THE *W*EST WAS THE GRADUAL
TRANSITION FROM *R*OME AS CITY IN *I*TALY TO *R*OME AS CAPITAL OF A
*M*EDITERRANEAN TERRITORIAL EMPIRE. *F*ROM A FACTUAL VIEWPOINT, IT WAS THUS
THE CONQUEST BY *R*OMAN LEGIONS *(*OCCASIONALLY BY MEANS OF DIPLOMACY*)* OF
COUNTRIES IN A REPUTEDLY BARBAROUS *W*EST AND IN THE *H*ELLENISTIC *E*AST –
CONQUESTS THAT, BETWEEN THE END OF THE *S*ECOND *P*UNIC *W*AR *(201)* AND THE
ANNEXATION OF *E*GYPT *(31–30)*, RESULTED IN THE FORMATION, UNDER THE AEGIS
OF *R*OME, OF THE MOST POWERFUL AND ENDURING TERRITORIAL EMPIRE IN HISTORY.
*B*UT – AND THIS IS ANOTHER ESSENTIAL HISTORICAL PHENOMENON – WHILE FOR THE
FIRST TIME THE *W*EST LAID HANDS ON THE *E*AST, IT WAS *G*RAECO-EASTERN
*(H*ELLENISTIC*)* CIVILIZATION THAT PENETRATED DEEPLY INTO THE *W*EST TO RESULT
IN A CULTURAL KOINE, OR COMMON LANGUAGE, THE CREATION OF A COMMUNITY OF
*G*RAECO-*R*OMAN CULTURE, DESTINED TO BECOME THE DISTINCTIVE MARK OF
WESTERN *E*UROPEAN NATIONS. *T*HE QUESTION OF *R*OMAN IMPERIALISM IS THEREFORE
OF FUNDAMENTAL IMPORTANCE, AND EQUALLY SO AN EXAMINATION OF ALL ITS
CONSEQUENCES.

ROMAN IMPERIALISM: THE GRIP OF THE WEST ON THE EAST

Much has been written about Rome's imperialism. There has even been speculation as to whether it really existed. But given that it did, when did it start? What forms did it take? Who should be deemed respon-sible? There is no lack of questions. What is certain is that Rome became a conquering power and that, at some point, there was a positive *will* for conquest and territorial expansion.

WHAT WAS ROMAN IMPERIALISM?

The word *imperium* is truly Latin, just as the concept it covers is really and initially Roman. And this concept led to the first true and lasting attempt at universal domination. But for some (Th. Mommsen, M. Holleaux, E. Badian), that imperialism was defensive rather than offensive: Rome responded to wars that were forced upon it – in sheer self-defense; the Roman Senate, in particular, had no expansionist policy. In the view of others, however (most recently W. V. Harris), the conquests were desired by all in Rome: by senators greedy for "glory" and the financial means necessary for their careers, by knights with an eye to financial exploitation of the conquered lands, and by ordinary citizens enticed by the prospect of looting and a share in the booty; war at that time appeared to be "a victory operation to beggar the loser and enrich the victor."

An unprecedented achievement, the Roman State was able to extend its domination over nearly all the inhabited world, and that in under fifty-three years. (Polybius, *Hist.* I.1)

[Other empires have existed] but *Rome* has subjugated more than just a handful of peoples. It has conquered almost the entire universe, so that there is no one today who can resist it and, in years to come, none can hope to surpass it. (I.2)

The problem of Roman imperialism was posed even in antiquity, in the first instance by Polybius, a Greek born about 200 and deported to Italy after the victory of Pydna (168), who meditated on the reasons for Roman successes, providing in his (universal) *History* a profound reflection on Rome, its past, its actions, and its destiny. Part of the Roman aristocratic world (in particular the Scipios' circle), he explained and, to a large extent, justified Rome's domination by the excellence of its institutions (which he judged well balanced) and by the superiority of its army, though adding – an important factor in a world permeated by the divine – "It is in the domain of religious concepts that the superiority of the Roman state is at its greatest" (VIII.56). Now, in the political morality of those days, anyone with any superiority whatsoever over his neighbors had the right, if not the duty, to make use of it. International law was not against it. Thus the superiority of the Roman people (*maiestas populi Romani*) went some way to legitimizing Rome's domination (*imperium populi Romani*).

Following Polybius, historians of the seventeenth and eighteenth centuries (Bossuet and Montesquieu among others) and even the twentieth (G. Colin, J. Kromayer, G. De Sanctis, etc.) accepted a premeditated, deliberate imperialism, evolved by a Senate constructing vast plans for expansion. Rome was supposed to have conquered the Mediterranean basin methodically: Latium first and then Italy, the western half of the Mediterranean next, and the eastern afterwards. This view is open to criticism:

- When it intervened in Illyria in 229 against the pirate state of Queen Teuta, Rome contented itself with simply maintaining bridgeheads there.
- Victorious over Philip V of Macedon at Cynoscephalae in 197, and then over Perseus at Pydna in 168, Rome could have annexed Greece at either time, but it did not do so until 146.
- In Spain, as early as 206, on the fall of the Barcine empire, Rome could have seized the country, whose natives, because of their hatred for the Carthaginians, would have given the Romans a warm welcome. It created a mere two provinces (Citerior and Ulterior) only in 197, and not until later did it set about a methodical conquest of the peninsula, completed only in 19 BC.
- In Africa, the Romans could have annexed at least the Carthaginian territories in 201. They did not do so until 146, and then contented themselves with what is today the north-east of Tunisia.
- In Egypt, if Rome had so desired, the country could have been annexed in 168; it became Roman only in 30, after the victory at Actium.

In fact, given the composition of the Senate and the mental attitude of the ruling classes, it would seem that hardly anyone in the governing circles of Rome at the end of the third century envisaged a commitment to a resolutely imperialist policy. At the time of the first war with Macedon (215–205), the only preoccupation was to prevent Philip V and Hannibal from joining forces. It was only after Zama, between 200 and 198, that Rome really began to take an interest in the affairs of the Greek world. Indeed, it was the Second Macedonian War (200–196) that really signed the birth certificate of Roman imperialism. But it is fair to say that the idea had been germinating in the minds of a few influential senators (the Scipios, for example) during the Second Punic War. At bottom, Hannibal himself was chiefly responsible for this: the outrage of the Punic presence on Italian soil, the threat hanging over the capital city, and the danger posed by the alliance of Carthage and Macedon were realities of a kind to spur certain senators to cast their gaze overseas. The attack made by Rome against Macedon in 200 was the start of a new policy.

But it was still essentially a defensive imperialism: before 148 the only annexations in the eastern Mediterranean were those of Zacynthos (Zante) and Cephallenia. It was "an imperialism as yet lacking self-awareness." Nevertheless, it should be noted that in this period, in 188, the Roman imperialist doctrine was explicitly formulated, thanks to the consul Cn. Manlius Vulso: in his view it was an urgent and absolute necessity for Rome both to ensure peace on land and at sea and to keep the entire East under surveillance (Livy XXXIX). Rome was to act as a universal "policeman," a policy which would lead to the establishment of protectorates over towns and of "client states" – and thence to annexation.

The era of annexations began in 148–146 BC: the reduction of Macedon to a Roman province, then the capture of Corinth and annexation of Achaea, and lastly the capture and destruction of Carthage, these signaled the great watershed. Henceforward a conquering brand of imperialism triumphed, leading in a little over a century to the formation of the Roman Empire. In 30 BC, the Mediterranean was virtually a Roman lake. The only piece missing was Mauretania, and that was won under Claudius (who also added Britain). Later, Trajan annexed Dacia, and for a time Mesopotamia further extended the eastern frontier.

Conquests from 200 to 148 BC
DEFENSIVE IMPERIALISM

As we have seen, Rome's conquests between 200 and 148 were extremely limited. But it is important to follow the way in which the Roman outlook developed through the course of them.

The Second Macedonian War (200–196 BC)

During the Second Punic War, Rome had struck up friendly relations both with Pergamum (to where in 205 a Roman embassy had gone to fetch the famous Black Stone of Pessinus), and with Rhodes, an important trading center. Now the king of Pergamum and the Rhodians warned that Philip V and Antiochus III of Syria had concluded a secret pact of alliance. In the light of this, and worried by other evidence of Macedonian imperialism, Rome, which had not forgotten the war with Pyrrhus, decided, in 200, to attack the king of Macedon and drive him out of Greece (where it had friends). Roman policy was to guarantee the security of the Italian peninsula, and to that end it now sought to remove the agressive king Philip from the Greek peninsula. But, it must be noted, to do so Rome itself turned aggressor. Nevertheless, victorious at Cynoscephalae in 197, Rome took virtually no territorial advantage from its success. One may recall the demonstrations of philhellenism made by the young and brilliant victor of Cynoscephalae, T. Quinctius Flamininus, who, in 196, made his famous declaration of independence, which so aroused the enthusiasm of the Greeks: "The Roman Senate and Titus Quinctius, consul, having vanquished king Philip and the Macedonians, leave free, without garrison, exempt from tribute, and in possession of their traditional laws, Corinthians, Phocidians, Locrians, Euboeans, Phthiot Achaeans, Magnesians, Thessalians, and Perrhaebians."

In fact, what the Greeks obtained was not total liberty (*eleutheria*), but rather a range of exemptions. Greece's status was actually that of a client state, a protectorate, with advantages for Rome. A center of espionage, advance post, buffer state: "free" Greece would act as a main road and a barrier, an arrangement set to guarantee Italy against the ambitions of Hellenistic monarchs.

By the same token, Rome found itself caught up in this arrangement. In 195, Flamininus was thus compelled to wage war against Nabis of Sparta, and then in 192–189 against the Aetolians, who had allied themselves with Antiochus (Battle of Thermopylae, won by M' Acilius Glabrio). The Third Macedonian War followed.

The Third Macedonian War (171–168 BC)

Philip V, who died in 179, was succeeded by the young Perseus. His keen interest in Greece, evident from very early on, made him a source of anxiety for Rome; his securing of ties with Syria (he became the son-in-law of Seleucus IV, Antiochus' successor), and his growing dealings with enemies of the king of Pergamum (Rome's friend), made him a threat, though hardly a serious one. It is clear that Perseus had no desire to fight Rome, and that in trying to win over the Greeks, the Achaean League in particular, he aimed at nothing more than to fulfill one of the traditional roles of the Hellenistic kings. But the dire warnings issued by Eumenes II of Pergamum, which were readily given credence by a Senate increasingly bent on managing the affairs of the Greeks, sealed his fate. For the second time Rome decided to intervene. After three indecisive campaigns in 171, 170, and 169, L. Aemilius Paullus carried off a victory at Pydna in June 168.

Following Cato's advice, the Senate was unwilling to annex either Macedon or Illyria (which had allied with Perseus); but it made terrible demands: though proclaimed free, the two kingdoms were carved up and subjected to the paying of tribute; royalty was abolished; that part of Epirus which had betrayed the Roman cause was devastated; and the Greek ruling classes who had failed it were purged. Rome thus continued to refuse any territorial annexation but increasingly behaved as Greece's suzerain.

The beginnings of economic imperialism (168–148 BC)

As early as the first half of the second century, crowds of Italian businessmen had followed in the legions' footsteps and spread all over Greece, where they were lumped together under the general term *Romaioi*. These *negotiatores* (businessmen, traders, and financiers at the same time) have been made known to us through epigraphy in Illyria, Epirus, and Thessalia (there is evidence of a community of Italians in Larissa at the beginning of the second century), and then at Delphi, in Boeotia, and above all in the Cyclades.

In 166, the Roman Senate took a decision of major importance: to turn the island of Delos into a free port, granting it to Athens as a colony. It was a matter both of rewarding Athens by giving it the holy island of Apollo, of punishing

Plate 5.1 Carthaginian silver coin from western Sicily, 3rd century BC.

Rhodes (which had failed to honor its alliance with Rome) by harming its trade, and as a means to this, of promoting the economic activity of the island. Indeed, this last was its chief effect: numerous Italian businessmen went to settle there and it would become the center of trade between the Hellenic East and the Roman West.

In the second half of the second century, associating in increasingly powerful groups, these *Romaioi* would swiftly attract the interest of Rome's ruling circles in their problems, carrying some weight in the counsels of the Senate and influencing its eastern policies. Then, and only then, were the bases of this economic imperialism laid down. But from about 170/169 there were noticeable changes in both tone and methods.

CONQUESTS FROM 148 TO 133 BC
CONSCIOUS IMPERIALISM

The years 148–133 mark a historical turning-point. That a brand of imperialism was being forged that would take Rome consciously toward Empire was evident in three events that occurred at the beginning of this period, events that, though certainly connected with external circumstances, also undoubtedly

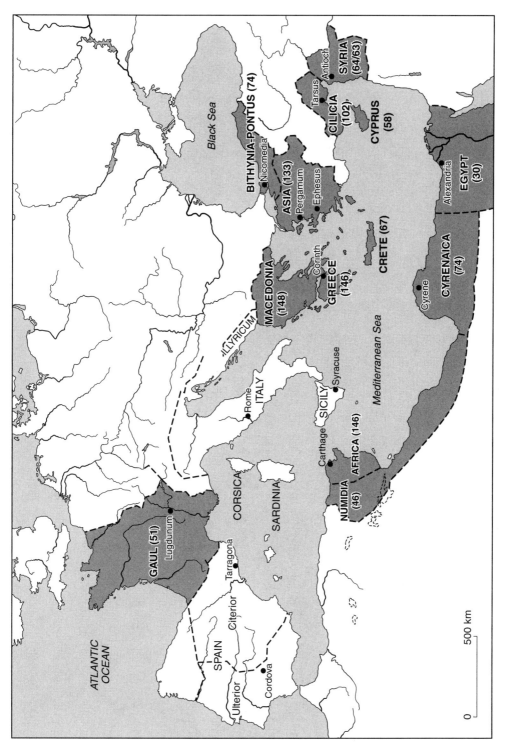

Figure 5.1 Roman conquests, 148–30 BC

displayed a new political determination on the part of Roman ruling circles to pursue an imperial course. This change was personified in 148, when although under the required age, Scipio Aemilianus (son of L. Aemilius Paullus and adopted son of the son of Scipio Africanus) was elected consul for the following year.

The annexation of Macedonia (148–146 BC)

In order to put an end to the venture of a certain Andriscus, an obscure Asian mercenary who had passed himself off as the son of Perseus and thanks to this subterfuge had rallied the majority of Macedonians behind him and found support in Thrace, the praetor Q. Caecilius Metellus launched and led an expedition, reinforced by Pergamum's fleet, and succeeded in bringing about his downfall. This time the Senate decided to reduce Macedon to the position of Roman province. A proconsul, resident in Thessalonica, was placed in charge of it. This was the first Roman province to be formed in the eastern basin of the Mediterranean. But soon, too, Greece's fate would be settled.

The rebellion and submission of Greece (147–146 BC)

The origins of the rising that occurred in Greece at this time are somewhat clouded. In this ruined country, given over to social struggles and nationalist agitation, every inter-city quarrel – they were traditional – ran the risk of degenerating into generalized conflict. In 151, the return of 300 Achaeans deported after Pydna, "decrepit old Greeks," to use Cato's words, but filled with hatred of Rome, did little to pacify men's minds. At all events, a row between Athens and Oropus over a question of customs rapidly escalated into a more serious conflict between the Achaeans, appealed to by Oropus, and Sparta, supported by the Roman Senate.

In 147–146, taking advantage of the fact that Rome was busily engaged in Spain and Africa, the Achaean strategist Critolaus, head of the anti-Roman party, stirred up trouble, promised the lower classes the abolition of debts, and succeeded in getting the vote for war against Sparta, Rome's ally. Two Roman legions, under the command of L. Mummius, were sent to Greece. Operations were short-lived. Critolaus was defeated and killed. His successor, Diaeus, had no better luck at Leucopetra. The last act was played out at Corinth, which had given a poor reception to a Roman embassy. In September 146, L. Mummius seized the town and, carrying out the Senate's official order to "destroy Corinth" (Livy, *Epit.* III), delivered it up to the mercies of his soldiers. The inhabitants were massacred or sold as slaves; the town was looted and burnt; the soil was vowed to the infernal gods. Great works of art were removed, dispersed, or destroyed. Polybius, who was on the spot, wrote: "I was there; I saw paintings trampled underfoot; soldiers sat down on them to play dice!"

No more than at Carthage was the destruction total, as modern excavations by American archaeologists have demonstrated. But the sacking of Corinth marked the end of free Greece. Under the name Achaea, it was henceforth a Roman province.

The Third Punic War and capture of Carthage (150–146 BC)

Several months earlier, in April of the same year, 146, Rome had similarly taken and destroyed Carthage. Since 195, Massinissa, the king of Numidia, had been increasing his attacks on Punic territories. Rome's arbitration (under the treaty of 201) had been generally conciliatory toward Carthage, although after 167, doubtless to reward Massinissa for his loyalty, it had been less so – it had thus allowed him to gain control of the ports of the Major Syrtis. It was chiefly the Roman embassy led by Cato in 153 which brought about an abrupt turnaround in Rome's attitude. Struck by Carthage's prosperity and its rearmament, Cato never ceased calling for its destruction: *delenda est Carthago*. War was declared

Plate 5.2 Punic Tower, Tunisia.

in 149 following a Carthaginian counter-attack on the Numidians. Conducted from 147 on by Scipio Aemilianus, who was consul at the time, it resulted, after a long, terrible siege and almost eight days of atrocious street fighting, in the fall of the Punic capital. In obedience to the Senate's orders, the inhabitants were reduced to slavery or forced to emigrate, the town was burnt (though not totally, as recent excavations have revealed), and the soil was declared *sacer*, or taboo, pledged to the gods for destruction. Punic territory (the north-east of Tunisia) became the Roman province of Africa, with Utica as its capital.

Thus, in the space of a few years there was a marked transition from the protectorate system, combined with more or less direct economic control, to a system of annexation pure and simple. The protectorate system was, however, by no means abandoned. Indeed, it was even strengthened, as in 136/135, when Scipio Aemilianus was sent to the East "to inspect the kingdoms of the allies" (the historian Justin). And meanwhile the activities of the *negotiatores* were developing everywhere.

The conquests between 241 and 271 BC	
241–121	**101–46**
Sicily: 241	Cilicia: 101
Sardinia: 238	Cyrenaica: 96–74
Corsica: 227	Crete: 68
Creation of two Iberian	Bithynia-Pontus: 64
provinces: 197	Syria: 64–63
Zante and Cephallenia: 168	"Long-haired" Gaul: 58–51
Delos, free port: 166	Cyprus: 58
Macedonia: 146	Numidia (*Africa nova*): 46
Achaea: 146	
Africa: 146	
Asia: 133–126	**46–27**
Transalpine Gaul: 121	Egypt: 30

The legacy of Pergamum

The Hellenistic kingdom of Pergamum had been formed in the third century on the west coast of present-day Turkey around the very rich Kaikos valley. Its successive rulers, Philetaerus, Eumenes I, Attalus I, Eumenes II, and Attalus II, had built it up into the most powerful realm in Asia Minor, its ports bursting with traffic and its sumptuously appointed towns almost all enlivened by pilgrims' sanctuaries of international renown. Troubled by their neighbors, the kings of Pergamum had maintained excellent relations with Rome. In 188, Eumenes II had placed himself under Rome's protection, but had at the same time preserved political sovereignty. Under Attalus II (159–138), that sovereignty had seeped away. With his successor, Attalus III, a peculiar, capricious person who suffered from a persecution complex, relations became closer than ever. In 136, when Scipio Aemilianus visited Pergamum, this Roman ambassador behaved as if he were in a conquered country. Attalus III died in the spring of 133. In his will, he bequeathed all his personal wealth and property, including his treasury and the territory of Pergumum, to the Roman people. To the town he gave its freedom. Some of the royal slaves were given their liberty. The rest were given to Pergamum.

This marvelous inheritance arrived just at the right moment for Tiberius Gracchus when he came to the tribunate in Rome. It only remained to make sure of its possession.

CONQUESTS FROM 133 TO 30 BC
THE GREAT IMPERIALIST POLICY

Once the inheritance of Pergamum was assured, annexations and campaigns intensified in both West and East.

Forming the province of Asia

In order to secure its possession of Pergamum, Rome finally had to send in troops. For Attalus' half-brother, Aristonicus, presenting himself as the legitimate heir of the Attalid dynasty, had challenged the will, and then occupied a number of towns, promising freedom to rural serfs and slaves. Rome succeeded, but it was not until 128–126 that M. Aquillius, assisted by ten senatorial commissioners, was able to constitute Pergamum as the province of Asia. Of all the empire's provinces, this was the finest and most sought-after by candidates for the proconsulship (a proconsul had the authority of a consul to command an army or govern a province).

The first interventions in southern Gaul

Rome's first interventions in southern Gaul came when it was called upon for help by its ally, the city of Massilia (Marseille), which was threatened by growing pressure from the surrounding natives, chiefly the Salyes or Salluvii of Entremont. The first expedition, sent in 125 under the consul M. Fulvius Flaccus, was followed in 124 by that of C. Sextius Calvinus against the Salyes and Vocontii. Entremont was taken and the leaders of the Salyes took refuge with the Allobroges. That was when the site of Aquae Sextiae (Aix) was

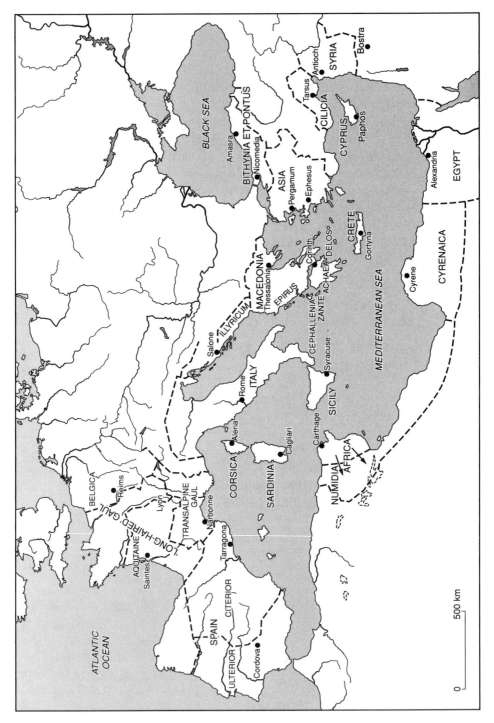

Figure 5.2 The Roman Empire in 27 BC

founded, a Roman garrison being set up there that made Rome master of the roads running east of the southern Rhône.

In 122–121, Cn. Domitius Ahenobarbus and Q. Fabius Maximus had to intervene against the Allobroges and the Arverni. And in 118, Narbo Martius (Narbonne) was founded, the first colony of Roman citizens in Gaul. Southern Gaul was formed into a Roman province. And through this, Roman Spain was linked by a land route with Italy, the Via Domitiana.

Intervention in Africa against Jugurtha (113–105 BC)

Rome engaged in a long and hard war against Jugurtha of Numidia to avenge the Italian *negotiatores* established at Cirta (Constantine) whom he had put to death. Pursued by Caecilius Metellus seconded by C. Marius, and then by C. Marius seconded by Sulla, the redoubtable warrior was finally overcome in the summer of 105. This was mainly thanks to the betrayal of his father-in-law, King Bocchus of Mauretania, who was persuaded by Sulla to hand him over. Rome did not annex Numidia, but numerous Italian businessmen established themselves there. Mauretania became a protected kingdom. And farther east, Leptis Magna (in present-day Libya), a free and friendly town, received a Roman garrison. This allowed Rome to control African trade as far as Tripolitania.

Intervention in Asia Minor and Cyrenaica (102–96 BC)

A few years later, in 102, in order to put down piracy in the eastern Mediterranean, a Roman expedition landed in Cilicia, where the highly indented coastline provided havens for pirates. Their bases were annihilated and the province of Cilicia was formed.

In 96, there was a new inheritance: the king of Cyrene, Ptolemaeus Physkon, bequeathed his territory to the Roman people. A new province was set up there. Its principal wealth lay in sylphium, a much sought-after medicinal plant.

The wars against Mithridates (88–62 BC)

The king of Pontus, Mithridates VI Eupator, was Rome's most formidable enemy in Asia Minor. Cicero described him as "our empire's most relentless adversary." Having gained mastery of the province of Asia, he there massacred all Italian nationals (30,000 according to some, 150,000 according to others). Following this bloodbath, which was unique in the history of antiquity, he claimed to be Asia's liberator. Between 88 and 62 it took three wars, demanding enormous efforts on Rome's part and the sending of its best generals (Sulla, Lucullus, and Pompey), to bring the matter to an end. In 63, Mithridates committed suicide. Pompey was in charge of reorganizing the Anatolian provinces of Asia, Cilicia, and Bithynia. These he protected on the Parthian side, toward the east, by vassal states acting as buffers.

The conquest of Syria (64–63 BC)

With Mithridates defeated, Pompey set out for Syria, which had been in a state of considerable disorder since 69, when Antiochus XIII was restored to the throne of the decrepit Seleucid empire: cities had been seized by tyrants; the depredations of pirates and highwaymen had gone virtually unchecked. Pompey's solution was characteristically direct – he declared Syria to be a Roman province. Deputations arrived meanwhile from Palestine, bearing gifts from Hyrcanus and Aristobulus, the sons of Jannaeus, who had been warring since 67 for the throne of the Maccabees. Pompey's lieutenant Gabinius had earlier intervened in favor of Aristobulus, who was supported by the Sadducees and was now under siege in Jerusalem. But Pompey chose instead to support Hyrcanus, who had the backing of the Pharisees and was thought to be more pro-Roman than his brother. Aristobulus agreed to submit, but his followers refused, and barricaded themselves in the Temple quarters of Jerusalem, which Pompey was therefore obliged to besiege (for three months). He recognized Hyrcanus to be High Priest and ruler, but not king, of Judaea.

The annexation of Cyprus (58 BC)

The island was stripped of its independence because its king, Ptolemy, had allegedly helped the pirates whose depredations had become commonplace during the war with Mithridates. There was no resistance: Ptolemy committed suicide; Cyprus was added to the province of Cilicia.

The conquest of Gaul (58–51 BC)

The region that the Romans called "long-haired Gaul" (*Gallia Comata*) was, according to Caesar, whose *Gallic War* provides a detailed, if sometimes self-serving, account of his campaigns there, divided into three ethnically distinct regions, each with its own languages, customs, and institutions: the south-west, between the Garonne and the Pyrenees, where the Aquitani lived; the center, which was home to various Celtic tribes such as the Aedui and Sequani; and the north, which was inhabited by the Belgae, mixed tribes of Celts and Germans. The Gauls were primarily an agricultural people who lived mostly in villages or small towns. There were a few mining and manufacturing centers on major rivers and trade routes, and several hilltop fortresses in the interior, including Bibracte (near Autun), Gergovia (near Clermont-Ferrand), and Alesia (near the headwaters of the Seine). The largest political unit was the tribal state (*civitas*), a loose confederation of more or less independent clans, which often fought among themselves.

When Caesar arrived in Transalpine Gaul in the spring of 58, the Helvetii of western Switzerland had begun to migrate west to escape the aggression of their Germanic neighbors, the Suebi. They had already assembled at the banks of the Rhône, having burnt their homes and villages behind them. Caesar refused to let them cross. Why he wanted to make war on the Helvetii is unclear: we might suppose that he saw in them an opportunity to win military glory; perhaps he genuinely believed that they were a threat to the security of the province. After some minor skirmishes, the Helvetii were decisively defeated at Bibracte. Envoys now arrived from many parts of central Gaul to request Caesar's help against Ariovistus, king of the Suebi, whose rudeness at a subsequent meeting with Caesar afforded him a suitable pretext for war. Somewhere along the eastern slopes of the Vosges (perhaps near Cernay), Ariovistus' army was routed; the survivors fled to the Rhine; Ariovistus died shortly afterwards.

When news reached Caesar in 57 that the Belgae were making military preparations, he advanced against them. Short of supplies, and overcome by mutual jealousies, they gradually dispersed. By the end of 57, the greater part of Gaul had been overrun.

In 56, while his lieutenants Quintus Sabinus and Publius Crassus reduced Normandy and Aquitania, Caesar marched against the Veneti, in Brittany. He had their leaders executed and the rest of the population sold into slavery. His next victims were the Usipetes and Tencteri, who had been driven across the Rhine by the Suebi. When they refused his offer of land east of the Rhine, he defeated them, and slaughtered their women and children. Late in the summer of 55, he launched his first attack on Britain, eager, perhaps, to lay claim to its reported mineral wealth. The invasion was short-lived, accomplishing little more than the submission of some tribal leaders in Kent. He returned in 54, defeated a Kentish army near Canterbury, and overwhelmed some Belgic tribes who had combined their forces under Cassivellaunus, king of the Catuvellauni.

By 52, Gaul was restless. Disturbances at Rome after the death of Publius Clodius touched off a rebellion across much of central Gaul, led by the Arvernian chief Vercingetorix, at whose hands Caesar suffered his first real defeat, at Gergovia. Later, near Dijon, he met up again with Vercingetorix, whom he forced into the hilltop fortress of Alesia. Though a large relief army came to his aid (250,000-strong, according to Caesar), Vercingetorix was eventually forced to surrender. Six years later, he was displayed in Caesar's triumph, and then executed.

It is clear that Caesar's conquest of Gaul was made easier by the disunity of the Gauls, and by the absence, until Vercingetorix, of an effective leader. It is undeniable also that, in opening up central Europe to Mediterranean civilization, it changed the face of history.

The annexation of Numidia (46 BC)

In the course of the civil war between Caesar and Pompey, Juba I of Numidia unwisely elected to side with the Pompeians who had occupied north Africa. When they were defeated by Caesar at Thapsus in 46, he paid with his kingdom.

It may be seen that imperialism became the concern of the great *imperatores* of the late Republic. It was then put to the service of their personal ambition. We shall return to this.

If Rome's conquest of the countries of the Mediterranean basin was a historical phenomenon of great importance in itself and for the destiny of the Western world, it was no less so for its many consequences at the heart of the imperial power.

THE ECONOMIC, SOCIAL, AND POLITICAL CONSEQUENCES OF THE CONQUESTS

The effects of the conquests were considerable in all aspects of Roman life, altering principally the conditions of the economy, of social life, and of political action. The Gracchan crisis, the slave wars, and the Social War all stemmed from the growth of empire.

NEW LIVING CONDITIONS IN ROME AND ITALY

The first fruits of the wars and victories reaped in Rome were economic; the rapidly following second growth social and political.

In the economy, several factors played their part, contributing to profound changes.

First, the looting of the countries, both traversed and vanquished. "So numerous were the spoils coming from wealthy nations that Rome was incapable of containing the fruits of its victories," notes the historian Florus (*Epit.* I.18). Tarentum and Syracuse paid a heavy tribute in works of art and money. To take but one example, in the course of his Asiatic campaigns Pompey drained the East of huge sums of money.

To the booty of war were added the indemnities imposed on the defeated rulers and the taxes levied on the provinces. This vast influx of booty and steady flow of gold brought about enormous movements of capital in a city hitherto devoted mainly to agricultural activities. They affected wages and the cost of living (generally by an increase at the expense of the poorer classes), but chiefly the financial world (devaluation of the denarius) and overall economic policy.

The long absences of Rome's citizen soldiers in distant theaters of war, preventing them for many years at a time from working their lands, as well as the army's need for vast quantities of cereals, oil, and wine, these things above all resulted in profound alterations in Italian agriculture. But the influx of slaves taken as prisoners of war (e.g. 50,000 on the taking of Carthage, 140,000 Cimbri and Teutons in 104) and of foreign corn newly made available, also left their mark. For the poorer peasants (the majority), there were only two ways

IVNIVS

Plate 5.3   A slave-boy named Iunius in a kitchen at Pompeii.

of coming to terms with the commercial unattractiveness of Italian cereals brought on by the increasing availability of foreign corn: to sell their land (hence the rural exodus and consequent proletarianization of the urban population, above all in the city of Rome), or to plant vineyards and olive groves as well, or instead, which were, however, costly replacements. The first resulted in the beginnings of the merging of properties, to the advantage of the largest beneficiaries of war (generals and *negotiatores*), the second in a diversification in the crops grown in Italy, bringing in its turn the development of rural commercial activity, with the organization of markets and the subversion or overcoming of the habit of self-sufficient living.

Development toward a trading economy was one of the new features of the second century. The opening up of Rome to the outside world, the activities of businessmen, the monetary influx, and increasing needs connected with the new conditions of living drove Romans and Italians to plunge into large commercial operations. As early as 218, a *lex Claudia* had attempted to prohibit senators from engaging in any lucrative activity based on trade – a law which they managed to get round by resorting to "puppets." Capital investment and financial loans (frequently at extortionate rates) became the major preoccupation of the wealthy. Delos emerged as a great trading center and huge slave market. The *Romaioi* were actively present in every Mediterranean port. They began forming joint stock companies in the hands of publicans (tax-gatherers), who put pressure on the provincials. Hatreds began to pile up.

The social and political transformations brought about by the conquests were no less important. The growth of slavery was perhaps the most spectacular phenomenon. In rural areas, the flood of slave labor contributed to the creation of a new type of agriculture and, at least in certain regions, to a preference for stockbreeding. In the towns, and above all in the city of Rome itself, the influx of domestic slaves altered the conditions of family life. And in time they would play a far from negligible role in cultural life, and not only as scribes, doctors, and teachers.

Another effect of the conquests, and of the profits they allowed to accrue, was the formation of municipal elites in Italy's towns. This became noticeable first in central southern Italy, where there was an acceleration in the growth of villages into urban townships, their municipalization bringing to them an administrative status that attracted the *nouveaux riches* (*negotiatores* or their relatives). These, soon, would become urban benefactors, defending and adorning their seats with defensive walls, forums, and temples.

From the second century on, these municipal elites, *domus nobiles,* as Sallust termed them, constituted a "reservoir from which part of the knights (*equites*) would be recruited" (who in their turn would help supply the senatorial order with fresh blood). They provided the Rome of the late Republic with the executives and elements of a new society, one which, at the very last, with the triumvirs and Octavian, would begin gradually to replace the established nobility.

In Rome, the second century saw the rise of the equestrian order to greater social, economic, and political prominence, a process aided by the ferment of conquest. Between the traditional senatorial nobility, whose wealth was founded on land ownership, and the lower classes, an equestrian "order" had formed during the course of the third century and was now rapidly gaining ground, the basis of whose wealth might be other than land. This was not a "middle class" (which did not exist in Rome), but a category of privileged citizens – senators' sons, officers, rich landowners, publicans – whose membership was signified by their entitlement to a horse supplied and maintained by the state (they were known as *equites equo publico*). In the second century, these knights, who still played a paramount role in the centuriate assembly at election times, aspired to take a more active part in social and, chiefly, legal affairs. They saw the fact that the courts were in the hands of senators as contrary to their interests. This was especially so when in 149 a *lex Calpurnia* set up permanent tribunals (*quaestiones perpetuae*) charged with judging promagistrates (governors of provinces), with whom knights engaged in provincial trading and financial business had fertile connections. The political power of the knights grew ever stronger from the time of the Gracchi.

There was an increased risk of conflict erupting because the senatorial class itself was undergoing changes. Although it still held the monopoly of high office (Senate and magistracies) and retained its land-based fortune and wealth (obligatory rating qualification: 400,000 sesterces, the same as for the equestrian order), the tendency to retain the gaining of high office within families to whose ancestors high office had once been given had led to the evolution of a group within it to whom the distribution of high office was increasingly confined, the *nobiles*. There were thus still patricians on the one hand and plebeians on the other. But now the group of the *nobiles* was on the increase, at first comprising former senior magistrates and their descendants, but by the end of the second century, limited to the descendants of former consuls. Therefore the same families (*gentes*) came to monopolize all the high offices. In the face of the new senators and the ambitions of the knights, this ruling social group appeared to be immobilized. At the same time, immense fortunes were being accumulated which did not always lie within their hands.

The tensions created by this increasing disparity between incomes and political weight among the upper social classes were accentuated by troubles among the free lower classes, whom the conquests had brought certain real social benefits (through the development of urban and even rural craftsmanship, and the boom in small trade thanks to the expansion of Italy's internal and foreign trading), but also undoubted ills, especially among the lowest ranks. Indeed, an *infima plebs* (free proletariat) was being formed in Rome, composed of those driven from the rural world, small shopkeepers (the *tabernarii*), the jobless, the unemployed professionals, the victims of slave-labor competition. They made up a "dangerous class" of people ready to form an army of rebellion.

But this period also saw the appearance of a social group that, at first in economic life, and then in the political world, proved to be increasingly happy and active. These were the freedmen: slaves, often men of quality or very astute, who had obtained their emancipation. Having become *liberti* (free citizens, but with reduced political rights), they stayed in the service of their former masters, as "clients" or supporters. Thus in the second century "clienteles" were formed serving chiefly the political interests of their "patrons" – at election times as their active partisans. When Gaius Gracchus came to the Forum, he was accompanied by some 3,000 friends and clients in procession. The pressures that could be exerted may be imagined.

Out of these new economic, social, and political conditions of life arose three great conflicts which deeply marked Rome's history and, to a certain extent, paved the way for the decline of the Republic.

THE GRACCHAN CRISIS (133–121 BC)

By 133 BC, at a point when the first grave political crisis of the second century was about to begin, three camps had formed among the leading political circles in Rome: the "conservative-liberals," like Scipio Aemilianus, victor of Carthage, who were prepared to make reasonable concessions to the aspirations of rising forces; the "reformers," such as the leader of the Senate, Appius Claudius Pulcher, and Tiberius Gracchus, who were influenced by the Stoics; and the "conservatives," like P. Scipio Nasica, the *pontifex maximus*, who put the safety of the state first and were ready to defend legality at all costs, even by force.

Evidently, the main line of opposition lay between those whose overriding aim was to maintain and ensure the safety of the state (*salus rei publicae*) and those whose watchword was the welfare of the people (*salus populi*). This opposition had become all the keener with the passage of the tabular laws, instigated by the people. The contentious innovation introduced by these was the replacement of the oral vote in the *comitia tributa* with a written vote (*tabella*), in 139 for the elections to minor magistracies, and in 137 for judgements – a secret ballot, in other words, with all that flows from that for good or ill. Now, in 133, the people demanded the same procedure for voting on laws.

At the same time, the "agrarian question," set out well by Appian in his *Bellum civile* I.7–8, was being much debated in Rome and Italy, both by those who wanted to protect their interests and by those demanding greater "justice." This question had in fact first been posed after Rome's conquest of the Italian territories, when a Roman territory (*ager Romanus*) had been formed and, within that *ager Romanus*, a public domain of the Roman people (*ager publicus*). In the *ager Romanus*, private appropriation of land was possible. In the *ager publicus*, it was exceptional; this patrimony of the Roman people, which was to assure them of income, was "allocated" either gratis (in exchange for services, or awarded to colonists) or for a fee. In theory, therefore, there was no full and complete ownership in the *ager publicus*, but only use or enjoyment (*possessio*), the state remaining the owner. In fact, with the passing generations, the *possessores* tended to look upon themselves as real landowners. And unwarranted acquisitions and usurpations of land had begun to occur. Furthermore, to the detriment of peasant smallholdings, large pastoral domains were formed there, their creation facilitated by the increase in slave labor. Thus between 145 and 133 the agrarian question reared its head sharply: with the state wanting to recover its property that had been wrongfully appropriated, and the occupiers ill-disposed to let themselves be stripped of what they saw as theirs; with peasants without land demanding some, and land without peasants given over to pasture.

Rome's domain (Ager Romanus)	
Late sixth–early fifth century BC	983 km²
340 (start of the Latin War)	3,098
Around 330	6,040
264 (after the conquests in Italy)	27,000
190 (after the Cisalpine conquest)	55,000
89 (after the Social War)	160,000
After 49 (Roscian law)	237,000

Civic population (adult males) (from the census figures)		
503 BC	120,000	
340	165,000	
264	292,000	
190	258,000	
124	394,000	
86	463,000	
70	910,000	
28	4,063,000	(with women and children)
AD 14	4,937,000	(with women and children)

Judging it to be the right moment, a young aristocrat, won over to the cause of the people, Tiberius Sempronius Gracchus, friend of the Scipios and son-in-law of the leader of the Senate, got himself elected tribune of the *plebs* for the year 133. Without delay he tabled a bill (the *rogatio Sempronia*) proposing the following:

■ A limit on individual possession of the *ager publicus*: 500 *jugera* (= 125 ha), plus 250 *jugera* per child, with a maximum of 1,000 *jugera* per family. It was thus a reward for having at least two children (and to that extent meant a stepping up of the birth rate) as well as a means of reconstituting a free peasant class without in any way affecting private property.
■ A college of three members (the *triumviri agris iudicandis adsignandis*) given the task of applying the law, with considerable powers to recover

land, judge the legitimacy of occupation, etc. This meant a reduction of the powers of the Senate, which until then had sole management of the *ager publicus*.

■ That lands reclaimed were to be distributed among "poor citizens," at the rate of 30 *jugera* per person, and these distributions were to be inalienable.

Presented to the people's assembly, the *rogatio* came up against the veto of another tribune, M. Octavius. During an impassioned session, Tiberius proposed the abrogation of M. Octavius' powers. When he had obtained his dismissal, the *rogatio* was voted and passed. The deposition of a tribune was an innovation (*res nova*), that is, for the Romans, a "revolution." Tiberius became a dangerous revolutionary. What is more, being downright provocative, he had himself elected one of the *triumviri* who were to apply the law, together with his father-in-law, Appius Claudius Pulcher, and his brother Gaius. To cap it all, he sought a second tribuneship, something completely at odds with tradition.

It was the signal for violence. The *pontifex maximus*, Scipio Nasica, rose against him. In the summer of 133, during a riot, Tiberius was assassinated and his body thrown into the Tiber.

The agrarian question was revived in 125 by Gaius Sempronius Gracchus. Elected tribune in 124 for 123, ten years after his brother, "against the Senate and in the most brilliant manner" (Appian I.21), "by an immense crowd that the Campus Martius could not contain" (Plutarch, *Gaius Gracchus* 32), he lost no time in once again bringing the agrarian conflict into the political arena. Naturally, he renewed the *rogatio Sempronia*, but skillfully, with certain shrewd amendments – for example, excluding from land recoveries parts of the Roman domain of particular interest to senators. He then decided to found colonies, two in Italy and one overseas, in Carthage. Above all, he caused a sensation with the *lex Sempronia frumentaria*, a corn law benefiting the proletariat of Rome (every citizen living there would receive a bushel of corn (40 lb) every month at a price reduced by state subsidy), and then with its immediate result, his reelection as tribune for 122. His opponents accused him of aiming for a higher and permanent tribuneship, a sort of "tribune monarchy." Meanwhile, a judiciary law had been voted which introduced into the courts as many knights as there were senators. This again serious innovation resulted in a rapprochement of the knights with the tribunes. And Gaius, politicly, also granted the knights the exploitation of the province of Asia (*lex de Asia*) and, in the theaters, reserved seats of honor for them next to those of the senators (*lex theatralis*).

Opposition raged, even among his friends. In 122, he was not re-elected tribune for 121, as he had wished. And in 121 a decree was passed putting an end to the attempt at colonizing Carthage. In response, he made the mistake of trying to resort to force. The Senate resorted to the ultimate senatorial decree, which enjoined magistrates "to do everything possible to prevent any misfortune befalling the Republic." In April 121, Gaius was murdered, together with 3,000 of his partisans.

Gracchan agrarian legislation was subsequently amended rather than abolished. And the question it tried to answer was to crop up again more than once in political life. But the Gracchan answer was also the occasion of the first violent political confrontations between citizens, and thus marked the first episode in the tragic civil wars that hastened the Republic's demise – a first episode made all the more dangerous by the start of the slave wars.

THE SLAVE WARS

The several serious slave wars that began their course at this time were provoked, first, by the sheer scale of the arrival of slaves, to start with mostly prisoners of war, and then bought in markets like that of Delos: a recent work estimates their number in the Italy of the second–first centuries BC at between 32 and 50 per cent of the population; secondly, by the harshness of some masters, mainly in the rural areas where in some parts slaves represented as much as 70 per cent of the population – their situation seems to have been especially painful in Sicily, under the iron rule of Greek masters; and thirdly, by the activities of ringleaders, most often of eastern origin.

The first of these slave wars was in Latium, where slaves employed as shepherds gladly and easily turned brigands, and the consuls of 143 and 141 had to use military force to quell them. But it was in Sicily, between 135 and 132, that the most serious revolts broke out, serious not only because of the number of rebels involved, but because of the strength of their organization, which took on the lineaments of a state. The first began in the region of Henna, under the influence of a slave of Syrian origin from Apamea, one Eunous, who claimed to be a soothsayer and devotee of the Syrian goddess Atargatis, but who also, and perhaps more usefully, called upon Demeter of Henna. There he had himself proclaimed king under the name Antiochus and set up his capital. A certain Achaeus (no doubt deriving his name from his Achaean origin) took a seat in his royal council. Another slave, a Cilician named Cleon, and his brother Comanus gained mastery of Agrigentum and placed themselves under the authority of Eunous. The rebels soon seized Tauromenium (Taormina), Catana, and Messina.

Sustained by the name of possession, home, and territory, and with religious backing, these collective revolts were difficult to suppress. It was not until 134 that Calpurnius Piso succeeded in recapturing Messina and was able, in 133, to begin the siege of Henna, and not until 132 that that town fell, with Cleon killed, and then Eunous, taken by surprise in a cave. It had been such a close shave that the Senate deemed it necessary to send a commission of ten senators to Sicily, with the task of reorganizing the province.

In 103, there was a rising of slaves in Campania, initially the individual undertaking of a Roman knight from Capua who was in love with a slave girl. The disturbances, however, reached Sicily. And at this point came the intervention of the Roman – or Italian – plebeians Varius and Salvius. The former had two rich landowners assassinated by their 30 slaves, while the latter, who claimed to be a seer, became king under the name of Tryphon, and was succeeded by a Cilician, Athenion, who claimed to be an astrologer. After several failures, the consul Aquillius managed to put down the insurrection in 101.

In Italy, the last and most famous of the slave revolts was that of Spartacus in 73.

This was different from the others: because of its proximity to Rome, which felt the threat all the more keenly; because of its origin, the actions of a Thracian gladiator which influenced the schools of gladiators in Capua; because of the personality of its leader, Spartacus, a man more Greek than barbarian; and because of the spontaneous nature of the movement.

The revolt opened with the occupation of the crater of Vesuvius and a victory over the praetor ordered to dislodge the rebels. Reinforced by the shepherd slaves of the Apennines, they then formed two groups, one commanded by Spartacus and the other by the Gaul Crixus. And the whole of southern Italy was pillaged.

Another difference from the Sicilian movements was that this one did not put on the mantle of a state. Spartacus' objective was to bring the slaves back to their home countries. On this point he differed from Crixus, who intended to remain in Italy.

In 72, both consuls were dispatched against the rebels. Crixus was killed. Spartacus then began to march north, as if he wanted to cross the Alps and take the Gaulish slaves home. After crossing Picenum, he vanquished the Cisalpine governor at Modena. Changing his tactics, he turned south toward Lucania, perhaps with the idea of taking the maritime route. A terrified Rome gave M. Licinius Crassus extraordinary command and six legions. Spartacus, seemingly cornered at the tip of Bruttium, managed none the less to escape in the winter of 72–71. Finally, with the help of Pompey, Crassus was able to defeat the rebels. Spartacus was killed, and 6,000 rebel slaves crucified along the Appian Way, between Capua and Rome. The remainder of Spartacus' army was crushed by Pompey on his return from Spain.

The revolt of Spartacus did not produce the same effects as the Sicilian wars. It brought no new legislation; the assurance of its total repression was enough. But the fear had been all the greater because fed by the memory and consequences of the Social War.

THE SOCIAL WAR (91–88 BC)

For three years Rome witnessed "the whole of Italy rise up against [it]" (Velleius Paterculus 2.15), the "great war" (as Diodorus Siculus called it). And for an apparently surprising reason: Rome's refusal to grant Italians the Roman citizenship they desired. In fact, the question had first been raised after the conquests in the third century. Since that time Italy had been a confused tangle of territories, with the privileges and rewards, rights and duties of the triumphant Roman state lying unevenly upon them.

In first place, of course, came Roman citizens. Full members of the civic body, they participated in all the state's activities; they enjoyed the benefit of civil and legal rights; since 167 (after Pydna) they had been free of the *tributum*, that is, direct taxation; and they were entitled to a share in booty, to agrarian allocations, and to distributions of corn. Next came the "Latins," who held a status half-way between that of citizens and that of *socii*, the third category. Inhabitants of Latin cities and colonies, the Latins shared the civil and legal rights of citizens (rights of contract, commercial and matrimonial), and were liable for certain fiscal and military dues (serving in auxiliary units). But these "allies with a Latin name" did not have all the political rights of citizens: in order to vote, they had to come to Rome and vote in a tribe drawn at random for each ballot. They aspired to full citizens' rights.

The *socii* or "allies" were peoples connected with Rome by a treaty that laid down their relations with the capital, which, in most cases, exerted close control over them. Although in general they had remained loyal during the Second Punic War, they had received no reward. Quite the reverse: since 177 they had been excluded from the possession of land which they had helped to win for or restore to the Romans. They continued to supply the Roman army with contingents that were indispensable to its wars of conquest.

In 123, Gaius Gracchus raised the possibility of granting citizenship to the Latins and Latin rights to the "allies." Not only did the Senate reject this proposal, but it was decided to expel from the capital those Latins and "allies" who had no voting rights. The matter resurfaced between 95 and 91, when new measures were taken to counter the infiltration of Latins and Italian "allies" into the city.

In 91, M. Livius Drusus, a "noble" demagogue, tabled a *rogatio* recommending, principally, a law that would grant citizenship to the Italians, as well as a new grain law. Immense hopes were raised among the Italians, but the senatorial oligarchy loosed their fury on Drusus. To support him, a commando group of 10,000 Marsi set off for Rome, intent on sacking the city. They were successfully persuaded to turn back. At the same time, the Senate rejected Drusus' *rogatio*, and in October 91 he was murdered in his own home. That gave rise to the revolt of the Marsi, and then of the Samnites, and soon of the whole of central and southern Italy. Thus began the Social War or war of the allies (*socii*).

This long and bitter struggle has sometimes been compared to the American Civil War. Great hatreds were unleashed: at Asculum (Ascoli) in Picenum, Roman women were scalped before being put to death; at Grumentum in Lucania, the small Roman garrison was put to the sword and the civilian population massacred. The Marsi and Samnites, most ardent of the rebels, precipitantly issued their own currency (a sign of sovereignty): among the Marsi this coinage bore the word *Italia*, and among the Samnites, in Oscan, *Vitalia*. Italian state institutions were set up and a capital, Corfinium, rechristened Italica. Faced with this secession and a "federal" contingent of some 100,000 men, Rome took fright. It decided on a very repressive measure (the *lex Varia*), and then dispatched its two best generals, C. Marius and L. Cornelius Sulla.

At the same time, by means of three laws, Rome gave evidence of its generosity by granting the essence of the Italian demands, notably by the *lex Julia* of 90: Roman citizenship was awarded to all the Latins and to the "allies" who had not taken up arms, or were willing to lay them down at that time. In December 89, the war seemed to have ended – though in a few places it was prolonged until 80.

On the face of it the "allies" had thereby won. But one vital question remained to be settled: how to integrate the new citizens (*novi cives*) into the civic body. Given the way voting proceeded in the *comitia*, and given the numbers of new citizens involved, their importance therein would be the greater the greater the number of the Roman tribes among which they were distributed. Seeing the danger of their presence in all or many of the 35 tribes upsetting the accustomed political arrangements, the Senate wanted to enrol them in only a few. Hence arose difficult disputes between *populares* and *optimates* (see glossary). It was not until a senatorial decree of 84 that the principle of their enrolment in the 35 tribes was conceded. And it was not until 70/69 that, under pressure from the *populares*, the related census-taking operations were completed – revealing that the adult male citizens at that time numbered 910,000, twice as many as before the war.

Apart from the coming about of those institutional changes that realized the hopes or fears of the advocates and opponents of this expansion, the main consequences of the Social War and of the enlargement of the citizen body (itself such a consequence) were, firstly, the wide diffusion of Roman law and the quickening of the process of Romanization in the peninsula that the Italians' access to Roman citizenship brought in its wake. Only the Cisalpine region remained a little apart, being still a province and administered as such until the time of Caesar. Secondly, as a result of the war, enormous "clienteles" were formed in Italy, for instance, that of Cn. Pompeius Strabo (father of Pompey the Great) in Picenum, where he owned vast properties. And finally, with the entry into the ruling classes of Rome of citizens from the Italian cities and colonies, a new society was in the making: moving gradually but relentlessly into the magistracies and the Senate, these new Italian Romans would eventually take over from the old Roman families.

As may be seen, the conquests had decisive effects on Rome's political, economic, and social development. Their consequences were no less important in the cultural and spiritual life of the Romans.

CULTURAL AND SPIRITUAL CONSEQUENCES

Direct contact with Magna Graecia and the Hellenistic world, the influx of foreigners, primarily slaves, into Rome and Italy, the increase in travel and trade throughout the Mediterranean, all these resulted in a transformation of the way of life on the peninsula, but chiefly in Rome, where in the second and first centuries BC a startling development is evident in its material culture as well as in the moral, intellectual, and spiritual life of its citizens.

THE DEVELOPMENT OF MATERIAL CULTURE

All aspects of the material culture of the peninsula at this time were affected by a trend toward grandiosity, luxury, and refinement.

In Rome, a town where architecture had largely remained simple and traditional, exotic stone temples were now being built, their bearing and manner announcing the sway of Greece, and conveying even the temptations of the East. Between 200 and 175, no fewer than fifteen temples were constructed. And between 146 and 121, a new series was built, featuring the Greek marble of Mount Pentelicus and the use of the portico. Other buildings began to give the city the look of a real capital; aqueducts, bridges, and roads enriched the urban plan. A new type of edifice, the basilica, appeared in Rome. The highly decorative Corinthian column became popular. And private houses became larger and more sumptuous, the number of great *domus* (private mansions), decorated with marble columns and possessing airy and ornate reception rooms, spurting at the end of the second century. In the Hellenized south of Italy at first, and then in central southern Italy, temples were built with vast sacred courtyards (*areae*) surrounded by colonnades – the temple of Apollo at Pompeii is a fine example. The most grandiose was the temple of Fortuna Primigenia at Praeneste. Built between 110 and 100, and then enlarged and embellished in the time of Sulla, it marked the triumph of macrotectonics and the baroque, with its great series of tiered terraces leading up to a *tholos* housing the sacred

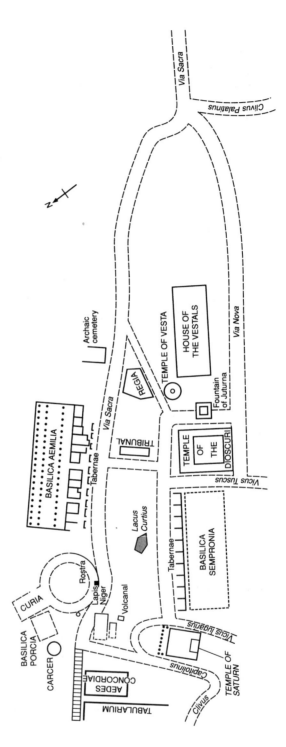

Figure 5.3 The republican Forum

Plate 5.4 Temple of Apollo, Pompeii. The statue of Apollo the Archer is a copy of a bronze statue found at the site, now in Naples Museum.

statue. Similarly, in the countryside large villas mushroomed, with porticoed gardens and gymnasia decorated with Greek works of art.

Matching the growing luxury of the public edifices and private dwellings, the settings of daily life, from the second century BC on there were luxurious developments in the adornments, clothing, and food of the Romans.

Back in 275, a consul had been excluded from the Senate for using a silver table service. Now engravers and silversmiths and other craftsmen began to manufacture in bronze and, sometimes, precious metals ornate vases and embellishments for beds and chests. In the same way, the coarse woollen tunic was replaced by tunics and togas of linen (from Egypt), and soon of silk (from the Far East). It is said that Lucullus had 200 purple cloaks. Roman cuisine was transformed as well. At the beginning of the third century, Romans were still mocked as "pultiphages" (porridge-eaters). A century later, bakers came on the scene. And now from far afield came peacocks, thrushes, guinea-fowl (from Africa), and pheasants (from Colchis), as well as the cooks to prepare them. The entire way of life of the Romans was undergoing a change.

AN INTELLECTUAL, SPIRITUAL, AND MORAL REVOLUTION

The second half of the third century had seen the appearance in Rome of the first generation of Latin literature, dominated by the personality of the Tarentine Livius Andronicus. In the years 215–160, the second generation was already triumphing. Naevius gave Rome its second national epic, devoted to an account of the war against Carthage. Roman history was born with Fabius Pictor. The comedies of Plautus emphasized the Italic and Roman nature of the theater. And, brought to Rome by Cato, Ennius, the first truly national poet, wrote, to the glory of Rome, 30,000 lines of a historiography entitled *Annales.*

Ennius provided the link with the "generation of 160" (P. Grimal's phrase). Led by the Scipios' circle, here we find Polybius, Terence, Laelius (the Wise), Pacuvius, the first tragic poet, Accius, perhaps the greatest of Roman tragedians, and lastly Lucilius, creator of the classical Latin satire.

In short, by the end of this period of exceptional intellectual expansion the main components of Latin literature had been born and were already in their various ways lustily proclaiming and refining the virtues and vices of Rome.

The Hellenization that so profoundly influenced the material culture of the Roman world flowed into its religion and morals through philosophy. We have already seen that, as early as the third century, Greek gods and rites had penetrated into the heart of Italy and Rome. With the Second Punic War and the upheavals and agitations it brought to the profaned peninsula there had come conspicuous developments in religious sensibility. It had been followed by a sort of fervent "national" reaction revealing itself in an invasive, luxurious, and often disorderly spirituality that manifested itself mainly at the time of the famous scandal of the Bacchanalia in 186 BC. In response to denunciations arising from a trivial event and calling the Bacchic mysteries into question, the Senate had been led to take extremely harsh repressive measures, resulting in over 7,000 men and women involved in legal proceedings and over 6,000 imprisoned or condemned to death, mainly in southern Italy and Rome, but also in Etruria. This affair revealed something of the extent of the popularity and influence of Dionysian mysticism.

To the same mystical trend, though flowing along different, even adverse channels, belonged the development of Orphism and Pythagoreanism, doctrines of purity combined with ascetic practices that enjoyed some success in Rome.

Meanwhile, the same movement of minds toward Greece brought into favor in Rome the schools of Greek philosophy, whose representatives there, mainly from Athens and Rhodes, increasingly attracted the young and the aristocratic. Such was the case with Stoicism, led by Panaetius of Rhodes, who, to counter the debasement of morals, recommended the practice of virtue, or rather of the four cardinal virtues: knowledge, justice, self-control, and courage. And so too with Epicureanism, a rival but aligned philosophy of virtuous contentment and atomistic explanation which achieved success in Rome at the end of the second century, and in the next century with Lucretius.

The significant shifts and evolutions in the morals of the Romans witnessed during the last two centuries of the Republic were what even ancient authors found most striking among the changes that had come with Rome's expansion. Polybius early on, and then later Sallust, Seneca, and Diodorus Siculus, not to mention Cato, vied with one another in denouncing the ever-increasing taste for pleasure as one of the major causes of republican Rome's decline. During his censorship, Cato had already taken measures against sumptuousness, particularly that of women, against luxury in food, etc. In 161, a law banned the fattening of chickens – and was met with hearty derision. But without doubt it was Sallust, in his *Conspiracy of Catiline*, who most strongly blamed moral reasons for the decline of the Republic, inveighing against not only the increase of luxury and the lust for pleasure, but also the gorgeous "contempt for the gods" and the impious corruption of men in power. A contemporary of Caesar, he himself had lived through the experience of Sulla and Pompey and the appalling civil wars that bathed Rome and Italy in blood. An observer of the political crisis of the Republic's last century, he well knew how to describe it.

Together with a great renaissance in literature and art, the conquests brought Rome the turmoil of serious disturbances in traditional political and social life and created the conditions for the overturning of ancient values. All that would explode in the first century BC.

6 / CRISIS OF THE REPUBLIC
The First Century BC

*T*HROUGH THE INSTITUTIONAL UPHEAVALS THAT IT HAD STARTED AND THE
RESORT TO VIOLENCE IT HAD PROVOKED, THE GRACCHAN CRISIS HAD
ALREADY SET IN MOTION THE GRAVE DISTURBANCES THAT ASSAILED THE ROMAN
REPUBLIC, VICTIM OF ITS OWN ITALIAN AND MEDITERRANEAN SUCCESSES. THE SLAVE
WARS AND, EVEN MORE, THE SOCIAL WAR SUBSEQUENTLY REVEALED ALL THE
WEAKNESSES OF A REGIME AND SOCIETY ESTABLISHED FOR A CITY-STATE, WHICH HAD
MEANWHILE BECOME A TERRITORIAL EMPIRE OF UNPRECEDENTED DIMENSIONS. IN THE
VIEW OF SALLUST AND VARRO, GAIUS GRACCHUS WAS AT THE ROOT OF THE CIVIL
WARS THAT BATHED THE LAST CENTURY OF THE REPUBLIC IN BLOOD. WE CAN AT
LEAST SAY THAT THE TRIBUNATES OF THE GRACCHI FORMED THE FIRST EPISODE OF
THE GREAT POLITICAL DRAMA THAT WAS TO SHAKE ROME, A DRAMA DOMINATED
BY ATTEMPTS TO SET UP PERSONAL POWER AND BY THE CONFLICTING AMBITIONS
OF MARIUS AND SULLA, POMPEY AND CAESAR, AND FINALLY MARK ANTONY
AND OCTAVIAN.
THE LAST CENTURY OF THE ROMAN REPUBLIC WAS IN MANY RESPECTS A DECISIVE
PERIOD IN ROME'S HISTORY: NOT ONLY BECAUSE IT WAS AN ERA WHEN, TO QUOTE
APPIAN, "VIOLENCE RULED EVERYTHING," THE FATE OF MEN AND OF THE RES
PUBLICA, BUT ALSO BECAUSE IT WAS A TIME WHEN TRADITIONAL VALUES WERE
COLLAPSING, OVERTAKEN BY NEW ATTITUDES OF MIND AND A DESIRE FOR NEW
STANDARDS OF LIVING.

PERSONAL AMBITIONS AND THE CIVIL WARS

The clash of personal political ambitions did not, of course, date from the end
of the second century BC, but at least until then it had occurred within the
framework of public institutions, in the Senate to influence or inspire important decisions, in the *comitia* to steer popular votes at the time of elections to
the magistracies. Now, feeling themselves less and less subject to institutional
rules increasingly held up to ridicule by all and sundry, those with political ambitions were more and more disposed to seek their achievement outside the
settled arrangements for gaining power within the Republic, and to this end

would have a remodeled instrument of personal advancement at their service: the army.

A NEW ROMAN ARMY

The republican army of the early days had been "national, based on the *census* and not permanent" (C. Nicolet). The whole military organization, as we have seen, was founded on the "Servian" constitution. The army was the state army; citizens served in it according to their wealth and were summoned to take part in campaigns as required. Since the third century, however, and above all since the Second Punic War, things had changed. The scope of the wars, the length of campaigns, the impoverishment of the lower classes (bringing disqualifications from the duty to serve), and the growing reluctance of citizens to do their military service (*militia*) had meant that the number of men who could be mobilized from the five classes had become painfully insufficient. It had therefore been found necessary to lower the minimum qualification of the fifth class and admit the *proletarii*. This was a development sanctioned by the reform instituted by Marius in 107, when he had a new method of enrolment adopted: voluntary service to complement compulsory service. Henceforward, volunteer *proletarii* could enter the legions; they would be paid, would be entitled to a share in the booty, and would receive an allocation of land at the end of their service. This reform had important consequences. From now on citizens from the lower classes, and especially those from rural areas, would supply the main body of recruits. An army of rich citizens would be replaced by an army of volunteers of proletarian rank. Soldiers would tend to turn professional and become ever more closely bound to their leaders, from whom they would expect everything – pay, booty, distributions of gifts at the time of triumphs, and plots of land when colonial allocations were being made. An *esprit de corps* would develop. The republican national army was replaced by the armies of Marius, Sulla, Pompey, and, above all, Caesar. These were armies that were totally devoted to their leaders.

MARIUS

C. Marius, a knight originally from Arpinum (Arpino) in Latium, owed his rise to his brilliant military qualities but also to the political backing of the Caecilii Metelli. It was they who, thinking they could use him for partisan purposes, had got him into the senatorial class and helped him on to become, successively, quaestor, tribune, and praetor (in 115). Having served his proconsulship in Spain, he later found himself once again in receipt of the patronage of the Metelli when Metellus, consul for 109, took him to Numidia as his senior legate in the war against Jugurtha. It was there that he decided, against his patron's advice, to stand for the consulship himself, and his break with the Metelli dated from that time. Elected consul for 107, he then began an astonishing consular career that lasted twenty years, until his death in January 86.

A "new man" (homo novus) as consul

A "new man," meaning that he had no noble ancestors who had held a senior magistracy, Marius was conscious that he owed everything to his personal and, above all, military qualities and particularly, as he said, to his integrity. "An uneducated man," his compatriot from Arpinum, Cicero, said of him, "but a real man!"

Elected consul for 107 in spite of opposition from the "old nobility," Marius was immediately seen as the man of the *populares*. His military reform, achieved in the face of the reluctance and opposition of traditionalists, naturally strengthened that impression. It took the disaster of Orange in 105 for a coalition of the *plebs* and *equites* to bring about his re-election as consul for a second term, even though he was busy in Africa against Jugurtha, and thus absent from Rome (which was a departure from tradition).

The wiping out of two Roman armies by the Cimbri near Arausio (Orange) had been the climacteric of the "great terror" that had set upon Rome in 113 when that German tribe had invaded Noricum, a fear fed by rumors about the numbers and strength of the barbarian force and by memories of the capture of the city early in the fourth century. In 109, the Cimbri had broken through to the Sequani (Franche-Comté), in 107 a group of Helvetii had entered the province of Transalpine Gaul, where a consul was killed, and subsequently the Volcae Tectosages had rebelled, forcing a consul to intervene and take Toulouse. It was then that the Cimbri, resuming their offensive, had come down the Rhône towards Orange.

Consul once again in 104, Marius set about the task of saving Italy from the danger of a German invasion. Made consul again each year until 100, he forged a powerful army, introducing a tactical recasting of the legion and a standardization of weaponry, and carried off successive victories against the Cimbri, despite their having been reinforced by the Teutons, at Aix (102) in Transalpine Gaul and Vercellae (101) in Cisalpine Gaul.

He had thus held six consulships altogether. Never had republican institutions been similarly mocked. His *auctoritas* was vast, and the temptation to employ it in the service of ambition immense. A disposition to allow the personal glory of victory to overflow traditional bounds had been evident back in 104. Returning to Rome to celebrate his African triumph he had picked the day of his entry into consular office, and without laying down the triumphal insignia, he had arrived the following day to sit in the Senate clad in the purple mantle of victorious *imperatores*. It was the first time that a military leader had insisted on wearing his triumphal apparel after the triumph. But Marius was no statesman; he made no use of his army to serve his personal ambition. Rather, he allowed himself to be used by the leaders of parties who were clever enough to involve him in their political struggles, and even to be led into civil war.

From 99 to 86 BC: the decline of Marius

Keeping his distance from the Social War as much as possible, Marius, who had had a house built close to the Forum, tried to enjoy the "warrior's rest" there in spite of the pressures brought to bear on him by his *populares* friends, led by two troublemakers, Saturninus and Glaucia, whom Cicero kindly described as "the ordure of the Senate." To escape from this Roman "climate," he managed to obtain an embassy (*missio libera*) to the East in 98. This was the occasion of his first encounter with Mithridates. And his row with Sulla stemmed from this new attraction for eastern affairs.

The conflict with Sulla (88) The Social War had just ended when another danger reared its head with the attack on the province of Asia by the king of Pontus, Mithridates VI Eupator. Who would take command of the expedition to be mounted against him? Sulla, to whom the Senate had legally entrusted this "province"? Or Marius, the experienced general, old it is true (he was then 72) and ill, but in a strong position because of his knowledge of the king and the support of the *populares*, who wanted it for him despite the Senate's decision?

The matter seemed on the way to being settled by the transfer of the command to Marius. But when, anticipating this, he had decided to send two military tribunes to take command of the army of Campania in his name, Sulla considered this a provocation and marched on Rome with his legions. He then persuaded the Senate to banish Marius, who, however, managed to escape to Campania. Though captured at Minturnae, where he was in hiding, Marius again managed to escape, fleeing this time to Ischia, whence he reached Africa to rejoin his old soldiers, who had been allocated land there through his good offices. Marius "took to the bush," but only for a while.

After Sulla's eventual departure for Asia to deal with Mithridates, the *populares* regained power in Rome. Marius landed in Etruria, recruited volunteers, joined forces with Cinna, one of the leaders of the *populares*, took Ostia, occupied the Janiculum and, at the end of 87, made his entry into Rome, which was given over to massacres. The senators hastened to revoke their banishment of Marius, while Sulla was declared a public enemy.

On January 1, 86, Cinna and Marius together took the consulship: it was the *imperator's* seventh time. On January 17, he died of pleurisy. Thus came the abrupt end, after a brief return to favor, of the "fortunate" general who for seven years had been master of Rome. He could have founded a military monarchy; he had not wished to do so. But he had prepared the mantle that would be donned by Sulla.

SULLA

The man who now came to dominate Roman political life, having faced down first Marius and then the *populares*, his political enemies, was of a quite different type. An aristocrat from an old patrician family, fond of pleasure, cultivated, even erudite, generous, charming, a successful man, a shrewd diplomat (it was he who had persuaded Bocchus, Jugurtha's father-in-law, to hand him over, though Marius took the credit), as well as an excellent military leader – in many ways L. Cornelius Sulla made a lively contrast to his older rival.

He had begun his political career fairly late. Quaestor in 108 (at the age of 30), he had served with distinction in Africa under Marius. Praetor in 97, he had caught the attention of the Romans by the sumptuousness of the "Apollo's games" he had given. Sent on mission to the East in 96, with the title of proconsul of Cilicia, he had had to deal simultaneously with Mithridates and the Parthians, Rome's perpetual rivals, on the subject of Armenia. From that emerged, on a diplomatic level, a pact of friendship between Rome and Parthia, which boosted his reputation as a wise diplomat, and on a personal level, a sense of merit or achievement that would give rise to sharp feelings of resentment when he saw Marius appointed over his head in 88 to conduct operations against the king of Pontus. From then on, Sulla found himself thrust straight into political agitation and civil war.

Agitation and civil war (87–82 BC)

In Rome, since the unmethodical attempt of the tribune M. Livius Drusus in 91 to resolve all the outstanding problems at once (the agrarian question, food distribution, the composition of the courts, relations with the "allies"), violence had made a comeback. Elected consul for 88, Sulla was, as we have seen, put in charge of operations in Asia, ensuring the favor of the powerful Metelli by marrying one of their family, Caecilia Metella. We have also seen how Marius provoked him by attempting to make certain, on his own behalf, of the six expeditionary legions massed at Capua, while in Rome a tribune of the *plebs* was maneuvering to deprive Sulla of that command. Gathering support among his legions, Sulla marched on Rome and seized it by force. For the very first time a Roman general under arms, with his legionaries, trampled the sacred soil of the city. This *coup d'état* laid the ground for many others. Sulla had shown the way.

After his departure (in March 87) first for Greece and then Asia, disturbances resumed not only in Rome, with L. Cornelius Cinna, but also in Italy, where partisans of Marius and Sulla were beginning to take opposing sides. Marius' return to the scene and his siege of Rome, horrifying in the heat of summer, were followed by terrible reprisals against Sulla's supporters: Rome lived in a bloodbath.

When the return of Sulla, the conqueror of Mithridates, became known, there was a short period of relative calm, dominated by the fear of reprisals. But then the violence resumed even more fiercely. Landing at Brindisi in the spring of 83, Sulla found himself confronted by a senatorial army, commanded by the consuls and with the mission of applying the senatorial decree which, at Cinna's instigation, had outlawed him. After bitter fighting which lasted through the summer of 83 and then the spring and summer of 82, Sulla gained control of Rome on November 1, at a cost of between 50,000 and 70,000 dead in the two armies and 3,000 executed among the 12,000 prisoners whom Sulla assembled on the Campus Martius.

The great proscription of 82 BC

Sulla also carried out a purge of Rome's ruling circles. Unable to obtain from the senators the legal means of doing so, he took matters into his own hands. He had the names of those he wished removed published in "proscription" lists, thus inventing "a new method of purging" (F. Hinard) or, perhaps, a "controlled purge," possibly intended to avoid even larger massacres. Sulla's proscription consisted of:

- The public display in the usual places (*proscribere* meant both to put on display and to proscribe) of an edict of the proconsul justifying the measures taken, before enumerating them.
- A ban on any shelter or help given to the named individuals, the threat of death for those who broke the ban, a reward of 40,000 sesterces for the denouncer or murderer of a proscribed person, and, similarly, emancipation for slaves who did so.
- A list of 80 members of senatorial rank, all Marian magistrates or former magistrates. A second and then a third list appeared subsequently with a further 440 names.

There were appalling scenes in Rome and Italy, notably at Praeneste, which had dared to resist Sulla in 83/82, and scandalous transfers of property (the confiscated possessions of the proscribed) and egregious acquisitions of wealth (from the same source).

The purge completed, it was necessary to fill the power vacuum.

Sulla's dictatorship (82–79 BC)

A *lex Valeria* conferred the dictatorship on Sulla, that is to say, full powers, but with no time limit – therein lay the institutional "novelty" or, if preferred, "revolution." It granted him:

■ The legalization of his past actions.
■ The right over life and death.
■ The right to share out the lands of the *ager publicus* and create colonies. This he did in Etruria, Umbria, Latium, Campania, and Corsica (at Aleria). It was a means of rewarding his troops and building up "clienteles" for himself.
■ The right to dispose of the conquered kingdoms.

Here we have "the first example of a law of delegation of sovereign authority (*lex de imperio*), on which imperial power would later be based" (A. Piganiol).

The years 81–80 were marked by intense activity on Sulla's part, both political and self-publicizing. Certain lost powers were restored to the Senate, and its authority was even strengthened: bills tabled by tribunes were to be submitted for its prior agreement, and the tribunes' right of veto was reduced. This has led some historians to see Sulla as a defender of the senatorial class. On the other hand, Sulla purged the Senate by proscription (as we have seen) and then raised the number of members from 300 to 600. That allowed him to fill it with his own men. Hence the accusation of his having "tamed" the Senate and of having, in effect, exercised a completely personal rule.

In the same spirit of either senatorial restoration or personal control, he increased the number of magistrates and reduced the judiciary power of the equestrian order, restoring court juries to the senators.

After celebrating a sumptuous triumph in 81, he surrounded himself with a train – which some called "royal" – of 24 lictors (consuls had only 12), while propaganda presented him as "Felix," the leader blessed by the gods, the particular protégé of Venus, and thus an eternal victor (the Greeks used the word *Epaphroditus* = protected by Aphrodite-Venus, translated by the Latins as *Felix* = fortunate). Here we have the first example of the use of a divinity to serve the personal ambition of an *imperator*.

Tired and ill, and perhaps believing that he had accomplished the essential part of his task by restoring order to Rome and reinstating its institutions, or, faced with an opposition that was once more rearing its head, having no desire to resort to fresh violence, at all events, in the year 80 (or 79 in the opinion of some historians) he abdicated and began to write his memoirs. He died in 78 in his sixtieth year.

For the "democrats" he was a tyrant *par excellence*, and that viewpoint was subsequently adopted by the nobility and developed by Caesarian propaganda eager to contrast Caesar with a Sulla-type dictator. But the historian cannot overlook the thoughtful changes that he effected in the state, the fact that he was able to "lay power aside" (as Plutarch says), and, perhaps above all, his work of urban renewal, both in Rome itself and in many towns in Italy, notably at Pompeii, where he created a *colonia Cornelia Veneria*. After him, Pompey had some difficulty in imposing his presence.

THE DOMINANCE OF POMPEY AND ITS HAZARDS (79–48 BC)

Born in 106/105, the son of Cn. Pompeius Strabo, master of Picenum during the Social War, Pompey had the early assistance of good fortune: first in inheriting his father's large clientele, and then in choosing to side with Sulla when he landed at Brindisi. His brilliant military qualities did the rest. In Africa, where he had been sent to fight the Marians, his soldiers acclaimed him with the title *Magnus*, "the Great" (the first to bear it since Alexander). And in 79, at the age of 26, he was able to celebrate his first triumph in Rome.

His successes under difficult conditions (79–61 BC)

Of equestrian origin, Pompey owed his first chances to the favor of Sulla. His first difficulties came with his inordinate ambition and total absence of scruples. And his qualities as a soldier and ability to make use of the dangerous situations of the moment won him his first successes.

Through seeking the consulship for 79 (while he was merely a knight and had therefore not been able to fulfill the prerequisite steps in a senatorial career), Pompey had fallen out with Sulla, who, for his part, was apprehensive of this over-young and ambitious man's popularity. Allying himself with the "nobles" against the dictator, he thus appeared, after Sulla's abdication, to be the man of the senatorial clan, an impression strengthened when he married Mucia, a close relation of the Metelli, and supported the candidacy for the consulship of M. Aemilius Lepidus, Sulla's relentless enemy. His course, however, took him away from these settled influences and returned him, eventually, clothed in the imposing mantle of a great military chief.

He first opposed Lepidus, an "utter scoundrel" (J. Carcopino) who, having failed to obtain a second consulship, tried to stir up Etruria and Cisalpine Gaul. Pompey succeeded in neutralizing him. Lepidus retreated to Sardinia, where he succumbed to disease.

Next, Pompey had to deal with Sertorius in Spain. An excellent officer of Sabine origin, who had joined the *populares*, Sertorius had been able to win the hearts and minds of the Spanish during his rule there from 83 to 81. When Sulla had sent Metellus to Spain to succeed him, Sertorius, backed by the provincials, had put up a resistance and soon dreamed of restoring popular

Plate 6.1 A scene from a play, with masked actors: a magician and his clients. The mosaic, signed by Dioscurides of Samos, is from Cicero's villa at Pompeii. National Archeological Museum, Naples.

government to Rome, starting from Spain. In 75, he successfully stood up to both Metellus and Pompey, the latter having arrived with reinforcements. Rome was threatened. In the end, armed with an *imperium infinitum majus*, i.e. an undefined and higher proconsular authority, Pompey managed to annihilate the threat of Sertorius, who was assassinated by one of his own lieutenants. He left the Iberian peninsula after taking measures to pacify the province, and had a memorial erected on the Perthus pass, its inscription attributing to him the capture of 870 "towns" (they were actually fortified sites belonging to the numerous tribes in the country). Crossing southern Gaul, where Marseille appointed him its patron, he returned to Italy, where he was required to combat Spartacus, hastening to help Crassus, who despaired of winning.

Victory was achieved in 71. After six years away, Pompey came back to Rome in a halo of glory, and still eaten up with ambition. It was an ambition that was beginning, with some justification, to alarm the Senate, and that would find its largest field of action in the East.

The agreement with Crassus and the consulate of 70 BC
Despite their initial disagreements, Pompey and Crassus, both thirsting after power, reached an accord to force the Senate to grant them the right to stand

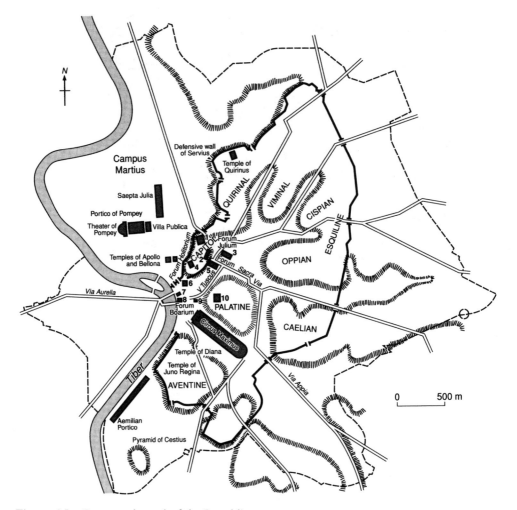

Figure 6.1 Rome at the end of the Republic

together for the consulate of 70. It was an absolutely illegal candidacy: on Crassus' part because he had just laid down the praetorship, a fact which imposed a legal time lapse before he could seek the higher office; on Pompey's, because he had still held none of the offices that had to precede the consulship.

The Senate's agreement rendered their candidacy legal. They had accomplished in fact a peaceful *coup d'état*, striking a serious new blow at republican institutions. The two consuls took advantage of their position to eradicate all the Sullan laws, one after the other:

- The tribunes regained their former powers.
- The censorship was re-established, and the new censors struck off 64 senators who were considered to be corrupt, the majority for profiting from the proscriptions.
- 100,000 Italian immigrants in Rome were inscribed on the list of citizens.
- At the time (autumn 70) of the trial of the notorious Verres, former propraetor of Sicily, who had been indicted by Cicero, the knights resumed their place in court juries, to the disadvantage of the senators. Pompey henceforward passed for a supporter of the knights, and he certainly treated their covetousness in the financial affairs of the provinces indulgently. It was an alliance that relaunched Rome's imperialism based on conquest.

Pompey in the East (67–61 BC)

Rome at that time found itself confronted with a triple danger abroad: in the Aegean, the depredations of pirates, who were severely hindering maritime trade; in Macedonia, the incursions of Thracian barbarians; in Asia, fresh threats from Mithridates and his son-in-law, Tigranes, king of Armenia. Leaving the governor of Macedonia the task of fighting the Thracians, Pompey first undertook to combat the pirates. In order to do so, and with the backing of a young senator called C. Julius Caesar, he had himself granted exceptional powers. The *lex Gabinia* of 67 conferred on him for three years supreme command over all the seas and coastal areas as far as 80 km inland, from the Bosporus to the Straits of Gibraltar (Pillars of Hercules), with an army of 20 legions, a fleet of 500 vessels, and the right to appoint his own legates, numbering 20. Never had one man alone, an *imperator*, combined such powers, powers placing Italy and Rome under his sole military authority. This gives some measure of the degree of decline in traditional institutions.

In a lightning campaign, from March to May 67, Pompey eliminated piracy from the Mediterranean. Following on its heels, he embarked on a campaign against Mithridates, this time armed with the *lex Manilia*, which confirmed his *imperium* for an unlimited duration, gave him full command of the war, and invested him with the power to conclude alliances and treaties. This was the occasion for Cicero to deliver his first great political discourse, the famous *De imperio Cn. Pompei*, in which he gave a brilliant eulogy of the qualities and "fortune" of Pompey, like Sulla a favorite of the gods, protected by Venus *victrix* (who grants victory).

It took Pompey a little over two years to overcome the king of Pontus, hold a court of twelve kings at Amisus, conquer Syria and take Jerusalem (above, p. 94). At the same time, this "empire-builder," as he has been termed, organized the East, with new provinces (Bithynia-and-Pontus, Cilicia, and Syria), surrounded by protected kingdoms and a string of states devoted to Rome. In this eastern activity he revealed himself to be a great administrator – and his work would survive.

He returned to Rome in 61, after conquering fourteen nations. Was he aiming at a "monarchy"?

Pompey's would-be "monarchy"

Enjoying unrivaled prestige, the victorious *imperator* could, perhaps, have gained sole control of the civil power. His vanity and ambition drove him in that direction. But he was careful to act within the constitutional framework which in Rome still conditioned the pursuit of power and kept in check the civil discord attendant on its too vigorous pursuit. Moreover, he was well aware that during his absence Caesar had been cutting the ground from under his feet. To avoid re-igniting the civil war, he dismissed his army and contented himself, for the moment, with demanding the honors of a triumph. For two whole days, September 28–9, 61, the greatest and most sumptuous triumph ever seen was celebrated. So that the memory should endure, building was started on the Campus Martius of the most extraordinary architectural complex ever erected in the city: the first permanent stone-built theater, with a temple to Venus *victrix* at its summit, and a garden surrounded by a colonnade, the whole ornamented with colossal statues representing the fourteen vanquished nations and one of Pompey himself, shown nude, in heroic vein, holding in his hand a globe, symbol of the world (*kosmos*) and thus here the emblem of the "master of the world" (*kosmokrator*).

Cicero and Catiline (64–62 BC)

In 64, an impoverished young noble, Lucius Sergius Catilina, campaigned for the consulship of 63, on a platform calling for the cancellation of debts, and with the backing, it seems, of Caesar and Crassus. He lost to Cicero (and the disreputable Gaius Antonius). The following year, after trying, again unsuccessfully, to win the consulship (of 62), he is alleged to have hatched a conspiracy that, according to Cicero and Sallust, aimed at nothing less than the violent overthrow of the government. An uprising is said to have been planned for October 28, but Cicero got wind of it and persuaded the Senate to issue its "ultimate decree" against Catiline, who then fled to Etruria, where his co-conspirator Lucius Manlius was raising an army. Several other conspirators were arrested, and, after a spirited debate in the Senate, summarily executed on Cicero's orders. Not long after, Catiline himself died in battle. A characteristically self-satisfied Cicero was proclaimed father of his country. It was the apogee of his political career. But the legality of his actions would later be questioned, and the ghosts of the executed would come back to haunt him.

The First Triumvirate (60–54 BC)

While Pompey was fighting in the East, Rome had experienced difficult times: rivalries between *populares* and *optimates*, personal conflicts and clashes of ambition between Caesar and Crassus, antipathies and maneuverings between Cicero, a "new man" but well received by the Senate, and demagogues such as Catiline.

In 60, Caesar returned from Spain, eager to hold both a triumph and the consulship of 59. As a commander, he was forbidden to enter the city to declare his candidature; he therefore asked the Senate for permission to stand *in absentia*. The not unreasonable request was refused. Pompey, meanwhile, was pressing his demands – that his arrangements in the East be ratified, and that land be given to his veterans. Crassus, on behalf of the publicans, was trying to persuade the Senate to revise the terms of the contract for collecting the taxes of the province of Asia. They, too, were turned down. It was because of the Senate's uncompromising and, in many ways, short-sighted position that the three men agreed to form a political alliance, which modern historians call the First Triumvirate. It was a private and, in the beginning, secret agreement, later shored up by the marriage of Pompey to Caesar's daughter, Julia. The triumvirs enlisted one of the tribunes of 58, Publius Clodius, to act as their agent. He pushed through a number of laws, including one that provided for the distribution of free grain, and even managed to remove Cicero from Rome, by proposing a law that outlawed anyone who had executed a Roman citizen without trial.

Caesar, too, left Rome in 58, to take up his duties as governor of Transalpine Gaul. Soon after, Clodius launched a series of public attacks on Pompey, some think at the behest of Caesar or of Crassus. Pompey was even obliged to hide out in his house for several months, and later, in 56, to organize a rival gang of armed thugs under the leadership of Titus Annius Milo. The Triumvirate seemed to be breaking apart, when the three arranged to meet at Luca (mod. Lucca), in April 56, where they managed to patch up their differences, agreeing, among other things, that Pompey and Crassus would be consuls in 55. But the Triumvirate soon collapsed altogether, when first Julia died and then Crassus was killed, fighting the Parthians at Carrhae, in Mesopotamia.

The road to war (53–49 BC)

Violence and disorder had now become commonplace at Rome, so much so that the consular elections of 53 had to be postponed. Early the next year, Clodius was murdered by Milo, and, in the rioting that followed, the Senate-house was burned down. A desperate Senate agreed to appoint Pompey sole consul. Their relationship increasingly strained, both Caesar and Pompey began to prepare, if not openly, for war. In December 50, one of Caesar's agents at

Rome, the tribune Marcus Scribonius Curio, forced the Senate to vote on his proposal that both men should disarm: only 22 senators were opposed, but they were able to arrange for a tribune's veto. In January 49, one of the tribunes, Marcus Antonius (Mark Antony), forced the consuls to read a letter from Caesar agreeing to the terms of Curio's earlier proposal; the consuls, with the support of an increasingly resolute Pompey, refused to allow the matter to come to a vote. It was now proposed that Caesar be declared a public enemy; the motion was passed, but vetoed by Antony. On January 7, Antony was warned to leave the Senate, which then issued its "ultimate decree." Caesar, who was at Ravenna, marched south to Ariminum; in doing so, he crossed the Rubicon river, the boundary between Cisalpine Gaul and Italy. It was, in effect, a declaration of war.

Technically, then, it was Caesar who was responsible for starting the war. But he did not want it, any more than Pompey did. We might point the finger instead at the 22 intransigent senators who voted against disarmament. Contemporaries understood that it was not principles that were at stake, but the honor and prestige of powerful and ambitious men.

Civil war (49–46 BC)

With just one legion, and with much of the Senate against him, Caesar seemed initially to be in a weak position. Pompey controlled most of Italy, Spain, and the East. But he had only two legions in Italy. And where Pompey hesitated, Caesar was decisive: after just two months of campaigning, Pompey was forced to abandon Italy for Greece. Since Caesar had no fleet, he went instead to Spain, to face the Pompeians who had assembled there, and whom he defeated in less than three months. Pompey himself was next, his army routed near Pharsalus (in Thessaly), in August 48. Pompey fled to Egypt, where he was murdered on the orders of its king, Ptolemy. Caesar followed, and lingered, captivated by the king's 18-year-old sister, Cleopatra. In October 48, in his absence, he was appointed dictator for a year.

Early in 46, he sailed to north Africa, where the remaining Pompeians had gathered. While he was besieging Thapsus, the Pompeian army arrived, only to be annihilated. The few survivors included Pompey's son Sextus, who escaped to Spain, where his brother Gnaeus had fled earlier. When news of his victory reached Rome, Caesar was appointed dictator for ten years. There were few complaints, and most of those seem to have been directed at his decision to install Cleopatra in his house on the Janiculum, together with her infant son Caesarion, whose father, it was widely believed, was none other than Caesar himself. The final campaign of the war brought Caesar back to Spain, where Pompey's sons had built up a sizeable army. The decisive battle was fought at Munda (near mod. Córdoba). Caesar then returned to Rome, where he remained until his death.

Caesar's dictatorship (48–44 bc)

Pompey had shown himself a brilliant general with outstanding qualities as a chief of staff and colonial soldier, but he was no statesman. Caesar was of a different caliber. Born on July 13, 101 (possibly 102 or 100), Gaius Julius Caesar belonged to an old patrician family allied with Marius. At the age of 17, he married Cornelia, Cinna's daughter. His links with the *populares* and their leaders were thus established very early on.

Caesar was also to show signs at an early age of an unscrupulous ambition, served by exceptional gifts and a complete confidence in his star, leading him as early as his seventeenth year to be appointed the *flamen* of Jupiter, and at 38 (and this in particular gave people food for thought) to get himself elected *pontifex maximus*, an office usually held by an experienced magistrate.

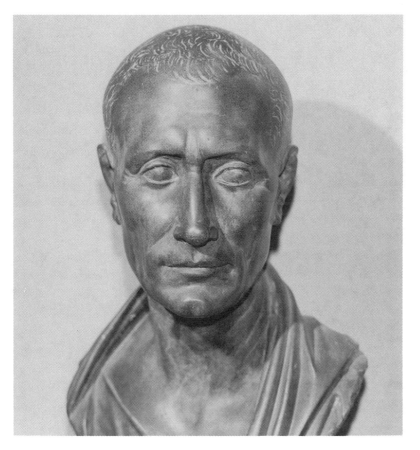

Plate 6.2 Bust of Julius Caesar. Vatican Museum.

His praise for the *gens Julia* on the occasion of the funeral eulogy for his aunt Julia (widow of Marius), which he delivered during his quaestorship, was also particularly revealing:

On her mother's side, my aunt Julia was descended from kings, and on her father's, her ties were with the immortal gods. Indeed the Marcius Rex family come from Ancus Marcius, and that was her mother's name; the Julii are descended from Venus, and we are a branch of that family. Thus with the sacred character of kings, who are the masters of men, she combined the sanctity of the gods, to whom even kings must submit. (Suetonius, *Caesar* 6)*

* According to legend, Venus loved a mortal, Anchises, and the fruit of their love was Aeneas, the Trojan, father of Iulus, mythical ancestor of the Julii. Hence Caesar's worship of Venus Genitrix.

CHRONOLOGICAL TABLE

July 13, 101 (?): Birth of C. Julius Caesar in Rome.

84: He marries Cornelia, Cinna's daughter. Appointed priest of Jupiter (*flamen Dialis*).

83: Birth of his daughter Julia.

80–78: Army service in Asia, then Cilicia.

78: Return to Rome.

75: Journey to Rhodes; taken prisoner by pirates.

73: Military tribune and *pontifex* (priest).

69: Funeral eulogy for his aunt Julia. He defies the Senate by having effigies of Marius paraded in procession. Quaestor in Farther Spain (Ulterior).

67: Rapprochement with Pompey and Crassus. He marries Pompeia, Sulla's granddaughter. Superintendent of the Via Appia.

65: Curule aedile; he gives sumptuous games (the *ludi Romani*) and a *munus* (gladiatorial fights) of 320 pairs of combatants.

63: Elected praetor at 38 (minimum age), he appears as leader of the *populares*. Elected *pontifex maximus*.

62: Praetor. The Clodius scandal; he repudiates Pompeia.

61: Propraetor in Farther Spain (Ulterior).

60: First Triumvirate of Caesar, Pompey, and Crassus.

59: Consul, great activity. He marries Calpurnia, daughter of L. Calpurnius Piso; Pompey marries his daughter Julia. The *lex Vatinia* confers the government of Cisalpine Gaul on him for five years, with three legions, then Transalpine Gaul, with a fourth legion.

Continued on p. 129

58–51: Proconsul in Gaul: the conquest of the Gauls:
  58: campaign against the Helvetii and Ariovistus;
  57: rising of the Belgae; campaign against the Suessiones and Nervii;
  56: campaign in Brittany, Normandy, and Aquitaine. Gaul appears to be conquered;
  55: crossing of the Rhine and the Channel;
  53: revolt in north Gaul; second crossing of the Rhine;
  52: deals with general insurrection led by Vercingetorix; defeat at Gergovia, victory at Alesia;
  51: the last rebellions; general pacification.
56: Renewal of the First Triumvirate at Lucca, with Pompey and Crassus.
54: Death of Caesar's mother and daughter.
50: Caesar stripped of his powers; break with Pompey; the Senate decides to recall him.
January 49: Crossing of the Rubicon, frontier between Cisalpine Gaul and Italy. March on Rome, evacuated by Pompey. Siege of Marseille and campaign in Spain against supporters of Pompey. Dictator for eleven days.
48: Caesar's second consulship. Victory at Pharsalus over Pompey (August 48). Pompey murdered. Siege and capture of Alexandria (October 48–March 47); Egypt a protectorate.
47: Lightning campaign against Pharnaces, king of the Bosporus; victory of Zela (August 47). Return to Rome: dictator for a year.
46: Campaign against Pompey's supporters in Africa: victory of Thapsus (April); in Spain: victory of Munda (March 45). Caesar's third consulship. Dictator for ten years.
45: Fourth consulship. Triumphs and honors from the Senate.
44: Fifth consulship. New honors, notably divine. Life dictatorship. Assassination (Ides of March).

Did Caesar, a true political genius, and a man persuaded in his early youth of the "inevitability of monarchy" (J. Carcopino), come to autocracy along a course mapped out in advance, his career planned and actions set? Or, fundamentally a realist and opportunist, was he driven there by circumstance and his own ambition? It is difficult to draw the line. At all events, his behavior seems at least to have evolved as events dictated.

Until 49, his main concern had been to avoid a precipitate return to civil war. Hence his compact with Pompey and Crassus. But during that time he had acquired in Gaul the inducements of glory and financial independence.

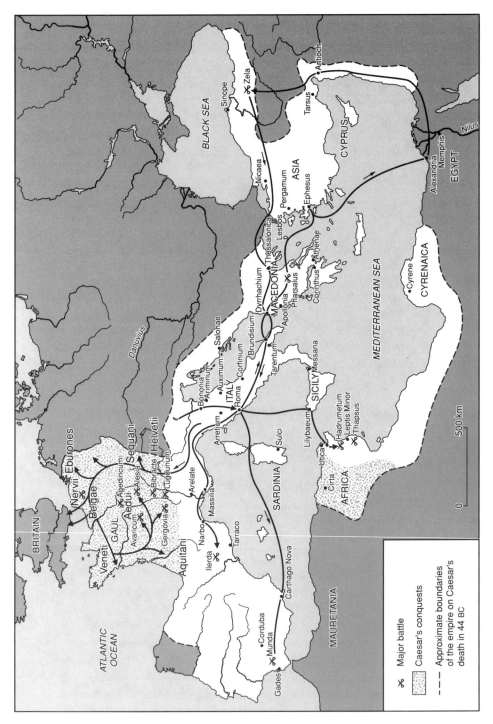

Figure 6.2 Caesar's conquests

By crossing the Rubicon, he became responsible for a new civil war. But while Pompey made the mistake of quitting Italy, *he* secured his position, both military and political, in both Rome and Italy: he promised the *plebs* a distribution of money, proceeded to distribute grain, and got the *lex Roscia* passed, a law giving Roman citizenship to all free men in Cisalpine Gaul, and thus creating a Roman Italy from the Alps to the Straits of Messina, at one stroke gaining himself a clientele among the Cisalpines and a source of recruitment to his legions.

The master of Rome, clothed in the glory of his victories, from 46 to 44 he set about amassing not only the honors due to the victorious general, triumphs and monuments, but the power unchained by institutional decay and civil discord and by his own activities and attributes – and the kingly, even divine emblems that came seemingly of their own accord. In August and September 46, he celebrated in great splendor his triumphs over Gaul, Egypt, Pontus, and Africa, and a fifth triumph in October 45 after the victory of Munda. Then, while monuments dedicated to his victories were appearing on all sides, he gradually built up his powers in the face of an apparently cautious Senate, resolved to vote without debate but at heart hostile. In 46 the dictatorship was given to him for ten years. And in February 44, a senatorial decree proclaimed him dictator for life. Since his triumphs he had lived in almost regal splendor: he wore footwear and a toga of purple, and on his head a laurel wreath; his effigy was engraved on coinage (a royal privilege), sometimes with a golden crown. The oath of loyalty was sworn on his name (a privilege reserved for Jupiter). His statue was placed on the Capitol, set beside those of the seven kings of Rome. He received the title *parens patriae* and seemed like a new Romulus, founder of the city. To be king, the only thing he lacked was the diadem of the Hellenistic monarchs.

Caesar's last months

In 44, Caesar was 57 years old. He was in full possession of his political, military, and intellectual powers. He enjoyed a reputation for invincibility, and now had 16 legions assembled in Epirus and Macedonia in preparation, it would seem, for a campaign against the Parthians. He appeared invulnerable, with his veterans, installed in Italy and the provinces, completely devoted to him. He appeared to enjoy a sort of moral inviolability.

However, the idea had been growing since 45 of getting rid of the dictator. Even Caesarians feared a new war with Parthia. Republicans grouped together around the ideal of *libertas*.

On February 14, at the time of the issue of the *senatus consultum* granting him lifelong dictatorship, he received the senators in front of the temple of Venus Genitrix (his ancestress) that dominated his Forum, sitting on a gold seat at the foot of his own statue. He at once promulgated three measures: a general amnesty, the dismissal of his personal guard, and the entrusting of his safety to the faithful fulfillment of the pledges of loyalty he had received. These were "royal" measures.

On February 15, there occurred the famous scene that took place during the Lupercalia festival: on the Rostra in the Forum he was offered the diadem – which he refused.

On March 15, the day of the Ides, during a sitting of the Senate being held on the Campus Martius in the curia of Pompey's theater (the last session before the launch of the Parthian campaign, fixed, it was said, for the 18th), a group of conspirators, led by Brutus and Cassius, murdered him, stabbing him 23 times.

The dictator's death started a new civil war, this one lasting thirteen years and marked by the horrors of another proscription, the first action of the Second Triumvirate. But at the end of it, it would begin to become clear that, in the space of a few years, it had been he who had laid down the principles of the Augustan Principate. He may thus be regarded as the true founder of the imperial regime. Suetonius made no mistake when he placed him at the head of his *Lives of the Twelve Caesars*.

The End of the Republic: The Second Triumvirate: Toward a New Order

The period 44–31 BC is framed by two major events: Caesar's assassination and the victory of Octavian at Actium. These two events encompass a time of immense importance in the history of Rome. The end of dictatorship, a thirteen-year crisis, the end of the civil wars and the advent of a personal regime benefiting the restorer of peace – this period thus witnessed at the same stroke the doom of the aristocratic Republic, with its boast of *libertas*, and the turbulent advent of that regime, commonly known as the Empire but in fact a "monarchy" in the etymological sense of the word, which, on January 16, 27, became the Augustan Principate. But, more than this, it also witnessed the advent of a new order or, better still, a new "culture." When Rome, hitherto dominated by Hellenistic civilization, became the great capital of the Empire, it acquired its own Graeco-Latin personality. Beginning in 31–27, Rome became itself.

The great crisis of the Second Triumvirate (44–31 BC)

The conspirators had planned to throw Caesar's corpse into the Tiber and proclaim the return of liberty by declaring all his measures null and void. But now, confronted by the hostility of the crowds, who had soon learned what had happened, they were forced to take refuge on the Capitol. Mark Antony, now the only consul and only legal authority, had gone into hiding in his house on the Esquiline. Lepidus, who had been the dictator's master of cavalry (*magister equitum*), had remained on the Forum, close to his troops, who were massed on the Isola Tiberina. Anxiety reigned everywhere.

From March 15, 44 to the autumn of 43, after some vacillation, positions gradually hardened.

Mark Antony obtained Caesar's papers, will, and riches and attracted the favor of the crowds by informing them of the contents of the will and organizing the funeral ceremonies for Caesar, whose eulogy he declaimed. A brilliant officer and a friend of the dead man, he seemed at the time to dominate the situation. Brutus, Cassius, and the other conspirators left Rome.

Octavius, Caesar's eighteen-year-old great-nephew, subsequently known as Octavian, was at Apollonia when he learned of his relative's death. As soon as it was announced that the latter had appointed him his "first heir" and had adopted him, he visited his adoptive father's veterans (now calling himself Gaius Julius Caesar Octavianus), who welcomed him as Caesar's successor. He recruited 3,000 men from among them, and set himself up as Antony's rival.

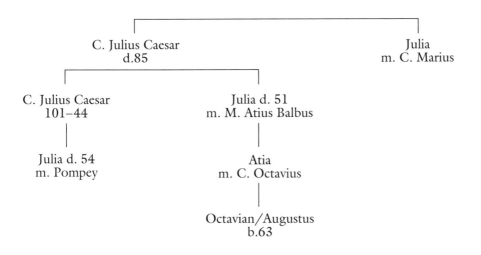

The former consul Cicero attempted a senatorial restoration by drawing closer to Octavian in league against Antony, whom he loathed (see his *Philippics*). The attempt would ultimately fail, but it succeeded in rousing the Senate against Antony and unleashing the War of Modena (the first of the five civil wars of 43–31). Antony was defeated and withdrew to Provence; but the two consuls in command of the senatorial armies were killed. Octavian, appointed propraetor despite his youth, was hailed as *imperator* by his troops. He had eight legions with him. Conscious of his strength, he marched on Rome, seized the state treasury, which he distributed among his men, organized elections, and got himself elected consul (breaking all the rules, of course).

In spite of Cicero, and even in opposition to him, this young "pre-Machiavelli" arranged a reconciliation with Mark Antony. This was concluded in the autumn of 43 through the mediation of Lepidus and a mutual friend, Asinius Pollio. This was the basis of the Second Triumvirate.

Following a meeting on the Reno near Bologna, a general agreement was concluded: a triple magistracy was instituted for five years for Mark Antony, Octavian, and Lepidus, to be renewed in 37 BC. On November 27, the *lex Titia* formally recognized the Reno pact. Thus, whereas the First Triumvirate had been a secret, extra-legal arrangement, the second was publicly sanctioned by a legal document. It was a decision imposed by reason of "the safety of the state." Its immediate consequences were:

■ A new proscription. The triumvirs sent paid assassins to Rome with the task of executing 17 opponents, including Cicero. A list was displayed as at the time of Sulla's proscription. Then a second. There appear to have been 300 victims in all: 150 senators and 150 knights. The chief victim was the republican Senate, certain of whose members had left Rome with Brutus and Cassius.

■ The distribution of the (Roman) world. Lepidus received southern Gaul and the Iberian provinces, with three legions; Antony "long-haired" Gaul and Cisalpine Gaul, with 20 legions; and Octavian Africa, Sicily, and Sardinia, with 20 legions. Italy remained undivided, and the East was for the time being in the hands of Caesar's murderers.

■ War against the murderers. In order to recover the East, with its wealth of men and money, Octavian and Antony set out together eastward, by the Via Egnatia. They carried off the victory of Philippi in October 42. First Cassius and then Brutus committed suicide.

This gave rise to a new distribution: Lepidus had to yield southern Gaul to Antony, who now became master of the whole of Gaul, and Spain to Octavian, who added it to Sicily and Sardinia. Africa (later) went to Lepidus, leaving him with only that province. Italy was still undivided. The triumvirs also shared out missions among themselves: it fell to Antony to raise in the East the money and troops necessary for a resumption of Caesar's plans against the Parthians; to Octavian to deal with Sextus Pompeius, son of Pompey the Great, who since 44 had occupied Sicily, and to allocate land to the veterans of Philippi. In fact, Mark Antony allocated himself the East with its riches and dreams of glory and profit; Octavian faced difficulties, but he had the advantage of being on the spot in Rome. Lepidus withdrew to Africa.

From 42 to 36 BC: each to his own task; the first signs of discord

Octavian first had to resolve the problem of the veterans, to whom land in Italy had been promised. Virgil's first *Eclogue* records the difficulties (a veteran had seized his estate at Mantua). Antony's supporters made the task no easier: the war of Perugia (in 40) against Antony's wife, Fulvia, and his brother Lucius was fuelled by the dispossessions that the settlement of the veterans involved. Antony then returned to Italy to recruit soldiers for his campaign against the Parthians, only to discover that the harbor at Brundisium (mod. Brindisi) had been closed to him by Octavian's troops. Angry, he effected a landing anyway, and laid siege to the port. When Octavian arrived soon after, war seemed imminent. But the soldiers on both sides, many of whom had served together under Caesar, refused to fight, leaving the generals little choice but to patch up their differences, in an agreement that came to be known as the Treaty of Brundisium (October 40). It added Transalpine Gaul to Octavian's command in the West, confirmed Antony's control of the East and Lepidus' position in Africa. To seal the arrangement, Antony, whose wife Fulvia had recently died, married Octavian's sister, Octavia. Virgil's fourth *Eclogue* celebrates the hope of a lasting peace.

It now fell to Octavian to deal with Sextus Pompeius. Disappointed at having been overlooked in the Treaty of Brundisium, an adventurer who behaved increasingly like a kind of pirate-king, Sextus had begun routinely to interfere with grain shipments to Rome, and to menace the coast of Italy. But when Octavian prepared to move against him, the popular reaction at Rome, where food shortages and riots had become commonplace, forced him instead to negotiate. Late in 39, the triumvirs met with Sextus at Misenum (near Naples), where they agreed to let him keep Sicily, and to give him Corsica and the Peloponnese as well.

But Sextus soon grew disillusioned, not least when Octavian suddenly divorced Sextus' relative Scribonia on the very day she gave birth to a daughter, Julia. (Octavian wanted to marry Livia Drusilla, mother of the future emperor Tiberius; her husband complacently went along with the new arrangements.) In 38, with Sextus having resumed his piratical ways, Octavian advanced against him, but was soundly defeated in a naval battle off the coast of southern Italy. By 36, Octavian was prepared to try again. While Lepidus occupied western Sicily, Octavian managed to lose another naval engagement, this time off the coast of eastern Sicily. But his admiral, Marcus Vipsanius Agrippa, was able to destroy much of Sextus' fleet at Naulochus, near the Strait of Messina. Sextus fled to Asia, where he was later executed, on Antony's orders.

Meanwhile, a dangerously self-important Lepidus claimed Sicily for himself. When Octavian objected, Lepidus ordered him to leave. But Octavian slipped into his camp, and persuaded his soldiers to desert. Lepidus was now stripped of his triumviral powers, and forced into retirement at Circeii (mod. San Felice Circeo), where he died 24 years later.

Octavian was received as a victor in Rome and given a tribune's powers. With his 45 legions (about 300,000 men) and a fleet of 600 vessels, he was now the unchallenged master of the West.

During his first stay in the East, Antony's chief concern had been to raise money, which he did by imposing onerous levies on the towns and through other oppressive demands. After a stay in Alexandria (on which much has been written concerning his relations with Cleopatra) and his rapid journey to Italy for the Brindisi meeting, he engaged in the planned campaign against the Parthians. It was a failure. He retreated to Alexandria, where he later celebrated a triumph, after his annexation of Armenia. This Alexandrian celebration scandalized the Romans, for whom a triumph outside Rome was inconceivable. It was then that ancient sources (favorable to Octavian) spoke of his "orientalization." He was said to have become Cleopatra's plaything, to have dreamed of making Alexandria the capital of the world, sharing the East with the queen of Egypt and her three children.

From 36 to 32 BC: toward civil war

In 37, the Second Triumvirate had been formally renewed. But by 36, the agreement was already beset with difficulties, with propaganda busily at work on both sides. The first signs of a break came in 35, when Octavian refused to send the agreed amount of military aid to Antony, who was preparing his revenge on the Parthians. Much of 33 was taken up in a war of propaganda, with Octavian generally getting the better of it. A letter that Antony had sent to the Senate in 34 requesting ratification of his arrangements in the East was conspicuously ignored. Octavia, who had returned to Italy late in 37, was now sent notice of divorce. Octavian's response was to get hold of Antony's will, which had been left with the Vestal virgins, and read it in the Senate: it provided for his children by Cleopatra, and ordered that he be buried at her side. Soon after, it was rumored that he intended to move the capital to Alexandria. On January 1, 32, Octavian officially announced the split.

The war of Actium (32–31 BC)

The year 32 was a difficult one for Octavian. With the Triumvirate officially at an end, he had no legal authority and took the precaution of leaving Rome, where his enemies were preparing his impeachment. At the beginning of February, he reacted by making a bid for power: he returned to Rome, convened the Senate, and made his appearance there surrounded by soldiers to lay before the senators his grievances against Antony. Panic-stricken, the consuls (two Antonians) fled to Ephesus with 300 senators.

In July 32, by senatorial decree, war was declared on Cleopatra and Antony was stripped of all his powers. Both sides made ready:

- In the East, a powerful army and fleet, mainly Egyptian, were assembled, while intensive propaganda was put out against Octavian.
- In the West, Octavian had himself elected consul for 31 and obtained, first in Italy and then in the western provinces, the swearing of an oath of loyalty to him, a move of great significance, making the entire West his clientele as well as giving him command of the war. A no less intensive propaganda campaign on his behalf accused Antony of every possible turpitude.

The two sides clashed in the Adriatic on September 2, 31, at the entrance to the Gulf of Ambracia, at Actium, below a promontory dominated by a temple to Apollo. It is a much debated battle, regarded by some as a tough engagement, and by others as involving no real test of strength. In any event, Cleopatra decided to return to Alexandria, and Antony followed her after ordering his army to retreat to Macedonia and then Asia. The following year, Antony and Cleopatra committed suicide at Alexandria. Caesarion and Antyllus, Antony's older son by Fulvia, were hunted down and executed. Egypt was annexed.

The victory was at least indisputable from the political and psychological viewpoint. Augustan poets celebrated it as a great and decisive military victory, *terra marique*, on land and at sea, won through the intervention of Apollo, and bringing the era of civil wars to a close. But in the view of history, far more important than the battle itself were the events that took place in its aftermath, events constituting the emergence of a new order. The lines of that new order soon became apparent and clearly revealed the profound transformations that had taken place in attitudes during the thirteen years preceding the military event.

TOWARD A NEW ORDER

In order to understand why in 27 BC, when they accepted Augustus as their sole leader, there was no muttering among the Romans, as there had been in February 44 when Antony had tried to place the royal diadem on Caesar's brow, one must be sensible of the changes that society and social life, the concept of political power, and even the concept of life itself had undergone since then. These were part of a development that had started well before that time, but which between 44 and 31 underwent such a marked acceleration that the period has been described as witnessing a "Roman Revolution" (R. Syme).

Social change in the late Republic

All classes of society had found themselves affected by the upheavals. Among the ruling classes, the strongest positions were beginning to be occupied by the "new senators" who had emerged from the municipal elites of Italy and the western provincial elites, replacing the tired old aristocracy, decimated by the civil wars and proscriptions, the patricians long since overtaken by plebeians. This was particularly apparent in the entourage of Octavian: almost all of his consuls and all of his "marshals" were Italians, as was his right-hand man Agrippa. The equestrian order too now jostled at the top, having constantly risen socially since Pompey and Caesar, whose "cabinets" had been filled with knights. The proscriptions had been the occasion of considerable profit for them. And their growing influence and confidence were displayed in the figure of Maecenas, a great Etruscan aristocrat, who preferred to remain a knight when he could have gained access to the senatorial class.

Among the lower classes the changes were no less, with centurions promoted to municipal senates and sometimes even to the equestrian order, and freedmen occupying increasingly privileged positions in economic and social life. A witness to this ascent was Horace, whose father was a freedman. Naturally, all these beneficiaries of social advancement were keen partisans of Octavian.

Private life: women and family

The re-ordering of social hierarchies had important consequences also for the position of women. A number of women of the politically active class were able to assert themselves in ways that were highly visible, and that seem not to have been possible in an earlier age, though even now they met with widespread disapprobation. Sempronia, whose husband was one of the consuls of 77, is said to have been involved in Catiline's conspiracy; she is described by Sallust (*Conspiracy of Catiline* 24–5) as smart, funny, and well-read, but altogether too skilled at singing and dancing. The "Lesbia" to whom the poet Catullus proclaims his devotion was, in real life, Clodia, sister of Publius Clodius, tribune in 58, a married woman so notorious for her very public love-affairs that Cicero could claim, apparently with a straight face, that her home served merely as a cover for "lust, extravagance, and every kind of unheard-of vice" (*In Defense of Caelius* 57). Male society, we might suppose, will have been more comfortable lauding the accomplishments of a woman like Turia, who is said to have risked her own safety to rescue her husband from the clutches of the triumvirs, and who may be the unidentified woman who was memorialized in a eulogy delivered by her husband, and later inscribed on stone at Rome (the so-called *Laudatio Turiae*), that also extols her more conventional attributes – modesty, obedience, affability, agreeableness, dedication to wool-working, sober dress. What Turia, or any other woman, might have thought of her husband's characterization of her is, unfortunately, unknown.

It is difficult to know also whether the public conduct of women like Sempronia and Clodia, whose exploits our sources take a considerable and unconcealed pleasure in recounting, should be understood to signal a broader change in the roles of women who were not part of the wealthy, governing class. No one, of course, would maintain that the behavior of ordinary British women is described by the conduct of the women of the royal family. In the absence of evidence to the contrary, we might suppose that the lives of most lower-class women, including slaves, were not so very different from what they had been. Free-born women continued to scratch out a living as laundresses, weavers, butchers, and fish-sellers, or in one of the occupations that are recorded on inscriptions at Pompeii: bean-dealer, nail-seller, brick-maker, even stonecutter. A number of poor women worked as waitresses in taverns, where they were probably expected, or obliged, to engage in prostitution on the side. In fact, for a lot of unskilled working-class women, prostitution was the only way to make a living, however inadequate. Many worked out-of-doors in the public archways (*fornices*). Slave-women were employed mostly in the homes of the wealthy, cooking, cleaning, weaving – in short, doing whatever they were told to do, which sometimes meant submitting to the sexual demands of their owners.

It has been suggested that it was also mainly among the poorer classes that new-born children were abandoned (in the Roman term, "exposed"), left in public places – either because their parents were unable to care for them or because they were unwanted – usually, it seems, with the expectation (or hope) that they would be found and raised as slaves. Many undoubtedly died. Apologists for the Romans have sometimes minimized the extent of the practice, but the evidence is conclusive: it was both widespread and widely accepted. It is reasonably clear also that daughters were abandoned more often than sons, perhaps because they might some day need a dowry, and could therefore be seen to be a potential drain on the family's financial resources. It is a cruel and often unremarked irony that the very institution of dowry, which served as the means by which some women acquired a measure of independence within marriage, may have condemned others to slavery.

It is unlikely that anything had a greater effect on the lives of upper-class women than the changes that occurred in marriage and divorce, mainly, it seems, in the period between about 150 and 50 BC. Where it had previously been customary for a woman to marry in such a way that she passed into the control of her husband, who then exercised over her a legal authority not unlike that of a father over his daughter, by the time of Cicero, if not earlier, most marriages were arranged so that instead of becoming subject to her husband's authority, the wife remained under her father's power. Why the shift happened is unclear. It is tempting, but probably wishful thinking, to suggest that it occurred because women wanted it to. Modern commentators are inclined to think that it was the product of an increasingly widespread desire to prevent women's share of their fathers' estates from passing out of their natal families. Whatever the explanation, the effect was to give women considerably more independence in marriage. It continued to be the case, however, even into the second century AD, that a woman's consent to marriage was not legally required. (It was sufficient that her father, or guardian, approve.) And wives were, on average, it seems, about ten years younger than their husbands – a disparity that, in the view of some moderns, is likely to have made them psychologically and emotionally subordinate. There is little reason to believe either that male expectations were now considerably less rigid or restrictive than they were in the time of Cato, who once complained publicly that women were violent and uncontrollable, and went on to say that if wives were ever given the same rights as their husbands, they would be unbearable.

An even more dramatic change took place in the rules governing divorce. For much of the period of the Republic, only husbands could initiate a divorce, and then only in certain circumstances. Originally, according to a law that our sources attribute to Rome's legendary founder, Romulus, divorce was permitted only in the event of poisoning (which probably means that the wife had taken or drunk something to induce an abortion), tampering with the keys, or wine-drinking (which was more or less synonymous with adultery). Sometime in the third century BC, a man named Carvilius Ruga was allowed to divorce his wife on the grounds that she was barren (inability to conceive was generally assumed to be the wife's failing). By the time of Cicero, however, divorce was easily accomplished, by either wife or husband, generally without financial penalties, and for almost any reason. It was, if the disapproving moralists of the Augustan age are to be believed, fairly common, at least in the political class. But though wives now possessed the right to end a marriage, few actually seem to have done so, maybe because women had very few opportunities to make an independent living, and perhaps also because custody of children was normally awarded to their father.

The legal independence of women was somewhat constrained also by the institution of guardianship. Like prepubescent children whose fathers had died, every adult woman who was not in her husband's control, or under her father's power – either because she had outlived him, or had been released from it – was required by law to have a guardian (*tutor*), whose main function was to authorize financial transactions she entered into that might result in loss to her (the signing of a contract, for example). The legal sources are explicit about the reasons women were thought to need guardians: they lacked judgment, and were easily duped. In most cases, it appears that the guardian was either the woman's husband or a male relative (often, it seems, an uncle). By the time of the late Republic, however, guardianship had become something of a formality, at least in some cases, so that an increasing number of women were able to manage their financial affairs more or less independently. And from the time of Augustus, free-born women who had given birth to three children, and freed-women who had given birth to four, were released from guardianship altogether.

In law, and probably often in fact, a woman's place in the home was emphatically subordinate to that of the *paterfamilias*, the male head of the household, who possessed almost unlimited authority over everyone who lived in it. He had the right to dissolve his children's marriages, and even to execute them (thankfully, few actual instances are recorded, and some of them are probably unhistorical). Those who were under his power (*potestas*) owned nothing in their own name; anything they acquired belonged to him. Under the law, then, it was theoretically possible for a senator whose father had not formally released him from his authority to be unable even to sign a contract.

In practice, however, the power of the *paterfamilias* was limited, in at least two ways. First, what the sources refer to as the "family council," which appears to have been made up of male relatives and to have served as a kind of advisory group to the *paterfamilias*, may sometimes have acted as a check on his authority. Second, and more importantly, the demography of the Roman family, which can now be reconstructed thanks to the pioneering studies of Richard Saller (and others), indicates that most Romans were probably not subject to their fathers' control at those times in their lives when they are most likely to have wanted to make independent decisions. Comparative evidence drawn from other, better documented, pre-industrial societies suggests that average life-expectancy at birth in the Roman world was probably of the order of 25 to 30 years. Infant mortality was undoubtedly very high: more than one-quarter of newborns are likely to have died before their first birthday. Half or more of all children probably did not survive past the age of 10. Those who did will have lived, on average, another 35 to 40 years. It is reasonably clear also that men's average age at marriage in the Roman world was, compared to many other pre-industrial societies, relatively late. Analysis of funeral inscriptions suggests that most men probably married in their late twenties (most women in their late teens or early twenties). So the difference in age between father and child will often have been as much as 40 years. This comparatively large generation gap, when combined with the figures given above for average life-expectancy at birth, means, among other things, that probably only one-fifth of men, and fewer than half of all women, were still under their father's power at the time they got married. And more than 95 percent of men will have been free from their father's control by the time they turned 40.

It may also be doubted that the traditional picture of the Roman household as consisting of several nuclear families ruled by an authoritarian, elderly patriarch corresponds, in any very precise way, to the realities of Roman family life. The image is derived mainly from what survives of Roman private law, easily our largest source of information about the family. But legal rules do not always reflect social practice. The literary sources, including Cicero, suggest that it was very unusual for adult sons to live with their fathers, or for adult brothers to set up a common household. And the many surviving funeral inscriptions on which the relationship between the commemorator and the deceased is identified rarely record extended relatives (grandparents, aunts and uncles, cousins). What really mattered to the Romans, it seems, were the relationships of the nuclear family, of husband and wife, and of parent and child.

It is impossible to determine (or even to estimate) the average size of a Roman family. The evidence that we do possess about the number of children the Romans had is entirely anecdotal, and tends to report the exceptional, like Gaius Crispinus Hilarus of Fiesole, who is said to have made a sacrifice at the Capitol in Rome on April 9, 5 BC, together with his 8 children, 27 grandchildren, and 18 great-grandchildren. It is notoriously difficult also to determine what attitudes or sentiments may have characterized the relationship of parent and child. It seems now to be fashionable to maintain that the Romans generally attached little value to children, and then mainly for the adults that they would grow up to be, or in the expectation that they would support their parents in old age. The philosophically minded, like the emperor Marcus Aurelius, were inclined to categorize children with barbarians, slaves, and animals, on the grounds that they were all irrational. But the grief expressed on tombstones set up to commemorate children is, in many cases, undeniably genuine. It was not uncommon for adults to show interest, and even to take pleasure, in the behaviors of childhood. Among the wealthy, about whom we are best informed, it seems to have been expected that fathers would play an active role in the education of their sons, especially when they were young. And small children were often referred to as *deliciae*, "sweethearts."

Intellectual life

In the cultural field, new lines of development appeared in sharp contrast with republican traditions.

One striking feature was the decline in the art of oratory. Hortensius and Cicero had gone. Political eloquence no longer had a place in the Senate. Refuge was taken in history (Sallust, Cornelius Nepos) and in science and erudition (Varro). But, chiefly, Latin found its voice among the young and brilliant Italian intellectuals who flocked to Rome eager to sing the praises of the new order: Virgil (from Mantua), Horace (from Venusia in Apulia), Cornelius Gallus (from Fréjus), Ovid (from Samnium), Tibullus (from the Tivoli region), Propertius (from Umbria), Livy (from Padua). These gathered around Maecenas, the friend of Octavian.

Since the era of Caesar, when the Epicurean philosopher Philodemus of Gadara had been much esteemed, a political and learned Epicureanism had

Plate 6.3 Virgil, seated, holds a copy of the *Aeneid*; he is flanked by the muses Clio and Melpomene. Roman mosaic from Tunisia, 2nd/3rd century AD. Bardo Museum, Tunis.

spread in high society, and a moral and vulgar Epicureanism among the body of the people. In Rome, peace was the principal aspiration. Civil war became more than ever an object of horror. Peace, and above all peace among citizens, was regarded as the supreme good, bringing with it order and prosperity. The deliverer of these blessings would be a "savior."

Religion itself did not escape this need for renewal. We have seen to what extent the *imperatores*, from Marius and Sulla to Caesar, had made efforts to "mobilize" the deities (Venus especially) in the service of personal ambition. Caesar had even enjoyed the benefit of being officially deified during his lifetime, as voted by the Senate at the beginning of 44. After his death, he had been recognized (in July 44) as *divus Julius* and admitted among the gods of Olympus, and the *lex Rufrena* of 42 had gone on to organize his cult throughout Italy. This shows that at the very end of the Republic, as well as in its heyday, religion remained indestructibly linked with political and civic life.

Octavian was fully conscious of this when he accumulated priesthoods and overlooked nothing in order to appear to be protected by the gods. Made a pontiff as early as 48 by Caesar, and becoming an augur between 42 and 40 and a member of the college of quindecimvirs in 37, he subsequently became a fetial, an Arval Brother, and a member of the Titian brethren, before being elected *pontifex maximus* in 12 BC. He thus sanctified his powers and, through them, his person. Victor at Philippi in 42 avenging Caesar's death (an act of *pietas*), he pledged a temple to Mars the Avenger. Victor over Sextus Pompeius in 36, he vowed a temple to Apollo, his appointed protector, on the Palatine – it would be Rome's most luxurious temple.

Octavian knew how to turn to advantage his contemporaries' aspirations for peace, their anxieties in the face of Antony's orientalizing ambitions, and the numerous prodigies happening in Italy and Rome, interpreted as divine warnings. With consummate skill and the effective support of his entourage, not to mention the poetic evocations of fashionable authors, he used them to appear in the eyes of all as the protégé of Apollo, the young god of order, the arts, and youth, the complete opposite to Dionysus-Bacchus, Mark Antony's patron and god of orgiastic excess. Fighting from the West against the East, he knew well how to give himself the image of the savior of traditional Rome, the restorer of ancestral values threatened by the oriental mirages of a "new Dionysus," the ally of troublesome Egypt. He knew to perfection how to play on national feeling and war-weariness. In this respect, Actium was a victory for Rome and the West, as much as for Octavian himself.

But it also spelled the end of the Republic.

PART II

Rome, Master of the World

SOURCES

It is essential that students familiarize themselves with the sources. This is made easier by the existence of useful and discerning collections, and by the availability of the principal literary sources in softback translations as well as in specialized bilingual editions.

LITERARY SOURCES

The literary sources all offer something of interest to the historian, from whose viewpoint, they may be divided into two groups, according to their literary genre.

Historians and geographers

There are six essential names. Without them our knowledge of the early Roman Empire would be much less than satisfactory.

Strabo (ca. 58 BC–ca. AD 25) This Greek from Asia visited a large part of the Empire and lived in Rome and Alexandria. A notable who rallied to the new Roman government, this father of historical geography wrote for the use of the ruling powers. His *General Geography* has come down to us almost in its entirety. In his view, geography was "the science of man's appropriation of the land, an inventory of his dwellings, his resources and the traces that he has left on it" (C. Nicolet). It was also a political subject: it made for better government and even explained the forms of government (physical size of a country, local resources, etc.).

Tacitus (AD 55/7–after 117) Tacitus had a brilliant senatorial career, a fine marriage, and good connections, and was a renowned orator, envied writer, and *grand seigneur*, with a sparkling style but doubtful objectivity. For the historian, there are four essential works: *The Life of C. Julius Agricola* (written in 98), in which Tacitus, acting as biographer and apologist for his father-in-law, describes the senatorial career of a great and loyal servant of the state, but also how Roman administration in Britain worked and the problems posed by Romanization in that province; *Germany* (written in 98), in which Tacitus "draws up an inventory of what still eluded the *Orbis Romanus* in the West" (P. Grimal); the *Histories* (12 books written between 105 and 109), covering a period of 28 years (69–96) in which Tacitus was both observer and participant, of which only a part has come down to us, recounting the events of 69 and the first nine months of 70; and the *Annals* (18 books written from 112/113 onwards), his major work, but with many lacunae, in which is unfolded the history of the Empire from the death of Augustus to that of Nero – despite its mutilations, it is our chief source for that period.

Suetonius (ca. 70–after 122)   A knight, a friend of Pliny the Younger, a prolific writer, a man who immersed himself in books and documents, Suetonius produced twelve portraits of emperors from Caesar to Domitian (*The Lives of the Twelve Caesars*). A recent study has shown that his information was better than had been supposed, and that his inquiring and painstaking mind, proceeding by small deft touches, made him not just a mere collector of anecdotes but a true historian.

Dio Cassius (ca. 160–ca. 235)   Among the historians, Dio Cassius, a Greek aristocrat from Bithynia, had one of the most remarkable public careers (he was twice consul). Retiring to Bithynia some time after 229, he there completed the *Roman History* he had begun at the beginning of the third century. This work, some eighty books long, retracing Rome's history from its origins to 229, has come down to us in a very mutilated form, with many books known only through the Byzantine abbreviators of the eleventh and twelfth centuries Xiphilinus and Zonaras. For the origins, the period of the kings, and the Republic, Dio Cassius relies fundamentally on earlier historians. As regards the Empire, his work and testimony are essential, in spite of some reservations (a taste for reworked discourse, for dreams, etc.).

Herodian (ca. 175–ca. 250)   A Greek from Syria, attached to the imperial administrative services, Herodian divided his life between the Roman court and the provinces: "My work," he wrote, "recounts those events following the death of Marcus Aurelius that I have personally witnessed or heard of, and also those in which I have taken part." His *History of the Roman Emperors* is a chronicle extending from 180 to 238. Rather than being a simple series of biographies, it sets out to define an ideal of government through a portrayal of the sovereigns.

Augustan History   This name is given to a series of 39 biographies of emperors, caesars, and usurpers, from the advent of Hadrian to 284, with an interruption between 244 and 259. They appear to have been written by six authors of the end of the third century and beginning of the fourth, but later studies have shown the work to be that of a forger who lived in the last decade of the fourth century or even in the fifth century, a pagan man of letters who frequented Roman senatorial circles. It is riddled with anachronisms, inventions, and fantasy, and is therefore extremely difficult to use as a source. Nevertheless, for the period up to the death of Caracalla in 217, it is a work that may be used for reference.

Beside these fundamental sources, the writings of other historians of antiquity seem secondary, even if they contribute a good deal on certain points – as do, for instance, the *Periochae* (summaries) of Livy's *Roman History*, the *Summary of Roman History* by Velleius Paterculus, Plutarch's *Parallel Lives* (*Galba, Otho*), the *Jewish War* by Flavius Josephus, and the *Book of the Caesars* by Aurelius Victor.

Literary and technical authors

Poets, orators, novelists, encyclopedists, grammarians, agronomists, engineers, military writers, philosophers, and jurists have an incomparable way of informing us about intellectual and daily life in Rome, how to build a temple or how to make a cadastral survey, Rome's congestion problems or the pleasures of hunting in the woods. These are the sources, in short, which allow us to picture Roman private life, its activities, schools of thought, and social practices. We shall meet them in the course of this work. Otherwise, it is advisable to use a history of Latin literature and launch boldly into a voyage of discovery, starting perhaps with the novels of Petronius and Apuleius.

Mention must also be made of the correspondence between a great administrator, Pliny the Younger, and his emperor, Trajan, and of Pliny's *Panegyric* to Trajan.

EPIGRAPHIC SOURCES

The early Roman Empire was the golden age of epigraphy. People wrote in every region (from Morocco to the Caspian, from Britain to the south of Egypt), on every kind of material (walls, lead pipes, pottery, wood, bones, and, above all, naturally, stone). The field covered by epigraphy is immense: private life, religious life, public life, military life, commercial activities, electoral campaigns, bankers' and potters' accounts, water supplies, the running of a great domain, customs tariffs, calendars, milestones.

There are several "great documents" which must be at least known, if not studied. For instance:

■ Three imperial texts, one by Augustus (the *Res gestae*), the second by Claudius (the *Claudian Table*), and the last by Hadrian (*Address to the Army of Africa*, known from the inscriptions of Lambaesis).
■ Legal texts, laws, and regulations: *Tabula Hebana*, the *Lex de imperio Vespasiani*, municipal laws of the Iberian peninsula.
■ Texts on economic history: mining regulations, the document on African agriculture, the *Table of Veleia*.
■ Texts on social history: a senatorial career, an equestrian career, the regulations of a college.

Arranged in series, inscriptions allow us to gain knowledge of a cult, the administrative personnel of the Empire, the distribution area of a pottery, the composition of a priestly college. In addition, they very often let us put a precise date on a monument, a dedication, an ex-voto or votive offering. They offer, moreover, the possibility of constructing genealogies, sometimes over several generations (e.g. the family of Septimius Severus). The use made of them is obviously enriched by other historical sources.

NUMISMATIC SOURCES

Because Roman coinage became the emperor's concern, its study is also of major importance to the historian of Rome. On the face was a likeness of the sovereign together with his titles, or that of a member of the imperial family. On the reverse was a depiction or symbol of an event, a monument, an idea, a god, a province – whatever the emperor wanted to make known to all. It was thus the simplest and most effective means of propaganda. The contributions to knowledge made by numismatics are extremely varied: economic and political history (diffusion, devaluation, network of provincial workshops, survival of the coinage of certain cities); religious history (cults favored by the emperor, the imperial cult); ideological history (the concept of imperial power); history of events (a victory, a river crossing, the conquest of a province); history of art (knowledge about a monument, a statue) – not to mention an extraordinary portrait gallery.

PAPYROLOGICAL SOURCES

Although the majority of the papyri that have relevance to the history of the Empire are concerned with Egypt, it would be wrong to think that they are relevant only to the history of Roman Egypt and its inhabitants. For in some ways Egypt reflected what was happening at the heart of the Empire: they may disclose the exact date of an imperial accession, the contents of a constitution, etc. Furthermore, many documents (contracts, loans, etc.) were of virtually the same form in the various provinces, and the papyri generated by the vast dealings between Egypt and Rome (through the *annona*, or year's grain supply, and trade in general) were on such a scale and so variously informative that it would be hard to imagine the history of the Empire without papyrology. Other very important papyri have been found elsewhere than in Egypt (Pompeii, Dura-Europus).

ARCHAEOLOGICAL SOURCES

To say that archaeological sources are essential to the study of antiquity would be an understatement. New techniques (underwater archaeology, aerial photography, spectroscopy, ground-probing radar, etc.), the refinement of excavation methods, and the amplitude of what has already been achieved have contributed in striking fashion to a better knowledge of life in the Empire (rural dwellings, history of the landscape, etc.). From pinpointing this or that trading circuit by a study of amphorae to establishing with certainty a picture of a monument or building, nothing escapes this field, and it is constantly growing: trade, merchandise, agriculture, the city of the living, and the city of the dead, relations between the town and its local region, military life, and so on.

7 / THE ROMAN WORLD IN 31–28 BC

*O*NLY HALF A VICTORY IN THE MILITARY SENSE, BUT PSYCHOLOGICALLY AND
POLITICALLY A TOTAL VICTORY, *ACTIUM* TOOK ITS PLACE AMONG THE
EXPLOITS OF *OCTAVIAN-AUGUSTUS* AS THE MOMENT WHEN THE *"PRINCE"* WAS
PRESENTED BY THE GODS TO MEN: *"THE SHIP OF AUGUSTUS [FLOATED] IN FULL SAIL
UNDER THE SIGN OF JUPITER. . . . PHOEBUS . . . ROSE ABOVE THE STERN OF
AUGUSTUS' SHIP . . ."* (*PROPERTIUS*, ELEGIES *IV.6.21–7*). BUT BEFORE LEGEND
COULD BECOME SUPERIMPOSED ON REALITY, THE WAR HAD TO BE BROUGHT TO AN
END AND THE HERITAGE THAT THE YOUNG CONQUEROR WAS BUSY REAPING HAD TO
BE GATHERED TOGETHER.

ACTIUM AND ITS AFTERMATH

On the evening of September 2, 31 BC, the prospects for Octavian's camp were encouraging rather than assured. Part of the enemy fleet had managed to flee, with Antony, Cleopatra, and the spoils of war, another part was still intact, sheltering in the Gulf of Ambracia, and there had still been no engagement with Antony's land army. It was a matter of urgency to obtain a victory and bring the war to an end.

ENDING THE WAR

The next day, Antony's fleet surrendered. A week later his deserted legions rallied to Octavian. The sailors and legionaries were incorporated into the armed forces of the victor. For Antony that spelled the loss of Greece, Macedonia, and Asia Minor, for they were thus left defenseless. Octavian went to Samos, but at the end of the autumn was recalled to Italy because of a simmering military rebellion and a reported plot. How did the defeated rulers use this respite? Returning like a conqueress to Alexandria, Cleopatra concocted fantastic schemes – to settle in Spain, to carve out a realm for herself in India. Mark Antony, a broken man, deserted by his Cyrenaican legions, went to Alexandria, where he lived in near-isolation.

Plate 7.1 Cleopatra and her son Caesarion make offerings to the goddess Hathor. The relief is on a wall of the temple of Hathor at Dendera.

At the beginning of the year 30, Octavian returned to the East, received the backing of the king of Judaea and, from Syria, made preparations for the invasion of Egypt. There were two armies: one in the west led by C. Cornelius Gallus, the other in the east led by himself. Cleopatra, trying to preserve the throne for her children, attempted to negotiate with Octavian, who coveted the treasure of the Ptolemies. She had a mausoleum prepared in which she threatened to have herself incarcerated and burnt together with the treasure if her conditions were rejected. At the end of July, Octavian's cavalry was at the gates of Alexandria. Despite an initial success, Antony was betrayed and was defeated on August 1. Believing the queen to be dead, he stabbed himself to death. Octavian played for time, negotiated with Cleopatra, put her out of action, and gained control of the treasure. A few days later, to avoid being put on display in the triumph of Octavian, Cleopatra in her turn committed suicide.

Cleopatra's son by Caesar and Antony's son Marcus were executed, and Egypt was reduced to a province, though with a special status: Cornelius Gallus, a knight, was its first governor, and senators were prohibited from going there without authorization. At the end of the summer of 30, Octavian left Egypt. He was master of the whole Mediterranean basin.

RE-ESTABLISHING ORDER AND PEACE

In the East

From Alexandria, Octavian proceeded to Syria, Asia Minor, and then Greece. On his way he reorganized everything that needed it. There was no upset: Antony's policy had been judicious, and Octavian-Augustus maintained its principles – to consolidate frontiers, to have regard for the differences between cities, and to make allies of local princes and kings.

■ Consolidating frontiers. Octavian's weapon here was diplomacy. It mattered little to him whether or not the kingdoms bordering the empire had supported Antony. He was ready to make sacrifices to ensure peace on his eastern borders. So he settled the confused problems of Armenia and unraveled as best he could the complex situations created by rivalries among the Parthians.

■ Respecting the differences between cities. Those cities that had declared themselves against Antony (Beirut, Aphrodisias) received privileges, and those that he had plundered had their debts remitted. Everywhere, they preserved their autonomous status (Antioch, Laodicea), as was apparent on their coinage. Many cities in Asia and Syria began to date events in their history by reference to the Battle of Actium.

■ Forming alliances. Although a few wayward or recalcitrant sovereigns were deposed and put to death (Alexander of Emesa), the majority had rallied in support fairly quickly in order to secure their chances of being pardoned, and like Herod submitted and swore fidelity to Octavian (Amyntas in Galatia, Archelaus in Cappadocia).

On January 1, 29, while at Samos, Octavian assumed his fifth consulship.

In the West

By way of Greece (he put Sparta back on its feet and gave it the task of organizing the "Actium" games), Octavian returned to Rome, arriving at the start of the summer of 29. The Senate and people had earlier awarded him exceptional honors: his name had been written into the Salian chant, all his actions had been ratified by a special disposition, tribunician power had been granted to him for life (in 30) and with a wider scope than for the tribunes of the *plebs*, and lastly, on January 11, 29, the doors of the temple of Janus on the Forum had been closed for the third time: for the third time in their history the Roman people had peace – a peace they owed to Octavian.

On August the 13th, 14th, and 15th, Octavian celebrated a triple triumph, over Illyria, Actium, and Egypt. Three days later he dedicated the temple to the Divine Julius on the Forum, on the very spot where the dictator's body had been burnt in March 44. And on August the 28th, the Curia Julia was opened. Henceforth in the Senate's meeting hall there stood a statue of Victory and an altar dedicated to the goddess. The purpose was to remind everyone of Actium and its victor.

THE MIRACLE OF ACTIUM

Immediately after the battle which rendered him master of the world, Octavian had two trophies erected: one in the temple of Apollo guarding the entrance to the Gulf of Ambracia; the other, opposite, on the actual site of his camp. The latter trophy, instead of being placed under the care of Venus or Victory, was raised to Mars, Neptune, and Apollo. It was a way of showing plainly that victory had been won both on land and at sea. The legend of Actium was beginning. It was supported by a series of politico-religious measures and was fed by an admirable literary and artistic propaganda.

Politico-religious measures

First it was necessary to give thanks to Apollo, Octavian's guardian deity, so the Senate took the decision to build a temple to Apollo on the Palatine near his residence. Secondly, facing Actium, the free, autonomous Greek city of Nicopolis (the town of Victory) was founded to serve as an immortal monument. So that it might become a dazzling center, it was allotted a vast territory. And near the town, a great shrine was dedicated to Apollo, containing a sacred grove and a stadium and gymnasium intended for the celebration of games that were to be put on an equal footing with the Olympic Games (the first were held in 28). Lastly, coins were minted bearing the figure of Victory carrying trophies.

Literary and artistic propaganda

Virgil, Horace, and Propertius turned the victory at Actium into an epic of Octavian. Several themes may be picked out from their poems: the victory had been total, on land and at sea; Octavian, represented in majesty ("he stands on the tall stern of his vessel, from his radiant temples springs a double flame," Virgil, *Aeneid* VIII.680–1), is his father's (i.e. Caesar's) worthy heir and the savior of his country; and in this national victory of West over East he has been aided by the whole of nature (wind, waves, animals) and by the nation's gods (Venus, Neptune, Minerva, Mars, and, above all, Apollo and Jupiter, whose earthly lieutenant Octavian is). As for art, both on the triumphal arch erected in the Roman Forum shortly after 31 and on various altars, the theme of victory constantly suggests the Battle of Actium.

This impressive ensemble of works connected with Actium reveals the main themes of an "Octavian" ideology, holding the idea of victory at its core. This was to be the heart of the imperial mystique. Octavian owed his victory directly to the Olympians and the auspices in his possession. By skillfully emphasizing the defense of Hellenism in the face of Egyptian barbarism, drawing a parallel between Salamis and Actium, Octavian opened up the possibility of reconciling the Greek Orient and the West: Virgil made Aeneas hold the Trojan games on the shores of Actium.

ROME AND ITALY

At the very idea that Cleopatra might set up an oriental monarchy in Rome, as Octavian's propaganda had put about, the whole of Italy rose up and gathered around its protector: in 32 it swore an oath of loyalty for the Actium campaign. This almost unprecedented revolutionary act turned all citizens into clients of Octavian. On his return from Actium, how did Rome and the peninsula appear?

ROME

The city was old. Behind it lay seven centuries of history. For a long time a city of peasants, it had undergone profound transformations affecting the surroundings and way of life of its population of citizens, slaves, freedmen, and foreigners; it had become a Hellenistic town. With its 800,000 (perhaps

1,000,000) inhabitants, it was the largest conurbation in the ancient world, but, or perhaps partly for that reason, it was far from being a beautiful city, one that might serve as a model, comparable with the great cities of the East, or be seen as a worthy capital of the world and a suitable dwelling-place for conquerors. Conscious of this disparity, Caesar had desired to ennoble the city and improve living conditions. His assassination and the civil wars had meant the shelving of these plans, but the problems did not go away.

The problems

- The city was no longer contained by the Servian defensive wall, which it largely overflowed, especially into the area across the Tiber. As a result, the old administration, with its four areas, was outdated. Rome was an open town.
- Provisioning was no longer at all adequate and, as the war against Sextus Pompeius had shown, this inadequacy could become crucial if supplies of the staple food, wheat, were disrupted. There was also insufficient water.
- Actual dangers: fire (in 31 the Circus Maximus was destroyed by fire), flooding of the Tiber (the last after the death of Caesar), theft, murder, and molestation, and popular disturbances.
- The upkeep of ancient buildings, which constantly needed repairs.
- The circulation of traffic was extremely awkward. Rome had never had any town-planning system and buildings were erected haphazardly. There was a shortage of space and the Forum was too small.

Caesar's works and projects

The dictator had realized the urgent need for reorganizing the city. In 45, he had issued a municipal regulation concerning the cleaning, maintaining, and paving of the streets. And in order to gain more space to work with, he had planned to make maximum use of the Campus Martius, even at the price of diverting the course of the Tiber. He had already embarked on a metamorphosis of the capital and to further that end set about a vast program of building and rebuilding: the Basilica Julia, Comitium, Curia Julia, Forum Julium, Villa Publica, Saepta Julia, the expansion of the Circus Maximus, and a plan for a theater, to mention merely the most striking components. Retarded by his death and the civil wars, all this work was still in hand at the time of Actium.

Octavian's achievements

Although he abandoned certain of Caesar's enterprises (diverting the river), Octavian pursued others (linking the Forum and the Campus Martius) and completed the construction of what had already been started (the Curia Julia was opened in 29, the planned theater would become the theater of Marcellus, etc.). Moreover, he undertook various other works, whether it was a matter of fulfilling vows (the temple of Mars Ultor, pledged in 42, that of Apollo on the Palatine, pledged in 36 and completed in 28), or of carrying out reconstructions and restorations (the temple of Apollo Sosianus in 34/33, the portico of Octavia perhaps in 33, repairs to eighty-two temples in 29 using the Egyptian booty), or of constructing totally new buildings (his own mausoleum in 29).

Octavian also actively encouraged private citizens to provide public buildings and amenities. The building activity of Agrippa in 33 was a fine example of such beneficence. Agrippa gave priority to the water supply to the capital: he added two aqueducts to the existing four, restored the latter to good working order, increased the number of water supply points, renovated the drainage system, and reorganized the water services, all at his own expense.

To keep in favor with the populace, Octavian paid great attention to everything connected with Rome's provisioning: in 29, he distributed 400 sesterces to each of 250,000 beneficiaries, and in 28 arranged exceptional distributions of grain. Lastly, he complemented the opportune with the diverting and began a policy of providing amusements (the first stone amphitheater was constructed in the capital). In the early twenties BC, the Great Rome of the Principate was taking shape.

ITALY

For the first time in a very long while Italy (the peninsula plus the Cisalpine region) saw an end to civil war, brigandage, disorder of all kinds. Following Actium and the isolation of Antony's Italian supporters, there had indeed been some intestine difficulties, of which the events that had brought Octavian back from the East at the end of 31 were an echo. And, certainly, towns in Italy loyal to Antony (like Bologna) had had to be punished, as well as his supporters among the Italian senators and men of note. But the feeling of a political and spiritual unity that had manifested itself at the time of the oath in 32 had been strengthened by the victory at Actium, to the point where it was possible to acknowledge the existence of "a dual nationalism, both Italian and Roman, which in the end became but one." It is true that, with the exception of a few Alpine tribes, all free men in Italy already had Roman citizenship and enjoyed important privileges. But this unity of citizenship and shared privilege involved no compulsory uniformity: each Italian Roman had two "countries," one his place of origin (colony or *municipium*), the other Rome, whose Senate administered Italy, which remained a federation of cities. Each region preserved its individuality: Etruscan was still spoken in Etruria, Greek in Magna Graecia, Oscan in Samnium, even though Latin was gradually prevailing throughout Italy.

In the economic field, efforts begun before Actium, their development already remarked on by the poets and stimulated by the arrival of the eastern booty (the monetary crisis faded), began to bear fruit. The last civil wars had accelerated the changes initiated in the preceding century: the numbers of small landowners continued to decline; tree crops (olives) and livestock (sheep, breeding of fine strains) developed to the detriment of cereal crops; there was growing specialization. These changes must not be exaggerated, however. In essence, agriculture remained much the same as in Cato's time: a subsistence economy with some specialization. There existed every type of holding (*latifundia*, small and medium properties) and every method of working the land (direct land development, use of slave labor, indirect farming by tenants and sharecropping). The only real novelty was the appearance of a new category of colonists, no longer free workers but slaves to whom the slaveowner rented land as if they were free men. The problem of settling veterans in Italy, with all the contentious transfers of property it involved, had been faced first by Octavian in the period following the death of Caesar. With the demobilization after Actium he faced it again.

Regionally, there was a considerable and marked diversity in what the land was given over to producing – here again, the result of much earlier developments, but clearer cut than the regional differences in types of holding and methods of working the land: some Apennine areas were still living a marginal existence; in the south of the peninsula, pasturage became predominant; Campania, with the best lands in Italy, preserved all its richness (corn, oil, wine exported as far as the Three Gauls) and all its joy of living, as evidenced by the luxury villas adorning its coastline; Latium and its surrounding terrain were devoted to market gardening and to keeping Rome supplied with food; Etruria, despite its wines and corn, was slowly declining. The new element was the entry into the Italian economy of the Cisalpine region, which indicates that that region had gone over to agriculture and livestock breeding for trade. The only two large Italian markets attested in antiquity were held in northern Italy (*Campi Macri* near Cremona, and Modena). If the situation as a whole was less somber than was sometimes believed, nevertheless Columella's comments seemed justified: there was a lack of capital to invest in agriculture because the profitability of land was dwindling.

In the field of rural and urban craftsmanship, Italy excelled because of the quality and variety of its products, some of which, such as the stamped pottery from Arezzo, flooded the markets.

But in the wake of Actium, Italy owed its true, dazzling revolution to the renewal of its political class. That was due to a triple phenomenon: the demographic disappearance or weakening of the families of the old nobility; the rise of new Roman nobles; and the appearance of a fresh generation of "new men," for the most part Italian, who gathered around Octavian. Frequently very rich, these new men were the ones who formed the young victor's most fervent supporters. To some extent, Actium can be regarded as the victory of a new Italy

Plate 7.2 A main street at Pompeii.

over an old Rome: not a single one of the great writers who contributed to the
legend of Actium originated from the city of Rome.

THE PROVINCES

Consisting of all the countries directly or indirectly subject to Roman law,
Rome's empire, in 30 BC, belonged to the Mediterranean world and was the
result of conquests. Some of its provinces were old (Sicily, Sardinia), others only
recently acquired (Egypt). Each was governed according to the particular status
it had been given at the time of its annexation. This world was thus extraordi-
narily varied and though it largely lacked unity and coherence these were not
desired at all costs. If we are seeking signs of unity and coherence on an Empire-
wide scale, then at best two major groupings can be distinguished, the very ones
in confrontation at Actium: the eastern half of the Mediterranean, where Greek

was spoken and a certain cohesion of civilization, practices, and customs was evident, chiefly in the towns, which were Greek or Hellenized; and the western half, almost barbarian, where Latin was the language most used, even though Romanization was extremely uneven, and where the freshness of "civilization" could render Rome's actions easier, faster, and more decisive for the future.

THE WEST

Sicily
The oldest province. After a period of prosperity between 43 and 36, it was visited with the punishments that Octavian inflicted on the cities that had helped Sextus Pompeius and with the brigandage that followed Naulochus. It only gradually recovered. Six colonies were founded in the coastal zones, but the ruined hinterland went to great estate owners. A Greek-speaking writer, Diodorus (Siculus) of Agyrium, wrote a *Bibliotheca historica*.

Sardinia and Corsica
The civil wars gave these two provinces a certain importance. There was fighting over their ports and their grain. Peace returned them to obscurity.

The two Spains
There were four influences at work in the Spanish provinces of Citerior and Ulterior: that of the old Iberian civilizations, the Greek influence around Emporia (present-day Ampurias), the Punic influence on the south coast, and the Celtic on the south-east coast. Since 39 they had had a single administration. Romanization was very uneven. It was strong in the south (no other province had as many colonies of citizens), but weak elsewhere, leading to incessant revolts. Moreover, in the north-west, in the regions inhabited by the Astures and the Cantabri, the conquest had not yet got underway. This resistance meant that the decade 39–29 BC was punctuated by military interventions – five triumphs over Spain were celebrated in those ten years. It was obvious that large numbers of soldiers would be necessary to settle the situation. Furthermore, those untamed regions in the north-west possessed vast mineral wealth, and into these, in 29, one of Octavian's trusted men undertook a first campaign.

Africa
As early as 40, the two African provinces (*Africa vetus*, the former territory of Carthage, annexed in 146, and *Africa nova*, the former kingdom of Numidia, annexed in 46 after Thapsus) were combined under the authority of the same governor, a proconsul residing in Carthage, which was refounded as a Roman

Plate 7.3 The theater at Mérida (ancient Augusta Emerita), Spain. Originally built in 24 BC, it was later reconstructed.

colony and reinforced by the arrival of 3,000 new colonists. The territory he administered stretched from the Minor Syrtis as far as the River Ampsaga (the Rummel Wadi), around which lay a land that enjoyed a certain autonomy, the Cirtian confederation (centered on Cirta). Outside the territory (*pertica*) of Carthage, and apart from a few pockets along the coastline (Utica) and in the interior (Cirta itself), Romanization was limited and tentative. It ran up against the obstacles of cultural reluctance (indigenous and Punic traditions remained very much alive) and military instability (the insecurity of the southern fringes as well as civil wars meant the celebration of three triumphs *ex Africa* between 34 and 28). Three threats existed: to the west, from the tribe of the Musulamii, and to the south from the tribe of the Gaetuli and the nation of the Gara-mantes. The importance of these African lands was immense: as grain-growing regions, they could provide greatly for Rome's food supplies. To the west of the Ampsaga lay Mauretania. On the death of the Moorish king Bocchus II, his kingdom came under the direct administration of Rome, represented by prefects. So it remained until 25 BC, when it was entrusted to Juba II, the son of the king defeated at Thapsus.

Transalpine Gaul

For almost a century there had been a Roman presence here. But until Caesar, Romanization had been relatively meager. Octavian continued the process, founding colonies (Béziers in 36, Orange in 35, Fréjus after Actium) and resid-ing there for a time (39–38). If one compares the excessive demands made on it in the pre-Caesarian period with the treatment it began to receive under Caesar, it is understandable that the transalpine area should have pledged a solid attachment to Caesar's adoptive son.

Celtic Gaul

Sporadic risings among the Treveri (31–30), the Morini (29), and the Aqui-tani (28) should not hide the reality that Celtic Gaul was satisfied with, or at least adapted to, the Roman presence. Caesar's expeditions had left the country so weak and drained that the peace that the Roman presence brought was cer-tainly much needed, if not wholeheartedly desired. In 40 (and until the begin-ning of 37), Agrippa had not only re-established order but also undertaken the development of the new province. A military show of strength, combined with a skillful policy of alliances with the Germanic peoples of the left bank of the Rhine, had sheltered the country from the incursions of the Germani from across the river. Moreover, the "Caesarian" foundations of Nyon, Lyon, and Augst blocked the access routes to the Rhône valley, which had been the favored passage to Italy for Germanic invaders. Roman policy was no longer exclusively Mediterranean. By preventing Gaul from being drawn into the Germanic sphere, it showed a concern for the mainland as well.

Plate 7.4 Triumphal arch built ca. AD 20 to commemorate the campaigns of the II legion *Gallica*. Orange, France.

Illyricum

This province, the pivotal point of the two Mediterranean basins, had been almost lost in the period after the death of Caesar. It had been allocated to Octavian following the agreement at Brindisi, and in a series of hard-fought campaigns (in which he was twice wounded), he had reconquered the country and even penetrated into Pannonia (35–33), although only the coastal regions remained really under Roman control.

All in all, Rome held on with fair success to its western conquests. In order, as it were, to round them off, only the north-west of Spain and the western and central Alps remained to be subdued; and the only significant threats to their settled state came from the nomads of the southern parts of the African territories and the Germani east of the Rhine.

THE EAST

Octavian's first concern, as we have seen, was to reorganize the East. He had to gain the confidence of the populations who had supported Antony, but at the same time, in order to dissociate himself in Roman and Italian eyes from the eastern tendencies of his adversary's policies, he had to preserve Roman forms of government there. All this he did with ingenuity and pragmatism, setting up or maintaining vassal states by annexation or diplomacy so that there was the least possible break between the Roman provinces.

Macedonia

Macedonia, the oldest Roman province on the eastern side, was of great strategic importance, both serving as a shield for Achaea, which it protected against the barbarians of the north, and controlling the Via Egnatia, which provided a vital link between West and East, the first big strategic route built outside Italy. Octavian immediately strengthened this province through diplomacy (placing a subject king, Cotys, on the throne of Thrace, to the north-east of the province), through force (in 29–28 the governor of Macedonia, M. Licinius Crassus, repulsed an invasion of the Bastarnae and Getae and launched victorious counter-operations), and through the settlement there of veterans of Philippi.

Achaea

What with civil wars, the passage of troops, looting, the burden of taxes, and the recruitment of soldiers, this province was in ruins after Actium. By taking prompt action, Octavian gave the towns new hope: in around 30, the plan for the new Corinth was laid down; Patras (before becoming a colony) received his attention; Sparta was rewarded for its loyalty; and Nicopolis was founded. By contrast, the rural areas, in the hands of great landowners who went in for livestock breeding, remained in a pitiable state.

The Asiatic provinces: Asia and Bithynia

Between 31 and 29, Octavian made two stays in these two provinces. At the time of Actium they had enthusiastically given him their support. In 29, they requested authorization to award Octavian divine honors.

Syria

A mosaic of territories of different status (cities, principalities, tetrarchies) more or less closely linked with Rome, the province of Syria had undergone changes under Mark Antony and had peace come upon it after Actium, but it preserved throughout its astonishing diversity. Most remarkable was the preservation of a series of vassal kingdoms – Galatia, Cappadocia, Paphlagonia, Commagene, Judaea, Armenia Minor, Pontus, etc. – which ensured the connection between the Asiatic provinces and Syria, and between the latter and Egypt. On the death of each sovereign, annexation took place, for the most part without clashes, almost as a natural course.

Egypt

In the aftermath of the conquest of Egypt, two problems arose for Octavian: to ensure its security and to organize the new province. Military expeditions in Upper Egypt and against the "Ethiopians" began in 30. Its administration was completely out of the ordinary. The creation both of its people and of its conqueror, the successor to the Ptolemies, Roman Egypt was not properly speaking a "province." In 30, with the exception of the Greek cities (Alexandria, Ptolemais, and Naucratis), its territory was placed under the management of a knight. And the outlines of Octavian's policy for Egypt began to emerge: to preserve, at least on the surface, the respect due to tradition; to disengage himself from the power of the priests and from customs deemed too alien or unseemly for a Roman; and to make sure that Rome made its mark on the heart of the system. Thus he preserved almost in its entirety the traditional administration, but Romanized his "coronation name," breaking with a thousand-year-old tradition. For "Pharaoh Octavian was declared to exercise his office in the name of a power that belonged to him alone, which no longer owed anything to Egypt and its traditions: he was Pharaoh, in this instance, as *Autokrator*, that is, in the name of the *imperium* conferred on him by the Senate and the People of Rome" (J.-C. Grenier). The exploitation of Egypt could begin.

Cyrenaica, Crete, and Cyprus

Tossed from one camp to another in the civil wars, these relatively recent provinces found stability after Actium. Cyprus was detached from Egypt in 31; Crete was grouped with Cyrenaica.

In August 29, as Octavian celebrated his three triumphs in Rome, the world he dominated was no longer the one that had existed two years earlier. There was the Roman world before Actium, and the Roman world after Actium. The end of the Roman Republic and of the Hellenistic era and the start of the imperial regime and of the unitarian organization of the world. Was it an official break? Perhaps. The ancient historians (Dio Cassius) regarded it as fundamental – an opinion shared by many moderns.

BEYOND THE FRONTIERS

Beginning in the years 76–75 BC, the increasingly frequent appearance of the globe on Roman coins leaves no room for doubt: Rome saw itself as the guarantor of order in the world. And the consciousness of it as a task grew. The peace of Octavian, far from being viewed as an inevitable outcome of the course of events, was seen as deliberately masterful. Later he prided himself on having reached the limits of the world. "Rome did not literally conquer the old world – yet, all the old world was able to come to it" (C. Nicolet). For between the

Roman world and the rest of the world there were numerous attractive connections, commercial, cultural, belligerent.

ON THE FRINGES OF THE ROMAN WORLD

In the north

Caesar had twice crossed the Channel and landed in Britain. Since then, contacts between the island and Roman provinces had been rare. But they did exist.
Rome followed the political transformations brought about by the wars
between the British kingdoms. In 34, 27, and 26, Octavian planned expeditions against the Britons. By contrast, Ireland remained completely set apart.

In the north-east: Germania

For the early authors, the term "Germania" covered the territories extending
from the valleys of the Rhine and Danube to the North Sea and the Baltic. The
eastern frontiers were not defined; but modern scholars agree that the valley of
the Vistula was probably the eastern boundary. Even before Caesar crossed the
Rhine, Roman traders had ventured into those regions. And following him,
Agrippa was the second Roman to cross the river at the head of an army. But
until the Augustan era nothing is known of the frontier system. It seems likely,
however, that the Rhine had almost no true defense. At the most it may be
supposed that, during his stay in 39–38, Agrippa had established the Ubii on
the left bank of the Rhine, in the area of the future Cologne, to hold in check
their brothers from across the Rhine. The movements of these western Germani
(the peoples between the Rhine and the Elbe: the Suevi or Suebi, Canninefates,
Chatti, Frisii, Marcomanni, Quadi, Batavi, etc.) were in certain cases beginning
to become stabilized. Their expansion henceforward was to the west into the
Celtic region and to the east into the territory of other, eastern Germani, themselves on the move from the Baltic toward the south-east, along the Elbe and
the Oder.

The Alpine peoples

These peoples controlled passage between Italy, Celticum, and Raetia, in particular the two passes of the Little St Bernard and the Great St Bernard, used
by numerous Roman traders, and between Italy and Transalpine Gaul.
Extremely divided amongst themselves, and keeping themselves apart from
foreign influences, they lived by porterage and by working a few mines and
breeding livestock.

The Danube basin

In the western part were Celtic peoples (in Raetia and Noricum) and Germanic
tribes; in the central part, Illyrians (Dalmatians and Pannonians) and more

Celtic peoples; farther east, Thracians (Moesians, Getians, Dacians) and Germani (Bastarnae). These Germani too were turbulent. They launched raids into the Roman provinces of the Balkans (for instance in Macedonia in 29–28), and organized themselves into "kingdoms" and leagues.

In the east: Parthians and Arabs

Parthia   Since the defeat at Carrhae, the Romans had regarded the Parthians as their chief enemies. Caesar and Mark Antony had both tried to keep them in check. Apart from a reciprocal desire to expand, there were two sources of conflict between the Arsacid empire and Rome: Armenia, constantly at stake between the two powers, and the Syrian frontier. The Parthian empire, which had provided itself with a new capital (a new town, Ctesiphon), controlled one of the essential stages of the silk route, which passed through its territory.

The Arabs   The Nabataean Arabs lived on the caravan routes converging on Petra, an immense distribution center of luxury products originating from the Indian, Arabian, and African worlds. The Kingdom of the Nabataeans was, in Roman eyes, the gateway to an idyllic country, *Arabia felix* (fruitful Arabia, present-day Yemen), and the land of the Gerraei, "the richest of all peoples," as Strabo called them – countries that fascinated Rome because of their wealth and importance in international trade.

In the south

Nubia   Lower Nubia was occupied by pillaging nomads from the eastern desert, the Blemmyes, who threatened Egypt from time to time. Farther south lay the Ethiopian kingdom of Meroe (present-day Sudan), a centralized kingdom strong enough to launch military operations as far as Roman Egypt. It was the southernmost land in Africa known to the Greeks and Romans, and was the great staging post between the Mediterranean world and black Africa. Gold and slaves made their way through it toward Aswan and Alexandria.

The Sahara   There is no specific word in Latin to designate this great desert. Latin writers spoke of the "lonely places" or "wilderness." The Nasamones lived near the eastern and southern shores of the Major Syrtis; the Garamantes farther west, in Fezzan; the Gaetuli led their nomadic life on the borders of Numidia and Mauretania; and still further west came the Pharusi. All were nomadic shepherds, their territories poorly known to the writers, with ill-defined boundaries. They occasionally harassed the settled inhabitants of their regions, particularly those in the coastal towns, and with caravans of donkeys and mules, crisscrossed the northern fringes of the desert, the Nasamones sometimes going as far as Chad and the Niger – the famous "ships of the desert" played as yet no commercial or military role.

Beyond

The Slavs, Balts, and Finns Living to the east and north of the Germanic peoples, they were as yet unknown to the Romans. The appearance of the Slavs in Latin texts would have to wait until Pliny the Elder (the Veneti of the Vistula) and that of the Balts and Finns until Tacitus (the Estes and the Fenni).

The Sarmatae The Sarmatians, Iranian nomads, lived to the east of the Bastarnae, though they were moving west and south, and in 30–29 stepped up their incursions across the Danube even as far as Macedonia. They were sometimes called the Scythians.

India and China If we are to believe Strabo, shortly after the annexation of Egypt, 120 vessels passed the straits of Bab el-Mandeb at the southern end of the Red Sea, the gateway of the sea route to India. Some went as far as the Ganges. And as early as the end of Augustus' principate, large quantities of pottery from Arezzo made an appearance in the region of Pondicherry on the south-east coast of India. Direct relations with China, the country of the Seres, though very limited, existed from the last quarter of the first century BC.

This world, which was still restricted and compartmentalized, would eventually assume a new coherence. In this regard "the foundation of the Empire produced considerable changes" (C. Nicolet). When we have described this foundation, it will then be time to take stock again of the world situation.

8 / AUGUSTUS
The Birth of the Imperial Regime,
29 BC–AD 14

O N *August 19, AD 14, at Nola in Campania, the emperor Augustus died in his seventy-sixth year. All Italy wept for the man who prided himself on having re-established peace on land and at sea, on having "expanded all the provinces of the Roman people situated on the frontiers of nations which were not subject to our Empire," as he stated it in his Res gestae, the catalogue of his actions, compiled by himself and finished a few months earlier, that was destined to be engraved on the bronze tables placed in front of his mausoleum on the Campus Martius (RG 13 and 26); the man who had desired but one reward, so he said, "to be considered the author of the best of regimes" (Suetonius, Augustus 28). In Rome, the senators outdid one another in heaping honors on their dead emperor. One even proposed "designating the entire period from the day of his birth till the day of his death, the age of Augustus" (ibid., 100). "It was tantamount to admitting," remarks R. Étienne, "that Augustus had left such a mark on his era that it belonged to him." How did the leader of a victorious faction become the "midwife" of the new regime that we call the Empire, but which the ancients, apart from the unofficial title of "Principate," always referred to as the "State" or "Republic"? Why did Rome come to recognize itself in this regime, and so become, according to Virgil, aware of its place in the universe and the mission entrusted to it by Providence? "Thou, O Roman, reflect that thy role is to lead the nations by thy authority; for this is thy skill, and also to keep peace under thy control, to be merciful to those thou hast subjected and to humble the arrogant" (Aeneid VI.851–3).*

THE FORMATION OF THE PRINCIPATE

Was it in 31, 29, 27, or 23 BC that the new regime was born? All four dates are given by historians. Their disagreement reveals the confusion thrown up by the long-lasting failure fully to recognize and take into account the monarchical nature of a government whose true manner of operation (as is now agreed) lay obscured behind an ambiguous and complex institutional façade. Also, rather than using the word "birth," we should perhaps speak of emergence, since the features of the Augustan monarchy that were adopted by its successors took shape gradually, bit by bit, within the republican institutional edifice. For the Principate was not created *ex nihilo* but slowly put in position using existing forms, and following no preconceived plan but, rather, added to and modified according to circumstance, adapted to Octavian-Augustus' will to power.

THE ORIGINS

Thematically-speaking, the origins of the Principate were somewhat indistinct, the elements and influences involved being so many and so various, but for clarity's sake certain broad distinctions may be made. In reality, of course, these disparate themes combined, their coherence ensured by the personality of Augustus and the length of his reign (44 years, starting from Actium).

The Hellenistic model   In the eastern half of the Mediterranean basin, the city-state of Rome had come into contact with the monarchies born out of the division of Alexander the Great's empire. These kingdoms, syntheses of Greek and eastern elements, were often theocratic in appearance, with bureaucratic administrations and a tendency to universality. If the inhabitants of the eastern side of the Mediterranean were convinced of the need for a large empire to be led by one man alone, Italian and Roman soldiers and traders, and even the populus at large, were at least becoming accustomed to the monarchic idea – a "modern" idea to the contemporary Roman (P.-M. Martin). The *imperatores* or generals themselves, at least since Scipio Africanus, had remained fascinated by the image of Alexander the Great. And Octavian was no exception: in the first fortnight of August, 30, in Alexandria, "he placed on public display the coffin containing the body of the great Alexander which he had removed from its vault, and showed his veneration by laying a crown of gold upon it and scattering flowers. When asked if he also wanted to inspect the tomb of the Ptolemies, he replied that he had wanted to see a king, not corpses" (Suetonius, *Augustus* 18). Furthermore, on his return from Egypt, it was on the model of Alexander's tomb that Octavian undertook the construction of his own mausoleum in the northern part of the Campus Martius. Circular in shape, this imposing edifice (87 m in diameter) thus proclaimed itself "the tomb of a monarch and his dynasty" (Le Gall and Le Glay). In addition, in his Forum in Rome, two pictures represented episodes from Alexander's life, and a colossal statue of the emperor as (it is thought) Alexander adorned his curia.

The extent of the conquests   The Republic had conquered an immense territorial empire. But it had rapaciously exploited its provinces, not knowing how to give them a sound organization or how to ensure that their inhabitants felt some sort of attachment to Rome. Taken as a whole, it was a fragile edifice. Yet at the same time the Roman state affirmed its claim to universal domination (a claim first asserted in the middle of the first century BC, as official documents and coinage bear witness). Now, did that geographical expansion, together with the associated desire to stabilize and confirm, as well as enlarge, the possessions it had brought that is implicit in this claim to universal domination, necessitate changes, for technical and administrative reasons, in the nature of government? Anciet authors (Strabo, Florus, Dio Cassius) thought so, and modern historians agree that it was reasonable to think that "sooner or later conquests would render the structures of republican government unsuitable" (M. Humbert). A parallel swiftly imposed itself: just as Rome was the center of power, so that power could be held only in the hands of one single person.

Exhaustion of the old institutions Torn apart by civil wars, pulled this way and that between rival generals, ridiculed by the very ones who should have defended them, the traditional institutions of the city-state lay prostrate, their vigor spent. They survived only through the use of exceptional measures. Since Cicero's death in 43 BC, no project, no reform, no program had kindled the enthusiasm of supporters of the senatorial Republic. They proposed no remedy other than a return to an earlier state. Even worse, the most daring champions of the Republic in the face of the challenge of personal rule, the murderers of Caesar, who claimed by that singular act to have brought the hope of restoration and renewal, were incapable of arousing a popular movement. Since the near-disappearance of the old republican nobility no one, with the exception of Octavian, had been able to call up a popular response to a claim to be defending the cause of republican liberty. Dating perhaps to 32 BC, the exclamation of the poet Tibullus, "I do not want to die young and for nothing" (*Elegy* I.10), is a true reflection of the universal belief in the inability of traditional institutions to renew themselves.

The evolution of attitudes In a rather confused way, without clear awareness of it, people's minds were becoming familiar with monarchical ideas. It was thus agreed that the victors owed their success to their good fortune, a gift from the lord of the gods granted on the intervention of a guardian deity, Venus. And it was right, therefore, that these exceptional men should receive earthly honors that went beyond the customary norms. People began to pray to the gods for the well-being of an *imperator*, as if the well-being of the state and the Roman people depended on that of one man alone. Changes too in notions concerning the ideal life opened the door to a monarchical order. Whereas formerly the citizen had found his happiness in and through public life, henceforward he sought it far from the Forum, in the peace of rural life or by giving up his life to the service of a general. The task of being a citizen was replaced by the ideal of a rustic existence or of commitment to serving a *dux* or general. The political orator was succeeded by the court poet. All this meant that, in opposition to the idea of inevitable decline, an idea eventually linked with the theory that, like human beings, cities undergo a biological cycle (birth, growth, maturity, decline, death), a new idea took root that "a city must be formed in such a way that it is eternal" (Cicero, *De republica* 3.23). There was the budding hope of a new order that would ensure peace and break the cycle of violence and civil war – a hope shared by all.

The teachings of the schools More than Platonism, more than Stoicism, more even than the influential, if ambiguous, reflections of Cicero, Epicureanism presented the institution of monarchy as a conquest for mankind. The disciples of Epicurus looked on it as a regime in which the citizen, relieved of the concern of participating directly in government, could devote himself entirely to the cultivation of his inner life, avoiding the snares of competition and rivalry that littered the public world. Several testimonies to that proposition have come down to us. One of the most striking consists of fragments of a political treatise, *The Good King according to Homer*, written by Philodemus of Gadara, possibly in 45 BC, demonstrating that good kings *could* exist. Enlightened by wise counselors, it is the duty of the good king to be moderate, to make sure that his personal conduct conforms to the rules of morality, to show himself to be just toward men and pious toward the gods, and to see that unity and peace exist between his subjects.

It may be seen that, under the influence of various forces, Roman society was ready to give itself to the providential man whose virtues would ensure peace. But that readiness had still to be tapped, and the aspirations that underlay it might yet need to be emphasized by skillful propaganda. This was something that Octavian understood perfectly.

INSTITUTIONAL COMPROMISE (29–23 BC)

Obstacles and advantages

The triumph of 29 meant the end of the war against Cleopatra and a return to a legal state. But of what kind? To have instituted a monarchical regime openly, Octavian would have had to overcome a number of formidable obstacles.

1 The title of king, or anything that might be a reminder of it (the name Romulus, wearing the diadem), still retained sufficient emotional charge in Rome to incite to murder: that was the lesson of the Ides of March.

2 The Senate, guardian of ancestral custom, the *mos maiorum*, had preserved its prestige, although its power was weakened. To overlook it, underestimate it, or in any way fall foul of it, would be to expose oneself to the hostility of

the great families, a hostility that was all the keener because they held the *res publica* to be their own personal property – and they had, moreover, extensive "clienteles."

3 The reputation and personality of Octavian did not go unchallenged. Like Antony in 43, he was accused of owing his success to a name, that of Caesar, and, certainly, looked at in a certain light, his personal military accomplishments were somewhat lackluster, and were indeed criticized. His family origins inspired malicious gossip and lies, but it was true that his father C. Octavius, initially a knight, had been the first in his family to follow the *cursus honorum*. And it was still remembered that during the civil wars Octavian had been a ruthless faction leader – cruel too, according to his opponents.

4 The institutional position of Octavian was ambiguous for the present and uncertain for the future. Since 32, his triumviral powers had in theory ceased. Three elements of power thus remained to him: the consulship, which he had occupied each year since 31 but which conferred no military responsibility on him; the sacrosanctity of the tribunes of the *plebs*, and tribunician power (i.e. the power of the tribunes without actually being one), both for life, received respectively in 36 and 30; and the oath of loyalty sworn to him by Italy and the western provinces in the autumn of 32. In 28, the crisis provoked by M. Licinius Crassus, grandson of Caesar's colleague in the First Triumvirate, revealed how precarious that position was. By asking to celebrate a triumph and lay down the arms of the slain general in the temple of Jupiter Feretrius, Crassus rivaled Octavian's military pre-eminence.

On the other hand, Octavian held some first-rate trump cards were he to seek the substance of monarchy, if not its appearance.

1 He was the (adoptive) son of a "god." This prestigious relationship linked him not only to Caesar, the only *divus* in Rome, but also to Caesar's ancestress Venus Genitrix. Two events brought his divine antecedents into plain view. In 29, the temple of the Divine Julius was dedicated in the Forum, and the new Curia, the Curia Julia, begun by Caesar, was inaugurated: before the façade of the temple was a platform decorated with the *rostra* or prows of the ships captured at Actium; at the far end of the Curia, a statue of Victory brought back from Tarentum by Octavian, and before it an altar, making it an object of worship. Both were ways of celebrating the father and at the same time recalling the merits of the son.

2 He stood at the head of a formidable and, as Antony's soldiers had rallied to him, single army of over sixty legions, as well as all the auxiliary troops. Although he quickly demobilized more than half of his legionaries and settled the veterans, his military power in real terms remained overwhelming.

3 He was immensely rich. His expenditure between 30 and 29 BC has been estimated at 1,000 million sesterces. That fortune came partly from inheritances from both his natural father and his adoptive father and partly from the

confiscation of lands and sales of enemy possessions, but above all from the Egyptian booty. He was the richest man of his time and could practice a policy of public benefaction on an imperial scale.

4 In 43 BC, Octavian had been acclaimed *imperator*. In 40, he had transformed this honorific title into part of his name, attaching it definitively to his person, like a real forename, doubtless to show "the possession of a primacy of honor and a superiority of power."

5 He seemed to be simultaneously the man of victory and the man of peace. Apart from his triumph in 29, a series of initiatives taken by the Senate while Octavian was in the East brought him the appearance of deserving this double merit. As we have seen, on January 1, 29, the Senate gave its *auctoritas* to all his acts up to that date, and on January 11 the doors of the temple of Janus were closed for the third time in the history of Rome, signifying the coming of peace. In addition, Octavian was saluted with the title "savior of the State." An arch in his honor was erected in the Forum, between the temple of the Divus Julius and the temple of Castor. And on this triumphal arch could be read the words *Respublica conservata*. Better still, on the occasion of the triumph, when according to tradition the magistrates and the Senate headed the procession, for the first time it was the *imperator*, Octavian, who led it.

So Octavian enjoyed numerous advantages. But more than this, he knew how to use them skillfully, taking decisions, or seeing that they were taken, apparently with the sole aim of restoring the past, while he tested out innovations of a seemingly minor nature but of decisive importance for the balance of power within the state. His political genius lay precisely in his grasp of the fact that, the better to establish his personal power, he had to preserve the Republic, even to consolidate the outward appearance of its institutions in order to empty them of their content. Between 28 and 23 BC, slowly and with pragmatism, an advantageous institutional compromise was visibly pieced together.

The forms of the compromise

In 28, Octavian inaugurated his sixth consulship, with Agrippa as his colleague. There was no military expedition – the two consuls stayed in Rome the whole year. Vested with censorial powers, they took a census (the last dated back to 70 BC), in which 4,063,000 citizens were listed, and employing the same powers, revised the senatorial rolls. Through this *lectio*, though the Senate's numbers still topped 600 members, 190 senators left the assembly. Moreover, this *lectio* had Octavian himself appointed *princeps senatus* (head of the Senate). He could now steer the assembly's decisions, since he would be the first to give his opinion when its deliberations got under way. In the same year, several moral and sumptuary laws were enacted, increasing the advantages that lay to "good citizens." The Republic of former years appeared to be restored: the coinage of the year 28 celebrated Octavian as *libertatis reipublicae vindex*, the champion of republican liberty.

At least, that is what Octavian proclaimed. On January 13, 27, he "transferred the Republic from [his] power into that of the Senate and the Roman people" (*RG* 34). It was ostensibly an abdication: Octavian handed over all his powers to the Senate – which, however, at once begged him to stay. Was it a sincere renunciation, a clever maneuver, the expression of a sense of duty pushed to the point of sacrifice, or the conscious fulfillment of a historic mission of restoration? Such are the chief explanations put forward by historians for that day, though it is also often treated as a piece of play-acting. At all events, an accommodation was reached marking a disposition of imperial authority that was to last several centuries. Octavian accepted, in response to the Senate's pleas, only a special commission giving him for a set period the authority of a proconsul over certain provinces. But these were the provinces where the bulk of the troops were stationed, so that he now possessed the legal authority he had lacked but with little diminishment in military power, and though this proconsular *imperium*, on the nature of which historians are still pondering, was specified to last for ten years, it would in fact be renewed, until his death, from one decade to the next, as a matter of course. For its part, the Senate kept the management, except in special circumstances, of the remaining, mostly pacified provinces with no army. Did this sharing out of provinces mean that the Empire would at heart be a diarchy? Mommsen and his disciple Kornemann believed so. But that argument has been largely abandoned, particularly since the discovery of five edicts of Augustus at Cyrene, attesting the intervention of the emperor in senatorial provinces, in this instance the province of Crete and Cyrenaica. Not only did his interference cause no problem, but the Cyreneans expressed their gratitude to the man who had shown concern for their fate. "Imperial intervention was an honor and they were conscious of its value."

On January the 16th, three decrees complemented the awarding of the *imperium*. The first accorded Octavian the title "Augustus." "Romulus" and "Quirinus," originally proposed, had been turned down: they carried too strong an evocation of royal power. "Augustus," by contrast, was a new term, borrowed from religious vocabulary. For Suetonius it was linked with augury; for Livy it was contrasted with *humanus*. The word achieves its full value when it is put together with *auctoritas*, signifying thus "the holder of *auctoritas*." From then on, everything that Octavian undertook would be "augmented" by a superior quality, related to divinity. He was already more than a mere man: "At that time," he wrote, "I was above everyone in authority (*auctoritas*), but I had no more power (*potestas*) than any of my colleagues in my various magistracies" (*RG* 34). In this way, his *auctoritas* ensured that his powers were superior to those of other magistrates. He thus became *Imperator Caesar Divi filius Augustus*, indicating his *imperium* by his *praenomen*, his divine kinship with his adoptive father, whose *cognomen* (*Caesar*) became a family name, and his new quality by his surname (*Augustus*).

The second decree awarded him the laurels and the civic crown, allusions to his triumph and his role as savior of the collective nation. By virtue of the third decree, a golden shield was to be hung in the Curia, inscribed with the words *virtus, clementia, iustitia, pietas. Virtus* was the quality of a truly manly man and here designated the excellence of the one who possessed it. *Clementia* suggested magnanimity, especially toward the defeated, together with moderation in the use of power and forbearance in the face of the faults and errors of others. *Iustitia* represented justice and equity. And *pietas* embraced all that each man owed to the deities, his family, and his *civitas*. Since the time of Scipio Africanus, those four virtues had been the ideal virtues of the Roman man.

The young victor thus rose above the state both as a being of divine nature (*augustus*) and a "sage" . . . and also as a Roman, possessing the virtues of national tradition. This was a particularly remarkable synthesis, causing Roman values as well as those of philosophy, and further still, those of the good king of Greek orators and poets, to work toward the glorification of the triumphal lord. A synthesis which obviously marked Augustus out as a king, but without the title. (P. Grimal)

Between 27 and 23 BC, Augustus strengthened his powers in practice without adding extra offices. He asked only to retain the consulship, which he assumed each year, thus enabling him to exercise a kind of supervision over Rome, Italy, and the various other magistrates.

Augustan government (23 bc–ad 14)

The new regime seemed to be established; so much so that Augustus was able to leave Rome for three years (27–24). However, in 23 the weakness of a system in which everything depended on the person of the emperor was exposed, in the first place by an obscure crisis that arose when disquiet linked with the trial of a provincial governor gave rise to a conspiracy in which the emperor's colleague in the consulship was compromised. This immediate crisis was resolved, but a dis-ease remained and this was aggravated by the rapid decline in Augustus' health that followed, to the point of death it seemed. The great uncertainty created by these events, either of which might have precipitated renewed dissension and civil war, brought about some important constitutional modifications to the regime.

In the first place, Augustus gave up the consulship – he resumed it only twice, in 5 and 2 BC, in order to present his grandsons and heirs to the people. It has often been thought that, in return, he had the benefit of an *imperium maius et infinitum*, an *imperium* exercised over the whole empire, but that he did is not at all certain: his renewable proconsular *imperium*, together with his accumulated personal *auctoritas*, would have sufficed to afford him powers of that scope. From 23 BC onward Augustus was therefore, in the absence of the consulship, no longer a magistrate in the technical sense of the term. He refused the dictatorship, life censorship, and consulship in perpetuity offered to him by the Senate and people, and accepted only special duties that were to some extent detached from the magistracy that supported them, such as the power of censorship in 19, 18, and 12, and the consular power for life, given to him in 19 (by refusing the permanent consulship, he left open both posts of consul, for such purposes as patronage, instead of monopolizing one himself).

His abandonment of the consulship was more than compensated for by the formal confirmation of his tribunician power, received officially on July 1, 23. (It was renewed each year on the same date, and the number of the renewal served to enumerate the years of his reign.) Though not a tribune of the *plebs* (he was not eligible, being patrician), Augustus now possessed all the tribunes' powers: sacrosanctity or inviolability, veto over other magistrates, the right to convene the Senate, the right to propose laws, and the *ius auxilii*. Better still, above that of all other tribunes, this power not only applied to the capital but extended to all of the Empire and its inhabitants. The *tribunicia potestas*, *imperium*, and *auctoritas* from that time onward constituted the three "granite pillars" of the new regime.

The final additions were made in 12 BC, when, on the death of Lepidus, Augustus was elected *pontifex maximus*, and in 2 BC, when he was hailed as "father of his country" (*pater patriae*) by the Senate and people, thus becoming a kind of "patron" on an imperial scale. The main features of the Principate were thus all in place. They would evolve according to the emperor and the circumstances, but the various constitutive elements of Augustan power would always be there. The institutions of the Republic (Senate, magistracies, *comitia*) persisted; Augustus himself was only a simple citizen. Remaining outside the state's institutions, he allowed them to continue functioning in their normal manner. But if he thought he should intervene he did so, and irrevocably. Two administrations and two powers were superimposed. But the imperial power always had the last word.

Symbolically, the dividing line between the age of the Republic and the Augustan age may be seen in the celebration of the Secular Games of 17 BC. These games marked the end of one *saeculum*, or era (defined as the utmost span of a human lifetime), and the beginning of the next, an event calculated to occur every 100 years. They had taken place in 348, 249, and 146. But the civil wars had prevented the holding of the games in the forties. By holding them in 17 (with the *saeculum* recalculated as 110 years), Augustus was therefore observing a tradition, but at the same time, in what the celebrations proclaimed – as Horace's *Carmen Saeculare* shows – he was profoundly reshaping it, and with the certainty that he was opening a new age.

THE EMPEROR AND HIS ENTOURAGE

AUGUSTUS

BIOGRAPHY (until 44 BC)

63: Born in Rome, on September 23. His father, C. Octavius, who died in 59, was a *homo novus*. His mother, Atia, was a niece of Caesar, who took an interest in her son at an early age and introduced him to Roman life – he entered the college of pontiffs in 48. Caesar also watched over his education, which was carefully conducted. Strong bonds of affection existed between the young man and his great-uncle.

46: Caesar had Octavian take part in his African triumph even though he had not been in the campaign. It was a way of designating him his heir.

45: He fought at Caesar's side against Pompey's supporters in Spain. In September, without telling him, Caesar adopted him and made him his heir.

44: He was in Apollonia in Epirus, as much to complete his studies as to prepare for the campaign against the Parthians, when he learned of the dictator's assassination. He decided to avenge him, and, in reply to his mother, who tried to dissuade him, he quoted a passage from the *Iliad*: "May I die now, for they have killed my friend and I was not there to defend him." He was in Rome by May. There then began one of the greatest political ventures ever: having set out to avenge his adoptive father, Octavian established a regime that was to last five centuries and left its decisive imprint on the history of mankind.

The man

Although there is no lack of written and sculptured portraits, it is difficult to picture Augustus. For the writings reflect two opposing propagandas, and the effigies, which range over a whole lifetime, are almost all deliberately idealized. From antiquity to the present day, however, one judgement persists: "Augustus is ambiguity" (R. Étienne). We are soon submerged in worn expressions which yet contain a germ of truth: good looks, frail health, self-control, energy, hard work, efficiency, organizational ability, simplicity of life in his Palatine residence,

Plate 8.1 Detail from the *Ara Pacis Augustae*, a great marble altar consecrated July 4, 13 BC on the Campus Martius at Rome. It depicts members of the imperial family.

strong will, prudence, morality, and vice. In short, a complex man whose greatness and genius shone most brilliantly in political action, its preparation, realization, and utilization.

His political ideas, born of a feeling of vengeance, inspired by the Caesarian heritage, and adapted to circumstances in order to win and preserve power, grew stronger during the course of his reign, and reached their apogee in an elevated and austere concept of the function of the state. Yet even before this majestical plane had been achieved, an early "Augustan" ideology had emerged. It was prepared by two poets, Virgil and Horace, and indicated perhaps a burgeoning sense of mission in Augustus himself between 36 and 31, the period that saw its emergence. The themes of the Augustan ideology were peace (one of the most characteristic monuments is precisely the *Ara Pacis Augustae*, the altar of Augustan peace), social order, a return to the Roman virtues (those of the golden shield), the restoration of traditional religion, the grandeur of Rome, and the defense of *libertas*. And to celebrate Rome's second birth, the return of plenty, the reign of perpetual youth, and the majesty of the *Imperator* – to this end poets, architects, sculptors, and artists of every kind placed themselves at the ruler's service. In all styles and at all levels of artistic achievement, these themes appeared again and again: never yet had the potency of the image been put to use so totally to announce the dawn of a new golden age, when happiness would not be given freely and without cost, but earned by effort and devotion to the affairs of the state.

HIS FAMILY

Augustus had become engaged in political life through a family drama; now he engaged his family (see the genealogical table) in his political struggles. He used it variously. The bond of marriage was most usefully employed to seal an alliance, ensure a succession, and neutralize possible opposition. Thus, in 40, he married his sister Octavia to Mark Antony to conclude the treaty of Brindisi; in 25, he had his only daughter, Julia, married to his nephew Claudius Marcellus, marking him out as his preferred successor; and in 12 BC, he forced his stepson Tiberius to separate from his wife in order to marry Julia, again for reasons of the succession (Marcellus, and then her second husband, Agrippa, having died). It was not, though, only because of their usefulness as instruments of policy that he had reason to treat family members in the light of political considerations. Thus, in 2 BC, reasons of state caused him to exile Julia, following a mysterious affair, perhaps a plot. There was nothing wholly new or surprising in all this – in the use he made of his family, Augustus was merely exaggerating the customs of his time. Somewhat more singular was his passion for his third wife, Livia, whom he married in 38. Belonging by birth and marriage to the loftiest republican aristocracy (the *gens Claudia*, from which came the Julio-Claudians), she had divorced her husband, by whom she was pregnant, in order to marry Augustus, who had himself just separated from Scribonia. "A Ulysses in petticoats," to use Caligula's words, as the trusted consort of the emperor, Livia came to play a notable political role, discreet as became a woman, but with important dynastic and even more closely political effects, particularly through her constant pushing to the fore of her sons Tiberius and Drusus Germanicus. Augustus adopted her in his will, under which she became "Julia Augusta."

THOSE CLOSEST TO HIM

Among those who worked closely with Augustus, two figures stand out because of the leading roles they played, Maecenas and Agrippa. A famous passage from Dio Cassius describes a debate, after Actium, between the two counselors in Augustus' presence. What was to be done? Re-establish the Republic, suggests Agrippa; think up a new regime, a monarchy in all but name, recommends Maecenas. Behind this dialogue, "imaginary but not necessarily untrue" (C. Nicolet), may be discerned the real influence of these two counselors, their tendency to take opposing views (exaggerated perhaps by the medium of the dialogue), and their absolute loyalty to Augustus.

1 Maecenas, who belonged to the equestrian order, which he never wanted to leave, was about ten years older than Augustus, and came from Etruria (his maternal family had formerly reigned over the city of Arezzo). A wealthy aristocrat with refined tastes, he was a disciple of Epicurus and a patron of the poets Virgil, Propertius, and Horace, whom he drew into the Augustan circle, with such lasting effects. But his service to Octavian-Augustus was above all as a diplomat (he negotiated the treaties of Brindisi and Tarentum) and as a kind of informal minister of the interior, his active and very well informed intelligence making him capable of thwarting conspiracies and ensuring order. Nevertheless, during his last years (he died in 8 BC) he fell into semi-disgrace.

2 Born in 64 of an obscure family, one that is with no important ancestors to boast of, Agrippa was with Octavian at Apollonia. From then on his destiny merged with that of the future emperor, on whose behalf he helped win the war of Perugia and carried off victories at Naulochus and Actium. Long viewed by history mainly in the light of his military activities, he has emerged from recent work with a richer and more rounded personality. A faithful supporter, a clever strategist, a great builder, a peacemaker as well as an administrator, a public benefactor, the author of an autobiography and some technical works – this rough, many-talented soldier devoted all his energies to the glory of Rome and its empire, the emperor, and the dynasty. His sterling qualities, his single-minded devotion, and the solid trust shown him by Augustus marked him out, on the death of the heir presumptive Marcellus, as the new husband for Julia, whom he married in 21. Five children were born of this union, including Gaius and Lucius Caesar. From 18 BC on, possessing tribunician power and the pro-consular *imperium*, he became Augustus' co-regent and colleague. His powers were renewed in 13 BC, but he died the following year on his return from a campaign in Pannonia.

A HIERARCHY OF OFFICES

The creator of a new regime hallowed by the traditional forms it claimed to have restored, Augustus also sought, through the forces of emulation and the law, a moral and social reformation that would both revivify the old and secure the new. To this end he aimed, in general terms, at a return to the morality of the ancients, the strengthening of social cohesion, and the re-establishing of state service as a high ideal.

The desire to recover the moral order was possibly combined with a concern to bolster the numbers of the established population. At all events, a series of laws in 18 BC and AD 9 denounced bachelorhood and adultery by women, and gave advantages to fathers of families. Similarly, the two forms of social mobility most likely to alter the established order, the emancipation of slaves and the

Table 8.1 Augustus and his family (from J. Le Gall and M. Le Glay, *L'Empire romain*, pp. 56–7)

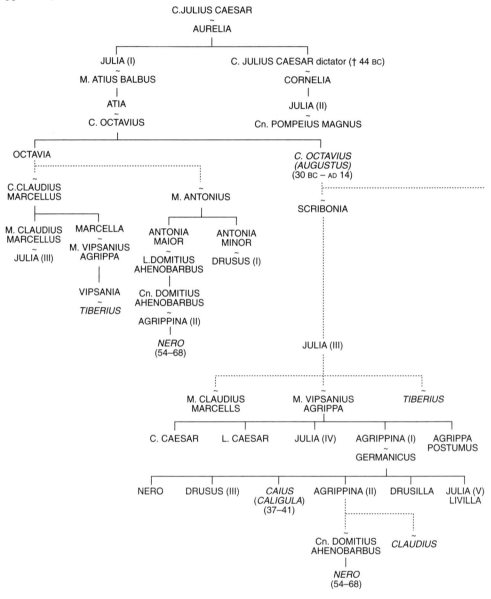

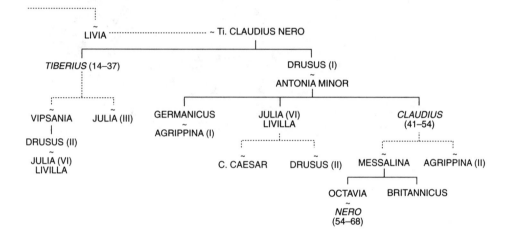

Plate 8.2 Pont du Gard, near Nîmes, France. About 275 meters long and almost 50 meters high, it was built in the time of Augustus. Water was carried above the top tier.

granting of citizenship to foreigners, were restricted and controlled, with a new social status created to capture that class of slaves manumitted outside these measures, the Junian Latins. These last two sets of arrangements meant that under the Empire Roman society come to be structured, on the legal plane, as follows:

- the two *ordines* (the senatorial and equestrian "orders")
- the Roman citizens of Rome, Italy, and the provinces
- the Latins
- the Junian Latins
- foreigners (*peregrini*)
- the *dediticii* (free men who could never become citizens)
- slaves.

Augustus brought his attention to bear chiefly on the two upper groups, the senatorial and equestrian "orders." He refined them, set out clear conditions of entry, and began to work on their development.

The Senate and the Outline of
a Senatorial Order

In the republican era there was no such thing as a senatorial order. The only condition demanded of members of the Senate was the possession of capital equivalent to the equestrian property qualification (400,000 sesterces). The son of a senator was a knight. He himself became a senator, if he so desired, on the day he began his first magistracy, the quaestorship. He then returned his public horse to the state. In the case of a "new senator," that is a senator not of the senatorial class but with at least an equestrian fortune if not a knight himself, entry to the Senate again coincided with his entry into the duties of the quaestorship. "The Senate was merely an assembly and the quality of senator remained individual" (A. Chastagnol). Beneath their toga, the members of the assembly wore on their tunic a broad band of purple, the laticlave. Now, after the death of Caesar a dual development was noticeable: the number of senators increased; and the sons of senators and the sons of knights improperly used the laticlave to make plain their ambitions. Such was the situation inherited by Augustus. He reformed it step by step, combining, as was his wont, the influences of the past and innovations, leaving compromises, contradictions, and ambiguities.

Wearing the laticlave In 18 BC, in parallel with the reduction of the Senate's numbers to 600, Augustus forbade the sons of knights to wear the laticlave, creating for them the angusticlave (a narrow band of purple), and reserved the use of the laticlave for the descendants of senators: "in order to familiarize them more rapidly with public affairs, he allowed the sons of senators to wear the laticlave and attend meetings of the Senate immediately they had received the toga of manhood" (Suetonius, *Augustus* 38). In the emperor's eyes, senators' sons were thus predestined to become senators. But, although therefore members of the senatorial "order," these young men remained knights. (The future emperor Claudius, for example, continued to belong to the equestrian order until in AD 37 Caligula appointed him as his colleague in the consulship and made him a senator.) In 18 BC, the *ordo senatorius* was thus as yet only an outline of what it later became, its single mark being the wearing of the laticlave, which only the senators and their descendants, from the age of 17, were authorized to do.

The institution of a senatorial property qualification Between 18 and 13 BC, a senatorial property qualification was fixed. It was now necessary for the sons of senators to have a capital of 1,000,000 sesterces if they wished to seek a quaestorship. This was to avoid corruption. For the same reason, if a man who was already a senator fell short of the required amount, he had to give up his senatorial office – unless the emperor made up the deficit. Here was a new means of controlling the budding *ordo* in addition to that which derived from the fact that it did not contain all possible candidates to the Senate and therefore lacked the additional power and security that such a monopoly would have offered. But the creation of a different and higher rating to that of the equestrian order raised a fresh barrier between knights and senators. And the inner coherence of the two orders differed considerably, to the advantage of the new one, for the descendants of senators tended to form a better-defined social group.

The "ius honorum"　In order to be able to enter the Senate, those who were not the sons of senators also had to possess, over and above the property qualification and an honorable name, the *ius honorum*, that is to say, the right to stand as a candidate for the first magistracy. It appears that this right was granted to all the Roman citizens of Italy and the Latin colonies, but denied to provincials other than knights and citizens of Roman colonies and Roman *municipia* or free towns.

The Senate　As under the Republic, admission to the Senate was by way of the quaestorship, but it was a process now largely subject to the will of the emperor. The terms on which the assembly functioned mostly remained the same as a century earlier. Augustus' reform in 9 BC – two sittings a month on fixed dates (with the possibility of meeting outside those days), the necessity of a quorum for all senatorial decrees, which sometimes became law – aimed at giving the Senate the best possible conditions under which to fulfill its traditional function and confirm its primacy in the hierarchy of society. To these improvements was added the constant concern of the emperor to favor the free exercise of senatorial initiative. The Senate was also the constitutional body that confirmed the powers of the emperor, providing the formal seal of legitimacy, it gained the right to set itself up as a tribunal to try its own members, retained the administration of certain provinces, had reserved to its members certain administrative posts (the prefectship of Rome, supervision of water, etc.), and participated in the emperor's *consilium* (15 senators chosen by lot). However, although the republican tradition continued in appearance, in reality the Senate was politically weak. Not only did it need to ask Augustus for help on several occasions, but it also lost control of foreign and military policy and a large part of fiscal policy (around 12 BC it was deprived of its right to strike coinage). Its members wavered between submission to the emperor and a sterile opposition of clumsy plots. Nevertheless, by a paradox that became more marked as time went on, "the Senate continued to be recognized as the symbol of the *res publica*" (J.-A. Talbert) and its prestige remained considerable.

MAGISTRATES AND COMITIA

Regular elections for the magistracies were re-established in 28 or 27 BC.
Though there was a shortage of candidates for the minor posts (quaestor,
tribune, aedile), the higher positions (praetor, consul) were much sought
after; they gave an entry, in effect, to the important offices in the administration of the Empire. The praetors saw their number increased (to 12),
and from AD 5 on, the use of *suffecti* (substitute) consuls became normal,
though it was the *consules ordinarii* by whose names years were recorded in
the *fasti*.

Though he seemed by this to have restored the freedom of election, Augustus
in fact controlled elections by means of two procedures, the *nominatio* (acceptance of the candidacy by the magistrate in charge of the election), when
the known wishes of the emperor were taken into account, and the *commenda-
tio* (recommendation of candidates by the emperor himself). The *comitia*, traditionally the primary electoral bodies, were therefore not reinvigorated by this
reinstitution of regular elections, and the *comitia centuriata* in particular suffered
a further substantial reduction in its political role after AD 5, when a complex
system of mixed "centuries" (senators and knights) was instituted to take part in
a *destinatio* (appointment) of praetors and consuls prior to the decision of the full
comitia (see the *Tabula Hebana*).

In the short term, Augustus' initiatives in this field not only hastened the
decline of the *comitia*, which lost all judicial competence, but also deprived the
traditional magistracies of much of their political and constitutional substance.
Even so, they remained in existence, the titles marking the stages in the *cursus*
or career progress of a senator, the structure of which gradually developed under
the early Empire.

THE EQUESTRIAN ORDER

Between the ancient *ordo* of the republican era and that organized by Augustus,
there were several points in common: the property qualification of 400,000 sesterces was retained; the annual procession on 15 July was revived; there was yet
an obligation to hold Roman citizenship; appointment was still by virtue of one's
qualities and worthiness to receive the title of knight, awarded now by the
emperor acting in the role of censor. Being a knight brought privileges: the right
to wear a tunic with a narrow purple band (angusticlave), a gold ring, reserved
seats for shows. But there was no legal heredity: except for the sons of senators,
who wore the laticlave, one was not born a knight; one became a knight. The
knights thus formed a group which, by its nature, was more open than that of
the senators. The geographic or social origin of the new knight mattered little;

SIMPLIFIED PLAN OF A SENATORIAL "CURSUS" UNDER THE EARLY EMPIRE

Laticlave military tribunate (starting with the Flavians, second office).
Vigintivirate: 20 posts (in decreasing order) (starting with the Flavians, first office):

- *Triumvir auro argento aere flando feriundo* (triumvir responsible for the melting and stamping of bronze, silver, and gold)
- *Decemvir stlitibus iudicandis* (decemvir responsible for trying lawsuits)
- *Quattuorvir viarum curandarum* (quattuorvir responsible for road maintenance)
- *Triumvir capitalis* (triumvir responsible for public prisons and executions).

(The post occupied often determined the course of the later career.)
Quaestorship: 20 posts, minimum age 25 years.
  In Rome and the provinces (responsible for finances in a senatorial province).
  Quaestorian function: legate of the proconsul in a senatorial province.
Tribunate of the *plebs* (10 posts) or aedile (6 posts).
  Patricians were exempt, hence a more rapid career.
Praetorship: from 10 to 18 posts, minimum age 30 years.
  Praetorian functions:

- legate of a legion
- proconsul of a praetorian senatorial province
- legate of a praetorian imperial province
- prefect of the treasury of Saturn, etc.

Consulship: minimum age 33 years. The first consulship was often as a *suffectus* or deputy consul.
Consular functions:

- curator of aqueducts, the Tiber, etc.
- legate of a consular imperial province
- proconsul of a consular senatorial province (Asia or Africa)
- prefect of Rome (generally after the second consulship).

what mattered most were his merits and his capacity to serve. For with this remodeled *ordo*, Augustus forged not only a body of active supporters, ready to uphold the new regime and likely to rally to it provincial notables and the most enterprising elements from the world of the *municipia*, but also an elite of diligent officials.

Of course, not all knights (perhaps between 10,000 and 15,000 men in all) entered the emperor's service. Many of them held aloof from the servitude of official appointments and went on living on their lands or by their commercial enterprises, enjoying their title as a means of becoming "patrons" and of strengthening their social standing. These we know of only through chance inscriptions. By contrast, those who followed an administrative career are relatively well known. Their *cursus* fell into shape gradually and continued to develop in diverse ways with changing circumstances. At the outset their administrative function in the civil sphere was essentially financial, involving in the main the management of Augustus' possessions (or those of the imperial family). The former senior officers or knights to whom he seems to have entrusted this task bore the title of *procurator* (agent or manager) and this term would be retained even when the business of the employees of the emperor in civil administration became increasingly diverse and of much wider scope. Depending on the provinces in which these men worked, a distinction was made: in the imperial provinces they were increasingly regarded as state officials; in the senatorial provinces they remained the emperor's private employees, which did not prevent them, when the need arose, from keeping an eye on the senatorial administration. However, as yet the imperial civil administration was at its small beginnings. For the Augustan era, fewer than 30 of these procurators are known to us.

The emperor similarly opened up career prospects for knights by devising posts that were to be reserved for them:

- Legion commands in Egypt, war fleet commands.
- Provincial governorships, e.g. in the Maritime Alps and Sardinia, though without the *imperium* or the right to impose the death penalty (*ius gladii*).
- Administrative posts in Egypt, where no senator had the right to go: the prefectship of Egypt (from 30 BC), then the summit of the equestrian career; and various posts replacing those of officials of the Ptolemaic monarchy, while keeping their titles (*idiologus, epistrategus*).
- Two posts of praetorian prefect (*praefectus praetorio*), created in 2 BC for the command of the praetorian cohorts.
- The post of prefect of the *annona* or grain supply (*praefectus annonae*), created at the end of the reign (about AD 8) for the securing of the provisioning of Rome. Rome's grain supplies had always been precarious. In 22

BC, Augustus had taken charge personally, before appointing former praetors and consuls to secure them. With the creation of this prefectship, a knight had that responsibility.

■ The post of prefect of the *vigiles* or Watch (*praefectus vigilum*). Republican Rome had had neither firemen nor a police force. A fire-fighting corps of 600 slaves had been set up in 23 BC, commanded by aediles. In AD 6, they were replaced by seven cohorts of *vigiles*, all freedmen, under the command of this prefect.

Thus a pool of candidates was gradually formed suitable to fill the growing range of imperial offices: the military posts in which they began their careers, and then those connected with the administration of justice and finances (tax farming and companies of tax-gatherers, though, did not disappear). We can see from all this that there was nothing systematic in the setting up of the new equestrian order, which was a continuation of the old one but now included all the elements necessary for the formation of a great body of state employees responsible to the emperor. Its members were at first in competition with the traditional senatorial administration, but they would gradually come to replace it, and so become incorporated into the first order of society.

THE ARMY AND ITS CONQUESTS

THE ARMY

Augustus took particular care over the army. A regime born of victory on the field of battle and proclaiming an internal and external peace of which the *Princeps* had made himself the champion could not overlook that body of men on whose loyalty and quality the securing of these things depended. Augustus himself was, moreover, singularly identified with the army. The soldiers swore to him alone the *sacramentum* or oath which, under the Republic, had bound the soldier to his general. It was he who chose the legions' legates and the governors with troops at their disposal (with the exception of the proconsul of Africa). And to him alone belonged every victory and triumph, his legates achieving success only by a kind of delegation, for all campaigns were fought in his name. This universal personal involvement, as well as his own inclinations, meant, on the other hand, that he was less personally involved in the field. Feeling more at ease in ensuring that discipline was observed than in directing operations, he relied on the able generals he knew how to surround himself with, some of whom came from the imperial family itself (Agrippa, Tiberius, Drusus). Augustus' military policy, traditionalist in some ways, innovatory in others, may be summarized, without undue distortion, under four headings.

Action on behalf of veterans

In the wake of Actium, troop numbers far exceeded both the requirements and the means of the Empire. There had to be large reductions, and the newly discharged soldiers had to be kept happy and their loyalty secured. In several stages, 300,000 men were returned to civilian life. Until 13 BC, they generally received land in a colony, settled principally in Italy, on the Iberian peninsula, or in southern Gaul; after that date, a sum of money. In AD 6, a special fund was created, the *aerarium militare*. It allowed a retirement pension to a soldier who left the service with the *honesta missio* (a "good conduct certificate") – for a legionary, 3,000 denarii (thirteen years' wages). Its funds came from two new taxes, the "twentieth" (5 per cent) on inheritances and legacies (*vicesima hereditatum*), paid by Roman citizens, and the "hundredth" (1 per cent) on sales by auction (*centesima rerum venalium*).

A permanent army

Although Augustus did not do away with the principle of obligatory military service for all qualified citizens (there were levies in AD 6 and 9), voluntary enlistment sufficed to provide the 6,000 recruits to the legions needed each year. The army became a professional body. Length of service reached or exceeded 20 years for legionaries, whose basic pay was 225 denarii a year. Recruitment included contributions from provincials who were Roman citizens but was fundamentally Italian. A standing legionary army was thus eventually formed. These legions each received a number and a name (for example, the Third Augusta, stationed at the time at Haidra), and were supported by auxiliary units.

Legions and auxiliary units

The distinction between legion and auxiliary unit as regards recruitment, command, the mission allotted to each, etc. already existed prior to Augustus but became more precise under him:

	Legion	*Auxiliary unit*
Numbers/ranks	5,000 footsoldiers 120 horsemen	generally 480 men horsemen: *alae* (wings) footsoldiers: cohorts foot + horse: mixed cohorts
Organization	10 cohorts (1 cohort = 6 centuries, except the 1st cohort,	cohort divided into centuries *ala* divided into squadrons

Continued on p. 192

	which comprised 5 centuries with double numbers)	
Legal status	Roman citizens, may not marry	foreigners except for command (and exceptions!)
Staff	1 legate (prefect in Egypt) 1 laticlave tribune 1 camp prefect 5 angusticlave tribunes 59 centurions, of whom one is a *primipilus* (chief)	1 prefect or 1 tribune (equestrian or senatorial rank) plus centurions, and decurions (for the horsemen)
Length of service	20–25 years	25 years minimum
Wage	225 denarii p.a.	75 denarii p.a.

The auxiliary corps as a whole equalled the legions in numbers of men, a total of very nearly 250,000. The auxiliary units were generally given names corresponding, originally, to the tribe or region they were raised from, for instance, the *ala Thracum* for the Thracians. When released from service, the auxiliary could have Roman citizenship; his son would therefore be able to enlist in a legion.

Allocation of troops

Here again Augustus introduced innovations and tested solutions. In particular, he gathered around him what was in effect the only garrison on the Italian peninsula, and set up a new strategic allocation of his forces in the provinces. In Rome Augustus could by the end of his reign rely on various bodies of troops. First there were the nine praetorian cohorts, formed in 27 or 26 BC to be the emperor's escort. The praetorians served for 16 years, earned a wage of 750 denarii a year, and received on their discharge an award of 5,000 denarii. These cohorts were mostly garrisoned not in Rome but in the cities of Latium. Only under Tiberius would they be concentrated in Rome itself and play a political role. Secondly, there were the three urban cohorts, created in around AD 13. They had the job of keeping order in the capital and were under the orders of its prefect. Their activities were not limited to simple daytime policing operations, however; if necessary they could be transformed into combat troops. Lastly, there were the 500 Germani who formed Augustus' personal bodyguard. By the end of the reign, therefore, "Rome's garrison" well and truly existed, even if its barracks were not all within the city walls.

By that time too, the legions and auxiliary corps, distributed among the various provinces, were with the exception of those forces in Africa, to be found only in the imperial provinces. Taking into account the three legions lost at the time of Varus' disaster in AD 9, which reduced the number to 25, on the death of Augustus the following allocation of the legions is accepted by historians:

Syria	4	Iberian peninsula	3	Pannonia	3
Egypt	2	Moesia	2	Upper Germania	4
Africa	1	Dalmatia	2	Lower Germania	4

Safety on the seas was not forgotten, even if after Actium the Mediterranean had become a huge "Roman lake." Two ports, Misenum and Ravenna, had the task of controlling, respectively, the western and eastern divisions of this inland sea. Each of the two fleets was placed under the command of a prefect of equestrian rank. Besides performing their policing function, these permanent fleets (a novelty) provided a pool of men, ensured the logistics of military operations, and transported troops and even the emperor himself on his journeys. In addition, local maritime fleets and river flotillas were gradually formed.

This deployment of forces was not without strategic purpose. There was still a need for pacification, consolidation, and further conquests to bring peace to the known world.

CONQUESTS AND PEACEMAKING OPERATIONS

Africa and Egypt

29–27 BC: The first prefect of Egypt, C. Cornelius Gallus, put down a rising in the south and concluded an agreement with the Ethiopians of Nubia: the First Cataract was to be the frontier, and the Ethiopians recognized the Roman protectorate.

25 BC: Juba II was made king of Mauretania and part of Numidia. Until his death in AD 23 he proved a reliable and loyal ally.

25–24 BC: A prefect of Egypt, Aelius Gallus, organized an expedition to southern Arabia (present-day Yemen).

22 BC: Following a new raid by the Ethiopians, a military zone, the *Dodekaschoenos* (= the twelve leagues), was organized south of the First Cataract. It gave Egypt 250 years of peace.

21–20 BC: Raid against the Garamantes of present-day Fezzan. L. Cornelius Balbus reached their capital. His aim was to establish the security of the desert.

AD 1–6 (or between 6 BC and AD 9): Revolts of the nomadic and semi-nomadic Berber tribes (Nasamones, Musulamii, Gaetuli), calling for large-scale military action.

Plate 8.3 A Roman warship, equipped with ram and prophylactic eye (the eye of Osiris). Mosaic from Sousse, Tunisia, late 2nd century AD. Sousse Museum.

The East

25 BC: Annexation of Galatia.

20 BC: Phraates IV, king of the Parthians, returned to Augustus the military standards taken from Crassus and Mark Antony. This scene was to become one of the images used to evoke the grandeur of the new regime. In particular, it is illustrated on the breastplate of the statue of Augustus (possibly posthumous) found at Prima Porta, near Rome. In the same year, Tiberius crowned Tigranes II king of Armenia. A client kingdom was thus restored in a disturbed and strategically vital region.

2 BC–AD 4: Following the death of Tigranes (in 6 BC), Armenia went through a new period of turmoil. A number of diplomatic and military offensives were launched. While returning from a campaign there, Augustus' grandson Gaius Caesar died from his wounds on February 21, AD 4.

AD 6: Judaea and Samaria were placed under a prefect resident in Caesarea and responsible to the legate of Syria.

The West

29–19 BC: Military campaigns on the Iberian peninsula, especially against the Cantabri and Astures. Augustus was there from 27 to 25. It was effectively his last military command. The fighting was hard, and despite the foundation of 21 new military colonies (for instance *Emerita Augusta*) the presence of three legions was necessary to ensure complete pacification.

12–9 BC: Perhaps with the desire to push back the Empire's frontiers as far as the Elbe and establish communications between the Rhine and the Danube, Augustus' stepson Drusus invaded Germania, gained control of the North Sea coast, and then thrust as far as the Elbe. On his return he died as the result of a riding accident.

9–7 BC: Tiberius continued Drusus' campaigns, even going beyond the Elbe as far as Brandenburg.

AD 4–6: Tiberius' campaign against the Marcomanni. In AD 6, a revolt on the Danube forced him to leave this front.

AD 9: The government of P. Quinctilius Varus provoked a rebellion in the territories occupied by the Romans in Germania. The Germani under Arminius defeated Varus, annihilating three legions and nine auxiliary corps in the Teutoburg Wald. As a result, the dream of a great Roman Germania crumbled. Even though in his *Res gestae* Augustus refused to admit the abandonment of these plans, henceforward the Romans hardly advanced beyond the Rhine.

AD 9–12: Returning from Pannonia, Tiberius restored Roman authority over the Rhine by expeditions into Germania.

The Danubian frontier

29–28 BC: Having repulsed an invasion of the Bastarnae and Getae, the proconsul of Macedonia subdued Moesia, and occupied the regions north of the protected kingdom of Thrace. Although no administrative organization followed, the Romans now controlled the lower Danube. This acquisition remained to be consolidated.

15 BC: In a combined operation, Tiberius, coming from Gaul, and Drusus, coming from Cisalpine Gaul, caught the Raeti in a pincer movement. They thus extended the Roman frontier to the upper Danube. The province of Raetia was created. The linking of this new province to the territories of Moesia to the south-east by way of Noricum and Pannonia was then embarked upon. Noricum was annexed in this same year and transformed into a province.

12–9 BC: Tiberius subdued Pannonia.

9–6 BC: Creation of the province of the Maritime Alps, and submission of the Cottian Alps, whose king, Cottius, took the title of prefect on behalf of Rome. A trophy erected at La Turbie, above Monaco, mentions the names of the 45 Alpine peoples conquered by Augustus.

AD 6 (date uncertain): Creation of the province of Moesia.

AD 6–9: Rebellion of Pannonia and Dalmatia in the province of Illyricum, a violent revolt that threatened Italy. Five legions were sent from the East. They were reconquered by Tiberius, and Illyricum was re-formed into the two provinces of Pannonia and Dalmatia (as they were later known).

Territorially, the Empire left by Augustus on his death was very similar to that of the third century AD. There would be rearrangements and some further conquests, but the essentials were already in place.

THE ADMINISTRATION OF THE EMPIRE

For all its constitutional suppleness, military vigor in expanding and defending frontiers, concentration of power and authority, and political inventiveness, the new regime in Rome was ultimately dependent for its success on its ability to control and administer the immense territories of the Empire, inhabited by approximately 50 million people. The façade of "republican" tradition behind which it concealed its monarchical nature meant that it could readily draw on the sturdy sense of public duty and respect for the state that imbued the *mos maiorum*; the creation of the two new "orders" and the emulation (or rivalry) thus engendered provided the seed-beds, spurs, and springs of action for the personnel it required; the desire for peace which all shared and which was beginning to take material form facilitated all its work; and the different but complementary ambitions raised by the imperial venture (some lying within the framework of Rome, others in the provinces, still others on the scale of the Empire) mostly suited its own: these helpful conditions and useful creations, as well as the fact that the victors felt no need to impose uniformity on outlooks and forms of behavior in the conquered regions (due to indifference rather than to respect for indigenous characteristics); the ease with which they settled themselves into administrations or social organizations that predated their own, which they then cheerfully made use of; their conviction that they were presenting a model of civilization, which they knew was imperfect but believed to be the best possible; and the easy concurrence of the local elites to whom they presented it, who were swiftly won over to this new way of life and coveted Roman citizenship: all these factors made the work of the new administration easier; but the somewhat idealized and oversimplified picture outlined below must not make us forget either the administration's numerical weakness (a few dozen men to a province), its scanty resources, or its brutalities. We shall look at three administrative levels: those of Rome, Italy, and the provinces.

ROME

In order that the city of Rome should better suit its place as the nerve center and showcase of the Empire, administratively conducive to the work of census-taking and the holding of elections, but also in keeping with the majesty of the new regime, Augustus transformed the capital in three areas.

Administrative organization

The administrative structures of the capital had remained archaic, illsuiting those changes which had made Rome the most heavily populated conurbation in the ancient world. Augustus altered them profoundly when he adapted them to the new realities. In 7 BC, he divided the urban territory into 14 districts (*regiones*), each in the charge of a magistrate chosen by lot from the praetors, tribunes of the *plebs*, and aediles. These districts were themselves divided (in total) into 265 quarters (*vici*). At the head of each *vicus*, *vicomagistri*, often freedmen, were entrusted with religious and administrative functions. The whole of the capital's administration came under a prefect of the city of Rome, of senatorial rank, an old institution from the republican era made permanent by the emperor. This *praefectus urbi* was assisted by other senators (with the title of *curator*) who supervised the aqueducts, public works and places, sacred buildings, the bed and banks of the Tiber, and the streets. And the urban cohorts, created near the end of Augustus' reign, were placed under his command. Similarly, as we have seen, Augustus created a prefect of the *annona* (grain supply), of equestrian rank, to solve the problems of provisioning, and set up cohorts of watchmen to combat fires and look after nocturnal policing.

Embellishment by monuments and new building works

Through the restoration and completion of monuments that neglect or civil war had damaged or left uncompleted, and through the creation of new works symbolizing the grandeur of the regime and celebrating the *Pax Augusta*, Augustus sought to make Rome the most beautiful city in the world, adorning it to such an extent that he could boast that he had "found it brick and left it marble" (Suetonius, *Augustus* 28). This was the dawn of an art, a style, a mode of town development, all devoted to the glorification of power. And it was the presence of this ingredient in all aspects of the work, from architectural theory (Vitruvius' *Treatise on Architecture*) down to the details of town-planning (Augustus was the first to regulate by law the height of private buildings), that gave this ensemble of activities its coherence. The emperor's personal domain was merged with public space: grounds belonging to him or his family were built on before being given to the Roman people, and areas that harked back to common history (like the Palatine) were annexed to the imperial *domus*. Urban spaces became the setting for the festivals of the new regime, the monuments translations into stone of what the poets glorified in their verses, allowing all to obtain a material understanding of its ideology. Four areas of the capital received Augustus' especial attention: the Roman Forum, the Forum of Augustus, the Campus Martius, and the Palatine.

Augustus' material transformations of the city of Rome, though in many respects revolutionary, were nevertheless rooted in tradition. He had the towers and gates of the Servian wall restored, and did not have the *pomoerium* moved: the *urbs* remained within its traditional boundaries, even though the administrative boundaries now extended far beyond them.

The political and administrative capital

Augustus also began to sketch in in Rome the outlines of those governmental and administrative arrangements that would, in a much more developed state, constitute the formal machinery of the central government of the Empire. Nothing was clear yet; but the following may be distinguished:

- A *consilium principis* or emperor's council formed in 27 BC. It comprised the consuls in office, a magistrate from each of the other boards or colleges of magistrates, fifteen senators chosen by lot, and friends of the emperor. It was a way of associating the Senate with imperial decisions. Its rapid turnover in membership (every six months for senators, every year for the other members) avoided any hardening of the institution's arteries. In AD 13, it was reorganized with a more monarchical bias: 20 ordinary members were appointed by Augustus for a year, but Tiberius had a permanent seat on it. There was also a more unofficial and informal imperial *consilium* that was summoned from time to time to assist the emperor in judicial or administrative matters. And it was this, rather than the regular senatorial *consilium*, that prefigured the imperial privy councils of later years, such as that formed by Tiberius.
- To link Rome with the Empire, Augustus restored the existing road system to good working order, created numerous other road networks with a real overall plan, such as the one which, centered on Lyon, served the Three Gauls, and organized a postal service for the sending out and circulation of official messages, the *cursus publicus.*
- The great departments of state of future centuries existed as yet, if at all, only in embyro. The Empire was still managed like a private business. The offices that served it were those of the imperial household, entrusted to its freedmen and slaves, and were as yet not well defined as regards their respective duties. Nevertheless, by the end of the reign a petitions office (*a libellis*), an official correspondence office (*ab epistulis*), a legal department (*a cognitionibus*), and a department which prepared papers and reports (*a studiis*) all operated in some form or other.

ITALY

Italy, inhabited by between 5 and 8 million people, enjoyed a special status: its free men were all Roman citizens; they paid no land tax; and, even though it

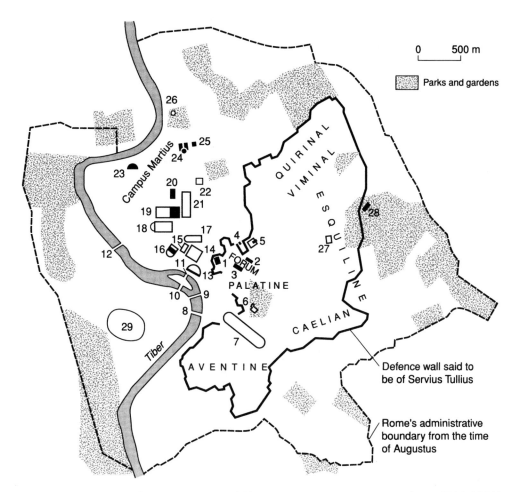

Figure 8.1 Rome in the Augustan period (from J.-P. Martin, *La Rome ancienne*, PUF, 1973)

was theoretically under the control of the Senate, its 470 or so *municipia* were all autonomous. Augustus divided it into eleven regions, no doubt for statistical and fiscal purposes, but also so that everyone could vote in his place of origin – until then it had been necessary to come to Rome to take part in the elections of the state's magistrates. For all that, Augustus scarcely ever intervened in its administration.

THE PROVINCES

As we saw, the settlement of 27 BC between the Senate and Augustus gave rise to a distinction between senatorial and imperial provinces.

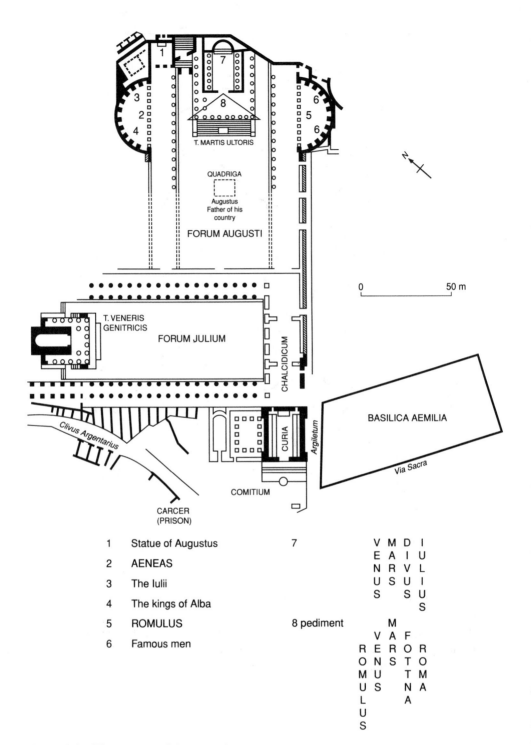

1	Statue of Augustus		7	V	M	D	I		
				E	A	I	U		
2	AENEAS			N	R	V	L		
				U	S	U	I		
3	The Iulii			S		S	U		
							S		
4	The kings of Alba								
5	ROMULUS		8 pediment		M				
				V	A	F			
6	Famous men			R	E	O	R		
				O	N	T	O		
				M	U	T	M		
				U	S	N	A		
				L		A			
				U					
				S					

Figure 8.2   The Forums of Caesar and Augustus

Senatorial provinces   The governors of these provinces, who bore the title of proconsul (as under the Republic), and were assisted in financial matters by quaestors, were chosen by the Senate from among former consuls (for Asia and Africa) or former praetors (for Achaea, Bithynia, Crete-Cyrenaica, Macedonia, Sicily, southern Gaul, Cyprus, and Baetica). But by a law of Pompey's which Augustus revived a magistrate had to have been out of office for at least five years before seeking one of these provincial posts, and it could be held for a year only.

Imperial provinces   The governors of the imperial provinces were chosen by the emperor, and whether they were former consuls or former praetors bore the title of propraetorian legate of Augustus (*legatus Augusti pro praetore*). Provinces with more than one legion were governed by a former consul. The length of a propraetorian legate's mandate depended on the will of the emperor. And he was accompanied by a procurator of equestrian rank who managed his finances, looked after the levying of taxes, and controlled the imperial assets (domains, saltworks, mines, and quarries). Certain recent imperial provinces did not have a legion, but simply auxiliary troops. They were then governed by a prefect of equestrian rank.

IMPERIAL PROVINCES		
Consular	*Praetorian*	*Equestrian*
Tarraconensis	Lusitania	Raetia
Syria	Aquitania	Maritime Alps
Dalmatia	Belgica	Noricum
Pannonia	Lugdunensis	Judaea
Moesia	Galatia	Sardinia-Corsica
Military districts of Upper and Lower Germania		

Egypt   Egypt's status was special. Legally it was annexed to the "Empire of the Roman People" (*RG* 27). But in practice it was treated as the property of the emperor, who ruled there, employing a prefect of Egypt as his representative, on much the same lines as his predecessors, the Ptolemies. Another original feature was that its capital, Alexandria, led an active, even turbulent, life separate from that of the province itself (*Alexandraea ad Aegyptum*).

This general organization of the Empire may appear somewhat rigid but was in fact flexible and capable of adapting to changing circumstances. For that there were several reasons. First of all, the administrative status of a province was never definitive. If need be, an imperial province could become senatorial (as happened with Baetica between 16 and 13 BC) or a senatorial province imperial (Illyricum in 11 BC). Secondly, the map of existing provinces was never inviolable. Illyricum, for example, was split into two provinces in AD 9, becoming Dalmatia and Pannonia. Similarly the organization of the Alpine provinces changed at different times.

But there were also reasons that had to do not with the way in which the provinces themselves were disposed but with the fact that the overall organization of the Empire into types of provinces did not fix the scope of imperial action, especially, or set up inviolable legal and administrative boundaries. The same laws, for example, could be applied to both types of province. In the time of Augustus, imperial instructions (*mandata*) and imperial edicts, like the one in 12 BC allowing the Jews to send money to Jerusalem, were addressed to all provinces. In the same way, decrees of the Senate were applied everywhere, such as the *senatus consultum Calvisianum* on extortion (4 BC). The Edicts of Cyrene, already mentioned, exemplify the emperor's intervention in the local organization of justice in a senatorial province. And in the matter of penal justice, the emperor's power was above that of all the governors, including those of the senatorial provinces, who were reduced in this instance to simple lower-court judges, and who were in any case themselves indirect "officials" of the emperor since they too, like the governors of the imperial provinces, received a salary disbursed ultimately by him. And finally, the financial districts for the direct and indirect taxes that had to be paid by provincials did not always fall within the boundaries of a single province.

If we were to look more particularly at the arrangements within the individual provinces, rather than at their overall organization, any such air of rigidity or uniformity would be even more thoroughly dispelled. Within these provinces there existed a great variety of administrative and social frameworks either inherited from the past, from the period of independence, or introduced since then, the extent and manner of their continuance or advance depending on the extent of Roman settlement, the density of towns, etc. In reality, each province or group of provinces was a special case: in the provinces of the Gauls, for example, the old tribal territories of the Gaulish peoples survived, with some modifications, as the basis of the provincial administration, under the name of *civitates* – there were 60 such "cities" for the Three Gauls, about 20 for Narbonensis – with their subdivisions of *pagi* and *vici*. Lusitania, on the other hand, like Baetica and Dalmatia, had imposed on it, for judicial purposes, an entirely alien division into *conventus*.

We might indeed almost go further, on looking even more closely into the provinces at the civil centers that abounded there, those worlds of variety, and say that each city was a special case and the Empire fundamentally a mosaic of cities.

Religious Policy

Augustus' religious policy was both traditionalist, involving a work of restoration and renewal of traditional religion, and innovatory, concerned with the foundation of the imperial cult. It was well considered and well thought out, and perhaps reflected the emperor's personal position regarding religion. The opposite of Caesar, who had been on the sceptical side, Augustus showed a pernickety fidelity, verging on credulity, toward the forms of ancestral religion. He disregarded no dream, considered every prodigy and auspice infallible, and took account of every omen – if he put his right foot into his left shoe in the morning, he saw it as a sign of disaster. His religious sensibility was thus down to earth; if he experienced any religious qualms at all, they had more to do with superstition than with metaphysics. So he would have kept his distance from religions of salvation with their mystical aspirations (although he had been initiated into the Eleusinian mysteries). Nevertheless, this *homo religiosus* was not a gullible innocent. He knew well how to exploit the religious side of an event for political ends whilst also drawing on it in a religious sense. For example, he banned Egyptian cults within the *pomoerium* in 28 BC after the conflict with Mark Antony and Cleopatra, while at the same time terracotta plaques showing Isis between two sphinxes were to be found in the temple of Apollo Palatine which abutted on his residence.

A WORK OF RESTORATION AND RENEWAL

- *Restoration.* In order to elevate the dignity of the priesthoods, Augustus assumed the principal ones himself. "I was *pontifex maximus*, augur, quindecimvir in charge of sacred ceremonies, *septemvir epulonum*, Arval brother, one of the *sodales Titii*, and a Fetial" (*RG 7*, 3). He also became a restorer of temples: 82 according to the *Res gestae*. Lastly, he imparted new life to rites that had fallen into disuse.
- *Renewal.* He associated with various of his secular reforms and policies the deities that matched them: the cults of Ops and Ceres with grain distributions, the cult of the Dioscuri with the era of youth. In addition, he attached singular favor and importance to certain gods and goddesses: Venus Genitrix, Apollo, Mars, and Vesta. Depending on the period, one or other of these divinities was brought to the fore by virtue of his or her potential political use.

However, major as it was, this work pales in comparison with the founding of the imperial cult.

THE FOUNDING OF THE IMPERIAL CULT

Its origins

The various arguments that are advanced concerning the origins of the imperial cult all carry the risk of reducing to a single explanation a complex phenomenon that requires a multifaceted explanation in order to account for the interplay of its very diverse elements. This is quite an easy trap to fall into since, according to the point of view adopted, one often finds quite good evidence that goes some way towards justifying the line taken but which encourages one to overestimate the weight to be placed on it in the overall evaluation of the data. Three main hypotheses have been proposed:

1. *Eastern origins.* In the Hellenistic world, kings, heroes, and leading politicians (Lysander, for instance) had received divine honors. The most obvious model for Rome was Alexander: called *neos Herakles* (the new Herakles) in his lifetime, he was the object of a cult after his death. Now, in the east such honors had already been paid to Romans by Greek cities: for example, Flamininus, Mucius Scaevola, Lucullus, and of course Caesar. Moreover, it was on his return from the court of Alexandria that L. Munatius Plancus had proposed the title *Augustus* with its divine associations. It has thus been thought that the beginnings of the imperial cult can be traced to the eastern part of the Empire.

2. *Roman and national origins.* On top of the kings, legendary or not, who had become gods, the century of the *imperatores* brought fresh examples of divine inspiration and superhumanity, and even an example of a mortal who became divine – Caesar. Augustus was the "son of the deified," and through Caesar was descended from Venus. But better still, he had the eminently useful example in Caesar's human life (44 BC) of a decision that oaths would be sworn by the *genius* of the dictator, a divine privilege.

3. *Indigenous origins*, in particular Iberian. On January 16, 27 BC, in the course of an extraordinary meeting of the Senate, a tribune of the *plebs* vowed himself to Augustus after the fashion of the Iberians and exhorted his compatriots to do the same. It was in the Iberian peninsula that the first municipal altar in the west in honor of Augustus was erected.

Its establishment

In seeking to understand why and how the imperial cult was established, we must therefore not underestimate (or overestimate) local initiatives, the cultic tendencies of the East, the attitude of Augustus and his followers, or the memory of Caesar (nor the negative one of Mark Antony). In order to gain an understanding of what was involved in its establishment it will be simplest to follow the chronology of its manifestations in the various parts of the Empire.

BC	Western provinces	Rome and Italy	East
32	The western provinces and Italy swear an oath of loyalty to Octavian.		
30		Honors to Octavian awarded by the Senate: ■ his name in the Salian chant; ■ libation to his *genius* at banquets.	Octavian as Pharaoh (Dendera). Many Greek cities begin a new era with Actium and take the name of *Caesarea*.
29			In response to requests from Greek cities, Octavian agrees that: ■ Roman citizens who live there will worship the Goddess Rome (*Dea Roma*) and the deified Caesar. ■ The Greeks will worship Octavian and Rome (Pergamum, Nicomedia, Ephesus, Nicaea).
28		Temple of Apollo on the Palatine; in its portico a statue of Octavian.	
27		*Augustus.*	
26	Altar at Tarragona (or 25).		At Mytilene, a temple and priests consecrated to Augustus.
25		Augustus refuses to have Agrippa's Pantheon dedicated to him.	
23		In Horace's *Odes*, Augustus appears as a god descended to Earth.	
19	Three altars to Augustus at Noega (*numen* or *nomen*?): *Arae Sestianae*.	The altar of Fortuna Redux is erected at Porta Capena in honor of Augustus' return.	In Samos, a monument to *Dea Roma* and Augustus is built.
15	Altar to Augustus at Merida.		
12	Pledge by Drusus of an altar at Lugdunum (Lyon) to Rome and Augustus; consecrated 10 BC.	*Pontifex maximus.* Association of the *Lares Compitales* and the *Genius Augusti*. Oath by the *genius* of Augustus; sacrifice to his *genius*; *Lares Augusti*.	
9	Altar of the Ubians (between 9 BC and AD 9).	Dedication of the *Ara Pacis Augustae*.	Reform of the calendar in Asia. It begins on the day of Augustus' birth.

Continued on p. 206

BC	Western provinces	Rome and Italy	East
8		Regular festivals for the anniversary of Augustus' birth. The month of *Sextilis* is renamed *Augustus*.	
6	In Baetica, Augustus is named *pater patriae*.		
3			Oath of the Paphlagonians to Augustus, his sons, his descendants, "By Jupiter . . . and by Augustus." Imperial temples and altars of Augustus are reported. The distinction between Greeks and Romans has disappeared.
2	Altar erected on the Elbe.	Dedication of the Forum of Augustus (*Mars Ultor*). From this date, development of the cult in Italy: ■ temple to Augustus and Rome, at Pola and Tarracina; ■ temple to his *genius* at Pompeii; ■ evidence of *flamines Augustales* in various cities.	
1			In Caria, mention of a priest of *Dea Roma* and Augustus.
AD	?Altar of the *gens Augusta* in Carthage.	AD 9 First public altar to the *numen* of Augustus.	
11–13	Altar of Narbonne to the *numen* of Augustus.		
14		Death of Augustus. Augustus deified by the Senate (apotheosis). A temple is vowed to him; dedicated in 37.	
15	Temple to Augustus at Tarragona.	At Nola, the house where he died is turned into a temple; at Bovillae, the place of origin of the *gens Augusta*, a sanctuary.	

From this chronology a few conclusions may be extracted.

1 The initiatives taken were extremely varied. They came from towns and communities (Tarragona, Narbonne, the towns in the East); members of the imperial family (Drusus), who acted, no doubt, with the emperor's consent; legions (the three legions of Asturia and Cantabria with the three altars of the legate Sestius); and individuals, often freedmen, who spontaneously participated in the cult (altar of the *gens Augusta* in Carthage).

2 The attitudes of the participants varied from one province to another, and from one social group to another: there was a world of difference between the thinking of a Roman senator, a Carian peasant, and an Egyptian *fellah*. And the forms taken by the cult also varied in this way: here, emphasis was placed on the association between the Goddess Rome and Augustus, there on his *genius*, elsewhere on his *numen*, or on the person of Augustus himself or the soteriological aspect of his birth date.

3 The less a region was Romanized, the more manifest the expressions of the cult. But if the East, where this type of worship eventually became commonplace, opened the way, the western provinces followed with enthusiasm, and Italy was not left behind: the Empire as a whole regarded Augustus as its savior. Looking beyond local and regional differences, and beyond the dwindling distinction made between a cult for Roman citizens and a cult for natives, one may see in all these manifestations of the imperial cult the possibility of the various parts of the Empire coming together to form a more unified whole, with the unifying effect of the cult itself one agent of this.

4 However, it is still impossible to compare, the cult that was thus being organized around the various altars, with a state religion. If the government permitted or encouraged these demonstrations of adoration and loyalty, the response far exceeded its expectations. They emanated almost always from private bodies, individuals, communities, with municipal worship, which was voluntary, providing a vigorous supplement to this activity. There were two exceptions in the West to this absence of state organization: the altar of the Three Gauls, situated at the confluence of the Saône and the Rhône; and the altar of the Ubians, on the Rhine, where a town (the future Cologne) was created around it. In these two cases, politico-religious institutions were set up, following the emperor's wishes, in a regional framework with a hierarchized priesthood, a dedicated group of buildings, a special territorial status, and regular festivals held during the year as well as annually, an organization perhaps modeled on that of the East, where there were to be found special provincial priests (the Asiarch, the Bithyniarch) elected for one year by an assembly of the delegates from cities in the province. This formula remained limited, however. To systematize it and extend it to the whole Empire was the task of Augustus' successors.

THE SUCCESSION

In order to secure his achievements, to make lasting the results of the colossal labor of political, social, administrative, and religious reorganization that this chapter has surveyed, Augustus had to secure the succession. And this required not only the transmission of what might seem untransmissible, a power that reposed largely on the prestige, the *auctoritas*, and the personal qualities of Augustus himself, but that it be achieved within the narrow margins for maneuver left him by the constitutional artifice that had hitherto been so advantageous to him. Publicly to appoint a successor was to admit the reality of a monarchy and to found a dynasty – something that Augustus in all his actions had refused to acknowledge. Yet to say nothing, to allow free rein to personal ambition, the vyings of clans, or the assertions of old institutions, would perhaps be to reopen the field to civil war and to look upon his achievements as temporary. Augustus was tormented by this dilemma, all the more so because he had no son of his own, and no principle of succession had ever been broached. It is generally agreed that he favored a system of associating his preferred successor with his government, thus indicating conspicuously where his choice lay while at the same time respecting constitutional forms and so providing a semblance of legality for the expression of his will and the workings of his *auctoritas*. A marriage or adoption would further underline his preference.

The first choice was the son of his sister Octavia, M. Claudius Marcellus. Born in 42, he was elevated at an early age to the pontificate, was married in 25 to Augustus' daughter Julia, and received an aedileship in 23, ahead of the normal age. But Marcellus died that same year. His ashes were laid in the future tomb of Augustus on the Campus Martius. Cautious or mistrustful, Augustus had also accelerated the career of his stepson Ti. Claudius Nero (the future Tiberius), like Marcellus born in 42. However, when Marcellus died, it was not Tiberius who was approached but Agrippa, to whom Augustus remarried Julia in 21. Their two sons Gaius and Lucius were born in 20 and 17. On the birth of Lucius, the two boys were adopted by Augustus, becoming Gaius and Lucius Caesar. They could succeed, together or Gaius alone, either their adoptive father or their natural father, who had become co-regent in 18. In 12, Agrippa died. Augustus forced Tiberius to divorce Vipsania, Agrippa's daughter, in order to marry Julia (in 11). Honors and offices were heaped on the new son-in-law. But in 6 BC, when he received tribunician power (as Agrippa had formerly) for five years, he asked for leave and voluntarily took himself off into exile in Rhodes, where he lived as a private citizen.

In 5 BC, with complete disregard for all the rules, Gaius was appointed consul (but for five years later), and the Roman knights proclaimed him *princeps iuventutis* (one of the noblest of the Roman knights, a title which came to denote the probable successor to the throne). Three years later, in 2 BC, Lucius received the same honors. The two brothers were given commands, and took part in the imperial council, doing their apprenticeship in government. But their education in office was never completed. Both died on official missions, Lucius in AD 2 and Gaius in 4. These two deaths once more called everything into question. The funeral honors paid to the two, such as the Maison Carrée at Nîmes, cannot conceal the confusion that followed.

Within the bosom of the imperial family there remained few capable of ensuring the succession. Augustus turned once again to Tiberius, adopting him in AD 4, but at the same time he adopted Agrippa Postumus, the last surviving son of Agrippa and Julia, born in 12 BC after his father's death, and ordered Tiberius to adopt Germanicus, the son of Tiberius' brother Drusus. Back in the saddle in the race for the succession, Tiberius was again vested with tribunician power. Agrippa Postumus on the other hand was subsequently repudiated and exiled because of his unhelpful character. And the order of succession then became clear: Tiberius, then Germanicus. In AD 13, Tiberius received powers equal to those of Augustus. Even if he had chosen Tiberius out of desperation, the old emperor knew that the succession was finally assured.

9 / THE JULIO-CLAUDIANS
The System under Stress, AD 14–68

"*I*NTERNALLY, ALL WAS CALM, THE NAMES OF THE MAGISTRACIES WERE
UNCHANGED; THE YOUNGEST MEN HAD BEEN BORN AFTER THE VICTORY
OF ACTIUM, AND EVEN THE MAJORITY OF OLDER MEN HAD BEEN BORN IN THE
MIDDLE OF THE CIVIL WARS; HOW MANY PEOPLE WERE LEFT WHO HAD SEEN THE
REPUBLIC?" WONDERED TACITUS (ANNALS *1.3.7*). IN OTHER WORDS, FEW
QUESTIONED THE NEW REGIME. IT WAS TESTED, MODIFIED, ADAPTED, BUT EVEN
AMONG THOSE WHO OFTEN SPOKE OF THE REPUBLIC HARDLY ANYONE PROPOSED ITS
RE-ESTABLISHMENT. GOVERNMENT BY ONE MAN ALONE WAS GENERALLY
ACKNOWLEDGED TO BE NECESSARY. DESPITE INTERNAL DIFFICULTIES, NEW
ANNEXATIONS, AND FRESH CONQUESTS, POLITICAL LIFE, DOMINATED BY THE MEMORY
OF AUGUSTUS, WAS THE PREDOMINANT ISSUE UNDER THE JULIO-CLAUDIANS. THE
PERSONALITY OF THE EMPEROR, THE INFLUENCE OF THOSE CLOSEST TO HIM (FAMILY,
COUNSELORS, EMANCIPATED SLAVES), HIS RELATIONS WITH THE SENATE, WHICH OFTEN
DETERMINED THE IMAGE OF A REIGN THAT HAS COME DOWN TO US (THE "GOOD"
AND "BAD" EMPERORS), HIS RELATIONS WITH THE VARIOUS PROVINCIAL ARMIES, THE
MANNER OF HIS ACCEPTANCE BY THE PLEBS, HIS INTEREST IN THE ADMINISTRATION
AND THE PROVINCES – ALL THESE ELEMENTS CAME INTO PLAY.

FOUR PERSONALITIES

TIBERIUS (AD 14–37)

Senatorial historiography presents this second Caesar as a bad ruler, even a tyrant, who imparted an autocratic form to the regime. Numerous studies have qualified those assertions – perhaps too much. At all events, it is clear that the government of the Empire suffered hardly at all from the moods of the emperor.

Portrait
Tiberius came to power at the age of 55. His merits were indisputable: he appears to have been one of the most capable and experienced men of his time, having already demonstrated his worth in all fields – military, administrative, and diplomatic, and was, moreover, a cultivated man – an excellent orator, a

fine Hellenist, passionately interested in astrology, in all lacking in neither intelligence nor character. Yet, paradoxically, this man of duty, republican by conviction, the scrupulous heir of Augustus, never succeeded in becoming popular with the Senate or the people, inspiring on the whole fear rather than love. Unsure of himself and awkward rather than hypocritical as it seemed, hurt by having been the perpetual second runner in the race for the succession, irritated by the senators' lack of spirit, and unwilling in his acceptance the constraints of public life, he became misanthropic, curt, and suspicious.

The principal events of his reign

Assuming power This was done easily enough. Augustus' will designated Tiberius and Livia as his principal heirs. Agrippa Postumus was executed without delay – there could thus be no dynastic chal-lenge. The Senate, the magistrates, the army, and the people swore an oath of loyalty to the new emperor. Imitating Augustus in 27 BC, Tiberius at first refused the duties offered to him before ultimately accepting them. After the official investiture, an enabling law was voted by the people, the *lex de imperio*. (This would increasingly become a simple formality at the start of a reign – it is known solely by the one that was voted for Vespasian.) Two mutinies on the Rhine and Danube were reported, both indirectly connected with the change of emperor. But Tiberius easily put an end to them. Once the first months of his assuming power were over, three phases of his reign may be distinguished.

15–23 During these years, the regime was fairly "liberal." They were years not without their difficulties, however. There was the conspiracy of Scribonius Libo in 16 to deal with, and the revolts of Tacfarinas in Africa (17–24) and of Florus and Sacrovir in Gaul (21). The expeditions in Germania in 15–16, led by Tiberius' adoptive son Germanicus, were inconclusive and costly. And then there were the family problems that arose due not only to Livia's cantankerous nature (she lived until AD 29) but to the rivalry that Germanicus' popularity provoked between Tiberius and the young general. When Germanicus died in Syria in 19, general opinion suspected that one of Tiberius' people had poisoned him in order to keep the succession for the emperor's son Drusus. Finally, at the end of the period, Drusus himself died, to Tiberius' deep sorrow.

23–31 This period was dominated by Sejanus. The son of a knight and himself a knight, he had family links with prefects of Egypt and with consuls. In 15, he was sole prefect of the praetorian guard. In this post he proved active and intelligent, but also extremely compliant in his dealings with Tiberius, who trusted him completely. As a result of his growing influence over the emperor, the Senate accorded him honors that exceeded those due to his office, and a court formed around him. He became the most powerful person in the regime after Tiberius. The death of Drusus in 23 may even have given him hopes of one day becoming emperor himself. His asking to marry Drusus' widow, a request refused by Tiberius (25), suggests that this may well have been so. His influence in Rome increased further when Tiberius, encouraged by his advice (given, perhaps, so that he might have a freer hand in the capital), retired to Campania in 26, shutting himself away on the island of Capri, which he virtually never left again. In 30, Sejanus was appointed consul for the following year with Tiberius as his colleague – an exceptional circumstance. But then, in that following year, Tiberius, from Capri, perhaps anticipating Sejanus' ultimate ambitions, perhaps urged on to act by a group of nobles connected with the clan of Germanicus, which was being persecuted by Sejanus (the affair remains obscure), brought about his downfall. In October 31, following a cleverly arranged scenario, Sejanus was arrested and executed. His supporters and children soon followed him.

31–37 From Capri, Tiberius continued to govern with the same fanatical attention to political affairs that he had shown before he retired there. In particular, he created lese-majesty procedures which allowed those suspected of "treason" (*maiestas*) to be taken and tried by the Senate, and if found guilty to have their goods confiscated, and their persons punished by death or exile. Bitter and cynical, the emperor nevertheless also continued to give careful consideration to the larger concerns of the state – he halted a financial crisis and neutralized the Parthian danger. In ill health, he died in March 37 at Misenum without having prepared for his succession. It seems that he was hesitating between his own grandson and his great-nephew, the grandson of his brother Drusus, Gaius Julius Caesar Germanicus, surnamed Caligula (who was rumored to have finished off the dying man).

CALIGULA (AD 37–41)

Little is known of Caligula's accession, simply that the new praetorian prefect, Naevius Sutorius Macro, played an important part in it and that the Senate and the people of Rome joyfully welcomed the man whom the crowd acclaimed with cries of "our baby" and "our star." The funeral rites of Tiberius, whose ashes were carried to the mausoleum without his being awarded an apotheosis, passed off without incident. His will had already been nullified in order to give maximum powers to the new emperor, on whom the right of command over the armies and government of the provinces within his scope had been conferred. Enthusiasm pervaded the entire Empire. Soldiers and civilians (Roman citizens and foreigners) swore the oath of loyalty. We have three testimonies to that, the first from Umbria in Italy, the second from Lusitania, the third from a small town in the Troad (present-day Turkey). Over and above the 2.7 billion (= thousand million) sesterces left to him by Tiberius, Caligula thus had available a vast capital of popularity.

Less than four years later, on January 24, AD 41, when Caligula was assassinated by a conspiracy of praetorian officers and imperial freedmen, no one grieved for him, neither the praetorians who acclaimed Claudius, nor the senators who waited and made speeches, nor the people of Rome who demonstrated in favor of the praetorians' candidate. "Caligula's memory, so it seems, met with popular indifference: neither outrage nor regrets are mentioned in our sources" (D. Nony). How had adulation turned to indifference in such a short space of time? The only voices from the sources that speak to us about this emperor paint so black a portrait that their value is questionable.

Explanations are not lacking, but there is now unanimous agreement only on the reasons for his popularity: his youth (25 years old on his accession), the popularity of his father, Germanicus, the length of Tiberius' reign (twenty-three years), his childhood in the legionaries' camps, which earned him his nickname Caligula ("little soldier's-boot," or "Little Boots"), the misfortunes of his family, victims of Tiberius and Sejanus, his relationship to Augustus and Mark Antony, his devotion to his family. Thereafter everything is open to argument. To give a few examples: for a long time it was suggested that a serious illness in October 37 could have explained behavior that was, to say the least, extravagant; now a more detailed analysis shows that his recovery from the illness marked no significant political change. His foreign policy seems incoherent, even grotesque if one thinks of his aborted attempt to land in Britain as recounted by Suetonius; but one may as well read into the account the wisdom of an emperor faced with an ill-prepared expedition as accept at face value the tittle-tattle of Suetonius. Some historians think that he contemplated the revolutionary introduction into Rome of the Egyptian cults of Isis and Serapis; for others the indications that he did are not convincing. Other explanations are more general, such as that given by Albert Camus, who envisaged Caligula as the systematic and insolent rejection of the falsehoods and hypocrisies of the system set up by Augustus; but again that is just one interpretation. At all events, we at least know, besides those facts noted above, that Caligula emptied the treasury's coffers, annexed Mauretania, remained in control of the governmental and administrative machinery, and displeased the Jewish people by wanting to install his statue in the Holy of Holies in the Temple at Jerusalem.

CLAUDIUS (AD 41–54)

An involuntary emperor: his accession

After Caligula's assassination, while the Senate was discussing the possibility of restoring the Republic, the praetorians were scouring the Palatine Palace for a member of the Julio-Claudian family. "A soldier searching hither and thither having chanced to see his feet (he had hidden in the folds of a hanging placed in front of a door), was curious to discover who it could be, recognized him, dragged him from his hiding-place and as the terrified Claudius threw himself at his feet, hailed him as emperor" (Suetonius, *Claudius* 10). Behind this anecdote lie three truths: Claudius had no desire to become emperor; he was the first emperor to be invested by the praetorians; and, through fear, he was also the first emperor to try to secure their loyalty by promising them a sum of money (*donativum*) – in his case, 15,000 sesterces each.

The man

Claudius was born in Lyon in 10 BC on the day his father Drusus consecrated the altar there to Rome and Augustus. With Drusus as his father, he was thus the nephew of Tiberius, the uncle of Caligula, and the younger brother of Germanicus. His career was very slow-moving. Everybody regarded him rather in the light in which his mother viewed him: "A caricature of a man," she said, "an abortion merely sketched by nature" (Suetonius, *Claudius* 3). Certainly, he was not steady on his feet, and he stammered. Besides, everyone doubted his intelligence. No one would have had the preposterous idea of entrusting him with important responsibilities, still less have imagined him capable of governing the Empire. He even remained a knight until Caligula took him on as his colleague in the consulship in 37. Living on the sidelines, Claudius developed a passion for philology (he invented three new letters for the Roman alphabet) and for history (he wrote a history of Rome in over forty volumes, one of Etruria in twenty, and one of Carthage in eight, the last two works being composed in Greek). This erudite emperor, who spent much of his time in the study and the office, where he kept company with the freedmen who worked there, was held up to ridicule by early writers. Seneca depicted his apotheosis as a transformation into a pumpkin (*The Apocolocyntosis of the Divine Claudius*), and he was constantly portrayed as a drunkard, the plaything of his freedmen Callistus, Pallas, Polybius, and Narcissus, and of his wives (he had four, two of whom have their place in history, one for her doubtless exaggerated escapades, Messalina, and the other for her political acumen, Agrippina, Nero's mother). Today, despite his weaknesses, this unexpected emperor is esteemed for the quality of his actions on both internal and external fronts. He transformed the central administration of the Empire into a great chancellery adapted to actual needs. He undertook all kinds of construction and public works (the draining of Lake Fucinus, and the building of aqueducts, the port of Ostia, and road systems). He looked favorably on the promotion of provincials (see the Claudian Table of Lyon), whom he introduced into the Senate. He was concerned about justice; he revived Augustus' religious policy; he showed an especial interest in the provisioning of Rome; and he founded numerous colonies

(Cologne). He took on the censorship in 47 and 48 (there had been no censor since 22 BC) and exercised it scrupulously; and he engaged in a varied and, generally speaking, inspired legislative activity. All in all, even if he was not conscious of it, since he was rather traditionalist in outlook, his actions were innovatory and even revolutionary.

The principal dates of his reign

41 Punishment of Caligula's murderers. Dynastic policy is affirmed (Livia awarded apotheosis). Claudius, though conscious of imperial dignity, rejects the title *Imperator*.

Free practice of the Jewish religion is confirmed; calm is restored in Alexandria, with its large Jewish population, following disturbances there brought on by the anti-Jewish policy inaugurated by Caligula.

42 Mauretania is organized into two procuratorial provinces, Caesariensis and Tingitana.

43 Beginning of the conquest of Britain (imperial cult at Camulodunum (Colchester)). Lycia, free since 168 BC, becomes, in conjunction with Pamphylia, a new imperial province of praetorian rank. The whole of Anatolia is henceforward integrated into the Empire.

Abolition of the Druidic religion.

44 Judaea once more becomes a Roman province.

The *aerarium Saturni* (the Senate's treasury) is taken from the control of the two *praetores aerarii* and returned to that of two quaestors, but they are to be chosen by the emperor. In other words, the *aerarium* comes under imperial control.

46 Thrace becomes a procuratorial province.

47 Claudius' censorship.

Cn. Domitius Corbulo in Frisia and Germania (Rhine–Meuse canal).

48 Claudius appears before the Senate, makes speech on the Claudian Table.

Intrigues by Messalina; Narcissus has her killed.

49 Claudius marries his niece Agrippina.

Seneca, recalled from exile, is appointed tutor to Nero, the son of Agrippina.

Extension of the *pomoerium* by Claudius.

Intervention in Commagene.

50 Nero is adopted by Claudius; he thus moves ahead of the emperor's own son, Britannicus.

51 Accession of the Parthian king Vologeses. From then on, Rome again senses danger from the Parthians, a feeling heightened by the intervention of Vologeses in the allied kingdom of Armenia.

54 October 13: Claudius dies, perhaps poisoned by Agrippina. He seems to have placed Britannicus side by side with Nero to succeed him. The Senate

decrees his apotheosis; Agrippina becomes the priestess of the Divine Claudius, as Livia had been of the Divine Augustus.

NERO (AD 54–68)

The son of Agrippina

The emperor Claudius' ill-luck at succumbing to a sudden violent, illness, or more probably poison, allowed Nero to become Rome's new emperor. He was aged nearly 17, making him the youngest of the emperors. The manner in which his accession took place reveals careful preparation. Claudius' death was kept secret and Britannicus was detained while Nero presented himself to the praetorians, accompanied by their prefect, Afranius Burrus. In return for the promise of a *donativum*, they acclaimed him emperor. In the afternoon, Nero went before the Senate, and there read out a speech prepared by Seneca in which he took up the Augustan theme of government shared equitably between the emperor and the Senate, a speech that made an excellent impression on the assembled senators. Thus, within the space of a few hours after the death of Claudius and without any problems, Nero had become emperor, easily outstripping those carrying forward the claim of Britannicus. Behind this easy assumption of power may be discerned the presence and intrigues of his mother Agrippina, one of Caligula's sisters. But his way was also eased by his resonant and inclusive ancestry, or at least, emphasis was placed on its most favorable parts to justify his claim. Through his mother and father (Cn. Domitius Ahenobarbus), Nero was descended from both the Divine Augustus and Mark Antony. And as the adopted son of Claudius, he thus united in his person the two rival branches of the imperial family, the Julii and the Claudii. His reign began under the most favorable auspices. But his birth, on December 15, 37 at Antium, had, or so the stories went, already been surrounded by presages, and only some of these were beneficent and marked the child with a royal sign; others were ominous and evoked the image of the monster emperor. These are, of course, legends, where consistency is not to be expected. Yet we shall meet with a similar difficulty in pinning the subject down when we look at the problem of Nero's personality and at what has been termed "Neroism," an original political path, closer to a way of life or an aesthetic ideal than to a political program.

The emperor's personality

Two somewhat contrasting pictures of the emperor Nero emerge from the evidence. On one side, the literary evidence is damning, rounding off in its portrait of Nero the image of the emperor-tyrant that started with Caligula. For these writers, Nero was "the enemy of the human race" (Pliny the Elder), a

Plate 9.1   Roman circus, lion killing man, 1st century AD.

monster who killed his half-brother, practiced incest with his mother before having her killed, eliminated his wife and his tutor, had himself married to one of his freedmen, was a ham actor, played at being a charioteer, and set fire to the capital, not to mention other crimes and acts of turpitude. Jewish and Christian writers were even more damning: Nero became an apocalyptic figure, the Beast of the Revelation, the Antichrist. On the other side of the coin, the image is that of the autocrat as artist, his striking enterprises those of a cultural revolutionary aiming "to make the Romans accept a mental outlook and scale of values vastly different from those they had known hitherto" (E. Cizek). The archaeological evidence reveals a man of taste, a lover of painting and sculpture, singing and music, who enjoyed architectural boldness and dreamed of transforming Rome into a "Neropolis," possibly modeled on Alexandria, at the heart of which would be the Domus Aurea (Golden House), an imperial palace conceived as a closed world, a truly marvelous scaled-down version of the external world. Somewhere between these two images the personality of the young emperor may perhaps be found: a ruler fascinated by Greece and the ways of the East but maintaining "Western" staff; a man both cruel and generous; a show-off, tormented and harrowed by fear; a megalomaniac and a dandy (short-sighted, he used an emerald as an optical aid); an occasional buffoon and permanent egotist but undeniably a cultured man; an amateur musician who took his lyrical pursuits very seriously, and a poet whose work, Tacitus tells us, was not to be laughed at; not the greatest artist of his time, as he liked to believe, but neither a talentless boaster. A man, then, with evidently genuine artistic passions but lacking in restraints of character. When he eventually became his own master, he sought to give an original turn to political practice by subjecting it to his aesthetic vision of the world, producing a popular, "show-business" politics. It is this deliberate confusion between art and politics that makes his reign so difficult to assess.

His reign

Taking their cue from authors of late antiquity, historians long considered that the first five years of Nero's rule (54–9) had been, as it were, a period of felicity terminated in March 59 by the murder of Agrippina, when the monster entered the scene. Today, if a political turning-point is sought, it is placed in 61 or 62, when Nero's attitude to the senatorial aristocracy hardened. Before that date the program announced in his inaugural speech before the Senate was applied. After it, the "political" path that he traveled was, with increasing regularity, the novel one he had begun on after the death of his mother of trying to inspire Roman society with his new values, offering it games, festivals, luxury, happiness, instead of martial contests, stern traditions, dull self-restraint, and security.

54 Two advisers to the new emperor: Seneca the philosopher; Burrus the prefect of the praetorian guard. For foreign policy, Agrippina.
   Start of the war in Armenia against the Parthians.
55 Murder of Britannicus.
   Reaction against the policies of Claudius; understanding with the Senate.
   Corbulo in the East against the Parthians. Talks with the latter.
58 Senate rejects a fiscal reform proposed by Nero.
   Corbulo drives the Parthians out of Armenia.
59 Murder of Agrippina.
   Beginnings of Nero's "axiological reform," or reform of values: introduces games called the *Iuvenalia* and creates the *Iuvenes Augustiani*, a select body of youths.
   Installation of Tigranes V as Rome's new vassal king of Armenia.
   Annexation of the Alpine kingdom of Cottius (perhaps as early as 58); transformed into a procuratorial imperial province.
60 First *Neronia* (quinquennial games), following a Greek formula. Baptized "Nero's Jousts," they include musical, gymnastic, and equestrian competitions.
   At the same time, baths and a gymnasium are inaugurated.
61 Rebellion by Boudicca (Boadicea) in Britain; Colchester and London are destroyed.

Plate 9.2 Mosaic of a charioteer wearing the colors of his sponsor and a leather helmet for protection. National Archeological Museum, Rome.

Replacement of government personnel.

War between Vologeses and Tigranes.

62 Death of Burrus; Tigellinus, the emperor's henchman, becomes praetorian prefect.

Seneca gradually withdraws from the court.

Lese-majesty trials are revived in the Senate.

63 Successful initiatives by Corbulo on the eastern front. The Romans recognize Tiridates, the protégé of Vologeses, as king of Armenia. End of the Parthian war.

End of the rebellion in Britain.

64 For the first time Nero appears on a public stage, in Naples.

July: the burning of Rome; plan for a new city; beginning of construction of the Domus Aurea.

Annexation of the kingdom of Pontus.

65 Piso's conspiracy; suicide of Piso, Seneca, Lucan, et al.

66 Arrival of Tiridates in Rome; there he is crowned king of Armenia and hails Nero as the god Sol.

Construction of the colossus of Nero, set up in the entrance to the Domus Aurea.

Closing of the doors of the temple of Janus: universal peace is proclaimed.

Nero leaves for Greece.

Rising of the Jews in Judaea.

67 Nero's exploits at athletic contest in Greece. Start of the digging of the Corinth canal. Greece is proclaimed "liberated." At the end of the year, return to Italy.

New wave of terror; suicide of Corbulo.

Vespasian fights the Jews in Judaea.

68 February: contacts between Vindex, legate of Lugdunensis, and other governors, such as Galba, legate of Tarraconensis, with the aim of overthrowing the emperor.

March: artistic triumph by Nero in Rome; uprising of Gaul with Vindex.

April: Galba rebels.

May: Vindex is crushed at Besançon by loyalist troops from Germania; rising in Africa of the legate Clodius Macer; Otho, legate of Lusitania, and Caecina, quaestor of Baetica, give support to Galba; in Rome, the praetorians also declare their backing for Galba; the regime collapses.

On June 9, declared a public enemy by the Senate, deserted by all but four servants, Nero kills himself on the point of being arrested. Almost his last words are: "What an artist perishes with me!" He was 30 years old. A period of civil war then begins.

CONSTANTS AND INNOVATIONS

It is sometimes difficult to judge what in the government of the Empire as it was carried on after his death was owed to Augustus and what to his successors. For a long time, the new regime was viewed as having been fully formed down to the last detail by the time of his death, with his heirs needing only to preserve and maintain their heritage and make it bear fruit. Today, historians are discovering that the Julio-Claudians were not mere followers-on. They too introduced innovations, even if they were frequently only deepening and consolidating Augustan achievements. Those achievements were often robust or resilient institutionally, but it also mattered that they were *his*. For, whatever their particular personalities, the Julio-Claudians were inclined to determine their actions in relation to those of Augustus, either clearly setting out to follow them or setting their face against doing so. "I regard everything that he did, everything that he said, as so many laws," asserted Tiberius. His successor, Caligula, thought otherwise: he "proclaimed that his [own] mother was the fruit of an incestuous act committed by Augustus with his daughter Julia; and not content with thus sullying the memory of Augustus, on the pretext that the victories of Actium and Sicily had been disastrous and lethal for the Roman people, he forbade their celebration by traditional festivals" (Suetonius, *Caligula* 23). We shall therefore look at the works of the Julio-Claudians in relation to those of Augustus, in terms, that is, of constants and developments, innovations and shifts, while bearing in mind that in so doing we are greatly simplifying matters.

CONSTANTS AND DEVELOPMENTS

Power and the dynastic idea

As we saw, Octavian-Augustus had made use of his relationship to the deified Caesar, and throughout his reign had tried to associate members of his family with the government of the Empire. The dynastic principle was thus already in evidence, but it had not yet emerged into the world of ideas as an acknowledged principle by which a claim to power could be justified. This development came under the Julio-Claudians. The fact that, with the exception of Tiberius, all the Julio-Claudians were of the blood of the Julii (a line that ended with Nero), may be taken as evidence that, as a justification for the possession of sovereign power, "dynastic heredity took the place of charisma" (J. Béranger). It was because he did not possess that blood (and it was pointed out to him that he did not) that Tiberius ostentatiously displayed his loyalty to his adoptive father: like Augustus, he initially refused the power that was offered to him, similarly affected a "democratic" simplicity, and considered that "the body of the State was one and must be governed by a single mind." There are many testimonies to this Tiberian ardor for celebrating the idea of dynasty. One of the most exceptional is the "Great Cameo of France" in the Cabinet des Médailles in Paris. Interpretation of this extraordinary sardonyx cameo raises many questions, but if, with the majority of scholars, one takes the middle part to show the living members of the imperial family, the upper part members who had been summoned to heaven, and the lower part vanquished enemies, then each person may be identified. In the center are Tiberius and his mother Livia. Then, starting from them, the imperial family is arranged as on a genealogical tree. Names and dates are still arguable, but there is no doubt that it is a glorification of the *gens Augusta*.

Caligula, Claudius, and Nero did not have this obstacle of not being "of the blood." They based their legitimacy on their relationship – grandson, son, and great-grandson – to Antonia Minor, the younger daughter of Octavian-Augustus' sister Octavia and Mark Antony. All three clearly affirmed their dynastic policy. Caligula laid the ashes of his mother and brother in Augustus' mausoleum, bestowed the title of *Augusta* on his grandmother Antonia, included his three sisters in his rule, and honored his uncle Claudius by appointing him as his colleague in the consulship. Claudius married his cousin Messalina, and then his niece Agrippina, in order to monopolize the "blood" of Augustus. At the start of Nero's reign Agrippina appeared on coinage with the new title *Augusta mater Augusti* (she had been *Augusta* since 50). Lastly, although Nero's first wife, Octavia, was *Augusta* only unofficially, his second, Poppaea, was so officially. The dynastic idea was becoming firmly implanted in people's minds.

Relations with the Senate

Augustus had sought to ensure that the Senate should preserve an appearance of liberty and power. The game had been played to perfection. It may be recalled that he misled some great historians, who spoke of a diarchy. In reality, Augustus ruled undividedly. His successors all pursued this line of collaboration with the Senate, at least initially.

Tiberius received his powers from the Senate and waited until it confirmed them and awarded him the *auctoritas*. This respect for what was in fact a simple formality (he had already obtained the army's oath) revealed his desire to see the Senate participate in government. Curiously, problems stemming from this willingness of his to cooperate arose more on the side of the Senate than from the emperor's attitude to it. Tiberius declined the titles of *Imperator* and *pater patriae* that the Senate proposed for him, keeping only that of *Augustus*. He showed great courtesy to the senators both individually and as a body. A senatorial decree (of *Larinum*) extended to their families the senatorial dignity. They were consulted on numerous points (taxes, buildings; the distribution, levies, and disbanding of troops). And he let them take decisions that went against his own views: "A good and helpful ruler," he said to the senators, "should be at the service of the Senate and all citizens" (Suetonius, *Tiberius* 29). In three fields (legislative, electoral, and judicial), he even strengthened the prerogatives of the Senate. It voted laws in the form of senatorial decrees, one of which laid down for the first time rules concerning private law; it gained the right to elect magistrates, a right hitherto reserved for the people; and it developed its role as a high court of justice, where the emperor intervened only in order to mitigate punishments. The cooperation, then, was exemplary, while it lasted. It ceased around the thirties, either because Tiberius, disappointed by the servile behavior of the senators and made increasingly mistrustful, gave up listening to their opinions, or because, in the face of the emperor's growing suspicions, the Senate, as much through weakness as through fear, gave itself over to the seeking out and eradicating of "treason" in its midst, decimating itself in the process.

Early historians trace a similar development in the relations between Caligula and the Senate: good to start with, poor later, the pattern found, rightly or wrongly, in the accounts of the reigns of nearly all the emperors blackened by senatorial historiography. It appears that relations between Caligula and the Senate started to go downhill following his authoritarian replacement of the two consuls on September 2, 39. It became clear at that point who the real master was. It was only from this date that it is possible to speak of "an attempt at imperial absolutism."

However that may be, Caligula did not upset the composition of the Roman Senate at this time by having a few knights, all of whom were Italian, admitted to it. Modern historians are far more inclined to call him "the real creator of the *ordo senatorius* in the full sense of the term" (A. Chastagnol), inasmuch as in 38 he had instituted the practice of granting the laticlave (the wearing of which had been confined by Augustus to senators and their descendants) to selected knights or notables of Italian or provincial towns, provided they met the property qualification and citizenship conditions, and so made it necessary henceforth to distinguish the senatorial order (2,000 or 3,000 individuals), to which the laticlave was the symbol of belonging, from the senatorial class itself (comprising the senators and their descendants). This grant of the laticlave, which came to be awarded, with solemnity, at any time during a reign and independently of the exercise of censorial powers, gave a man by this means admitted to the senatorial order, usually before the age of 25 and if he had been a knight having severed all links with the equestrian order he had just left, the possibility of seeking the quaestorship, exercising it, and thus gaining access to the Senate. One consequence of prime importance was that the careers of young members of the senatorial order and those of young knights would in future be quite distinct and free from confusion.

The policy of Claudius toward the Senate was both conciliatory and authoritarian. It was conciliatory, firstly, in that there was an undeniable return to Augustan practices, with the recruitment of AD 42, involving the voluntary resignation of those who no longer reached the required property qualification and their replacement by knights, and with the rebirth of the censorship, which Claudius himself held for eighteen months in 47–8; and secondly, in that there was a clear desire to honor the assembly by insisting on treating it as a responsible body, a desire evident in a speech, known through a papyrus, in which Claudius urges the senators not to be puppets, as well as in his requests for their opinions and advice and in the freedom allowed to senatorial decrees. The authoritarian side to his policy came because Claudius, perhaps under pressure from his freedmen but more certainly for practical and administrative reasons, wanted to have a degree of direct control over the Senate. He thus removed its right to grant its members leave, appropriating it for himself, and he appointed the quaestors in charge of the *aerarium Saturni* (the Senate's treasury). But, chiefly, he used his censorial authority, by which the *album senatorum* was produced, directly to modify the composition of the Senate. This method of recruitment, the *adlectio*, was a matter of the direct appointment of a "new man" to the Senate by classifying him in the *album* above the entry magistracy, from which he was exempted. Under Claudius, we know of three *adlecti* among the tribunes of the *plebs*. Similarly, the emperor strictly separated the obligations of future senators and those of knights by setting out precisely the military duties that a young knight had to fulfill – command of a cohort, command of an *ala*, legionary tribunate.

Nero's relations with the Senate followed the pattern of agreement at the start of the reign, mistrust and discord later on. Until 62, the emperor showed favor to the senators, helping them financially to hold games or to keep their property qualification. For its part, the Senate intervened in institutional and social matters, and concerned itself with maintaining order in Italy (as in the famous quarrel between Pompeians and Nucerians). The Senate's refusal in 58 to accept the fiscal reform proposed by the emperor signaled the start of a change in attitude. In 62, the first lese-majesty case in the reign took place. From then on the authority of the *patres* weakened as Nero eliminated or disregarded the great senatorial dynasties. One example sums up this development – the use of the title *Imperator*. Like his predecessors, Nero had refused it as a "forename" at the start of his reign. In 66, however, *Imperator* appeared in inscriptions. It made Nero the equal of Augustus.

Foreign policy

"Augustus," says Dio Cassius, commenting on the recommendations made by the old emperor to Tiberius in the field of foreign policy, "was of the opinion that they should be content with the present boundaries of the Empire and not in any way seek to extend them; for if they did, he claimed, it would be difficult to keep what was gained, and there would be a risk of losing what they already possessed." There were three parts to this policy: a consolidative rather than expansive military presence at the frontiers, active diplomacy, and the system of client kingdoms. Those three lines were followed, with slight or not so slight variations, by the Julio-Claudians. The most faithful was Tiberius: expeditions to intimidate the Germani but not to conquer, clever diplomacy in the East, and a solid network of client states along the Danube. Caligula may have had plans for a great expansionist policy in the West, but the evidence is too fragile for certainty. Claudius and Nero partly distanced themselves from the Augustan watchwords. A sizeable breach on Claudius' part was the conquest of Britain. Nero, on the other hand, was forced by circumstances to inter-

Plate 9.3 A cavalryman's tombstone from Gloucester, 1st century AD. It reads: "Rufus Sita, cavalryman of the 6th Thracian cohort, lived 40 years, served 22. Erected by his testamentary heirs . . .".

vene in the East, but he took the opportunity it presented, envisaging at first the pursuit there of an "energetic strategy" of expansion before making do with an original solution of "semi-expansionism." In the West, apart from his annexation of client kingdoms (one of the causes of Boudicca's rebellion), what he did accorded with Augustus' policy.

Opposition

In seeking constants and developments in this area, we are concerned not directly with imperial policies but rather with opposition to them, or to the regime, the Roman presence (in the provinces), the imperial family, or the emperors. Enduring opposition the nature of which did not change from the reign of Augustus to that of Nero came from within two groups, the provincials and the aristocracy of Rome, though in each it took a very different form. The people of Rome, by contrast, were either indifferent or brought to the boil only by concerns of a narrowly emotional or material kind (love for Germanicus, fear that the emperor would desert Rome; the provisioning of the capital, the cost of living), so that their "opposition," when it arose, tended to be fickle and weakly political, its particular nature depending on whatever it was that occasioned it and the circumstances of the moment. It was in tune with this that they increasingly showed their feelings toward the government, bad or good, in the theater or at the circus, applauding the actors detested by Caligula or giving Nero a triumph that they later regretted.

Revolts and internal risings under the Julio-Claudians		
17–24	Tacfarinas	Africa
21	Risings	Thrace
	Florus and Sacrovir	Gauls
25	Risings	Thrace
36	Revolt of the Cities	Cappadocia
39–40	Disturbances	Judaea
42	Insurrection	Mauretania
52	Disturbances	Judaea
61	Boudicca's revolt	Britain
66	General rising	Judaea
68	Vindex's revolt	Gauls

The provincials   In the Empire as a whole during this period, revolts and risings were in the end few and very local, the movements of opposition that underlay them never really worrying the government, only the local authorities. Moreover, the situations were different, and the seriousness of the disturbances and the Roman commitment varied considerably. Nevertheless, the nature of this opposition remained the same. What was disputed was not the regime but rather the Roman presence, which was constantly and forcefully brought to mind by the burden of taxation, the (often mythical) memories of the period of independence, and the difficulties of adapting to a modern administration (taxes, censuses, land surveys, etc.).

The aristocracy   Opposition was keenest among the great senatorial families. The Empire had after all been built against them. It was thus within the bosom of the aristocracy that plots and conspiracies were hatched, above all if those families were close to the government. Scions of the Junii Silani, the Silii, the Scribonii Libones, the Calpurnii Pisones, and the Annii were the ones to be found from reign to reign in the opposition lists until the extinction of the family by assassination or suicide. An enduring influence on this opposition was Stoicism. Curiously, it found in this not a political argument (since Stoicism would rather have been favorable to the monarchy) but a moral code. Nevertheless, the doctrine produced its own lineage of opponents: Caecina Paetus and Arria in 42; their daughter Arria and her husband Thrasea under Nero; then *their* daughter and her husband Helvidius Priscus under Vespasian. Throughout this period, then, the Roman aristocracy produced a constant stream of opponents, the nature of whose opposition little varied from reign to reign. Recent work has, however, doubted that these various opponents can properly be said to have constituted "an opposition."

For there to be an opposition, there must be a real will for change; coherence and principles are necessary. None of that can be discerned in the behavior of the malcontents and rebels . . . The system as such is not in question, and discontent does not focus on basic problems but on people. Blame is laid on the emperor, his vices, his entourage, his colleagues, and his freedmen. (A. Giovannini)

INNOVATIONS AND SHIFTS

Strengthening the role of the military

On the death of Augustus, Tiberius, as commander-in-chief, gave orders to the praetorian cohorts and wrote to the provincial armies "as if he already held the principate," notes Tacitus, adding: "He never showed any hesitation except when it was his turn to speak in the Senate" (*Annals* 1.7). Prudent and clear-thinking, the heir presumptive (the Senate had not yet played its part) knew where the true source of power lay. During his reign the praetorian cohorts, reinforced by the urban cohorts, were installed in the "camp of the praetorians" (*castra praetoria*), just north-east of Rome. Moreover, the office of praetorian prefect gained in prestige, and with Sejanus, and also with his successor Q. Naevius Cordus Sutorius Macro, the responsibilities of the prefect continued to expand. Indeed, it was thanks to Macro as praetorian prefect, already Tiberius' principal colleague, that Caligula attained the Empire.

The example, though embellished by the curlicue of sometimes not waiting on the death of the emperor before making, or helping to make, a new one, was followed in the praetorian camp and imitated in others. In 39, the commander of the Rhineland legions plotted against the young emperor. He failed. But in January 41 the tribunes and centurions of the praetorian cohorts succeeded, slaughtering Caligula and hailing Claudius as emperor. He was taken to the camp of the praetorians, an act which became a ritual at the start of a reign. Together with the imperial palace on the Palatine and the Curia, the "Castra" was henceforth one of the places of central importance in Roman political life. Again, it was a praetorian cohort that acknowledged Nero after Claudius' death and carried him in a litter to the camp, where, as Claudius had, he granted a *donativum*. And it was the rising of the armies of the provinces, followed by the treason of the praetorian prefect, that brought about Nero's flight and suicide. The entry of the army onto the political scene as a separate player and even a "king-maker" was one of the most important new elements in the transformations of the first century.

Overall, however, the army remained loyal to the Julio-Claudian house. The only emperor among them to have lost its respect was Nero. A tribune of a praetorian cohort, implicated in Piso's conspiracy, revealed the reasons why before he was put to death. When Nero asked him why he had forgotten his military oath, he replied: "I hated you! No soldier could have been more loyal to you as long as you deserved to be liked. I began to hate you when you proved to be the murderer of your mother and your wife and became a chari-oteer, a ham actor and an arsonist" (Tacitus, *Annals* 15.67).

Extension of the imperial cult

The "imperial cult" under Augustus, which as we have seen was largely spon-taneously organized, involved both the apotheosis of a dead ruler, the deified Caesar, and the worship, through his *genius* or his *numen*, of a living one, Augustus. These two aspects to worship within the cult did not disappear under the Julio-Claudians, but the apotheosis of Augustus, decreed by the Senate, the innovations of Caligula and Nero, and the development of a dynastic aware-ness, so altered the cult that it became, in effect, a new religion, certainly now official, though with more-intense popular echoes than has been allowed for by historians.

The dead emperors   After Augustus, Claudius alone among the Julio-Claudians attained the rank of god. Nevertheless, the honors that Tiberius awarded the Divine Augustus served as a model for his successors. They deserve going into in a little detail.

1 The ritual of apotheosis begun for Augustus reached its peak in the second half of the second century but all along kept the same sequence of events. First the corpse (later, a wax effigy) was placed on a high pyre erected on the Campus Martius. Then, after the priests had consecrated the site, the various bodies of society walked in procession around it, and an eagle was released from the pyre, supposedly bearing away the emperor's soul. After the cremation, the ashes were

collected (by Livia in the case of Augustus) to be placed in the tomb (in later times, the body itself was placed there). For the same person could be honored as both a divinity and a dead human being, a concept that delighted a few sceptical minds in Rome: "I feel that I am becoming a god," the emperor Vespasian is supposed to have said jokingly on his deathbed.

2 A temple to the Divine Augustus was begun in the Forum, south of the Basilica Julia (it was inaugurated in 37, under Caligula). And priests were pledged to him: a *flamen augustalis* (the first was Germanicus); and a college of *sodales augustales* recruited from members of the imperial family and the greatest Roman *gentes* (this college is not to be confused with the *seviri augustales*, who were already, under Augustus, in charge of the imperial cult in the towns of Italy). These were all the elements of an official state cult and were features of virtually every Roman deification.

3 Similarly, a domestic cult of Augustus grew up. It was born within the imperial family, with Livia as its priestess, and was then taken up by the great families of Rome.

On the death of each important member of the imperial family (except for Livia), an upsurge of the imperial cult occurred: for instance, on the death of Germanicus in 19, and on the death of Caligula's sister Drusilla, deified in 38.

The living emperors The temperament, personal beliefs, and policy of each emperor determined the form of the honors rendered to him, or perhaps one should rather say the form of those that he accepted.

Tiberius, with a few exceptions in the East (for example, at Claros in Asia), always refused the divine honors offered to him. Two testimonies are particularly eloquent regarding his attitude. To the magistrates of the city of Gythium in Laconia who, shortly after the death of Augustus, had decided to bestow divine honors on Augustus, Livia, and himself, Tiberius gave his consent for Augustus, reserved his reply for Livia, and refused for himself. Similarly, in a speech delivered to the Senate in 25, in response to a petition from the provincials of Baetica who wished to erect a temple in his honor, he declared that he was a mortal and above all desired temples and statues in the hearts of men. However, starting from the time of the conspiracy of Sejanus, a development took shape. On coins and in official inscriptions, a deified *Providentia* was associated with Tiberius. She "became the profoundest expression of the strength of imperial power protected by the gods" (J.-P. Martin). By suppressing Sejanus and his supporters, Tiberius placed the world and the divine will in accord.

The short reign of Caligula poses an unresolved problem. For some, he was the first emperor to want to impose a theological and theocratic conception of government. He is said to have appeared dressed as Bacchus, Apollo, and even Jupiter. Moreover, in 40 he ordered a statue of himself in the guise of Jupiter to be installed in the Temple at Jerusalem. For others, who do not dispute these facts but explain them either as "the follies of a poseur" or as to do with the imperatives of Egyptian politics, Caligula would in no event have tried to institute an eastern-style despotism and, during his lifetime, impose his worship on the Romans. He was here, they say, the object of spiteful and slanderous criticisms from those whose insolence far removed them from the Roman ideal of *gravitas*. At the most he accepted, like Augustus, that a cult with an altar and possibly a priestly brotherhood should be consecrated to his *numen*.

Claudius, infatuated with religious sciences (he reorganized the *haruspices* and the worship of Cybele, and persecuted the Druids), shared the attitude of Tiberius but also resumed the provincial and western religious policy of Augustus: Britain, newly conquered, had its temple of the imperial cult in Colchester.

Nero seemed indifferent to traditional Roman religion. On the other hand, being extremely superstitious, he consulted astrologers, did not hesitate to resort to magical practices, and turned to eastern cults. He also made use of the opportunities of the imperial cult, gathering and encouraging divine associations to himself. Although inscriptions ascribe to him the prerogatives of a Hercules, a Mars, a Jupiter, he was chiefly, and from the very first months of his reign, associated with Apollo – the very voice of the emperor was claimed to be divine. Historians are divided on whether all this marked a new, individualized, and exaggerated form of the imperial cult that was intended to bring about the institution of a sort of absolute monarchy underpinned by a sun-god theology. Evidence for it has been found in the colossal statue of himself as Helios, in the construction of the park of the Domus Aurea, in his personal mythology relating to his birth, in the issues of coins on which he wears a radiant crown, symbol of the Sun, and in numerous inscriptions which make him out to be a new Apollo. But there are not only queries about the inspiration, origins, and line of descent (Greek, Egyptian, Alexandrian . . .) of this new form of the imperial cult, but also doubts about whether it is not more a matter of over-bold extrapolations by speculative historians.

For the sake of convenience we have made a distinction between the cults of the dead and living emperors. It must not, however, be supposed that there was any opposition between the two. Quite the reverse. Veneration for the dead emperors strengthened the authority of the living, who were all potentially "deifiable." In any case, the association of the dead and the living in the imperial family made itself: it appeared, as we have seen, on the Great Cameo of France; it is to be found again in a sanctuary at the gates of Rome, with the first appearance, under Tiberius, of the concept of the *domus divina* ("divine house") embracing the dead and the living in the same community; and it triumphs in the sumptuous Sebasteion of Aphrodisias in Caria.

A "spiritual revolution"?

The imperial cult and the Christian faith were born at much the same time, both witnesses to a "spiritual revolution" in the mediterranean world according to the great Italian historian Santo Mazzarino, who, employing a modicum of rhetorical license, compares the "gospel of Augustus" with that of Jesus in order to underline the soteriological expectations that pervaded the ancient world in the first half of the first century AD. The argument that they were competing cults has received spirited support. What is undeniable is that there was a conflict. But that came later.

Jesus Near the end of Tiberius' reign a man named Jesus died on the cross in Jerusalem. Those whom he had drawn to him, the disciples, members of the Jewish community, were disoriented after his death. The prefect of the province of Judaea, Pontius Pilate, whose existence is attested by an inscription, very probably submitted a report on the matter to the emperor, but it appears that no echo of this local news item reached wider circles in Rome.

The case of the Jews The Jews were the only people in the Empire whose beliefs were completely alien to the ideology of the imperial cult. To take part in an act of worship purely as part of the imperial cult (or any other pagan cult) was blasphemy for a Jew. Death was preferable. This exclusive faith was not confined to Palestine; the Jews of the diaspora, scattered throughout the Mediterranean basin, also retained the faith of their ancestors. To serve the singular needs of this tenacious people, whose monotheism, dietary prohibitions, and other rites and customs (such as circumcision) also tended to single them out from the other inhabitants of the Empire, a series of privileges had been obtained from the Roman authorities, chiefly in the religious domain. Under the Empire, they preserved the council of the Sanhedrin (their supreme court of justice, presided over by the High Priest, with competence to deal with all cases coming under Mosaic law) and their religious organization was secure. For the purposes of the imperial cult, all they were required to do was to offer a daily sacrifice to their God for the emperor. (This was the compromise that Caligula wanted to challenge.) But even though for Rome the Jewish religion was permitted and legally recognized, a Jew, even if a Roman citizen, had great difficulty in obtaining a magistrate's office or holding an imperial post. This unusual status within the Empire was compounded by a special politico-religious situation which divided the Jewish people into several sects or parties according to the positions they adopted with regard to the Law, the Temple, and the priesthood.

Parties/sects	Social situation	Religious nature	Attitude to Rome
Sadducees	Great priestly families	Bound to the letter of the Torah; importance of priests and Temple	Fairly definite collaboration; divided in 66/7, some for revolt, others for conciliation
Pharisees	Less homogeneous recruitment: lower classes and comfortably-off	Written and oral tradition; study of Scriptures; importance of rabbis and schools	Reserve; cautious participation but dissociated themselves from opponents
Essenes	Known from the Dead Sea scrolls; lived in communities far from Jerusalem	Eschatological glorification that must end in the victory of Good over Evil	Hostility; participation in revolt of 66
Zealots	Of the people	Same doctrine as Pharisees, but awaited a Messiah to liberate them from Roman domination	Active hostility; preached rebellion in 66

These were the four great Jewish sects or parties defined by Flavius Josephus. On the fringes of official Judaism there was an intense religious ferment, the numerous prophetic and popular movements maintaining a constant turbulence increasingly marked by its fundamentally anti-Roman nature.

Jesus and his disciples   Jesus seems to have rejected these divisions, and to have kept aloof from both the Zealots and the Sadducees. The Sadducees attempted to have him condemned by the Roman governor by making the Sanhedrin treat him as an agitator, imparting an immediate political dimension to his messianic claims. Hence the trial conducted by the Roman authorities and the *titulus* "King of the Jews" affixed to the cross. For the Romans, the founder of the new religion thus appeared as a rebel, a troublemaker, in short a "zealot," so that, even though Jesus had continually stated that his kingdom was not of this world, and that those things that were Caesar's should be rendered unto Caesar (in other words, that taxes should be paid), at its very inception "Christianity presented features which had to make it suspect or disturbing in Roman eyes" (C. Lepelley).

Jews and Christians The great innovation of the early Christian communities was to have extended their proselytizing to the Jews of the diaspora, and then to the pagans. The internal conflicts that arose over the accommodations involved in this converting of the pagan world may be simplified as the conflict between the Judaeo-Christian Peter and the Apostle of the Gentiles Paul. The victory of the Pauline tendency meant that the Christian communities gradually cut themselves off from the Jewish colonies of the diaspora, the largest of which was in Rome (30,000–50,000 members), while in Jerusalem they dissociated themselves from the Jews at the time of the revolt in 66. But when they broke their links with Judaism, the Christians were no longer covered by the official privileges conferred by Rome on the Jewish people. Their religion, not connected with any state or people, ardently preached, and aiming at universalism, became illegal and illicit, even though in its monotheism and rejection of any concession to the imperial cult it was the direct heir of Judaism.

Christianity and the Roman state There was no animosity to the Roman state on the part of Christianity: a Christian had to obey the emperor and his officials, respect the existing social order, including the position within it of Christian slaves, and trust in imperial justice (as did Paul, who as a Roman citizen appealed to the imperial tribunal). This was a matter not of mere strategy on the Christian side, but of profound belief. The kingdom of God in fact was yet to come, and would be signaled by the return of Jesus and the resurrection of the dead. This expectation of the "eschatological second coming" was a passionate experience, and the event was regarded as imminent. Consequently, the temporal world took second place: "Our city lies in the heavens," said Paul. Such an affirmation was outrageous in the ancient world, where the bond linking a citizen to the state was paramount. On its side, the Roman state took little interest in the Christians. At first they were confused with the Jews, as in the first allusion to Christianity we possess in a non-Christian document: "Claudius expelled from Rome," notes Suetonius, "the Jews who were constantly agitating under the influence of *Chrestus*" (*Claudius* 25). This sentence has provoked countless commentaries. But there is now general agreement in recognizing in that agitation the result of Christian preaching among the Jewish colony in Rome in 49 or 50. Thirteen or fourteen years later, the distinction had been made: after the Great Fire of Rome of 64 "Christians were put to the torture, a kind of people addicted to a new and harmful superstition" (Suetonius, *Nero* 16). A longer passage in Tacitus confirms and explains these words (*Annals* 15.44). Two points that arise from his account should be borne in mind. First, the Christians were hounded only in Rome, and not so much because they were Christians as because they were accused (falsely) of a heinous crime (setting fire to the capital). Secondly, public opinion loathed them. Nevertheless, there was no law to punish adherence to the Christian faith. Under Nero there was no persecution in the strict sense. But a long period of insecurity was beginning for Christ's followers.

DEVELOPMENT OF THE ADMINISTRATION

Augustus had organized an efficient administrative apparatus adapted to the scale of the Roman world and centered on Rome. Its ability to administer the vast regions under Roman control depended on its flexibility, adaptability, and capacity for transmitting orders and gathering knowledge of and then deploying the resources of the Empire. That it was capable of keeping the emperor supplied with overall information can be seen from the *Breviarium imperii* that Augustus left on his death, a document providing a complete list of military resources and dispositions, and diplomatic and administrative obligations, and indicating as well "the Treasury's reserves and state revenues." The perfecting of this administrative apparatus continued under the Julio-Claudians, with a concomitant increase in the power of the state. The growth of the imperial departments that this involved could be seen in the urban geography of Rome, where many of the (still surprisingly small number of) state officials were to be found (for all its growth, the Roman state was not comparable in size to a modern state). It was visible first and foremost in the extension of the palace area on the Palatine. From the residence of Augustus and his family and staff, confined to the north-west quarter, it expanded through successive stages to occupy the entire hill, which became a sort of imperial city (see next chapter, fig. 10.1).

CENTRAL ADMINISTRATION

The changes made by the Julio-Claudians that transformed the administrative apparatus left by Augustus into a true central administration were essentially the work of Tiberius and, chiefly, Claudius.

Tiberius Under Tiberius, the emperor's council as it had functioned under Augustus disappeared, to be replaced by a circle of "companions" (*comites*), more informal than the old "senatorial" *consilium* but apparently more efficient. Above all, though, Tiberius filled in some of the outlines of the central administration adumbrated by Augustus, keeping vigilant watch over the way the various services worked, and making improvements by placing men of consular rank at the head of some of them and by increasing the number of technical posts.

Claudius Claudius was the true organizer of the central administration, which he entrusted to his freedmen. Thanks to them, the bureaux, though preserving, on the whole, a domestic character, became real ministries, rendering the emperor independent of the Senate and the knights.

- Narcissus became the private secretary in charge of imperial correspondence (*ab epistulis*).
- Pallas looked after the bureau *a rationibus*. By virtue of this, he found himself at the head of finances, which were divided between several departments but which Claudius began to dominate by the creation of a central fund, the *fiscus Caesaris*. Surpluses from provincial revenues were channeled into it. Moreover, the free distributions of grain, formerly funded by the Senate's finances, were henceforth the responsibility of this *fiscus Caesaris*.
- Callistus was in charge of the bureau *a libellis*, receiving requests and petitions addressed to the emperor. In fact, he was a sort of minister of justice.
- Polybius, lastly, was responsible for the bureau *a studiis*, which carried out various inquiries and compiled records and files.

These departmental heads were helped by assistants, the *adiutores* (slaves or freedmen), aided by numerous other employees (*scrinarii*).

Contrary to what Latin historians (Suetonius and Tacitus) suggested, the policies of Claudius were not at the mercy of his freedmen's moods. They, moreover, fulfilled their tasks unfailingly. But their wealth and power aroused rancor and jealousy among the senators.

PROVINCIAL ADMINISTRATION

Under the Julio-Claudians, there were few fundamental changes to the Augustan organization of the provinces; the changes were mainly alterations and rearrangements due to annexations or conquests. (With one exception, Lycia-Pamphylia, the new provinces increased the domain of the imperial provinces.) However, taken as a whole, an improvement in provincial administration was noticeable. Governors were generally controlled by provincial assemblies, such as the Assembly of the Three Gauls. And the number of known procurators' posts doubled: 23 under Augustus, 25 under Tiberius, 27 under Caligula, 38 under Claudius, and 46 under Nero. Here again, the reigns of Tiberius and Claudius were important.

Tiberius gave his attention to creating a more just administration. During his reign, several governors were sentenced for misappropriation of public funds and abuse of power. And he was aware of the cost of crushing provinces under too great a burden of taxation: "A good shepherd," he said, "shears his sheep; he does not flay them" (Suetonius, *Tiberius* 32). He also kept the governors he valued in their posts for long periods: C. Poppaeus Sabinus stayed as governor of Moesia for 24 years. Tiberius' concern for provincials was further revealed by the financial aid he gave at times of disaster and by reforms of customs districts.

Claudius, born in Lyon, could hardly deny the interests of the provinces and provincials. He did not do so, and was even accused of wanting to "put a toga on every Greek, Spaniard, Gaul, and Briton." His provincial policy had four principal aspects:

- The founding of colonies and the creation of *municipia* on a regular basis and a vast scale, linking his policy to those of Caesar and Augustus. Favored regions were Britain, Germania, Mauretania, Pannonia, Dalmatia, Thrace, Cappadocia, and Syria.
- A generous policy of naturalization, the extent of which is shown in several documents: full rights for the Alpine peoples, and for the provincial elites; request for the right to enter the Senate for notables of the Three Gauls who already had full Roman citizenship; individual grants of citizenship for easterners; naturalization of auxiliaries after they had served out their term. Citizenship, however, was not cheapened: it was removed from provincials who did not know Latin, and those who were found to have wrongfully assumed full rights were executed.
- Reinforcement of the powers of imperial procurators, in both senatorial and imperial provinces.
- A policy of major works (roads, aqueducts).

The Julio-Claudians' experiments with the Augustan system produced satisfactory results in every field. Theirs was a period rich in innovations, trials, errors, and corrections; and one that was decisive on the administrative level. It witnessed the apogee of Italy in relation to the provinces and contained the seeds of future developments: the might of the army, the conflict with Christianity, and the expansion of the provinces. At its end there arose again the vexed question of the succession. But the Republic had finally been laid to rest; it survived as a mythical reference point, but no one challenged the Empire.

10 / THE FLAVIANS
Consolidating the Imperial Order, AD *68–96*

*T*HE DEATH OF NERO OPENED A PERIOD OF CRISIS LASTING ONE AND A HALF
YEARS. IT WAS SERIOUS NOT ONLY BECAUSE OF ITS GEOGRAPHICAL EXTENT,
AFFECTING ROME, ITALY, GAUL, THE GERMANIES, SPAIN, AFRICA, SYRIA, JUDAEA,
AND EGYPT, BUT ALSO BECAUSE OF WHAT WAS AT STAKE, BECAUSE OF THE FORCES
ENGAGED, AND BECAUSE OF ITS POSSIBLE CONSEQUENCES. IT WAS A CRISIS THAT LAID
BARE THE CONTRADICTIONS AND AMBIGUITIES OF THE SYSTEM SET UP BY AUGUSTUS,
AND ONE THAT IN MANY RESPECTS CAME CLOSER TO A RETURN TO THE REPUBLICAN
CIVIL WARS, WHOSE MEMORY STILL OBSESSED PEOPLE'S MINDS, THAN DID OTHER
DRAMATIC EPISODES IN THE HISTORY OF THE EMPIRE. CERTAINLY, THE FIELD OF
BATTLE WAS ON AN EMPIRE-WIDE SCALE. BUT WAS THE CONFLICT SO DIFFERENT FROM
THAT BETWEEN CAESAR AND POMPEY? IT CERTAINLY BECAME APPARENT THAT AN
EMPEROR COULD BE CREATED ELSEWHERE THAN IN ROME. BUT WAS THAT REALLY A
NOVELTY? AND WHO DID ALL THIS? GOVERNORS AND LEGIONS. IN OTHER WORDS,
ROMAN CITIZENS, ALMOST ALL ITALIAN. FEW PROVINCIALS TOOK PART IN THIS
ITALIAN WAR, IN WHICH, AS IN FORMER CIVIL WARS, THERE WERE SOME REMARKABLE
INSTANCES OF VIOLENCE. THE PROVINCIALS WAITED. A SIGNIFICANT POINT IS THAT
ONCE TENSIONS HAD BEEN RELEASED IN MASSACRES, THE DYNASTY WHICH RE-
ESTABLISHED COLLECTIVE HARMONY, AS AUGUSTUS HAD BEEN ABLE TO DO, BELONGED
TO THE ITALIAN MUNICIPAL "BOURGEOISIE." THE CIRCLE OF LONG-ESTABLISHED
ROMANS WAS BROKEN. BUT THE PROVINCIALS STILL REMAINED ON THE OUTSIDE.

RETURN OF THE CIVIL WARS?

In order to get a better grasp of the possible interpretations of this complex
crisis, we shall need to look first at the key events and personalities.

EVENTS AND MEN

Galba (June 68–January 69)

Born in 3 BC, the scion of an old patrician family, Sulpicius Galba had been held
in esteem by all the emperors and had had the classic and in his case brilliant

career of a loyal and highly regarded senator. In 68, having been proconsul of Africa under Claudius, he was the governor of Tarraconensis, an elderly, rigid, and stern figure – the antithesis of Nero. Having learnt that Nero wanted to have him assassinated and having been invited by Vindex to be the new emperor, he too had rebelled. After the death of Vindex, he had headed the revolt, while remaining in Spain, where he received news of the death of Nero and his own acceptance as emperor by the praetorians and the Senate. In October, he arrived in Rome, where he committed one political blunder after another:

- In order to restore the finances, he refused to give the promised *donativum* ("I do not buy my soldiers, I choose them"), but he granted benefits to his supporters from the Gauls.
- He executed Nero's colleagues and massacred Nero's troops in Rome.
- He took action against those accused of "treason," merely on the evidence of informers and without going through the Senate.
- He left matters to his "pedagogues," three very mediocre persons.

In under six months Galba managed to alienate almost all classes in Rome: the praetorians, the Senate, and the people, who missed Nero. He showed the same tactlessness and shortsightedness in his treatment of other parts of the army, recalling a popular legate from Upper Germania and sending the only legion loyal to him to Pannonia. He thus had no one to help him when the legate of Lower Germania, A. Vitellius, was proclaimed emperor by his troops on January 2, 69. His only response was to adopt L. Calpurnius Piso and on January 10 designate him as his successor. Five days later the praetorians hailed Otho as emperor and killed Galba and Piso. Galba was "worthy of ancient times," observed Tacitus. Two emperors remained – in other words, one too many.

Otho (January 15–April 14, 69)

Born in 32, a patrician but of a recently ennobled family, Otho had been Poppaea's husband before Nero, which is why he had been sent to Lusitania as governor in 58. He stayed there ten years, and was the first to support Galba, whom he hoped to succeed. He was worth more than is suggested by his reputation as one who liked the high life; his provincial government had been good, and his policies were not without intelligence.

On the evening of January 15, the Senate awarded him tribunician power, the name of *Augustus*, and all the imperial honors. The legions of the Danube, the East, Egypt, and Africa soon all gave him their backing. And he astutely rallied the praetorians to his cause by a *donativum*, and the people by reinstating the memory of Nero. He undeniably enjoyed a measure of popularity.

In February, Vitellius' troops invaded Italy. Against his 60,000 men, Otho could range, immediately, only a much smaller force. He nevertheless set out without waiting for the legions from the Danube. From this haste came two tactical errors. The first was his seeking a decisive battle before he could fight on equal terms, leading to the defeat, in his absence, at Bedriacum in the north of Italy, near Cremona, on April 14. The second was his precipitate suicide on the day after he learned of the defeat.

Vitellius (April 15–December 20, 69)

Born in 15, Vitellius, a big, strong, jovial man, had been consul, and procon-sul of Africa, before being appointed by Galba to head the army of the Rhine. Having been hailed as *imperator* by his soldiers, as we have seen, he happened to be in Lyon when his lieutenants informed him of the victory at Bedriacum and Otho's suicide. By the 19th, the Senate had recognized him as emperor, Vitellius appearing as the avenger of Galba. Without hurrying himself, his troops looting and pillaging with gusto on the way, he took the road for Rome. He sent the Othonian legions back to the provinces and dismissed the praeto-rians, whom he replaced with his own soldiers. And at the beginning of July he entered Rome amidst a force of 60,000 men.

Meanwhile, in the East, the legate of Syria, the prefect of Egypt, and the commander of the troops in Judaea, T. Flavius Vespasianus (Vespasian), took counsel together, contacted the Danubian troops and those of client kingdoms and the governors of other provinces, and in Alexandria on July 1, 69 the legions under the prefect of Egypt acclaimed Vespasian emperor. Not much is known of the reasons for this conspiracy or of its organization, nor has the choice of Vespasian been fully explained. At all events, the legions of Egypt, Judaea, Syria, and the Danube rallied to him. Vespasian himself secured control of Rome's grain supplies at Alexandria, while his son Titus took his place in conducting the war against the Jews. In the autumn of 69, Flavian troops entered the north of Italy. And on October 24, Vitellius' forces were crushed at Cremona. Spain, Gaul, and Britain joined Vespasian. In Rome, Vitellius real-ized that he could not win, and tried to negotiate, in particular with the prefect of the city, Vespasian's brother. But the praetorians and the people of Rome, absolute hardliners, opposed any agreement with Vespasian or his supporters. On December 18, Rome was the stage for a battle waged between the two sides. The Capitol, to which Vespasian's supporters had withdrawn, was burnt and the prefect of the city was killed by the crowd, but Domitian, Vespasian's other son, managed to escape by loosing himself, suitably disguised, among a fleeing band of priests of Isis. On December 20, the armies of the Danube made an assault on the capital. Vitellius was killed, and the Senate acknowledged Ves-pasian as emperor. He waited until peace had been re-established in Rome before leaving Alexandria. This absence of haste also indicated common sense.

Passions had to be extinguished for the capital to be rebuilt and the achievements of Augustus to be restored.

INTERPRETATIONS

Because this crisis was so complex, there are many possible interpretations of it. It has been argued, for example, that at its heart lay social antagonisms which expressed themselves through intermediary champions, with Vitellius representing (involuntarily) the lower classes and Vespasian the upper ranks. Nevertheless, certain things are clear:

■ It was not a constitutional crisis – no one dreamed of re-establishing the Republic. It stemmed from the failure of one man, Nero.
■ The memory of Nero continued to divide political life. Behind the differences in attitude to his memory it is possible to see an opposition between two conceptions of government: one popular and monarchic, with Otho and Vitellius; the other more senatorial, with Galba and, to a certain extent, Vespasian.
■ The role of the praetorians was effaced by that of the armies from the provinces, among whom we must make the distinction between legionary and auxiliary troops. Furthermore, each great corps of the army had its own quite distinct personality (the Rhine army was very different from the Syrian army), provoking rivalries between them. Yet the organization was the same, commanders were shaped in the same mold, and recruitment was not basically different, even though for the eastern part a higher number of local soldiers was noticeable.

THE "BOURGEOIS" EMPIRE OF VESPASIAN AND TITUS

At the end of 69, the Empire presented a sorry spectacle. At least that is the impression given by the famous opening passage of Tacitus' *Histories*. And, indeed, difficulties of all kinds might have led one to fear the worst. There was nothing to encourage a hope of better times to come. The emperor was not in Rome and the most sacred sanctuary lay in ruins. The war against the Jews was getting bogged down, the provinces were in a state of agitation, and nations were in rebellion or making agreements with the barbarians. Bands of unmanageable soldiers, deserters from routed armies, roamed the land, and even the victorious armies were disturbed and divided. Administrative problems crowded in because of unsettled and contradictory appointments, and the air was laden with the bitterness and resentment of the defeated. In reality, however, the ills were not as deep as they seemed. Within two years Vespasian had restored the situation.

THE MEN

Vespasian (69–79)

Vespasian was 60 years old when he became emperor. He came from a family of municipal notables (his father belonged to the equestrian order) in the Sabine region of Rieti, and had begun his career in the equestrian order. Having received the laticlave in 35 or 36, he was a praetor under Caligula, legionary legate during the conquest of Britain, in which he took part, consul in 51, and proconsul of Africa in 61 – a solid rather than a dazzling career. His elder brother, by contrast, pursued an outstanding senatorial career, leading him as far as the prefectship of Rome. Vespasian had, however, given proof of his energy, so that when a vigorous leader was being sought at the time of the Jewish revolt in 66, thoughts turned to him. Moreover, remarked Suetonius, there seemed little to fear from him, "seeing the obscurity of his birth and name" (*Vespasian* 4).

Modest, realistic, cautious, an efficient general with a sound knowledge of the mysteries of administration and finance, Vespasian knew how to select his colleagues and make an exact assessment of the situation. Already among those closest to him in 69 was his son Titus.

Titus (79–81)

Born in 39, Titus was raised at court with Britannicus. Unlike his father, he received a careful and thorough education – he shone in music and writing verse. His career brought him military postings in Germania, Britain, and then Judaea at his father's side. During 69, he played a considerable part in the negotiations between the members of the conspiracy. When his father went to Alexandria, he naturally assumed leadership of the troops that remained in Judaea. An ambitious man, he made plain his intention of succeeding his father. That was thought shocking – before becoming emperor, Titus had not been regarded as "the love and delight of the human race." However, it was perhaps because Titus existed and had a brother that Vespasian was chosen as emperor. The succession would be more or less assured, so that the choice gave promise that there would be no new period of civil conflict.

The dynastic concern suggested to explain the choice of Vespasian was also to be found in political life during his reign. In 69, Titus was named *Caesar* and *princeps iuventutis*. Father and son together assumed the consulship in 70, 72, 74, 75, 76, 77, and 79. And in 73–4, they both held the censorship. Moreover, Titus was included in the tribunician and proconsular powers of the emperor, and better still, although a senator, was the sole commander of the praetorian guard from 71. Suetonius' judgement that he became "the partner and even guardian of the emperor" is understandable. When, on the death of

Table 10.1 The Flavians (from G. Townend, *JRS*, LI (1961), pp. 54–62)

T. Flavius Petro   Vipsanius Pollio

T. Flavius Sabinus ~ Vipsania Polla

daughter
died aged
1 year

T. Flavius Sabinus
3 – con. 45,
prefect of Rome, d. 69

T. FLAVIUS VESPASIANUS
~
Flavia Domitilla

Flavia Sabina
~
L. Iunius
Caesennius Paetus
(con. 61)

T. Flavius Sabinus
(con. 69, II, 72)
~
Arrecina

L. Iunius
Caesennius Paetus
(con. 79)

T. Flavius
Sabinus
(con. 82)
~
Iulia Titi

T. Fl.
Clemens
(con. 95)
~
Domitilla

T. Flavius
Domitianus
Caesar

T. Flavius
Vespasianus
Caesar

(adopted by Domitian)

TITUS FL. VESPASIANUS
(39–79–81) ~ Arrecina Tertulla
~ Marcia Furnilla

Flavia Iulia (= Iulia Titi)
~
T. Fl. Sabinus

Flavia Domitilla
~
Q. Petillius Cerialis
(con. 70, 74)

Flavia Domitilla
~
T. Fl. Clemens

T. FLAVIUS DOMITIANUS
(51–81–96)
~
Domitia Longina

Flavius

his father, Titus became emperor (June 24, 79), he was certainly the best-prepared man for the task. His reign, however, was short – he died on September 13, 81. Perhaps that is why, even though a bias toward the East comparable to Nero's has been detected in him, and the episode of his passion for Berenice is but one of its aspects, such a wonderful memory of him was preserved. But it is also no doubt the case that his reign was embellished by senatorial historiographical tradition in order to make the horrors of his brother Domitian's "tyranny" stand out more sharply.

Domitian (until 81)

Vespasian's second son, Domitian, was born in 51. Unlike his brother's childhood, his own was unhappy, and his education was neglected. In December 69, caught up in the turmoil of civil war, he owed his life to his sang-froid and astuteness. Emerging from hiding after Vitellius' death, he represented the imperial family in Rome, since his father and brother were still in the East. He was named *Caesar* and *princeps iuventutis*, and for 70 received the praetorship with the consular *imperium*. He then wished, in his father's absence, to run the government, and was outraged when he was given a mentor, the former legate of Syria, C. Lucinius Mucianus, whom Vespasian trusted completely. Kept away from real power under Vespasian and Titus and excluded from military expeditions, he succeeded by his careless and vindictive behavior in annoying his father and falling out with his brother. However, he was a member of all the major religious colleges, his name accompanied those of Vespasian and Titus on public monuments, and he became consul six times during his father's reign, though only once as an *ordinarius*. Despite all these honors, Domitian considered that his family had acted unfairly to him. And although associated with the government, he remained apart; and during the principate of Titus, was even involved in conspiracies, trying to rouse the armies against his brother and playing with the idea of leaving Rome to join them.

RESTORING PEACE

The most urgent need was to remedy the ill consequences of the civil war and restore peace. This was the task of Mucianus in the West, and Vespasian and Titus in the East.

In the West

Mucianus first re-established order in Rome itself. There were no reprisals against the vanquished troops; and the victorious troops were sent back to their provinces. A commission was set up to return goods stolen during the war. And on Vespasian's orders Mucianus embarked upon the reconstruction of the temple of Jupiter Capitolinus, the dedication taking place on June 21, 70. In the West, the only trouble to persist was the Batavian rebellion. Taking advantage of Rome's troubles, the Batavians had revolted at the instigation of Civilis. Early in 70, various Gaulish tribes (the Lingones and Treveri in particular) joined Civilis and proclaimed an "Empire of the Gauls." Relying on the auxiliary troops, reinforced by Germani from across the Rhine, and profiting from the uncertainty of the legions, they took Xanten, Mainz, Bonn, and Cologne. But each group was fighting from a different motive: "the Gauls in the name of liberty, the Batavians in the name of glory, and the Germani for loot" (Tacitus, *Histories* 4.78). Worried about the alliance with the Germani, the States of the Three Gauls met at Reims to establish a common position. They freely chose to give up their independence in order to remain loyal to Rome. Besides, eight legions were marching against the rebels. Before the end of 70 calm had descended once more on the Rhine frontier.

In the East

The main problem in the East was the Jewish War. Since 66, the situation had continually worsened. From rioting in Caesarea it had developed into a rising in Jerusalem and then into open war with Rome. The army commanded by Vespasian in Judaea numbered about 60,000 men. At the beginning of the summer of 68, the insurgents controlled only Jerusalem and its region as far as the west shore of the Dead Sea. Then came the death of Nero, the civil wars, and Vespasian's departure for Egypt. Roman operations were suspended. They resumed in the spring of 70 under the leadership of Titus. He had at his disposal four legions, auxiliary corps, and men levied from the garrisons of the Euphrates and Egypt, and had the mission of "ending the affair as quickly as possible and at all costs" (Le Glay and Le Gall). The Siege of Jerusalem lasted five months. The Temple fell on August 30, then the lower town, and finally the upper town on September 25. The entire place was pillaged and set on fire. Elsewhere, several strongholds still held out. Masada, the rebels' last bastion, was not taken until May 2, 73. For the Jews, the consequences of the war were profound. Judaea, which became a praetorian province, was in ruins, its population diminished by a third, and a new diaspora took place. The Sanhedrin vanished. The Temple building was destroyed and the liturgy of the Temple was abolished. The construction of a new place of worship was prohibited. And the didrachm (the tax the Jews paid to the Temple) was henceforth to be paid to a new fund, the *fiscus Judaicus*, to the profit of the temple of Jupiter Capitolinus.

When Vespasian left Alexandria for Rome in September 70, peace had been virtually re-established in the East. The following year, together with Titus, he celebrated a triumph over the Jews. On the arch of Titus in the Roman Forum, pictures of that triumph may still be seen: on one side, Titus in triumph on his chariot; on the other, the procession carrying on stretchers the menorah, or

Plate 10.1 Arch of Titus, built in AD 81 in the Roman forum. Roman soldiers return from the sack of Jerusalem in AD 70 carrying the spoils, including the menorah from the Temple.

seven-branched candelabrum, the shew-bread table, incense vessels, and silver trumpets of the Temple.

RESTORING CONFIDENCE

Once peace was restored it had to be preserved. To this end, Vespasian set about removing the weaknesses that the crisis had brought to light. First, it was imperative to re-establish imperial authority, to unite the inhabitants of the Empire under it and obliterate the memory not only of the time of Nero and of the terrible year just past, but also of his own upstart status. Secondly, he had to reconcile the different parts of the Empire with one another, stabilize the provinces, and strengthen the administration. Lastly, there was a need to ensure the security of the Empire as a whole, by consolidating its fringes.

Re-establishing the authority and prestige of the imperial office

Establishing the present   On July 1, 69 at Alexandria, it may be recalled, Vespasian had been acclaimed emperor by the legions under the prefect of Egypt. It was thus a provincial accession, somewhat inglorious all in all, that elevated to the purple a wily general who did not even originate from the capital and was a plebeian to boot. "Vespasian lacked prestige and a kind of majesty, because of his unexpected and still recent elevation," wrote Suetonius (*Vespasian* 7). However, a visit to the temple of Serapis, followed by two miracles of healing performed by Vespasian, and an inspired discovery of a cache of ancient vases that each displayed his likeness, soon revealed him as the choice of the god and gave him those missing qualities. His elevation by *coup d'état* was thus transformed into a kind of religious enthronement. But, in spite of that, Vespasian's power did not rest on any legal foundation. Only on the death of Vitellius did the Senate consecrate Vespasian his successor. In other words, it was an investiture that had been postponed for six months. Now, traditionally, that investiture started a new reign, of which it marked the birth date (*dies imperii*), even if the assembly was ratifying a choice that had not been its own. Vespasian, however, flouted protocol, made the deed and the law coincide and decided that his *dies imperii* was the day when the army, and not the Senate, had chosen him, July 1, 69. All the acts of the period until the investiture had to be legalized after the event. The "law on Vespasian's *imperium*" (*lex de imperio Vespasiani*) – a document on the nature of which there is still doubt – includes a clause of retroactivity. The seven other known clauses enumerate the laws relating to the *imperium* and the tribunician power. Up till then the conferment of titles and powers had been fragmented. Here, all the powers were accorded *en bloc*, with details and new features that emphasized the absolutist aspect. At the same time, the imperial title was fixed in its canonical form: *Imp(erator) Caesar Vespasianus Aug(ustus)*. The first term is abbreviated, like a *praenomen*; the second, with gentilitial value, links the emperor to the founders of the regime; the third, his personal name, allows the emperor to be identified; the fourth transmits to the title-holder the religious aura of the first Augustus. Thus past and present are combined, the past embodied in the present.

Connecting with the past   The circumstances surrounding Vespasian's accession to power recalled that of Augustus. A chronological coincidence (into which the ancients read predestination) accentuated the parallel: 100 years had passed since Augustus' victory at Actium. It was an opportunity not to be missed. Several monetary issues of 70–1 were directly and consciously inspired by Augustan coinage: while Augustus had been given the title *Vindex* (champion) of liberty and the Roman people, Vespasian became *Adsertor* (savior/protector) of public liberty. Like Augustus at the beginning of his principate, Vespasian occupied the consulship on an almost permanent basis. And just as Augustus had raised an altar to Peace, so Vespasian, between 71 and 75, had a temple to Peace built, celebrating his victory over the Jews, with its façade facing the Forum of Augustus. Indeed, throughout the Flavian period the inspiration of Augustan art would be exploited – the bas-relief of the Chancellery Palace can be seen as its final flourish. This faithfulness to the achievements of Augustus had already been foreshadowed in the law on Vespasian's powers in 69. It was even further enriched by acts and measures that allowed Vespasian to appear as the heir of those good Julio-Claudians Tiberius and Claudius. Claudius was especially honored (Titus had been raised at his court, which may have made him more independent of Roman circles than his father). Not only did Vespasian, like Claudius, take on the censorship and extend the *pomoerium* (a measure not without fiscal repercussions), but he also rebuilt the temple to the Divine Claudius on the Caelian hill. This was also a way of distancing himself from Nero, who had transformed the earlier temple into a *nymphaeum*. This anti-Neronian policy was further revealed in the dismantling of the Domus Aurea, its baths being rearranged to become those of Titus (the first to prefigure the great *thermae* of the second century) and its drained lake making way for a gigantic amphitheater, the Colosseum. Rome was thus handed back to the Romans. In order that this revived Rome (the theme of one of the first of Vespasian's issues of coinage) might be strengthened, it was necessary to safeguard the future.

Preparing for the future   With great self-assurance, Vespasian "dared to tell the Senate that his sons would succeed him or he would have no successor at all" (Suetonius, *Vespasian* 25). We have seen how, at the end of 69, his two sons were each named *Caesar* and *princeps iuventutis*. This dynastic policy extended to other members of the *domus divina*. The daughter of Vespasian, and later Titus' daughter, received the title *Augusta*. Under Domitian, the family residence on the Quirinal became the *templum gentis Flaviae*. And a special college, the *sodales Flaviales*, was established to render worship to the deified members of the family.

The better to entrench this restored power, Vespasian made use of the imperial cult, which he developed and organized on the provincial level, at least in the West. Thus, in Baetica, proconsular Africa, and southern Gaul, in none of which had the imperial religion gone beyond municipal level, he instituted in each a provincial *flamen*, whose duty, at the head of the *concilium*, was to celebrate the official cult of the emperor by sacrifices and games. On one point, however, Vespasian (and his sons) departed from the religious attitude of Augustus. Whereas Augustus had suppressed the Egyptian cults, Vespasian

Plate 10.2 Interior of the Colosseum at Rome, dedicated in AD 80. The floor (*arena*) has been excavated to reveal the vaulted subterranean structures.

linked them with the destiny of his family. On two occasions they had played a considerable role in the dynasty's history, favoring Vespasian's accession and allowing Domitian to escape from the Capitol. And on the eve of their triumph, Vespasian and Titus spent the night in the temple of Isis on the Campus Martius, a temple which was represented on the reverse of coins in 71, and which Domitian rebuilt after its destruction in the great fire of 80.

Reinforcing the Empire

In the main, Vespasian's attempts, continued by Titus, to strengthen the basis of the Empire and restore its fortunes involved actions to remedy and consolidate delicate or deteriorating situations in three areas of administration.

Provincial reorganization No emperor since Tiberius had possessed as good a knowledge of the provinces as Vespasian. He had spent time in Thrace, Crete-Cyrenaica, Gaul, the Germanies, Britain, Africa, Syria, Judaea, Egypt, Greece, and Asia. His structural, constitutional, and administrative modifications to the organization of the provinces were to the end of increasing the Empire's security and improving its tax system:

72 Annexation of the Commagene region, joined to Syria.

Annexation of Armenia Minor, incorporated with Cappadocia, which, joined to Galatia, became a consular (imperial) province with two legions.

Creation, in the south of Anatolia, of the praetorian imperial province of Cilicia.

Reconstitution of the province of Lycia-Pamphylia (date uncertain).

77 Rhodes, Samos, and Byzantium lost their liberty. The first two were attached to Asia; the last to Bithynia.

Financial reorganization   "The State needs 40 million [or billion?] sesterces in order to survive," Vespasian is said to have estimated at the start of his reign (Suetonius, *Vespasian* 16). It was a tough challenge. He rose to it with ingenuity, setting about the task with both ferocity and method. To increase revenues he did away with the exemptions granted by Nero and Galba, together with the franchises enjoyed by certain free cities; increased taxes in the provinces; created a *fiscus Alexandrinus*, a *fiscus Asiaticus*, and a *fiscus Judaicus*; instituted new taxes in Rome (including a toll on the city's urinals); continued to levy in peacetime the exceptional taxes levied in wartime; and even tried to launch a state loan. However, he was not a miser; though careful about not wasting money, he spent freely on large-scale works both in Rome (the Capitol, Colosseum, Temple of Peace, granaries, etc.) and throughout the Empire (numerous roadbuilding enterprises). He also helped senators to meet the senatorial property qualification and paid an allowance to impoverished former consuls, gave aid to towns destroyed by fires or earthquakes, and set up academic chairs financed from the imperial revenues. Furthermore, to simplify the financial departments, he incorporated the wealth of the Julio-Claudians with that of the crown (*patrimonium*).

Economic reorganization   During the period of the disturbances, lands in many areas had allegedly been fraudulently seized by private owners. Vespasian initiated the drawing up of cadastral surveys to establish the exact status of these lands, determine who the owners were, and establish the total land taxable for each. Inscriptions discovered in Italy and many provinces (for example, the survey of Orange) show that this gigantic and lengthy task was effected throughout the Empire. He also took an interest in the lands of the public domain that had not been allocated after centuriation, the *subsiciva*, which he put up for sale or rent. In northern Italy he paid subsidies to revive agricultural life, while in the provinces he regularized the administration of the imperial domains and set out precisely, at least in Africa (*lex Manciana*), the rights and duties of the *coloni*.

Watching over the Empire's safety

A well-informed soldier, Vespasian knew better than anyone that he had to secure the safety of the Empire. Once the Empire's internal troubles had been quelled and discipline had been restored to the army by regroupings of the legions and the purging of the praetorian cohorts, and having strengthened the fleets (mainly those in the East) and reorganized the provinces in the light of strategic concerns, he set about consolidating the fringes of the Empire, either by means of expeditions and peacemaking operations, or by fortifying them.

Expeditions and peacemaking operations

■ Africa: expedition against the Garamantes, who had come from Fezzan to harass the towns of Tripolitania.

■ Britain: three great legates (Q. Petilius Cerialis, Sex. Julius Frontinus, and Cn. Julius Agricola, the father-in-law of Tacitus) resumed a forward policy toward Wales and the North of England, bringing both under control, and then continuing northward; in 81, Agricola took up his position on the line of the Forth–Clyde isthmus.

■ Germania: the weakest point on the frontier was the angle formed by the valley of the Upper Rhine and the upper course of the Danube; from 73 onwards, a series of actions resulted in a cautious advance: the Black Forest was occupied.

■ The East: in 75, Vespasian rejected an alliance with the Parthians against the Alani; Vologeses, king of the Parthians, in frustration attacked Syria; he was repulsed, and died soon afterwards; the initiative now lay with Rome.

Fortifying the frontiers With the systematic installation of the legions along the frontiers (except the legions of Jerusalem, Alexandria, Tarraconensis, and Dalmatia), a static line of defense was gradually set up at each frontier, comprising a road network, and a range or series of fortifications between which the legions could thus smoothly move, the whole allowing Rome to have in-depth defense along a tract of ground stretching around the boundaries of the Empire (the obvious drawback being that, once that strip of ground had been passed, a potential enemy would be well inside a province, with no troops ahead). The defensive imperative for secure places and good communications in the face of possible invasions or incursions by organized forces is understandable. But the fortified zone could also keep surveillance on nomads, filter barbarian groups, and even supervise trade between the Roman world and the world beyond. This type of defense system gradually acquired the name *limes* (this meaning of the word is attested for the first time by Tacitus in 98).

■ *Africa* The first two Flavians set up a *limes* intended to provide better control of the line of the Aurès. The camp of the Third Augusta was transferred from Haidra to Tebessa, farther west, with a detachment at Lambaesis. Moreover, auxiliary units were installed to the west and south of the Aurès.

- *Britain* A series of forts and fortresses marked the progress of the legions westward and northward, in particular, two legionary camps at York and Chester.
- *Germania* In Lower Germania the *limes* rested on the old legionary camps at Xanten, Bonn, and Neuss and the new camp at Nijmegen; in Upper Germania, on those of Mainz, Strasbourg, and Vindonissa. Under Vespasian, these camps and the fortresses that accompanied them were in the main restored to good order, structures of wood and earth being replaced by stone walls. In parallel, Vespasian established new forts on the right bank of the Upper Rhine (for example, Heidelberg), and founded *Arae Flaviae* (Rottweil), perhaps in 73, to keep watch on a road that connected the Rhine and the Danube through the Black Forest, while another route, farther north, also protected by forts, linked Mainz with Augsburg, the capital of Raetia.
- *Danube* Vespasian, and then Domitian, reorganized the Danubian fleet, created auxiliary camps, and considerably strengthened the Danubian frontier.
- *The East* Client kingdoms no longer existed here. The Euphrates became the eastern frontier of the Empire. With the creation of Greater Cappadocia, Rome henceforward possessed a solid line of defense stretching from the Black Sea to the Arabian desert, connected internally and with the rest of the Empire by a well-protected and well-constructed system of strategic routes, and manned by the six legions permanently posted there as well as numerous auxiliary units.

In 78, an inscription in honor of Vespasian accorded him the title of "restorer" and *conservator* – two fully justified epithets. The "emperor of good sense," who had wanted to die on his feet, was deified at the end of the spring of 80. When Titus died, he too was deified – in the month following his death. By contrast, the last Flavian, Domitian, received not an apotheosis but a *damnatio*.

DOMITIAN AND TYRANNY (AD 81–96)

At least one person was not upset by the death of Titus, and that was his brother and heir, Domitian. It was even claimed that he had poisoned him. What is certain is that Titus, though on his death-bed, had not actually given up the ghost before Domitian left him to go to the praetorians' camp, where he had himself hailed emperor and distributed a *donativum*. The next day, September

14, 81, the Senate conferred full imperial powers upon him. At the age of nearly 30, the new emperor had no time to lose. Since the accession of his father, and even more since that of his brother, he had been associated with honors but kept away from government. And he fully intended to rule.

His reign lasted fifteen years. On September 18, 96 he was stabbed to death. The conspiracy included his wife, Domitia, the two praetorian prefects, members of the palace, and a few senators. One of these senators, M. Cocceius Nerva, had been designated in advance as the new emperor. Domitian, once dead, and after his *damnatio memoriae* (the erasure of his name was one of the most systematically carried out), was presented as the "bald Nero" and "a particularly cruel wild beast." Against him then were ranged Pliny the Younger and Tacitus (both senators who had made their careers during his reign), Juvenal, and later Dio Cassius. In his lifetime he had at least had flatterers (Statius, Martial). In the end, the most balanced judgement lies with Suetonius. He emphasized his qualities as a ruler, his sense of duty, his attention to the conduct of his magistrates and provincial governors, and his innovations, as well as the decline in his character that led him from being a lenient and generous man to becoming increasingly cruel and grasping. Above all, he reveals the two centers of opposition to the emperor, intellectuals and senators, the two being frequently closely related.

Even at the start of his reign Domitian was the object of sneers and slanders. He did not possess an easy temperament, being vain and mistrustful, unwilling to suffer either comparisons with his brother or criticisms of an absolutism that became daily more obvious. By stages, he came to engage in a policy of repression that merely had the contrary effect of nurturing conspiracies, upon which it in turn fed, and eventually grew so that it justified everyone's fears. Three stages may be picked out. Between 81 and 89, the two sides watched each other – a fashionable literary opposition of malcontents, and conspiracies by political factions in 83 and 87, met with a brutal response from the emperor, but nothing irreparable occurred. Then, in 89, the legate of Upper Germania, L. Antonius Saturninus, rebelled, having himself proclaimed emperor and bringing with him two legions and some Germani. This usurpation was vigorously put down. Lastly, after a hesitant effort at rapprochement with the Senate, Domitian engaged in a trial of strength with it at the end of 93, leading to a bloody persecution of senators, the expulsion of philosophers from Rome and Italy, and proceedings against Jews and Christians. Even the imperial family was not spared. It was because she felt herself under threat that the empress encouraged the decisive plot. In all, there were perhaps fewer death sentences than has often been thought (probably about twenty, over half of which resulted from the application of the law of lese-majesty that had been revived) and only three years of tyranny. They, and they alone, captured the attention of second-century historians, at the expense of the view of him as an emperor who in other respects continued Flavian policies, but who showed himself an innovator as well.

THE EMPEROR OF CONTINUITY

In essence, the government of Domitian scarcely differed from that of his father and brother.

The institutional field

He amassed consulships (seventeen in all, ten of which were during his reign). In 85, he had himself granted censorial powers, altered to censorship in perpetuity the following year. He was acclaimed *imperator* twenty-two times, and he celebrated three triumphs. His "council of friends" was of high quality: in the main, he preserved his father's entourage, and for a long time adopted the same attitude as his predecessors toward the Senate.

Building activity

Besides restoring the areas of the Capitol and the Campus Martius that had been damaged or destroyed by the fire of 80, he followed up and completed the building works begun in the two preceding reigns: the Flavian amphitheater (the Colosseum, which he complemented with a school of gladiators, the *Ludus Magnus*), the baths of Titus, and the temple of the Divine Vespasian at the foot of the Capitol. Moreover, he developed further this Flavian policy of large-scale building works, undertaking, notably, the arch of Titus, the temple of the *gens Flavia* on the Quirinal, the Campus Martius stadium (the present-day Piazza Navona follows its shape), the Forum Transitorium (between the Forum of Augustus and the temple of Peace), which Nerva later inaugurated, and the Domus Flavia on the Palatine (see figure 10.1), an imperial palace occupying the entire central part of the hill and for the first time joining the private residence and official palace to create "the architectural representation of monarchic absolutism."

Administration of the provinces

"[Domitian] put so much zeal into suppressing the scheming and intrigues . . . of provincial governors that they were never again more impartial or just, whereas after him we have seen a great many of them accused of all kinds of crimes" (Suetonius, *Domitian* 8). We have, for example, epigraphic testimony to a former governor of Baetica, accused of embezzlement, being sentenced to pay damages to the wronged provincials. The application of this apparently unusual surveillance was perhaps one of the causes of the antagonism between the Senate and the emperor. Quite a number of other testimonies to Domitian's intervention in the life of the provinces have come down to us. Not

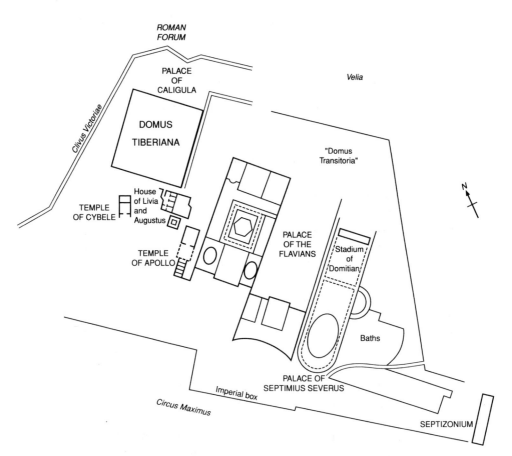

Figure 10.1 The imperial palaces

only did he actively pursue the renewal of land surveys and settle the difficult matter of the *subsiciva* to the satisfaction of the cities, but he also advanced many detailed measures to improve the well-being of the provincials, as well as measures that may have been intended to strike a balance in the production of certain crops at Empire level. An inscription from Pisidia, for example, reveals the measures taken by a governor to combat speculation and ensure the supply of cheap grain to the inhabitants; and the edicts on viticulture that have come down to us from this time, of perhaps AD 92, seem to have had the ultimate aim (though the matter is still debated) of reducing the number of vineyards in order both to increase grain production in Italy and the provinces, and to defend the income and value of lands belonging to the great owners. Lastly, inscriptional evidence also suggests that it was perhaps Domitian who was responsible for the creation of the post of city curator, officials of the central government appointed to help with the problems of provincial cities.

Frontier safety

In this domain also, continuity would have triumphed if new factors – the pressure of the Germani on the Rhine, risings by Decebalus and his Dacians – had not obliged Domitian to modify the family policy.

Britain   Agricola's thrust northwards continued. He occupied a large part of Scotland, built a legionary camp on the Tay (Inchtuthil), defeated the inhabitants of the Highlands at the Battle of Mount Graupius, and succeeded in taking his fleet round the north coast of Scotland. In 84, Agricola was recalled. The province was at peace, but Scotland remained outside the Empire.

The Germanies   A Germanic people, the Chatti, living in the region of the Taunus mountains, threatened and harassed the Roman settlements of the Rhine valley and Vetteravia (Wetterau). Domitian launched a powerful campaign against them, led in 83 by the emperor himself and completed by peace-making expeditions. This, and a second campaign in the region of Upper Germania, in 89, following the revolt of Saturninus, had five main results: the Chatti were repulsed and driven from the Rhine valley; Lower and Upper Germania were formally established as provinces; the territory controlled by Rome on the right bank of the Rhine, upstream from Mainz, was increased southward and eastward to form the Tithelands (*Agri Decumates*), which were attached to Upper Germania; the *limes* of Upper Germania was completed, with an almost continuous line of defense now set up from Koblenz to the neighborhood of Stuttgart; and the Rhine–Danube links were solidly secured.

Danube   In these regions the Julio-Claudians had made use more of diplomacy and the transfer of populations than of armed force. But the appearance on the scene of an organized Dacian nation, and of the Sarmatians, nomadic peoples from the borders of Europe and Asia, with their mixed populations, altered the geopolitical situation along the river. In 85, the Dacians crossed the Danube, invaded Moesia, and killed its governor. An initial Roman expedition (85–6) ended in a defeat in which a praetorian prefect died. Others followed (87–8); and an important victory (88) resulted in a compromise peace (89). Meanwhile, Moesia had been divided into two provinces, Upper Moesia (four legions) and Lower Moesia (two legions). The Dacian peace did not mean, however, that operations on the Danube were halted. From 89 to 92 they moved farther west, against the Quadi, the Marcomanni, and the Sarmatians. These difficult operations involved the Roman forces in fierce fighting, with on one occasion a whole legion being wiped out. And they had, moreover, no certain outcome. On the eve of his death, Domitian was arranging a third Pannonian expedition.

The East   There was little change here. Domitian strengthened the *limites* or defense systems, and a Roman expedition reached as far as the eastern end of the Caucasus, as a Latin inscription from the Baku region bears witness.

Not only had Domitian preserved what he had inherited, he had also consolidated it. And in at least three areas he had also made innovations.

The innovator

Absolutism

"Dictating a letter which his agents were to circulate, [Domitian] began in this manner: 'Our master and our god commands the following'" (Suetonius, *Domitian* 13). These two titles, *dominus et deus*, were not held officially; they publicly expressed the emperor's wish to be no longer merely the first citizen in the state but an absolute monarch, in almost eastern style. He avoided any display of familiarity with his subjects and wanted to give his person a sacred character, as is indicated, for example, by the layout of the imperial palace, his constant wearing of the triumphal purple, the qualities attributed to him by his poets (his eyes held a mysterious power, his hands were divine, etc.), the placing of his equestrian statue in the center of the Forum, the association of his image with those of the gods on the forecourt of the temple of Jupiter Capitolinus, and the institution at court of eastern rites (the kissing of feet, for example). A century later, such manifestations caused hardly any surprise, but at the time they offended the majority of senators.

Military policy

For the first time since Augustus, the pay of the praetorians, legionaries, and auxiliaries was increased by a considerable amount (about a third). The legions and praetorians were consequently favorable to him, and after his death the troops wanted to avenge him.

Administrative policy

With Domitian, the policy began of replacing freedmen in the central administration with knights. Thus, the management of the bureaux *ab epistulis* and *a patrimonio*, the latter a bureau controlling the tax of 5 per cent on inheritances, was transferred to the knights. Furthermore, under Domitian senior officials found themselves provided with an assistant of equestrian rank, who would at the same time keep an eye on them.

A Developing Municipal Life and
a Changing Society

The supplanting of a dynasty of Roman aristocrats by a family of Italian municipal notables was in itself a social revolution, a sign of the politico-social transformations that the Augustan "Roman revolution" had brought in its wake.
The Flavian era, besides, witnessed the confirmation in the Empire as a whole
of a model way of life, that of the city, while society in general went through
the beginnings of a very profound change.

Municipal life

Among the things separating barbarians from civilized men was the city. Living
in clans and tribes, barbarians had no knowledge of it. Of course, they were
aware of common customs and of gods, but they possessed neither limited and
demarcated territories nor stable institutions generally connected with an urban
center. Now, although this knowledge of a municipal life was but one of the
marks of a civilized man, to live in a city was in itself a prize worth seeking. It
was more than just a stage in the eventual advance to a superior type of civilization; it was also a point of arrival, the outcome of a conversion to another
way of living. Hence the teaching about the city that is to be found constantly
at work in the West, urging the provincial to follow the Roman example, to
adopt a Roman system of values: "In fact, in the West, identity was not defined
against Rome but in Rome" (F. Jacques). Although the situation varied from
one province to another, and sometimes from one region within a province to
another, in this matter of the city and city life the distinction between East and
West kept all its weight. Fundamentally, with the exception of a few cities (and
by no means the lesser ones) of Greek or Punic origin, municipal life in the
West began with Rome, whereas in the East, with a few exceptions, it had pre-
existed the arrival of Rome and was therefore rich in tradition, and more intense
and more varied than in the West. Here we have space to draw only a general
picture of municipal life in the Empire – all the more so since the connected
topics of urbanization and Romanization must be included. But it should be
borne in mind that the life of each city was a singular phenomenon and that,
in many respects, the Empire remained a patchwork of particular and multi-
form cities, not all of which are even known.

The status of the cities

Leaving aside those peoples and populations judged by the Romans to be incapable of self-government and of living in a city, and with the exception again
of Egypt, the inhabitants of the Empire lived in communities or areas belong-

ing to one of three juridically defined and denominated types of "cities": pere-grine cities, *municipia*, and colonies.

Peregrine ("foreign") cities These were communities and their territories as they had existed at the end of independence, or as they had been remodeled by the Romans after conquest but without their having been therein granted either Roman or Latin rights. These cities preserved their own laws, and their inhabitants remained *peregrini*, although groups of Roman citizens could, of course, live there. At the start of the Empire, they represented the majority of provincial cities and were divided into three categories according to their status *vis-à-vis* Rome. These differences were to last a long time despite a development toward uniformity:

- *Stipendiary cities* These were the most numerous. They were subject to Rome and paid a tribute (*stipendium*). In theory, the provincial governor had legal control over all their affairs.
- *Free cities* These were theoretically autonomous and juridically outside the provinces. Actually, their rights were conceded by a unilateral act of Rome. Some, though it became increasingly an exception, were exempt from paying tribute.
- *Federated free cities* These were that minority of free cities which signed a treaty with Rome putting them on an equal footing with it.

The municipia A *municipium* was a city that superseded a pre-existing community of *peregrini* (and might even retain some of its institutions) through a grant by Rome to that community of either Roman or Latin rights. The distinction between these two classes of provincial *municipia*, Roman and Latin, resulted from the historical conditions under which the rights had been granted. At first, as at the time of the organization of Italy after its conquest, Rome had granted Roman rights to *municipia* situated in the provinces. Thus Italica, in Baetica, founded in 206 BC and peopled by ex-soldiers, became under Caesar a *municipium* with Roman rights. The last known *municipium* of Roman citizens was Volubilis, which was awarded that rank by Claudius in AD 47. Starting with Claudius then (or perhaps Vespasian), there were no further creations of *municipia* with Roman rights (although the early ones did not disappear), and the provincial communities that newly became *municipia* were all initially granted Latin rights. In these *municipia* with Latin rights, municipal office gave access to Roman citizenship. Thus, from the Roman viewpoint, there were two sorts of inhabitants of *municipia* with Latin rights, those who, over and above citizenship of their own little city, managed to become full-blown Roman citizens because of the office they had held, or individually through the emperor's generosity, and those who, while remaining *peregrini*, benefited from the advantages of Latin rights (not all aspects of which are known).

The colonies   Unlike the creation of a *municipium*, the founding of a colony was the creation of a new town, with the introduction of colonists (*deductio*) into lands seized from conquered cities or peoples. It was most frequently created *ex nihilo*; but if not, then it was religiously and legally severed from the earlier settlement. The colony adopted full Roman rights; and if it also received the privilege of Italic rights (*ius Italicum*), it was thereby put in the same category as Italian soil, and was thus exempt from land tax. In southern Gaul (Nîmes), however, there still existed a particular type of colony with Latin rights, where, as in Latin *municipia*, the majority of inhabitants were *peregrini*.

In this way a hierarchy was established and there was emulation between cities. The peregrine cities aspired to become *municipia* with Latin rights, and the *municipia* with Latin rights aspired to obtain Roman rights. They also increasingly asked for the title of honorary colony, that is, a colony that had not been founded, and without a settlement of colonists. It was probably under Vespasian that Bordeaux passed from the status of stipendiary peregrine city to that of Latin *municipium*. And it was Vespasian who changed the status of Leptis Magna (ca. 73–4) from free peregrine city to Latin *municipium*. Moreover, by granting Latin rights to all the communities of Spain at the beginning of the seventies, Vespasian may have forged the link between *municipium* and Latin rights. Employing stereotyped municipal constitutions which each city personalized, native Spanish cities were allowed to claim the status of Latin *municipium*, as we are informed by a series of laws (laws of Salpensa, Malaca, Irni) discovered in Baetica. However, we do not know whether there was an automatic connection between the granting of Latin rights and the move to a form of municipal organization.

The cities were also sometimes subdivided into districts of various kinds, each with a fairly broad autonomy, such as the *pagi*, *vici*, *castella*, and *oppida* in the West, the names of such subdivisions varying according to the province. Moreover, stable judiciary districts wider than the city sometimes existed, like the *conventus*, which grouped several cities together and which, under the Flavians, were extended to cover the whole of the Iberian peninsula.

Municipal institutions

Generally speaking, there was no intermediate administrative level between city and province. For the majority of the Empire's inhabitants, the city was the backbone of political life (and of life generally). Not only did these basic cells look after local administration, levying the greater part of the taxes that were

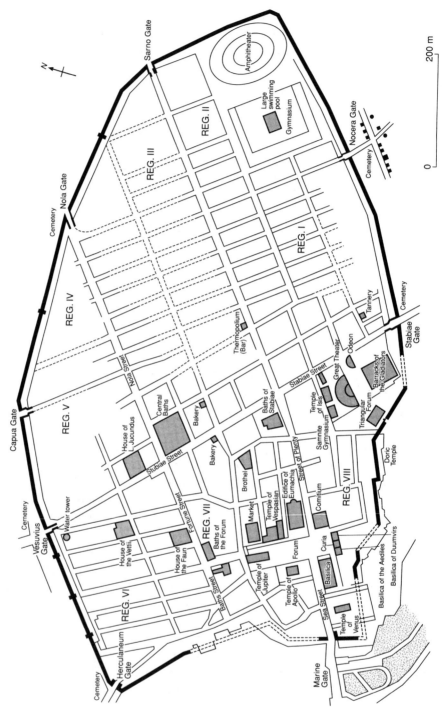

Figure 10.2 Plan of Pompeii

then passed on to the provincial collector, attending to the building and upkeep of roads, etc., they also took care of justice at lower court level. Their institutional machinery, and the men who ensured that it functioned well, gave municipal autonomy its vitality and efficiency.

What those institutions were, depended on the status of the city. Peregrine cities kept their native magistracies and particular laws. Thus, Athens maintained its institutions, its archons, its calendar, and its festivals; only the military magistracies disappeared or were altered – the hoplites' *strategos* now had the task of supervising grain supplies. Elsewhere there was the same conservatism: Punic *suffetes* and Celtic *vergobrets* survived, either under their own titles or Latinized into praetors or *magistri*. Nevertheless, the indigenous cities, and more especially those of the West, which were less ancient and less resistant, seemed to be drawn to the model of the *municipium* or the colony.

The institutions of the *municipia* and colonies were modeled on those of Rome. The civic body (*populus*) was defined as a *respublica*. Divided into *curiae*, which assembled in *comitia*, it elected the city magistrates according to the most detailed procedures (law of Malaca). In order to be a candidate, a man had to be free and a local citizen, possess a property qualification, which varied according to the wealth of the city, and be at least 25 years old. Furthermore, for certain posts, financial pledges were required, since there was a personal responsibility in management. The whole range of municipal offices, each tenable for one year, and all unpaid, formed a municipal *cursus honorum* of, usually, three stages, each of two posts: first, those of the two quaestors, who looked after financial matters; secondly, those of the two aediles, who regulated and controlled food supplies, the markets, buildings, roads, etc.; and, lastly, those of the *duumviri*, the two supreme magistrates, who were in charge of justice and responsible for conducting a census of the population every five years.

To assist these magistrates, there was a local senate, the size of which varied in relation to the importance of the city. Its members, the decurions, were recruited from the former magistrates and wealthy local worthies, and though formally making up an advisory body, were in reality in charge of all the municipal departments. It was the decurions who decided, by decree, whether an embassy was to be sent, a statue erected, a bridge built, an entertainment organized, a public building demolished, etc. And they were the ones who elected the city priest in charge of the imperial cult. They were also collectively responsible for the gathering of the imperial taxes, and in the event of any shortfall on the part of their fellow citizens, they had personally to make up the amount that was lacking. Frequently interconnected by marriage, these local notables, who were certainly rich but whose qualities were not based on wealth alone, formed a pool from which the emperors could draw new members of the equestrian order.

SOCIAL CHANGES

The most profound of the social changes witnessed by the Flavian era, eclipsing in importance the decline with the passing of the Julio-Claudians of the senatorial aristocracy, with its love of luxury, noisy exuberance, and crazy pretentiousness, the almost total disappearance of the ancient families of the republican era, the slow but continuous rise of the knights, and the lowering of the influence of the freedmen, was the rise of the provincials, who, under the Flavians, came for the first time into the limelight, which had come to be dominated by the Italians, who had now indeed even taken their place at the very head of the Empire. The emergence of the provincials came about at this time for three reasons. In the first place, the return of peace and the stability of the new administration allowed the provinces to acquire an economic and cultural dynamism superior to that of a weary Italy, which had known its political peak at the very time when it lost its pre-eminent economic position. Secondly, the effects of the accelerated Romanization that had taken place under the Empire in the western provinces, which for historical and political reasons had been favored since Actium, now made themselves felt – so much so, that the West, at the end of the first century AD, was prevailing over the East. Lastly, Flavian policy conduced to their rise. The granting of Latin rights to the provinces of Hispania, more frequent recourse to the *adlectio*, a policy of winning over the Gauls, the setting up of urban centers in Germania and in Africa (where a town, Hippo Regius (Annaba) received the title of honorary colony), and the granting of favors of every kind in the East, all allowed the other advantages accruing to the provincials, basically either descendants of Italian immigrants or prominent natives, to be used by them to their great advancement. Here are a few examples taken from different fields of the rise of the provincials and the provinces during the Flavian era:

The political field   The proportion of provincials in the Senate increased notably until, under Domitian, it reached almost a third of the assembly. Of these known provincials, most originated from the Iberian peninsula or southern Gaul, although over a third were eastern in origin. Again, out of 259 senators and knights from Gaul (including Narbonensis) during the period between the end of the Republic and the end of the second century, 55 came between the end of the Republic and the death of Nero, 75 between the death of Nero and the end of the reign of Domitian, and 81 in the whole of the second century.

The military field   Here, the same phenomenon is evident, but is even more marked. From the time of Vespasian, although not because of any action by the government, not many of the rank and file legionary soldiers were from Italy. The number of non-Italians correspondingly forged ahead. In the western part of the Empire, they came from the richest and most Romanized senatorial provinces, southern Gaul, Baetica, Africa, and Macedonia, and even from the imperial provinces where regional recruitment was beginning to develop; in the eastern part, recruitment was mostly regional. Only the praetorian and urban cohorts continued to be composed principally of Italians.

The economic field   The decline of Italy from its position of eco nomic pre-emi-nence, revealed by the abandonment of Pompeii, Herculaneum, and Stabiae, three towns destroyed by the eruption of Vesuvius on August 24, 79, but nevertheless lying in the rich region of Campania, seems accentuated because of the dynamism of the provinces, chiefly those in the west. In this respect, the case of the wine trade between southern Gaul and Italy tells a story. The first evidence of Gaulish wine imported into Italy is datable to the first half of the first century AD. Before that time, the flow of trade must have been largely from Italy to Gaul. Then the boom in vineyards in the south of Gaul, and the appear-ance in Narbonensis of a few workshops producing amphorae, reduced imports of Italian and Spanish wine into Gaul, in the first place late in Augustus' reign. And, later, the trade circuit was reversed. Whereas no Gaulish amphorae were found in the Claudian level of the deposit of the Castro Pretorio at Ostia, they formed 40 per cent of the wine amphorae of the Flavian level (against less than 30 per cent from Italy and less than 15 per cent from Spain).

The religious field   In this area, the emergence of the provinces is less evident. It is clearest in the success in Rome of cults from the East. Rome's adoption of foreign cults is not, it is true, peculiar to the Flavian period. Nevertheless, under the Flavians the thrust of eastern cults was marked. First, the Flavian emperors were not unmindful of what they owed to the gods of the Nile – in the Domus Flavia on the Palatine, for example, a chapel of Egyptian worship housed the imperial devotions. Also, under the Flavians the first dedications to Mithras appeared in Rome, and Statius makes the first reference in Latin litera-ture to bull sacrifice. Lastly, there were converts to Judaism (or, less probably, Christianity) within the imperial family, exposed and persecuted by Domitian in 95.

The intellectual field   Though the provinces of Spain were best represented, with Columella, Quintilian, and Martial, also important were Greece with Plutarch, Phrygia with Epictetus, and southern Gaul with Tacitus (his first work is dated to 98).

What the provincials still lacked, supreme power, they would gain in the next century, with the same twist that we have seen for the Italians, with the decline of economic power preceding political dominance.

For a long time, the Flavian dynasty were appended to the Julio-Claudians, or seen as their essential but less-interesting complement. Moreover, hemmed in between a flamboyant Nero and an all-conquering Trajan, and handicapped by the rather dull common sense that has been attributed to the first of them, they did not stimulate much research. That period seems to be over, and it is realized that the dynasty played a decisive part in the history of the Empire: "I am inclined to think," says R. Syme, "that the epoch of the Antonines began with Vespasian."

11 / THE ANTONINE EMPIRE, AD 96–192

*I*N THE EYES OF ITS CONTEMPORARIES, IT WAS A GOLDEN AGE, HAILED AS SUCH BY
SEVERAL ISSUES OF COINAGE. NEVER HAD THE ANCIENT WORLD KNOWN ITS LIKE.
"THE UNIVERSE HAS BECOME A SINGLE CITY," EXCLAIMED AELIUS ARISTIDES, A
GREEK-SPEAKING RHETOR WRITING AROUND THE MIDDLE OF THE SECOND CENTURY.
HE ADDED, *"THE WHOLE WORLD IS IN FESTIVE MOOD. IT HAS ABANDONED ITS
WEAPONS OF WAR TO GIVE ITSELF UP TO THE JOY OF LIVING."* HIS EULOGY OF ROME,
WHICH GOES BEYOND MERE SYCOPHANCY, SINGS THE PRAISES OF THIS COHERENT
EMPIRE WITH ITS PERFECT ADMINISTRATION, WHICH, LIKE A FRESHLY POLISHED
WINEGLASS, EMITS A SINGLE NOTE, AND WHICH UNANIMOUSLY OBEYS THE *"SUPREME
GOVERNOR, PROVIDER OF ALL THINGS."* APPIAN, HIS CONTEMPORARY, A GREEK FROM
ALEXANDRIA, REFLECTING ON THE CONSEQUENCES OF THE ROMAN POLICY OF
CONQUEST, AFFIRMS THAT *"THE CAPITAL WAS RENDERED FAR MORE BEAUTIFUL,
INCOMES WERE CONSIDERABLY INCREASED, AND A SURE AND LASTING PEACE
INSTITUTED TO CREATE PERMANENT HAPPINESS."* SOME YEARS LATER, AN EMPEROR
WHO WANTED TO PROVE HIMSELF THE EMPEROR OF PEACE, MARCUS AURELIUS,
BECAME THE EMPEROR OF WAR, THE ONE WHO, IN HIS OWN WORDS, HUNTED THE
SARMATIANS AS A SPIDER HUNTS FLIES. THE SUBJECT OF WAR HAD DISAPPEARED FROM
ARTISTIC PRODUCTION FOR HALF A CENTURY, NOW IT BECAME TOPICAL AGAIN. BUT
WHAT DIFFERENCES ARE TO BE SEEN ON TWO MONUMENTS OF THE SAME KIND BUT
SEPARATED BY THIS PERIOD, THE COLUMNS OF TRAJAN AND MARCUS AURELIUS!
*"TRAJAN'S COLUMN GLORIFIES AN OFFENSIVE BATTLE, WHILE THAT OF MARCUS
AURELIUS REPRESENTS A DEFENSIVE BATTLE"* (B. ANDREAE). THE EMPIRE DESIRED
PEACE; WAR WAS FORCED UPON IT.

"ITALO-PROVINCIAL" EMPERORS

It is usual to consider the dynasty of the Antonines (a term formed retrospectively using the name of the fourth emperor) *en bloc*, with a prologue (Nerva), four acts (Trajan, Hadrian, Antoninus, Marcus Aurelius), and an epilogue (Commodus). But within it, a "Spanish" dynasty (the first three) may be distinguished from the Narbonensian dynasty that follows. At all events, the actions of all the men, except perhaps those of Trajan and (even more) Hadrian,

Plate 11.1 Detail of Trajan's Column, Rome, showing the building of a fort. The column was erected in AD 113.

give the impression of being of less account than the silent movements that ran through the century, whether they were signs of prosperity or causes of trouble.

NERVA (96–98)

Even before Domitian's assassination, Nerva had been designated to succeed him. There was no power vacuum: on the eve of the murder the Senate confirmed the conspirators' choice. It was a choice without risk; Nerva was reassuring. He was rich without ostentation, had reached the age of 70 but seemed in good health, was the descendant of an old family of the republican nobility but had no children and little ambition. A prudent career had allowed him to win the respect of a succession of emperors and the esteem of the Senate. Skillfully and firmly, he contained the anti-Domitian reaction and restrained the grumblings of the praetorians, defusing *coups*, quelling, possibly, a military uprising in Upper Germania, and forming amicable relations with the Senate. And he came up with some bright ideas in agrarian and fiscal areas which his successor continued. He also, according to Tacitus, united two incompatible things, the Principate and liberty. And an inscription indeed proclaimed that he

Plate 11.2 A food shop at Ostia, ca. 2nd century AD.

had restored liberty on September 18, that is to say, the day of his accession. In the following year, the fragility of this position was exposed when a mutiny by the praetorians humiliated the emperor in his palace, revealing both a weakness (the succession) and a threat (the attitude of the army). Nerva escaped from both by a clever stroke: on October 28, 97, after a ceremony at the Capitol, he announced that he was adopting the legate of Upper Germania, M. Ulpius Traianus (Trajan). The Senate immediately conferred the title of *Caesar* on Trajan *in absentia*, and awarded him tribunician power, the proconsular *imperium*, and the *cognomen* of *Augustus*. Heir designate (but did he know?), Trajan thus found himself in association with the Empire. At Nerva's request he remained on the Rhine. Three months later Nerva died (January 27, 98), and the news of his death was soon after announced to Trajan in Cologne by P. Aelius Hadrianus (Hadrian), Trajan's great-nephew. Nerva had been a sensible, clear-sighted, and realistic interim emperor. Through force of circumstance, he had (unlike the Flavians) chosen his successor by adoption, and had chosen not a relation (though he had some) but a man selected on merit and for his capabilities, thus creating a precedent that could perhaps shield the Empire's destiny from the quirks of fate, if only it were followed. For some, this edifying story of adoption is suspect, and the choice of Trajan supposed instead to have been imposed by a group of soldiers and Spaniards. But even if that were so, it was a clever appointment. Trajan had the military prestige to bring the praetorians to heel, and enough connections to obtain the backing of the different armies. As he was a provincial, the provinces and world of the *municipia* could support him. The son of a senator, and a traditionalist by nature, he would not clash with the Senate. What is more, he was popular. Unanimity was plain concerning the new emperor.

Trajan (98–117)

Before his accession

Trajan was born in around 53 at Italica, in Baetica, to a family of colonists who had reached indisputable notability in this, the oldest Roman foundation on the Iberian peninsula. His father had had a brilliant career, crowned by the proconsulship of Asia in 79–80. Trajan was therefore not a "Spaniard," a native of Spain. Nevertheless, for the first time a man from the provinces was emperor. His career, which developed entirely under the Flavians, was marked by a predilection for military posts, thus, for example, he remained a legionary tribune for 10 years instead of the customary one year; and throughout his *cursus*, he showed his unfailing loyalty to the ruling emperor (in 89, he fought Saturninus' rebellion), winning at the same time a justified reputation as an army leader.

The man

Camp life had left its marks on Trajan. Nevertheless, he was not the drunken ruffian he has sometimes been made out to be, as one may conclude from the quality of those close to him (Dio of Prusa, Pliny the Younger, Frontinus, Neratius Priscus, the great jurist, whom he had in mind to succeed him, Licinius Sura, a clever politician and discerning man of letters, Apollodorus of Damascus, his architect). He was not indeed a refined intellectual – but then he never pretended to be one. He was a soldier and administrator, and his tastes inclined to simplicity. The replies he gave Pliny bore the stamp of common sense, efficiency, and respect for law and justice. A man of experience and good will, he led a simple life removed from all magnificent show, was affable in his manner, and made rapid and clear-sighted decisions. He also knew the value of the gesture that strikes the imagination and consolidates popularity, such as his solemn entry into Rome, made on foot, without protection, amid a jubilant crowd (and he reached the imperial palace in the same way), and his swimming of the Euphrates, when over the age of 60. Deferential to the senators and magistrates and courteous to those under his administration, he nevertheless agreed,

PRINCIPAL EVENTS OF TRAJAN'S REIGN

Date	Internal politics	External politics	Civilization
99	Trajan's arrival in Rome (between spring and autumn). Distribution of a *congiarium* to the people.	*En route* for Rome, he consolidates the frontiers of the Rhine and Upper Danube.	
100	Trajan's third consulship. Trials of provincial governors.		Foundation of Timgad. Pliny the Younger: *Panegyric of Trajan*.
101	Trajan's fourth consulship. Extension of the *alimenta* (tables of Veleia, and Beneventum) (around 101).	First Dacian War.	
102	Triumph of Trajan: surname of *Dacicus*, second *congiarium*.	End of the First Dacian War.	Commencement of the laying-out of the port of Ostia.
103	Trajan's fifth consulship. Division of Pannonia into Upper and Lower Pannonia (between 103 and 106).		
105		Second Dacian War.	Bridge over the Danube at Dobreta (Turnu Severin).
106		Capture of Sarmizegethusa, suicide of Decebalus, capture of 50,000 Dacians, vast booty (Dacian gold). Annexation of Arabia, which becomes a province (roughly present-day Jordan).	Bridge of Alcantara. Construction of a road between Damascus and Eilat. Roman fleet in the Red Sea.
107	(before 107) Law obliging senators to invest one third of their wealth in Italy. 123 days of festival and games to celebrate the second Dacian triumph. Third *congiarium*.	Dacia, Roman province. Indian embassy to Rome.	Beginning of major public works in Rome. *Via Traiana* Beneventum–Brindisi. Trophy of Adamklissi. Trajan's Baths: Aqua Traiana. Tacitus, *Histories*.

Continued on p. 272

Date	Internal politics	External politics	Civilization
ca.110		Break with the Parthians over succession to the throne of Armenia.	
111			Pliny legate in Bithynia.
112	Trajan's sixth consulship. His father and sister are deified.		Pliny's letter on the Christians to Trajan. Dedication of the Forum of Trajan. The ancient Red Sea–Nile canal is restored.
113			Dedication of Trajan's Column.
114	Thrace becomes a praetorian province for strategic reasons. Title of *Optimus* for Trajan.	Start of war with the Parthians. Invasion of Armenia, which, annexed to Armenia Minor and Cappadocia, becomes a Roman province. Campaign in northern Mesopotamia, capture of Nisibis.	Dedication of the Arch of Beneventum.
115	Jewish rebellion in Cyrenaica, Egypt, Judaea, and Mesopotamia.	Temporary occupation of Dura-Europus on the Euphrates.	
116	Trajan receives the title *Parthicus Maximus*, which he retains even after his death.	Invasion of Adiabene, a district of Babylonia across the Euphrates. Capture of Seleuceia, Ctesiphon, and Babylon; Trajan reaches the Persian Gulf. He contemplates a province of Assyria and one of Mesopotamia.	
117	End of the Jewish revolt. Hadrian, governor of Syria. Trajan dies at Selinus *en route* for Rome, on 9 August. His ashes, carried to Rome, laid in the base of Trajan's Column.	Parthian counter-offensive. Victory of Trajan, who has to give up the idea of a Roman settlement in Assyria and Lower Mesopotamia.	Tacitus, *Annals*.

Table 11.1 Trajan and Hadrian

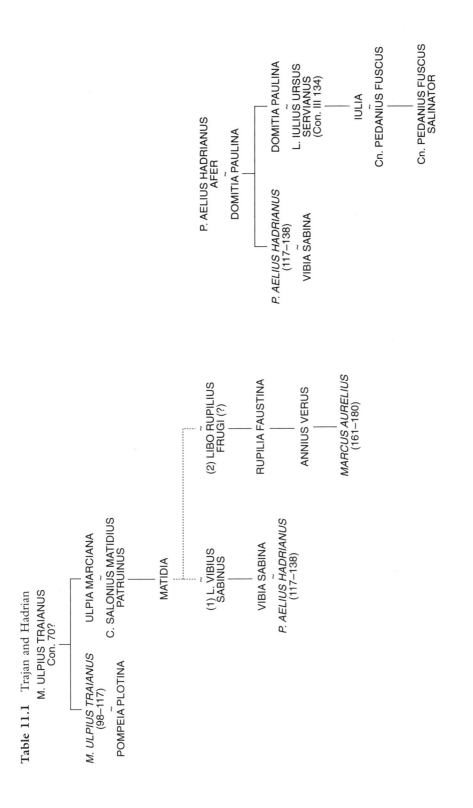

in 114, to be known as *Optimus* (the Best), a title he shared with Jupiter. For despite his off-hand ways, Trajan had a very lofty conception of his office and its duties and did not yield one iota of his powers. Lastly, if the accounts of his feats and exploits during the campaign against the Parthians in 116–17 are to be believed, he also possessed more than a touch of that imaginative, "Alexander-like" military daring that was almost obligatory for any great captain worthy of the name.

The causes of his conquests

The three cases (Dacia, Arabia, and Mesopotamia) were different.

■ The causes of the Dacian wars are obscure. The Dacian danger had existed since Domitian. Possibly Decebalus tried to create an anti-Roman coalition. The alliances he concluded with other barbarian peoples, and perhaps with the Parthians, would lead one to suppose so. Certainly, it does not appear that Trajan, who "did not fear war but did not seek it" (Pliny the Younger), at first thought of altering the Danubian frontier and collecting as his prize the gold mines of Dacia. Fear of the barbarians, a feeling of insecurity, and perhaps a desire for military glory seem to have been the motives for the initial Dacian expedition.

■ The kingdom of the Nabataeans threatened the sole direct land link between Egypt and Judaea, by way of Gaza. Moreover, it imposed a tax on Roman traders on their way to the Red Sea. Here, then, the motive was strategic (to do away with the need to rely on the Gaza corridor), but chiefly economic and political.

■ Three kinds of explanation have been put forward for the Parthian wars. For the ancients, it was a matter of Trajan's personal ambition, his desire to equal the exploits of Alexander and take up on his own account the dreams of Caesar and Mark Antony. Strategic considerations have also been thought to be not insignificant: the putting to rights of the frontiers, and the creation of a protective glacis beyond the Euphrates to give better protection to Syria. Lastly, economic reasons have been suggested, to do with controlling eastern trade routes and large-scale commerce with the Far East.

The exercise of power

"Here is something that I hear for the first time, that I learn for the first time, that the emperor is not above the law, but that the law is above the emperor," Pliny the Younger declared in his *Panegyric*. It is from the time of Trajan and his government that modern historians begin to speak of a liberal Empire, guided by a sort of official Stoicism. One may wonder, however, whether these historians may not have fallen into the verbal trap of arguing in nineteenth-century terms, such as "liberal," about a period in which those terms have little

Plate 11.3 Nabathaean rock-hewn temple, 40 meters high, at Petra, modern El Deir (The Monastery), Jordan. 1st century AD.

or no real application, and also whether they may not have overlooked the truth that the second-century emperors (including Trajan) in fact possessed more power than a first-century emperor, but also, because of the very success of the regime set up by Augustus and the acquired custom of "having only one master to serve," met with less opposition, so that, in comparison with the past, the representations of power could more afford to lay claims to its limitedness and subordination to higher principles, even though its substance had not lessened at all – quite the reverse. We may judge the exercise of this power in four areas.

Ideology The *Panegyric of Trajan*, a speech of thanks delivered by Pliny the Younger, and the *Discourses on Royalty* by Dio of Prusa (later known as Chrysostomos, "Golden Mouth"), set out, in fairly similar terms, the major features of the ideal ruler. This ideal emperor-king is chosen by divine providence and acts in harmony with the supreme god. He governs, in Pliny's view of the emperor, in accordance with the political "platform" proposed by the senatorial party, and his life is devoted to the work of fulfilling the duties of his office. Father and benefactor to his subjects, he leads free men and not slaves. And his friends as well as the nobility must participate in the administration of the state.

This formulation of general (and also Stoic) standards may reflect a victory of the cultivated classes in the Empire, for whom the accomplished *homo Romanus* had become the inhabitant of the *orbis Romanus*. And in many aspects, the exercise of power by the soldier-king embodied by Trajan matches this model. His virtues in the exercise of political power and his successes in military command bear witness to "the victorious *numen* that shone within him and was the basis of his authority over the earth" (J. Beaujeu). Echoing Pliny and Dio, the more original, "Jovian" theory of the government instituted by Trajan goes a step further. Inspired by the example of Domitian, but nevertheless setting aside all idea of deifying the emperor, it claims that, with Trajan, the emperor becomes the agent of "Jupiter on earth, vested with his power and charged with governing all men in his name, now that the Empire is tending to envelop all the inhabited world: he is the earthly viceroy of the sovereign of the universe" (*idem*). On the attic of the Arch of Beneventum, on the town side, Jupiter welcomes Trajan, to whom he proffers his thunderbolt.

Relations with the Senate   Trajan showed real consideration toward the Senate, expressed by many attentions on his part (in his presence at sittings, in his choice of consuls, in his allowing the genuine election of magistrates by the Senate, etc.). But he placed great emphasis on provincial entries into the assembly, so that under him about 45 per cent of the senators were provincials. And his considerateness led to no renunciation of even the least of his powers: his censorial powers were tacitly acknowledged, and in exceptional circumstances he interfered in senatorial provinces (e.g. by sending Pliny to Bithynia-Pontus).

Administration   The prominence given to the emperor's friends and to his council, which was still informal, was one of the main features of Trajan's administration. Among his "friends" were several groups: the "marshals," the Spaniards, the intellectuals, and the technicians. They had in common, not only an ability in administrative matters, but also a loyalty to Trajan that brought some of them to their death at the start of the following reign. Secondly, the development of the administrative machinery, to the benefit of the knights, whose *cursus* was fully established, continued under Trajan. Thus, the number of known equestrian procurators went up from 64 under Domitian to 84 under Trajan. And except for the bureau *a libellis et censibus*, the great central offices were now all run by knights.

Finances   The tense financial situation that had marked Domitian's reign continued, despite the contribution of the booty from the Dacian wars and the gold mines of that country. At the start of Trajan's reign, outstanding debts to the state and the coronation gold exacted from the provinces on the accession of a new emperor could be remitted, to popular acclaim. But construction work, a larger administration, military expeditions, and soldiers were very expensive.

Plate 11.4 Roman brick architecture at Trajan's markets in Rome, constructed ca. AD
100–12.

All in all, there were few novelties in the field of financial administration. The
changes that occurred were more in the nature of developments, alterations,
and rearrangements, though there were a few innovations (a tax of 5 per cent
on inheritances by officials, the end of farming the *portorium* (customs), now
entrusted to *conductores*, who retained either a percentage or a fixed sum).

Trajan's reign left a dazzling memory. To emperors of late antiquity, the wish
was expressed that they should be "more fortunate than Augustus and better
than Trajan." This renown rested not only on his last great conquests and the
monuments and embellishments of the capital and the Empire, but also on the
change in the style of government to one more in sympathy with the spirit of
the times. But, by a very revealing paradox, Trajan, who prepared his campaigns
so meticulously and ran his administration with such precision, neglected to
settle the succession. That was done for him.

HADRIAN (117–138)

The accession

On August 8, 117, did Trajan on his deathbed in Selinus in Cilicia designate Hadrian his successor, as the official version would have us believe? The early authors doubted it. And it is true that the circumstances are confused. The letter announcing the adoption to the Senate was signed by Plotina, Trajan's wife; on August 9, at Antioch, Hadrian learned of his adoption, and on the 11th it was announced that Trajan had died. The army immediately acclaimed Hadrian emperor, and he wrote to the Senate assuring it of his respect and asking it to confirm the imperial titles. This was done. So what actually happened? Was there some help from Plotina and the praetorian prefect, who was known to support Hadrian? Did it come to him for reasons of state? Was it awarded to him for family reasons (he was Trajan's only male relation, his great-nephew and ward, and the husband of his great-niece)? A recognition of the *de facto* power that Trajan had given him by entrusting Syria to him, a key position in the opinion of the dead emperor? The result of a life spent at Trajan's side – he had been his *comes* (companion) during the First Dacian War? Besides, was it not well known that Trajan had given him a ring which he himself had received from Nerva? None of these arguments taken in isolation is convincing. But taken as a whole they may settle doubt concerning Trajan's intentions. All the more so because the career of the new emperor seems to have been encouraged throughout by his great-uncle.

His career before his accession

Like Trajan, Hadrian belonged to a family of Italians who had emigrated to Spain. His date of birth is certain: January 24, 76, but not his place of birth: perhaps Italica but more probably Rome. His career was that of a senator, with numerous honorific posts. In 108, he was *consul suffectus* at the age of 32 – not the usual age, but not exceptional for one so close to the emperor. And in 111 or 112, he was elected archon in Athens, a rare honor. The most remarkable feature of his *cursus* was his almost continuous proximity to Trajan. He was hardly ever away from the center of power. He followed Trajan to Germania, was imperial quaestor while the emperor was in Rome, accompanied him to Dacia, and then to the East. And like the emperor's councilors, though they were older and had more experience, he was one of the senior administrative staff.

The man

Hadrian's personality (popularized in a novel, *The Memoirs of Hadrian* by M. Yourcenar) divides historians. For some he was an inquisitive, unstable "intellectual," rebelling against authority and tradition, practicing several forms of art, but rather as a dabbler, an admirer of the beauties of nature, but as a man vain, cruel, and obstinate. In contrast with this extreme view (that of R. Syme), the numerous other judgements range from an almost unconditional admiration to the adoption of an ancient author's definition, according to which Hadrian was *varius, multiplex, multiformis*. And it is true that it is difficult to encapsulate his personality in a single definition. A good example of a work of his that may be seen as an expression of his personality but which is (therefore) difficult to interpret is his palace at Tivoli near Rome, which he had built in two stages (118–25 and 125–33) and which comprised a dozen or so great complexes numbering about thirty buildings. Interpretations of this differ widely, but roughly speaking, they fall into three categories: the collections of a dilettante and souvenirs of a traveler; a sort of résumé of the Empire over which Hadrian reigned; or a setting for and instrument of imperial deification. Nevertheless, this example included, there are details enough in the evidence, and in the various interpretations that it has been subject to, to allow a closer view of the man, whose personality astounded even his contemporaries, though they did not greatly appreciate him. In his favor were his superior intelligence, a variety of gifts, his unfailing physical vigor, a vast if slightly pedantic culture, a good knowledge of the provinces, and a solid grounding in the arts of war (witness his speeches from the Lambaesis inscriptions). His tastes were for a simple life, which by no means ruled out refinement in certain areas. He had a liking for taking part in debates with professionals, and immersed himself in intellectual disciplines (geometry, music, architecture, etc.). He relished the hunt, and indeed for him hunting assumed a symbolic value, it was the manifestation of the imperial *virtus*. His enjoyment of traveling led him to travel almost as a tourist (climbing to the summit of Etna, making a detour in order to visit a monument); and he admired Greece to the point of being nicknamed *Graeculus* by the Romans. Moreover, he seems to have been possessed by a real spiritual concern. It took several forms. Besides the usual interest in astrology and respect for traditional religion, he showed great enthusiasm for Greek cults (in particular that of Demeter at Eleusis, and Asclepius at Pergamum), as well as an infatuation with Egyptian cults that led him to bring to birth a new cult, that of Antinous, a young slave in the emperor's service who, having been drowned in the Nile, came, with the encouragement of Hadrian, to be worshiped as a god. The emperor's failings were on a par with his qualities. He was authoritarian, egoistic, vain, touchy, devious, and jealous of his power, and had alternating fits of hard work and dilettantism.

The exercise of power

A more marked authoritarianism Although Hadrian may not perhaps have been responsible for the murder at the start of his reign of the four ex-consuls,

PRINCIPAL EVENTS OF HADRIAN'S REIGN

Date	Internal and external politics	Hadrian's journeys (sp = spring, s = summer, a = autumn, w = winter)	Civilization
117	Disturbances in the provinces (Mauretania, Britain, Danube). Abandonment of Trajan's eastern conquests.	s: Antioch. a: departure from Syria: Tyane, Ankara. w: Nicomedia or Byzantium.	115–120 Beginning (at the latest) of the construction of the new camp at Lambaesis.
118	Hadrian's second consulship. Troubles caused by the Roxolani on the Danube. "Conspiracy of the four ex-consuls," all four executed by the Senate, an act perhaps inspired by Hadrian.	w/sp: Moesia. sp: Pannonia. July 9: Rome.	Start of work on the villa at Tivoli, and rebuilding the Pantheon.
119	Hadrian's third consulship.		
120	Creation of four judiciary districts of Italy, entrusted to former consuls (the *IVvir consulares*). Dacia is divided into two provinces, Upper and Lower. Then, in *c.* 123, the former is subdivided into two with the creation of Dacia Porolissensis.		Suetonius, *The Twelve Caesars*.
121	Reinforcement of the Rhine and Danube *limites*.	May–August: departure from Rome for Gaul. w?: in Lyon.	
122	Beginning of Hadrian's Wall. Death of Plotina.	sp: Upper Germania, Raetia, Noricum, Lower Germania. s: Britain. a: return via the Three Gauls, and Narbonensis (Nîmes, Avignon, Apt). w: Tarragona.	
123	Restoration of the sanctuary of Augustus at Tarragona. Peace with the Parthians.	w: Tarragona. w: Mauretania? (or 128). s: departure for Syria. s?: on the Euphrates. s/a: inspection along the *limes* of the Euphrates, in Cappadocia. w: return to Bithynia.	

Continued on p. 281

Date	Internal and external politics	Hadrian's journeys (sp = spring, s = summer, a = autumn, w = winter)	Civilization
124		sp/s: visit to Asia (Pergamum, Ephesus). a: Rhodes, Eleusis. w: Athens and journey through the Peloponnese.	
125		w/sp: journey in central Greece (Delphi). March: initiation at Eleusis. s: return to Rome via Sicily (Etna); Rome/Tivoli; journeys in Italy.	
126			
127			
128	July, speech to the army of Africa.	s: Sicily, Africa, ?Mauretania (or 123). s: Rome. a/w: Athens, Eleusis.	
129	Large-scale building works in Athens.	w: Athens. sp: Ephesus. sp/s: Asia, Phrygia, Cappadocia, Cilicia. a/w: Antioch.	
130	Jerusalem becomes *colonia Aelia Capitolina*.	w: Antioch. sp: Palmyra, Arabia, Judaea. s: Alexandria, trip on the Nile. a: Thebes (colossi of Memnon), return to Alexandria.	?Start of work on Hadrian's Mausoleum. Death of Antinous and founding of Antinoöpolis (October 30).
131	Edict of the Praetor given definitive form.	sp: departure from Alexandria, coastal journey along the coasts of Syria and Asia. s/a: ?Thrace, Media, Dacia, Macedonia. w: Athens.	Inauguration of the Olympieion (Athens).
132	Jewish revolt in Judaea known as that of Bar Kochba. The cause was the plan to build a Roman town at Jerusalem, now *colonia Aelia Capitolina*.	Return to Rome. (The journey to Judaea is not certain.) Tivoli.	

Continued on p. 282

Date	Internal and external politics	Hadrian's journeys (sp = spring, s = summer, a = autumn, w = winter)	Civilization
134	Recapture of Jerusalem.		Inauguration of the Aelius bridge (present-day Sant'Angelo in Rome). Dedication of the temple of Rome and Venus (Rome).
135	End of the Jewish revolt. Judaea becomes the consular province of Syria-Palestine.		
136	Start of Hadrian's illness. Problem of the succession: adoption of L. Ceionius Commodus, who becomes L. Aelius Caesar.		
138	L. Aelius Caesar dies (Jan. 1). Adoption of T. Aurelius Antoninus (the future Antoninus Pius), who himself has to adopt L. Verus and M. Annius Verus (the future Marcus Aurelius).		

Trajan's supporters, his rule was nevertheless marked by a tightening of control. His resolve to govern directly, and (a novelty) to intervene in every area, can be seen in the codification of the social hierarchy that he initiated, with the intention of rationalizing and moralizing social relations; in the doubtless legitimate but misunderstood attempt to lighten the workload of Roman magistrates by dividing Italy into four judiciary districts, each entrusted to a *consularis*; and in his strained relations with the Senate (which decreed his apotheosis only on the orders of his successor).

His journeys Hadrian spent a dozen of the twenty-one years of his reign traveling throughout the Empire, accompanied, apparently, by part of his council. These journeys were far from being the whims of an aesthete, they were rather a method of government. First, they enabled Hadrian to make sure of the frontiers and see to their reorganization, and at the same time to check on the morale of his troops, their loyalty, discipline, and capabilities (under his reign, *Disciplina* became a "personified abstraction" who was worshiped). Secondly, by journeying through the provinces he could oversee the management of the governors, and closely assess its quality. Lastly, it was an opportunity for him to meet provincials, take stock of the condition and needs of cities, and help them by, for example, providing material aid in the form of financial benefits or construction works, appointing *curatores* to supervise their affairs, or granting them the status of colony. Under him, the political integration of Greek-speaking elites was fully achieved.

Change of strategy   Trajan's conquests were too widely spread to be held with any success in an Empire whose reserves in terms of manpower were virtually the same as in the Augustan era. So, in the East, Hadrian "completed the strategic withdrawal initiated by Trajan" at the very end of his reign (E. Luttwak), and the new provinces of Armenia, Assyria, and Mesopotamia were abandoned as early as the end of 117. Elsewhere, Hadrian pursued a policy of consolidation: the Empire had to be ready to defend itself.

Imposing legislation   In particular in the domain of civil law. The "Edict of the Praetor" had been the principal source of private law. In theory, this "catalogue of all actions open to litigants" as formulated by the *praetor urbanus* (M. Humbert) was in effect only during the year of office of the magistrate who made it public on taking up his post, but it was customarily renewed by his successor, so that a substantial body of rules remained in existence, yet with the constant possibility of development. With the extension of the imperial law, this edict became petrified. Hadrian took note of this and appointed a jurist to give it a definitive form. The "perpetual" edict would remain the basis for the taking of legal action by private citizens until the sixth century. Hadrian's legislative acts embraced all sectors of society. They concerned soldiers, criminals, and slaves, but also re-established the wearing of the toga, denied full rights of citizenship to children of a union between a Roman and a foreign woman, and fixed numerous economic regulations in the imperial domains.

A masterful administration   Under Hadrian, the imperial council became a permanent organ of central government, with jurists among its members, as well as senators and knights, the jurists selected for their abilities and divided into two categories according to their remuneration. Under Hadrian too, the knights, whose *cursus* was now established, completed their run of conquests. They supervised all the great offices of the imperial bureaucracy, and obtained as well new financial posts (such as that of the *advocatus fisci*, an official charged with representing the interests of the tax administration in lawsuits). With 104 known equestrian officials, organized in a hierarchy that permitted military and civil advancement, the administrative machine worked well. The number of posts was not very high, but then: "This astonishingly limited number of staff was without doubt one of the fruits of the *pax Romana*" (H. G. Pflaum).

Plate 11.5   Gateway to the Roman fort at Chester on Hadrian's Wall.

Hadrian arranged the succession in such a strange way that it still arouses the curiosity and exercises the ingenuity of scholars. Following the death of L. Aelius Caesar, his first, unfortunate (or shrewd?) choice, he adopted T. Aurelius Fulvius Antoninus Boionius Arrius, who in his turn had to adopt a child of seven, L. Verus, and a young man of not yet seventeen, M. Annius Verus (the future Marcus Aurelius), his nephew by marriage. From that time (February 25, 138) Hadrian, increasingly ill, handed over the office of imperial power to the one who would replace him. He died at Baiae on July 10, 138.

ANTONINUS PIUS (138–161)

Stability, prosperity, happiness, harmony: these are the words constantly used to praise the reign of the man who gave his name to the dynasty. Yet this reign, which marked the apogee of the Empire, may seem insipid, lacking in artistic

Plate 11.6 Coin of Antoninus Pius, emperor AD 138–61.

imagination, anodyne – rather like the image of the man himself, of whom little is really known. He was born in 86 at Lanuvium in Latium, but part of his family originated from Nimes. It was an illustrious family: one grandfather had been prefect of Rome, the other proconsul of Asia. They were also rich. With brickfields in the Roman region and vast properties in Italy, Antoninus was one of the wealthiest senators in the mid-second century, and his fortune had been further increased by marriage. We know next to nothing of his *cursus* before he became emperor, except for his consulship in 120, his appointment as one of the four *consulares* of Italy, his proconsulship of Asia (133–6), and his membership of the imperial council.

The sources never run short of eulogies on his qualities as a man. What we know of him and his tastes (simple and rustic) is all in the same vein. The idealized portrait of him at the helm of state by Marcus Aurelius (*Meditations* 1.16) reveals no failing: the statesman appears to be as one with the private man. We may find this perfection irritating, but not one of his contemporaries makes the slightest criticism. All seem to have subscribed to the recommendations Marcus Aurelius set for himself: "In all things act as a disciple of Antoninus: look at his efforts to suit his actions to reason, his equitableness in all things, his piety, his gentleness, his scorn for empty reputation, his desire to grasp reality . . . May your last hour find you with a conscience as pure as his" (*Meditations* 6.30).

Table 11.2 The Antonines

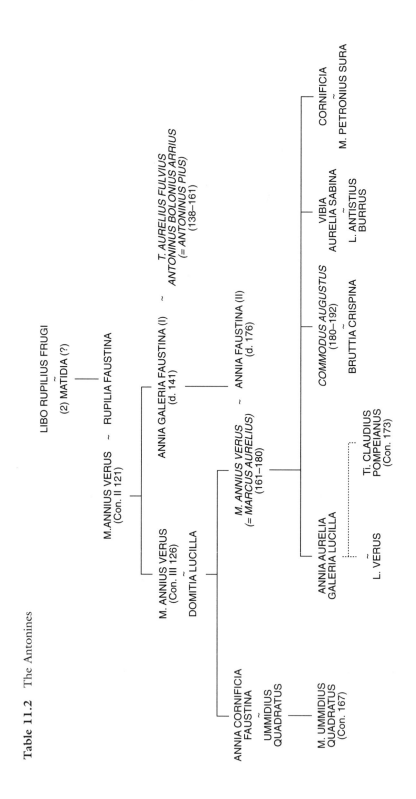

Antoninus died on his Lorium estate on March 7, 161. It is said that one of his last utterances was the watchword given to the tribune of his praetorian guard: "Aequanimitas" (equanimity).

There were few outstanding events in this long, peaceable, and prudent reign, during which (in 148) the 900th anniversary of Rome's founding was celebrated. No senator was put to death, the state's reserves increased, the various parts of the administrative machinery functioned smoothly (although the four consular governorships of Italy, an unpopular creation from the start, were abolished), eastern cults made headway (the first *taurobolium* known in the West, at Lyon, is dated to 160) but were linked with the imperial cult, the rise of the jurists continued, and the provinces grew richer. There were some dark patches, however.

- In Britain, between 141 and 143, a new wall was built, between the Clyde estuary and the Firth of Forth, and thus farther north than Hadrian's Wall. Why this further outpost of the Empire? Was there a rising of the Brigantes? A revolt by the inhabitants of the Lowlands? A strategic review? We do not know. But around 154–5 the coinage celebrated a fresh subjection of Britain. At the same date or soon after, Antoninus' Wall was abandoned, but it was repaired about 158, before being gradually abandoned once more from 159 on.
- In Egypt, around 142–4, a peasant revolt broke out, probably economic in origin.
- Disturbances in Mauretania around 145 required reinforcements to be brought from the Rhine and Danube frontiers.
- Military expeditions were organized in Dacia in around 156–7.

All in all, none of this was serious: a few small risings broke out around the Empire and were easily controlled. But what would happen if graver threats occurred simultaneously at several points on the *limes*? Not at all military by temperament, rather stay-at-home to boot (he was the only emperor not to leave Italy), and not very imaginative, Antoninus was incapable of foreseeing the possibility of that danger.

MARCUS AURELIUS (161–180)

Now, that unto every one is most profitable which is according to his own constitution and nature; and it is my nature to be rational in my actions and sociably and kindly disposed toward my fellow members of a city and commonwealth; as an Antonine, my city and my country is Rome; and speaking as a man, the whole world. Those things that are expedient and profitable to these cities are the only things that are good and expedient for me.

There can be nothing more unequivocal than these declarations from the *Meditations* (6.39). Everyone must submit to the guidance of his conscience; everyone must carry out his duty as his conscience teaches him. And when one is a Roman and an Antonine, one owes it to oneself to be a good Roman and a good Antonine. For Marcus Aurelius, to be emperor was first and foremost a duty. It was also, in the unlikely event that world order no longer existed, up to him to persist, to put the world in order: "If God exists, then all is well; or if all things go by chance and fortune, yet mayest thou use thine own providence in those things that concern thee properly, and then art thou well" (*Meditations* 9.26). This sense of duty and concern to maintain order seem to have been the determining factors in the deeds of Marcus Aurelius.

Up to the accession

He was born in Rome in April 121 and named M. Annius Verus. His family, which had consuls on both sides, came from Baetica (on his father's side) and was related to the family of both Trajan and Hadrian. Three features of his childhood and upbringing should be noted.

1 Hadrian noticed him very early on and granted him distinctions that were exceptional for his age: at six he became a knight, and at seven he entered the brotherhood of the Salians. Then at fifteen he was betrothed to the daughter of Hadrian's short-lived intended successor, L. Aelius Caesar. Lastly, in 138, he was adopted by Antoninus. Henceforward, he was known as M. Aelius Aurelius Verus. At the age of nearly seventeen he knew that he was later to be the head of state.

2 From his infancy he was brought up as a ruler. He had nineteen teachers in all, and they were of the best. One of them, M. Cornelius Fronto, who taught him Latin rhetoric, remained in the emperor's service until his death, in around 166. Between teacher and pupil a correspondence was kept up that has come down to us. The pupil was of a rare seriousness. At fourteen he opted for Stoicism. And all his life he remained loyal to its moral code, practicing spiritual exercises to that end which he consigned to a collection of note-books traditionally called the *Meditations*. Written in Greek, these note-books are the last great testimony of ancient Stoicism.

3 During Antoninus' reign, Marcus pursued an accelerated *cursus*, becoming quaestor in 139 and then serving as consul with Pius in 140, shortly before his nineteenth birthday. He stayed in the emperor' s entourage, marrying his daughter Faustina in 145, by whom he was to have fourteen children. And in 147 he received tribunician power and the proconsular *imperium*.

Rarely had an emperor been so well prepared in the theory of government. What he lacked was practical experience: he had had no military command, had made no tour of the provinces, and had no acquaintance with provincial administration. Frail in health, Marcus Aurelius would wear himself out in the task of government, which he tackled with good will and conscientious vigor. The man who dreamed only of books was forced to spend the greater part of his life among soldiers, spending 17 out of the 19 years of his reign on campaign.

Lucius Verus

In 138, together with Marcus Aurelius, Antoninus had had to adopt a child of seven, L. Ceionius Commodus, son of the dead L. Aelius Caesar. He had studied under the same teachers as Marcus Aurelius, but the results were not the same. Sturdy and cheerful, he was a young man who loved life. Perhaps he was not merely the jolly fellow so often described, but of the two (adoptive) brothers Antoninus preferred the elder, who was also his nephew by marriage. So Ceionius Commodus stayed in the background and did not become *Caesar*.

On his accession, Marcus Aurelius got the Senate to agree that his brother should be associated with him on an equal footing, with the same titles, except that of *pontifex maximus*, which could not be shared. Here was an original arrangement: for the first time a collegial administration was at the head of the Empire. Commodus became *Imperator Caesar Lucius Aurelius Verus Augustus*, remembered by history under the name Lucius Verus. Theoretically, then, the brothers had much the same powers, but in fact Marcus Aurelius always kept a pre-eminence unchallenged by Verus. Although he was not a hindrance to Marcus Aurelius, neither was he a great support. However, the philosophical emperor allowed him to marry his daughter Lucilla in 164. It was necessary to produce solid evidence of the harmony between the two emperors, celebrated by an issue of coinage in 168.

Continuing wars

Since 117, the Empire had lived in almost total peace, but in 161, war returned, brutally and on all fronts. In Britain it was mere unrest, in Raetia and Upper Germania an incursion by the Chatti. But the main event at the beginning of the reign was in the East.

War against the Parthians (161–166) Vologeses III, king of the Parthians, launched a double offensive against Armenia and Syria. The legions were beaten, one being massacred at Elegeia. In response, three legions were transferred from the Rhine and the Danube to the East under the command of L. Verus, who installed himself at Antioch and entrusted the direction of operations to some remarkable generals, such as Avidius Cassius, a Syrian. In 163, Armenia was reconquered and the Parthians driven out of Syria. In 165, Avidius Cassius took the offensive, invaded Mesopotamia, and set up a Roman protectorate there, penetrating as far as Media. In 166, a peace treaty was concluded with the Parthians, and Dura-Europus was reoccupied. Two consequences: in the East, a great military command including Egypt was entrusted to Avidius Cassius; and from the East, the army brought back the plague to the West. It was to ravage the Empire for fifteen years.

Meanwhile, in the same year, 166, Marcus Aurelius raised two legions which he installed in northern Italy. For a new danger threatened, this time on the Danube, where the provinces were reorganized and put in the hands of experienced generals. In 168, Verus having returned, Marcus Aurelius announced to the Senate that the two emperors would have to leave Rome in order to settle matters on the Danube.

The Danubian Wars   The various episodes of these wars are imperfectly known, and their chronology is far from certain, but it is clear that they had their origin in the slow movements of the Germanic peoples. Very probably for reasons of overpopulation, the Germani from Scandinavia (Gepidi in the second century, Goths before them) had begun to move southward, crowding out of central and eastern Europe the eastern Germani (Burgundii, Vandals, Semnones), who in their turn pushed against the western Germani (Marcomanni, Quadi, Suevi) and a Sarmatian people (the Iazyges), who, confined in an inner Germania reduced in size by the advance of the imperial frontier, both saw only one solution: to take refuge in the Empire, by agreement or by force. Several wars resulted. It would not do to study them in detail here, but they may be broadly grouped in two series, separated by a precarious period of respite between the spring of 175 and the autumn of 177.

The first wars (167–175)
- 167: The plague devastated and terrified Rome, where old purificatory religious ceremonies occupied the emperors. The Langobardi invaded Pannonia. And the Iazyges attacked the Dacian gold mines. The situation was restored, but not decisively.
- 168: The Marcomanni and other peoples created trouble on the Danubian frontier. The emperors went to Aquileia and negotiated with the tribes, who desired peace. There was an inspection of the Pannonian *limes* (Marcus' first journey outside Italy), and the *praetentura Italiae et Alpium* (advanced defense line of Italy and the Alps) was set up, a military zone north of Aquileia, where the emperors stopped, until the ubiquitous plague forced them to leave this port.
- 169: Lucius Verus died. Marcus Aurelius returned to Rome for the funeral and apotheosis. Intent on preparing a large campaign with the idea in mind of subduing permanently the troublesome regions to the north of the Danube, but at the same time faced with a financial crisis, he took urgent measures to secure the means he required (raising troops that included brig-

ands and slaves, auctioning the imperial tableware). By the autumn, he was once again on the Danube.

■ 170: In the spring, there was a strong Roman offensive across the Danube. It was a disaster. Northern Italy was (very probably) invaded by Quadi and Marcomanni, who may have thrust as far as Aquileia. And Costoboqui (perhaps from the north of Dacia) invaded Macedonia and, in a spectacular raid, reached Eleusis. Backed by excellent generals (Pertinax and the emperor's new son-in-law Pompeianus), Marcus Aurelius repulsed the invaders. A new great command was established in the three provinces of Dacia (*Tres Daciae*) and Upper Moesia.

■ 171: Marcus Aurelius at Carnuntum in Pannonia. Realizing that the Marcomanni were the main danger, he drove out the last invaders, made peace with the Quadi, and organized a large-scale expedition against the Marcomanni. Barbarians were settled in regions depopulated by war and plague.

■ 172: The Romans entered Marcomanni territory, won a victory, and then attacked the Quadi. During this campaign there were apparently supernatural occurrences of lightning and rain. A treaty was agreed with the Marcomanni: they were forbidden to form alliances amongst themselves, and they promised to trade under Roman control, to hand over booty and hostages, and to keep at least 5 miles from the Danube. (A rebellion in Egypt of the *boukoloi*, herdsmen of the Delta; incursions of the Moors into Baetica; disturbances in Armenia.)

■ 173: A succession of small engagements. Marcus Aurelius stayed at Carnuntum.

■ 174: A new war against the Quadi and a campaign against the Iazyges, who were defeated in a savage war.

■ 175: A fresh assault on the Sarmatians. Marcus Aurelius seemed determined on creating new provinces out of these regions. However, when he learned that the governor of Syria, Avidius Cassius, had proclaimed himself emperor and that the eastern provinces had rallied to the usurper, a peace was arranged with the Iazyges.

The second Germanic war (177–180)   Even less is known about this second series of operations along the Danube than about the first. Everything started up again: guerrilla warfare, banditry, in-security. The situation deteriorated to such an extent that the presence of the emperors became necessary (from January 1, 177, Marcus Aurelius' son Commodus was co-emperor). They left Rome in August 178 with an impressive headquarters staff. The following year a victory was achieved, probably over the Quadi. The barbarians seemed to be wearing themselves out. The Iazyges not only remained calm but found advantages in being on Rome's side. It was found to be possible to Romanize the

Marcomanni. And the Quadi were contemplating emigrating northwards. Thus, in the spring of 180, the creation of two new provinces beyond the Danube did not appear quite so utopian. But on March 17, 180, two days before the opening of the new military campaign, Marcus Aurelius died on the Danube, at Vindobona (Vienna). He was almost 59.

We must assess the importance of these wars. Militarily, the breaches of the Empire's defenses, though serious, were less catastrophic than was then believed, yet these threatening barbarian invasions so newly close to home, the terrible plague, and the endless wars were such a decisive time in Rome's history that many historians see the Empire's crisis as beginning with the reign of Marcus Aurelius. Without entering a debate that turns on one's approach to the philosophy of history, we can agree that the government had lost impetus, and that there was widespread anxiety. In its most elementary form it showed itself in the persecution of the Christians, who were held responsible for the gods' anger. At its highest level of expression, it may be seen in art. For instance, the sarcophagus of Portonaccio (dating from 190, slightly later therefore), which represents a battle against the barbarians. Here there is no longer any question, as in earlier art, of grasping and rendering in its entirety and perfection the movement of bodies in space. The artist preferred the seething mass of tangled combatants framed by the great figures of the barbarian princes who had been taken prisoner, "exhausted, emaciated creatures, stamped with grief and humiliation, born of a new awareness of the frailty of the human being" (B. Andreae). It is as if Rome were now sharing the sufferings of the conquered.

SIMPLIFIED PLAN OF AN EQUESTRIAN "CURSUS" IN THE SECOND HALF OF THE SECOND CENTURY

Equestrian militiae: one year in each office (from the age of 25):

- prefect of a cohort
- angusticlave tribune of a legion
- prefect of an *ala*
- sometimes, a fourth year, as prefect of an *ala miliaria*

Procuratorships hierarchized by remuneration:

- 60,000 sesterces per annum
- 100,000 sesterces per annum

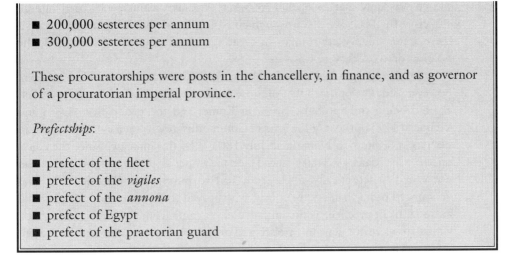

- 200,000 sesterces per annum
- 300,000 sesterces per annum

These procuratorships were posts in the chancellery, in finance, and as governor of a procuratorian imperial province.

Prefectships:

- prefect of the fleet
- prefect of the *vigiles*
- prefect of the *annona*
- prefect of Egypt
- prefect of the praetorian guard

The exercise of power

If war was the major preoccupation of Marcus Aurelius' government, the running of the Empire was by no means neglected. The tenor was conservative, but with some new aspects.

The overall running of affairs was inspired by the example of Antoninus, the model for Marcus Aurelius, or governed by the functional development of the imperial administration's major offices. Relations with the Senate were good, in spite of the reinstatement of the *consulares* of Italy under the title of *iuridici*, chosen from former praetors. There was a further increase in officials of equestrian rank (there were now 125 known procuratorial posts, the chief one with an annual salary of 300,000 sesterces). The position of the imperial council was confirmed (a list of members for July 177 is known from the Table of Banasa). There were measures to limit fraudulent claims to Roman citizenship and to resolve fiscal problems. Talented men were promoted, these frequently of modest social origin (Pertinax, Pescennius Niger) or from the provinces (Pompeianus, Severus). And there was a further extension of imperial legislation (over 300 known laws, half of which concern women, children, and slaves).

Out of respect for Hadrian's intentions, Marcus Aurelius had associated Lucius Verus with the government of the Empire. This experiment in collegiality was repeated: on January 1, 177, Marcus Aurelius' son, Lucius Aelius Aurelius, born in 161 and *Caesar* since 166, became *Augustus*, with the same powers and the same subordination (he was not *pontifex maximus*) as Lucius Verus had had. The succession was secure. This innovation of the unequal sharing of supreme power was accompanied by a trial delegation of powers. The most obvious instance is that of Avidius Cassius, who received supreme command over all the provinces in the East. The risk of usurpation that this carried was duly met in April 175, when Avidius Cassius proclaimed himself emperor. In this case, the army remained loyal and there was no civil war. If there were military advantages in creating great positions of command, the political drawbacks were obvious.

In the preceding reigns there had been some Christian martyrs. Their renown, however, did not approach that of those in Marcus Aurelius' reign (the most celebrated being the apologist Justin in Rome, and the group from Lyon and Vienne in 177) or those at the start of Commodus' reign (such as the first African martyrs at Scillium in Numidia in July 180). Why this increase? Since the edicts on the Christians of Trajan and Hadrian, imperial policy toward them had not varied. Theoretically, a governor had to punish any Christian who was denounced other than anonymously, who proved to be such, and who persisted in his faith. In practice, as the initiative never came from the public authorities, Christians were not generally persecuted or systematically sought out. Each affair was a special case that depended on the state of relations between Christians and non-Christians at that particular place and time and on the attitude of the governor. Like other pagan intellectuals (for example, Celsus, whose *True Account* was written in about 178), Marcus Aurelius felt no sympathy for Christians. He blamed them for their obstinacy in exposing themselves to death and, far from seeing it as an act of courage, condemned it as fanaticism. Nevertheless, he had no desire for confrontation with the Christians because of their beliefs; what occurred was merely the application of the law currently in force. The main causes of these martyrdoms are to be sought elsewhere. There were three.

1 The spread of the new religion. It reached the western provinces and penetrated intellectual and military circles. In expanding, the Church encountered its first heresies, such as Montanism in Phrygia and Rome, which glorified and encouraged the thirst for martyrdom during the 170s.
2 Popular hatred. Not very well known, living apart, the Christians of this anguished period were blamed for every ill.
3 The Christians' refusal to recognize the gods of the Empire and the divinity of the emperor, which automatically placed them among the subversive elements of society, since their loyalty thus seemed conditional.

COMMODUS (180–192)

The succession

For the first time an emperor had been born to the purple. His education had been meticulous, he had been prepared for his office, and, since 177, he had been co-emperor. On the death of his father, he became sole emperor without the slightest difficulty. There had been a return to the principle of a hereditary monarchy: whatever the new emperor's defects, he was Marcus Aurelius' only surviving son. Although, by all accounts, his personality counted for less with his father than his heredity, historians have argued over the question whether Marcus Aurelius made the best choice. Actually, the question is pointless. "There could be no better choice than the son of the man whom the gods had placed at the head of the Empire. Marcus Aurelius could not hesitate" (J.-P. Martin).

The chief events of his reign

- 180: Influenced by some of his father's friends, Commodus stayed on the Danube, negotiated a victorious peace with the Quadi and Marcomanni, and then returned to Rome in October.
- 182: A plot by Lucilla, Commodus' sister, which almost succeeded with the help of certain senators. From then on, Commodus distrusted the Senate and lived in fear of assassination. He inaugurated a reign of terror, had friends of Marcus Aurelius executed, and let others govern on his behalf in order to give himself over to debauchery.
- 182–5: Government by the prefect of the praetorian guard Tigidius Perennis. Competent in military matters, he kept an attentive eye on the frontiers, but he also engaged in personal politics; he apparently favored the knights over the senators and even tried to elevate his son to the purple. He was murdered by the soldiers.
- 185–9: Government by the chamberlain Cleander, a former slave promoted to the rank of knight. While Commodus took no interest in anything but chariot races and gladiatorial fights, Cleander sold offices, debased the Senate and the magistracies, had important people killed, and had himself appointed praetorian prefect in 189, before being executed on Commodus' orders to pacify the starving and rebellious Roman crowd (end of 189 or the spring of 190).
- 190–2: Conspiracies real or imagined, murders, favorites, concubines (especially Marcia), and intrigues formed the political fabric of these years. Commodus increasingly revealed signs of a religious mania whose first symptoms had appeared early in his reign. He claimed to be Hercules, refounded the city of Rome as the *colonia Commodiana*, and gave legions, fleets, the city of Carthage, and the months of the year names that he claimed as his titles, such as *Exsuperatorius* ("he who prevails over all"), a title reflecting the influence of eastern astrology and Greek theological thought. Holding himself to be the first among the gladiators, he insisted that the ritual procession of January 1, 193 should be transformed into a procession of gladiators, after which (although this is disputed) various people were to be put to death. Three of his intended victims, including Marcia, stole a march on Commodus-Hercules, poisoning and strangling him on December 31, 192.

The exercise of power

The madness of Commodus had significant repercussions only in the capital; the Empire suffered hardly at all. The administrative machine worked by itself; the imperial council and central offices took decisions and the emperor added his signature. There was one modification however: the post of praetorian prefect became the most elevated, its holder a sort of vice-emperor who directed the imperial council. Troubles in Britain were reported, and the frontier was withdrawn to Hadrian's Wall; likewise in Gaul, with bands of deserters led by a certain Maternus. The supposed economic crisis of the time is now often regarded as beginning about a decade later. In fact, the reign of Commodus is not very well known. The sources in general merely list him among the bad emperors – yet his successor, Septimius Severus, insisted on declaring himself a brother to Commodus.

With the death of Commodus a dynasty and an era came to an end. A period of crisis began, the most serious since the year of the four emperors.

ITALY IN DECLINE, THE PROVINCES EXPANDING

By giving a new administrative structure to the provinces and Italy, Augustus had upset the traditional relations between the peninsula and its conquests. Until that time the provinces had been exploited for the benefit of the victors. Starting with the Julio-Claudians, the new status of the provinces allowed them to develop in their own way, almost on an equal footing with Italy. But the consequences of this change – the relative decline of Italy and an uneven but general expansion of the provincial world – did not begin to show until the time of the Flavians. Under the Antonines, they were plain to see, and were reflected in the geographical origin of the imperial families.

ITALY

Peopled entirely by Roman citizens (among its free inhabitants), divided since the time of Augustus into eleven regions, administered by the Senate and senatorial magistrates, and benefiting from a privilege that exempted it from land tax (*tributum*), Italy, which also maintained an active municipal life, from which the Flavian dynasty had emerged, was distinct from the provinces, and occupied a privileged position that had ensured its prosperity in the first century. However, in the second half of the century, it had begun to show a lassitude, even a decline, which became more marked in the second century.

Signs of decline

They can be picked out in every domain.

Administration and law   Imperceptibly, those features of the peninsula in the domain of administration and law that had made it entirely distinct from the provinces became blurred, more for technical reasons than by political will. To ensure better administration and better justice, Hadrian created four judiciary districts entrusted to former consuls. The measure was so unpopular that his successor revoked it, before Marcus Aurelius re-established it in a weaker form with the *iuridici*, former praetors and all Italian. Similarly, for trials beyond the competence of municipal magistrates, it was the praetor, the prefect of the capital (in a radius of 100 miles around Rome), or the praetorian prefect who stepped in. Since the reign of Marcus Aurelius, the praetorian prefect had also been responsible for maintaining order in the peninsula. Lastly, the upkeep of roads and riparian lands was supervised by senators or knights.

Politics   Under Trajan, around 45 per cent of the senators were provincials, and under Commodus around 60 per cent. In the pressure groups that formed within the Senate, the Italians had little influence, except under Antoninus.

Military domain   Until the time of Marcus Aurelius there had been no great troop concentrations in Italy, apart from those stationed in Rome and the ports of the praetorian fleets. The barbarian threat on the Danubian frontier compelled troops to be stationed in the northern part of the peninsula, though not permanently, it is true. Secondly, Italians virtually disappeared from the legions. Starting from Hadrian's time, the movement was very clear, and was to be found at all levels of the military hierarchy. Among the ordinary, rank and file legionaries, Italians became rare (those that there were often came from Cisalpine Gaul), and among centurions and *primipili*, Italians were henceforth in a minority. In fact, Italians who chose the armed profession preferred the Rome garrison.

The economy   The economic decline of Italy during this period, known to the ancients and given varying interpretations in modern times, took different forms according to the region, economic sector, and type of property, but it was noticeable as early as the beginning of the second century and was accompanied by the problem of a workforce that had become scarce, expensive, and, according to Pliny the Younger, lacking in ability or, as modern historians suggest, not properly used. Generally speaking, those regions of Italy with products in competition with those of the provinces (pottery in the case of Etruria, wine and oil in that of Campania) suffered a decline, while those which preserved a local market (Latium and Rome, for instance) or made gains (such as Cisalpine Gaul with the development of Aquileia and its region) maintained their activities without slackening. Hence, the picture of the Italian economic decline is a fragmented one, so much did local conditions play a determining role: the Apennine territories, which lived somewhat apart, the rural areas in the south, and those of Campania appear to have been the most affected. In

Plate 11.7 A butcher's shop. Relief from Dresden.

nearly all the regions where the decline was apparent (in Etruria, for example), there was a perceptible retreat into self-sufficiency or stagnation rather than a brutal collapse. With the expansion of interprovincial trade, Italy, besides, no longer played the role of middleman that it had once enjoyed. It no longer had anything to sell to the East, and had precious little to offer the West.

ROME UNDER THE ANTONINES

The fabric of the city of Rome, with its rich monumental inheritance, was renovated by the building works of the first Antonines (chiefly Trajan and Hadrian). The political, intellectual, artistic, and chief consumer center of the Empire, it was a cosmopolitan city of around a million people, with a hierarchized social stratification that reflected imperial society (slaves, freedmen, *peregrini*, *humiliores*, *honestiores*). Built without any overall plan, and with construction work permanently going on, it juxtaposed private houses of one or a few storeys (*domus*) and multi-storey apartment blocks (*insulae*), residential quarters and working-class quarters. The city was an interlacing of narrow, cluttered, twisting streets (about 85 km), public and private buildings, open squares and gardens. Despite the spectacles provided by this leisure capital, despite the abundance of water and a more or less satisfactory drainage system (for surface water), and despite the "lungs" provided by the Tiber, life seems to have been hard for the common people and turbulent for the great, but everyone was proud to live in this city *par excellence*, the center of power, where everything converged – men, products, religions.

The intellectual field   A lack of intellectual dynamism and a flagging of the creative spirit became increasingly evident in Italian circles during the century. The Italian literary vein dried up: men compiled, summarized, and began to repeat the ideas of former times. There are some memorable names, though in some instances they still belonged to the first century, by virtue of their education: Tacitus, Pliny the Younger, Suetonius, Juvenal, Aulus Gellius. But it is significant that Marcus Aurelius wrote his *Meditations* in Greek, the language of philosophy certainly, but also of intellectual renewal. The only thing to offer resistance was the law, in which field Roman jurists, despite tough competition from the Greek schools, still preserved their supremacy. In particular, manuals of jurisprudence were drawn up, such as the *Institutes* of Gaius (perhaps a Greek!).

A relative decline

The image of an Italian decline, which is fair when looked at overall, needs not only to be corrected for the effect of the growing prosperity of the provinces producing an appearance of absolute decline, but to be modified in a number of other ways as well. First, it took place on a number of time scales, though generally it was more perceptible at the end of the second century than at its start. Secondly, the wealth of the regions not having been identical to begin with, a region in crisis like Campania could still be richer than one that had always been neglected. Thirdly, certain economic sectors (brickworks, metal industries, luxury crafts, grain growing, and wool weaving) maintained their position or even advanced, and building activity in the cities and municipal benefaction showed no signs of faltering right up to the reign of Marcus Aurelius and even beyond. Furthermore, one must take into account Italy's amenities (roads, monuments, baths, standard of living, etc.), which were more complete and more established than those of the provinces and required upkeep (generally carried out) rather than addition. Lastly, one should not overlook the importance of the prestige that remained bound up with the land and history of Italy, with the Latin language learnt in the provinces, and with the presence in Italy of the great centers of political decision-making. For all the factors leading to decline, there remained stimulating factors in Italian economic life: the influence of the capital and its satellites, the ports, the numerous towns that still existed, and the linking of Italy, by way of Cisalpine Gaul, with a market that, in the second half of the century, began to escape the pull of the Mediterranean and to turn toward continental Europe. Moreover, the Antonines, except for Hadrian, always paid great attention to the position of Italy, which they wanted to support. In this respect, Trajan's policy was significant, even if it is hard to discern the results. The price of land had gone down. By obliging senators to invest one third of their wealth in Italian land, the emperor sought to increase the value of properties in Italy. Working in the

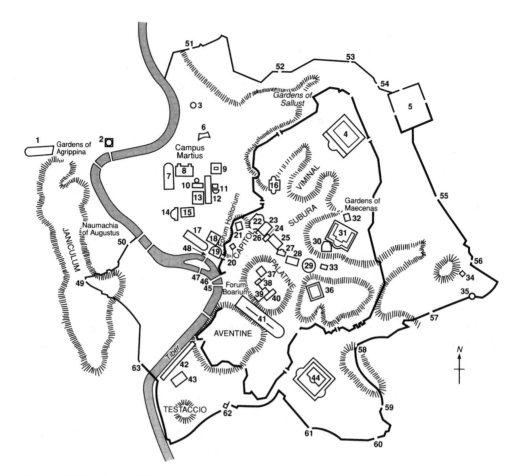

Figure. 11.1 Imperial Rome

same direction, Trajan developed one of Nerva's creations, the *alimenta*. These were permanent loans at around 5 per cent granted by the imperial tax administration to Italian landowners. Interest was collected by the public administrations of cities, who distributed it to poor children (first boys, then girls). It has been suggested that it was a sort of land bank intended to encourage peasants to develop their lands, but it is more realistic to see the *alimenta* as a work of public assistance, or poor relief, perhaps meant to combat population decline, with the ultimate aim of ensuring the military recruitment of Italians. At all events, the imperial initiative led to a host of similar, private foundations.

THE WESTERN OR LATIN EMPIRE

Since Actium, on the psychological level, and since the dual chancellery (Latin and Greek) instituted by Claudius, on the administrative level, one may legitimately make a distinction between two sides: the West, where Latin was the sole official language, and the East, where Greek competed with it.

Roughly speaking, the boundaries were administrative: south of the Mediterranean the dividing line coincided with the frontier between proconsular Africa and Cyrenaica; to the north, the northern frontiers of Macedonia and Thrace, although the Moesias, Latin-speaking (above all, the army), also spoke Greek. It was possible to get on in the world without speaking Greek (although Romans of the cultivated classes were bilingual); it was impossible without a knowledge of Latin.

In the second century, the western provinces reaped the benefits of the Flavian initiatives and the *pax Romana*. For all of them, the Antonine era was, to varying degrees, a period of great prosperity. It is true that during the last quarter of the century there were sporadic signs of a developing climate of uncertainty – for instance, those caches of coins that archaeology has revealed in Gaul, hidden in the reign of Commodus. Nevertheless, the West's political supremacy, only marginally disturbed by Avidius Cassius' bid for power in the East, was undeniable. It was accompanied by great administrative stability: with the exception of Dacia, and some alterations of status linked with problems of security (under Marcus Aurelius, Baetica was for a time an imperial province, and Noricum and Raetia, from being procuratorian, became praetorian provinces), the western provinces each retained the same administrative status as in the preceding century. But, first and foremost, these provinces enjoyed unprecedented economic success, which showed itself in the expansion of cultivated land in rural areas and the embellishment and expansion of towns, which at that time reached the summit of their splendor (Lyon, for example) and often found themselves cramped within their original boundaries (like Cuicul (Djemila), in Africa, a colony founded under Nerva, which was already overflowing its early walls). The western provinces also now possessed an intellectual life which, at least in Africa, went beyond the general mediocrity and with Florus, Fronto, Apuleius, and Tertullian, one of the leading Christian writers in the Latin tongue, took over from Italian literature as the main, if not copious, source of brilliance in Latin writings. Finally, throughout the West, and apparently more there than in the East, the local elites who aspired to Roman citizenship were everywhere achieving their desire, either by personal promotion (auxiliaries, magistrates, and even decurions since Hadrian) or by collective advancement (honorary colonies). It was bestowed without necessarily supplanting the traditional or customary rights of the local community: the Table of Banasa shows that in 177 the chief of the Zegrenses tribe in Mauretania Tingitana both obtained full citizenship rights and retained the traditional right of his tribe.

The islands

Sicily, a senatorial province, remained a land of large cereal-producing estates (especially imperial ones). Since the time of Augustus, its inhabitants had benefited from Latin rights, and the exploitation of republican times had ceased. There was a strong Romanization, but Apuleius indicates that people there still spoke Greek and Siculian alongside Latin. The three main towns were Syracuse, the capital, Catana, and Tauromenium (Taormina), which, with its famous theater, dates, as we know it, from the Antonines.

Sardinia was generally administered by the Senate, and Corsica by an equestrian procurator. Each in its own rhythm, these two islands participated in western expansion. In both cases, urbanized coastal regions (Olbia, Cagliari, and Porto Torres in Sardinia; Aleria and the east coast of Corsica) were in contrast with a hinterland where life carried on as in the times of traditional societies. Sardinia exported metals and grain; Corsica made the most of its resources of coniferous trees and tar.

The Iberian peninsula

The Iberian peninsula comprised three provinces, one senatorial (Baetica), the other two imperial (Tarraconensis, where the Seventh Gemina was stationed, and Lusitania), each divided into *conventus*. By the start of the second century, it had undergone three waves of Romanization (the Second Punic War, Caesar and Augustus, the Flavians), and was now looked on as one of the leading provincial areas, having given the Empire not only great writers but also the first non-Italian emperor. It was fortunate enough to possess some significant advantages. It was the only large portion of the Empire remote from a dangerous frontier. Its rivers were accessible far into the interior, its plains were fertile, its mountains contained minerals that had for centuries made it the Eldorado of antiquity, its coastal waters teemed with fish. And it had old civilizations, vitalized by Phoenician, Greek, and Punic contributions. But it had also turned these things to good account. Thus, it exported grain, excellent olive oil, and wine, and its flocks were plentiful. Works producing garum (a thick sauce prepared from pickled fish) dotted the southern coasts. Mining territories, with special procurators, were formed in the north-west, the south-west, and Baetica. And the towns were so numerous in the south and in the valley of the Ebro that they could rival the three capitals, Cordoba, Merida, and Tarragona, not to mention Italica, which neither Trajan nor Hadrian neglected.

The Alpine provinces

These were procuratorian and followed the same pattern as each other. There were few novelties, but rather a consolidation of the features of the preceding century: a mountain economy (wood, honey, cooperage, cheeses, etc.), porterage, tolls on the mountain passes.

The Three Gauls (Lugdunensis, Aquitania, Belgica)

These comprised about sixty "cities" which gathered once a year, in a sort of federal district at Condat on the slopes of the Croix-Rousse between the Rhône and Saône facing the colony of Lyon, to celebrate the cult of Rome and Augustus, and to deliberate in a Council of the Gauls. In this sense, they indisputably formed a political and territorial entity. Within this, the weight of the Roman army was felt more and more the closer one was to the Rhine, especially through its influence on economic production – thus, cereals and wool produced by the villages of the north (present-day Artois and Picardy) were steered toward the legions of the Rhine. In the second century, the Three Gauls enjoyed a dazzling material prosperity, based on their varied agricultural produce (grain, wood, abundant livestock, wines, textiles), modern techniques (scythes, "harvesters," marling), good, sound craftsmanship (pottery, textiles, metalwork), a road network improved by Antoninus, navigable rivers, and active traders (such as the merchants of Lyon and Trier). This material prosperity was enhanced by the splendor of the towns, in the front rank of which was Lyon, which the Antonines showered with favors; then came Trier, Bordeaux (which, during the second century, became the capital of Aquitania), Autun, Reims, and, in their wake, the large towns of Metz, Poitiers, Limoges, and Lutetia. In the southwest, the center, the west, and the north, where towns were very sparse, there were immense empty spaces. Nevertheless, this urban disposition was to a great extent the model for the present-day network of towns and cities.

There is no doubt that the Three Gauls were not only among the richest provinces in the Empire but also, because of the diversity and complementary nature of their riches, the best prepared to live independently. Yet their loyalty to the regime was total. Farmers, traders, artisans, urban notables, and native chiefs were committed to the peace that secured their incomes, protected them from the Germani, and ensured their social position. Paradoxically, therefore, very few Gallo-Romans, originating from these regions, are known to have had the desire to play a political role at Empire level. A municipal or guild setting seems to have attracted them much more. And peace, material prosperity, and urban splendor had not brought a spirited intellectual life, which, if it is to be judged by what it produced, was in fact barely mediocre.

The two Germanies

These two military provinces formed the shield for the Gauls. Lower Germania, to the north, extended east only to the banks of the Rhine and IJssel, and had Cologne as its capital. Upper Germania overflowed into Switzerland, Burgundy, and Franche-Comté on the left bank of the Rhine, on which bank its capital (Mainz) lay, and covered to the east the Taunus mountains region and the *Agri Decumates*. In these provinces, the army left its mark everywhere: towns arose from the legionary camps, permanent or temporary; forts and fortresses gave birth to little villages; tanneries, brickfields, farms, and every kind of craftwork all served the army; political life was linked with loyalty to the generals. At the end of the second century, it was no longer a Roman army in the Germanies, but the Roman army *of* the Germanies. Trade with independent Germani and contacts with the Danubian pro-vinces and Britain all played a part in the area's development.

Britain

This province contained three colonies (Colchester, Lincoln, Gloucester), some twenty "cities," *municipia* (including London, where the governor resided), and three legions, whose presence made it, in relation to the size and population of the province, the largest garrison in the Empire. In reality, two Britains were living side by side: in the south, a country Romanized by veterans, with villas and a few centers of Roman urban life; in the north, a military zone. There were also mines, chiefly of silver and iron, and there was extensive trade with the Rhineland by way of Boulogne, the British imports through which in the second century eclipsed those of products from southern Gaul and Italy. Like the Three Gauls, Britain began to live on its own economic development.

Dalmatia

The territory of Dalmatia was broadly the same as that of present-day ex-Yugoslavia. Since the Flavians, there had been no troops stationed there on a permanent basis, but it remained a consular imperial province. The governor resided at Salonae, which blossomed around the mid-second century, at which time it possessed some 60,000 inhabitants, an amphitheater, and a baths. In the last quarter of the century, a new equilibrium appears to have established itself. Until then, the coast, which had been colonized very early on and was thoroughly Romanized, had been the wealthiest region. At this time, however, it appears to have entered a period of stagnation, to the advantage of the interior, a reservoir for army recruits, which rose to the height of its prosperity.

The Danubian provinces

Lying along the banks of the river, these provinces were crisscrossed by military flotillas. There was one province on the left bank, Dacia. All the others lay on the right bank.

Dacia   The administrative status and internal arrangement of Dacia changed several times until, under Marcus Aurelius, it was organized in three sectors, each supervised by a procurator, under a single governor of consular rank. Heavy colonization began in the reign of Trajan. Civilians and ex-soldiers from all over the Roman world settled there. The Dacians were attracted by Roman civilization and "Romanization took place there rapidly and in depth" (E. Cizek). The former capital, Sarmizegethusa, became a Roman colony between 108 and 110. But the governor resided in another large town, Apulum. The province had the advantages of a good road network and mines, but these mines yielded less than had been hoped.

Raetia   Snugly fitted in between the *Agri Decumates* to the north, Upper Germania to the west, and Italy to the south, Raetia, a poor and barely Romanized imperial province, became praetorian in status under Marcus Aurelius. It had two towns of importance: the capital Augsburg, a Roman foundation that enjoyed its greatest prosperity in the second century, and Regensburg, where the legion commanded by the legate was stationed.

Noricum   The administrative development of Noricum paralleled Raetia's. But this province was richer (iron mines, chiefly exploited in the second century, and earlier Romanization) and it carried more weight on the strategic level because of its role as a communications center: its capital, Virunum, and the town of Celeia (Celje, in Slovenia) were the junctions commanding the roads to the Danube and Aquileia.

The Pannonias   Emerging under Augustus from the dismemberment of Illyricum, Pannonia was divided by Trajan: to the west, with its northern frontier resting on the Danube, Upper Pannonia (capital, Carnuntum, 40 km east of Vienna); to the east, Lower Pannonia, bounded by the river, whose line it followed (capital, Aquincum, Budapest). In the center of the Danubian *limes*, these two provinces (four legions in the second century) occupied a vital position, and would constantly grow from the time of the Severi. But it was in the second century that their nature was definitively established. It involved four elements:

1 Romanization was early, with strong urban development under the Flavians (Siscia/Sisak and Sirmium, two colonies that enclosed the River Sava) and under the first Antonines (Carnuntum and Aquincum became *municipia*; Poetovio and Mursa, colonies that kept watch on a more northerly line than that of the Sava, the Drava). As early as in Trajan's time, each of these provinces had a *concilium*.

2 The integration of the indigenous peoples was successful. They adhered to the municipal system, and many of them served in the army. At the beginning of Trajan's reign some Pannonians reached praetorian rank.

3 There were few large landed estates, but very many small and medium-sized properties belonging to veterans and native free peasants. Both were influenced by the presence of the armies and maintained a particular outlook, little removed from that of the "soldier-peasant."

4 Trade, which was in the hands of foreigners, was lively. There was the old north–south amber route as well as the new Danube route, with many traders from Cologne and Trier, and with outlets from the eastern provinces via Sirmium.

The Moesias   Created by Domitian, the two consular provinces of Moesia straddled the Latin and Greek worlds. To the east, Lower Moesia opened on to the Black Sea, where Greek towns preserved their autonomy (Tomi, Callatis); to the west, Upper Moesia adjoined Lower Pannonia. Under the protection of the omnipresent army, a basically agricultural economy developed under the Antonines. The primary function of the towns was military, whether it was Viminacium (a *municipium* under Hadrian), Trajan's headquarters at the time of the First Dacian War, or Oescus, also on the Danube, a colony under Trajan and former legionary base.

THE EASTERN OR GREEK EMPIRE

Compared with the West, the East gave the appearance of being a more unified entity. The reality was different: the ethnic and cultural diversity was perhaps even greater. Like the western provinces, those of the East enjoyed a dazzling prosperity in the second century, but the equality of achievement of the two parts of the Empire in the middle of the century actually masked an unequal dynamism. The western provinces reached their peak at this time, and this achievement was not prolonged much beyond the end of the century, except in Africa, while those in the East, despite a few bad patches, maintained their economic expansion, extended their intellectual pre-eminence, and, in the following century, became the vital center of the Empire. So the province-by-province study of the East will be integrated into the picture of the Empire in 235 (see below, ch. 13).

The reasons for prosperity

The overall expansion of the East to the detriment of a West grinding to a halt in its "golden age" can be distinguished in the second half of the Antonine century. But the reasons for it lie further back. Before we come to these, we must first note that those eastern lands were all countries with ancient civilizations and had, to all intents and purposes, never stopped being rich, so great was the capital that still lay in the memory, knowledge, and experience of men in every area (technical, commercial, social, political, economic, and spiritual). It was just that piracy and brigandage, conquest and pillage, civil war and destruction had all weakened and divided these regions, bringing a measure of decline.

The first reason, or cause, was the restoration of confidence following the annexations and alterations of the first century AD, which events, together with the various expeditions to the frontiers and outside the Empire, had brought about at the dawn of the Antonine century, not only almost complete internal peace and stability (with the exception of the Jewish revolts, and endemic but feeble brigandage in Roman Egypt, Thrace, and the north-east of Cappadocia), and the disappearance of all the client states west of the Euphrates (the last being the Nabataean kingdom, annexed in 106), but also a more honest and careful administration (see the correspondence between Trajan and Pliny), and an increase in wealth due to the presence of the troops – all results likely to restore confidence throughout the whole of the East. But there were also the particular local effects on commerce. In Syria, for example, in the wake of Trajan's Parthian expeditions, "commercial relations with the Parthian Empire resumed with an increased intensity and profit" (J.-P. Rey-Coquais).

The second cause of eastern expansion in the second century was the creation by Rome of a policy adapted to the East that encouraged, or at least did not discourage too much, the reinvigoration of its intensely urban life. The extent of the East's urbanization was remarkable not only in terms of the number of towns and cities to be found there, and of their size (in the Augustan era, Alexandria had over 600,000 inhabitants and Antioch around 300,000, and many in Asia Minor over 50,000), but also in terms of the centrality of the position they had achieved, culturally and historically. The city and the town lay at the very heart of the history of the East, where from the beginning towns had fulfilled administrative, economic, and religious functions. Although these towns, different in their founding, their development, and their functions, some marked by indigenous tradition, the majority stamped with the pattern of Hellenistic urban life and art, had entered a period of relative or absolute decline (of the 53 towns known in Boeotia in classical times, 10 had disappeared by the end of the republican era), the peace and stability brought by the Empire had produced a check on this, although not everywhere (in Boeotia only 32 remained in the second century). They had revived, for example, those faltering cities which, under Augustus, through self-interest as much as vanity, set about honoring the emperor with monumental buildings, in order to obtain from him advantages that would allow them to outstrip a rival. It then became clear that, confronted with these numerous, heavily populated towns, often haughtily proud of their past, yet also anxious to gain Roman favors and preserve their privileges, Rome could not conduct a policy comparable to the one it had used in the West.

There are too many missing parts for us to know all the aspects of the policy that Rome adopted in the East. It seems to have revealed itself in two complementary ways. First, in Rome's showing, within its provincial framework, a respect, real or pretended, for the institutions that had pre-existed Roman government, as long as they supported it. Secondly, in its presentation of a model state – its own – which could be adjusted to suit different places and circumstances, the better to achieve its spread. A clear (if extreme) example of the first type of case was that of Egypt. Apart from the introduction of a few high officials and a poll tax (payable by all, except Greeks and Romans, between the ages of 14 and 60), as well as a modification of the status of lands and the creation under Hadrian of the Greek city of Antinoöpolis, there were no basic changes in the institutions of the Ptolemaic period. Similarly, in the Hauran, where Rome could not rely on a network of cities but where numerous rural communities existed, doing a fairly adequate job of self-administration, Rome encouraged these villages to provide themselves with more-structured institutions, and granted the largest of them the privileged rank of *metrokomia* (mother-village). Again, it is revealing that the number of free and autonomous cities (e.g. Laodicea under Hadrian) was far higher in the East than in the West.

An example of the second type of case is Patras, whose resettlement took place through a combination of Greek populations founded as a Roman colony, whereas farther west and north, in Nicopolis, the foundation established by Octavian after Actium had been created not as a colony but as a "Greek city." In interior Anatolia, tribal communities formed themselves into a new city, and Anatolian towns that in earlier times had preserved their status of sacerdotal state became ordinary *poleis* during the first century (Hierapolis in Phrygia). In Pisidia, the veterans of the Augustan colonies were rapidly absorbed by the native milieu, and in the Biqa' valley, indigenous and Roman colonial communities (there was a *pagus Augustus*) closely adjusted their lives to one another to their mutual benefit.

The final factor that gives us a better understanding of the East's expansion in the second century is the attitude of the emperors. As we have seen, once the confrontation with Mark Antony was over, Augustus took care to repair the disastrous consequences of the civil wars and to restore friendly relations with Greece and the East. He had in any case been drawn along that path by the rapidity with which the eastern cities had greeted his victory and was drawn further along it by the eagerness with which they promoted the imperial cult (the first sanctuaries of Rome and Augustus were set up at Nicomedia and Pergamum). His solicitude for the eastern provinces (aid for Corinth, for Paphos when it was devastated by an earthquake, for Athens, etc.) was in turn met by evidence of loyalty and enthusiasm on their part (temples, towns that changed their name, etc.). This double movement continued and spread during the first century AD. Claudius took a special interest in Apamea, which named itself Claudia Apamea in his honor. And in 77, Corinth, ravaged by an earthquake, was treated with great generosity by Vespasian, in whose honor it changed its name to the colony of Julia Flavia Augusta Corinthiensis, a change that might have appeared no more than a simple form of adulation had it not been accompanied by an architectural reorganization of the town center, henceforth dominated by buildings connected with the imperial cult. The East increasingly asserted its Roman nature.

Since it had been building up for a century, the prosperity of the eastern part of the Empire perhaps rested on foundations that were firmer than those of the western part, or at least on foundations that lay more outside Roman tradition. At all events, its frequently dazzling outward signs affected all sectors of human activity.

The signs of prosperity

Profusion of public buildings   The construction of public buildings was carried out swiftly and on a large scale, with occasional disasters (e.g. the collapse of the theater in Nicaea). The motivation behind these constructions was rarely of an economic kind. The reasons put forward were, first, "reasons of aesthetics, health, and prestige" (P. Gros). What occasioned the work varied, ranging from the presence of an emperor (from Athens to Jerash in Jordan, from Ephesus to Pergamum, new buildings marked out the journeys of Hadrian), through benefactions by ultra-rich notables (Herodes Atticus in Athens and Corinth, Vedius Antonius at Ephesus, Maleus Agrippa at Palmyra) and competition between towns (Nicomedia and Nicaea, Prusa and Apamea), to reconstructions after earthquakes. The range of edifices constructed was accordingly extremely wide. Three new features should be noted. First, in the second century, the imitation of Roman building forms (baths, triumphal arches, amphitheaters, drains and aqueducts, covered markets) was far more important than it had been. Secondly, there was an evident taste for gigantic proportions, expressed in imposing colonnaded avenues, and in colossal constructions often connected with the imperial ideology. Lastly, a composite but harmonious art was developed and employed in these works, in which, to varying degrees, three influences may be distinguished – Hellenistic, Roman, and indigenous (witness Ephesus, Aizanoi, and Baalbek). One point remains open: was this proliferation of constructions necessarily a sign of economic growth? It seems not, but one must qualify according to the cities and their regions.

True economic wealth   Although it is true that some regions merely struggled to get by (Boeotia, eastern Anatolia), the dominant impression of the East during the Antonine period is one of undeniable prosperity, even opulence, in the agricultural, artisanal, "industrial," and commercial sectors, with the long-distance trade with China and India exclusively eastern and going via Petra, Palmyra, or Alexandria, depending on routes and products. In the commercial sector, the Syrians in particular were outstanding. They dominated small- and large-scale commerce, and were to be found all over the Empire, from Cadiz to Cologne, Ostia to Lyon. In Lyon, the funerary inscription of a merchant from Laodicea specifies that he had come to bring to "the Celts and the lands of the West all that God had chosen to give to the lands of the East, fruitful in all produce."

Intellectual renaissance   In the second half of the Antonine century, the East enlightened the Mediterranean world in all areas of intellectual life. In history, with Philo of Byblos, Plutarch of Chaeronea, Arrian of Nicomedia, Appian of Alexandria (and Pausanias, the traveler). And in rhetoric, with Herodes Atticus, Dio of Prusa, Aelius Aristides, Lucian of Samosata, and Maximus of Tyre. The Easterners were equally masters in medicine, with Galen; in astronomy, with Ptolemy; and as novelists, with Longus of Lesbos and Philostratus of Athens. And when Trajan wanted to engage an architect, he chose a Syrian, Apollodorus of Damascus. Even the law, until that time the unchallenged domain of the Latin West, was invaded by eastern schools, such as that of Beirut.

A new feeling: being a Greek-speaking Roman   While in the first century certain Greek writers had still scornfully surveyed the Roman barbarians from the West and cultivated the memory of the past, that attitude disappeared in the second century. In no way did it mean abandoning one's city of origin, but the feeling of belonging to the *orbis Romanus*, the Roman world, was much stronger. Aelius Aristides, a Mysian, proclaimed it in his *Eulogy of Rome*: there are no longer any but Romans who speak Latin and Romans who speak Greek. This was not rhetorical flattery, but simply a common-sense observation. Syrian villages built Roman baths, and there are records of over 350 monuments connected with gladiatorial fights and *venationes* (animal fights) in the eastern Greek world: leisure activities and games took their inspiration from the Roman model. On a more exalted plane, in 193, when he was old, nearly blind, and more than ever resolved to live in retirement, it was proposed to Ti. Claudius Pompeianus, who was one of Marcus Aurelius' sons-in-law, but also the son of a knight of Antioch, that he should be emperor. He refused. But by the contrast it set up with the usurpation by Avidius Cassius (another Syrian) that had occurred some years previously, the proposal assumed symbolic value: it was no longer inconceivable that the emperor should be an Easterner.

A MEDITERRANEAN ECONOMY

Economic thinking existed among the Romans, but its reasoning was not the same as our own. In Rome, economic thinking "was never anything but part of an all-encompassing reflection which in reality placed the state, in its entirety, at the heart of everything; it was seen to be the unrivaled place for human relations, and its cohesiveness and values had to be preserved at all costs" (C. Nicolet). It was the moral equilibrium of the state that mattered. There would always be confusion between morality and economy. Thus, the wealth brought by trade could be regarded at the same time as an economic resource, a sign of political domination, and a source of moral corruption.

That said, economic history itself has made enormous strides in the space of a few years. Though it is not possible to have a general overview of the whole Empire (economic studies being most frequently regional), one may nevertheless assemble enough information to look at the major economic sectors. There is no question here of our presenting the results in their entirety. Rather, we shall be giving a few broad indications, both specific and general, concerning economic life in those sectors in the second century of the Empire.

Before we do so, we should recall that the conditions of economic life were extremely favorable to its blossoming. There was peace. There was a network of roads that were continually maintained and improved, a spread of rivers that allowed access to the interior from the Mediterranean, the sea itself, which had become safer, though it was not much frequented between November and March (the sea is closed, said the Romans), and ports that were constantly being developed (Ostia, Carthage, Alexandria, Leptis Magna, Seleucia of Pieria, etc.). There was the very extent of the Empire, offering a huge range of varied and complementary resources, and there were vast centers of consumption (Rome, the large towns, the frontier zones). There was the continuing advance in luxury and the evolution of a society which consumed more and more, together with an almost stable currency (despite a weakening under Marcus Aurelius), and a population increase that encouraged the opening up of new lands. All in all, it was an era of such obvious economic prosperity that its material effects impressed even a Christian writer of anti-establishment temperament: "We note with certainty," Tertullian wrote in around 210,

that the world daily grows better cultivated and better supplied with everything than it used to be. Everything is accessible, everything is known, everything is used; delightful rural domains have forced famous deserts to retreat, furrows have tamed the forests, herds have put wild animals to flight; stretches of sand have been sown with seed, roads are opened through the rocks, marshlands are drained, there are now as many towns as there once were houses . . . Everywhere there are dwellings, peoples, cities, life.

Plate 11.8 Mosaic in the Square of the Corporations at Ostia, depicting a lighthouse, a dolphin, and two ships with large steering oars. 2nd/3rd century AD.

AGRICULTURAL LIFE

The foremost economic activity was agriculture, the foremost source of wealth land. Of the Empire's 50–60 million inhabitants, at least 90 per cent made their living from the land. An aristocrat's resources were measured in landed property: one could be both rich in land and an upright, worthy man. Moreover, the emperor was the chief landowner. No more perfect happiness in the world could be imagined than a peasant's life. The good peasant lives far from towns, says Dio of Prusa in the *Euboicus*, and Pliny the Younger, while hymning the solitude of the forests, was none the less an efficient and practical farmer.

Rome's imprints

With the expansion outside Italy of centuriation and the appearance in the provinces of a type of farmhouse built in stone, the *villa*, Rome's presence there could be seen in material form in the rural landscape. Centuriation was the dividing of land into regular plots (*centuriae*) on a grid based in theory on north–south and east–west lines. With both a fiscal and land demarcation purpose, these "centuries" were introduced throughout the Empire following

Plate 11.9 A Roman matron and her servant bathing a baby. Detail of a sarcophagus, 2nd century AD. Capitoline Museum, Rome.

the same system. In contrast, the *villa* could be flexibly adapted to local traditions, different climates, and the area of its land, the *fundus*. Whether it emerged from the influence of the conqueror or demonstrated a Romanization of those who had been conquered, this sign of Roman colonization, generally constructed on a symmetrical plan and built on a carefully selected site, most often comprised two parts: the dwelling of the master or his representative (*pars urbana*) and farm buildings (*pars rustica*). Nearby there is often evidence of the presence of indigenous inhabitants, sometimes scattered, sometimes grouped together. From Tunisia to the London basin, from Picardy to the Hungarian plains, aerial photography has enabled us to discover thousands of such villas.

Movements during the century

Four major developments became evident in agricultural life during the second century, apart from its growing prosperity. First, the huge estate (*latifundium*) was replaced by small and medium-sized holdings within the framework of large-scale property. The sharecropper colonist thus made his appearance, and we can follow the development of this kind of colony thanks to Pliny the Younger and three documents found in Tunisia (inscriptions of Henchir Mettich, Ain Djemala, and Souk el Khemis). Secondly, an expansion of cultivated areas is noticeable – for example, in North Africa, the *Agri Decumates*, Dacia, and the Fens in England. Thirdly, alongside large-scale farming devoted mainly to the growing of cereals, a type of farming that was in decline, an intensive and more dynamic type of farming was to be found, diverse in its products and activities but centered on a principal crop (vineyards, orchards, olive groves) and livestock breeding. Lastly, the second century seems to have been one of agricultural science. The great landowners read treatises by agronomists, looked beyond providing for their own consumption to the commercialization of their surpluses, sometimes specialized, and even, in some cases, regarded land as an investment and no longer merely a form of property that brought social status.

Ways of working the land

These depended on the size of the property. In charge of the vast imperial domains (*saltus*) which went beyond the territory of the cities, were procurators, either one or two (equestrian) procurators per province for the imperial possessions in that province, or one procurator (freedman) per great domain. The procurator was assisted by a *conductor* (farmer general), who leased out land to colonists, the real farmers, who paid rent and were obliged to supply a certain amount of free labor. The domain itself was divided into four: one part was cultivated for the procurator, another by the colonists for themselves, the third comprised pasture lands, and the fourth was land left fallow. The organization was the same for a large private domain, but the procurator was replaced by a *villicus* or steward. At the other end of the scale, the small freeholding was directly worked by the owner (veteran, native inhabitant), with or without the help of slaves. Between these two types of holding was a whole range of others combining the various different elements, and involving as well the use of day-laborers.

Provincial variety

The provinces varied enormously in how prevalent the various types of ways of working the land were within their regions and in the precise form that they took. These were matters linked to the status of the lands (in Syria, towns and temples owned huge properties which they administered themselves, and agricultural slavery was little developed), to native traditions (small and medium-sized properties seem to have predominated in western Gaul, Asia, Pannonia, etc.), and to the vicissitudes of history (settlements of colonists and veterans, confiscation of lands by the emperor).

"Industry" and commerce

"Industry"

"Industrial" production grew without technical progress: improvements were made on what already existed. As it increased, this production diversified and, above all, tended to become less concentrated, remaining, in most cases, in keeping with the size of the province. For these reasons, domestic industry, that is, the manufacture of products in a domestic setting, maintained its strength (such was the case in rural areas, where people spun, forged metal, wove, etc.) and urban crafts were vigorously developed. On the other hand, a relatively heavy, though still in modern terms modest, concentration is noticeable in the case of certain activities which were created around a heavy or very localized raw material (mines, quarries), or which were involved in the mass-production of one model (lamps, crockery), or which required a high degree of skill (glass-making). Let us look more closely at two areas of production, mines and manufacturing industries.

Mines and quarries (in Latin, a single word *metalla*) were spread through-out the Empire (see figure 11.2) and were worked intensively in the second century. Since the first century AD, the largest deposits had belonged to the state (or to the emperor personally). Depending on the region and the mine, it could either be exploited directly by the government, or be leased to individuals or companies. One equestrian procurator per province supervised the mines, which were sometimes divided into sectors, each entrusted to subordinate procurator (freedman). These mining districts led a special existence, known to us through inscriptions (the bronze tables of Vipasca in Portugal): they came outside any municipal structure and were directly administered by imperial officials. Though there were miners who were free men, the majority were slaves and convicts. But these two sources of labor were inadequate for the demand, and working conditions and tools did not improve, so that labor for the mines became increasingly scarce.

Manufacturing industries (see figure 11.2) may be placed in two categories: common and specialized. In the first group belong textile production (wool, linen), dyeing, shoemaking, furniture-making, building trades, etc. In the second, luxury industries (cotton, goldsmithing, silk, perfumes, glassware, papyrus paper, parchment), almost all of their products originating from Asia, Syria, and Egypt; food industries (garum, oils), essentially situated in a relatively few geographically extensive "production areas"; metalwork, relatively scattered, because there were countless small deposits of iron and copper; and

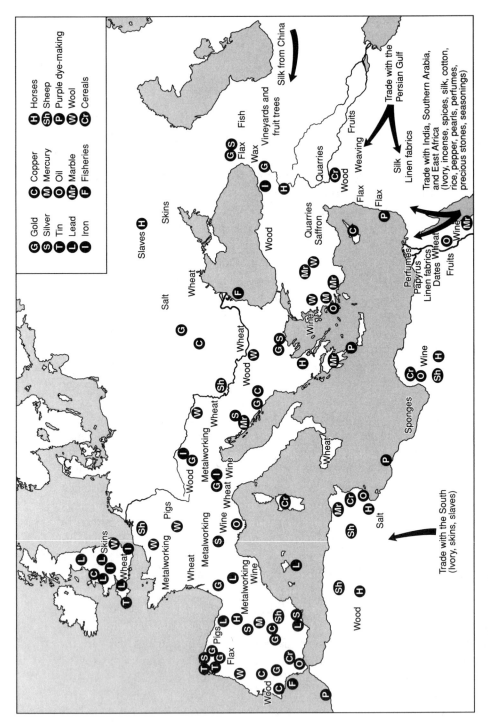

Figure 11.2 The Empire's resources

lastly pottery, which made the fortune of Gaulish craftsmen gathered together in large centers, first in workshops in the south of Gaul (Montans, La Graufe-senque, Banassac) from 30 BC to AD 120 for their greatest output, then in workshops in central Gaul, which had a period of industrial production from Vespasian to Commodus (Lezoux), and lastly in workshops in the east of Gaul which opened at the end of the first century AD and in some cases survived until the third century (Mittelbronn, La Madeleine, Rheinzabern).

Commerce

Trade was the Empire's second source of wealth. Ancient routes brought into use again, powerful infrastructures, general peace, and the existence of numer-ous products, all favored a great expansion in trade. Since the middle of the first century AD, Italian merchants had lost control of the Empire's trade to Easterners (Jews, Egyptians, Syrians), both within the Empire and beyond the frontiers (see figure 11.3).

Internal trade A Mediterranean world with a few Atlantic and continental links, the Empire could meet all its needs with the exception of exotic products. Trading circuits produced three maps. First, there was local, regional trade, a permanent retail trade, existing in every city, but about which very little is known. Then came inter-regional trade centered on the large ports (Carthage, Narbonne) and towns situated at communications junctions (Lyon, London). Lastly, "centralized" trade that converged on Rome, with four mar-itime routes of prime importance: Alexandria–Rome, Carthage–Rome, south-ern Gaul–Rome, and Iberian peninsula–Rome. One may then understand the fundamental position occupied by certain ports, like Alexandria, the largest exporting port in the Roman world. In the second century, a new circuit began, abandoning the Mediterranean to follow the Rhine and the Danube, thus putting Britain in contact with the Black Sea. Transported goods were surpluses produced by the provinces or imported from abroad. For Rome they obviously corresponded to its provisioning in goods of all kinds in the framework of the *annona* (grain, oil) or outside it. Quantities are difficult to estimate, but an annual figure of about 190,000 tonnes of grain for Rome seems acceptable.

External trade This took four different directions:

1 Countries of northern Europe. Amber, slaves, hides, furs, and dried fish were bought there. Finished goods (gold and silver vessels, glassware, and pottery) were exported to them. The big frontier post was Carnuntum on the Danube, with Aquileia as its Mediterranean opposite number.
2 Countries north of the Black Sea. Traffic went by way of Olbia and Tanais and was mainly in horses, slaves, and jewels.

Figure 11.3 Trade routes (from P. Petit, *La Paix romaine*, PUF, 1967)

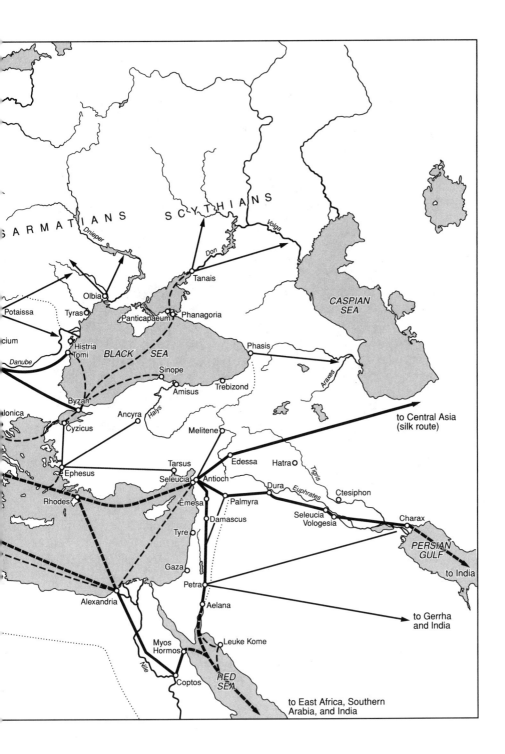

SARMATIANS

SCYTHIANS

Dnieper

Volga

Don

Potaissa

Olbia

Tyras

Tanais

CASPIAN
SEA

cium

Histria
Tomi

Panticapaeum

Phanagoria

Danube

BLACK   SEA

Phasis

Sinope

Araxes

lonica

Byzan'

Ancyra

Halys

Amisus

Trebizond

Cyzicus

Melitene

to Central Asia
(silk route)

Ephesus

Tarsus
Seleucia

Edessa

Hatra

Antioch

Dura

Tigris

Rhodes

Emesa

Palmyra

Euphrates

Ctesiphon

Damascus

Seleucia
Vologesia

Charax

Tyre

PERSIAN
GULF

Gaza

to India

Petra

Alexandria

Aelana

to Gerrha
and India

Myos
Hormos

Leuke Kome

Nile

RED
SEA

Coptos

to East Africa, Southern
Arabia, and India

Plate 11.10   The Capitol at Ostia, Rome's principal port, as seen from the forum.

3 Countries of black Africa. A modest amount of traffic came via Nubia and the Nile Valley; the rest by way of the desert (Fezzan) and Leptis Magna, although "we must resign ourselves to ignorance of the Saharan commercial routes in antiquity" (J. Desanges).

4 Countries of the Far East and Southern Arabia. This was the supreme example of large-scale trade, which allowed the acquisition of incense from Arabia, silk from China, and pepper from India, with additional merchandise (precious stones, skins). Three routes were used (see figure 11.3), ending at Antioch and Alexandria, craft center, transit and export port, the only harbor complex that by its activity could supplant Ostia's.

This external trade was hardly two-way. Rome paid in gold. For a long time this was described as a "haemorrhage" of gold, but it is now known that reflections of this kind were in-built in the Roman tradition of discourse against luxury, and that the 100 million sesterces involved did not put the Empire's economy in danger.

In the trading cities, mainly in the West, craftsmen, merchants, and shippers got together in guilds formed on the model of municipal *curiae*. These guilds also had a religious aim, promising their members proper funerals, and they played a not inconsiderable role in the lives of their cities, as did, for example, the guild of wine merchants in Lyon.

THE ARMY

With Augustus, a new army had been born – the imperial army. His successors had transformed this "experimental army" into a "standing army" (P. Le Roux) with one principal mission, to defend the Empire against any external aggression; a secondary function was to ensure order within the frontiers (keeping watch on roads, controlling nomads, preventing piracy, etc.), with subsidiary functions in administrative tasks, official mail, public works.

ORGANIZATION AND RECRUITMENT

Organization

Rome's garrison
- Ten praetorian cohorts under the orders of the praetorian prefect, basically made up of footsoldiers. Each cohort comprised 500 men. They used a camp situated on the Viminal, to the north-east of the capital.
- Three or four urban cohorts, each of 500 men. The term "urban" refers not so much to their mission as to their original garrison. In fact, even though they fulfilled a "policing" role in the capital, they were true military units (they took part in the Dacian campaigns) and gradually became indistinct from the praetorian cohorts, whose camp they shared.
- Seven cohorts of the watch. They were first of all firemen. However, these cohorts of 1,000 men, commanded by the prefect of the watch, became militarized during the second century.
- In addition, there were various corps whose task was to protect the emperor – his personal cavalry (*equites singulares Augusti*), body-guards – as well as special servicemen (looking after foreign residents, commissariat for the distribution of grain), and seamen.

The army of the provinces With the exception of the single urban cohorts set up under the Flavians in Lyon and Carthage, the army of the provinces consisted of legions and auxiliary units.

The legions There were 28 or 30 (according to the period), each of about 5,000 men, and in all representing the elite of the provincial army. Composed of footsoldiers and 120 horsemen, each legion was organized in ten cohorts of three maniples or six centuries apiece, except for the first cohort, whose five centuries were double the size of the others. A legion was designated by a number and a name (e.g. the Third Augusta), and as its emblem and principal standard it had an "eagle" (*aquila*), which was an object of veneration and was in the charge of a standard-bearer (*aquilifer*). It was commanded by a *legatus* of senatorial rank (except for legions stationed in Egypt), assisted by a laticlave tribune (also of senatorial rank), a camp prefect, and five angusticlave tribunes (knights). Subordinate to this headquarters staff, 59 centurions supervised the troopers, themselves hierarchized according to three criteria: fatigue duties (exempt or not), pay (from basic to triple), merit gained from the exercise of an office. Each legion had its music (to give commands), its instructors, health officers, engineers, caterers, security officers, and administrative personnel.

The auxiliaries These troops had the task of assisting the legions, but could be used separately. Divided into corps of 500 or 1,000 men (theoretically), in total they may nearly have equaled the number of legionaries. There were three kinds of auxiliary corps. The first kind, the *alae* or wings, were formed of horsemen, and the second, the cohorts, of footsoldiers (there were, however, also mixed cohorts, comprising infantry and horsemen). They were both commanded by a knight (prefect or tribune). The *numeri*, the third type of unit, were troops of indigenous and national soldiers who kept their ethnic character (language, uniform, weaponry) and were designated by the Romans according to their origins: the Moors, the Palmyrans, etc.

The navy There were two chief naval ports, Misenum and Ravenna, which sheltered the two great praetorian fleets, which patrolled, the one the western Mediterranean, the other the eastern. Provincial squadrons ensured the Roman presence on peripheral seas and the great rivers (fleets of Britain, Germania, Pannonia, Moesia, Pontus, Syria, and Alexandria). In total, this was a large network of naval bases, with naval resources of around 250 vessels and 45,000 men. For a long time, the military usefulness of this navy was questioned by historians. However, a recent thesis (M. Redde) has shown that, on the contrary, its military mission was of prime importance, and that its strength and technical standards commanded its enemies' respect. Besides performing a deterrent role, the imperial navy ensured army logistics, transporting troops, horses, arms, and food supplies, fought on the rivers of the frontier defense line, the *limes*, took part in combined operations, and, at least in the second century, made all its men undergo training for fighting on land.

The vexillationes In exceptional circumstances (a mission, war, building works, etc.), legions, auxiliaries, and fleets dispatched fairly large detachments known as *vexillationes*, from the standard (*vexillum*) around which these soldiers were assembled.

Taking all its forces together, the Roman army in the middle of the second century could line up around 350,000 men, whose supreme leader was the emperor, the only one entitled to celebrate a triumph.

Recruitment

- *The officers* They came from the senatorial or the equestrian order. Not specialized, men of peace as well as men of war, they regarded military activities as a temporary episode in their careers.
- *The centurions* In the second century, the majority were provincials (chiefly from the western and Danubian provinces). Most frequently they were the sons of municipal notables, fully Romanized from the earliest times, who reached this grade without always going through the ranks. A minority were soldiers' sons.
- *The legionaries* It was compulsory for them to be Roman citizens. Early in the second century, a uniform development began: "Regional recruitment slowly and gradually moved to local recruitment, through an intermediate phase during which soldiers came from cities that were ever closer to the fortress" (Y. Le Bohec). Take, for example, the Third Augusta, which was stationed in Africa: the first century belonged to the foreigners (Italians and Gauls); at the beginning of the next, Africans entered the legion, but still in smaller numbers than the foreigners (Bithynians, Danubians, Syrians); by the end of the second century, however, the Africans predominated: they were at first from Mauretania, but later from Numidia, where the legion was stationed. As for the legionaries' social origins, it seems (though studies are scarce) that they belonged to the elite of the plebeian *humiliores*, a choice reflecting the imperial policy of recruitment.
- *The praetorians* At the beginning of the second century, 89 per cent were Italian. This figure barely changed under the Antonines, but, to the extent that it did, Dalmatians and Pannonians made the principal gains.
- *The auxiliaries* These might be either Roman citizens or *peregrini*. Between the reign of Hadrian and 170, the first were as numerous as the second, who received citizenship on completion of their service. The net of recruitment was widely spread. Auxiliaries came chiefly from Tarraconensis, Belgica, Lugdunensis, Thrace, Pannonia, and Syria. It appears that, unlike the legions, there were auxiliary corps that did not gradually move toward local recruitment, so that overall among the auxiliaries there was a balance between local and external recruitment. There were three reasons for this: wherever they were stationed, the *numeri* were always barbarian troops; prudently, barbarian recruits were always sent far from their homeland (e.g. no Briton was

garrisoned in Britain); and certain specialized units always came from the same region (e.g. archers from Palmyra).

■ *The seamen* Many non-citizens (*peregrini* for the most part) but the question of their recruitment is not yet settled.

To ensure that numbers in the whole imperial army were kept up, it was necessary to recruit at least 18,000 men a year (service was voluntary although in theory the obligation to bear arms had never been abolished). This was, it would seem, an easily achievable figure, yet the authorities sometimes had difficulty in assembling such a contingent. Was it the length of service that put people off? This was sixteen years for the praetorians, twenty years (in theory) for the legionaries (more in practice), twenty-five for the auxiliaries, and twenty-six for the sailors.

STRATEGY, TACTICS, AND TRAINING

When, under the Flavians, the legions were put back on the Rhine, the rudimentary winter camps, built of wood and earth, were replaced by camps built in stone. This change in building methods was perhaps the first evidence of a new strategy. The "hegemonic" Empire of the Julio-Claudians was being succeeded by the "territorial" Empire, defined by its strategy of defending the perimeters, by setting up along them a permanent line of defense: "having attained the 'scientific' frontiers, no further operation was envisaged, in any case not beyond the range of fixed bases" (E. Luttwak). After Trajan's expeditions, this concept of preventive defense was imposed along all the frontiers, that is to say, 10,200 km including Dacia (9,600 without), plus 4,500 km of coastline. This system was known as the *limes*.

Tactical aspects of frontier defense

The various fixed parts of the *limes* were initially conceived of as a way of countering minor threats (infiltrations, raids, etc.), and not as a way of providing total protection against large-scale attacks. Thus, they served as points of departure for mobile forces setting out to intercept the attacks in advance or to cause them to be aborted. The battlefield thus lay beyond the frontier, rather than within it. These fixed "back-up" structures were:

■ A physical barrier (wall, palisade, earthwork and ditch) following the "frontier" of the Empire, as in Britain (the two Walls), Upper Germania, Raetia, Romania, and North Africa (the *Fossatum Africae*). But this was not continuous and was not a crucial part of the *limes*: the Empire never surrounded itself with a "great wall of China."

- Watchtowers and forts with outposts, which kept watch and gave warnings. The zone of external surveillance could extend as far as 80 km from the frontier.
- A system of visual communications (smoke, torches), which worked in two directions: along the frontier (even if there was no physically constructed line of defense) and across the frontier, between the outposts and the interior fortresses.
- Military bases: guard posts, auxiliaries' forts, legionary camps, all situated, in general, well behind the lines.
- Roads, which formed an essential element of the system. Some were at right angles to the frontier, which they crossed; others were parallel to it. The denser the network, the greater the strategic importance.

These material parts of the *limes* were merely the skeleton of the system, which was fleshed out with the activities of patrols, diplomatic missions, trade, and constant troop movements, and involved a whole host of local adaptations, with here a river used, there a mountain or desert.

Strategic aspects of frontier defense

Rome's military forces were spread unevenly along the frontiers and were divided into provincial or regional armies (*exercitus*) which, in Hadrian's time, began to acquire a measure of autonomy. Each of these armies was organized around a nucleus of legions permanently stationed in a province, reinforced by auxiliaries, and sometimes too by naval forces, which were also deployed around the perimeter of the Empire, except for the two central fleets.

Given the geographic configuration of the Empire, the slowness of internal communications (Cologne was sixty-six days' march from Rome, Antioch one hundred and twenty-six), the considerable distances between the various sectors, and the fact that reserves were very limited, the choice of a policy of regional deployment was, it seems, inevitable. But it was also admirably suited to allowing adaptation to regional frontiers, chosen, it would seem, not solely for topographical and tactical reasons, but also for strategic purposes. Thus, at the end of the reign of Antoninus there were 28 legions. The allocation of the legions is shown in the box on page 326.

Training

"Their nation," wrote the Jewish writer Flavius Josephus in the first century, speaking of the Romans, "does not wait until hostilities begin to give the men their first lesson in arms . . . they undergo continual training and never wait until the last moment to confront an unexpected danger." In the second century, his remark was more topical than ever. For it was, in fact, only continuous and intensive training that could maintain the fighting potential of an army that

Britain	3 legions
Rhine	4 legions
Lower Germania	2 legions
Upper Germania	2 legions
Danube	10 legions
Upper Pannonia	3 legions
Lower Pannonia	1 legion
Upper Moesia	2 legions
Lower Moesia	3 legions
Dacia	1 legion
Orient	8 legions
Cappadocia	2 legions
Syria	3 legions
Judaea	2 legions
Arabia	1 legion
Egypt	1 legion
Africa	1 legion
Iberian peninsula	1 legion

(from E. Luttwak, *La Grande Stratégie de l'Empire romain*, Paris, 1987, p. 70)

had to stay for an indeterminate period in military life during a time of almost total peace. It was necessary to make ready for victory and for this it was necessary to keep up the morale and proficiency of the troops by means of practice. The importance that the government attributed to the training and professional specialization of the soldier is witnessed to by the speech addressed to the troops in Africa by the emperor Hadrian found inscribed on a column at Lambaesis.

WEAKNESSES

Numerical weakness This could be partly offset by high standards and good training, but even so could constitute a serious handicap, especially in long-lasting wars, given the difficulty met with in keeping up even existing numbers.

The financial burden Maintaining such an army was a heavy expense. Estimates are only approximate, and are based on pay. But it is thus calculated that the cost of a legion was in the region of 2.25 million denarii per annum. And the entire cost of the army, if the navy cost as much as, or slightly less than, the auxiliaries, would be somewhere between 140 and 145 million denarii per annum (other, lower estimates vary between 80 and 90 million). At any rate, the army figured in the state budget as the main charge, between 40 and 50 per cent. (By way of comparison, the cost of the great powers' armies, before the industrial revolution, represented a minimum of 60 per cent of the budget.)

The system itself The Empire's military might was first of all a diplomatic instrument: the threat of its use dissuaded the enemy, who in the second century never produced a force likely to worry the legions. But beyond the frontiers it would take only the appearance of a federation of tribes or another empire to outface the *limes*, conceived as a deterrent to threats on a small scale: the extreme overstretching of the units did not in fact allow the detachment of a large part from one front to be sent elsewhere. The system lacked flexibility. What would happen if organized frontier peoples attacked at the same time at two very distant points?

*   *   *

The army under the Antonines attained its objective: to ensure permanent security for the populations living within the Empire's frontiers. In that, it was playing a part in the supreme designs of the Empire itself: to create a new society in which the barbarians within the frontiers, increasingly integrated into the Roman world and increasingly cut off from the barbarians outside, were to become heartfelt citizens of the vast Empire.

RELIGIOUS LIFE

"It was a true melting-pot," observes an American historian speaking of the Roman Empire and its religions. "Even if you skim lightly through the Roman Empire, or however cursorily you look at its religious diversity, you cannot fail to be struck by the proliferation of beliefs." It is a proliferation that must be preserved in its entirety on pain of failing to appreciate its vitality. In his study (*Paganism in the Roman Empire*), Ramsay MacMullen refrains from analysing the "constituent parts, [the] particular cults, their derivations and specific nature," in order to deal with the complete system and its exchanges. Doubtless he was right; but it is still necessary to know something of the essential features of its main components: traditional Roman religion, the imperial cult, and indigenous cults, some of which passed beyond their region of origin.

Traditional Roman religion

In his capacity as head of the Roman religion, Augustus restored and revived it. Henceforth, the emperor was the sole master of both the sacred and the profane: the auspices of the magistrates were thus subordinate to the auspicial pre-eminence of the emperor. But far from impoverishing traditional religion, this modification seems to have enriched it. Three general characteristics mark its development during the second century.

Continuity

For a long time, historians presented the traditional religion of the imperial epoch as in decline, anaemic, and virtually moribund. But now, rereadings of the texts, a better use of inscriptions, and a more-expert analysis of the relations between religion and civic activities have led them to place greater emphasis on the durability and continuity, that is, the permanence, and even the vigor of that religion.

Permanence, in so far as the old forms of worship continued to be practiced, expressing the age-old piety of Rome. Permanence also from the point of view of ritual, in so far as the liturgy itself did not basically alter. Festivals and sacrifices continued to be celebrated until the Christian era, with a fervor attested by all the documents and monuments, without doubt even greater fervor than during the rifts in the last centuries of the Republic, for piety was the very foundation of the imperial regime. Lastly, permanence in religious relations. As under the Republic, worship was safeguarded by the elite, the combined action of magistrates and priests, above whom was now placed the sovereign pontiff, the emperor.

The ancient rites (those of the Salii and Luperci, for instance) were still scrupulously celebrated, the proceedings of the Arval Brothers were still strictly recorded, Jupiter continued to be the most popular god in the pantheon (often, it is true, in implicit association with imperial worship), and the conduct of the devout pagan does not seem to have changed: "Pious travelers," notes Apuleius (*Florides* I), "if they come across some sacred wood or holy place in the course of their journey, are in the habit of making a vow, offering a fruit or sitting down for a moment."

The role of the emperors

Until the time of Commodus, the Antonines regarded themselves as guardians of the state: "Thus their chief preoccupation was the safeguarding of the material and moral heritage of Rome . . . they devoted themselves to preserving what seemed to them to be essential: the gods and the rites whose existence, in Roman eyes, affected that of Rome and the Empire, and the fundamental values of Graeco-Latin civilization" (J. Beaujeu). Their action took various forms:

- Honoring the priesthoods. Following Augustan tradition, the emperor not only was *pontifex maximus*, but also held several priesthoods concurrently. Nerva, for example, belonged to the four great colleges (pontiffs, augurs, quindecimvirs in charge of sacrifices, *epulones*); Hadrian had the young Marcus Aurelius entered in the college of the Salians at the tender age of seven (a unique privilege); and Commodus, having just become *Caesar*, was also received into the four great colleges (in 175), as his father had been too in 140. The emperor was indeed always admitted to those four colleges. But Marcus Aurelius also revived the ancient rite of the Fetial declaration of war.
- Controlling the priesthoods. Whether it was a matter of appointing someone to an individual priestly office, or of filling places in colleges or sodalities, the emperor, in fact if not in law, could appoint his own choice.
- "Promoting" a god. Trajan, for example, was devoted to the Hercules of Gades (Cadiz), the Latin name for the Phoenician tutelary divinity Melqart. Rather than impose this foreign god on Rome, he preferred to make the Roman Hercules benefit from his fervor. Vows, medals, games, and his representation on the Arch of Beneventum all demonstrate the particular favor accorded to Hercules during Trajan's reign.
- Honoring the whole range of traditional gods. Trajan's coinage reveals a great deal here. Nearly all the great deities of Rome are represented. If the effigies of Jupiter, Rome, Vesta, and Victory are the most frequent, those of Apollo, Ceres, Diana, the Dioscuri, Flora, Hercules, Janus, Juno, Mars, Mercury, Minerva, Nemesis, Neptune, Quirinus, Saturn, the Sun, Venus, and Vulcan are also to be found, as are those of Aeneas and personified abstractions such as *Concordia*, *Libertas*, *Pietas*, and *Spes*. The legends of archaic Rome were still held in honor under Hadrian and, above all, Antoninus, who attached remarkable importance to the old cults of Latium and the deities of rural Italy.
- Building and restoring. In this area, Hadrian well deserves the title of "champion of traditional religion" (J. Beaujeu), his claim here resting not only on such celebrated Roman monuments as the Pantheon and the temple of Venus and Rome, promoted now to the rank of official deity, but also on, for example, the renovated temples of his small home town, Lanuvium, in particular that of Juno Sospita, the most venerable of all the Italian shrines to this goddess.

The century of virtus and pietas

It was not by chance that, even before Trajan made his entry into Rome (summer 99), the Senate issued an *as* showing Victory with a shield, modeled on the reverse side of those struck under Augustus. The shield of Augustus was a potent symbol of the victor armed with virtue. On it figured both of these virtues, *virtus* and *pietas*, which now, with the Antonines, made a considerable advance.

- *Virtus*, the foremost of the Augustan virtues, manifested itself especially in combat. Under Trajan, it eclipsed *fortuna* and *felicitas*. Henceforward, it was no longer these two which ensured victory, but rather the personal *virtus* of the emperor. With Hadrian, the idea of *virtus* was altered. The purely military aspect became less prominent, and *virtus* was tellingly revealed in the hunt: official imagery glorified the emperor's hunting exploits (as in the eight medallions on the Arch of Constantine), likening them to bold displays of *virtus* on the field of battle.
- *Pietas* was invoked as early as Nerva's time. And it was the quality that Pliny acknowledged in Trajan, piety toward his family and the gods. But with Antoninus, *pietas* reached its zenith. Its effigy appeared in the first issues of coinage in his reign, and the emperor himself chose his *cognomen* of *Pius*, for he wanted "to personify in the eyes of the world that virtue, which was innate in him, and spread it around him like the essential seed of moral life" (J. Beaujeu). *Pietas* became the ideal proposed by this ruler to his century and the fundamental principle of the regime.

IMPERIAL RELIGION

Created by Augustus, organized by Vespasian, the imperial cult was simultaneously individual, municipal, provincial, and imperial, addressed to dead emperors but by no means neglecting the living ones, whether or not in worship they were associated with the Goddess Rome. In the second century, the imperial cult underwent a notable expansion. There were several contributory factors.

The Jovian theology of the Principate   Augustus had already harked back to Jupiter, but discreetly. With Trajan, a close association was forged between the first among the Romans and the first among the gods. When Trajan went to the Capitol on his entry into Rome, even before he had received the imperial titles the crowds had acclaimed him, says Pliny the Younger, with cries of *Jupiter Imperator*. It was a presage. From that time on Jupiter was ever-present. As we have seen, he is represented on the Arch of Beneventum delegating his powers to the emperor; Trajan became viceroy on earth for the master of the universe. Far from disappearing with Trajan, this dogma, clear and solid, was confirmed with his successors. An eagle proffers a scepter to Hadrian, *Providentia* lends her thunderbolt to Antoninus, and Jupiter himself helps Marcus Aurelius in his struggles against the barbarians. It will come as no surprise, therefore, to see numerous new temples to the Capitoline Triad being built in provincial towns between 150 and 170. Rather than representing a relative weakening of the imperial cult, this marked the complete assimilation of the deified emperors to Jupiter Optimus Maximus, the most popular of all the gods.

The cult of dead emperors   In 183, out of the sixteen deified persons officially honored by a cult, twelve were Antonines – the emperors Nerva, Trajan, Hadrian, Antoninus, and Lucius Verus, together with various sisters and wives. Whether deliberately or by a sort of natural development, the *Domus augusta* occupied an increasingly eminent position in religious life. A temple was erected for nearly every deified member, and further sodalities (for Hadrian and Antoninus) were created.

The success of the provincial and municipal cult   Whether in the setting of a province or of a city, the imperial cult was successfully transplanted. Ways and means varied depending on the province, with the assemblies variously formed (*concilium, koinon*) and the districts often peculiar to the province (the Three Gauls, the numerous reorganizations of Syria), but the loyalty of the population expressed at these assemblies seems to have been much the same everywhere.

A popular cult?   The popularity of the imperial cult was in doubt among historians for a long time. It was thought that because it was official, it could only be superficial. It now seems, on the contrary, that the "love of Augustus" was firmly entrenched in hearts and minds. The divine and quasi-divine attributes of the emperor's deeds were venerated, sacrifices were made for the emperor's health, and evidence shows that in both town and country, in both Italy and the provinces, this was more than mere affectation among the Empire's inhabitants.

INDIGENOUS RELIGIONS

Under this general term, we include all the religions in the Empire except "Italian" religions. This simple statement makes clear the vast range of the subject, which cannot be tackled here as a whole, even superficially. To go into it in detail would necessitate a tour of the Empire, province by province, even region by region. And no overall view is really pertinent: these religions had no links with universalism and were rooted in a precise area, history, and society (though some journeyed far from home). The most we can do here is to present a few evolutionary features that they (or some of them) had in common.

Continuity

If the idea of a rebirth of indigenous cults in the second century must be set aside (there had been no obliteration in the first century, or even necessarily a decline, but the second century, which produced a greater number of documents, gives the illusion of a renaissance), that of their succumbing to an advancing Romanization has to be qualified. Studying the north-west of the Iberian peninsula, A. Tranoy notes that "the religious policy of the Roman government permitted and facilitated the development of local religions in so far as they accepted a gradual assimilation with Roman deities." This statement, with a few qualifications, could be applied to other provinces. For example, while the coming of the Romans to Gaul had been the death of "the Druids' most authentic rites [human sacrifice, display of the heads], as well as their clergy and lore," "Celtic polytheism, though it had lost its myths, none the less expressed itself through, and was enriched by, various kinds of representations and inscriptions drawn from its contacts with Roman polytheism" (P.-M. Duval). Again, in Africa, despite all the apparent Romanization, "Saturn, the simple Latin translation of Ba'al-Hammon, remained an African god to the very end" (M. Le Glay). Nowhere did Rome seek to impose a form of religious life (with the exception of the disallowing of human sacrifice, banned in the first century). The cult of Rome and Augustus was no threat to indigenous cults. Often the two were even associated. Of course, the Romans had their reservations, the most obvious relating to Egypt. They scorned gods with animal bodies, finding them bizarre and ridiculous. But they left anyone who wished to worship them free to do so. All in all, in this encounter of polytheisms, continuing indigenous religions trace an invisible frontier – that of the Romanization of souls.

Interpretatio

"Among the Naharvali [an independent Germanic people], a sacred wood is to be seen, the place of worship of a very ancient cult. Its lord is a priest dressed as a woman, but it is said that the gods of the place are Castor and Pollux, according to the Roman interpretation" (Tacitus, *Germania* 43.4). Tacitus' phrase "the Roman interpretation" reveals the way in which a foreign observer understands an unknown god by likening it to, or identifying it with, a god that he knows. So we see a dual phenomenon, of major importance in the history of indigenous religions. Working one way is the *interpretatio Romana*, which dresses a native god in Roman guise, or sees a native god as a Roman god in local or native guise (Caesar, to take an example from an earlier period, had named the Gaulish god of trade and industry "Mercury"). Working the other way is the *interpretatio Gallica* in Gaul, *Africana* in Africa, or *Iberica* in Spain, for example, through which a Roman god comes to be clad in Gaulish, African, or Iberian style. In fact, these two processes often occurred simultaneously. The historian stresses the alteration that is of interest to him. Here is an example given by P.-M. Duval for Gaul, that of *Mars Vesontius*. The name could designate:

- the Roman Mars honored in the town of Besançon;
- a great native god whom the Bisontini identified with Mars; or
- a local native god likened to the Roman god.

If these examples are multiplied, one may understand both the richness and complexity of this phenomenon.

Established indigenous religions

This term covers the majority of the indigenous religions. We are speaking, as we have said, of non-Italian religions, testimonies to which, in the vast majority of cases (Gallo-Roman, Iberico-Roman, etc.), are to be found in their places of origin. All preserved their native identity, which survived, more or less altered, in Roman guise. Two examples follow.

Gaul Over 400 sanctuaries are known, most frequently in the vicinity of a spring, a cave, or a cliff, or on a peak, in a mountain pass, or at a river crossing. These sanctuaries took various forms. Some, for example, were chapels (*fana*) with a gallery in which people could circulate, others comprised several buildings and received many pilgrims (e.g. the sources of the Seine). Ex-votos and offerings, which are being increasingly studied, reveal the indigenous nature of the worshipers. Only 4 per cent of the Gaulish inscriptions addressed to native gods come from people whose names are not Gaulish. The divinities worshiped in these places are only partly known. They are represented in peculiar poses (cross-legged), and are often accompanied by animals. Frequently linked to naturist cults, they were gods and goddesses of the waters, of the fruitful earth, livestock, and trade. For example, the typically Celtic Mother-Goddesses, who bore a Latin name, the *Matres* (sometimes distinguished by a pertinent adjective of native origin), were mostly represented in a group of three, with a child and a horn of plenty.

Africa Here the case was very different. The native pantheon was dominated by a great god, "the" lord of Africa, whom the Romans assimilated with Saturn. Omnipotent, father of the gods, lord of the world, fauna and flora, protector of the dead, flanked by the sun and the moon, he was, contrary to his Roman name, in fact far removed (argues M. Le Glay) from the Graeco-Roman god who succeeded Janus. His cult, his sanctuaries and their decoration, the sacrifices offered to him (especially the *molk* sacrifice, the bloody offering of the first-born, and its substitute, *molchomor*, the sacrifice of a bull or a ram), and the standing of his worshipers (country-dwellers) – these provide clear evidence of his indigenous nature, revealing him as a Punico-Berber god, the heir of Ba'al, who had resisted all attempts at Romanization. This makes it easier to explain his success in north-western Africa and his lack of success elsewhere.

Dynamic indigenous religions

These are those indigenous religions (a minority on the scale of the Empire but one of great importance) that spread to Italy and Rome, and to nearly all the western provinces, from their native areas in the East. These "foreign" religions, as the Romans termed them, called "eastern" religions by Cumont, would be better termed "religions of eastern origin or Graeco-eastern religions" (R. Turcan), for their cults were not directly transposed from East to West, but were modified by contact with Greek religion and adapted to local conditions.

It has been noted that the dates when these religions made their appearance in Italy (and the same phenomenon is to be found in the provinces) are spread over several centuries, and that the political, psychological, and sociological circumstances of their arrivals were very different (for example, official for Cybele, private for Isis). The apparent coherence of this block of eastern religions is an illusion of perspective contrived for polemical reasons by a fourth-century Christian author, Firmicus Maternus, the first person to classify them as a distinct group. This tradition, brilliantly renewed and kept alive by Cumont, has led modern historians sometimes to ignore the specific characteristics of these religions and include them all in the same category, of "religions with mysteries which, issuing from naturist or animal-worshiping cults . . . to start with, seem to have evolved toward a spirituality with nuances that varied according to environments or individuals, but generally held together by a doctrine of the soul liberated after death from its mortal bonds and henceforth promoted to a happy celestial eternity" (R. Turcan).

The reasons for the success of these cults in the West also divide historians. It has traditionally been explained by the presence there of people who had adopted these cults in the East, followed by the conversion in the areas of the West where they resided of Romans and indigenous peoples, both of whom found in what they had to offer a spirituality lacking in their own religions. The presence of devotees from the East can be argued for from the nature of these cults. For these Graeco-eastern religions, which formed small communities distinct from the city, involved a religious commitment – even an initiation – at the end of which the believer shared in a revelation, and this commitment, which was not open to all, presupposes a spiritual and theological preparation organized by a specialized and sometimes learned clergy. Conversion was aided by seductive ceremonies and festivals, made so by the glamor of their music and processions, and was encouraged by an appealing individual morality produced by these religions that stressed the merits of purification, and by the promise of immortality they sometimes gave their followers, so that, in comparison with the colder, more external Roman religion, for example, which satisfied neither conscience nor intelligence nor even the feelings, they succeeded in convincing people of their excellence – although a conversion did not have to involve the abandonment of traditional religion.

PRINCIPAL EASTERN RELIGIONS

Name of god/goddess	Origin	Appearance in Italy and development
Cybele and Attis	Asia Minor	204 BC in Rome; development under Claudius; first mention of a *taurobolium* in AD 160.
Isis and Serapis	Alexandria	Before 105 BC in Pozzuoli; early first century BC in Rome; expansion under Caligula and (mainly) the Flavians.
Dea Syria (Atagartis)	Hierapolis-Bambyke (Syria)	As early as the end of the second century BC in Sicily; first century BC in Italy.
Jupiter Heliopolitanus	Heliopolis-Baalbek (Lebanon)	Developed from the time of Augustus in the East (Baalbek a Roman colony; theological creation around 16 BC); expansion in the West in the second century AD.
Jupiter Dolichenus	Doliche-Duluck (Turkey)	The type of god appeared in the first century AD; in the West under Hadrian; shrine in Rome in the middle of the second century.
Mithras	Iran	Under the Flavians, first epigraphic and literary attestations.

Other historians think that there were few conversions: "Under the follower of Isis in Ostia was hidden the man or woman from Alexandria or Antioch, or perhaps the descendant of a family originating from one of those towns. Similarly, the follower of Isis in Lyon concealed not a convert, but an immigrant" (R. MacMullen). In that case, "It is probable that the religious history of the West, more than would seem at first glance, is closer to that of the East, the same calm reigning in both parts of the Empire." If so, it was slaves and their descendants who provided the mass of adherents of these cults. For example, in Campania, Etruria, and Apulia, three-quarters of the signatories of inscriptions dedicated to Isis were slaves and freedmen; in Rome, the Veneto, and

Plate 11.11 Dancers in an erotic revel, 2nd century AD.

Sicily, they form three-fifths. In all, nearly half the followers of Isis in Italy had non-Italian origins.

Nevertheless, it is undeniable that there were conversions. For instance, in Spain, Gaul, Africa, Mauretania, Germany, and even in Britain, Isis went beyond the port districts and commercial towns frequented by Graeco-Egyptians and reached the indigenous populations. Similarly, the cult of the Great Mother (Cybele) found fertile soil in Gaul, where over 60 altars for bull sacrifice have been found, more than in any other region of the Empire. Perhaps the indigenous worship of the Mother-Goddesses had prepared the ground for the cult of Cybele. So we are led to steer a middle course: the presence of Easterners, transmission, often through relays of eastern origin, in Italy (Campania) and Romanized regions of the western provinces, followed by local diffusion. But it is still necessary to make a distinction, when we come to the specific sphere of influence of each cult, between the dynamic and the not so dynamic. If the worship of Isis, Cybele, and Mithras, for example, spread widely in the West, the Syrian gods, by contrast, remained marginal and were almost always honored only by migrants and foreign residents.

The spread of these various religions was advanced in a number of ways. A cult might be encouraged by the emperor, directly through personal belief or for political reasons, or indirectly through his entourage (wife, artists, slaves, and freedmen) and the court. Moreover, the adherents of these religions often linked their cults with the imperial cult, very often from civic solidarity – this was rare, however, among the devotees of Alexandrian cults. Imperial officials and soldiers, too, at all levels of their hierarchies, were important agents of diffusion. The soldiers reveal a marked preference for Mithras, Jupiter Dolichenus, and Jupiter Heliopolitanus. Leaving aside Rome and Ostia, the map of the spread of these three cults, even though civilians were also involved, virtually matches that of the military zones (apart from anything else, the civilians were often connected by their activities to the service of the armies and the imperial machinery). Lastly there are the traders, who were nearly all eastern. Their gods traveled with them. They were to be encountered in the ports (Pozzuoli, Ostia, Carthage, Marseille), along the rivers (the valleys of the Rhône, the Rhine, the Danube, the Guadalquivir, the Ebro) and along the land routes (Alpine passes, the Rhône–Rhine axis), in cosmopolitan and commercial towns, and at road junctions in general (Lyon, Poetovio, Trier).

All in all, the worshipers of these gods were people, eastern or not, who were continually on the move or cut off from their city of origin, who needed gods that could go outside the limits of the city, that were omnipresent, and little communities where comfort and safety could be found. Watching over individuals and in charge of the world, these eastern gods, removed from their native lands, intimately present in the hearts of their devotees, and endowed with limitless powers that transcended all the functions of the gods in the classical pantheon, were truly in keeping with the Empire.

12 / THE AFRICAN AND SYRIAN EMPERORS, AD 193–235

THE CRISIS OF 193–197

Circumstances had compelled the conspirators to make the utmost haste. On the very night of Commodus' murder (December 31, 192), they persuaded the prefect of Rome, P. Helvius Pertinax, to accept the purple, took him to the praetorian camp, and then before the Senate. The praetorians acclaimed him *imperator* under pressure from the mob and on the promise of a *donativum*; the senators in the flush of their deliverance from a tyrant for whose *damnatio memoriae* they at once voted, and from esteem for Pertinax, who received the imperial titles and, contrary to tradition, immediately assumed that of *pater patriae*. He was 66 years old. A native of Liguria and the son of a freedman, he had first followed an equestrian career before being admitted to the Senate among former praetors by Marcus Aurelius, and thanks to his qualities had eventually reached the peak of the senatorial career as prefect of the city. Worried by the condition of the imperial finances, attentive to the economic situation, and anxious about the barbarian threat, the new emperor was determined to apply measures likely to restore the might of the state. To do that he had to take the praetorians in hand. On March 28, a party of them broke into the imperial palace and, despite his courage, Pertinax was assassinated. He had ruled for just 87 days.

This abrupt mutiny, without any precise aim, had no political pretensions. Uncertain what to do about their crime, and since the Empire could not remain without an emperor, the praetorians let it be known that they would offer the post to the highest bidder. There were two competitors. For 5,000 sesterces per praetorian more than his rival (in all, 25,000 sesterces to each), the secondcomer, the ultra-rich senator M. Didius Julianus, won. Originating from Milan (where he was born in 133 or 137), and with family ties in Africa, he had pursued an exemplary senatorial career, culminating in the proconsulship of Africa (189–90). He was one of the most senior of the men of consular rank, and had both wide experience and good contacts. However, given a cold welcome by the Senate and jeered at by the people, Julianus, as emperor, could count on no one in Rome except the praetorians. And in the Empire itself, his support was even more tenuous. At the end of April, he learned that military risings had occurred in Pannonia and Syria, and that L. Septimius Severus and C. Pescennius Niger, respectively, had been proclaimed emperor by their armies. At Julianus' insistence, the Senate declared the two men to be public enemies and offered an amnesty to their troops. Four years of conflict began.

Septimius Severus and his Sons

On April 9, 193 at Carnuntum, the governor of Upper Pannonia, Septimius Severus, was hailed as emperor by his troops. He presented himself as the avenger of Pertinax, whose surname he adopted among his personal names. From the beginning of the month, he had been in contact with the legates of the neighboring provinces, with the result that in the following days the 16 legions of the provinces of the Rhine and Danube rallied to his cause. To avoid any disagreeable surprise, he neutralized the governor of Britain, D. Clodius Albinus, also an African, by offering him the title of *Caesar*, which designated him as Severus' chosen successor. Three additional legions and numerous auxiliaries were thus ranged on Severus' side. Before he had begun marching on Rome to win over the city and the Senate, he learned that, in Antioch, Pescennius had also been declared emperor, dragging all the East and Egypt into this venture. During these preparations for war, one of Severus' character traits was clearly revealed: caution (guile, his enemies would say) allied with the iciest determination.

The African emperor: Septimius Severus (193–211)

The man in 193

Septimius Severus was born in April 145 in Leptis Magna, Tripolitania. On his mother's side he was descended from Italian immigrants (the Fulvii) who had married natives who had obtained Roman citizenship; on his father's side, from a family of Libyco-Punic origin (Roman citizens since the first century) which had divided into two branches, one Italian, the other African, and which had entered the senatorial order in the generation of Severus' father, though his father himself did not belong to it. There had been notable men on both sides. For example, his paternal grandfather had been both suffete (*suffes*) and prefect of Leptis before becoming its first *duumvir* when the city became a colony under Trajan (see genealogical table 12.1). Members of this ramified family helped one another. One of Severus' father's cousins, for example, arranged for him to receive the laticlave. Around 164, Severus began a senatorial *cursus honorum* that led him to a consulship in 190 and the governorship of Upper Pannonia in 191. Points to note from these years are the following:

- He received the training of a jurist and rhetor (as well as Punic, he spoke Latin and Greek) in Leptis, and then in Rome. Oddly enough, this emperor who did much for his soldiers did not serve as a military tribune and received an important command only when he became governor of Upper Pannonia and its three legions came under his orders. First and foremost, he was an energetic administrator.
- He knew the Empire well. In the emperor's service, he had been posted to Tarraconensis, Sardinia, Africa, Syria, Lugdunensis, and Sicily. He had also spent two years in Athens, in a kind of semi-exile (183–5).
- The year 180 stands out for its importance for the future. A legate of a legion in Syria in this year, he became a friend of his superior, Pertinax, the future emperor, and at Emesa he met the Great Priest of the Sun, Julius Bassianus, and his daughters, Julia Domna and Julia Maesa (see genealogical table 12.2). In 187, he married Julia Domna (his second marriage), by whom he had two sons, Bassianus (Caracalla), born in Lyon in 188, and Geta, born in Rome in 189.

Some further aspects of his character may be picked out. He had a strong affection for his family and city of origin, and a facility for building relationships and making good use of them. His faith in astrology was complete, with astrological considerations often dictating his actions (for instance, his marriage to Julia Domna), and he possessed as well both religious curiosity (he was a devotee of Serapis and may have been initiated into the mysteries of Eleusis), and an evident interest in intellectual life and in antiquities.

Table 12.1 Septimius Severus

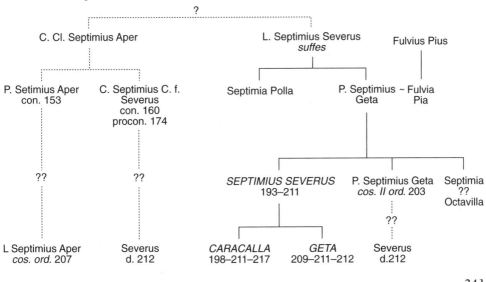

The victor in the civil war

The conqueror of Didius Julianus   In May, Severus left Carnuntum for Rome and marched through Italy without meeting resistance. On June 1, he was at Interamna, about 80 km north of the capital. The Senate acknowledged him as emperor and sent him a delegation. Julianus, abandoned, was killed the same day. And the praetorians guilty of the murder of Pertinax and putting the Empire up for sale were seized. On June 9, having first dismissed the whole of the praetorian guard, Severus entered Rome at the head of his troops. To the Senate he promised not to put any senator to death without its consent, and set himself to reorganize the Rome garrison, to arrange for the obsequies and apotheosis of Pertinax to be solemnized, and to supervise the provisioning of Rome, of which he was in total control. He could then turn his attention to Pescennius Niger and in July 193 he duly left Rome for the East.

The conqueror of Pescennius Niger   Born between 135 and 140, Pescennius rose to senatorial rank having followed an equestrian career. In 191–2, he was appointed legate of Syria (because of his mediocrity, according to Dio Cassius). Popular both with the army and in Rome, he represented a formidable threat, with his nine legions, the support offered to him by Egypt (one of the two main sources of Rome's grain supply), and the proposed backing of the eastern monarchs and the Parthians. Furthermore, he had already taken the offensive in Thrace and captured Byzantium. Septimius Severus and his marshals laid siege to that town (which capitulated at the end of 195, after two years), and won victories at Cyzicus and Nicaea in late 193 and early 194. These two victories opened up Bithynia and Asia and brought Egypt and Arabia to the Severan side, as well as some Syrian towns (Tyre, Laodicea), which were immediately punished by Pescennius. Pescennius, beaten again at Issus (April 194), retreated to Antioch, which was overrun and captured by Severan troops, and then sought refuge near the Euphrates, possibly among the Parthians. During his flight he was captured and executed. In under two years, Severus had reestablished the unity of the Empire. But Syria, wealthy, well populated, and defended by three legions, might – and experience would prove that it still would – remain over-inclined to support every imperial ambition. It was therefore divided. The northern part, with two legions, received the name "Syria-Coele" (literally "Hollow Syria"), with Laodicea as its capital, which was also rewarded by being granted the title of colony with the *ius Italicum*, whereas "Niger's city," Antioch, was punished by being given the status of a township in the territory of its rival (until 202). The southern half, with one legion, was called "Syria-Phoenicia," with Emesa or Tyre as its capital (no one is sure which). Lastly, in order to visit exemplary punishment upon peoples who had supported Niger, and to establish a more secure line of defense in the east than that of the Euphrates, Severus conducted two campaigns against the Osroëni, the Adiabeni, and the "Scenite" Arabs. He subsequently annexed the kingdom of Osroëne, with the exception of a small enclave around Edessa which he left to the sovereign, and turned it into a procuratorian province extending as far as Nisibis and the Tigris.

The conqueror of Clodius Albinus   During 195, a new imperial title appeared on coinage: Septimius Severus figured as a son of the divine Marcus Aurelius. Shortly afterwards, his own son Bassianus (Caracalla) became *M. Aurelius Antoninus* and received the title of *Caesar*. This indicated in the clearest possible way that Clodius Albinus, *Caesar* since 193, was *de trop*. On his side, Albinus (born around 150) displayed all the splendor of an emperor and, because of his nobility and character, was urged by a number of senators to establish himself in Rome. On learning of the appointment of a new *Caesar*, he claimed the title of *Augustus*. On December 15, 195, Albinus was declared a public enemy. He left Britain with his troops (it is not entirely clear whether this weakening of the Roman military presence there enabled the Caledonian tribes to invade), and, having reached Gaul, rallied almost the whole of that country to his cause, won over Tarraconensis as well, and set up his headquarters in Lyon. Opposing him were the armies of the rest of the Empire. At the beginning of 197, Severus took the initiative, advanced into Gaul from Upper Germania and fought the decisive battle near Lyon. On February 19, the defeated Albinus killed himself. Lyon was pillaged and burnt, Albinus' provincial partisans were hunted down and executed, and, in Rome, 29 senators were put to death. The confiscations of property were so large that procurators were appointed to record and administer them. Septimius Severus was now sole master of the Empire.

The reasons for Severus' victory
- The African connection played its part, in strengthening ties and granting the support of certain commands. But Clodius Albinus, another African, might equally well have benefited from it, as the names of the executed senators and the confiscations in Africa bear witness.
- Severus' troops were greater in number and better trained than those of his rivals. (The Danubian legions henceforth also outstripped those of other sectors, in particular those of the Germanies, in their influence and political clout.) And although the strategic ability of Severus himself was, it seems, mediocre – according to Dio Cassius, the Battle of Lyon was the first big engagement in which he had personally taken part – he had been able to gather round him some remarkable marshals, the nucleus of a new aristocracy.

Figure 12.1 Senatorial and imperial provinces around 200 (from F. Jacques and J. Scheid, *Rome et l'intégration de L'Empire*, PUF, 1990)

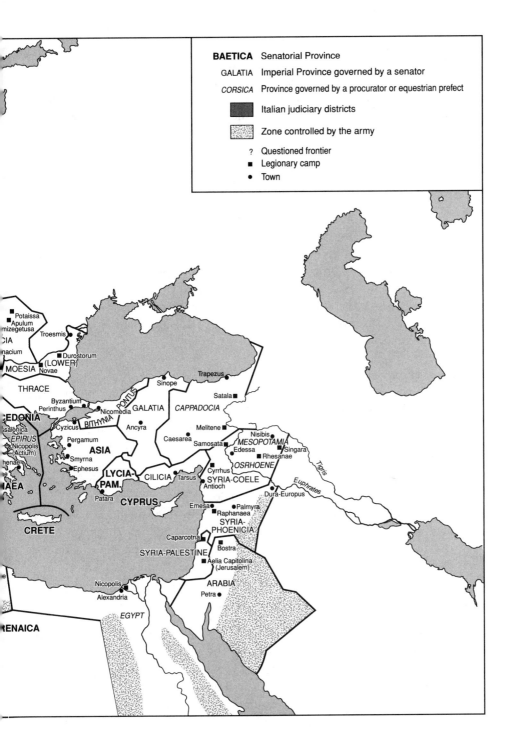

BAETICA Senatorial Province

GALATIA Imperial Province governed by a senator

CORSICA Province governed by a procurator or equestrian prefect

Italian judiciary districts

Zone controlled by the army

? Questioned frontier

■ Legionary camp

● Town

■ Potaissa
■ Apulum
■ mizegetusa
Troesmis ■

:IA
nacium
■ Durostorum
(LOWER)
MOESIA Novae

THRACE

Byzantium
Perinthus
:EDONIA
ssalonica
Cyzicus
Nicomedia
Nicopolis
(Actium)
henae
e

Pergamum
ASIA
Smyrna
Ephesus
LYCIA-
PAM.

IAEA

Patara

CRETE

PONTUS

GALATIA *CAPPADOCIA*

Ancyra
Caesarea

CILICIA Tarsus

CYPRUS

Sinope

Trapezus ●

Satala ■

Melitene ■
Samosata ■

Cyrrhus
SYRIA-COELE
Antioch

Emesa ●
Raphanaea ■
SYRIA-
PHOENICIA

Caparcotna ■
Bostra
SYRIA-PALESTINE
■ Aelia Capitolina
(Jerusalem)

Nicopolis
Alexandria

EGYPT

:ENAICA

Nisibis ■
MESOPOTAMIA
Edessa ■ ■ Singara
OSRHOENE ■ Rhesanae

Dura-Europus

● Palmyra

ARABIA
Petra ●

Tigris

Euphrates

■ Even if cruelty and guile are clichés in describing the Africans, Severus made effective use of both qualities. His intransigence and cruelty were particularly evident in his rejection of any idea of negotiation or power-sharing (proposed by Julianus and Niger) and in the violence and ferocity of his reprisals after the capture of Byzantium and Lyon; and in the light of his public praise for the harshness and cruelty of Marius, Sulla, and Augustus they took on the aspect of policy.

■ Coinage, pamphlets, copies of imperial proclamations distributed to the troops and the populace, and the diffusion of prophecies and presages – the use of these as means of propaganda was nothing new, but they were employed by Severus with unprecedented intensity.

■ Severus, who Dio Cassius says was the most intelligent of all the claimants to the throne, outdid the others politically, first by presenting himself as the avenger of Pertinax, and then by playing on the divisions of his enemies. He also had a better appreciation of the scale of the Empire, made use of all the means at his disposal, and was able to inspire a sound team of administrators and generals.

Features of the war years

■ The Senate, with its many volte-face, its indecision and sudden repudiations, disappeared completely as a political force.

■ The provincial armies, and no longer the praetorian guard, were the determining force in the choice of an emperor. The soldiers of the Danubian frontier had become masters of the Empire.

■ The conflicts of these years took on the appearance of interprovincial wars; and at regional level, rivalries between cities played a leading role.

■ Among the provinces involved in these conflicts, three provinces or groups of provinces assumed particular importance: Britain, the Danubian provinces, and the East. They definitively signposted the new trade route (Rhine–Danube–Syria) that counterbalanced the Mediterranean axis (East–Rome–West).

The guarantor of the Empire's integrity

The Second Parthian War (197–199) No sooner had Severus returned to Rome than he left again for Syria (June–July 197); for the Parthians had invaded Mesopotamia. Immediately on his arrival in Syria, he set out for the troubled region. Crossing the Euphrates, he advanced towards Nisibis, where the Parthians abandoned their siege. In the autumn of 197, he occupied Babylon, which had long been deserted, captured Seleucia and then crossed the Tigris and took Ctesiphon, which was sacked. On January 28, 198 (exactly 100 years after Trajan's accession), like Trajan, he was proclaimed *Parthicus Maximus*. On the same day, his elder son, Caracalla, received the title of *Augustus* and his younger son, Geta, that of *Caesar*. Returning from this Parthian expedition, he had a failure at Hatra, a stronghold and city used by caravans between the Tigris and Euphrates, which he still did not succeed in capturing at a second attempt (winter 198–9), although its king made an act of submission. Then, resuming his plan for reorganizing the eastern frontier, he created the new province of Mesopotamia, east of Osroëne, between Syria-Coele and the Tigris. Like Egypt, it was to be governed by a prefect of equestrian rank (residing at Nisibis). For strategic reasons, he also rearranged the provinces of Syria-Phoenicia and Arabia, after which he made stops in Palestine and Egypt.

Egypt (199–200) In many respects, his journey through Egypt recalls Hadrian's, combining tourism, religion, and administrative inspection. In the administrative field, he made innovations, giving a municipal Senate (a *boulê*) to Alexandria and the main cities in Egypt, and for the first time allowing Egyptians to enter the Roman Senate.

In late 200 or early 201, he reached Syria once more. There, at Antioch on January 1, he assumed the ordinary consulship with Caracalla (it was the first time that two emperors were ordinary consuls simultaneously, and away from Rome). During this stay, he also reviewed and annulled the sanctions taken against the cities that had helped Niger. Then, by way of Asia Minor and the Danube, he returned to Rome (April or June 202), which he had left five years earlier. There he celebrated the ten years of his reign, his *Decennalia*.

The African journey (202–203) Known only from an allusion in a disputed document, the existence of this journey is not accepted by some historians. Those who do, place it in 202 and early 203, basing their supposition on coinage, inscriptions, and archaeological testimony. Its route is largely hypothetical, but it would seem that during this journey Leptis Magna, Severus' birthplace, received the *ius Italicum* (the third city in Africa to obtain it, after Utica and Carthage), a number of indigenous cities in the north-east of Africa Proconsularis became *municipia*, and some existing *municipia* there became colonies. It may have been at this time too that Numidia, which existed as a province in fact before it did so in law, its legate having taken (or been given) civil, judicial, and religious powers in addition to his military command of the Third Augusta, became an autonomous province, detached from Africa Proconsularis. However, other dates have been put forward for this change: 198 or 199 in the view of some, 206–8 in that of others, and a third group say no earlier than 221. At all events, "under Septimius Severus, military organization in Africa was brought to its peak" (Y. Le Bohec).

His stay in Rome (203–207/8) This would be the longest stay that Severus made in the capital. In June 203, the emperor was in Rome, probably for the dedication of the triumphal arch erected in his honor on the Roman Forum. In the following year, he presided at the Secular Games, which were being held two *saecula* (each of 110 years) after the games of Augustus. In the ceremonial hymn (*carmen saeculare*), prayers were offered to Hercules and Bacchus, the gods of Leptis Magna. People came to these games from all over the Empire to celebrate the end of one *saeculum* and the beginning of another. Caracalla and Geta, consuls for 205, inaugurated the inevitably happy and fruitful new age. In Rome, too, Severus settled, by murder (205), the ambitions of the praetorian prefect, Plautianus, Caracalla's father-in-law, had the temple of Peace restored, began several new buildings, updated a marble map of the city (*forma Urbis*) (numerous fragments of which have come down to us), and wrote an autobiography (of which nothing has survived).

War in Britain (208–211) In 207, the Maeatae (peoples who lived near Antoninus' Wall), reinforced by the Caledonians, rebelled, and the governor of Britain apparently appealed to the emperor. There is no knowing whether this revolt required the presence of Severus, or whether he was finding inactivity burdensome. By taking his two sons with him, he perhaps hoped to remove them from the soft living of Rome. He may have thought that the army, in the inactivity of peacetime, would lapse into habitual idleness. Possibly, he wanted to achieve a victory over the still untamed northern barbarians. All these explanations were put forward by the early writers. Whatever the truth of the matter, Severus gladly seized the opportunity and placed himself at the head of an *expeditio felicissima Britannica* (208). He assembled a mighty army and fleet. They made a great impression on the rebels, who sued for peace. Severus refused. He seems to have been resolved to complete the conquest of the island. Textual sources are imprecise. But there appear to have been two campaigns, with the emperor setting up his headquarters in York (Eburacum). The first took place in 208–9. Starting from north-east of the Forth–Clyde line, Severus skirted the Grampians on the eastward side and ventured as far north as the Moray Firth, an itinerary marked out by the camps that have been discovered. A truce was concluded. Severus and his elder son assumed the title *Britannicus*, and Geta was promoted *Augustus* (209). There were thus now three emperors. During 210, disturbances began again. Severus, who was ill, entrusted Caracalla with the task of leading a punitive expedition. The winter of 210–11 was spent preparing the expedition. Septimius Severus died on February 4, 211 at his York headquarters. Tradition has it that he left this advice to his sons: "Live in harmony, make the soldiers rich, and don't give a damn for anything else." And, touching the urn destined to receive his ashes, he is reported to have said: "You will contain a man whom the universe has been unable to contain."

The exercise of power

Vitality, drive, activity – these words recur constantly in descriptions of the achievements of Severus, who, by his personal endeavors, or because he was in harmony with his era, brought about great changes in the way that power was exercised and in doing so gave emphasis to certain aspects of the regime, military, dynastic, anti-senatorial, and absolutist.

A military monarchy   Though he had not had much military training, his two years spent at the Danubian frontier (191–3) and the four years of civil war had made Severus familiar with camp life, and this, together with the experience and advice of his marshals, the information gleaned from the campaigns of Marcus Aurelius, and the knowledge that he owed the throne to the legions, had also made him aware of the weaknesses in the military machine, and that it was a matter of urgency to improve a system that had become unsuited to the new defensive situation. Whether the various measures formed part of a coherent whole or were taken in response to specific problems is of little importance, so greatly did the breadth of the reforms that he undertook alter the Roman army and steer it along new paths of development. Three areas were affected by these changes.

The organization of the army   In 193, Severus reorganized Rome's garrison. The praetorian cohorts were brought to a strength of 1,000 men (10,000 in total) and these were no longer recruited in Italy or even in the old Romanized provinces, but rather selected from the best of the provincial legions (Illyrians, Thracians). The numbers of each of the urban cohorts were trebled, from 500 men to 1,500, while the watch cohorts remained unchanged (7 cohorts of 1,000 men). Furthermore, between 193 and 197, Severus raised three additional legions (bringing the number up to 33), the three Parthian legions, all commanded by knights, and while two were stationed in Mesopotamia (the First and Third), the Second was based at Albano, near Rome. This means that, if we add to all these forces based in or near Rome the 1,000 *equites singulares Augusti* (the emperor's personal cavalry), charged with the ruler's close protection, Severus came to have at his disposal in the heart of Italy an army of 30,000 men (compared with 11,500 formerly). He thus had the means of forestalling any usurper's plans and of keeping an eye on Rome, and, above all, a massive reserve force giving him room to maneuver if, having crossed the frontier, barbarian elements ventured into Italy. Thus began the concept of a centralized campaign army (in Caracalla's reign, the praetorian guard and the Second Parthica were both put into combat). Severus also allotted a considerable role to large expeditionary corps organized for a single expedition and composed of detachments (*vexillationes*) commanded by *duces* or *praepositi* appointed by the central government – strong detachments from

Germania's four legions, for example, were employed in the Second Parthian War. Similarly, he seems to have stepped up the use of auxiliaries (such as the corps of Osroënian archers) alone, independently of the legions, and in large numbers. Although Severus was accused of deliberately barbarizing the Roman army, recent studies have shown that he did nothing of the kind, that Italians never completely disappeared, especially among the centurions and officers of equestrian rank, and that what happened was that the most Romanized sources of troops were used less and less, and that senior officers began to rise from the ranks.

The strategy on the frontiers The main objective of this strategy was, of course, to secure the Empire's defense, but this required that the safeguarding of one sector could be achieved without having to weaken another even though resources were limited and the location and intensity of the dangers varied. Hence the series of measures taken by Severus intended to adapt the system more closely to the threats that were presently feared, in the East against the Parthians (an overestimated danger) and on the Danube and Rhine against the Germani. Everywhere, there was a reinforcement of existing fortifications, communication systems, and glacis (Africa, Rhine, Danube). Two new legions, the First and Third Parthica, were installed in the East (this front, with 11 legions, henceforth rivaled that of the Danube with its 12 legions). Administrative and territorial modifications were made. Regular expeditions were undertaken, and, as we have seen, considerable use was made of special corps of *vexillationes*, brought together as the need arose to strengthen a threatened sector. Lastly, in the same period, completing a development commenced a century earlier, regional recruitment seems to have become the rule – in Africa, for instance, among the soldiers of the Third Augusta, "foreigners" were in the minority, which had not been the case at the beginning of the century, and the Africans were predominant.

Military life An improvement in the soldier's lot was an essential part of dealing with the continuing recruitment crisis. To make army life seem more attractive and so to encourage recruitment, Severus put in motion a train of reforms the like of which had not been seen since the time of Augustus, bringing social, economic, and honorific benefits to soldiers, and a measure of what might be termed "democratization" to the army: pay, which had not changed since Domitian's time, was increased; a military *annona* was organized (without creating a new tax – part of the old civilian *annona* was automatically diverted to the army); soldiers were permitted to live with their families outside the camp; and they were accorded the right to form colleges even during their years of service (until then only veterans had had this authorization); centurions were given direct access to the equestrian order (without, that is, having to go through the primipilate); *principales* (non-commissioned officers or soldiers exempt from fatigue duties) were allowed to wear a gold ring (formerly, the distinctive right of knights); and veterans were given immunity from personal municipal charges.

A hereditary monarchy As much through opportunity (one of the three legions in Upper Pannonia had been commanded by Pertinax) as from conviction (he had been one of Pertinax's lieutenants), Severus had presented himself as the avenger of Pertinax, whose panegyric he had delivered on the day of the apotheosis. This, however, was but the first step needed to legitimize his *coup d'état* and consecrate the founding of his power. He had also to establish a connection with the Antonine dynasty itself. This he did by means of a fictitious and retroactive adoption. In 195, he declared himself the son of Marcus Aurelius and brother of Commodus. Henceforward, his portraits resemble those of his "ancestors," and inscriptions trace his genealogy back as far as Nerva, making him the latter's descendant to the fifth degree. It was then unthinkable that he should long remain the brother of a non-deified emperor. In 197, that matter was rectified by Commodus' apotheosis. Securing thus the position of his family in the past, Severus also wanted to gain a place for it in the future and proclaim the dynastic nature of the imperial power. As we have seen, in 195 Caracalla was given the name Marcus Aurelius Antoninus, and in the same year was named *Caesar*. In 198, he became *Augustus*, while Geta was raised to the rank of *Caesar*. And, in 209, Geta in his turn became *Augustus*. There were then three *Augusti* at the same time, even if, in practice, they were not equal in rank.

This dynastic policy extended to the entire imperial family, the *domus divina*. As *Augusta*, Julia Domna was associated with government. Like the emperor, she was called *Pia* and *Felix*, but also "mother of the *Augusti*," "mother of the camps," and "mother of the Senate." With her two children, she accompanied Severus on all his expeditions, to the East as well as to Britain. The images and names of the imperial couple and their sons were on display everywhere, on coins, on monuments in Rome (the arch in the Roman Forum, the arch of the moneychangers in the Forum Boarium) and in the Empire (the four-façaded arch of Leptis Magna), and even on the flaminical crown. Simultaneously the heirs of the Antonines, to whom reference was constantly made, and midwives to a new age, whose birth was marked by the Secular Games of 204, Severus and his family emphasized the hereditary aspect of imperial power. Both branches of the family, African and eastern, reaped the benefits of imperial favor. The emperor's brother and the brother-in-law of the empress, for example, would not have had as much success as they did in their careers without such favor. But the most significant case is certainly that of C. Fulvius Plautianus. Originally from Leptis Magna, and connected by marriage with Severus' family, this knight became prefect of the praetorian guard in 197, and remained in the post until his death. The emperor's trusted man, he supervised all the troops stationed in Italy, obtained the consular robes and the right to sit in the Senate, and, managing to marry his daughter to Caracalla, entered both the imperial family and the patriciate – before being assassinated (January 205) on his son-in-law's orders and with the connivance of the emperor.

With Severus, this dynastic intent, which merged with the desire to restore the prestige of the Roman state, steered not only the imperial office but also the imperial cult in a more absolutist direction, giving new impetus by this turn to an institution that was showing signs of flagging (in particular, the *seviri augustales*). The cult of the living emperors thus became more closely bound up with that of their dead predecessors. Vested by Jupiter (*aurei* of 194 show the god proffering the globe of the world to the emperor), Severus was not regarded as a living god, but he was frequently likened to a god (Jupiter, Helios) in the attitudes and attributes of his figure in his portraits. Together with the rest of the imperial family, he already belonged to the same world as the gods. He had his statue placed in the Augusteum at Ostia beside those of the divine emperors (and his relations by "adoption") Antoninus Pius, Marcus Aurelius, and Lucius Verus; and by giving his son Caracalla the exact *tria nomina* of Marcus Aurelius he conferred on him "a kind of pre-deification" (R. Turcan). The qualifications "sacred" and "divine" began to be applied to everything pertaining to the emperor, henceforward called *dominus* as a matter of course. For example, there were numerous dedications, to various gods, made *in honorem domus divinae*. Moreover, astrology, of which Severus was an ardent follower, became more closely linked with the imperial person. In the imperial palace on the Palatine, Severus held audience under a ceiling on which his personal horoscope was painted, thus attributing a cosmic sacredness to his power. In addition, the Septizonium (inaugurated in 203), the monumental freestanding entrance to the palace, turned toward Africa, presented a façade with niches where the seven planets were arranged around the monarch, represented as the Sun. There was nothing basically new in all this. But what had formerly been considered a sign of tyranny or the manifestation of a deranged mind was now accepted by all. If the contrast between the Principate (from Augustus and the Julio-Claudians to the Antonines) and the "Dominate" is slightly artificial, it nevertheless reveals quite well how mental attitudes had altered.

An anti-senatorial monarchy From the first years of his reign, and above all after the senatorial purges that followed the defeat of Albinus, Severus' relations with the Senate were strained. This situation is perfectly symbolized by the siting of his triumphal arch in the Roman Forum: facing the temple of Concordia, it stands between the Rostra and the Curia, both of which it dominates.

Although the Senate continued to benefit from its great social and cultural prestige, the signs of its political enfeeblement were legion: Severus' choice of the prefect of the city in 193: one of his loyal supporters; the regulation and limitation of that office, senatorial *par excellence*; the massive confiscation of senators' possessions; the rehabilitation of Commodus; the importance assumed by the African clan among the imperial legates and other top people; the installation of a legion in Italy and the acknowledgement of the army's essential role there; the fact that the emperor permanently bore the title of proconsul in Rome and Italy even though they were officially outside the provincial system; and his choice of new senators, promoted either by *adlectio* or by the award of the laticlave: all partisans of Severus, most often from equestrian circles.

The acceleration in the Senate's political decline may equally be observed in the confirmation of the ascendancy of the equestrian order. To this order were entrusted the three new legions and two recent provinces. It was granted numerous procuratorial posts, of which there were increasingly many (Severus himself created more than any other emperor – 50 posts between 197 and 211). Because of the admission into it of a good number of centurions, the honors and titles distributed to members of the equestrian order were more numerous than ever. And the position of praetorian prefect, now invariably held by those of equestrian rank, had become the second most important in the Empire: the praetorian prefect, in addition to possessing immense power in virtue of his military functions, was head of the imperial administrative staff, leading criminal judge in place of the emperor for all Italy (except Rome and central Italy), appeal judge for all sentences issued by provincial governors, and a member of the emperor's council, of which he was leader. Moreover, the position (which regularly had two joint-holders) came to be occupied by men of great worth, such as the jurist Papinian, a Syrian relative of the empress, whose students Ulpian and Paul, themselves great jurists, later became praetorian prefects.

It has been noted that, in the hierarchy of equestrian officials, the upper and lower ranks were those most affected by Severus' actions. It was as if he wanted to increase social mobility, the clearest case being that of the legionaries. It seems, too, that a popular social policy was emerging, one that favored the less powerful – and again, by the contrast that it set up, pointed to the acceleration in the political decline of the Senate. The emperor, for example, recommended that prefects of the city should listen as much to the complaints of slaves as to those of their masters, generally gave a favorable response to petitions from peasants against local governors, and protected professional colleges against abuses. This aspect of imperial favor relating to the people was also to be found in official art: the frontal arrangement of the bas-reliefs on the arch in the Roman Forum or that of Leptis Magna, the replacement of a deep landscape with superimposed episodes in several rows, the hieratic, simplified, and expressive aspect of characters and scenes, all proclaimed a new artistic taste, far removed from the intellectual art appreciated by the senators, and intended to recount imperial exploits directly to the people.

An absolute monarchy Starting with Septimius Severus, the imperial regime's inherent absolutism, hitherto concealed behind a screen of institutions and customs (although that was increasingly tending to crumble) was revealed with complete openness. For instance, the emperor's speeches to the Senate became the official source of law. And the jurists surrounding the ruler put their knowledge to the service of his authority: "What pleases the emperor has the value of law," "the emperor is above the law," they said. Thousands of petitions (about 1,500 a year) flowed from all over the Empire to the emperor's council. And the number of imperial offices and employees also grew. The Empire started to become bureaucratized. Thus the *res privata* (the administration of the emperor's personal wealth), swollen by the confiscation of his opponents' possessions, expanded to the point where it became a real department on its own account, distinct from the possessions of the crown (the *patrimonium*). Further examples were the development of the services connected with the *annona*, state intrusion into the organization of trade and craft companies, and the expansion of the phenomenon of peasant associations, all of which were favorable to the growth of the central offices.

IMPERIAL CONSTITUTIONS

The first imperial edicts appeared with Augustus.

In the middle of the second century, jurists allowed imperial constitutions an authority comparable with that of the law.

In the third century, Ulpian identified the imperial will with the law.

There were four types of imperial constitutions:

1 *Imperial edicts:* texts of general application promulgated by the emperor by virtue of his *imperium*; they were obligatory throughout the Empire.

2 *Decrees:* decisions passed by the emperor (or his council) in civil or criminal trials; in principle, their force was restricted to individual cases, but in practice they had a formative effect on jurisprudence, and judges took a lead from them.

3 *Rescripts:* these were written replies given by the emperor to requests emanating from individuals in difficulties over points of law, whether litigants, or judicial officials in complicated cases; from the time of Hadrian, and above all under the Severi, they were a very important source of law; in theory, their effect was confined to the question posed, but, like the decrees, they assumed a normative value.

4 *Mandates:* instructions of an administrative nature addressed to magistrates or officials delegated by the emperor.

(from M. Humbert, *Institutions politiques et sociales de l'Antiquité*)

The birth of an unaccustomed style of court life is further witness to the absolutism of Severan power. Whether it was on the move or in one place, his court was characterized by an increasingly meticulous etiquette based on the eastern model: throne, crowns, robes, attitudes were all codified and the *adventus Augusti* (arrival of the emperor) unfolded according to a ceremonial of unprecedented formality. This new style also marked Severus' apotheosis. The ceremony itself was not new. Its ultimate aim had not basically changed, and was still the deifying of the dead emperor. Nevertheless, although the tradition persisted, various elements prefiguring the third century have been noted in it.

Two enemy brothers and an empress mother: Caracalla (211–217), Geta (211–212), Julia Domna

Born one year apart (188, 189), the two brothers loathed each other. The elder, M. Aurelius Antoninus, had very little taste for intellectual matters, despite having received a thorough education. His main interest was in military life. He was loved by the soldiers, who gave him the nickname "Caracalla," after the Gaulish cloak he liked to wear. Sickly, touchy, violent to the point of cruelty, irascible, hated by the senators and by literary tradition in one accord, he played the roughneck soldier, venerated Alexander almost fanatically, was a devotee of Serapis, whose vicar he considered himself to be, and was constantly in search of healing gods and miraculous cures.

Having always progressed at a slower pace than his elder brother, L. Septimius Geta is portrayed as more gentle and reflective by those early authors contrasting the two brothers. It appears that the senators were fairly favorable to him, and his mother also showed him preference.

As beautiful as she was intelligent (all the writers hymn her beauty, which is confirmed by a Munich bust), the empress Julia Domna (perhaps around 40 in 211) exercised considerable influence on the emperor before being supplanted by Plautianus. Giving up political life for the time being, she applied herself to literature and philosophy, was the leading light in a salon that was a meeting-ground for scholars, jurists (Ulpian, Papinian), doctors (Galen), and writers, surrounded herself with Easterners, promoted her family (in particular, her sister Julia Maesa), and kept careful watch on the future of her sons. With Plautianus out of the way, she resumed her place alongside Severus, whom she accompanied to Britain.

The combined reign of the two brothers (February 4, 211 to February 26, 212)
The end of the campaign in Britain Caracalla made peace with the Caledonians, withdrew the frontier (at this time or shortly afterwards) to

Plate 12.1 A doctor inspects the eye of a seated woman. Detail of a sarcophagus of the Sosa family from Ravenna, 3rd/4th century AD.

Hadrian's Wall, and divided Britain into two provinces, Upper Britain in the south, with two legions and a governor of consular rank, probably installed in London, and Lower Britain in the north, governed by a former praetor, with one legion (in York) and numerous auxiliary troops.

The funeral ceremonies The return of Severus' ashes to Rome and his apotheosis created the illusion of an understanding between the two brothers. Issues of coinage saluted Concordia between the two *Augusti* under the approving gaze of Julia Domna. In reality, each was contemplating ridding himself of the other. On February 26, 212, the empress made an attempt to reconcile them. It was in vain: Caracalla had his brother killed in their mother's arms. Before the praetorians, and then before the Senate, he justified his conduct on the ground that his brother had been plotting against him. And in order to convince them, he promised the praetorians money and the Senate an amnesty for exiles. Executions (20,000 people, according to Dio Cassius) and confiscations took place. Geta's supporters and other possible competitors (including a grandson of Marcus Aurelius) were eliminated. The memory of Geta was damned – on a painted medallion originating from Upper Egypt and representing the imperial family, Geta's face has been scratched out. Nothing was ever again allowed to recall his existence. For Julia Domna, matters were simplified: she would look after internal and administrative affairs and leave the waging of war to her son.

Caracalla's reign (February 26, 212 to April 8, 217)

The army With a more easygoing recruitment policy, an increase in pay of perhaps 50 per cent, and a raising of retirement gratuities, soldiers benefited from the reign, to the extent of the state's incurring an additional expense, according to Dio Cassius, of some 70 million denarii per annum, which Julia Domna deplored, but which must be set against an inflationary background.

The administration With a reorganization of the districts of the *res privata* and the responsibilities of the *iuridici*, as well as the appearance of a "controller," Italy lost a few more of its privileges. Additional procuratorial posts were created (16 between 211 and 214). And there was a further increase in the number of central officials. These actions bear witness to the continuation of Severan policy that, on the whole, characterized the management of the state during this reign.

Fiscal measures and monetary reform It seems that, in 194, Severus had carried out a devaluation of the denarius. Its silver content had been lowered in two stages to reach less than 50 per cent. This devaluation of the basic currency had been a success. If the situation still gave cause for concern, on the death of Severus the state's coffers were in a healthy condition. However, the new military and administrative expenses, the subsidies to be paid to the barbarian princes for their allegiance, and the expenditure on the large-scale public works that were undertaken (e.g. the Aventine baths, road maintenance) required the adoption of further measures. Certain taxes were increased (those on inheritances and enfranchisement went up from 5 to 10 per cent, but these affected only Roman citizens), extraordinary levies, such as the coronation gold (a "voluntary" contribution theoretically paid at the time of an accession), became more frequent, and the practice of exacting taxes in kind or in labor was extended. These fiscal measures were accompanied by a dual monetary reform. Firstly, the gold coinage was devalued, with the weight of the *aureus* going down by 17 per cent and the *aureus* itself rated at 50 denarii (25 in the Augustan system). Secondly, a new coin was created, the Antoninianus. This silver coin, heavier than the devalued "traditional" denarius, but also of low standard (ca. 50 per cent), was worth 2 denarii in use ($1\frac{1}{2}$ in real value) and was struck between 215 and 219. The later drop in its weight and standard (5 per cent) explains its disappearance (though this was not permanent).

The Antonine Constitution of 212 This enactment (known also as the Edict of Caracalla) extended the right of Roman citizenship to all communities within the Empire. Here is the text of this major decision: "I give all foreigners on earth [i.e. in the Roman Empire] the right of Roman citizenship, at the same time safeguarding that of their own cities, except for the *dediticii*." In other words, all the free inhabitants of the Roman world who had by this edict become Roman citizens were able to preserve their native rights and customs as long as they wished. Thus, Egypt after 212 has yielded numerous documents in which the new Romans have maintained their local traditions, Greek or Egyptian: "The papyri have established one point: the change, at least in the beginning, was chiefly psychological and honorific. Egypt's social structure, class relations, and restrictions showed no basic modification" (N. Lewis). Only the *dediticii* (who were perhaps irregular freedmen, though there is disagreement over the exact meaning of the term) did not benefit from this advantage, even when they too had become Roman citizens. This edict, then, a measure which marked the success of the Romanization policy, saw itself as realistic: it did not seek to impose Roman civil law, and did not need to.

The motives behind the Antonine Constitution have been widely argued, and with all the more asperity because the early authors had little to say about it. Several reasons underlay the edict. First, an economic and financial reason, already mentioned by Dio Cassius: foreigners-turned-citizens had to pay an inheritance tax, the one that had been increased. Then, too, the point of view of jurists and administrators must be taken into account: an Empire in which the status of the inhabitants was more uniform would lighten the task of the offices and courts. Finally, it is impossible to overlook the concern for religious unity proclaimed by the emperor in his preamble, which many historians think might well have provided the principal motive.

Frontier defense "I want to end my days at war," Dio Cassius makes Caracalla say. And indeed, from 213 until his death, the emperor fought uninterruptedly on every frontier:

213: Campaign against the Alemanni, mobilizing large forces (including the reserve force based in Italy) on the Rhine and Danube. Victorious on the Main, Caracalla took the name *Germanicus Maximus* and secured twenty years of peace on the western front.

214: Inspection along the Danube, and departure for the East following the route taken by Alexander the Great.

215: At Antioch, he received proposals for peace from the Parthian king. In Alexandria, where for reasons that are not clear (perhaps fear of a rebellion behind him during a Parthian campaign or rancor against a disaffected population) he came into conflict with the people, who were massacred.

216: In Syria, the cities of Emesa and Palmyra were promoted to Roman colonies with *ius Italicum*. Edessa in Osroëne became a colony. War was declared on the Parthian kingdom, an army was sent to Armenia, and the emperor led expeditions into Adiabene and Parthia, where he won the title of *Parthicus Maximus*.

217: On April 8, near Carrhae, he was stabbed to death by an officer of the praetorian guard on the orders of its prefect, M. Opellius Macrinus.

MACRINUS, ELAGABALUS, SEVERUS ALEXANDER

MACRINUS (217–218): AN INTERLUDE

The soldiers, who did not suspect a conspiracy, acclaimed the prefect of the praetorian guard emperor. It was the first time a knight had attained the throne. Born in Caesarea (Cherchel) in Mauretania in 164, Macrinus had been a lawyer, and then procurator of Plautianus' possessions. He had subsequently followed a civil equestrian career, during which Caracalla had noticed him. In 212, he had become praetorian prefect. His reign as emperor was given up to seeking support in order to confront the urgent demands of the moment: to rally the soldiers, persuade the senators, neutralize the Parthians, and break the ambitions of the Syrian princesses who were related to the Severi.

In order to win the loyalty of partisans of the Severi (especially the soldiers), he took the *cognomen* "Severus," had Caracalla proclaimed *divus* by the Senate, and bestowed the *cognomen* "Antoninus" (like Caracalla) on his young son Diadumenianus, together with the title of *Caesar*. But at the same time, in order to win over the opponents of the Severi, he repealed Caracalla's measures (reducing the inheritance tax to 5 per cent once more), paid the Parthian king an indemnity of 200 million sesterces to maintain the Roman–Parthian frontier and unchanged areas of influence (Armenia), and reduced the pay of new recruits by half. This retrenchment brought on disaffection in the ranks of the legions left undispersed in Syria. Moreover, his obscure origins and his clumsy tactics (his refusal, though justified, to come to Rome, the appointment of his colleague in the praetorian guard to the prefectship of the capital, etc.) alienated the little sympathy he had been able to arouse in the Senate. He thus found himself quite incapable of opposing the machinations of the Syrian princesses.

On the death of her son, after trying to incite the troops that Macrinus had sent as much to keep an eye on her as to honor her, Julia Domna starved herself to death at Antioch. But the *Augusta* left an elder sister, Julia Maesa, who had two daughters, Julia Soaemias and Julia Mamaea. All three were descended from the great priestly family of Emesa who ruled over the temple of the local god, Elah-Gabal. Similarly, all three belonged to the *domus divina* of Caracalla, and nurtured lofty ambitions. They possessed immense wealth, the legitimacy of blood relations, a solid network of loyal supporters, and two heirs: the son of Julia Soaemias, Varius Avitus Bassianus, and the son of Julia Mamaea, Gessius Alexianus. The former was born in 204, the latter in 205 or 206. Thus, both were first cousins once removed of Caracalla, but Bassianus held the priesthood of the god of Emesa. Artfully superseding the rivalry between the two sisters, the boys' grandmother allowed the rumor to be put about that Bassianus was the adulterine son of Caracalla, and that she had a great quantity of gold at her disposal. In April or May 218, Bassianus was acclaimed emperor by the Third Gallica under the names of his alleged father, M. Aurelius Antoninus. On June 8, the armies of Macrinus and Bassianus came face to face near Antioch. Macrinus was defeated. He fled but was caught a few days later while trying to get back to Europe. His corpse was left on the spot so that the new emperor might contemplate it when he took the road to Rome. "The Severan dynasty retrieved the imperial throne, but from being African it had become completely Syrian" (Le Gall and Le Glay).

ELAGABALUS (218–222): THE EAST IN ROME

It is under the name "Elagabalus," taken from the god of Emesa, that the new emperor is best known. A sculpted and inscribed relief discovered near Emesa (Homs, in Syria) explains it as meaning "mountain god." At Emesa, religion had a very marked solar nature, so the "mountain god" was also a sun god known as Sol Elagabalus.

Table 12.2 The dynasty of Septimius Severus

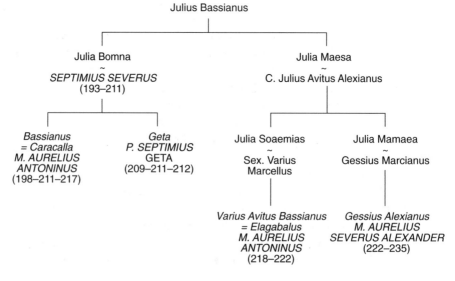

The temple idol was a huge conical black stone, said to have fallen from the skies, which coins represent with an eagle on the front of it or perched on its summit. God of the summits? Sun god? At all events, in Rome no one knew if he should be regarded as Jupiter or the Sun, and "Elagabalus" was often translated as "Heliogabalus." There, at times of religious ceremonies, to the strains of flutes and trumpets, clad in a purple and gold Phoenician robe, the high priest, now emperor, would dance before this god.

Several aspects of his astounding reign should be remembered.

The new emperor's arrival in Rome

After a short stay in Antioch and a purge of Macrinus' colleagues in the administration, the Syrian princesses and their offspring set off for Rome. The journey took a year, and assumed the air of a religious procession because of its route and because they brought the black stone with them, since the young emperor did not wish to be parted from his idol. In the summer of 219, Elagabalus made his solemn entry into Rome. He seemed to have only one preoccupation – to install his god.

A Syrian high priest

On the Palatine, near the imperial palace, the emperor had a temple built for his god, the Elagabalium, inaugurated at the latest in 221. Inside, he is said to have assembled the emblems of Rome's traditional religion (the Vestal flame, Palladium, Salian shields, black stone of Cybele), as if he wanted to centralize the sacred and subordinate all other cults to the god of Emesa, who also now married Tanit-Dea Caelestis of Carthage. For the first time, a kind of henotheism emerged at the heart of the Empire.

The princesses in power

The Syrian princesses were the ones who governed, especially Julia Maesa, Elagabalus' grandmother, and Julia Soaemias, his mother. They are even said to have taken part in sessions of the Senate. Julia Maesa's most important decision was to have Elagabalus adopt his cousin Gessius Alexianus (in 221). The future of the dynasty was thus assured. In 222, the emperor and the new "Caesar of the State and Elagabalus" were consuls together.

Numerous difficulties

The financial situation deteriorated, the Germani were aggressive once again, the hostility of the army and praetorians to the emperor was added to that of the Senate, and Julia Mamaea plotted in the interests of her son. Moreover, Elagabalus' bizarre and provocative behavior, his excesses, eccentricities, marriages, debauchery, and passion for courtesans and exotic animals, and his way of offering important posts to his favorites (the prefect of the watch was a former coachman, the prefect of the *annona*, a former hairdresser, and the prefect of the city, a former dancer) all affronted the Romans, fueled malicious gossip, and isolated the emperor. A refusal to sacrifice at the Capitol, a plan (real or imagined) to exile the Senate, and attempts to oust his cousin and rival provoked an uprising of the praetorians, plotted, it seems, by Julia Mamaea. Elagabalus, his mother, and those loyal to them were massacred in March 222. Their decapitated bodies were thrown into the Tiber, and their memory damned. Alexander was proclaimed emperor: "At the time he was young, and obeyed his mother and grandmother as if they were his tutors," noted Herodian.

Severus Alexander (222–235), the good pupil

The more that ancient sources condemn Elagabalus, the more they heap praise on the new emperor and father of all the virtues. Only Herodian has reservations, showing the gentle and amiable reader of Plato and Cicero as pusillanimous, weak, cowardly, and lacking in authority. But, in any case, it was not this fifteen-year-old who governed; it was the Syrian women, Julia Maesa and Julia Mamaea, the latter on her own after her mother's death (in 223 or 226). Rejecting the escapades of the preceding reign, the new government subscribed to the Severan tradition, as expressed in the adoption of the *cognomen* "Severus," slipped into the emperor's names, *M. Aurelius Severus Alexander*.

Internally

The new policy was marked by a more or less sharp reaction in three domains.

Moral reaction   Palace mores returned to an honest simplicity, and scandalous promotions were canceled, although a good many of the top people in Elagabalus' entourage remained in place, for example the prefect of the city, Valerius Comazon. Moreover, the jurists, students of Papinian, returned to the seat of power and gathered around the Syrian princesses. They included Ulpian (who died in 223, assassinated by the praetorians, whose prefect he was), Paul, and Modestinus, and it is probably to them (Ulpian had already affirmed that in the matter of natural law all men are equal) that a clearly perceptible humanitarian policy is due, including the limitation of lese-majesty cases, improvements in the condition of slaves, and the revival of food-providing institutions.

Senatorial reaction   According to the *Augustan History*, Severus Alexander restored to the Senate its political importance. For a long time, historians accepted this view. Nowadays, only one fact seems to point in this direction: the institution in 222 of a regency council (probably temporary) composed of 16 senators. Otherwise, it is not measures favorable to the Senate that are discernible, but rather, in the Severan tradition, reforms strengthening the equestrian order. The *cursus honorum* for senators, for example, was tightened, prefects of the praetorian guard were legally admitted to the Senate, and, in place of senators, knights were appointed to govern imperial provinces.

Religious reaction   All the statues and emblems that Elagabalus had assembled around the black stone of Emesa were returned: the Palladium went back to the temple of Vesta, Juno Caelestis to her temple in Carthage, and even the black stone to its temple at Emesa. The gods of the capital had their rights re-established and Jupiter the Avenger was placed in the former "Elagabalium." Severus Alexander wanted, besides, to be seen as welcoming all gods. He is said, though it is doubtful, to have worshiped Alexander the Great, Apollonius of Tyana, Abraham, Christ, and Orpheus in the palace shrines to the household gods. It is, however, certain that Julia Mamaea met leading Christian authors such as Origen and Julius Africanus, and that Hippolytus of Rome, a presbyter, dedicated a treatise on the Resurrection to her. Another of the century's trends, syncretism, thus revealed itself in place of Elagabalus' henotheism.

Externally

Externally, new threats loomed. In the East, the Sassanid Persians were driving out the Parthians. These nationalists wanted to re-establish the Persian empire within its former boundaries. They were fanatics who relied on a holy book, the *Avesta*, to impose the religion of Zoroaster, which was exclusive and intolerant. At their head was a remarkable prince, Ardashir (Artaxerxes). In 211/12, he had seized power in Persia, and since then had striven to re-create the former Achaemenid empire. In 227, he became the king of Persia. He organized a strong, centralized, even totalitarian state, in which Mazdaism, the religion taught in the *Avesta*, was the official and compulsory religion, and whose army included an impressive heavily armored cavalry, the cataphracts. In 230/1, the Persians invaded Mesopotamia and launched raids into the Syrias and Cappadocia. It was up to the emperor to intervene. He did so, but unwillingly and after attempts at negotiation. In late 231, he was at Antioch. Reinforced by large contingents drawn from the armies of Europe, the expeditionary force was divided into three corps. In the north, one was to attack Media through Armenia, Rome's ally. In the south, a second was to force its way down the Euphrates as far as its mouth. Between the two, the central corps, commanded by the emperor, was to make a frontal attack on the enemy troops. Only the army in the north fulfilled its mission, although it had difficulty getting back. The other two had to retreat. All in all, it was a half-success transformed by imperial propaganda into a victory. Back in Antioch, the emperor, who was preparing a new expedition against the Persians, learned that the Germani had crossed the Rhine and the Danube, attacking camps in the Taunus, and putting

Raetia and Noricum under threat. His presence on the Rhine was necessary. Oddly enough, Ardashir failed to take advantage of the situation. Severus Alexander returned to Rome, and then left for Upper Germania.

Operations against the Alemanni began in 234. The emperor and his mother were in Mainz, where an army was assembled with numerous auxiliary corps (for the first time, cataphracts are mentioned among them). A bridge of boats was built on the Rhine, and a few small local successes were achieved, but the emperor vacillated and deferred the launching of a large expedition. Bewildered, the soldiers mutinied, under the leadership of a Thracian, Maximinus. The emperor did not react. He let himself be killed in his tent by the mutineers (at some time between February 18 and March 9, 235). His mother and entourage were similarly murdered. Thus the reign of the Severi, both African and Syrian, came to an end.

PROVINCIAL UPSURGE AND THE ORIENTALIZATION OF THE EMPIRE?

Africans, Syrians, and a Thracian at the head of the Empire: it is obvious that the provinces, and more especially those in the eastern part of the Empire, were providing political and military personnel who aspired to the highest offices. This pre-eminence is also apparent in the intellectual field. For example, we find Aelian (?170–?235), a Latin from Praeneste who would never leave Rome, writing his *Animal Stories* in Greek. We shall look, in turn, at the progress made by the East in the religious and intellectual life of the Empire under the Severi.

RELIGIOUS LIFE

The easternization of Roman religion has often been attributed to the Severi. We have perhaps traveled too far along that path, as several British researchers have pointed out. But it is none the less true that, under the influence of the court and the empresses, as well as the traders and jurists, there was a noticeable expansion of the "eastern" religions in this period. In the countries where they had already been introduced, they gained more power, and they spread to places that they had not reached before. However, apart from the instance of Elagabalus, the connection between these religions and imperial activities was not always clear. Here are a few examples.

■ Everywhere, it could be seen that Cybele had returned to favor. Bull and sheep sacrifices became more numerous at the end of the Antonine era and during the period of the Severi, and were frequently associated with the imperial cult.

- The cults of Isis and Serapis benefited from imperial favor. On Julia Domna's denarii, Isis suckles Horus, with the legend "Felicity of the century," an allusion to the motherhood of the empress. Caracalla vowed a special cult to Serapis, who in 212 figured on the reverse of his coinage. He was also known as the "Well-beloved of Serapis," and had a grandiose temple built to this god on the Quirinal.

- Jupiter Dolichenus reached his apogee under the Severi, before declining (if the inscriptions are to be believed) around 220. But as he was closely connected with soldiers, and therefore recruited his faithful mainly from military circles, he was more or less confined to the various frontier defense lines.

- It was under the Severi that Mithraic dedications "for the safekeeping of the emperor" were most numerous. But that needs to be put in context in two ways. All inscriptions, of whatever kind, followed the same line, and of all the gods invoked for the safeguarding of the *Augusti*, Jupiter Optimus Maximus was by far in the lead.

- There could hardly be a better indication of the link between the actions of the Severi and the easternization of religion than the promotion of the local gods connected with the origins of the imperial family: Aziz of Emesa, honored at Intercisa for the protection of Severus Alexander; Liber Pater and Hercules of Leptis Magna, whose Latin names conceal the Semitic gods Shadrafa and Melqart.

Clearer than the connections between imperial activities during this period and the progress of the "eastern" religions are the trends in religious thinking revealed by these easternizing activities. Put simply, these trends can be seen as exemplified, respectively, in the two religious policies of Elagabalus and Severus Alexander. With Elagabalus, to the benefit of Sol (Helios), the increasingly popular idea was affirmed of a single god with manifold powers, of whom the other divine figures were merely expressions. The Sun was the great god who would benefit from the vast syncretist movement of the third century. With Severus Alexander, another sort of syncretism was displayed, one which placed the gods on the same level, without favoring one or excluding another, because, as the third-century philosophers saw it, they were all reflections of the higher divinity that they were seeking to define. At the heart of these two trends, the position occupied by philosophers grew ever larger as philosophies became increasingly imbued with the religious spirit.

Finally, the last aspect of the easternization of religious life was the expansion of Christianity. Until, in 202, Septimius Severus banned Jewish and Christian proselytism – the first formal legal act directly aimed at the Christians – the legal situation of Christians had not altered since the time of Marcus Aurelius. Was there also a Severan edict of persecution? Despite a passage from the *Augustan History*, it would not appear so. There are known to have been martyrs at this time, in Carthage and Alexandria in particular, but they were the result of local pogroms (actions by mobs, overzealousness on the part of governors), and not the application of a general decree, which no Christian author indicates the existence of. Apart from the measure of 202, the Severi showed a marked, and occasionally even benevolent, neutrality towards Christianity. Contemporary testimony reveals the growing number of Christians in every region and every class of society. A text from the end of the second century is quite precise: "Christians are not distinct from other men by either their country, their language, or their clothing . . . There is nothing singular about their manner of living . . . They conform to local customs as regards their garments, their food, and their way of life." They thus took part in economic, even political, life, but they also wanted to live as Christians, and this was not without its problems, over such matters as the use of the baths, attendance at certain spectacles, and the teaching of children. On the whole, however, apart from intransigent Christians (like the Montanists, or the writer Tertullian, who founded his own sect) who preached withdrawal from society and urged people to reject every sort of occupation, Christians shared in the daily life of their compatriots. In addition, they had the sense of belonging to another community, a community of faith, that was constantly growing and becoming better organized (with the first Christian cemeteries in Rome, the appointment of deaconesses, the appearance of Christian art, parishes, lower-order clerics). Missions went out from three important centers: Rome, already at the head of all the churches, Carthage, and Alexandria. But it was the East that remained the first Christian land in order of importance: the last king of Osroëne had himself baptized; at Dura-Europus the first building identifiable as a Christian church made its appearance; and in Alexandria the Didascalia, a school of Christian philosophy, flourished.

INTELLECTUAL LIFE

Taken as a whole, the intellectual life of the Empire was borne along by the intellectual currents of the East and the court of the Syrian princesses, a real workshop for ideas. Not a single area escaped the impress of the Greek-language authors. In history, Dio Cassius and Herodian dominated their period. Dio was from Nicaea, Herodian perhaps from Asia Minor. Both (but chiefly Dio Cassius, who was twice consul) held positions of high responsibility and were privileged witnesses of the period of the Severi, emperors whom they served before returning, at the end of their life, to their country of origin, there to record their experiences of the world. In the field of law, with Papinian and his students, who, as we have noted, impressed their views on the emperors, the school of Beirut was unrivaled. In philosophy, yet again the contribution of the East was of paramount importance. Since philosophies presented fewer certainties, people turned to the past to seek precepts and models, often all the more enthralling because they were hidden, and revealed to the initiated alone. For instance, Philostratus of Athens wrote the *Lives of the Sophists* and, at the request of Julia Domna, a *Life of Apollonius of Tyana*, a neo-Pythagorean miracle-worker of the second half of the first century AD who honored the supreme deity by the purity of his heart and knew all that could be known. The story, riddled with anachronisms, achieved great success: the mixture of the marvelous and the irrational revealed in this biography was in keeping with the spirit of the times. Less imaginative, but proceeding from the same approach, were the compilations of Diogenes Laertius of Cilicia (*Lives, Doctrines, and Opinions of Illustrious Philosophers of Each Sect*) and Athenaeus of Naucratis (*The Sophists' Banquet*). The era also produced some outstanding philosophers: Alexander of Aphrodisias, known as the Exegete, who drew up the texts of the Aristotelian tradition, with variants and an ample commentary; Sextus Empiricus, a Greek doctor who, as a perfect sceptic, criticized all philosophical sects, to end up with a philosophy of experience; and Ammonius Saccas, the first great neo-Platonist, who founded a philosophical school in Alexandria around 200 and had as his disciples Plotinus (204–70) and Origen (ca. 185–after 251), the two greatest thinkers of the third century and amongst the greatest in the ancient world. With this neo-Platonist and this uncompromising Christian, one enters a different intellectual universe.

The final contribution of the East to the intellectual life of the Empire was the appearance of a very important Christian literature written in Greek. This literature had been in existence since the late first century, but it really took wing at the end of the Antonines' reign and under the Severi, with four authors: Irenaeus, originally from Asia, the second bishop of Lyon and founder of Catholic theology (who died, probably as a martyr, in the reign of Septimius Severus); Hippolytus, a Roman presbyter (ca. 170–235), who composed, in Greek, the earliest exegetical treatise to have come down to us; Clement of Alexandria (ca. 150–ca. 215), who wrote under the Severi, a convert of staggering erudition who did not hesitate, as he said, "to make use of the finest elements of philosophy and culture" (*Stromateis* I.1.15) in order to elaborate what was the first great synthesis of Christianity and philosophy; and Origen, the author of a gigantic *oeuvre* (perhaps 2,000 books, of which 800 titles have come down to us), exegetist, philosopher, philologist, biblicist, ascetic, mystic, preacher, and teacher, in all "one of the mightiest geniuses of early Christianity" (C. Mondésert). Alongside these giants of Greek Christian literature, stands the imposing figure of Tertullian (ca. 160–ca. 220), a writer in the Latin tongue. An African, fanatical, intransigent, a polemicist crossing swords with everyone, he was also a remarkable writer and theologian. With these writers, Christianity took on an intellectual dimension. Therein lay the fundamental novelty, the issue largely of that melting-pot of cultures, the East.

Two hundred and twenty years and seven months or so after the death of Augustus, the dynasty of the Severi was tragically extinguished. On the face of it, the Empire was little changed at the end of that period. The constituent elements of imperial government and the survivals from past centuries were still in evidence. But, in fact, the Empire had evolved greatly. Managing to avoid equally well becoming ossified and being torn apart through brutal changes, it had adapted itself to new situations with extraordinary flexibility, and rare good fortune. It had been able to integrate the elites of the provinces with its senators and knights, and to maintain the prestige of a political body without power – the Senate. Absorbing assassinations of its rulers and two civil wars, it had extended Roman citizenship to all free inhabitants of its lands without, for the most part, suppressing their attachment to their own small homeland, and had brought security and a certain prosperity to almost everyone. Of course, the system had shown some weaknesses. Perhaps it worked badly. But at least it *worked*. The modest tomb of an African killed in 238 at the time of the revolt against Maximinus, who was deemed barbarous and tyrannical, is far more eloquent on the subject of Rome's success than any long discourse. There we may read: "He died for the sake of Rome."

PART III

Another Roman World
(Third to Fifth Century)

The Nature of the Times

The period that began in the year 235 can no longer be studied as it was some decades ago; adances in research have radically altered historians' ideas about it. Of course, in the main, it matches the three clearly defined stages attributed to it by tradition. We must therefore look for innovation not in chronological divisions but in the characteristics of each of these periods.

Thus, the years 235–84, which currently are generally regarded as the last part of the early Roman Empire, were marked by numerous serious crises affecting all areas of public life (politics, defense, the economy, society, collective attitudes, etc.). But today there is more emphasis on the limits of these crises, which varied in gravity according to regions and periods – Africa and the Iberian peninsula, for instance, suffered less than Gaul. Moreover, the general crisis of the times met with a sustained reaction on the part of the "Illyrian" emperors.

What used to be, and sometimes still is, called the "late Empire" began in 284. This term ultimately acquired a pejorative sense and became a synonym for a general profound decadence or decline. Researchers these days stress, on the contrary, the renaissance that occurred in a large number of areas, where a different order was being established. Consequently, some scholars now prefer to speak of "late antiquity" rather than the "late Empire." The state was reorganized; political power, the army, and civil institutions presented a new face, underlain by a strengthened monarchy, more imbued with the sacred and even more personal than in preceding centuries. Several sectors of the economy regained their dynamism, while social contrasts were accentuated but without giving rise to serious troubles. Culture and religious life also experienced a new upsurge, and the conflict between Christianity and paganism imparted great vitality to both.

In the last quarter of the fourth century, we may observe the appearance of a separation of destinies dividing East from West. A fresh crisis, both serious and deep-rooted, began in the West, illustrated by two dates: in 406, the Vandals, Alani, and Suebi crossed the Rhine, and no one could stop them; and, in 410, Alaric seized Rome. Nevertheless, a certain amount of vitality existed here and there, and bodies such as the Church, for example, succeeded in adapting to the new conditions created by history, thus prolonging "late antiquity." In contrast, the East witnessed the birth of a new civilization, that of Byzantium, though its passage into the world was certainly not an altogether easy one.

The Diversity of Sources

As for the preceding periods, historians have at their disposal a variety of sources, and these must, of course, always be approached in a critical light, since they all present problems of one sort or another.

Literary sources

The most useful, because the most explicit, are the literary sources. Here, the "primary" sources (when the author has lived through the events he describes) are to be compared with the "secondary" sources (experiences at second hand), and also Latins contrasted with Greeks.

Among the authors who devoted themselves to the traditional literary genres, reference will be made first and foremost to the historians Ammianus Marcellinus and the anonymous writer(s) who gave us the *Augustan History*. Characteristic of the times, just like the series of dates provided by the *Chronicler of 354*, are the abridgers Aurelius Victor, Eutropius, and Festus, with this genre occupying a place of growing importance in literary output.

Next, the productions of orators and letter writers may be used, the various *Panegyrics*, *Discourses*, and *Letters* of Libanius, Julian, and Symmachus, as well as the correspondence of the poet Ausonius for the daily lives of eminent men. There is also much to be gained from Augustine's correspondence, which has been enriched by recent discoveries.

But the great novelty of this period was the extraordinary development of Christian literature. The Arian crisis allowed Eusebius of Caesarea and Athanasius to display their talents. And a number of regional or local "schools" blossomed in Cappadocia (Basil, Gregory of Nazianzus, Gregory of Nyssa), at Antioch (John Chrysostom), at Alexandria (Origen, Claudian), in Africa (Cyprian, Arnobius, Lactantius, Augustine), and in Spain (Orosius and Prudentius). Somewhat apart from this movement, because of the importance of their theological message, St Ambrose, bishop of Milan, and St Jerome, a Dalmatian, were illustrious among those usually known as the Fathers of the Church.

Peripheral literature can also be of use – Jewish (the *Talmud of Babylon* and, chiefly, *of Jerusalem*), Syrian, and Armenian – or later literature (Byzantine).

Official documents

A mass of information may also be gleaned from legal compendia. The Code of Theodosius, a compilation carried out between 429 and 438 at the request of Theodosius II, reveals part of the imperial legislation promulgated from the time of Constantine. Of later date, Justinian's *Corpus Iuris Civilis* left us, first, the *Digest* (of 533), a collection of extracts from the works of jurists who were accepted as authorities and who had lived between the second century BC and the fourth century AD, in particular Gaius and some Severan jurists, Paul, Papinian, Callistratus and, chiefly, Ulpian, and secondly the Code of Justinian (of 534), which gathers together imperial *constitutiones*, the earliest of which go back to Hadrian.

A similar preoccupation, the concern to record acquired experience, gave rise to an official document, the *Notitia Dignitatum*. This catalogue of the Empire's administration and forces was drawn up perhaps as early as the end of the fourth century, and was certainly revised up to the middle of the fifth.

THE "AUXILIARY SCIENCES"

Research by scholars and archaeologists has given rise to several disciplines described as "auxiliary sciences" (though this expression is sometimes criticized). If, in some instances, they clarify knowledge provided by the early authors, in other cases they reveal areas that had been hitherto unknown.

Epigraphy is the study of texts inscribed on durable materials (stone, bronze, wood, terracotta). This source is no less rich for the fourth century than for earlier times; even better, it has left long inscriptions, sometimes composed in flowery style. These inscriptions may come from private individuals, and be carved for all time (funerary or honorific inscriptions), in which case we have to balance the said and the unsaid: in epitaphs, all husbands are loving and all wives faithful. But that is not to say that one must give uncritical acceptance to official inscriptions, for example legal ones, which were displayed in order that their contents might be brought to the attention of the public (we shall return later to Diocletian's edict on maximum prices, the table of Brigetio, the rescript of Hispellum, and the album of Timgad, in particular).

Always fruitful, papyrology, working with documents coming mainly from Egypt, but also sometimes from Syria (Dura-Europus), tells us about daily life in the provinces – prices, municipal institutions, religion, etc.

Of more general interest (in the geographical sense), numismatics, the study of coins, which were also abundant in the fourth century, allows us to follow the economic situation by highlighting a double development, in weight and denomination. It also throws light on imperial ideology – rather than "propaganda," for it is not certain that the users even analysed the wording and subjects engraved on what is after all merely a simple instrument of trade. Lastly, a map of buried hoards of coins can perhaps enable us to follow one or several invasion routes.

It is even harder to present archaeology, since the mass of data is overwhelming. This one word in fact covers very varied disciplines, with thousands of objects ranging from the fibula (brooch) and belt-buckle to the villa and the town, by way of pottery and every kind of monument. Mention will be made later of statuary (*The Tetrarchs*, now in Venice), monuments (the arch of Thessalonica), residences (Piazza Armerina, Montmaurin), palaces (Salonae, near present-day Split), churches (Saint-Clément, Saint-Martin-aux-Monts), and camps (Luxor, forts in Syria), etc.

This picture will give us some understanding of what, when they survey the sources, is such an enthralling task for historians, especially when they study the third and fourth centuries. In order to re-create the past, they must make use of all types of data available to them, but not without a preliminary critical "screening": they must know what they can and cannot expect from the data. This is where the chief difficulty lies, however, and it is twofold: many documents are only poorly known, and even more have never been studied scientifically. Much research still remains to be done.

13 / EQUILIBRIUM, AD 235

*B*Y THE TIME THAT THE LAST OF THE SEVERI DIED IN 235, THE EMPIRE HAD
ATTAINED A KIND OF EQUILIBRIUM (THESE DAYS IT IS NO LONGER BELIEVED
THAT THE ACCESSION OF SEPTIMIUS SEVERUS IN 193 MARKED THE START OF A
GREAT AND CONTINUING CRISIS). THE ALARM AND THE TERRIBLE YEARS OF
MARCUS AURELIUS WERE FORGOTTEN, AND THE DIFFICULTIES THAT CROPPED UP
HERE AND THERE WERE GENERALLY PERCEIVED AS FAIRLY NORMAL AND TEMPORARY
NUISANCES. AS FOR THE PESSIMISM THAT IS TO BE DISCERNED AMONG WRITERS, IT
STEMMED FROM A LITERARY COMMONPLACE – PRAISE FOR TIMES GONE BY. OF COURSE,
THAT EQUILIBRIUM WAS IN FACT THREATENED; BUT AT THE TIME NO ONE WAS AWARE
OF IT, APART FROM CERTAIN CULTIVATED INTELLECTUALS WHO FELT THEY WERE
LIVING IN A PERIOD OF CRISIS WHICH APPEARED TO THEM TO BE BOTH BIOLOGICAL
AND MORAL.

A Fragile Balance

Institutions

The Empire stretched from Scotland to the Sahara, from the Atlantic Ocean to
Mesopotamia. One city, Rome, had conquered this immense expanse, supporting itself, successively, on those it had vanquished, Latins, then Italians,
then various provincials. Its leader, the emperor, and he alone, guided political
life: the state became more and more an absolute monarchy.

The territory was still divided into provinces, some dependent on the Senate,
others on the emperor. The senatorial provinces were administered by proconsuls, the others either by imperial propraetorian legates who had come from
the Senate (for the larger imperial provinces, and those where legions were garrisoned), or by equestrian prefects or procurators (for the smaller ones, where
garrisons consisted only of auxiliaries).

Nevertheless, government left a certain amount of autonomy to the local
communities, the "cities," which formed the cells of this immense body
(colonies, *municipia*). The small clusters of habita-tion, *vici, pagi, castella*, etc.,
were subordinate to these larger ones, and semi-nomadic peoples who escaped

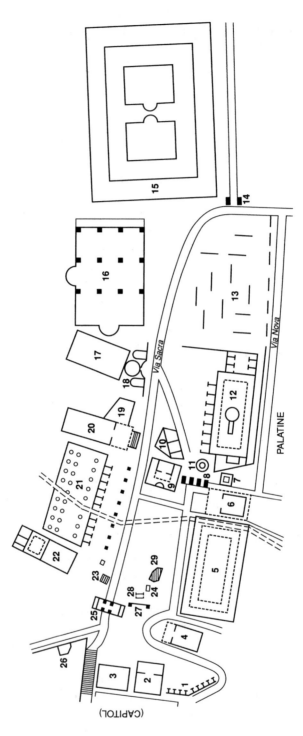

Figure 13.1 The Roman Forum in the imperial period

urban regulations were monitored by prefects. Since 212, all free men had been Roman citizens.

Society

Having on the whole remained relatively stable since the time of Augustus, society was tending to open up. Senators had lost their political role, although they kept their position in provincial administration and the army. In the imperial council and the important departments of state, their role had diminished, to the advantage of the knights, who were well in the ascendant. Moreover, provincial elites were increasingly coming to the fore, their members entering the Senate and the equestrian order. In the second century, there were signs of a reaction against this mobility. Another thing that fomented disunity was the rise of Christianity.

The economy

Although the institutional order within which the economy operated can readily be described, more caution is needed regarding the economy itself, as statistics are lacking.

Food supplies were still assured, in the main, by bread-making cereals, the "grain" which, in combination with vineyards and olive groves, which were progressing, formed the celebrated "Mediterranean triad." The breeding of livestock and regional differences, often linked with climate, must also be taken into account.

The period witnessed a great development in trade, helped by the famous Roman roads, as well as in craft products, which, in a few large concentrations, bordered on industry.

All these activities were set in motion by a rudimentary form of capitalism. We must, however, avoid anachronistic terms such as "primitivism," "modernism," and, with even greater reason, "underdevelopment." A regional description will show things more clearly.

Rome and Italy

The capital of the world, Rome had preserved its traditional institutions, apart from the *comitia*, which had disappeared long before. The Senate, which still played the political role that the emperor was pleased to allow it, at least served as a permanent municipal council. Magistrates, too, still existed: quaestors were concerned with the finances, aediles with the police and buildings, and praetors administered the law; the consulship was no longer anything but a reward

Figure 13.2 The Roman Empire and the barbarians in 235

SARMATIANS

GOTHS

CIA

Sarmizegetusa

Danube

ESIA

sus Serdica LWR.

opopolis

DONIA Adrianople

THRACE

hessalonica

Smyrna
Aphrodisias
Athenae Ephesus

SEA

Crete

ENAICA

ALEXANDRIA

Dnieper

Bug

Dniester

BOSPHORUS

Chersonese

PONTUS EUXINUS

Volga

Don

Ural

CASPIAN SEA

Caucasus

COLCHIS

IBERIA

Artaxata

Marcianopolis

Byzantium
Chalcedon
Nicomedia
BITHYNIA

Nicaea

Ancyra

GALATIA

Caesarea

LYCAONIA
PISIDIA
ISAURIA
PAMPHYLIA
LYCIA

Rhodes

Cyprus

PAPHLA-
GONIA

PONTUS

LITTLE
ARMENIA

CAPPADOCIA

COMMAGENE

Tarsus
CILICIA

Issos

ANTIOCH
Laodicea

SYRIA-COELE

Tigranocerta

Amida

Edessa
Carrhae

OSRHOENE

MESOPOTAMIA

Nisibis

ADIABENE

Hatra

PERSIANS

Dura-
Europos

CTESIPHON

Palmyra

Emesa

Heliopolis
Damascus

Tyre

SYRIA
PHOENICIA

Caesarea
Jerusalem

Bostra
Gerasa

PALESTINE

ARABIA

Petra

EGYPT

Nile

RED SEA

BLEMMYES
Syene

Seleucia
Babylon

Euphrates

Tigris

for men who had passed through the three preceding stages of the senatorial *cursus* and deserved well of the state, i.e. the sovereign.

The emperor had long since tightened his control by means of appointed representatives. The streets of Rome were maintained by a quattuorvirate. Curators were paired with the aediles and looked after buildings and aqueducts. And prefects supervised provisioning (prefect of the *annona*), the maintenance of good order in general (prefect of the city), and nocturnal policing and fire-fighting (prefect of the watch or *vigiles*).

The large number of staff was made necessary by the immensity of a city with widely varying economic functions and an overabundant population: besides being the political capital, it was the financial, commercial, and artisanal capital, and provided a multiplicity of "services," as modern economists say. Epigraphy clearly shows that Rome was no "city of idlers": it teemed with life, and all sorts of active people made their living there – shopkeepers, craftsmen, soldiers, servants, and all the staff needed for the leisure pursuits of the masters of the world.

Associated with Rome in its extraordinary imperial venture, Italy profited from its situation in the field of institutions rather than in the matter of its material prosperity. The cities it comprised in fact enjoyed a great degree of autonomy and were for the most part subject only to the fairly relaxed control of the Senate and magistrates of Rome, and to the activities of the four *iuridici*, imperial nominees whose exact function eludes us.

For the beginning of the third century, Italy's economic situation is most frequently judged quite harshly: a fairly general decline is noted, marked by depopulation and regional imbalances. But we must not look too much on the black side; the peninsula's reaction in 238 was not that of the moribund. Four regions stand out.

For Latium, it is enough to mention the name of Rome to grasp its importance. But that is not all: Ostia was certainly the busiest Italian port in that period, and numerous towns dotted the territory, Praeneste, for example, and Tibur, Alba, and Tusculum.

Campania had lost its splendor, and no longer possessed its remarkable balance between crafts and agriculture. It had chosen quantity rather than quality for its oil and luxury wines, Falernian and Massican, harvested on the borders of the region. The main centers were Capua (for what was left of its crafts), Misenum, Cumae, and Pozzuoli for their ports, and Naples for its cultural role.

A fairly similar but certainly less prosperous region was Etruria. Populonia had lost its "industrial" base; the territory of Cosa was going through a rural crisis; and we must mention also Veii, the port of Luna, and Carrara for its marble. Etrurian wines remained a much sought after product, except for that of Veii, where the wine was very poor.

From all the evidence, the Cisalpine region did the best. It produced wheat and wine, and raised cattle as well as the sheep which provided the raw material necessary for textile production, attested at Milan, Padua, and Verona. Aquileia continued to develop as a commercial center. And the other large towns of the region were Mantua, Piacenza, Modena, and Bologna.

THE WESTERN PROVINCES

The provinces in the West, which supplied Rome with emperors, Spanish under the Antonines and African under the Severi (which is evidence of their strength at all levels), had played an extremely important role during the first two centuries of the Empire. Italy's relative decline serves only to highlight their dynamism.

Before we come to the three main groups (Africa, the Iberian peninsula, and the Gauls), several minor provinces must be picked out: those of the islands in the Mediterranean and Atlantic. Sicily, a senatorial province, which still produced wheat, had Palermo and Syracuse as its chief centers. Sardinia, an imperial province, exported cereals, lead, gold, and silver; three towns stood out, Olbia, Cagliari (Carales) and Porto Torres (Turris Libisonis). More cut off from the great trading circuits, but like Sardinia an imperial province, Corsica was covered in forests. Lastly, Britain, divided into two imperial provinces under Septimius Severus or Caracalla, was also divided into two zones: a military sector in the north, with York (Eburacum) and Hadrian's and Antoninus' Walls, and a civilian region in the south, around London and Colchester (Camulodunum). In addition to the usual products, wheat, livestock, and pottery, it exported metals, in particular those of north Wales.

From the administrative standpoint, several units may be distinguished within Roman Africa. Africa Proconsularis, whose name expresses its status, covered present-day Tunisia, the west of Libya, and an eastern fringe of Algeria. Numidia, entrusted to an imperial legate, spread around its two major towns, Constantine (Cirta) and Lambaesis, where the Third Augusta was stationed. The two Mauretanian provinces, both governed by equestrian procurators, and thus also imperial, had as their principal centers Tangier (Tingi) and Volubilis in Tingitana, Cherchel (Caesarea) and Bougie (Saldae) in Caesariensis.

It has recently been discovered that some African pottery was made locally, but that discovery scarcely alters the classic picture: Africa was essentially an agricultural region. In terms of its economy, it was "wheat country" (valley of the Medjerda, the High Steppe, the High Plains), producing vast quantities of grain, which it exported either in the form of the *annona* or for commercial purposes. Olive oil production, which yielded a relatively mediocre product, nevertheless continued to develop; and, together with viticulture, it completed the "triad." Racehorses and wild beasts for the amphitheaters were also exported to Rome and Italy.

Furthermore, Africa was a highly urbanized region, especially in the north-east (Zeugitana) around Carthage, one of the largest cities in the Empire. Even ordinary tourists know the immense areas of ruins that stretch around Proconsular territory or the modern towns which have covered sites of antiquity, Utica, Hippo, El-Djem, Dougga, not forgetting Tebessa and Hadrumetum; in Tripolitania (in 235, still part of Africa Proconsularis) let us mention Leptis Magna and Sabratha; in Numidia, Timgad and Lambaesis in the south, Djemila and Constantine in the north; and the centers in Mauretania named above.

The Iberian peninsula, though larger than Roman Africa, was divided into only three provinces, shared between the Senate (Baetica) and the emperor (Citerior or Tarraconensis and Lusitania). Its economy also appears more balanced, since there was greater diversification. The "Mediterranean triad" was to be found along the eastern and southern coasts, especially in Baetica, where large amounts of wheat, wine, and oil were produced, the last two with a regard for quality; they ensured the prosperity of Seville, Cadiz, and Cordoba. The Atlantic regions seem to have been less prosperous, given over more to raising livestock (horses in the north and on the Meseta, sheep in the south). Lusitania yielded olive oil, but had opted for quantity.

The most original feature of the peninsula lay in its mineworkings: gold in the north-west (supervised by the Seventh Gemina, stationed at León, whose Latin name was Legio), gold, silver, and lead at Cartagena, copper at Cordoba, mercury at Almaden, iron, and tin. The main towns were agricultural centers, but they could also be administrative centers, like Merida, or ports, like Barcelona and Tarragona.

From the administrative viewpoint, the Gauls bring the Iberian peninsula to mind, with a rich senatorial province in the south, Narbonensis, and a range of imperial provinces, some civil and administered by legates (Aquitania, Lugdunensis, Belgica), others military and also entrusted to legates (Upper and Lower Germania), as well as the small procuratorian districts of the Alps (Maritime, Cottian, Graian, and Pennine).

Agriculture, moreover, showed the same contrast as on the Iberian peninsula, with a Mediterranean front, where cooking was done with oil, and wine was drunk, beyond which, in the north, on the Atlantic coast and inland, butter and beer were predominant. As a whole, the Gauls produced plenty of wheat, partly thanks to efficient technical means (scythe, harvester, and wheeled swing plough). Horses were bred, and pigs, left in semi-liberty in the forests, provided some renowned delicacies.

Gaulish pottery manufacture had definitively emigrated toward the Argonne region and the Rhineland, where it joined metalworking and glass-work. But

Plate 13.1 Mosaic from Moknine, Tunisia, mid-3rd century AD. The "Telegenic" troupe kills leopards at a beast-hunt. Magerius, for whom it is staged, pays each performer 1,000 denarii, which a servant carries in bags on a plate. Sousse Museum.

the Gaulish isthmus, between Britain and Germany to the north and Italy and Spain to the south, played an important commercial role. Its chief feature was its road network, complemented by navigable rivers, the Seine, Saône, and Rhône. From Boulogne, traders from Britain could reach Lyon, where they met those from Cologne, Trier, Strasbourg, Bonn, and Mainz, and from Germania across the Rhine, as well as from Mediterranean lands, coming by way of Marseille and Arles.

In Narbonensis, the Rhône valley was lined with towns, Vienne, Orange, Arles, and Nîmes, and it was matched by the Mediterranean front, with Agde and Marseille, a network completed by Narbonne and Toulouse. The Rhineland, too, was highly urbanized, with town development there connected with the presence of legionary camps, but Belgica was less densely populated (Reims, Metz), like Aquitania (Saintes, Bordeaux) and Lugdunensis (Autun and, of course, Lyon). As for the little Alpine provinces, they lived on a mountain economy, controlling the Alpine passes and, from Nice-Cimiez, access to the coast.

To the north, the Latin West was extended eastwards by the string of provinces along the Danube, that great river not only making a barrier against invasion but also, by lengthening the Rhineland route, forming a major line of communication. In 235, these were all imperial provinces with legions, and therefore governed by imperial propraetorian legates.

Straddling Switzerland and Bavaria, Raetia, a poor plateau, possessed only two large centers, Augusta of the Vindelicians (Augsburg) in the south and Castra Regina (Regensburg) in the north.

Immediately to the east, Noricum lived better, thanks to the breeding of livestock, salt production, and, chiefly, the supplying of iron from Styria and of lead. There were several important centers, Virunum, Celeia, Solua, and Lauriacum.

Lying at an angle to these provinces, Dalmatia and Pannonia had attained an importance that became more marked in the following decades. Economic life prospered: on the coastal strip with crops of the Mediterranean type, and in the interior with the profits of livestock breeding added to those of forestry. If the mining resources – iron, gold, silver – are also taken into account, as well as the trade in slaves imported from across the Danube, the density of population will be understood. The vigor of this population is explained by the presence of legionary camps in the north, at Vienna (Vindobona), Carnuntum, Brigetio, and Aquincum; Salonae, situated in the south, was more civilian in character.

One province alone lay on the left bank of the Danube, Dacia – so Romanized that it became our modern Romania. Besides cereals, it continued to supply gold, iron, and salt, and had a large population. Its main city was Sarmizegethusa.

Lastly, on the right bank of the lower Danube, Moesia belonged partly to the Greek world, the East, mainly on its Black Sea coast, where the old Greek colonies of Tomi and Callatis lay. These ports were used for exporting the grain surpluses produced by the plains of the interior.

THE EASTERN PROVINCES

The Greek-speaking East, like the West, had been organized in several great provincial areas, four of which stood out clearly: the Balkan peninsula, Anatolia, Syria, and Egypt.

Subject to Mark Antony's rule during the civil war that had ended in 31 BC, these regions had not always been looked upon with favor by the central government under Augustus. But Athens, Macedonia, Pergamum, the land of the Galatians, Syria, and Egypt had the benefit of a still considerable cultural and economic heritage, and in 235 found themselves in a pretty good overall situation.

Augustus had left to the Senate the two provinces in the Balkan peninsula, Achaea (all the southern part) and Macedonia. Later, Thrace had been annexed, and in the reign of Trajan was entrusted to an imperial propraetorian legate. But within this imposed administrative framework lay a number of regional distinctions set up by history and geography.

Within the province of Achaea (from which the imperial equestrian province of Epirus had been separated), Aetolia was a sparsely populated and depressed region, given over to brigandage, its economy dependent on meager cereal crops, wine, and top-quality olive oil. This seems to have been equally the situation of Attica. Hymettus honey and cultural tourism, based mainly on Athens, would do little to change this state of affairs, although the immense wealth of one such as Herodes Atticus in the second century had shown that a certain prosperity might exist. The island of Euboea possessed several trump cards, in the form of marble from Carystos, livestock, and the purple dye obtained from a type of shellfish, the murex. The Peloponnese appears to have been little more prosperous than Attica, but one may note the presence of some very wealthy and important men, especially in Sparta, Patras (Patrae), and above all Corinth, the province's capital. North again of Attica, the regions of Boeotia and Phocis seem to have attained a satisfactory level of prosperity, mainly based on abundant and relatively diversified agricultural production (wheat, vines, olive trees, chiefly around Lake Copaïs). Thebes remained the principal town.

Macedonia's antechamber, Thessaly, maintained its reputation as good country, specializing in horse-breeding. This was also important in Macedonia itself, where gold and silver mining supplemented agricultural production. Famous cities like Pella, Thessalonica, and Philippi dotted a territory crossed by a major route, the Via Egnatia.

As we saw, the kingdom of Thrace had been annexed to the Empire after all the other regions just listed. Despite the mountains that occupied part of its territory, this province possessed a healthy economy. Agriculture produced grain surpluses, horses were bred, pottery manufactured, and the subsoil yielded gold.

The Balkan peninsula thus had both weak and strong points. A very different situation obtained in Anatolia, where, together with its Persian and Hellenistic heritage, geography formed a unifying element. The country is a vast plateau, massive, high, and arid; the climate one of extremes, dry all year round but very hot in summer and very cold in winter, with Mediterranean weather showing itself only in the narrow coastal plains. The wealth of the past and its traditions enabled the effects of this harshness to be overcome. Temples, often places of pilgrimage, were the owners of immense domains and centers of craft production, and they also acted as banks. This arrangement dated back to early antiquity, like a good part of the urban fabric and road network, much of which had been established under the Persians and Alexander's successors, if not earlier.

Confined to the western end of Anatolia, the senatorial province of Asia corresponded to the ancient kingdom of Pergamum. It was one of the richest regions of the Empire. And its level of urbanization dazzlingly reflected its preeminence. Besides the capital, Ephesus, where the proconsul resided, mention must be made of Pergamum, which still produced *pergamena* (parchment), Miletus, Smyrna, Aphrodisias of Caria, Halicarnassus, and Clazomenae. Agriculture flourished in the coastal plains, the valley of the Menderes, and in the islands, particularly on "Chios, the isle of wines." The textile industry was supplied by sheep-breeding with its raw material. And the marble mines were still exploited.

Immediately to the north, Bithynia-Pontus, now an imperial province, benefited from its exceptional position between Europe and Asia, and between the Black Sea and the Aegean. To the income derived from the land, it added that from the sea, both fishing and trade, all of which constituted the prosperity of Nicaea, Nicomedia, Prusa, and Prusias.

In the remainder of Anatolia, divided into imperial provinces, men experienced harsher living conditions because of the climate. There is scarcely any evidence of wine and oil production outside the coastal plains. Galatia, less urbanized than the more temperate regions (its chief city Ancyra), was divided into large domains devoted to the raising of sheep for wool. The same applies to Cappadocia. But this also housed several great legionary fortresses, such as the one at Melitene, and the soldiers' pay favored the growth of a monetary economic sector. However, one can overstress the province's military function: civil centers like Tyana also played an important part in the life of the province. Lycia-Pamphylia seemed like an extension of Galatia, but with access to the Mediterranean. This fortunate situation was not without influence on its agriculture and trade. One man, Opramoas of Rhodiapolis, and one city, Xanthos, illustrate clearly enough the prosperity it had attained in the second century. Lastly, Cilicia, whose capital was Tarsus, produced goatskins from which a cloth (*cilicium*) was made, and saffron, as well as wine and oil on the plains.

Syria had a history at least as ancient as that of Anatolia and from this, as well as from its geography, came its particular diversity. Like Cappadocia, this imperial province was situated facing the Parthians, and it too had been supplied with legions, at Cyrrhus, Laodicea, Raphaneae, and Emesa. From here, the conquests of Septimius Severus had extended the Roman world as far as the Tigris, adding to it the province of Mesopotamia. Agriculture was developed in various ways. A Mediterranean fringe provided grain, wine, and oil.

The mountains, which were carefully maintained, supplied wood for ship-building. And in the east, cultivated oases dotted the desert. Meager rainfall enforced operations to collect, conserve, and distribute water, with the Euphrates and Orontes playing an important role here. Men's long experience was also an advantage to the craft industries. Textiles (linen and wool) bene-fited from the great inventiveness of the dyeworks (purple, extracted from the murex). Silk was imported from China. Glass was probably a local invention. These activities fed a coastal and caravan trade that was the fruit of over 1,000 years' experience. Consequently, Antioch was one of the largest cities in the Empire. Other centers also deserve mention, especially Apamea, Seleucia, Emesa, and the caravan cities in the east, Dura-Europus and Palmyra.

In the south-west, Phoenicia had been detached from Syria by Septimius Severus. Its agriculture was Mediterranean along the coast and mountainous to the east, where the cedars of Lebanon and other species of trees grew that were used in the naval dockyards. Here, too, traditions over 1,000 years old made the traders of Beirut and Tyre wealthy.

Farther south, two small provinces were caught between the sea and the desert. Judaea-Palestine lived very poorly, and religious or "national" motives were not entirely to blame for the risings in 66 and 132. An economy that was too exclusively agricultural (the Jordan valley) and overpopulation aggravated those difficulties. However, Caesarea and Jerusalem managed to attain a minimum of prosperity. East of the Jordan, Arabia had done better thanks to a greater diversification. The Hauran produced good harvests of wheat, and oil production had been well developed. Livestock-breeding, practiced by the semi-nomads, complemented these agricultural resources. Perfumes and incense were exported. And the caravan trade assured Bostra and Petra of a splendid income.

To the south-west, we come next to the last of the great provincial areas of the Roman world, Egypt, which from an administrative viewpoint had been reduced to the ranks, only the title of its governor, the "prefect of Egypt," dis-tinguishing it from other imperial provinces.

"Egypt," wrote Herodotus in the fifth century BC, "is a gift of the Nile," meaning the god Nile, for the river was regarded by those who lived along its banks as a beneficent god. By 235 AD, nothing had changed, the peasants still expected everything from it. In August, the floods arrived regularly and deposited a silt that fertilized the edges of the desert. The country was in fact divided into three zones, the valley, the delta, and the oases, and together these produced great harvests of grain as well as wine and oil, flax, and, above all, papyrus, which sustained a craft. Crafts, in fact, were well developed in this province, which was dominated by a real "industrial triad," papyrus, textiles (linen and wool), and glass. To these must be added the (relatively meager) production of a few mines, and the luxury goods (perfumes, fabrics, and jewels) from Alexandria, one of the principal cities in the Empire but always a purely Greek city, like Naucratis, Ptolemais, and Antinoöpolis.

To return to the islands of the Mediterranean, Cyprus, close to Syria, was a senatorial province, making its living from the sea (fishing, coastal navigation) and from agriculture on its plains. Crete, which must have had similar means of existence, had been linked administratively with Cyrenaica, forming the senatorial province of Crete-Cyrenaica.

Cyrenaica, situated in North Africa between Egypt and Africa Proconsularis, completes our circuit of the Empire. Here, there were both nomads and settlers, with traditional cultivation carried on around the towns (Cyrene) and trade from the ports (Apollonia).

Various governmental means were used to manage interprovincial relations and to smooth out the differences between the various parts of the Empire stemming from history and geography. It is difficult, however, to speak of the unity of the Empire in the third century without mentioning its neighbors.

Beyond the Limes

The development of Roman military strength on the frontiers of the Empire reveals which enemies were feared by army headquarters. Here we can distinguish three major sectors.

(1) Possibly the most dangerous adversaries, in proportion to their numbers, were the Britons living beyond Hadrian's and Antoninus' Walls. Picts and Scots might attack equally by land or sea. Against them it had been necessary to mobilize (and immobilize) three legions, almost one tenth of the imperial army.

On the Continent, beyond the Rhine and the Danube, lived the Germani. The size of their population and their effectiveness in combat made them fearsome enemies. Until the third century they had lived divided into small, very aggressive peoples, fortunately, for the most part, without any real coordination. But at the beginning of the century, leagues were formed. The Alemanni faced the angle formed by the upper courses of the Rhine and Danube. And the Franks waited behind the middle and lower Rhine. Moreover, the Goths (another Germanic people), organized notably by King Kniva, were coming down toward the south and south-east. It is possible, though not certain, that the movements of peoples at that time in the Far East had profound and swiftly propagated consequences on this frontier. What is certain is that the situation was deteriorating.

The imperial army headquarters had not failed to notice this deterioration, and military numbers continued to be reinforced on the lower Danube.

Whereas the Germanies were defended by only four legions, thirteen ensured the security of the provinces situated between present-day Switzerland and the Black Sea.

In the north-east, the Sarmatians were also on the move and increasingly often leaving the steppelands. They then either settled in the Empire or merged into the horde of Goths or, as in the case of the Iazyges and Alani, tried to preserve a certain autonomy.

(2) The second major source of danger lay in the east. Perhaps less formidable on the battlefield than the barbarian leagues, Persia was nevertheless the only large organized state likely to countervail against the might of Rome, and the number of legions charged with keeping it under surveillance had hardly stopped growing since the time of Augustus – it was now ten. The threat was made all the more apparent by the fact that the heavy trade in expensive and precious goods from the Far East passed in part through Persian territory. Moreover, between Persia and Rome lay a constant source of discord, Armenia.

During the reign of the Severi, Persia had undergone a profound upheaval. Between 212 and 227, the Arsacid Parthians had been replaced by the Sassanid Persians: Artaban had been driven out by Ardashir (a descendant of Sassan), who had mapped out a precise program on two levels.

Politically, he intended to pursue a fierce nationalism. He aspired to re-establish the Achaemenid imperial tradition and gain control of the territories formerly dominated by Darius and Xerxes. He relied on solid institutions: the king, an absolute and divine monarch, was aided by a great commander and a high priest; territorial government was assured by the traditional satraps (military governors), who were more closely supervised than ever. The development of a heavily armored cavalry (cataphracts) rendered this enemy even more fearsome in Roman eyes.

In the religious field, the new government revealed itself as intolerant, even fanatical, imposing a kind of reformed Zoroastrianism as the state religion. Zoroastrianism or Mazdaism was Persia's oldest religion. It had been preached by Zoroaster, also called Zarathustra, and honored the god Ahura Mazda, the "Wise Lord." But other beliefs existed in the Persian lands. In the east, Buddhism was widespread. This was a form of wisdom, rather than a religion. It sought to teach people to perceive the reality behind appearances, and to break the cycle of reincarnation by the practice of virtue and asceticism. In the west, lived large numbers of Jews (Babylonia was one of the great centers of the diaspora) and also, even at that early date, communities of Christians. And between 241 and 275, Mani preached a new dualistic theology of redemption, derived from Zoroastrianism, based on an insistent belief in two fundamental spirits, one of good, Ahura Mazda, and one of evil. He suffered persecution because of his teachings and died on a cross.

(3) The Roman emperor had fewer worries when dealing with his southern frontier. Possible enemies there had no political unity and little demographic potential, and represented a military danger only through their mobility and nomadic way of life.

The Nobades and Blemmyes, well attested south of Aswan, posed a possible threat to Egypt. The decline of the kingdom of Meroë had been matched by the development of the state of Aksoum, where Hellenism spread, but which turned rather more to the Red Sea and trade than to Egypt and war. Lastly, in north-west Africa, the Berbers, chiefly Garamantes and Maures, lived on either side of the *limes*, on the edges of the desert or in the mountains. These days credence is no longer given to the idea of a "camel revolution," the sudden spread of that animal in the third-century Sahara, a spread that might have been connected with rebellious elements being driven into this arid zone. The chief danger lay in the close interweaving of these peoples with those already settled: one of the soldiers' tasks was to keep watch over the comings and goings of the nomads, and to guide traders safely through their lands.

BALANCE AND DISEQUILIBRIUM

In 235, the Empire appeared to have achieved equilibrium. Despite some difficulties, order and prosperity ruled fairly generally. One might, however, pick out two possible sources of anxiety.

For one thing, the East and the West, which formed two distinct entities, had not progressed at the same pace. The Latin West had perhaps started off earlier than the Greek East, in the time of Augustus. But, precisely because of that, the phase of expansion had lasted a long time and was running out of steam, whereas the East experienced a great dynamism in the second century and early in the third.

For another, although the frontier system that separated Rome from the barbarians was still working satisfactorily, the Persians and Germani were altering and improving their own political, social, and military structures. On both sides of the Empire, difficulties appeared as early as under Marcus Aurelius; by 235, the last of the Severi had had to fight successively against the Persians and the Alemanni.

Severus Alexander's killers, his own soldiers, were unaware that they were opening a new era.

14 / A DISINTEGRATING ORDER, AD 235–284

*F*ROM 235, THE EMPIRE PLUNGED INTO A CRISIS DESCRIBED BY CONTEMPORARY
AUTHORS IN TRAGIC TONES. INDEED, THERE CAN BE NO DENYING ITS GRAVITY
AND GENERAL NATURE. RECENT RESEARCH, HOWEVER, TENDS TO SET CERTAIN LIMITS
ON THIS DISINTEGRATION AND NOTES THE EXISTENCE OF A REACTION. PERHAPS IT
WOULD BE BETTER NOT TO YIELD TO THE ABSOLUTE PESSIMISM OF THE WRITERS OF
THAT PERIOD.

SINKING INTO CRISIS (235–260)

Of course, the Empire did not suddenly collapse. Its fall was gradual, slow, and
prolonged. We must first look at this decline in its broad outlines, following its
chronology; for its rhythm is marked by the reigns of the emperors. Let us not
forget, however, that documentation relating to this period is particularly in
need of corroboration.

Senatorial tradition depicts Maximinus Thrax (235–8) as a rough soldier who
had emerged from the depths of society: a shepherd who became a soldier, and
then an officer, and then ascended all the ranks of the hierarchy. What is certain
is that, having become emperor, he associated his son with him as *Caesar*; and,
having waged a long, hard war against the Alemanni, installed himself at
Sirmium in order to keep a watch on the Dacians and Sarmatians and to make
ready for a counteroffensive against them. Some sources also mention persecution directed at the Christians, especially church leaders, portraying it as
the inadequate response of a simple mind confronted with a complex problem.

Maximinus also reacted in another way: to satisfy the needs of war he
demanded that taxes should be levied very strictly. By doing so, he unleashed
the events of 238. It was at first a general rebellion of the Africans, both rich
and poor, peasants and town-dwellers alike. At El-Djem (Thysdrus), an overde-
manding procurator was murdered by some young men of good family.
Stunned by their own audacity, they could see no salvation except in taking the
initiative. They proclaimed the proconsul of the province and his son emperors (we know them as Gordian I and Gordian II). At first, the Third Augusta
recognized their legitimacy; then, at the instigation of its legate Capelianus (a

senator), it ended the rebellion in a bloodbath of the short-lived emperors and those loyal to them.

Next, Italy rebelled. The senators, appalled by the base origins of Maximinus, and further exasperated by his tax policies, decided to give the provincials their support. They deposed the man they regarded as a tyrant, and mobilized against him all the forces of the peninsula, which at the time was less ruined than has sometimes been described. For good measure, they entrusted the government to two of their own number, Pupienus and Balbinus. Maximinus then had to decide whether to turn his back on the barbarians and immediately march on Rome. When he later met with stout resistance on his way through Italy, the soldiers put everyone in accord by assassinating Maximinus, together with his son, and not long afterwards Pupienus and Balbinus as well.

Power then fell into the hands of Gordian III (238–44). This choice was satisfactory to all concerned: to the senators because the newly elected man, the grandson of Gordian I and nephew of Gordian II, was one of their own people; to the soldiers because, on account of his youth, he was under the thumb of their chief, the praetorian prefect, who was no longer only a war commander but also the emperor's deputy and head of the entire army. In one sense, Gordian III was the candidate of an alliance, and a fairly wide alliance at that.

In fact, responsibility for running the Empire fell in 241 to the praetorian prefect, Timesitheus, whose daughter the emperor married. There was no shortage of work to be done. In 238, the Carpi and Goths had attempted to cross the Danube. The Goths were again repulsed in 242, while the Persians were defeated in 243. Gordian III was still on the Syrian front, at Dura-Europus, when he was assassinated.

His successor was Philip the Arabian (244–9). The new emperor made various efforts to consolidate his power. He associated with him his small son, aged barely six, and gave responsibility for eastern affairs to his brother Priscus, who received the title *rector Orientis*, these two measures clearly showing that Philip understood the importance of the succession, and had sensed that the destinies of the two parts of the Mediterranean world were starting to diverge. With an eye to propaganda, he also had Rome's millennium celebrated in great style, on April 21, 248, hoping thereby to strengthen his position.

But war continued to cause increasing difficulties. Philip had hardly become emperor before he had to buy peace from the Persians. In this way he hoped, first, to settle his position among his own followers, and then to gain the opportunity for military intervention elsewhere. For in the same year (244), the Alemanni invaded Alsace, and the Carpi and Goths were once again in evidence on the lower Danube.

The counteroffensives against the barbarians were made all the more tricky because in several places usurpers were declaring themselves, Uranius in Syria,

Pacatian in Moesia, Jotapian in Cappadocia, and then Decius, on the lower Danube, where he had repulsed the Goths.

Decius, however, is not properly to be numbered among the usurpers, since he succeeded in seizing power from Philip and his son and keeping it for over two years. To give the impression that all was going well, he had baths constructed on the Aventine in Rome, and to make sure that all would go well, he unleashed a wave of persecutions against the Christians. This inaugurated a period of about ten years during which followers of the "new faith" had at times to undergo great suffering.

But Decius' own gods turned a deaf ear. The plague spread through the Empire, and the Goths through the Balkans. In 250, the Goths crossed Lower Moesia, and reached Beroea in Macedonia and Philippopolis in Thrace. And then, during the summer of 251, they subjected the Roman army to a disastrous rout in the Dobruja (eastern Romania). Decius died in the battle confronting the enemy, which saved him from being assassinated.

The Empire was plunged into crisis. The barbarians became more and more of a threat, reigns increasingly unstable. Trebonianus Gallus (251–3) was partnered by his son Volusianus and only feebly applied the measures aimed at the Christians. He doubtless had other worries, for by then wars were ravaging even the interior of the Roman world. In an extraordinary exploit in 253, Franks and Alemanni crossed the Rhine, pierced the *limes*, and pillaged Gaul and then Spain before returning home. And the Goths were embarking on new expeditions in the direction of Greece and Asia.

Let us make brief mention of the Moor Aemilianus (253), the governor of Moesia, who held on as emperor for just three months even though he had been recognized by the East. For his attaining power was evidence of the new importance assumed by his country's cavalry in the ranks of the Roman army. In fact, consequent upon developments in recruitment and tactics, Moorish horsemen represented an essential element of Rome's fighting forces. This military role, in a period of military crisis, allowed them to play a political role and favor the promotion of their compatriots.

The Empire, meanwhile, had not yet plumbed the depths of its misfortune. It experienced its most trying times under Valerian (253–259/60), an ill-starred senator of illustrious origin. Barbarian assaults were launched on several points along the frontier. The Goths had attacked Greece and Asia in 252–3; in 256 they returned, and again in 258. In 253 and 256, the Franks and Alemanni returned to Gaul in search of riches; Valerian sent his son and partner Gallienus against them, and he succeeded in driving them back. The Saxons made their appearance on the shores of the North Sea, and Berbers were in revolt from 253 to 260. That was not all. In the East, the troops of Sapor (or Shapur) fell upon the province of Syria on at least three occasions, even reaching Antioch. The violent persecution of the Christians in 257 and 258 no more solved the

Plate 14.1 Roman soldiers fighting barbarians: detail of a sarcophagus. National Archeological Museum, Rome.

Empire's problems than did the action of Ingenuus, the governor of Pannonia, who proclaimed himself emperor (258–60) after repulsing the Quadi and Marcomanni.

The most tragic phase of the crisis came in around 260, with invasions and usurpations mounting up in a disastrous tally. The Roxolani and Sarmatians had descended on Pannonia. The Alemanni, having invaded Gaul, had threatened Italy, where Gallienus halted them only in the north of the peninsula. Under the sovereignty of Odaenathus, Palmyra seceded. In the East, again, there were at least two usurpers, Macrianus and Quietus. On the Danube, after defeating the Roxolani, Regalianus proclaimed himself emperor. In Cologne, Postumus also had claimed the throne, but confined his empire to Gaul. Valerian the Younger, son and grandson of the official rulers, was assassinated.

But more was to come. The supreme humiliation occurred: the emperor Valerian, who had been captured by the Persians (perhaps in 259), was put to death (in 260 at the latest), and his remains (or the slave's garment he had been forced to wear) put on display in the principal towns of Persia (the bas-relief of Bishapur allows a better comprehension of this affair). Sapor was able to boast about this total victory in the famous inscription of Naqs-i-Rustem, known as the *Res gestae Divi Saporis* (by analogy with the *Res gestae Divi Augusti*).

We shall now turn to the character, as well as the limits, of the crisis that these dramatic events disclose.

THE NATURE AND LIMITS OF THE CRISIS

The main characteristics of the third century's great crisis have long been known.

(1) To a large extent it was a crisis of military origin. For the first time the enemy had attacked persistently and nearly simultaneously on two fronts. The Germani had to be driven back in the north, on both the Rhine and the Danube, and the Persians in the east. The emperors had continually to chase back and forth from one end of the Empire to the other, depleting one province to defend another. Such a situation encouraged peoples to rebel who would otherwise have remained peaceable.

Defeat revealed two further weaknesses in the Augustan strategy. First, when they had penetrated the *limes*, the barbarians met no other obstacles. The army had been deployed in a thin "curtain" separating the Roman from the barbarian world. Secondly, for both economic and demographic reasons, commanders had no reserves of men at their disposal. The policy of quality in recruitment limited choice and imposed the payment of suitable wages.

(2) The defeats brought about a political crisis. To foreign war against barbarians was added civil war between Romans. Holding their supreme leader responsible for their woes, the soldiers frequently intervened. They eliminated the titular ruler and appointed his successor following a familiar procedure: the praetorian prefect had the emperor assassinated, took his place, and appointed a praetorian prefect who, in his turn, became emperor in this way. The Empire, deprived of a dynasty, had become "an absolute monarchy tempered by assassination," hence the brevity of the reigns. Moreover, such a situation aroused the desires of ambitious men with troops at their disposal, leading them to proclaim themselves emperor, sometimes not unsuccessfully – a legitimate emperor was often nothing more than a victorious usurper. Under these conditions, nobody enjoyed the continuity necessary for a policy of recovery.

(3) The defeats also brought in their wake an economic crisis. In antiquity it was traditional for invaders to loot. Booty was their avowed aim, and what they could not carry off they destroyed. Thus, when they had taken everything they could, the barbarians sacked the towns, destroyed the herds, and burned the crops. Moreover, lack of security cut the trade routes, with disorder bringing the rebirth of brigandage and piracy.

The development of coinage allows us to trace the development of misfortune – indeed, through the stoppage in trade that they caused, the invasions were themselves a prime factor in inflation, added to which were the rash promises made to soldiers by usurpers, the expenses inherent in long, hard wars, and payments made to the barbarians. But the Empire's monetary situation had, in any case, long been unstable. Trading beyond the frontiers had been poor, and the wages paid to the army even in normal times were already devouring most of the state's budget.

Gold disappeared, hoarded by the wealthy. The silver Antoninianus dwindled in weight and standard: from $5.18\,g$ and a standard of 450 per 1,000 in Caracalla's time, it fell to $2.80\,g$ and 50 per 1,000 under Gallienus. Even the bronze coinage was affected. The usurper Tetricus issued small bronze coins in Gaul which barely covered the little fingernail. Workshops stopped minting coins. Trade reverted in part to natural economy, by barter. Military pay itself was affected, and the *aerarium militare*, whose duty it was to pay out a sum to each veteran pensioned off, disappeared in the middle of the third century.

(4) As might be expected, these economic difficulties resulted in a social crisis. The poor were further impoverished, directly by the invasions, but also by growing tax pressure. The inscription carved at Scaptopara in Thrace during the reign of Gordian III was echoed in the laments of the imperial colonists living at Aragoe in Phrygia during the reign of Philip – everyone was protesting against excessive demands. Municipal worthies, made responsible for the levying of taxes, at first slowed down and then completely halted their acts of public benefaction. The rich, though not all of them, also had to suffer the misfortunes of the times. Lastly, signs of a period of crisis, brigandage, piracy, and the plague reappeared.

(5) These misfortunes, worsened by contemporaries' perception of them, provoked a moral crisis. Not knowing how to ward off fate, men lived in a state of disarray. Their uncertainties were transposed to the religious plane, but very few questioned the will of the gods, still less their existence. The query was simple: "Why don't the gods (who indubitably exist) give us better protection?" The reply was self-evident: "The peace of the gods has been shattered because in the bosom of the Empire lives an impious sect that does not worship

them." It may be guessed that this referred to the Christians. Hence the persecutions.

In 250–1, the emperor Decius commanded a general sacrifice to the state gods. Some terrified Christians "fell by the wayside" (they were called the *lapsi*) and accepted what was proposed to them – the granting of an official document (*libellus*) that showed that they had performed what had been required made them *libellatici*, a term of contempt used by Christians who had not yielded. There was a new wave of harassment in 252–3, but it was relatively moderate. The worst occurred in 257–8. Under the influence of Macrianus, his "minister of finance," Valerian resumed the persecutions. In 257, he banned Christian worship and ordered the members of the Church hierarchy to make sacrifices to the gods of the Empire. In 258, he had the refractory dignitaries executed, and stubborn rich Christians were deprived of their possessions. It was in this persecution that St Cyprian, bishop of Carthage, died.

TWO FURTHER CAUSES OF THE CRISIS?

The war on two fronts thus resulted in the disorganization of the Empire's political, economic, and social life, and in a period of persecutions. Perhaps two other causes of crisis should be added to these fairly generally accepted origins.

1 In the first place, it may be argued that what economists term the "current circumstances," especially of the western provinces, should be taken to have some bearing. Since the period of Augustus, the economy had continually grown, and at an increasingly rapid pace: the slow expansion of the Julio-Claudian era had been followed by the acceleration due to the operations of the Flavians, with the peak achieved under the Antonines and Severi. Now, a long rising phase of expansion is usually followed by a sharp downward phase of contraction, and it may be that a downturn of this kind underlay the crisis. However, we lack the day-to-day accounts that would enable us better to define this cyclical phenomenon for this period. Moreover, it is not absolutely certain that ancient economies even followed that pattern. All we have, therefore, is a hypothesis.

2 In the second place – and this point seems more sure – the third-century crisis seems also to have been a crisis of adaptation. The political, administrative, and military institutions of the Empire dated in broad outline from the period of Augustus, who had himself received the heritage of the Republic. Now completely original problems were presenting themselves. The Principate had been succeeded by the Dominate, war had broken out on two fronts, and nobody knew what attitude to adopt to the Christians, who had to be integrated somehow since they could not be destroyed. The Roman spirit was steeped in the law. To bring new solutions to new problems, it felt the need for new institutions.

The crisis

Military crisis (invasions)→$\left\{\begin{array}{l}\text{political crisis (government instability)}\\\text{economic crisis (ruin)}\\\text{social crisis (impoverishment)}\\\text{moral crisis (doubt, persecutions)}\end{array}\right.$

+ crisis of adaptation and (perhaps) of "current circumstances"

THE LIMITS OF THE CRISIS

Recent research has made it necessary to establish clearly the limits of this third-century crisis.

(1) There is first the matter of chronology. Today, it is no longer accepted that the period of the Severi was part of this unhappy time, apart from a few exceptional episodes. Indeed, for many provinces it marked a peak, for example in the economic field.

Difficulties did not begin until 235, and the Empire then sank into crisis until 260. Nevertheless, even in the midst of its worst problems, government did not remain inactive. To the military reaction must be added other measures, such as the creation of outlying mints as early as 250.

(2) We must also take geography into account. The most dangerous enemies were the Persians and the Germani, especially the Franks, Alemanni, and Goths. The provinces most exposed to their attacks suffered more and earlier than the others. Egypt, for instance, was not seriously affected until around 260, when the countryside was depopulated, sub-desert land was abandoned, and the Faiyum region was hit. Moreover, even in the face of the enemy, some sectors were better able to resist than others. Olbia on the Black Sea, for example, was finally abandoned to the invading barbarians only at the end of the third century.

Among the regions least touched by the crisis were the Iberian peninsula, especially Lusitania, then in full expansion, and Africa, especially central and southern Proconsularis, although Mauretania Caesariensis suffered a wave of rebellions and these overflowed into Numidia (there is evidence of disturbances still taking place in 260).

The usurpations and secessions, notably those of Postumus in Gaul and Odaenathus at Palmyra, reveal both the weakness of central government and the strength of the provincials' will to resist the invasions. It was not by chance that the two most important secessions erupted where the pressure was greatest: in Gaul, confronted with the Germani, and at Palmyra, confronted with the Persians. In 260, Postumus made himself master of the Gauls, and then gained the adherence of Britain and the Iberian peninsula. He was not rising against Rome, he said, but against the barbarians. The secession lasted until 274. The rule of Odaenathus and his wife Zenobia extended over Syria, Palestine, Arabia, and southern Anatolia.

One may even wonder whether some large landowners in sheltered provinces were not able to derive profit from the misfortunes of others, selling scarce goods at exorbitant prices. At the end of the crisis, quite a few found themselves richer than when they started. This might explain the origin of certain vast fourth-century fortunes, for example that of the Anicii.

(3) Not all sectors of activity were affected with equal severity. There was some redistribution of wealth. Life changed. Towns surrounded themselves with defensive walls – covering, it is true, an area smaller than in preceding centuries, but they were nevertheless able to build them. Moreover, although it did not reveal itself in any striking fashion until the following century, there was the beginning of a return to the land, with the powerful installing themselves more permanently in their landed properties. Lastly, despite the persecutions, or perhaps because of them, Christianity continued to make progress. In the later third century, Dionysius of Alexandria (who wrote apologetics and pastoral poetry) and the "school" of Antioch contributed to the deepening of the doctrine. Gnosticism, which first came into prominence in the second century and was now flourishing, having divided into many sects, may itself be interpreted as a sign of vitality – this heterodox theology set out the perfect knowledge (*gnosis*) of a God who was pure spirit, and affirmed that the quest for the good leads to the rejection of the material, the source of all evil.

But the best proof of the vitality of the Roman world was supplied by the attitude of the central government.

THE REACTION OF THE IMPERIAL GOVERNMENT (260–284)

In fact, the period between 260 and 284 was marked by a sustained reaction to the crisis. Gallienus himself, who lived through some very dark days, did not remain inactive – contrary to what senatorial tradition would have us believe. And his successors, the "Illyrian" emperors, so called because of the geographical origin of most of them, gradually restored the situation.

Gallienus (259/60–68), who in 253 had become a partner in his father's rule, indeed inherited a disastrous state of affairs, above all in the military field and in all parts of the Empire. Pirates pillaged the coasts of the North Sea, the Franks had entered Gaul, and the Alemanni had reached northern Italy. There was also unrest in Africa (the Moors) and Egypt (the Blemmyes). And in the East, after the death of Odaenathus in 167, his widow, the famous Zenobia, assumed power on behalf of their young son, Vaballathus. Palmyra had seceded the better to defend itself against Persia, and also to extend its trading ascendancy, but there was a pro-Roman faction, both among the desert Arabs and in the town itself.

The plunge into crisis (chronology)			
Dates	Emperors	Usurpers	Enemies
235–8	Maximinus		Alemanni Dacians and Sarmatians Carpi and Goths
238	Gordian I and Gordian II Pupienus and Balbinus		
238–44	Gordian III	Sabinianus (?)	Carpi and Goths Persians
244–9	Philip the Arabian	Uranius Pacatian Jotapian	Persians Alemanni Carpi and Goths
249–51	Decius		Carpi and Goths
251–3	Trebonianus Gallus	Aemilianus	Goths Persians Franks and Alemanni
253–259/260	Valerian	Ingenuus Odaenathus Postumus	Goths Franks and Alemanni Saxons Moors Persians Quadi and Marcomanni Roxolani and Sarmatians

But whatever senatorial tradition may say about him, Gallienus was a resolute emperor. He personally took part in campaigns, and above all reorganized the army. He was responsible for the creation of a mobile reserve, composed of *vexillationes* of cavalry commanded by *duces* (generals) and quartered notably at Milan, and made systematic recourse to the *protectores* as bodyguards. Moreover, when the senators balked at rendering themselves vulnerable to the chances of war, their military posts were abolished. As a result, the prefect of

Reaction to the crisis (chronology)			
Dates	Emperors	Usurpers	Enemies
259/260–8	Gallienus	Macrianus	Franks and Alemanni
		Quietus	Persians
		Regalianus	Goths
		Aureolus	
		Postumus → Laelianus	
		→ Marius	
		Odaenathus → Vaballathus	
		(Zenobia)	
268–70	Claudius II	Marius → Victorinus	Alemanni
		Quintillus	Goths
		Vaballathus (Zenobia)	Persians
270–5	Aurelian	Victorinus → Tetricus	Franks and Alemanni
		Victory over Tetricus	Carpi and Goths
		Victory over Zenobia	Sarmatians
275–6	Tacitus	Florian	Goths
			Franks
276–82	Probus		Franks and Alemanni
			Vandals
			Goths
			Blemmyes
282–3	Carus		Sarmatians
283–5	Carinus		Persians
283–4	Numerian		

the camp (*praefectus castrorum*), who had become first officer, was transformed into legion commander (*praefectus legionis*), and provincial legates gave way to equestrian governors (*praesides*). No one knows for certain where the new soldiers came from, but they were probably recruited from the sons of military men, from farmers, barbarians, and chiefly the inhabitants of Illyria, which soon became the pivot of the Empire.

Gallienus, the last great ruler to emerge from the aristocracy, considerably strengthened imperial absolutism by imparting to it a theocratic character, symbolized by the diadem. It became an abstract and eternal figure.

This cultured man, who was strongly philhellenic, had been initiated into the Eleusinian mysteries. He lived surrounded by a court led by the empress Salonina, where the neo-Platonist philosopher Plotinus was conspicuous. His reign witnessed a blossoming of culture and the arts. The use of Latin, which was expanding, spread to the lower Danube. Painting (the "Vault of the Flavii" in the Catacomb of Domitilla) and, even more, sculpture produced some masterpieces (the arch on the Esquiline, imperial busts, and sarcophagi, which reached their peak with the Ludovisi or "consul's" sarcophagus at Naples).

In 260, to gain an advantage, or perhaps from conviction, Gallienus discontinued the persecutions of Christians, issuing a decree of toleration that opened a 40-year period known as the Church's "little peace."

In 267, the external situation again gave trouble. The Goths reached Athens, and Illyria was invaded. But there was also soon a fresh internal threat. Aureolus, commander of the troops in Milan, proclaimed himself emperor. Gallienus, besieging him there, was assassinated by his own officers in 268.

His successors pursued his work of re-establishing order. These "Illyrian" emperors came, in the main, from the ranks of the army.

Claudius II (268–70), known as Gothicus, partly put the situation to rights. He freed northern Italy from the Alemanni, who had once more invaded, by crushing them near Lake Garda. He also liberated Illyria by a great victory over the Goths near Naissus (270), which earned him his nickname. He nevertheless had to put up with the (fleeting) usurpation of Quintillus, and failed to prevent the empire of the Gauls passing from Marius to Victorinus. Worse still, he was forced to let Zenobia extend Palmyra's domination toward Egypt and Asia Minor.

It fell to Aurelian (270–5) to carry on the task of restoration, but in the military field Rome still had numerous active enemies. In 270, the Franks attacked on the Rhine; Alemanni and Juthungi reached the Po valley; Marcomanni, Vandals, and Sarmatians entered the valley of the Danube, where the Goths were defeated in 271; and it was probably during this reign that Dacia was finally abandoned for good. However, two lasting military successes must be credited to this ruler. He became the *restitutor Orientis* (restorer of the East) after vanquishing Zenobia, and without combat obtained the surrender of Tetricus, the last emperor of the Gauls. He thus fully deserved the triumph celebrated in Rome in 274.

This tremendous war activity did not prevent his attending to works of construction and reform. Indeed, it was Aurelian who had Rome encircled by a new defensive wall, long sections of which may still be admired. And in the provinces, he tried to restore the economic situation by the creation of mints and the circulation of a new Antoninianus.

But Aurelian is best remembered as a man of solar theology. His desire was to rebuild the moral unity of the Empire around the sun god, and in 274 he put forward to his contemporaries a quasi-monotheism, or henotheism, something still alien to collective attitudes, though the forms of the cult remained close to traditional paganism (rites, the institution of priests of the Sun).

For contemporaries, it seems, the main feature that marked the brief reign of his successor, Tacitus (275–6), was a supposed late flowering of senatorial authority. Under his rule, or the one that followed, the *iuridici* of Italy created by Marcus Aurelius were replaced by *correctores* (a form of controller who ensured that everything was "correct" or in order). What is certain is that this emperor was faced with difficult problems, the first of which was Florian's usurpation. Even more serious, in 275 the Goths fell on Asia and the Franks on Gaul.

It was thus a burdensome legacy that came down to Probus (276–82). This vigorous officer drove the Franks and Alemanni out of Gaul, the Burgundii and Vandals out of Raetia, and lastly the Goths and Getae out of the Danubian provinces. He went to Asia, and then to Egypt to fight the Blemmyes. Under his rule an episode occurred that was of little importance in itself but is suggestive of the state in which the Empire and its navy found themselves: Franks who had been deported to the shores of the Black Sea seized some vessels, sailed across the Mediterranean, looting on the way, passed the Straits of Gibraltar, and returned home by way of the Atlantic. To these misfortunes must be added the usurpation by Proculus and Bonosus in Gaul.

The energetic Probus had another good general as his successor, Carus (282–3), who was partnered in his government by his two sons, Carinus (283–5), who set off to repulse the Sarmatians, and Numerian (283–4), who went with his father to do battle with the Persians. Carus had just taken Ctesiphon from them when he died. Numerian was withdrawing westwards when he was assassinated. Carinus in his turn was killed in Moesia, after being defeated by Diocletian. At that point another chapter opened in Rome's history.

*   *   *

The Germani and Persians had severely damaged the organization of 235. Imperial power had needed to be strengthened, the army to acquire greater mobility. The economic system had been disrupted, as had social structures and collective attitudes.

There were still many problems to be resolved, and a whole new development had to be taken into account. It was up to the conqueror of Carinus to take charge of setting up a new order.

15 / A DIFFERENT ORDER, AD 284–361

*T*HE DISORDER AND DESTRUCTION OF THE THIRD CENTURY INVOLVED THE
 SETTING UP OF A FRESH ORDER, AND ALLOWED THE BUILDING, OR
REBUILDING, OF A DIFFERENT WORLD. USING AND SYSTEMATIZING THE WORK OF
THEIR PREDECESSORS, DIOCLETIAN AND THEN CONSTANTINE REORGANIZED THE
STATE, THE ECONOMY, AND SOCIETY. A NEW EQUILIBRIUM WAS ACHIEVED IN THE
MID-FOURTH CENTURY UNDER CONSTANTIUS II. IN THE SAME PERIOD, THERE
BLOSSOMED A MATERIAL AND SPIRITUAL CIVILIZATION THAT WE RECOGNIZE
NOWADAYS AS BOTH ORIGINAL AND BRILLIANT.

DIOCLETIAN AND THE TETRARCHY (284–305)

Born around 245 in Illyria into a humble family, Diocletian pursued a military
career that eventually placed him at the head of Numerian's *protectores*. After
the assassination of this emperor in 284, he was merely the last in a long line
of usurpers, but he was clever enough to profit from the void created by the
third-century destruction, and also from the public-safety measures taken by
his predecessors, the "Illyrian" emperors, of whom he was also the last. Using
ingenuity and empiricism, he reaped the benefit of a long period (20 years) in
power. His policies, apparently contradictory, made him a reformer, even a
creator (civil institutions, the army), on the one hand, and on the other a reactionary, in the precise sense of the term (in the religious field he wanted to
return to an earlier situation). He was none the less the savior of unity.

A NEW POLITICAL REGIME

The better to solve military problems he established the Tetrarchy (also known
as the "First Tetrarchy"). With no preconceived plan, he proceeded gradually
and as circumstances demanded.

On November 20, 284 Diocletian, proclaimed *Augustus*, became emperor.
In the spring of 285, he got rid of Carinus, then appointed Maximian first as
Caesar and then (April 1, 286) as *Augustus*, his associate but nevertheless sub-
ordinate. In 293, Galerius and Constantius Chlorus both became *Caesares*.

Hierarchy of the Tetrarchy

East

DIOCLETIAN
Augustus, Jupiterian (Nicomedia, Antioch)

West

MAXIMIAN
Augustus, Herculean
(Milan, Aquileia)

GALERIUS
Caesar (Sirmium)

CONSTANTIUS CHLORUS
Caesar (Trier)

Plate 15.1 Palace of Diocletian, emperor AD 284–305, at Salonae, near Split, Bosnia.

Each of these four received a town of residence, respectively Nicomedia, Milan, Sirmium, and Trier. However, they remained in close contact and were bound together in various other ways. A religiously based hierarchy was instituted: Diocletian, "Jupiterian," prevailed over Maximian, who was merely "Herculean" (in both cases it was the office that was sacred, not the person). Family links were also forged, either real (fathers- and sons-in-law) or fictitious (by adoption). The absolutism of power was in no way less than it had been in the preceding centuries, but the two *Augusti* committed themselves to abdicating simultaneously after twenty years, in favor of the two *Caesares*, on condition that they then in turn appointed two seconds-in-command. The succession was thus settled, or so it was hoped. Diocletian was consequently the savior of unity, as symbolized by the sculptured group of *The Tetrarchs*, preserved in Venice, and the reliefs on the arch of Thessalonica.

ITS CONSEQUENCES

This political system produced good results in the military field, where there were three imperatives: to cut down the number of usurpations, to pacify provincial uprisings, and to repulse external enemies.

In the West, Maximian overcame the Bagaudes, a name given to Gaulish peasants who, unable to pay their taxes and condemned by the law, had turned to brigandage to escape punishment. Then Constantius Chlorus successfully fought Carausius and his successor, Allectus, who had formed an independent state for themselves in Britain and had even extended it to the Continent. Maximian once again drove the Franks and Alemanni from the field, and then went on to Africa to re-establish order (296–8).

It was Diocletian himself, and then Galerius, who repulsed the Iazyges and the Carpi on the lower Danube. Diocletian had had to go to Egypt, where he vanquished the Blemmyes and quelled the usurpers Achilleus and Domitius Domitianus. When Narses, king of Persia, attacked on the Euphrates (297), Galerius was again called on. He seized Nisibis and Ctesiphon, and defeated the nomadic Saraceni. The Peace of Nisibis (298) acknowledged the Empire's possession of five provinces beyond the Tigris.

The tetrarchic system had made these victories possible; they were facilitated or, at least, accompanied by the reorganization of institutions.

In fact, Diocletian undertook the creation of a new army. He increased the number of soldiers, chiefly in the frontier army, favoring quantity over quality, created smaller legions, and set up a different hierarchy, placing *duces* (divisional generals) over the prefects of legions.

He divided up the provinces (they went up from 47 to 85) following the example of the legions, brought Italy into line with the common regime, and grouped the provinces, together with the divisions of Italy, into 12 dioceses,

Plate 15.2 Gold medallion of Constantius Chlorus, minted at Trier, AD 297, to celebrate his victory over Allectus in AD 296. Constantius and his navy approach the gates of London, welcomed by Britannia.

each under the control of a *vicarius* (deputy). Each province was administered by an equestrian governor, except for Asia and Africa Proconsularis, which kept their proconsular status.

He similarly modified the central administration, where posts were created for *magistri* (heads of department).

He took even greater interest in finance. In 294, he reformed the monetary system, based on gold (the *aureus*), silver (the *argenteus*, which definitively supplanted the Antoninianus), and issues in good-quality bronze. In 301, his edict on maximum prices attempted (less unsuccessfully than has sometimes been thought) to fix an upper limit on prices and wages. Lastly, he set up a new fiscal organization, attested as early as 297 in Egypt, based on payment per head and per plot of land.

The last great persecution of the Christians is also attributed to Diocletian. Its true authors were in fact Maximian and even more Galerius (Constantius Chlorus, on the other hand, proved very moderate). At first, isolated measures targeted the army (the affair of the Theban legion in 285–6, and isolated martyrs, such as the recruit Maximilian, the veteran Typasius, and the centurion Marcellus). In 302, the soldiers were ordered to offer sacrifices. And then in 303 and chiefly in 304, four general decrees were promulgated: confiscation of holy books, destruction of churches; imprisonment of community leaders; freeing of those who recanted; organization of sacrifices throughout the Empire.

The Christians were not, however, the only ones to be targeted. In 297, in connection with the war against Persia, and again in 302, the state had also turned on the Manicheans.

After celebrating their 20 years in power (*vicennalia*) in 303, Diocletian and Maximian, partly pressed by Galerius, abdicated simultaneously on May 1, 305. Diocletian retired to his palace at Salonae.

Diocletian (chronology)	
284	Death of Numerian; Diocletian Augustus
285	Defeat of Carinus; Maximian Caesar
286	Maximian Augustus
293	Constantius Chlorus and Galerius appointed *Caesares*
294	Monetary reform
296	Reconquest of Britain
297	Persian attack; law against the Manicheans
298	Peace of Nisibis
301	Edict on maximum prices
303	*Vicennalia*
303–4	Principal persecution of the Christians
305	Abdication of Diocletian and Maximian

CONSTANTINE (306–337)

Before re-establishing single government, Constantine, who also benefited from a long term of office, for the most part took up and completed, or extended, Diocletian's reforms. He departed from them radically, however, in the religious field.

The son of Constantius Chlorus and Helena (possibly a former tavern waitress), Constantine was born at Naissus around 280. Like Diocletian, he was both a soldier (war in Egypt in 295–6, then against the Sarmatians) and a pragmatist. There was nothing of the theorist about him, and his powers of conceptualization appear to have been very limited. Despite long sessions of explanation, the bishops who advised him do not seem to have been able to

Plate 15.3 Bronze head from a colossal statue of Constantine, emperor AD 306–37.

make him grasp the difference separating orthodoxy from Arianism. In short, he was a man "with a narrow forehead but a powerful jaw" (J.-P. Callu).

SEIZING POWER

But he had first to obtain that power which had not in fact been destined to be his. In 305, Galerius became *Augustus* in the East and Constantius Chlorus in the West. For their respective *Caesares* they took Maximinus Daia and Severus. But in 306 the death (from natural causes) of Constantius Chlorus decided the army in Britain to proclaim his son Constantine emperor. React-

ing against this, the praetorians in Rome chose Maxentius, the son of Maximian, while Severus was assassinated. The following year, Maximian came out
of retirement to take up office again.

Galerius arranged a conference at Carnuntum (308). That gave rise to the
constitution of the "Second Tetrarchy," which left the East to Galerius and
Maximinus Daia, and entrusted the West to Constantine and a newcomer,
Licinius. Maximian and Maxentius, however, maintained their claims, and
Domitius Alexander declared his own in Africa. Thus there were then seven
emperors. The delinquent offspring of the Tetrarchy, this "Heptarchy" bore a
close resemblance to anarchy.

Death, more often than not by murder, clarified the situation. Maximian was
the first to die, in 310, followed by Domitius Alexander and Galerius. In 312,
the victory known as that of the Milvian Bridge (today's Ponte Molle on the
Tiber), but in fact at Saxa Rubra, enabled Constantine to eliminate Maxentius,
and a victory at Adrianople in 313 gave Licinius success over Daia. However, it
was not until 324 that Constantine was able to rid himself of Licinius (Battle of
Adrianople), thus finally re-establishing single rulership, to his own advantage.

REFORMS

These conflicts did not prevent Constantine from carrying out the reforms
referred to above.

In the military field, he organized a new officer corps (*magistri, comites*, and
duces); and he developed the mobile field army or army of the interior, the
comitatus, to the detriment of the frontier army. These alterations came into
effect before 325.

He also transformed the administration of the Empire. At the center, it had
once again become a monarchy: the Caesars, much subordinate to the Augustus, enjoyed very little power. And the sovereign made use of a larger number
of staff, who were also far more hierarchized: the prefect of the sacred chamber
(sacred = imperial), the quaestor of the palace, *comites*, and *magistri*. Likewise,
at regional level, Constantine introduced innovations. The praetorian prefects
lost their former functions. While retaining their title, they now became responsible for territorial prefectures, which grouped together dioceses that were
themselves collections of provinces.

And everywhere slunk the dreaded spies, the *agentes in rebus*.

RELIGIOUS POLICY

Constantine achieved his renown above all for his religious policy.

The first problem, one which still divides historians, concerns his conversion.
He appears to have been originally a follower of the sun god, and a vision of

Apollo led him to henotheism (almost monotheism). But then, on the eve of the Battle of the Milvian Bridge, a second vision, Christian this time, caused him to make his troops carry a *labarum*, a standard on which were embroidered a *chi* and a *rho*, the first two letters in Greek of the name of Christ, the combination of these two symbols, one superimposed on the other, evoking the rays of the Sun. We do not know precisely when it dawned on Constantine that Christ was not to be regarded as a version of his former favorite god (certainly not before 322). Nor do we know whether he eventually gained a clear understanding of Christian orthodoxy. But he certainly received counsel from Pope Miltiades and Ossius of Cordoba, a wealthy and cultured Christian. It is true that he had himself baptized only on his deathbed, but that was not out of the ordinary for that period (although the fact that it was done by an Arian bishop has caused much ink to flow).

At all events, the conversion was preceded by an attitude of genuine sympathy for Christianity. Galerius had issued a decree of toleration in 311, and Maximinus Daia one of persecution in 312. By the Edict of Milan in 313, Licinius and Constantine established the "peace of the Church": freedom of worship was assured and confiscated possessions restored. Furthermore, the government intervened in two Church conflicts: Donatism was condemned as a schism by the Synod of Arles in 314, and Arianism as a heresy by the Council of Nicaea in 325.

THE FOUNDING OF CONSTANTINOPLE

The emperor also lent his name to the foundation of Constantinople. The decision had been made in 324, and the inauguration took place on May 11, 330. The new town, which covered the former Byzantium, imitated Rome: it lay on seven hills, was divided into fourteen regions, and possessed a forum, a capitol, and a Senate.

Although it was merely the second capital of the Empire, headed at first by a proconsul and not a prefect of the city (its true period of expansion dates from Constantius II), there should be no misconception over the significance of this measure. It was not an act of public benefaction, or an aesthetic choice, but the result of a careful consideration of a profound change in the disposition of affairs: the Empire's center of gravity had shifted eastward in every area, politics, the economy, religion, culture.

Constantine gave early attention to his succession. In 317, he appointed three *Caesares*, Crispus (whom he had executed in 326, on moral grounds, or to limit the risks of anarchy, or for both reasons), Constantine (II) the Younger, and Licinius the Younger, to whom he added Constantius (II) in 324, Constans in

Table 15.1 Constantine and his children

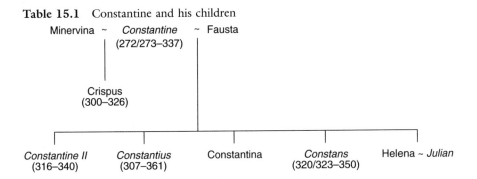

333, and Dalmatius in 335, after celebrating the 30 years of his official reign (*tricennalia*).

His work accomplished, he died on May 22, 337.

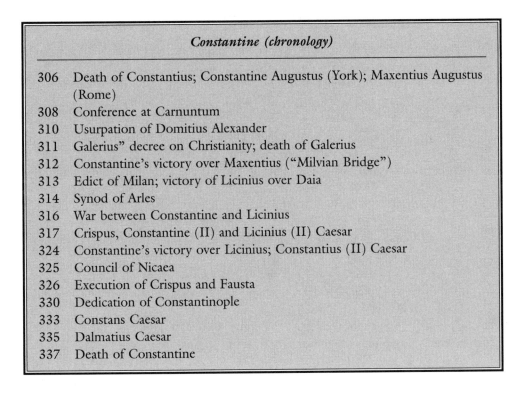

Constantine (chronology)
306 Death of Constantius; Constantine Augustus (York); Maxentius Augustus (Rome)
308 Conference at Carnuntum
310 Usurpation of Domitius Alexander
311 Galerius" decree on Christianity; death of Galerius
312 Constantine's victory over Maxentius ("Milvian Bridge")
313 Edict of Milan; victory of Licinius over Daia
314 Synod of Arles
316 War between Constantine and Licinius
317 Crispus, Constantine (II) and Licinius (II) Caesar
324 Constantine's victory over Licinius; Constantius (II) Caesar
325 Council of Nicaea
326 Execution of Crispus and Fausta
330 Dedication of Constantinople
333 Constans Caesar
335 Dalmatius Caesar
337 Death of Constantine

The sons of Constantine (chronology)	
337	Accession of Constantine II, Constantius II and Constans
338	Siege of Nisibis
340	Death of Constantine II
343	Constantius II in Adiabene
350	Usurpation of Magnentius; death of Constans
351	Battle of Mursa
353	Death of Magnentius
354	Execution of the Caesar Gallus
355	Julian Caesar
357	Battle of Strasbourg; Constantius II's journey to Rome
360	Julian acclaimed *Augustus*
361	Death of Constantius II

CONSTANTINE'S SONS (337–361)

In the middle of the fourth century, the history of the Empire was dominated by three problems: government, Christianization, and the barbarians.

From the political viewpoint, the major undertaking of the era was the re-establishment of a single ruler, in the first place by the elimination of all the legitimate emperors until only one remained. In 337, after three months of intrigue, Dalmatius was assassinated. The Empire was then divided into three: Constantine II, who was in authority over the imperial college, took charge of Gaul, Britain, and Spain; Constans of Africa, Italy, and Illyria; and Constantius II of the East. In 340, Constans reunified the West, to his own advantage, after Constantine II, who had sought to expand at his expense, had been defeated and killed. In 350, he in his turn was defeated and killed, by the usurper Magnentius, who was himself beaten at Mursa in 351 by Constantius II, although not eliminated until 353.

Constantius II is regarded as the first Byzantine emperor. He held a sacred nature from the God of the Christians, and exerted an absolute and tyrannical power that manifested itself in hieratic attitudes and justified every sort of cruelty. He lived surrounded by a court filled with eunuchs (the lord chamberlain Eusebius), which was a hotbed of intrigue. The emperor's council had become a "consistory" (those taking part had to "remain standing" in the presence of the imperial majesty). He gave pride of place to the East, and despite the solemn nature he imparted to his visit to Rome in 357, there must be no illusions on this point. He appointed two *Caesares*: Gallus, a cousin, whom he soon had executed, and another relation, Julian, whom he dispatched to Gaul to restore order there.

Two dangers threatened the Empire at this time.

1 The religious question divided consciences. Whereas Constans had sincerely supported the orthodox party, notably under the influence of Athanasius, Constantius II had ended by supporting Arianism, with equal sincerity. To this risk of conflict between Christians was added the real conflict that set Christians against pagans (edict of 356). We shall return later to these issues (chapter 18).
2 War began again. Persia had attacked in Armenia at the end of Constantine's reign and in 337 Sapor II targeted Roman Mesopotamia. In Gaul, the Caesar Julian fought a series of campaigns against the Germani. The army of the West had suffered heavy losses at Mursa, but this did not prevent Julian from achieving a great victory (Battle of Strasbourg in 357) over the Alemanni, who had been ravaging Gaul since 352.

When Constantius II asked Julian for reinforcements to help him to repulse the Persians, the troops assembled at Lutetia (Paris) staged a *coup d'état*: despite himself, Julian was proclaimed emperor (360). Constantius II died very opportunely (361).

THREE EMPERORS AND THEIR ACHIEVEMENTS

The period from 284 to 361 was dominated by the three personalities of Diocletian, Constantine, and Constantius II. The measures each took contributed to the birth of a different Roman world, with new institutions, a fresh economy and fresh social structures, and a new civilization. In spite of everything, the dangers, mainly from barbarians, had become less pressing.

16 / DIFFERENT
INSTITUTIONS
Reorganization

*I*N THE FOURTH CENTURY MORE THAN EVER, THE ROMAN EMPIRE REMAINED AN
ABSOLUTE MONARCHY. THE FICTION OF THE PRINCIPATE HAD BEEN ABANDONED,
AND THERE WAS NO LONGER ANY HESITATION IN SPEAKING OPENLY OF THE
DOMINATE. THE SOVEREIGN MADE HIMSELF UBIQUITOUS BY MEANS OF A METICULOUS
BUREAUCRACY, AND THE ARMY WAS STILL A FUNDAMENTAL INSTRUMENT OF POWER
IN HIS HANDS. HOWEVER, IN THE FACE OF MOUNTING DIFFICULTIES HE WAS
INCREASINGLY CONSTRAINED TO SHARE HIS GOVERNMENT AND POWER.

CENTRAL GOVERNMENT

THE EMPEROR

Inscriptions and coins bear the range of titles by which the emperor let it be
known what he wanted from his sacred power. As under the early Empire, but
with even fewer limitations, this was exercised in three principal areas.

1 In civil matters the emperor was the law, and he intervened personally.
   Through his edicts, which were applicable throughout the Empire, through
   his orders to governors, and through his responses to the petitions of private
   persons as well as to embassies from the towns, he was the fount of law and
   its determining factor, and was therefore fundamentally responsible for ensuring the maintenance of order and social stability – this point formed one of
   the fundamental elements in Roman collective attitudes. To this end, the sovereign appointed his representatives in the provinces, the governors, and set
   the amount of taxation.
2 As regards the army, which was one of his main supports, if not *the* main
   one, he was its supreme commander, awarding honors and promotions, and
   determining the level of pay. His special charisma assured Rome of victory.
   Like Mithras, the pagan emperors bore the title *invictus* (unconquered),
   while from 324 Constantine, and from 337 his sons, had themselves called
   "victor," abandoning only the polytheistic reference.
3 Religion, another fundamental element in the collective attitudes of the
   times, also came into it, firstly, as has been said, because success in combat

was a gift from the gods and the manifestation of celestial support, but also because, for the pagans, the safeguarding of Rome and the good fortune of the Empire depended on the "peace of the gods." The pagan emperors demanded that the sacred nature of their office be recognized, but imposed nothing concerning their person: people were at liberty to worship them or not, as they pleased. Obviously, the same did not apply to Christian rulers, who considered themselves only God's "vicars" – which, incidentally, diminished their absolutism not one iota. But the "peace of God" followed on quite easily from the "peace of the gods," the smooth progress of affairs bestowed by the celestial protector or protectors.

Given these conditions, it may be seen how a usurper was to be recognized: he acted like a tyrant, abused his power in regard to his subjects; an impious man, he did not respect the gods; consequently, he was doomed to defeat. At least, that is how the victor's propaganda represented him.

This strengthening of absolutism was reflected in the elaboration of an etiquette that had already existed under the early Empire. The sovereign no longer had anything in common with ordinary mortals. He lived in a palace (Milan, Aquileia, Nicomedia, and Antioch notably). When he made his (epiphanic) appearances, he wore the insignia of his office, a diadem and a cloak adorned with precious stones; and, before any audience, he was separated from the public by a curtain. Later, it was required that he be venerated ("the adoration of the purple" had been demanded since 291) and addressed as "lord," *dominus*. A ceremonial character was also conferred upon certain regular actions of his, such as a speech (*adlocutio*) or an entry into a town (*adventus*).

CENTRAL ADMINISTRATION

To take his decisions and transmit his orders, the emperor had at his disposal a central administration that was much larger than in preceding centuries and was becoming "militarized," at least in its vocabulary.

Diocletian had in the end made few innovations in this field. The creation of the Tetrarchy had brought in its wake the creation of four councils, already called "sacred"; the multiplication, if not the emergence, of the notorious spies known as *agentes in rebus* dates back to this period; and *vicarii* (vice-prefects) were appointed to administer the newly created dioceses (groups of provinces). For the rest, Diocletian had retained the praetorian prefects, veritable prime ministers and ministers of war simultaneously, and above all had changed titles: *magister memoriae* and *magistri scriniorum* in the chancellery, *rationalis rei summae* and *magister rei privatae* in finances. These important personages, ministers of a kind, ruled like despots over their departments.

It was Constantine who did most in this field: from his time date the appearance of new high offices, and a new praetorian prefectship, now territorial, which will be discussed later in this chapter.

The imperial household, overall control of which was entrusted to the prefect of the sacred bedchamber (*praepositus sacri cubiculi*), was divided into two, the sacred chamber properly speaking, in the care of the *primicerius* or "chamberlain," and the palace, entrusted to an aide-de-camp (*castrensis*).

The administration, in the precise sense of the word, was divided into offices (*scrinia*), each under the command of a head or master (*magister*), who was himself subordinate to the quaestor of the palace, a person with extensive authority who replaced in this role the old praetorian prefect, and to a *primicerius*, or superintendent, both of whom in addition controlled the "school" (*schola*) of notaries. The principal departments dealt with archives, correspondence, petitions, and official journeys. The proliferation and the power of the bureaucrats were two characteristics of the new government.

Similarly growing in importance, the police were responsible to the commander of the imperial guard, that is, the master of the offices (*magister offi-*

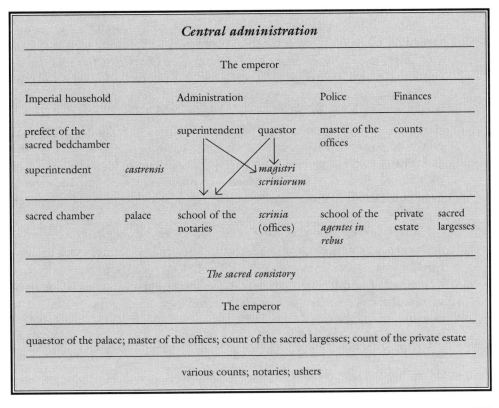

Central administration						
The emperor						
Imperial household		Administration		Police	Finances	
prefect of the sacred bedchamber		superintendent	quaestor	master of the offices	counts	
superintendent	*castrensis*		*magistri scriniorum*			
sacred chamber	palace	school of the notaries	*scrinia* (offices)	school of the *agentes in rebus*	private estate	sacred largesses
The sacred consistory						
The emperor						
quaestor of the palace; master of the offices; count of the sacred largesses; count of the private estate						
various counts; notaries; ushers						

ciorum). They were furnished by the "school" of *agentes in rebus*, at least on the political side – every potential plotter was kept under surveillance.

Lastly, the two main treasuries, the Private Estate and Sacred Largesses, were each entrusted to a "count" (*comes*).

On the fringes of these "ministries," the "emperor's council" (*consilium principis*) was still active. Beside the seated emperor would stand the quaestor of the palace, the master of the offices, and the two counts assigned to finances. Various other counts were also summoned to attend, together with notaries and ushers.

LIMITATIONS

The reinforcement of the imperial power and its administration explains why the sovereign's authority was exercised without encountering many limitations.

Free men, the plebeians, were rarely able to have their say. They could barely make themselves heard, except in Rome and Constantinople, and only then by mutterings and demonstrations, for instance at chariot races at the circus, though these were not altogether negligible.

Of the former Senate nothing remained but its name: the assembly was used only as a municipal council for Rome, or Constantinople. The *cursus honorum* or political ladder still survived, but quaestors, aediles, praetors, and consuls carried on no real activity, contenting themselves with bearing titles that were void of power. Under Constantius II, three such career structures led to the consulship – civil, military, and bureaucratic. Valentinian I, doubtless to better the demarcation of hierarchies, classed senators in three levels, *illustres* (illustrious) at the apex, *spectabiles* (worthy of respect) in the middle, and *clarissimi* (honorable) at the lowest. Nevertheless, though not possessing real political power by virtue of their magistracies, some senators possessed great wealth and senators were occasionally able to wield a certain moral authority (as in the affair of the altar of Victory, which a Christian emperor wanted to remove from the Curia), limiting factors which, again, may not have been entirely negligible.

It was, however, mainly the force of circumstances that set limits on the imperial power. The difficulties linked with the extent of the territory and the barbarian menace often imposed collegiality. And even though heredity became increasingly the rule, the question of the succession still caused difficulties, so that the emperor had sometimes to tread carefully lest discontent led to usurpations.

Another element that enfeebled power was the finances, which were still precariously balanced and were organized on a system that was extremely bureaucratic, and thus not very profitable.

FINANCES

Under the heading of expenditure, the army took first place, followed by the administration, the court, imperial benefaction, and the "ruling populace" who had conquered the world, in other words the plebeians of Rome joined now by those of Constantinople.

As regards revenues, each reign added a new measure, further complicating a structure that from the start had not been exactly simple.

The *annona* still existed. The word indicated both a tax and the department responsible for levying it. Originally this land and personal tax, paid at least partly in kind, was intended to assure free men in the capital of the essential minimum of food. The military *annona*, which could be paid in coin (*adaeratio*), was the part of that payment hived off to the benefit of the army, beginning from the start of the third century. During the fourth century, yet another part was allocated to administrative staff. In the last two cases, it was hoped to compensate for dwindling salaries. The officer in charge, the prefect of the *annona*, eventually yielded his power to the praetorian prefect, assisted by the prefect of the city, the association of shipowners, and a large staff. Under Diocletian, the method of levying such taxes was altered and the system of *iugatio–capitatio* perfected, extending now to Italy. The *iugatio* applied to land. But historians are divided about the *capitatio*: for some it had a strictly personal nature, whereas others consider, perhaps rightly, that it was a land tax calculated on a personal basis (the tax assessor took account of the number of people working on an estate). Depending on the province, only the *iugatio* counted (Syria), or only the *capitatio* (Gaul), or both methods of calculating were used (Asia Minor). Soldiers and veterans benefited from an immunity, but only for part of the *capitatio*. Responsibility for levying these two categories of revenue was at first entrusted to the master of the Private Estate (*magistri rei privatae*), who was subordinate to the *rationalis rei summae*, a sort of finance minister. The property qualification assessment was revised every five years under Diocletian, and then, beginning with Constantine, through a cycle of fifteen years ("indiction").

Another tax on land, the tribute, also persisted, and Theodosius again demanded that it should be paid in coin. In Constantine's time, someone had the idea of making the rich pay up. The senators were asked for the *gleba* ("land"), municipal men of importance for "coronation gold," which with Valentinian became obligatory, and merchants for *chrysargyre* ("gold and silver").

The anonymous author of *De rebus bellicis*, writing in the late fourth century, who is generally considered to have an open and inventive mind, suggested a lowering of taxes by means of a reduction in expenditure and, above all, waste. He does not appear to have been heard.

LAW AND JUSTICE

A high level of sophistication is to be found in the field of law and justice, and here the Roman tradition was truly respected. We know how a legal matter proceeded. Henceforth, only the procedure called "extraordinary" (*extra ordinem iudiciorum*, "outside the order of private judges") was applied, as only the administrative authority took a hand in it. Minor cases were heard by municipal magistrates. Every affair of any importance was within the competence of the governor of the province. And an appeal could be made only before the emperor or his representative, the praetorian prefect. Furthermore, any official in authority had jurisdiction.

The main points of the laws promulgated during the time of Constantine and his successors are to be found in the compilation of the Code of Theodosius made between 429 and 438.

THE ARMY

The third-century crisis, which had brought about profound alterations in the state, had likewise affected the army, all the more so because it had been first and foremost a military crisis.

From an organizational viewpoint, the heritage of Gallienus must not be overlooked: he had developed the cavalry and created a mobile reserve to the rear of the frontier zone. Nor must we forget the role played by the army in public life, and above all in politics, where it had created and destroyed emperors. However, the strengthening of the sovereign's authority, and the parallel decline of that very army, had caused it gradually to lose its power, although it remained the case that the mere presence of a garrison was enough to alter the economic, cultural, and religious life of the surrounding area.

UNDER DIOCLETIAN

Diocletian was the creator of the new army (although we should note that some historians attempt to play down the importance of his reforms, to the advantage of Constantine).

His actions were inspired by what he had deduced from the failures of the third century and the two principles emerging from them: quality had to be replaced by quantity as the overriding consideration in the recruitment of soldiers, and men by stone in the matter of defense. Without going so far as to quadruple the numbers of men, as Lactantius accused him of doing, he certainly considerably increased, and perhaps even doubled, them.

He reorganized the different types of units, to the undeniable advantage of the frontier army. New, smaller legions of no more than 1,000 men came on the scene (some legions however retained their 5,000 combatants), and two legions were posted in each frontier province. Their total number at the time went up from 39 to 60. The *alae* (wings) and *vexillationes* (detachments) of the cavalry assumed greater importance, from the point of view of numbers and prestige, as revealed in their pay (see below). The auxiliary infantry of the cohorts was still in evidence, and agreements were made with neighboring peoples, who supplied temporary troops (*gentiles*).

In contrast, the place of the field army created by Gallienus seems to have been reduced, even to nothing, according to some historians, who think that it was gleaned in times of major wars from the troops assigned to the frontiers. Such a choice, reactionary in the precise sense of the word, would not have been surprising on Diocletian's part. At all events, the campaign army, if it still existed, played a minor role during his reign.

On the other hand, he found it to be necessary to build up the navy once more, not only restoring it but even improving it after the decline it had experienced during the third century. It had a presence in the Mediterranean and on the rivers, and a new squadron was installed at Constantinople. According to an argument recently put forward, its numbers reached over 10 per cent of the entire Roman army, that is, 45,000 men out of 435,000.

Pay, which helped to ensure the prosperity of military regions, also revealed the lines of the new hierarchy: horsemen of the *alae* obtained parity with legionaries (1,800 pieces of silver per annum), and thus remained well above the cohort footsoldiers of the auxiliaries (1,200).

The addition to personnel posed the question of recruitment. The principle of compulsory military service remained in force but, as under the early Empire, volunteers provided the initial source of recruits. When there were not enough of them, it was decided that large landowners, by virtue of the extent of their estates, should supply men or, failing that, money (*aurum tironicum*). Soldiers' sons, "born in the camp," formed a good part of the troops, and when there was a shortage of traditional recruits, barbarian volunteers were accepted. These choices are good evidence that considerations of quality were way behind those of quantity – but it is not at all certain that, in the long term, this policy produced good results.

The state proved hardly more careful (though how could it?) with officer material, at least at the lower levels. Since the middle of the third century, senators had no longer wished to carry out military duties. Commanders of units (prefects of legions, prefects and tribunes of *alae* and cohorts, the commanders of *vexillationes*) came from the equestrian order or rose from the ranks. The *limes*, the Empire's military frontier, was divided into short sectors each entrusted to a *praepositus*, and a province's army might, as an exception, be placed under a general (*dux*). Further up the ladder, the *vicarius* was in charge of the troops in his district, and higher still were the praetorian prefects.

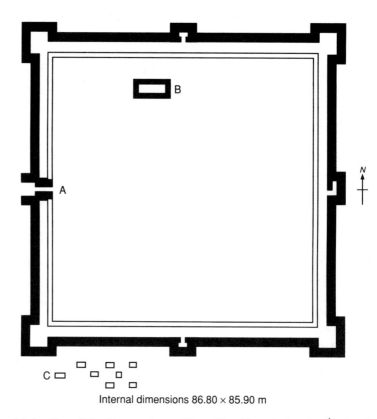

Internal dimensions 86.80 × 85.90 m

Figure 16.1 Plan of the Centenarium of Aqua Viva (from L. Leschi, *Études d'archéologie, d'épigraphie et d'histoire africaine*, Paris, 1957)

At the very summit, the supreme command belonged to the emperors, the Tetrarchs.

To make up for the mediocrity of the men, defense works were stepped up. The Empire had for a long time erected physical barriers, "linear defenses," in places where no natural obstacle thwarted the barbarians (the walls of Hadrian and Antoninus in Britain, the "Devil's Wall" in Germania). Those that already existed were now repaired or brought back into commission, and others were constructed. Moreover, many new fortresses were built, usually of modest size (they were called *centenaria*, a mysterious word), like the one discovered in the south of Algeria at Barika in the locality of Aqua Viva ("Living Spring"). These new camps were provided with rectangular corner towers that protruded externally; and accommodation abutted on the enclosing walls, as did sometimes the *principia* (headquarters). These characteristics define what archaeologists still occasionally refer to as the "Diocletian type," although it is now known that the development of this type of fortress predates the period of the Tetrarchy.

One of the pioneers of aerial photography, R. P. A. Poidebard, discovered in the Syrian desert several dozen of these enclosures which dated from the beginning of the fourth century, a strategic arrangement that had been complemented by a new road, the Strata Diocletiana, which ran from Damascus to Mesopotamia.

UNDER CONSTANTINE

Diocletian's military measures were completed or, on some points, reversed by those of Constantine.

The different types of units were reorganized. First, a new imperial guard had to be created, after the disbanding of the praetorian cohorts and the *equites singulares*, both of whom had sided with Maxentius. Thus, a corps of officers was set up, the *protectores et domestici*, and the five Palatine "schools" (*scholae palatinae*).

Little by little the *comitatus* was formed, perhaps from what Diocletian had left. This field army, or army of the interior, very mobile and intended for rapid intervention, comprised legions and *vexillationes* of horsemen. Special care was taken with its recruitment and training, so that it formed an elite.

By contrast, the frontier army, which was still made up of legions, auxiliaries (*alae*, cohorts, *numeri*), and *vexillationes*, seems to have been neglected. Constantine has been accused of having "barbarized" the *limitanei*; but, as we have seen, this kind of reproach had been commonly leveled against the emperors in the third century.

The new types of units called for a new type of officering. Certain commands were assigned to particular army corps (for example, the *comitatus* infantry), others to a geographical area (for example, Gaul). This cross-checking of authority, which complicated military operations, must also have hampered excessive ambition and thus attempts at *coups d'état*.

On the other hand, civil and military powers were definitively and completely separated. Praetorian prefects and *vicarii* (vice-prefects or deputies) were restricted to purely administrative and judicial functions, and only for part of the Empire. Similarly, provincial governors were released from all concerns of a military nature.

The imperial guard was therefore handed over to the master of the offices (Palatine schools) and the count of the *domestici* (*protectores et domestici*). Two masters of the militia, one for the infantry and the other for the cavalry, were placed at the head of the *comitatus*. Three other masters of the militia shared the Empire (the East, Illyria, and Gaul). The groups of provinces received counts, and the provinces dukes. This last institution, already in evidence under Gallienus and Diocletian, was thus generalized. The institution of the *praepositus limitis*, the officer responsible for a sector of the *limes* of a province, was also generalized. In contrast, the commands of units (prefects, tribunes, and *praepositi*) were left untouched.

All these reforms came about gradually – the first of them undertaken as a result of the *coup d'état* of 306. But in this area everything was completed by 325.

UNDER CONSTANTINE'S SUCCESSORS

Under Constantine's successors, modifications were of a minor nature.

The army corps were still further hierarchized. Within the *comitatus* a distinction was made between the Palatine and the ordinary units; legions (infantry) and *vexillationes* (units of cavalry) could come into either category. The frontier army, which was static, comprised, in descending order, *pseudocomitatenses* legions, *riparenses* legions and units of cavalry, and auxiliaries (*alae*, cohorts, and *numeri*). But it also relied a great deal, probably too much, on the "federates," barbarian peoples loosely bound to the Empire by a treaty.

The navy must not be omitted from this picture; it fulfilled its missions until at least the end of the fourth century.

Lastly, the policy of fortifications was continued. Even under Valentinian, large-scale works were carried out in Germania to strengthen Gaul's security. The establishment of Sponeck at Kaiserstuhl in the Black Forest was part of this system.

In the *Notitia Dignitatum* one may find lists showing that at the beginning of the fifth century all units were still at their posts, at least on paper.

As time passed, recruitment had recourse more and more frequently to the barbarians, chiefly the Franks. They gradually invaded the hierarchy, reaching even the highest ranks.

THE ROLE OF THE ARMY

The historical significance of the army cannot, however, be reduced to its purely military function and activities. As under the early Empire, it played an important role in the life of its times.

From the material point of view, the presence of soldiers still had the same consequences (peace, prosperity), but the nature of army pay had changed. The proportion paid in cash, the *stipendium*, was charged to the central treasury (*aerarium*), which had it distributed through the financial authorities in the provinces (*thesauri*) under the aegis of the count of the Sacred Largesses. Distributions in kind, the military *annona*, were carried out in the name of the praetorian prefect and deducted from the *arca*. In addition, soldiers and veterans benefited from tax exemptions, described on the bronze table found in Pannonia at Brigetio.

The army in the fourth century

Units

Imperial guard	Army of the interior (comitatus)	Frontier army (limitanei, riparenses)
Protectores et domestici Palatine schools (5)	Palatine and ordinary legions; Palatine and ordinary *vexillationes*.	*riparenses* and *pseudo-comitatenses* legions; *vexillationes, alae,* cohorts, *numeri*; peasant auxiliaries; *gentiles*.

NB: (1) Legions numbered either 1,000 or 5,000 men; (2) The navy still existed: ca. 10 per cent of total numbers.

Officers

Diocletian	Constantine and his successors	Extent of authority
Emperor	Emperor	Supreme command
Praetorian prefects	Masters of the militia (*comitatus*), infantry, cavalry	Emperor's direct aides
Praetorian prefects	Master of the offices and count of the *domestici*	Imperial guard
Vicarii	Masters of the militia, the East, Illyria, Gaul	Regional commands
Dukes	Dukes	Provinces
Praepositi limitum	*Praepositi limitum*	Sectors of the *limes*
Prefects, tribunes, *praepositi*	Prefects, tribunes, *praepositi*	Units

In the spiritual field, it appears that the army had developed little and remained one of the bastions of paganism and tradition. Tertullian, it is true, had already said, under Septimius Severus, that Christians were cluttering the camps, but he was no doubt exaggerating. And the martyrdom of the Theban legion, which Maximian is supposed to have annihilated to punish it for its faith, needs to be reduced to more modest proportions: at the very most a cohort was involved in the emperor's condemnation. Soldiers more willingly took sides with the persecutors than with the persecuted. Even so, geographical distinctions must be made: more Christians were to be found in the garrisons of the East than in those of the West.

De Rebus Bellicis

After all the reforms of Gallienus, Diocletian, and Constantine and his successors, the situation of the army in the late fourth century, above all in the West, nevertheless appeared sufficiently grave to move some intellectuals to reflect. Two works, arguing for contrasting solutions, call for our attention.

Vegetius proposed a pure and simple return to the past. He sketched a picture of the Roman army of the early Empire, at least as he believed it to have been, in the hope that this description would lead to a rediscovery of the key to success.

The anonymous author of *De rebus bellicis*, on the other hand, showed himself to be more innovative. To start with, he introduced the military problem into the overall questions of his time, and neglected neither the political nor the social aspect. He went on to suggest unprecedented alterations. For example, raising pay must improve the quality of recruitment and give greater motivation to the fighting troops. New fortifications would allow a saving in human lives. More intensive recourse to war machines would give the Empire superiority over the barbarians.

The Roman army of the fourth century does indeed seem to have lost part of the efficiency possessed by its forerunner in the early Empire. And this development was no doubt due to a certain weakening in recruitment, itself the consequence of the financial difficulties of the state. The author of *De rebus bellicis* had the right idea about these matters.

Territorial Authorities

The state had to ensure order on the frontiers and within the Empire. To this end, and in keeping with the Roman taste for law, it resorted to a complex system of institutions, partly inherited from the early Empire – although the same name often masked a quite different institutional structure.

The organization of land areas into provinces still existed, but Italy itself had lost all its privileges and had been brought into alignment with the administrative model used in other parts of the Roman world. Diocletian had broken up the provinces, raising their number from 47 to 85. We know that Byzacena and Tripolitania, taken from Africa Proconsularis, were created between 294

The dioceses after 381		
Prefectship of the praetorian guard (praetorium)	*Number*	*Names*
The East	4	Thrace, Asia, Pontus–The East, Egypt
Italy	6	Macedonia, Dacia, Pannonia, Africa, Italy, Rome
Gauls	3	Gauls, Spain, Britain

and 305. The first *praeses* (ruler) of Byzacena bore the additional title *perfectissimus*; his successors, between 313 and 322, became *clarissimi*, and were sometimes called "consulars." In contrast, all their known counterparts in Tripolitania remained *perfectissimi*.

The governors received the title of *praesides*. Those in Asia and Africa Proconsularis remained proconsuls, others were called "consulars" or "correctors." Under Constantine they finally and completely lost their military powers. All that remained to them was an important judicial role, which they long performed – their presence is still attested at the beginning of the fifth century, chiefly in Africa.

It was also Diocletian who grouped the provinces into dioceses. Heading each one was a *vicarius*, an important official who was officially or technically a deputy of the praetorian prefect. The number and composition of these dioceses varied as time went on, although the number stayed in the region of 13.

In order fully to understand the overall structure of the dioceses, one must know that the implication of the expression "prefectship of the *praetorium*" changed radically. After 324 the title survived, but it covered a completely different function, with the holders of this office now confined to purely administrative and judicial activities, and their areas of responsibility restricted to groups of dioceses, forming territorial prefectures. There were most often three praetorian prefectships: the East, the Gauls, and Italy; but sometimes a fourth was added, Africa-Illyria. The arrangement of 381 was created in the wake of the invasions of 378–80.

The hierarchy of province–diocese–praetorian prefecture no doubt matches a desire for uniformity, which may be taken for rationalization. But this arrangement also expresses the wish of the imperial power not to entrust extensive authority to anyone other than the emperor himself. Here, too, there was a fear of usurpation.

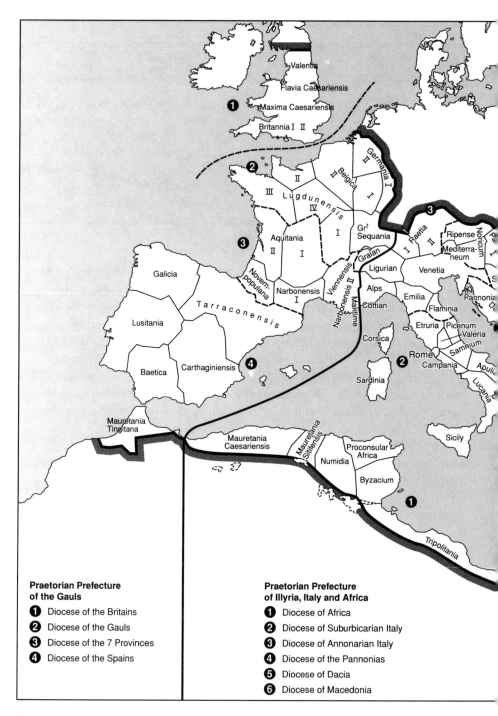

Figure 16.2 The Empire's territorial administration in the fourth century (from R. Rémondon, *La Crise de L'Empire romain*, PUF, 1980)

Legend:
- Boundaries of the provinces
- Boundaries of the dioceses
- Boundaries of the praetorian prefectures
- Frontiers of the Empire
- Line of the "partitio imperii"

5

esia

Dacia Ripensis

Moesia II

Dardania

Dacia Medite-rranea

Thrace

Hemus

Macedonia

Rhodope

Europe

1

Constantinople

Bithynia

Hellespontus

Phrygia I

Scythia

Paphlagonia

Helenopontus

3

Pont Polemoniacum

Armenia Major

ntus

Thessaly

Asia

Lydia I

Phrygia II

Galatia

I

Cappadocia

Armenia I

Armenia II

Arzanene

Mesopotamia

Achaea

Caria

Pisidia

Lycaonia

Cilicia I

Cilicia II

Osrhoene

Euphratensis

Crete

Pamphylia

Lycia

Isauria

2

Cyprus

I

Syria I

Syria II

eses passed
e East in 395
ecture of Illyricum)

Phoenicia

Phoenicia Libani

4

II

Arabia

I

Libya II

Libya I

Egypt

5

P a l e s t i n e

III

Augustamnica

I

Praetorian Prefecture of the East

1 Diocese of the Thraces
2 Diocese of Asia
3 Diocese of Pontus
4 Diocese of the East
5 Diocese of Egypt

Thebais

I

II

0   500 km

CITIES AND MUNICIPAL LIFE

The Empire was still an immense body whose cells were the cities. The study of these cells and their activities, municipal life, forms one of the main centers of interest of current research, the most recent work coming out of which has tended to cast doubt on the exaggeratedly pessimistic traditional picture of deserted *curiae*, impoverished municipal worthies, and the disappearance of autonomy under the weight of bureaucracy.

THE TWO CAPITALS

We shall begin with two special cases. Despite the general trend toward administrative uniformity, the two most important cities, the two capitals, largely preserved their peculiar administrative status.

In Rome, the Senate, as we have seen, found itself reduced to the role of a municipal council, and the "treasury of Saturn," which still existed in the fourth century, was no longer anything more than the city's funds.

The people of Rome had played no real administrative part for a long time; the plebeians still wanted only "bread and circuses," and their expressions of dissatisfaction were confined to demonstrations at such venues as the circus.

The real administration was in the hands of a range of high officials, the prefects of the city, of the *annona*, and of the *vigiles* (night police and firemen), as well as such other officials as the curators of the aqueducts and public works. But among these it was the prefect of the city who came to play the leading role. Still very rich, and often from the old aristocracy, he accumulated powers. At the end of the third century, he administered the city of Rome and the port of Ostia, and exercised his jurisdiction to a distance of the hundredth milestone around Rome. Constantine made him the city's grand master. Already chief of police and president of the Senate, he also became, after 331, the superior of the curators and other prefects. But he possessed no legislative power and was himself kept under the eye of the prefect of the *praetorium*, an official appointed and dismissed by the emperor.

Constantinople, conceived by its founder as an imitation of Rome, was thus also endowed with a staff of high officials and a Senate, though this conferred less prestige on its members than the Roman one. But it was only the second capital of the Empire and because of that, to begin with, it received no prefect of the city, but rather a proconsul. As for its plebeians, they had been put on an equal footing with those of Rome.

ITALIAN AND PROVINCIAL CITIES

The civic arrangements of the rest of the Empire, that is, Italy and the provinces, had been drawn up on a common model. However, this standardization did not prevent a difference in status. There were three separate cases:

1 Non-urbanized peoples, tribes, lived within the *limes*. Subject to their own laws and ruled by their chiefs, *principes* or *reguli*, they were nevertheless under the firm control of the governor.
2 Settlements that were not deemed worthy of complete autonomy, known as *vici*, *pagi*, or *castella*, were dependent on their nearest large center for a number of their needs, especially for the exercise of justice.
3 The true cities, all similar, came into a single category, that of the *civitas*, although some, from vanity, retained their former title of colony or *municipium*. They had autonomy and the complete range of civic institutions.

It was precisely these institutions, broadly still those of the early Empire, but modified by developments, as is to be expected, that gave evidence of an astonishing vitality.

■ The assembly of the citizens, the *populus*, still existed. It is attested in Africa until the end of the fourth century.
■ The municipal council (*curia*), the *ordo* of the *curiales* (the new name for the decurions), played a more important role. In order to be admitted to it, one had to have a property qualification, although the principle of heredity was also involved. The members of this assembly had become responsible for the collection of taxes and for that reason were generally detested. This obligation weighed heavily enough on some for them, at least during difficult periods, to take refuge in the desert, or in the clergy, all the more so since membership of the assembly was not confined to the rich.
■ A variety of municipal posts existed, one greater even than under the early Empire. The head of the magistrates, the curator of the city, had become the real mayor of the town, the *duumvir* serving only as his aide. The aedile and the quaestor no longer did anything much, except, as regards the second, in the financial field. The state also instituted the posts of "defender of the city" and, from 368, "defender of the *plebs*," magistrates who had the duty of affording protection against oppressive provincial government. But the best protection lay in the backing of a good patron, especially against the abuses of tax collectors (*exactores*). Naturally, the most popular choices were priests – *flamines*, pontiffs, and augurs, and sometimes Christian clergy.

An inscription found at Orcistus in Phrygia (Anatolia) provides a good illustration of the importance of these institutions. The township, formerly a city,

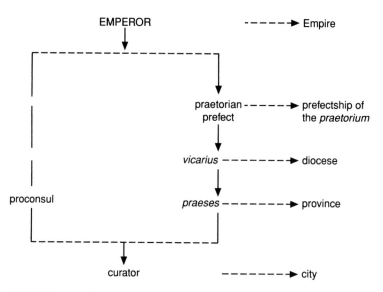

Figure 16.3 Territorial government

had been reduced to the rank of *vicus* and placed under the authority of its neighbor, Nacolia. It addressed a petition to Constantine, who re-established it in its former position of *civitas*. It could thus regain the bodies it had lost, *ordo, populus*, and magistracies.

Municipal life displayed a vitality that can be measured, thanks to epigraphy, by following the development of public benefaction (see chapter 17).

An examination of municipal life, as it was lived in these latter years, shows that the fourth-century towns could enjoy prosperity and that Romanization was doing better than has often been believed. However, geographical, chronological, and social distinctions need to be made.

An Absolute Monarchy

The Empire of the fourth century, like the early Empire, was ruled by an absolute monarchy. But power now made itself more present, pressing, and oppressive. The number of employees in the service of the state, although it did not reach the figures of the twentieth century, certainly increased. Bureaucracy became more meticulous and officious. And military men and state officials occupied a growing place in society.

17 / A DIFFERENT SOCIO-ECONOMIC WORLD
Recovery and State Control

Perceptible in the last quarter of the third century, economic recovery was confirmed in the period of Diocletian. Signs of a fresh crisis, however, made their appearance after Julian's reign (361–3). The particular situation created by this expansion (the boundaries in time and space of which we must mark), but also the legacy of the disorders of the third century, and the demands of the state, both civil and military, together explain the characteristics peculiar to fourth-century society.

THE ECONOMIC RECOVERY

The character of economic life in the fourth century has more to do with the conditions in which it developed than with production itself.

CONDITIONS

Because of the gaps in documentation, it is difficult to give precise answers to the question of the "conjuncture" or combination of circumstances that provided the general conditions of economic life. Nevertheless, one may trace a few of the main outlines, thanks to two special measuring instruments, public benefaction and coinage.

Acts of public benefaction varied in inverse proportion to taxation, usurpations, and invasions, so forming a good indicator of the prosperity of different periods and different regions.

In chronological terms, the case of Africa as shown by public benefactions is well known. Recovery showed itself as early as 276, and was very clear under Diocletian. Civil war then caused a slowing down, which was followed by a new boom under Constantius II, and this reached its peak under Julian. Prosperity was then maintained until the time of Theodosius, but the late fourth century witnessed a return of crisis, which was plainly marked under Honorius.

As for geographical variation, the study of public benefactions allows us first to pick out the most threatened regions. Gaul, Britain, and the provinces bordering the Rhine and Danube were particularly affected by the barbarian invasions. Egypt, except in Alexandria, had never developed a very active municipal life. Italy and Spain kept themselves going fairly well. In Anatolia, and also in the Syria of Libanius at Antioch, men still took a passionate interest in the affairs of their town. Africa too offers a good example of a healthy municipal condition. Three hundred and thirty-two construction sites have been counted there for the fourth century; and, in Proconsularis and Numidia, even the mountain areas were Romanized. On the other hand, these African projects were generally works of restoration, and the Mauretanias and Tripolitania did not keep up with the general trend.

As to the coinage, four dates mark important moments for the historian: 274, 294, 301, and 311. These punctuate the setting up of a new monetary order.

Under Aurelian, the failure of the Antoninianus had become obvious. Gold and silver (real currency) had disappeared and bronze (fiduciary currency), being over-plentiful, had lost all credibility. Aurelian, taking note of the new state of affairs and acknowledging the force of circumstances, deprived the Senate and the cities, with the exception of Alexandria, of the right to issue coinage, and had his own coins struck, mainly in provincial workshops, and with greater regularity. Gold reappeared, the Antoninianus was improved, and confidence in bronze was restored.

The first really major reform of the coinage took place under Diocletian in 294. A new system was set up, with new weights and new denominations. (The official maintenance of the bimetallic coinage in this system should not hide the fact that, because of the greater dynamism of the East in commercial affairs, gold, which the East favored, assumed an increasing role in trade.)

The institution of this system provoked a serious financial crisis marked by a general rise in the cost of living. The state made efforts to react. In 300, it had an inquiry held throughout the Empire to establish the value of goods and labor. Then the edict on maximum prices (301), which we know from inscrip-

Diocletian's monetary system (294)			
Metal	Name	Weight (in grams)	Remarks
Gold	*Aureus*	5.45	1/60 pound
Silver	*Argenteus*	3.41	1/96 pound
Bronze	*Follis*	>9	
	Neo-Antoninianus	2.90	1 neo-Antoninianus (real currency) = 2 denarii (account value)

tions, fixed a maximum for all prices and wages. The text of this edict, in Greek and Latin, was to be displayed in every province, and anyone contravening the regulations contained in it was liable to the death penalty. Whatever commentators may have written, this measure enjoyed some success: the rich were content because it contributed to stabilizing prices, the poor because it readjusted the lowest wages.

The development that followed confirmed the trend that had begun toward the primacy of gold in trade, which was achieved around 309 and then embodied in official practice by Constantine, who decided in 311 to create the gold *solidus*, a coin of 4.55 g (1/72 pound) destined for a long future.

The monetary system of late antiquity stabilized. A sector of natural economy survived in the *annona*, and the monetary economy, which predominated, remained everywhere officially subject to the rule of the bimetallic system, even though it remained the case that the most used precious metals were silver in the West (outside of trade) and gold in the East.

Other conditions accompanied the fourth-century economic recovery. Unsurprisingly, there were few technological innovations. The only advance that deserves notice here is the spread of the water mill.

This advance was perhaps connected with a decline in population in those regions. Early authors frequently bewailed the depopulation that caused shortages of labor. Unfortunately, in the absence of population statistics, it is difficult to know what weight to attach to this stock literary theme.

We have a better knowledge of the system of "colleges" or corporations, a social structure that formed a setting for economic life. A legacy from the early Empire, it underwent two major modifications in the fourth century, due in the main to Constantine: constraint and compulsory inheritance. These decisions are explained by the importance of certain associations, especially that of the shipowners, for the provisioning of the two capitals. However, numerous workers, even in the towns, eluded this structure; and even in the case of the trade corporations, it is essential to make a distinction between the political intentions, as revealed in the laws, and what really happened.

ACTIVITIES

As a whole, these conditions seem to have been less favorable to economic activity than those of the early Empire.

Agriculture   Wheat still formed perhaps 90 per cent of food consumption, and certainly still employed 90 per cent of the agricultural workforce. Vineyards and olive groves had however made progress. Vineyards were still spreading everywhere, but especially northward, while olive groves, which were far more delicate and susceptible to climatic conditions, were developing mainly in Africa,

Plate 17.1   Mosaic of a Roman country estate in Tunisia, 4th century AD. Bardo Museum, Tunis.

which produced large surpluses for export, as discoveries of stamped amphorae bear witness. In the north, however, people went on drinking beer and cooking with butter. And livestock raising saw no new developments, apart from the propagation of the dromedary in Africa.

The change which had the greatest effect on agricultural life was the continuing concentration in the ownership of the land (for example, to the benefit of the Anicii family). Historians and sociologists (M. Weber as early as 1896) have long been analysing this process. But some of the effects had been noted by the early authors, who lamented the fact that rural areas were becoming deserts and that some apparently productive lands had been abandoned.

There was still great diversity in the way the land was worked. Livestock raising was still partly carried on by semi-nomadic populations. For settled peoples, there was at first a great expansion of the colonist system, which after the third-century crisis became the usual form of working the land. The sons of *coloni*, though, in fact, their tenure of the land tended to be held by right of inheritance, were still tenants and remained sharecroppers, with the supervision of the master that this entailed at least enabling them to escape the supervision of the state. Recent research stresses that they were less attached to the soil than had once been believed, and notes a decline in the number of small-holdings. The "Albertini tablets," wooden tablets that derive their name from their discoverer, show the persistence of this type of farmworking in Africa until the Vandal period.

Though often subjected without distinction to the colonist regime, barbarians installed in the Empire were differentiated on the legal plane. (1) The *dediticii,* those who had been conquered, had to pay capitation and perform military service; they lived on imperial or private estates. (2) The "federates," those who had obtained a treaty (*foedus*) with Rome, had received the right of ownership (*commercium*). (3) The *laeti* or "fortunate" (the Franks came into this category) provided recruits in exchange for land; they therefore occupied a position midway between the *dediticii* and federates. (4) The *gentiles* (notably Sarmatians) enjoyed the same status as the *laeti*.

These newcomers brought an advantage, for they supplied a reinforcement to the workforce, but they also posed a problem, for they no longer became assimilated.

Craftsmanship The work of extracting precious and non- precious metals, stone and marble, etc., resumed its normal operation after the reunification of the Empire and the restoration of state authority.

Manufacturing activities, by contrast, had undergone considerable changes. Pottery production, in particular, had been dispersed, with local, more mediocre products having everywhere replaced the fine stamped pottery of the early Empire, and with the large Gaulish workshops having been swept away in the upheavals of the third century (with the exception of new centers of production in the Argonne). More generally, there were still private corporations of craftsmen. But they were increasingly subject to the requirements of the state, and independent businesses now coexisted with imperial workshops.

Trade State intervention in trade also became more insistent than before. A number of dealers were compelled to join corporations (*collegia*), where it was easier to keep an eye on them. Besides the *mercatores* (wholesale dealers, or merchants), who had to pay the *chrysargyre*, these included the mariners, water-carriers, and shipowners who ensured Rome's food supplies, working with the department of the *annona*.

The return of peace favored trade. The barter system was still in use, although the monetary sector had never completely disappeared. Road and sea routes resumed the same traffic as under the early Empire. But although the West experienced a certain recovery, it was the East that showed the greatest dynamism (Byzantium): all roads no longer necessarily led to Rome.

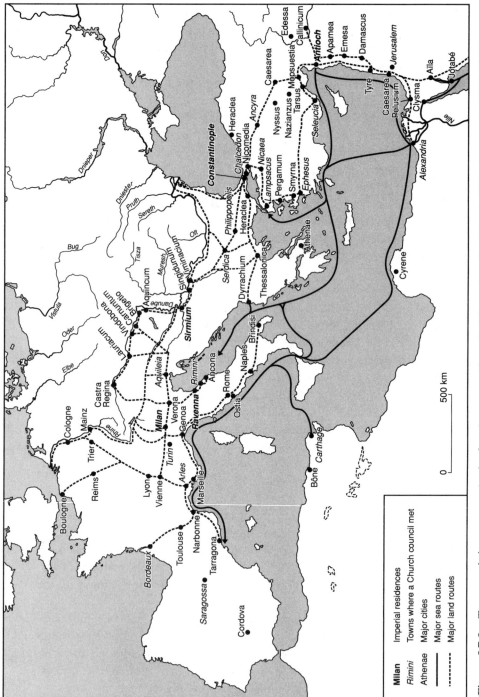

Figure 17.1 Towns and the economy in the fourth century (from R. Rémondon, *La Crise de L'Empire romain*, PUF, 1980)

Legend:

Milan Imperial residences
Rimini Towns where a Church council met
Athenae Major cities
Major sea routes
Major land routes

0 500 km

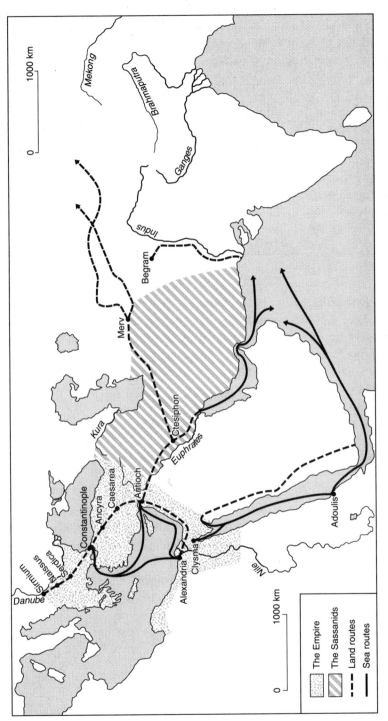

Figure 17.2 Communication routes in the late fifth century (from R. Rémondon, *La Crise de L'Empire romain*, PUF, 1980)

On land, some new routes were developed. In northern Italy, Milan and Aquileia now played a leading role, and not only strategically. And a great northern road ran along the Rhine and Danube. Each region had its backbone: Tarragona–Cadiz in Spain, Carthage–Tebessa in Africa, Arles–Lyon–Boulogne or Trier in Gaul, the old Via Egnatia from Dyrrachium to Thessalonica in Macedonia, Nicomedia–Mopsuestia and Ephesus–Tarsus in Asia Minor, the coastal road and Strata Diocletiana (Damascus–Mesopotamia) in Syria, and lastly the valley of the Nile in Egypt.

Goods carried by sea used a more centralized network: Ostia was linked to Tarragona, Carthage, Cyrene, Alexandria, Antioch, and Ephesus. But the Red Sea, the Black Sea, and the Adriatic, by their comparative dynamism, threatened to alter the traditional balance.

Society and the State

Main features

Society in the fourth century was more a society of orders than it had ever been. By means of ever-increasing legislation, the emperor defined the various hierarchies and the places within them with ever-increasing precision. From the juridical point of view, there was a fundamental contrast between the elite of *honestiores* and the mass of *humiliores*, who did not have the right to equal treatment in the courts; for the same crime, the first were less severely punished than the second.

It was also undeniably a class society. The concentration of landed properties already mentioned brought about a concentration of riches. An increasingly restricted minority grabbed a growing portion of the available possessions.

But the most striking feature was to be found elsewhere: for the government, by its actions, seemed to be intent on forming a society of castes. The compulsory inheritance of occupation or place imposed by certain laws, for example, tended in this direction. Nevertheless, social mobility still existed, for many were not affected by such legislation, and it was also sometimes possible to evade it, even though an all-too-present bureaucracy, or rather the spying of the notaries and *agentes in rebus*, made this increasingly difficult. In the face of the constraints imposed by this bureaucracy, and also the tax system, notables sometimes had no alternative but to enter the clergy or flee to the desert. Individual peasants, among others, might gain protection through patronage, entrusting themselves and their possessions to the governor, to high officials, or even to military officers, whose tenant farmers they became. The state attempted to limit this practice, even to ban it, but often in vain. For most strata of society, however, the thing that counted was hierarchy.

Social elites

Two features define the social elites: their role in the service of the state and their wealth, which, as has been said, continued to grow.

At the apex was the emperor, together with his family, an extremely tiny minority, who possessed honors but, even more, power and immense fortunes.

Running these a close second were "the rich," a group that was hardly less limited. Landed property owners in the main, they were able to extend their influence, not only over several cities but even over several provinces, gathering vast clienteles. Probus, for example, a member of the Anicii family, who held a praetorian prefectship almost uninterruptedly from 367 to 384, owned estates everywhere, enabling him to offset the disadvantages of climatic hazard, for it was always fine *somewhere* on his properties, so that he was assured of obtaining at least one good harvest each year. Symmachus, who belonged to the more recent nobility, similarly possessed vast wealth.

The poet Ausonius was somewhat lower on the scale of riches. The owner of eight estates distributed across Aquitaine, he was, according to Robert Étienne, a provincial notable, and represents the more dynamic section of the municipal councils of the provinces, men who maintained great geographical mobility and could sometimes still penetrate to the heart of the Roman aristocracy.

The wealth sometimes survived well into the fifth century. The *Life* of Melania the Younger and the notes Palladius devoted to her acquaint us with the elites living in Spain at the time: immensely rich, they owned vast estates and revealed themselves as still very attached to classical culture. The hagiographers tell us that this saint plundered her inheritance to give to the poor. In the same period in Gaul, Sidonius Apollinaris of Lyon distinguished himself by the same characteristics of wealth and learning. In addition, he strove to serve both the Church (becoming bishop of Clermont in 472) and the state.

Together with the possession of wealth, it was this service to the state in an official capacity which set one up to become a senator. Of course, birth still counted: theoretically, a *nobilis* had to be the son of a noble, although some newcomers had managed to work their way into the circle. Connections through family, revealed by biographical and career studies, still bound the senators together. Birth, wealth, and power – if they had these they might be tempted into the political game, as in their interventions in the usurpations of Maximus and Eugenius, and their opposition to the emperor in the affair of the altar of Victory (see ch. 19). Consequently, their relations with the current emperor were subject to variation – poor with Diocletian, the "hammer of the aristocracy," but far better with Constantine.

Here we must make a distinction between the two capitals of the Empire. The Roman Senate, the membership of which Constantine raised from 600 to about 2,000, made up of a minority of true Romans and a majority of Italians and provincials, still enjoyed great prestige, particularly the elite of this body – a prestige to which certain customs contributed, such as the holding of games on appointment to the rank of praetor, and the consuls' giving carved ivory tablets (diptychs) to a few privileged friends as New Year presents.

The senators of Rome commanded respect by their attachment to classical culture, which was still based on values such as *otium* (the refusal to do exacting paid work) and paganism (though Christianity slowly spread among the senatorial families).

An internal hierarchy was expressed in titles. Every senator had himself addressed as *clarissimus* ("most illustrious"). Constantine created the non-hereditary dignity of *patricius* (patrician) for the outstanding among them. And then, in the mid-fourth century, in the time of Valentinian I, senators were divided into three grades, *clarissimi* on the lowest rung, *spectabiles* at intermediate level, and at the summit *illustres*, who were few in number, spread then among only nine families. The instituting of this classification was no doubt connected with the fact that recruitment at that time had developed, with bureaucrats from Ravenna and German military men having come to join traditional Roman aristocrats. The title *clarissimus*, moreover, swiftly suffered devaluation, being conferred even on the elite of municipal notables.

Belonging to the Senate of Constantinople bestowed less prestige. For one thing, the institution was of recent date, something which mattered a great deal to the collective attitudes of the time. For another, entry to this assembly was comparatively easy. Certainly, the law demanded the exercise of an office; but it was necessary to allow co-optation. As a result, under Constantine and Constantius II, men who had emerged from the people, stenographers, fullers' sons, and so on, were to be found there. And again under Constantius, it was

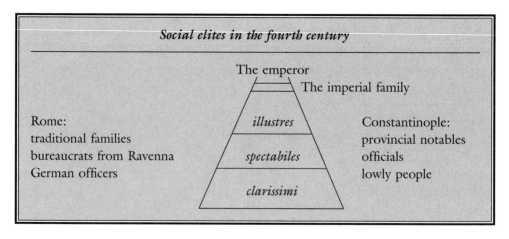

Social elites in the fourth century

The emperor

The imperial family

Rome:
traditional families
bureaucrats from Ravenna
German officers

illustres

spectabiles

clarissimi

Constantinople:
provincial notables
officials
lowly people

possible to become a senator and citizen of Constantinople at the same time. Themistius attempted to raise the standard of recruitment, calling on intellectuals and provincial notables as members, as the correspondence of Libanius shows.

Belonging to the Senate conferred greater prestige than did membership of the equestrian order. The knights had nevertheless assumed a large share in public life. In the course of the third century, and during the crisis, they had monopolized military duties; and at the beginning of the fourth century, when the bureaucracy started to develop on a large scale, they grabbed the posts of heads of department. As a result, under Diocletian, the smooth functioning of the state rested to a great extent with them.

Paradoxically, it was between 312 and 326 that the equestrian order vanished. Early in the fourth century, many knights attained the rank of senator; and then, in 326, the main equestrian title, *vir egregius* ("distinguished man"), was abolished. There were then a good many equestrian *clarissimi*, and although the equestrian title *perfectissimus* survived, it was reserved for the holders of a few rare offices.

Historians have pondered over the causes of the disappearance of the equestrian order, and some have deemed it inexplicable. In fact, it would seem that it died of its own success and from the desertion of the state by the senatorial elites. The role played by knights, from Valerian to Diocletian, forced the state to recognize their merits; and the awarding of a prestigious title, without necessarily adding the material advantages linked with it, enabled the government to escape cheaply. This is a well-known governmental practice.

THE MIDDLE CLASSES

Here, the historian comes up against a difficulty of method, for the very notion of the "middle" classes raises a problem in the absence of statistics (the opposite situation, it is true, would cause other kinds of difficulty). Amount of wealth and participation in local government are taken into account, but the choices that are made are always to some extent arbitrary.

Among the easily identifiable groups are the *curiales* (members of a city council or *curia*), the new name for the former decurions. From the economic point of view, they are defined as landowners whose estates rarely went beyond a city's boundaries. Because of that, they had a certain heterogeneity – some lived fairly comfortably, others on the edge of poverty. All one needed to become a *curialis* was to own 25 *jugera* (6.25 ha), and the term in the end became a simple synonym for *possessor* (hereditary owner). Their situation deteriorated because, to the consequences of the third-century crisis and obligatory benefaction, were added the burdens laid on them by the tax system. In each city, a commission of ten members from among the decurions (*decemprimi* in

---

The ordo salutationis *(provincial hierarchy)*

Governor

Senators
Governor's cabinet
Former priests of the imperial cult
(Christian priests, excluded under Julian)
Personnel of the provincial administration
Simple *curiales*

---

the West, *dekaprotoi* in the East) had been charged at the end of the second century with the collection of taxes due from their municipality. Members of the assembly ended up being responsible for these payments out of their own pocket, so that they found themselves trapped between the government and their own citizens, who regarded them as "petty tyrants" (Salvian). The honor became a burden, as revealed by a play on words: *honos-onus*, "honor (is) burdensome." Some chose to flee, others entered the Senate or the clergy. Their plight varied greatly according to imperial policy: if Constantine persecuted them, Julian made efforts to lighten their burden.

To counterbalance those duties, prestige and honor accompanied the title of *curialis*, as is shown in the letters of Libanius, who lived in Antioch. The most comfortably-off, called *principales*, could enter the senatorial order, or could at least receive the title *clarissimus*. A famous inscription found at Timgad in Numidia indicates into which order those who had come to greet the governor had been admitted. This *ordo salutationis*, dating from the time of Julian, reveals the hierarchy that had been established in the province and in the municipal council.

Entry to the *curia* was prepared for by enrolling in a body of young people, the *iuvenes*. Here sons of notables, whether *honestiores* or *humiliores*, received paramilitary training, especially in the amphitheater – an inscription from Saldae (Bejaia) tells us that they were capable of manning the walls in the absence of regular troops and of repelling an enemy attack. They also celebrated pagan cults, and particularly honored Mars and Jupiter, thus transforming into sacrifices the executions of condemned men that took place in the arena.

Besides the landed property owners, other groups belonging to the middle classes sometimes saw their members gain entry to the *curiae*. In the lead were the more modest officials who had some learning and were close to the government, which gave them some prestige. It is known that their numbers were increasing. To these should be added members of the liberal professions, lawyers, doctors, teachers, men esteemed for their culture but usually fairly poor, although the state financed a few professorial chairs.

The position of the Christian clergy depended to a great extent on the attitude of the emperor. Emperors favorable to the new religion granted them exemption from duties (*munera*), and privileges such as the right to use the official postal service, the *cursus publicus*. The Christian clergy was a heterogeneous body, including among its members not only sincere believers, but also "escaped" *curiales*. Municipal priests enjoyed greater dignity than monks, at least in the eyes of their contemporaries.

The last group to be examined here are the soldiers. They served as government auxiliaries, which justified giving them a regular wage and exemption from certain charges. Their importance had grown with their numbers, but the entry of barbarians into the camps proportionately diminished the prestige traditionally attached to their profession. With the soldiers, we in fact arrive at the edges of the lowest strata of society.

THE LOWLY

The idea of the "lowly" or "humble" is equally difficult to define, again because of the gaps in documentation. But, while bearing in mind the limitations of this subject, we can say that the term covers all those who lived in poverty or were excluded from power.

Here we must contrast the working classes with the "dangerous classes." The former – unfortunately, the least known of all – made up the greater number, and included shopkeepers, artisans (either settled or itinerant), and peasants, the vast majority of whom had the status of *coloni*. The state embodied in corporations those crafts or trades that were essential to it for the provisioning of the capitals or for armaments. And it was a novelty of the time that barbarians were settling in the Empire but no longer seeking to integrate.

Slavery persisted, but its role in production had dwindled still further. It provided some farmworkers, craftsmen, and tradesmen, as well as domestic servants and prostitutes. The Church, which had never condemned the institution, had eventually resigned itself to its existence, confining itself to recommending masters to practice Christian charity. But harsh treatment increased, as legislation bears witness. Heavy lead collars have been found, kept for slaves who had once tried to flee and had been recaptured, bearing the inscription: "I am a fugitive slave; return me to my master."

The periods of crisis drove many men onto the roads to form the "dangerous classes." Among them one could encounter charlatans, magicians, astrologers, vagabonds, and brigands. The Bagaudes, led by Aelius and Amandus, had ravaged Gaul between 284 and 286.

Africa witnessed the development of the *Circumcellio* movement, about which much ink has flowed. The "Circumcellions" were agricultural day laborers, "ones who lurk around the storerooms," especially in the slack seasons. They came to light first in a religious context, supporting the Donatists, which earned them the condemnation of the orthodox (Optatus of Milevis, and later St Augustine). Then, chiefly between 340 and 347, the movement was transformed into a peasant revolt, largely through the impetus provided by Axido and Fasir. Crossing Numidia, the Circumcellions incited slaves to rebel and terrorized masters and creditors, which caused the Donatist bishops themselves to call on the army. In the light of this unexpected turnaround, they again gave a religious coloring to their actions, making a cult of their dead, whom they elevated to martyrdom.

Fourth-century society appears in the end to have been closely bound up with political power, which had a finger in every pie and imposed virtual state control. It also seems to have been fragmented into groups, or cells, rather than carefully arranged in horizontal layers. Another feature of the period was the new balance between town and country.

TOWNS AND VILLAS

On this subject there is a traditional image of the fourth century: the decline of the towns and a retreat to the countryside. Recent research has called that picture into question.

URBAN CENTERS

In fact, generally speaking one notices a continuance of urban life, though obviously accompanied by changes. The third-century crisis had caused much destruction and many material difficulties, and had brought about the creation of new administrative structures. After the return to calm, towns displayed new features.

■ Many towns surrounded themselves with a rampart or defensive wall, although it is now known that these walls were not all built at around the same time, but rather at various times during the second half of the third century and during the course of the fourth. Moreover, not all were built in haste using materials taken from previous buildings.

■ In general, these structures enclosed a more limited surface area than that occupied under the early Empire, either because the town was smaller or because part of it was left outside. In some cases, we may note a revival of the suburbs in the fourth century; in others, it seems that excluded areas were abandoned for good (for example, at Aix-en-Provence, where the dead were buried in a place that had formerly been part of the town).

- The setting up of schools, encouraged and assisted by the municipal authorities, reflected the desire to defend classical culture and tradition. The survival of Roman paganism and the rebirth of native cults expressed the same sentiments.
- The expansion of Christianity brought about the appearance of groups of episcopal buildings (cathedral, baptistery, and bishop's residence).

There were limits to this revival, however. Some areas were never rebuilt, there is no evidence of any new town, and restorations of monuments by far outstripped the building of new ones. Moreover, crisis reared its head again at the end of the fourth century, above all in the West.

The two largest cities were, of course, the capitals. In the middle of the fourth century, Rome still preserved its unchallenged primacy. The emperors continued to strive to beautify it (Diocletian's and Constantine's baths, the grandiose basilica of Maxentius and Constantine), and in the midst of pagan Rome a Christian Rome was born. The first Roman churches, the *tituli*, were in fact private homes used for worship – there were 25 at the beginning of the fourth century. In Constantine's period came the great basilicas, St Peter's and chiefly the Lateran, then later Santa Maria Maggiore. Outside the city, catacombs such as those of Domitilla and St Callistus enabled all the Christian dead, and especially the martyrs, to be honored.

The Empire also possessed other great cities that were at least as dynamic as they had been formerly.

In the East, Alexandria, still cosmopolitan (Greeks, Syrians, Jews) and prosperous (craftsmen, trade), remained a cultural capital. The spread of a Christianity at first heterodox (Gnosticism) and then more traditional (Dionysius, Athanasius) was marked in the landscape by the appearance of catacombs west of the town, and later mainly by churches.

It was in the fourth century that Antioch reached its peak, its population estimated to have been then between 150,000 and 200,000. It owed its rise to the fact that it sometimes played the role of capital, and to its economic activities, notably trade with Mesopotamia and the non-Roman East. Like Alexandria, Libanius' Antioch was characterized by its cosmopolitanism and the presence of a good number of Christians.

The West also had its large centers, at the head of which was Carthage, which archaeologists continue to excavate. Its vitality may be explained chiefly by the dynamism of its port, which provided part of Rome's food supplies. Large dwellings have been found there (the "hunting house," probably the headquarters of an equestrian club, the "house with the *cachette*"), and many large

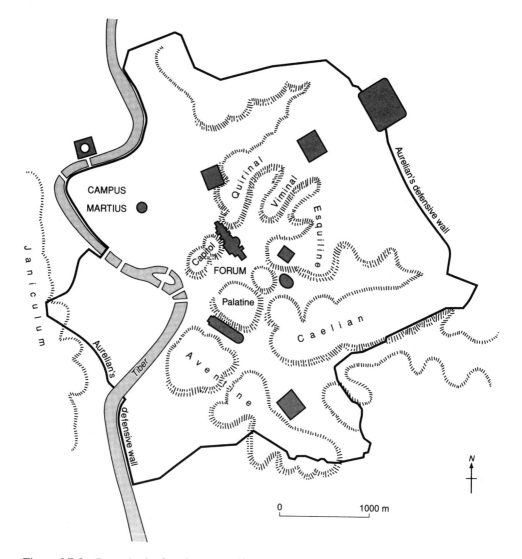

Figure 17.3 Rome in the fourth century (from A. Aymard and J. Auboyer, *Rome et son empire*, PUF, 1980)

and beautiful mosaics (the mysterious "lady of Carthage"). And in the time of St Augustine the town had no fewer than 12 churches.

Europe, in the far north, could pride itself on Trier (Augusta Treverorum), an imperial residence from the time of Constantine, where palaces, basilicas, temples, and then churches were built. A mint and arms-makers (siege weapons and shields) contributed to its prosperity. The praetorian prefectship of the

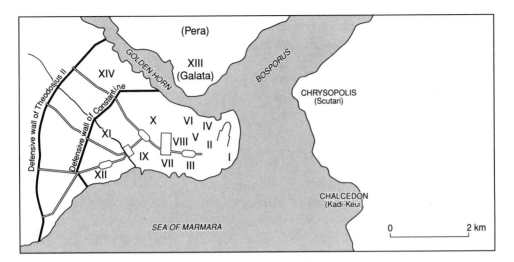

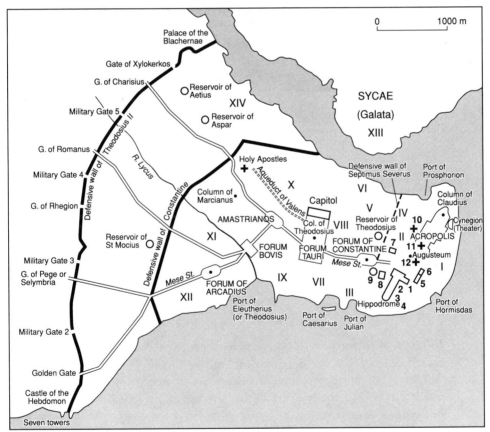

Figure 17.4 Constantinople in the fifth century (from R. Rémondon, *La Crise de L'Empire romain*, PUF, 1980)

Plate 17.2   Roman mosaic from the hunting villa of the emperor Maximian, built AD 293–305. A bullock-cart carries wild animals to the amphitheater. Piazza Armerina, Sicily.

Gauls had its headquarters there, and when in the fifth century that was transferred to Arles difficult times ensued.

Another great western town was Milan (Mediolanum). It owed its expansion to its situation in the center of a prosperous region and the easy communications it offered with the frontier regions on the Rhine and Danube. It too was used as an imperial residence.

RURAL CENTERS

In terms of the growth of economic centers, the most striking feature of the fourth century was the development, mainly in the West, of the rural villa. Although one must certainly not picture a vast exodus from the town to the country, it is none the less certain that this expansion reveals a shift of numerous centers of gravity.

In Africa, archaeology tells us of many fortified farms, or villas with towers, as depicted in the great mosaics of Carthage and Tabarka. In Sicily, there is the vast dwelling decorated with beautiful mosaics at Piazza Armerina, said by some commentators to have been occupied by Maximian until 309 – although there is nothing to prove that it was in fact used as a retreat for the Tetrarch. Then there is the famous villa of Montmaurin in southern Gaul, which covered 4 ha for its central part, including over 200 rooms, and 18 ha overall. And many other examples of this type of residence could be quoted, such as the "small inheritance" of Ausonius or the villa of Nennig – the movement indeed reached as far as the Germanies.

EXPANSION AND LIFESTYLES

The fourth century experienced an economic recovery accompanied by a reorganization of society, both developments marked by much greater state intervention. Although many traditions endured in the ways that life was lived, with the town preserving a great importance, the powerful paid more attention to the countryside than ever before. This material expansion, with its limitations, was not, however, the only upheaval in an era that also had its renaissance.

18 / A DIFFERENT CIVILIZATION
Between Paganism and Christianity

*F*OR SOME DECADES NOW, HISTORIANS STUDYING THE THIRD AND FOURTH
CENTURIES HAVE FOR THE MOST PART BEEN REACHING THE SAME
CONCLUSION: AFTER THE CRISIS OF THE THIRD CENTURY, THE LIMITS OF WHICH MUST
BE CLEARLY DEFINED IN THIS AREA TOO, WE ARE IN THE PRESENCE NOT OF A DECLINE
OF CIVILIZATION, BUT OF A REBIRTH.

THE CHARACTER OF THE TIMES

THE FOURTH-CENTURY RENAISSANCE

First of all, it will be noticed that the military, political, and economic difficulties of the third century did not bring about a general decline in intellectual and artistic activities. Quite the reverse. In certain fields, creative artists improved their production techniques still further. This is especially so in the case of sculpted busts and sarcophagi. Some historians even consider the period to mark a kind of climax in those fields. The fourth century then witnessed a continuance of this flowering of technique, chiefly in mosaics: immense tessellated pavements, characterized by their size, the heaviness of their ornamental foliage, and a growing indifference to perspective, adorn the grand residences. The mosaics produced in North Africa, notably at Carthage and Tabarka, have encouraged a belief in the existence of an African school, to which the decoration of the villa at Piazza Armerina in Sicily, among others, has been attributed (at least five master craftsmen worked there early in the fourth century). We must, however, note the limits of this renaissance, which did not equally affect all sectors of intellectual and artistic production, as we shall see later.

ELEMENTS OF UNITY

Because of the many unifying elements that survived, it is certainly still possible to speak of "Roman" art and literature.

Fundamentally, classical culture remained an ideal to which all subscribed. Homer, Cicero, and Virgil were unreservedly admired. For a very long time

Rome had been the model. And consolation for the real or imagined ills of the present was sought in a quest for the past. One consequence was that the restoration of monuments and reading the works of earlier authors tended to prevail over the creation of new works.

Studies went through four grades: a young man passed through the hands of a *litterator*, or primary school teacher; a *grammaticus*, or secondary school teacher; a rhetor, or teacher of rhetoric; and lastly a specialist teacher (law, philosophy, etc.). Students, like those of Libanius, generally belonged to the privileged social groups. Schools multiplied. For rhetoric, there was a choice between numerous centers, both in the West (Rome, Autun, Bordeaux, Milan, Carthage) and in the East (Athens, Constantinople, Antioch, Alexandria). For law, one still had to go to Rome or Beirut. The state created chairs and granted exemptions.

This spread of education did not prevent the proliferation of the irrational – far from it. Many lives were ruled by astrology, which on the basis of the observation of the regular movements of the heavenly bodies claimed that the lives of men are ruled by those movements. The observation of nature also encouraged a belief in magic, which claimed to be able to compel the gods through the action of spirits. Alchemy sought to transform base metals into gold. And theurgy promised miracles and arranged apparitions. Spell-casting tablets multiplied during the fourth century. At a mystical ceremony a magic text was inscribed on a papyrus, or a tablet of wood or metal, chiefly lead, and then placed in a tomb or shaft. From these we can discover what preoccupied people's thoughts – love, revenge, winning on the horses, and bumper harvests.

The attraction of the irrational spared no one, and spread to the highest levels of state and society. The emperor Constantius II lived permanently in superstitious fear. He banned anyone from casting his horoscope, on pain of death. And Julian, an intellectual if ever there was one, believed in theurgy.

A BREAK IN UNITY

Though all minds shared the same taste for the past and the irrational, some elements of diversity were beginning to spread. Under the early Empire, unifying trends had prevailed: Rome, the emperor, and his family formed universal examples. A change in artistic production has been noted that came about in Constantine's period, which was one of transition. In the middle of the fourth century, there was great variety in works, not only between one region and another, but also between one studio and another.

Moreover, certain facts of life that had their origin in the early Empire became more pressing during the fourth century. Firstly, artists and intellectuals were trapped between independence and servitude. Few had the means to be truly free; most were dependent on patrons. And all had to reckon with the weight of political power, the Church, and dominant attitudes, constraints that were all more stifling than in the preceding centuries. Secondly, a choice had increasingly often to be made between Greek and Latin. The Empire remained officially bilingual, but the inhabitants of the East became less interested in Latin, while fewer and fewer westerners used Greek.

Lastly, there was the conflict that set pagans against Christians, the element of diversity that most marked the spirit of the times, collective attitudes, literature, and art. However, the struggle did not prevent them influencing each other. The pagans, turning away from the cheerfulness of popular Epicureanism, vied in austerity with Christian morality, justifying this attitude now by neo-Platonism rather than Stoicism. Meanwhile, the Christians tried, by "baptizing" it, to save everything that could be saved in pagan art and thought.

PAGANISM ON THE DEFENSIVE

Here one must beware of a facile anachronism: at the beginning of the fourth century all was not lost for paganism, which later even found itself in the role of persecutor once again, and which could rely on an increasingly elaborate philosophy.

THE DIVERSITY OF PAGANISM

The same pantheon was to be found as under the early Empire, with the same rites, though with variations. If indigenous gods and traditional Roman gods (Jupiter) appear to be less venerated, that is perhaps because many of their worshipers lived in rural areas, where the custom of employing inscriptions and sculptures was less strong.

The imperial cult persisted and developed, passing through three phases. At first it preserved all its vigor, all its political and religious implications, and was even reinforced under Diocletian. Next, under Constantine, it was maintained, but its content was not clearly defined, although its celebration could still include gladiatorial combats as well as sacrifices (the rescript of Hispellum, which created and organized this kind of celebration in Umbria at the time of Constantine and his sons, corresponds with this phase). Lastly, in the official Christian era, it was emptied of all sacred content and transformed into a civic and social demonstration. Even before then, in the time of Diocletian, the Council of Elvira had permitted Christians to be pagan priests, allowing them to fulfill the civil, public part of their office, provided they abstained from performing sacrifices. And long after the Christianization of the Empire, *flamines* and *sacerdotales* are attested in Africa, up to the time of Vandal domination, although by then those titles meant nothing more than that one belonged to an elite.

Pagan fervor also affected the eastern cults, which reached their peak early in the fourth century. At that time, they had more followers than ever, but only in urban and military circles, and became even more elitist. That aspect was strengthened by the adherence of intellectuals like the emperor Julian, who imparted a philosophical form to the myths.

The attack on paganism came mainly from a few emperors, and was thus an intensely political phenomenon. Although he did not completely adopt the Christian faith until fairly late, and had never fully understood Christian doctrine, Constantine, in 331, dealt paganism an unobtrusive but much harsher blow than has sometimes been thought. Inspired by piety, or the chance of advantage, or perhaps by both, the law of that year ordering an inventory of temple possessions resulted in confiscations that enabled Constantinople to be built. It destroyed paganism's economic power, a weakening that had considerable consequences.

His son Constantius II was bold enough to attack pagan practices themselves. By a law of 356, he ordered the banning of sacrifices and the closure of certain temples. That decision, however, seems to have applied only to the East.

Under Valentinian I and Valens, there was a period of toleration; the first, despite his faith, did not wish to interfere in religious affairs, and the second was more concerned with heretics and schismatics than with pagans.

The imperial measures against paganism do not appear to have met with all the hoped-for success, since they had to be renewed. They recur in a group of measures taken by Gratian and chiefly by Theodosius, the great enemy of paganism. In 381, sacrifices involving bloodshed were forbidden once again. In 385, the ban was extended to the reading of entrails. This policy encouraged fanatical Syrian monks who in 386 set about destroying pagan sanctuaries, provoking a protest from Libanius (his discourse *On Behalf of the Temples*). The Syrians had their imitators in Egypt and Africa. Finally, in 391, the emperor banned the celebration of pagan cults in Rome and Alexandria, and in 392 throughout the Empire.

Paganism had hardly any true martyrs. Nevertheless, a pagan backlash occurred. Intellectuals displayed their contempt for Christianity as a religion that was deemed foreign, simplistic, and popular, not to mention dangerous to the state. They proclaimed their respect for tradition, and showed their capacity for renewal through philosophy, which developed a "henotheism," that is to say, a conception that was still polytheistic but in which one god dominates the others to such an extent that it verges on monotheism.

	The persecution of paganism
331	Inventory of temple possessions, confiscations.
341	First ban on pagan sacrifices.
356	In the East, ban on sacrifices, closing of temples.
381	Ban on sacrifices.
after 382	Paganism rejected as state religion: the altar of Victory is removed from the Curia.
385	Ban on sacrifices and examination of the victims' entrails.
386	Destruction of temples in Syria, Egypt, and Africa.
391	Ban on private pagan worship in Rome; destruction of the Serapeum in Alexandria.
392	Ban on all forms of pagan cult in the Empire.
399	Destruction of rural pagan temples and the temple of Caelestis in Carthage.
435	Renewed ban on pagan sacrifices.

Here we must establish some geographical distinctions. It is agreed that the West remained more faithful to tradition, especially Gaul and Illyria, but with Africa showing itself more receptive to Christianity.

Similarly, in social terms, some groups showed greater attachment to the past, expressing in this their rejection of Christianity. But these displayed no unity. They included aristocrats from the highest nobility (Symmachus) and intellectuals (Iamblichus, Libanius), but also humble peasants (the word *paganus*, rural dweller or peasant, eventually came to designate the "pagan") – an inscription from Arykanda in Lycia informs us of a petition got up by such folk against the Christians. It was the same with the soldiers, especially in the West – Constantine's army at the "Milvian Bridge" and Julian's in Gaul certainly did not worship Christ. This is doubtless explained by soldiers' attachment to tradition, and the fact that recruitment took place chiefly in rural areas and among barbarians.

Consequently, this pagan resistance was fitful (see also chapter 19). Julian's policy, which re-established paganism in 361 and persecuted Christians from 362, did not outlive him. The affair of the altar of Victory lasted from 382 to 402, the resistance of the Senate in this matter, led by Symmachus, marking paganism's last great battle. The usurpation of Eugenius (393–4) must be placed in this context. He was supported, if not pushed, by pagan aristocrats hoping for the re-establishment of their religion. The Battle of the River Frigidus, in which Eugenius died, marked the end of polytheism's political and military hopes.

Having lost its wealth in 331 and the state (finally) in 394, paganism took refuge in the souls of soldiers and peasants and the hearts of a few intellectuals. It had nevertheless achieved some important work in the fourth century, in both the literary and the artistic field.

THE WORKS OF PAGAN INTELLECTUALS

When we look at the written works, the first distinction that imposes itself is language.

In the main, philosophers resorted to Greek. In Gallienus' court, Plotinus gave birth to the neo-Platonism that pervades his *Enneads*. He influenced the Athenian rhetorician Longinus and had many disciples, chiefly Porphyry and Iamblichus. This doctrine, characterized by an elevated spirituality and austere morality, permeated the entire fourth century.

The emperor Julian was also among the Hellenists. This intolerant writer wrote theoretical treatises (*Against the Galileans, On Helios, the King, On the Mother of the Gods*), speeches (*Panegyrics*) and letters. He will be mentioned again in chapter 19.

He was at least regretted by Libanius. This teacher of rhetoric from Antioch, moderate in all things, left chiefly speeches (65 are known, including *On the Death of Julian*) and letters. Thanks to him we have been able to describe the student world and municipal life of his homeland, but his works contain many other riches.

The output of works in Latin was far larger and may in the main be separated into three genres, oratory, history, and poetry.

Oratory is illustrated by *Twelve Latin Panegyrics*, a collection of eulogies of emperors composed in a fairly pure Latin, for the most part in Gaul, notably by Eumenius of Autun. In the late fourth century, Symmachus, who attained the prefectship of Rome in 384, was renowned not only for his wealth but for his eloquence, which pervaded his speeches and letters.

History inspired Latin writers even more. The *Augustan History* is presented as a series of biographies aiming to extend the work of Suetonius. These are ostensibly composed by six senators living under Diocletian and Constantine. We now know that, in fact, the whole work was written in about 400 by a modest *grammaticus* who was expressing the viewpoint of the moderate pagan aristocracy. Aurelius Victor aspired to continue the work of Livy. Prefect of Rome under Theodosius, he wrote a work on the *Caesars*, which was abridged in an *Epitome*, as was often done at the time. It was the historical works of Tacitus that were used as a model and starting-point by Ammianus Marcellinus, an army officer from Antioch. His *Histories*, extend-ing Tacitus' narra-tive up to 378, show him to have been a moderate pagan.

In poetry, three names attract attention. According to certain authors, Auso-nius was converted to Christianity; but there is no trace of this faith in his little poems (*The Moselle*, *Roses*). Originally from Bordeaux, he had been private tutor to Gratian, who made him governor of Gaul and later of other provinces. Clau-dian, though born in Egypt, wrote biting satires in Latin, in the service of Stili-cho (see chapter 19). Rutilius Namatianus, a Gaul from a great family, returning from Rome to his native country in 417, related his *Return* in a poem in which he eulogizes Rome and its civilization.

Lastly, in Macrobius we have an author who is quite apart. A friend of Sym-machus, he left in the *Saturnalia* a series of dissertations that aim to summa-rize his encyclopedic knowledge.

ART IN PAGAN TRADITION

We must first recall the renaissance that took place in Gallienus' time in spite of the crisis. As we have seen, it was outstanding chiefly for the production of busts and sarcophagi. The sarcophagi fall into two major categories, those fea-turing a philosopher, and Dionysiac sarcophagi, which are characterized by a "lively baroque style of ornamentation" (R. Turcan) for the rich, and by a *pointilliste* style and strigils (or scored lines) for the less well-off.

Artistic development did not cease in the fourth century. Under Diocletian, Rome remained the city of cities (Diocletian's baths). But the provincial palaces (Diocletian's residence at Salonae) and great country villas (Piazza Armerina with its famous mosaics) assumed importance. At the time, there was both a court art (*The Tetrarchs*) and a private art (sarcophagi were now adorned with scenes from everyday life; the Dionysiac carvings, still baroque, showed processions).

Rome maintained its urban pre-eminence in the time of Constantine (arch and baths), but Constantinople gained the rank of second capital, and towns such as Trier, Arles, Autun, Antioch, and Alexandria underwent great development.

The late fourth century produced several major works. African mosaics, already flourishing at the beginning of the century, continued to do well (Carthage, Tabarka). Sculpture is illustrated by the *Colossus of Barletta*, which probably represents the emperor Honorius (395–423). And a new form of art, ivory work, made its appearance with the celebrated consular diptychs, New Year gifts given by consuls to their friends.

However, it would not be fair to reduce fourth-century civilization to its pagan aspect. Christianity, too, contributed much. But it cannot be understood without some account of Judaism.

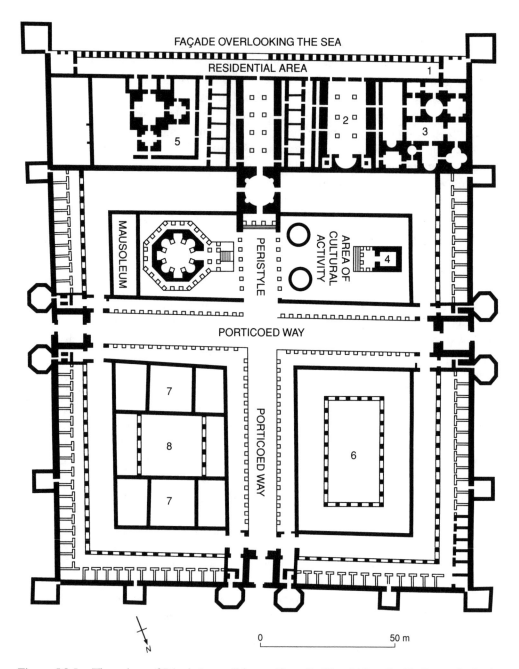

Figure 18.1 The palace of Diocletian at Salonae (from R. Bianchi-Bandinelli, *Rome, la fin de l'art antique*, Gallimard, 1970)

Plate 18.1 Arch of Constantine in the Roman forum, constructed AD 312–15. The emperor makes a state sacrifice of the ox, boar, and ram. The panel was taken from a monument of Marcus Aurelius, with the face of the emperor recut to represent Constantine.

JUDAISM BETWEEN THE EMPIRE AND THE CHURCH

In Roman eyes, belonging to Judaism meant belonging to both a nation and a religion. The defeats of 68–70 and 132–5 had two consequences for Judaism. First, Pharisaism prevailed, combining strictness in the monotheistic faith and rites with toleration in politics (although Rome had been universally detested

Plate 18.2 Ivory leaf of a diptych, ca. AD 450, showing the apotheosis of an emperor, possibly Antoninus Pius.

by its adherents). Secondly, the diaspora grew and spread. It had always been strong in the East in Mesopotamia, and thus among the Persians, and in the Roman sphere at Alexandria and Antioch and in Anatolia and Greece. It now reached the West – although Rome itself had had a large Jewish colony for a long time – with Italy and Africa (Carthage) seeming to have received more Jews than Spain and Gaul. Each community (this is the primary meaning of the word "synagogue") had a hierarchy of dignitaries: the *archon* (leader), clerk, and "father" and "mother" of the synagogue (honorific titles).

From the economic point of view, there is nothing to make us think that the Jews were any different from the other inhabitants of the Empire. They expended their energies in the religious field. It was agreed that the writing down of the Law had been completed. From the second to the fourth century, a commentary was undertaken, and together these went to make up the *Talmud*. This work of commentary was carried out by two schools, one at Tiberias, the other in Mesopotamia, who collected the opinions of the rabbis and rearranged them into several treatises. The first produced the *Talmud of Jerusalem* (in fact, of Tiberias), and the second the *Talmud of Babylon* ("Talmud" thus refers to the *Gemara* as well as to the whole).

The Talmud

Talmud =
1 *Mishna* ("recital" of the Law) + *Gemara* ("commentaries" on the Law)
2 *Halaka* ("rules" of conduct) or prescriptive parts + *Aggada* ("story") or narrative parts
Midrash = collection (of homilies)

The synagogues (the word means both the assembly and the place in which it meets) resembled vast private homes; but there was a room for prayer, with benches, and a throne for the rolls of the Torah. The one at Dura-Europus is from before 256; those at Tiberias and Hammam-Lif in Tunisia seem to be later. The cemeteries were catacombs (Villa Torlonia in Rome) or groups of underground chambers (Palestine, Gamarth near Carthage).

The aesthetic quality of Jewish art, which borrowed much from paganism (mosaics of Hammam-Lif), influenced Christianity. Among its iconographic subjects, only the seven-branched candelabra (*menorah*) remained a purely Jewish symbol (it is found on mosaics and lamps); Old Testament scenes (paintings at Dura-Europus) were also used by Christians.

Relations between the Jews and Christians had always been bad, and did not improve in the fourth century. Before the time of Constantine, the Jews had sometimes been the persecutors; subsequently, they often became the persecuted.

CHRISTIANITY TAKES THE OFFENSIVE

Between Christians, Jews, and pagans, relations were complex, turning now to confrontation, now to appeasement, with the three religions always influencing one another. Everything depended on the balance of power. The "new faith" achieved swifter and greater success in the East. Persecuted under the Tetrarchy, the Church found "peace" under Constantine, and then in its turn changed into an agent of persecution, chiefly under Gratian and Theodosius, as we shall see in chapter 19.

THE DEVELOPMENT OF DOCTRINE

The Christians believed that Christ is God. It had then to be explained how he could be simultaneously also the Son of God and part of a Holy Trinity completed by the Father and the Holy Ghost. Their strict monotheism forbade any compromise with paganism in such matters, as well as any worship of the gods in Rome's traditional pantheon and any acceptance of the imperial cult.

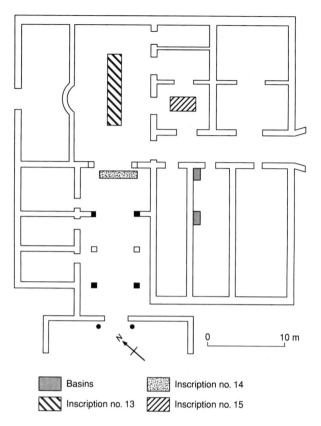

▩	Basins	▦	Inscription no. 14
▧	Inscription no. 13	▨	Inscription no. 15

Figure 18.2 Plan of synagogue at Hammam-Lif

Their fundamental beliefs were set out in two series of books. They preserved the message of the Jewish scriptures in the Old Testament (on condition that it was interpreted according to the teachings of Christ). Christ's teaching, the "Good News" (*evangel*), and some treatises that accompanied it, formed the New Testament. How-ever, the Christians rejected any contribution from Judaism later than the birth of Christ, placing the *Talmud* on the same level as pagan mythology.

The richness of the theory and the dynamism of the religion brought about a deepening of the doctrine, embodied most enduringly in the works of the Fathers of the Church, notably Basil, John Chrysostom, Gregory of Nazianzus, and Augustine (d. 430). The golden age of this movement, to which we shall return later, occurred in the second half of the fourth century. Points of argument could be debated in assemblies that brought together the elite of clerics, in regional synods and councils, or in ecumenical councils, which assembled, in theory, bishops from "the whole world." Such a burgeoning, however, also brought divergences in its wake, leading to schisms and heresies.

A break with the Church over disciplinary matters was called a "schism": a minority would break away to signify its disagreement over a practical measure. African Donatism came into this category. One Caecilian had been ordained bishop of Carthage in 312. Because one of his consecrators had previously "yielded" sacred objects at the time of a persecution and was therefore a "traitor," some members of the African Church considered the ceremony to be worthless, and eventually elected Donatus as a rival bishop. The movement spread. The Donatists denied that sacraments given by "traitors" had any validity. They provoked riots over the possession of churches. And, reinforced by the Circumcellions, they waged a real war of religion (347). However, contrary to what has sometimes been written, their movement never had an ethnic or a social flavor. They had been condemned in 314 at the Synod of Arles; they were then attacked by Optatus of Milevis in around 360–5, and later by St Augustine; and the great episcopal conference of 411 in Carthage ended in the dissolution of their movement.

The fourth century was also marked by heresies, or breaks with the Church over theological matters. The most important was Arianism. Arius, a priest in Alexandria, claimed that only the Father was God, and the Son merely a man. He was condemned by the Council of Nicaea in 325, but his message spread. It reached the West much earlier than has sometimes been said, extending through northern Italy, Illyria, and the Danubian provinces, and secondarily in Gaul and Spain. The doctrine was deepened in the middle of the fourth century, notably by the theologian Maximinus. It reached the Goths as a result of the preaching of Wulfila, beginning in 350, but it was not the Goths who brought Arianism into northern Italy (on their arrival in the fifth century it had long been present there). After numerous debates and conflicts, Arianism was definitively condemned, and ultimately disappeared.

The Arian heresy

1 Strict Arians (homoeans)	Father is God, Son is man, Son subordinate to Father.
2 Extremist Arians (anomoeans)	Father is totally different from Son.
3 Strict Nicaeans (homoousians)	Father and Son: same substance.
4 Moderate Nicaeans (homoiousians)	Father and son alike but not consubstantial.

A different source of heresy left its mark on the fifth century, the Monophysite argument. Egyptian clerics had affirmed "the single composite nature," human and divine, of Christ (Monophysitism). In Antioch, Nestorius took the side of the duality of Christ's nature, saying that Christ possessed both a human *and* a divine nature. Two ecumenical councils were convened. The first, at Ephesus (431), condemned Nestorianism; the second, at Chalcedon (451), rejected Monophysitism.

The ecumenical councils

325	Nicaea	Arianism	Condemned (homoousian success)
360	Constantinople I	Arianism	Accepted (homoean success)
381	Constantinople II	Arianism	Condemned (return to Nicaea)
431	Ephesus	Monophysitism	Adopted (Nestorianism condemned)
451	Chalcedon	Monophysitism	Rejected

CHRISTIAN PRACTICE

Christians followed these arguments with passionate interest. In social terms, the majority belonged to the poorer classes, *tenuiores* and slaves who expected alms from their more fortunate brothers. Notables had, however, joined them. There is evidence of these early in the fourth century, when some Christians wanted to enjoy the prestige attached to the title of *flamen*, and on this point consulted the Council of Elvira, which gave them permission on condition that they refrained from making sacrifices. In the bosom of the Church, the rich formed only a minority, whether clerics like St Cyprian or laymen. They were those who could have the advantage of a "privileged burial," for example having their tomb placed under a mosaic inside a church.

All were united for a certain number of ceremonies that punctuated Christian life. Several sacraments existed at that time. Entry into the community could be marked by baptism, which was, however, commonly deferred until one's deathbed, as in Constantine's case, because it erased sins. But infant baptism was also already in existence. In all instances, baptism involved immersion in a vat of water. The eucharist, a communion meal at which bread and wine were consumed, regularly gathered the faithful together, and penance was performed in public.

Other ceremonies drew the pious to make pilgrimages to *loca sanctorum* or *martyria*, and the councils of the Church made efforts to replace the *concilia* of the imperial cult.

The organization of the Church was hierarchical and, as usual in the Roman world, employed institutions modeled on those of the state. The clergy comprised numerous grades, first and foremost the hierarchy of bishops. The pope, the bishop of Rome, continued to extend his authority, although this was still largely moral, based on his prestige alone. The primates, from 381, controlled several provinces, and the metropolitans a single province. The local bishop carried out his responsibilities in a city, over which he had an almost monarchical power. With his subordinates, he formed a sort of select assembly similar to the *curia*. Ordination was perceived as entry into an *ordo*, and the state reinforced this structure by granting exemptions from duties and awarding civil jurisdiction. A regular *cursus honorum* was set up, as is shown by the inscription of Flavius Latinus in Brescia: starting as an exorcist, he became a priest and finally a bishop. The three upper grades in the hierarchy of the clergy subordinate to the local bishop were priests or elders, deacons placed in the service of the bishop, and subdeacons. The lower grades were divided into four levels: acolytes to assist the subdeacons, exorcists to drive out the devil, lectors to read during ceremonies, and porters to attend to material tasks. The laymen, the faithful, among whom there were some privileged members, including ascetics, confessors, virgins, and widows, corresponded to the *populus*.

On the fringes of the Church's organization in the cities, monasticism began to expand. Founded by St Anthony (d. 356), at first it was most successful in the East. Anthony himself lived as a hermit in the Theban desert of Egypt. Extreme ascetics called the stylites lived on the tops of pillars. Saints Pachomius and Basil, on the other hand, recommended a communal life (cenobitism), an idea which spread in Upper Egypt, east of Alexandria, and in Palestine, in the form of the *laura* or groups of recluses' cells.

The life of the Church had sometimes been troubled by persecutions. These had often had to do with politics: rejection of the imperial cult and traditional gods had placed authority in jeopardy. The legal aspect had always been involved: by stubbornly continuing in their faith, Christians had been disobeying the emperor and the governor. Sometimes, competition between religions had played a part (Cybele, Judaism), as had communal enmity and the provocation of tactless fanatics. But though at first the persecuted, Christians later became the persecutors, of Judaism and, above all, paganism, as we shall see in chapter 19.

Nothing, however, could prevent Christianity from penetrating literary and artistic production.

Plate 18.3 Early Christian baptismal bath in the Basilica, originally a Roman temple, at Sbeitla (Roman Sufetela), Tunisia.

CHRISTIANITY IN LITERATURE AND ART

The new religion imposed itself first in the field of literature, by way of an output that was soon plentiful and often polemical, for it felt obliged to do battle against Judaism, paganism, and heresies.

Writing in Greek, there are four distinct groups of Christian authors.

1 Origen, born in Alexandria, emigrated to Palestine, most probably to Caesarea and Tyre. He wrote erudite treatises on the scriptures, and a work of apologetics *Against Celsus*, criticizing pagan neo-Platonism.
2 The Arian conflict was in part the inspiration for the works of both Eusebius and Athanasius. Eusebius (265–340), bishop of Caesarea in Palestine, has left *Speeches*, religious treatises (*Evangelical Preparation*), and historical works (the *Chronicles* retrace the history of the world, and the *Ecclesiastical History* is concerned with Church government and the persecutions). The commitment of Athanasius (295–373) against the Arians revealed itself more plainly. This bishop of Alexandria was an unbending opponent of the heresy that was born in his own city.

3 The Cappadocians. Born in Caesarea, St Basil (330–79) studied at Athens and Antioch, notably under Libanius, and became a bishop. He fought against Arianism and made efforts to organize monasticism. His friend St Gregory of Nazianzus (329–90) had been a rhetorician before he too became a bishop. He was above all a contemplative, and wrote *Speeches* and *Letters*. St Gregory of Nyssa (340–94) was Basil's brother. In his writings he sought to use Platonic philosophy in the service of Christianity.

4 The school of Antioch was made illustrious mainly by St John Chrysostom (345–407). This son of a master of the militia was possibly a student of Libanius. Bishop and monk, moralist and preacher (his name means "golden mouthed"), he was the author of many works, including speeches, treatises, and letters.

In the case of Latin authors, there are also four distinct groups – although let us first mention St Hilary of Poitiers, who also fought against Arianism.

1 The African school proved especially fruitful. St Cyprian, bishop of Carthage, who was martyred in 258, left letters and treatises. Arnobius, who lived in the time of Diocletian, was a convert, and a rhetorician by profession. He attempted to prove that the ills of the period were not attributable to Christianity, and pointed out the absurd features of pagan mythology. His student Lactantius, who went on to teach in Nicomedia, composed a *History of the Persecutions* and a work *Concerning Divine Institutions*. Undoubtedly, the most important member of this group was St Augustine. Born a pagan at Thagaste, in the province of Africa Proconsularis but in Numidian country, he studied at Carthage, Rome, and Milan, where he became a rhetorician in 383. He was converted, returned to Africa, became the bishop of Hippo in 396, and died in 430. He left a considerable number of works directed against the Jews, pagans, heretics, and schismatics, chiefly the Donatists, the most outstanding of his works being *The City of God* and his *Confessions*.

2 History was not neglected. Orosius, a Spanish priest of passionate temperament, took up Arnobius' arguments in favor of his religion and against polytheism, while Eutropius, under Valens, wrote an *Abridged History* which began with the founding of Rome.

3 Besides those already mentioned, the group of the Fathers of the Church includes two more great names. The illustrious St Ambrose (ca. 330–97), bishop of Milan, dominated both Church councils and emperors (Theodosius). He was the author of *Funeral Orations*, a *Treatise on the Duties of the Clergy*, and a collection of sermons, the *Hexameron*. No less famous was St Jerome, who was born around 340–50 in Dalmatia or Pannonia. After studying in Rome, he withdrew to the Syrian desert and later founded the

monastery of Bethlehem. He left extensive works (lives of saints, letters, and, above all, the Vulgate, the Latin translation of the Bible). He died in 420.

4 Christianity inspired poetry as well, chiefly the barbarian verses of the *Instructions* and *Carmen apologeticum* by Commodian. Prudentius (348–410), a Spanish lawyer, was converted at the age of 57; he "wove the crowns" for the martyrs in his *Peristephanon*. Sidonius Apollinaris, bishop of Clermont-Ferrand in 472, also left poems as well as a collection of letters.

The emergence of Christian art is not seen until after that of Christian literature. This delay can be accounted for in several ways – biblical mistrust of visual art, the caution necessary in a hostile environment, and also poverty. In Rome, the great Christian buildings did not begin to be built until the time of Constantine. But before then the conversion of a few wealthy people brought about a change in the nature of Christian art, as did the needs of worship and catechesis, as well as the unobtrusive influence of paganism. For Christian art had initially been produced first and foremost for ordinary people.

Among the iconographic subjects, the best known, apart from the dove, is the fish, the Greek word for which, *ichthus*, comprises the initial letters of the words of the phrase *(I)esous (Ch)ristos, (Th)eou h(u)ios, (s)oter* (Jesus Christ, son of God, savior). Other subjects were borrowed from Judaism (Isaac and Daniel) and paganism (the Good Shepherd), but received a new meaning (the sacrifice of Isaac prefigures that of Christ).

Christian art became renowned in the same fields as pagan art. Painting was used very early on, in the church and baptistery of Dura-Europus before 256, and in the Roman catacomb of Domitilla. Sculpture produced sarcophagi illustrated with scenes from the Old Testament, sometimes separated by columns, or ornamented with simple strigils. The sarcophagus of Junius Bassus, found in Rome and dated 359, sets biblical and evangelic subjects side by side. Mosaics, chiefly African, enabled figured representations and inscriptions to be brought together. They were used in particular for the tombs of leading clerics and wealthy people who had themselves buried in a church ("privileged interment").

Little by little, all forms of pictorial art were thus represented. There was also the gradual development of a Christian architecture. The church was at first a room in a house, then the house itself, and finally a special building constructed on a basilican plan. With the development of large Christian communities, the episcopal group was born, comprising at least three distinct parts – a cathedral, a round or octagonal baptistery, and the bishop's house. Rome saw the construction of the basilica of the Lateran and its baptistery (around 319), then Santa Maria Maggiore, St Peter's (in the Vatican, after 326), St Paul-without-the-Walls (with some rebuilding under Valentinian II), and Santa Pudenziana

Plate 18.4   Christian mosaic, ca. 4th century AD, from the catacombs of Hermes in Sousse, Tunisia. The dolphin and anchor symbolize Christ on the Cross; the fish represent his faithful followers.

(late fourth century). Constantinople did not follow this example until later, like Alexandria, Trier, Aquileia, and Milan (church of San Nazaro, basilica of the Martyrs). In Palestine, it was St Helena, Constantine's mother, who built the church of the Nativity in Bethlehem and the sanctuary of Golgotha in Jerusalem. The latter, which covers an area of 36 × 140 m, includes a church of basilican plan with five naves and an exedra. Conceived as a place for the worship of Christ the Martyr, it was built against the mount of Calvary. The whole also included a rotunda, corresponding to the Holy Sepulcher, and a baptistery.

Cemeteries were at first on the surface (Vatican), then subterranean chambers or *hypogaea*, and lastly catacombs (in Rome, St Callistus, Domitilla). Their decoration was particularly careful and abundant.

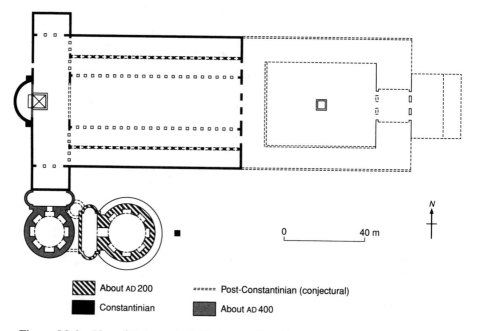

◿◿ About AD 200	====== Post-Constantinian (conjectural)
■ Constantinian	▦ About AD 400

Figure 18.3   Plan of Constantine's Vatican basilica (from R. Bianchi-Bandinelli, *L'arte dell'antichità classica*, Gallimard, 1976)

BOOM AND DECLINE

In the fields of religion, intellectual life, and the arts, the situation was not as has been described for the economy. Pagans, Jews, and Christians were in opposition to one another, but were also mutually enriched. Without doubt, however, it was paganism and, to a lesser degree, Judaism which were the eventual losers, although their decline was by no means total – far from it.

From the point of view of language, one could already distinguish the Latin West and the Greek East. When these actually divided, the break chiefly affected the West, especially after the events of 406 and 410, but these dates have little significance for Christianity, and chiefly concern political and military matters.

19 / THE END OF THE ROMAN WORLD?

*T*HERE IS NO EASY WAY TO FIX A DATE AT WHICH TO CLOSE A HISTORY OF ROME. ONE CAN BUT OBSERVE A COMPLEX PROCESS THAT DIFFERED ACCORDING TO THE SECTORS OF ACTIVITY AND THE REGIONS INVOLVED. HOWEVER, AT LEAST THE SYMBOLIC IMPORTANCE OF CERTAIN EVENTS, AND THE EMERGENCE OF A CRISIS STARTING IN *364*, MUST BE NOTED.

JULIAN (361–363)

The man Christians called "the Apostate" had a tragic destiny, perceived as such even in the sixteenth century. Modern thinkers explain it variously: for psychologists, he was an unbalanced hothead; psychoanalysts emphasize the traumas he suffered in his childhood; historians see him as an exceptional man who had to try to resolve many serious difficulties.

HIS EDUCATION

The grandson of Constantius Chlorus, Julian was born in 331, and for his tutors had Eusebius, bishop of Nicomedia, and the Scythian eunuch Mardonios.

His childhood was spent on the estates of Chalcedon, where he studied Homer, and at Macellum in Cappadocia, where he came under the influence of the Arian bishop George. Constantius II, who distrusted everything and everybody, exiled him to Nicomedia. There he discovered the works of Libanius and, following a vision, was converted to paganism.

This aristocrat was first and foremost an intellectual with a passion for Hellenism, especially neo-Platonism (Plotinus, Porphyry, and Iamblichus). His conversion came in a period of difficulty for Christianity (Catholics against Arians) and during a renaissance of culture in the East.

He left plentiful literary works, which are both profound and yet not without a touch of humor, for example the *Misopogon*, a satire against the inhabitants of Antioch who had made fun of his beard, and the *Caesars*, in which he eulogizes Marcus Aurelius and criticizes Constantine.

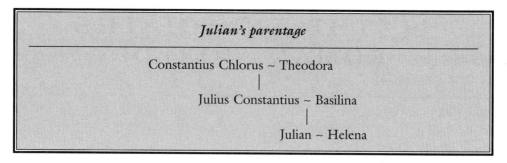

Julian's parentage

Constantius Chlorus ~ Theodora
|
Julius Constantius ~ Basilina
|
Julian ~ Helena

JULIAN CAESAR

In 355, under the pressure of events, Constantius II appointed him *Caesar*. The danger came not only from within, with six usurpers having declared themselves, but above all from without. Sapor II was preparing a new offensive in the East despite the threats that lay over his northern frontier. And in Europe there were as many dangers as there were peoples. There was fear of the Franks on the lower Rhine, the Alemanni in the angle of the Rhine and Danube, the Quadi and Marcomanni facing Pannonia, and the Goths on the lower Danube, not forgetting the Huns (the advance guard of the Turks), who were driving the Scythians before them.

Julian left for Gaul in 357. There he won a great victory over the Alemanni near Strasbourg, and made incursions into Germania. He set up his winter quarters at Lutetia, where he read Caesar and Plutarch, and was there when Constantius II asked him to bring reinforcements to the East. The army refused to leave and proclaimed him emperor. He hesitated, then accepted, and was marching on Sirmium when Constantius fell ill and died.

JULIAN AUGUSTUS

Julian had defined his political philosophy in a eulogy of Constantius II entitled *On Royalty* and published in 358. To the virtues of piety, justice, and clemency, borrowed from Roman tradition, he added that of kindness, an addition dictated by his humanism.

Above all, his religious policy is known. A devotee of theurgy and initiated at Eleusis, a worshiper of the Sun (*Discourse on King Helios*) and Cybele (*Discourse on the Mother of the Gods*), he first restored paganism by decree, and then attacked Christianity (treatise *Against the Galileans*): Christians were banned from teaching, holding public office, and performing funerals in daylight.

A few other reforms, sometimes considered only secondary, were made: he simplified court etiquette, alleviated the tasks of the *curiales* by quashing exemp-

Plate 19.1 Statue of Julian the Apostate. Louvre, Paris.

tions from taxes and reducing coronation gold, and did away with the authorization that had been given to private citizens to use the state postal service, the *cursus publicus*.

Meanwhile, he had to confront the Persian problem inherited from Constantius II. He marched against Sapor II, advanced toward Ctesiphon, but then had to retreat. During this episode he was mortally wounded. Only a legend nurtured by Christians ascribes to him the famous last words: "You have won, Galilean!" Nevertheless, once again an emperor had died confronting the enemy.

Those in command named Jovian as his successor. This Pannonian officer, a moderate Christian, capitulated to Persia: he abandoned the left bank of the Tigris, which had been occupied since 298, and gave up all influence over Armenia. He also annulled Julian's measures against the Christians. He died in 364, the year after becoming emperor.

THE START OF A NEW CRISIS (364–395)

The period that then began was marked by a crisis similar to that of the third century. Its origins, too, lay in wars. But the fresh wave of invasions was, though there were exceptions, more a matter of slow and gradual infiltrations. The barbarians admired Rome, yet showed themselves unable or unwilling to assimilate with it. This situation brought about a division of the Empire; but while the West then foundered in disorder, the East rode out the storm and made ready for the emergence of a new civilization.

The single unifying element came from the dynastic policy that was followed at the time. From 364 until the beginning of the fifth century, the same blood ran through the veins of all the emperors except Theodosius.

For convenience' sake, three periods may be distinguished, each marked by a personality, those of Valentinian I, Theodosius, and Stilicho.

THE PERIOD OF VALENTINIAN I

Valentinian I soon opted for a division: he kept the West, with Milan as its capital, and in 364 entrusted the East to his brother Valens, who installed himself in Constantinople. In 367, his son Gratian was proclaimed a third *Augustus*, and sent to Trier. He was only eight years old, but was betrothed to Constantia, the daughter of Constantius II, which conferred additional legitimacy on the dynasty.

Valentinian I (364–75) acceded to the Empire at the age of 44. This Pannonian officer, a tolerant Catholic, was vigorous and honest, quick-tempered and cultured (he chose Ausonius as tutor to Gratian).

He made efforts to improve the situation of all strata of society. To win over the Senate, he instituted the *defensor senatus*, but a split developed and this brought executions in its wake, which explains the criticisms leveled at him by the aristocratic Ammianus Marcellinus. He also tried to improve the lot of the *curiales* by transferring to the state part of their responsibilities in the areas of taxation and the official postal service. He took an equal interest in the plebeians, increasing free food distributions in Rome, and appointed a *defensor plebis*, a lawyer acting for the city's poor. But he was unable to do anything against the owners of great landed estates or against corruption.

The gravest difficulties came from the barbarians, and Valentinian I's period was marked by several wars. The Scots and Saxons who were ravaging Britain were repulsed in 368–9 by the Spanish officer Theodosius. In 366–74, Valentinian I fought in person in the Gauls against the Alemanni, who finally obtained a treaty after suffering defeat. Africa, too, was troubled by raids, directed at the ports of Tripolitania (364), and by the rebellion of Firmus (372–5), a movement combining indigenous demands, weariness with taxation, and religious confrontation, Donatist in this instance. This situation was brought under control by the same Theodosius, who was beheaded shortly afterwards for an unknown reason.

In the East, responsibility for running affairs had been handed over to Valens (364–78), a fanatical Arian. The crisis there seems, paradoxically, both more complex and less serious than in the West. In 365, there was a usurpation in Constantinople. The claimant, Procopius, was related to Julian, and his movement was simultaneously political and religious. Moreover, social difficulties became apparent in outbreaks of brigandage.

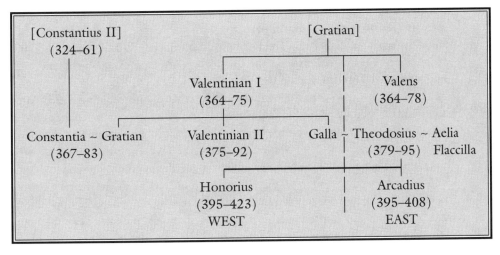

But it was the accompanying military problems that were the main cause for concern. In 372–3, the war against the Persians resumed. In 374–5, the Quadi and Sarmatians were defeated by Valens and Theodosius (the son of Valentinian's Spanish general). And all the while it had been necessary to fight the Goths (who were themselves harassed by the Huns), as attested in 364 and 367–9 (when they ended by negotiating). Finally, in 378, Valens was defeated and killed by the Goths at Adrianople. It was the first great defeat for the Empire since the third century, but the scale of the disaster must not be exaggerated, as Ammianus Marcellinus did. The East was still capable of hitting back.

THE PERIOD OF THEODOSIUS

At this point the Empire was once more divided into three. The young Gratian, based in Trier, found himself compelled to face the Alemanni in that same year, 378. In 375, Valentinian II had succeeded his father, but he was only four years old and was placed under the tutelage of a Frankish general, Arbogast, who took Milan for his capital. From there he kept watch on Illyria and protected Italy. This moderate pagan is said to have been a morally upright man. Meanwhile, the younger Theodosius, a man endowed with a powerful personality, impressed everyone. He had attained the rank of master of cavalry, and was appointed *Augustus* in 379 after the disaster of Adrianople. To legitimize his dynasty, he married one of Valentinian I's daughters, Galla, the future mother of Galla Placidia, then set himself up in Trier. Of Spanish origin, he was a good general and an orthodox Christian, fervent according to some, fanatical in the opinion of others. He had to confront the two great troubles of the Empire's crisis, barbarians and usurpations, to which he added religious conflict.

On the military plane, Theodosius achieved success in three theaters of operations. After a new thrust, the Goths were settled in the Empire in 380, with a treaty (*foedus*) – although this particularly unstable race became restless again in 386. In 387 and (by the Treaty of Constantinople) 390, Theodosius came to an agreement with Persia on the division of Armenia. And, in the end, war and victory restored peace on the Rhine.

Theodosius showed himself much more active in the religious field. After Constantine's conversion, his reign marked the most important change in the relations between the government and the gods; for the state now renounced paganism. As early as 379, Gratian had refused to wear the mantle of *pontifex maximus*. Then, in 382, he had rescinded the privileges granted to pagan priests and had ordered the altar of Victory to be removed from the Curia. A symbolic value was lent to that removal, with the result that senatorial opposition, led by Symmachus, united against it. But the strongest measure against paganism came directly from Theodosius. In 391–2, under the influence of St

Ambrose, he banned private pagan worship, and prohibited the adoration of statues and the performance of pagan rites.

Theodosius had also to solve problems of an internal nature, notably two attempts at usurpation. In 383, a pretender made himself known in Britain. This was Maximus, who soon extended his authority over Gaul, where he eliminated Gratian and proclaimed himself *Augustus*. At that point, Theodosius could do nothing to stop him. In 388, Maximus defeated Valentinian II and ousted him. But Theodosius was now able to take action – he did so and was victorious.

The ban on paganism in 391–2 provoked discontent that crystallized around a new usurper. In 392, Arbogast had Valentinian II strangled, and proclaimed Eugenius emperor. This reaction by traditionalism lasted until just after the Battle of the River Frigidus (394), when Eugenius and Arbogast were defeated.

Theodosius had associated his two sons with his rule: Arcadius had taken charge of the East; Honorius of the West (under the supervision of the Vandal general Stilicho). Theodosius died in 395. By then, Christianity had won, peace reigned, and the Empire was divided.

THE PERIOD OF STILICHO

Stilicho now came to the fore. Flavius Stilicho was born in around 360 to a family of Vandals who were settled in the Empire and had been converted to Christianity, but were Arian in tendency. There has been much argument about this man: he is sometimes presented as a barbarian friend of the Goths' leader, Alaric; others see him as a Roman and the defender of the city. In fact, he behaved like a Romanized barbarian, as is evidenced by his career and his relations with Claudian.

The poet Claudian, originally from Egypt, had remained a pagan, although he had lived in a largely Christian court. He gave up his mother tongue, Greek, for Latin, and for ten years, from 394 to 404, acted as Stilicho's spokesman, a task which inspired part of his abundant polemical and other writings.

Stilicho had a family connection with Theodosius, whose niece Serena he had married. The famous ivory diptych of Monza represents him and his wife with one of their children, Eucher. Appointed in 395 to supervise the education of Honorius, who lived in Milan, he became even closer to the ruling dynasty in 398, when his daughter Maria married the young emperor.

Pedagogy and intrigue, however, were not the main part of the Vandal Stilicho's activities; he was chiefly concerned with war. First there was an internal conflict. In 395, Stilicho had to face the rebellion of the count of Africa, Gildo, who, at the instigation of Eutropius, the favorite of Arcadius, sought to gain independence for the provinces of Africa. Gildo, the brother of Firmus, whom he had betrayed, blocked the provisioning of Rome. He repulsed the troops

Plate 19.2   Thirteenth-century book painting of Attila besieging Aquileia.

sent to fight him in 397, but was in his turn betrayed by another of his brothers, Maczel. He was captured and executed in 398. The role played by Eutropius in this affair shows that relations between Rome and Constantinople were far from friendly. Campaigns fought by Stilicho in Thessaly (395) and the Peloponnese (397) aimed at weakening the influence of Arcadius more than at driving out the Goths who had infiltrated there.

While the imperial forces weakened themselves in internal struggles, the barbarians were preparing to launch fresh attacks. In the East, Eutropius had to repulse the Huns in 398 – though this fearsome race continued to make news. In 401, Alaric's Visigoths were beaten by Stilicho near Aquileia. And in 406 it was the turn of the Ostrogoths under Radagais to experience defeat at his hands (near Florence). But the danger was coming nearer to Rome. The Romans, however, felt reassured by Stilicho's actions. They gave him a triumphal welcome on two occasions, in 403 and 406. Statues were erected to him and inscriptions carved in his honor.

THE END OF ROME?

For historians seeking the end of Rome, the point at which to end a history of Rome, the question, At what moment did it happen? gives rise to two prior questions: What happened? and How did it happen? In short, what, how, and when?

Several answers have been given to the first question, the "what?" of the scholars. There are three substantial arguments.

Many writers have long talked about decadence. Even in antiquity this idea was a literary commonplace, and the Christians reinforced it: the end of Rome was a punishment sent by God. During the Renaissance, moral reasons were again sought; Biondo and Machiavelli added the decline in population; and in the eighteenth century, Montesquieu and Gibbon did not dissent from this general approach. More recent writers blame the failure of institutions to adapt, or a general crumbling of institutions, as according to J. Carcopino, who thought that the Roman Empire died a natural death. Lastly, a book by M. Le Glay returns to the idea of decadence – though in relation to the Republic rather than the Empire.

The "assassination theory" is newer. Finding that the situation in the provinces, as revealed by archaeology, appears in a less somber light than it had previously appeared in, A. Piganiol in 1947 advanced the original proposition that the barbarians killed a perfectly healthy Roman world. H.-I. Marrou, who had spoken of decadence in 1938, retracted in 1949, and sided with the opinion of Piganiol, who was however criticized by Carcopino. This theory postponed any crisis or decline until the early Middle Ages, which is disputed by medievalists.

Finally, several recent researchers, perhaps inspired by a conception of progress as something that cannot be halted by any constraint, have tried to show that there was no decline, still less a decadence, but merely a succession of transformations.

To get a better answer to the first question, the second must be asked: How did it happen? The fourth century was in fact characterized by its complexity: features of the early Empire coexisted with new elements; and the latter may be seen as creative, and thus elements of strength, or as tending to weakness and crisis. The complexity even forces us to make distinctions and to give our attention to three sets of contrasts.

East and West, indeed, cannot be regarded in the same light. While the Byzantine Empire was being born in the East, provincials in the West saw the state growing weaker and the army unable to prevent the barbarians crossing the Rhine in 406 or capturing Rome in 410. The might of the Germani partly explains this decline. The reinforcements they received through further migrations from the east and their improved organization in federations of peoples contributed just as much to their success as did the enfeeblement of Rome by bureaucracy and the economic crisis, the lack of currency and an imbalance between town and country.

The second contrasting pair, town and country, experienced opposing and no longer complementary fortunes. It is widely agreed that there was at least a comparative preservation of the towns, but the unequal distribution of taxes weighed more heavily on rural dwellers than on townspeople, and on the poor more than on the rich (at all events, that is how people saw things). At the same time, a privileged minority were squandering increasing sums as if there were no tomorrow.

Lastly, we must distinguish between two cultures, paganism and Christianity, which were certainly not totally alien to each other but had sometimes clashed bitterly. Pagan tradition survived in cultural circles, to be sure, but only by becoming the subject of study; it no longer created anything, apart from academic works (Martianus Capella). In contrast, Christianity continued to progress, and this expansion was accompanied by new forms of art and thought. Moreover, according to Piganiol, this religion "favored the formation of an internationalist ideology that knew no boundaries."

Of course, all these changes did not come about simultaneously. Hence the third question: When?

In the late fourth century, an economic crisis occurred and was accompanied by a slowing down in public benefaction. East and West were already following their separate destinies. Thereafter, a few major events have captured the attention of historians. These occurred at the beginning and end of the fifth century.

Stilicho's last years were marked by a drama that began on the night of December 31, 406, when the Vandals, Alani, and Suebi crossed the Rhine, which had frozen over. They traversed Gaul, Spain, and Africa (crossing the Straits of Gibraltar in 429). Nothing could stop them.

This invasion led to Constantine's usurpation in Gaul, a fresh offensive by Alaric's Visigoths, more successful this time, and a general reaction: the councilor Olympus, the emperor's sister Galla Placidia, and the army united against Stilicho, who was arrested and beheaded, together with his wife and children, on August 23, 408. Galla Placidia then revealed herself as a major figure at the center of her times.

The death of Stilicho did not prevent Alaric from taking Rome in 410; the city was sacked, and this pillaging also marks an essential date for our consideration. From then on, the Roman West had in actual fact become the barbarian West.

For the main part of the fifth century (from 410 to 471–2), the destinies of the two parts of the Empire diverged.

In the West, the weak Honorius (d. 423) had enabled Constantius to come to the fore (411–21), fleetingly as Constantius III (421). Next it was the turn of Valentinian III (425–55) to be eclipsed, this time by the master of the militia Aetius. Their initial adversaries were the count of Africa, Boniface, and then

Plate 19.3 The Roman Forum, seen from the Capitoline hill.

Attila, king of the Huns, who was defeated in 451 at the Campus Mauriacus. But the central government functioned only in fits and starts: the Visigoths moved from Italy to Aquitaine; the Franks and Burgundians installed themselves in Gaul; Vandals, Alani, and Suebi pursued their ventures. From 457 to 472, it was a Suebian, Ricimer, master of the militia, who imposed his protectorate on the West.

In the East, and even though the situation sometimes had characteristics similar to those described for the West, the general situation, both internal and external, improved under Theodosius II (408–50), chiefly thanks to the many undertakings of Anthemius. It was then that the Code of Theodosius was worked out. The lull on the frontiers even allowed internal conflicts to arise: the murder of the pagan philosopher Hypatia by the Alexandrian mobs in 415; the Monophysite dispute (the Monophysites believed in the "oneness" of Christ's nature, while Nestorius maintained that Jesus possessed both a human and a divine nature); the Council of Ephesus, in 431, which condemned Nestorianism. But then, between 450 and 471, the East experienced the same fate as the West, with one difference: it was a member of the Alani, Aspar, who imposed his protectorate.

The end of the century was marked by two events with a strong symbolic content.

In 475, Orestes, Attila's former secretary, had driven the emperor Nepos out of Rome and given the purple to his own son, Romulus Augustulus. The Scirian Odoacer, who had also frequented Attila's court, became king of the Heruli and asked for federate status. When he was refused, he drove Romulus Augustulus out and sent the imperial insignia back to Constantinople (476). Odoacer became "patrician" and "king of barbarian peoples," carving out a domain for himself in Italy, Sicily, and Dalmatia.

The emperor Zeno, in 488, gave the Ostrogoth Theodoric the task of reconquering the West; after the assassination of Odoacer in 493, Theodoric made himself master of Rome and Italy, and henceforth the Roman West became *in law* the barbarian West.

The fifth century did not mark the end in every field, for there was a legacy.

In the East, a new Roman Empire was built up, linked with Byzantine civilization, and this lasted until 1453. In the West, the idea of empire remained very strong. This is borne out by the creation of the German Holy Roman Empire and the diffusion of the title "Caesar," which lasted in Russia until 1917 (abdication of "Tsar" Nicholas II), until 1918 in Germany (abdication of "Kaiser" Wilhelm II), and as late as 1946 with the Tsars of Bulgaria.

At the end of the twentieth century, several European countries still bear the imprint of Rome, though contemporaries do not always realize it. The people speak a Latin-based language, the principles of their law come from Roman law, their town layouts and rural landscapes are 2,000 years old. Their daily life, their festivals, their forenames bear the stamp of Christianity. Their art, literature, and philosophy since the Renaissance – which was the rebirth of Rome – were often inspired by the works of the Republic and the Empire. Their values (liberty, justice, law, honor, courage) are also 20 centuries old.

In a way, Rome still survives; Rome lives on in them.

CHRONOLOGICAL TABLE

MILITARY EVENTS	POLITICAL AND SOCIAL EVENTS	CULTURAL AND RELIGIOUS EVENTS
BC	BC	BC
	2nd millennium Arrival of the Indo-Europeans in Italy.	
	8th century. The Etruscans in central Italy. Greek colonization in Sicily and south Italy.	
	754/753 Foundation of Rome (according to tradition); the first villages.	
	753–717 The Latin and Sabine kings.	
	650–510/509 The Etruscan kings (Servius Tullius).	
540 Battle of Aleria between Etruscans and Carthaginians.		
	509 Expulsion of the Etruscan kings. Annual magistrates (praetors, then consuls) replace them.	**509** The first Capitoline temple.
497 Battle of Lake Regillus		**496–484** First temple to Saturn, at the foot of the Capitol. Temple of Ceres, Liber, and Libera. Temple of Castor and Pollux in the Forum.
494 Secession of the *plebs*.		
485? Coriolanus' victory over the Volsci.		
474 Cumae, Greek victory (Syracuse) over the Etruscans and Carthaginians.	**471** The first tribunes of the plebeians.	
	451–450 Law of the XII Tables.	

MILITARY EVENTS	POLITICAL AND SOCIAL EVENTS	CULTURAL AND RELIGIOUS EVENTS
405–395 Siege and capture of Veii. ca. 400 The Celts in north Italy. 390 The Gauls sack Rome.	440 *Lex Canuleia*: equality of patricians and plebeians. Creation of the censorship. 421 The first quaestors.	
341 First Samnite War. 340–337 Revolt and end of the Latin League (the Latin War).	367 Death of Dionysius of Syracuse. Licinio-Sextian plebiscite: sharing of the consulship between patricians and plebeians. 348 Agreement between Rome and Carthage.	367 Camillus' temple of Concordia at the foot of the Capitol. 362 The first *ludi scaenici*. 348 The first Secular Games.
327–304 Second Samnite War.	338 Antium (Anzio), Roman colony. 335 Foundation of Ostia. 328 Rome in control of Latium, Etruria, and Campania. 312 Via Appia, Rome–Capua. 312–308 Censorship of Appius Claudius. Ovinian plebiscite. 306 Roman–Carthaginian treaty.	
298–291 War on Tarentum and Pyrrhus. 272 Capture of Tarentum. 264 Capture of Volsinii. 264–241 First Punic War.	300 *Lex Ogulnia*: the pontificate open to plebeians. 270–265 Rome in control in Italy except Cisalpine Gaul.	275 Theocritus at Syracuse. 272 The Romans in contact with Greek civilization. 264 First gladiatorial fights in Rome.

256–255 Regulus' expedition in Africa.

242 Victory in the Aegates Islands.

240–237 Rebellion of the mercenaries against Carthage.
238 Carthage yields Corsica and Sardinia to Rome.
237 Hannibal founds the Barcid kingdom in Spain.

230 Illyrian pirates raid in the Adriatic.

225 Roman intervention in Illyria. Gaulish offensive in north Italy.
221 Hannibal in Spain.

219–202 Second Punic War.

218 Roman defeat at the Trebia.
217 Trasimene.
216 Cannae.
215–205 First Macedonian War against Philip.
213 Hannibal takes Tarentum.
211 Recapture of Capua.
210 Scipio in Spain, recaptures Cartagena.

244 Brindisi a Roman colony (Brundisium).
242 The first non-Roman (*peregrinus*) praetor.
241 Reform of the *comitia*.

227 Sicily, first Roman province. Creation of the provinces of Corsica and Sardinia.

219/218 *Lex Claudia* on trade.

217 Fabius Cunctator dictator.

215 First companies of *publicani* (tax-gatherers).

ca. 254 Birth of Plautus at Sarsina (Umbria).

241 Via Aurelia (Rome–Pisa).
240 The first tragedy in Latin (Livius Andronicus of Tarentum).
239 Birth of Ennius near Tarentum.

235 First play by Naevius.
234 *On Agriculture* by Cato the Elder.

220 Via Flaminia (Rome–Ariminum). Building of the Circus Flaminius in Rome.
219 First Greek surgeon in Rome.

217 First Plebeian Games.

212 *The Menaechmi* by Plautus.

MILITARY EVENTS	POLITICAL AND SOCIAL EVENTS	CULTURAL AND RELIGIOUS EVENTS
207 Victory of the Metaurus.		
205 Peace with Philip V of Macedon.		
204 Scipio in Africa.		204 *Miles gloriosus* by Plautus.
202 Victory of Zama.		201 Birth of Polybius.
200–196 Second Macedonian War.		
198 Flamininus in Greece.		
197 Victory of Cynoscephalae.	197 Spain a Roman province (two praetors).	
	196 Flamininus proclaims Greece's freedom.	
	195 Consulship of Cato.	193 Construction of the Emporium (port) at Rome.
192–188 War against Antiochus III of Syria. Victory of Thermopylae.		190 Birth of Terence.
189 Victory of Magnesia.		189 Tragedy by Ennius.
188 Treaty of Apamea.	187 Trial of Scipio.	186 Last comedies of Plautus.
	186 Affair of the Bacchanalia.	185 Basilica Porcia on the Forum.
	184–182 Censorship of Cato the Elder.	181 Temple of the Erycine Venus on the Capitol. Birth of the philosopher Panaetius.
	183 Death of Scipio and Hannibal.	180 Birth of Lucilius at Suessa Aurunca.
	180 *Lex Villia Annalis* on the *cursus honorum*.	179 Basilica Aemilia in the Forum.
		173 Epicurean philosophers driven from Rome.

172–168 Third Macedonian War.	166 Delos a free port.	170 Basilica Sempronia in the Forum.
168 Victory of Pydna over Perseus.		167 Polybius at Rome as a hostage.
		166 Terence's *Andria*.
		160 Terence's *Adelphi*.
154–152 Campaign by Marcellus against the Celtiberi.		155 Embassy of the Athenians Carneades, Diogenes, and Critolaus.
150 Massinissa's war against Carthage.	149 Death of Cato. Creation of the *quaestiones perpetuae*	150 Cato's *De agricultura*.
149–146 Third Punic War.	146 Roman provinces of Macedonia and Africa.	
147–139 War with Viriathus in Spain.		146 Secular Games.
146 Capture of Carthage.		146 First use of Greek marble for Roman temples.
146 Rome's war against the Achaean League. Capture of Corinth.		145 Panaetius in Rome.
		144 Aqua Marcia.
	140 *Lex Aebutia* on formulary procedure.	142 Pons Aemilius.
137–133 Scipio Aemilianus against Numantia.	134 Tribunate of Tiberius Gracchus.	
135–132 Slave War in Sicily.	133 Agrarian reforms (*lex Sempronia*). Legacy of the kingdom of Pergamum to Rome.	131 *Satires* by Lucilius.
	124 Tribunate of Gaius Gracchus.	
125 Legions in Transalpine Gaul.	122 Foundation of Aquae Sextiae (Aix-en-Provence).	
	120/119 Creation of the province of Gallia Narbonensis	

MILITARY EVENTS	POLITICAL AND SOCIAL EVENTS	CULTURAL AND RELIGIOUS EVENTS
	119/118 Foundation of Narbo Martius (Narbonne).	116 Birth of Varro.
	119 Tribunate of Marius.	
	113 Creation of the province of Asia.	
113 Invasion of Noricum by the Cimbri and Teutones.		
112 Massacre of the Italians in Cirta.		109 Pons Milvius.
107 Military reforms of Marius.	107 Marius' first consulship.	
106 Marius against Jugurtha.	106 Birth of Pompey.	106 Birth of Cicero at Arpinum.
105 Roman defeat at Orange.		
103–102 Second slave war in Sicily and Campania.		
102–101 Victories of Marius at Aquae Sextiae and Vercellae.	100 Disorders in Rome (Saturninus). Expedition against the Cilician pirates; creation of the province of Cilicia.	101? Birth of Caesar.
	89 *Lex Plautia Papiria*: citizenship rights to Italians who desire them.	98? Birth of Lucretius.
91–88 Social War.	88 Sulla's consulship; end of the Social War.	
89 Massacre of Italians by Mithridates.	87 Marius' seventh consulship.	87 Birth of Sallust. Birth of Catullus at Verona.
85 Sulla negotiates with Mithridates.	82 Sulla's measures against the reforms of the Gracchi.	
82 Sulla returns to Rome. Anti-Marian proscriptions.		
80 Rising by Sertorius in Spain. Third war against Mithridates.		

73–71 War with Spartacus; Pompey victorious.

67 Pompey against the pirates.

63 Pompey defeats Mithridates.
61 Germani (Helvetii) in Gaul.

58–50 Gallic war.

54 The disaster at Carrhae.
53 Rebellion of Vercingetorix.

49 Caesar crosses the Rubicon.

48 Pharsalus; Pompey defeated; assassinated in Egypt.
47 Caesar victorious at Zela.
46 Caesar defeats the supporters of Pompey at Thapsus.
45 Caesar's victory at Munda.

42 Philippi, defeat and death of Brutus and Cassius.

37–36 War against Sextus Pompeius.

74–67 Creation of the provinces of Crete and Cyrenaica.
74–62 Provinces of Bithynia and Pontus.

63 Creation of the province of Syria.
60 First Triumvirate.
59 Consulship of Caesar.
56 Lucca agreements.

52 Assassination of Clodius. Trial and exile of Milo. Pompey sole consul.
51 Celtic Gaul becomes a Roman province.

49 Marseille becomes a Roman town.

46 Caesar dictator for ten years. Foundation of Arles.

44 Caesar dictator for life. Ides of March, assassination of Caesar.
43 Second Triumvirate. Foundation of Lyon.

40 Peace of Brindisi.

70 Birth of Virgil near Mantua. Cicero's *Verrines*.
65 Birth of Horace. Poems by Catullus.
63 Cicero's *In Catilinam*.

59 Birth of Livy.

55 Pompey's theater, the first stone-built theater in Rome.
54 Basilica Julia in the Forum. Birth of Tibullus.
52 Cicero's *Pro Milone*.

51 Caesar's *Gallic Wars*.

47 Birth of Propertius.

44–43 Cicero's *Philippics*.
43 Birth of Ovid.

40 Sallust's *Jugurthan War*.
39 Virgil's *Eclogues*.
38 Horace presented to Maecenas.
36 Varro's treatise *On Agriculture*.
35/34 Horace's first book of *Satires*.

MILITARY EVENTS	POLITICAL AND SOCIAL EVENTS	CULTURAL AND RELIGIOUS EVENTS
31 Victory at Actium. **30** Occupation of Egypt.	**30** Octavian in Egypt; suicide of Antony and Cleopatra. Egypt becomes a Roman province. **29** Octavian's triple triumph.	
29 Beginning of the Spanish campaigns.	**28** *Census* and *lectio senatus* of Octavian and Agrippa. Octavian becomes *princeps senatus*. **27** "Sharing out" of the provinces between the Senate and Octavian, who receives the title "Augustus." **25** Galatia becomes a Roman province.	**29** Virgil: the *Georgics.* Dedication of the temple to the deified Caesar. Start of the imperial religion. Building of the first stone amphitheater in Rome, and Augustus' mausoleum and triumphal arch.
25 Start of the Alpine campaigns. Expedition by the Romans in Arabia. Indian embassy to Rome. **20** Return of the insignia by the Parthians.	**23** Political crisis in Rome. Augustus quits the consulship, receives tribunician power for life, renewable each year.	**27** Dedication of Agrippa's Pantheon. **25** Foundation of Aosta and Merida. Livy begins his *Roman History* around 25. **20** "All roads lead to Rome," capital of the Empire. **19** Death of Tibullus and Virgil.
	18 Agrippa associated with the Empire. Julian laws on morals.	**17** Secular Games. Horace: *Carmen saeculare.*
15 Combined campaigns of Tiberius and Drusus in the Alps. **12** Tiberius in Pannonia. Drusus' campaigns in Germania.	**15** Raetia and Noricum Roman provinces. **12** Augustus, *pontifex maximus.* Death of Agrippa.	**11** Marcellus' theater. **10** Dedication of the altar of the Three Gauls. **9** Dedication of the *Ara Pacis Augustae.* **8** Death of Maecenas and Horace.

8–6 Tiberius' campaigns in Germania. 7/6 Surrender of the Alps. 2 Revival of the Armenian question. AD 4/6 Tiberius' campaigns in Germania. 6–9 Dalmatian–Pannonian rising; Tiberius' campaign. 9 Varus' disaster. 10/12 Tiberius' campaigns in Germania. 14/16 Germanicus' campaigns in Germania. 17 Germanicus in the East (to 19). Tacfarinas' rising. 21 Revolt of Sacrovir and Florus. 34 The Parthians control Armenia. 39 Caligula in Gaul, on the Rhine.	7 Creation of the 14 districts in Rome and perhaps the 11 regions in Italy. 2 Augustus, Father of his Country. AD 4 Adoption of Tiberius by Augustus. 6 Judaea becomes a Roman province. 10 Province of Pannonia. 14 Death of Augustus. Accession of Tiberius. 15 Sejanus, prefect of the praetorian guard. 17 Province of Cappadocia. 19 Death of Germanicus. 26 Tiberius in Campania. Pontius Pilate prefect of Judaea. 31 Downfall and death of Sejanus. 33 Financial crisis in Rome. 37 Death of Tiberius. Accession of Caligula. 41 Assassination of Caligula. Accession of Claudius. 42 Organization of Mauretania into two provinces.	6 Trophy of La Turbie. 2 Dedication of Augustus' Forum. AD 8 Ovid exiled to Tomi. 17 Death of Livy and Ovid. ca. 25 Death of Strabo. ca. 30 Preaching and death of Christ. 32 Temple of Bel at Palmyra. ca. 34 Martyrdom of Stephen. Subterranean monument of the Porta Maggiore.

MILITARY EVENTS	POLITICAL AND SOCIAL EVENTS	CULTURAL AND RELIGIOUS EVENTS
43 Start of the conquest of Britain.	43 Establishment of the port of Ostia. 45/6 Province of Thrace. 47/8 Censorship of Claudius. Discourse of the Claudian Table. 54 Death of Claudius. Accession of Nero. 55 Death of Britannicus. 59 Assassination of Agrippina.	47 Reconstruction of the college of *haruspices*. Reform of the cult of Cybele. ca. 49 "Apostolic Council" of Jerusalem. Seneca appointed Nero's tutor. 50 Foundation of Cologne. 54 Expulsion of the Jews (Rome). 60 First celebration of the *Neronia*.
58–9 Campaigns of Corbulo in Armenia. War against the Parthians. 61 Boadicea's rebellion. 63 End of the war against the Parthians. Agreement on Armenia. 66 Revolt of the Jews. Start of the Jewish War. 68 Rising of Vindex in Gaul, Galba in Tarraconensis. 69 German–Gaulish rebellion of Civilis. 70 Capture of Jerusalem. Assembly of Reims and end of the "Gaulish Empire."	64 Burning of Rome. Monetary reform. 65 Piso's conspiracy. 66 Nero in Greece. 68 Suicide of Nero. Accession of Galba. 69 Year of the four emperors: Galba, Otho, Vitellius, and Vespasian, who triumphed. 71 Titus associated with government.	64 Start of building of the Domus Aurea. 65 Suicide of Seneca and Lucan. 66 Suicide of Petronius. before 70–80 The Synoptic Gospels. 70 Destruction of the Temple (Jerusalem).

74–90 Subjection and organization of the *Agri Decumates*.

83 Domitian's campaigns in Germania.
85–6 War against the Dacians.
ca. 85 Formation of the first *limes* (frontier defense line) in Upper Germania.
89 Rising of Saturninus.
89–92 Campaigns on the Danube.

96–7 Operations in Germania.

98 First attestation of the word *limes* as meaning a defense system.
101–2 First Dacian War.
105–6 Second Dacian War.
106 Annexation of Arabia.

72–78 Reorganization of the East.
73/74 Vespasian and Titus appointed censors. The Iberian peninsula receives Latin rights.

77–84 Agricola in Britain.
79 Death of Vespasian. Accession of Titus. Vesuvius erupts.
81 Death of Titus. Accession of Domitian.

ca. 85 Creation of the two provinces of Germania.
86 Moesia divided into two.

92 Decrees on viticulture.

96 Assassination of Domitian. Accession of Nerva.
97 Poor relief project.
98 Death of Nerva. Accession of Trajan.

102–5 Development of the port of Ostia.

71 Rebuilding of the temple of Jupiter Capitolinus in Rome.

74 Expulsion of philosophers and astrologers (Rome).

79 Death of Pliny the Elder.

80 Dedication of the Colosseum.
80–120 Literary activity of Plutarch.

ca. 88–97 Clement I, Pope.

92 Quintilian, *Institutio oratoria*.
94/5 Expulsion of philosophers (Rome), including Epictetus.
ca. 95 St John's Gospel and Revelation.

98 Tacitus, *Agricola*, *Germania*.
100 *Panegyric of Trajan* by Pliny the Younger. Foundation of Timgad.

MILITARY EVENTS	POLITICAL AND SOCIAL EVENTS	CULTURAL AND RELIGIOUS EVENTS
	107 Dacia becomes a Roman province.	109 Tacitus, *Histories.* Trophy of Adamklissi. 112 Dedication of Trajan's Forum. Pliny's letter on the Christians. 113 Dedication of Trajan's Column.
114–17 Parthian wars. 115–17 Jewish rising in the East. 117 In the East, the evacuation of Trajan's conquests. Frontier on the Euphrates.	114 Trajan receives the title of *Optimus.* Armenia becomes a Roman province. 117 Death of Trajan. Accession of Hadrian. 118 Execution of the four ex-consuls.	117 Tacitus, *Annals.* 118 Start of work on Hadrian's villa at Tibur (Tivoli). Rebuilding of the Pantheon.
122 Hadrian's Wall. 123 Peace with the Parthians.	120 Creation of the *consulares* of Italy. 121–5 First journey by Hadrian in the provinces. 128–34 Second journey of Hadrian in the provinces.	120 Suetonius, *The Twelve Caesars.*
132–35 Revolt of Bar Kochba.	138 Death of Hadrian. Accession of Antoninus.	130 Jerusalem becomes *colonia Aelia Capitolina.* Death of Antinous. 131 Perpetual Edict of the Praetor. 134 Dedication of the temple of Rome and Venus (Rome).
142 Building of Antoninus' Wall.		143 Aelius Aristides, *Eulogy of Rome.*

161 Parthian invasion of Syria and Armenia.	161 Death of Antoninus. Accession of Marcus Aurelius, who has Lucius Verus as his associate.	160 First known *taurobolium* (sacrifice of a bull) in the West. ca. 160 Gaius, *Institutes.*
162 Campaigns of L. Verus in the East.	163 Institution of the *iuridici* in Italy.	
167–75 First "Germanic" War.	167 The plague in Rome and in the Empire.	ca. 170 Appearance of Montanism. 177 Persecution in the Empire (martyrs of Lyon).
175 Revolt of Avidius Cassius. 177–80 Second "Germanic" War.	169 Death of Lucius Verus. 177 Commodus appointed co-emperor.	ca. 178 Celsus, *The True Account.* between 180 and 196 The Aurelian column.
180 Peace with the Quadi and Marcomanni. 186 Rising of Maternus.	180 Death of Marcus Aurelius. Accession of Commodus.	
193 Two military rebellions: Septimius Severus, Pescennius Niger. 194–5 First war against the Parthians.	192 Assassination of Commodus. 193 Pertinax becomes emperor and is killed. Didius Julianus buys the Empire. 194 Septimius Severus sole emperor. 196 Clodius Albinus declares himself *Augustus.*	197 Tertullian, *Apologetica.*
197 Clodius Albinus beaten at Lyon. 197–200 Campaigns of Severus in the East and journey in Egypt.	198 Caracalla becomes *Augustus.*	ca. 200 Christian School of Alexandria (Clement, Origen). Neo-Platonic school (Ammonius Saccas). 202 Ban on all Jewish and Christian proselytism.
208–11 Campaigns in Britain.	209 Geta becomes *Augustus.*	

MILITARY EVENTS	POLITICAL AND SOCIAL EVENTS	CULTURAL AND RELIGIOUS EVENTS
	211 Death of Septimius Severus. Caracalla and Geta co-emperors. Assassination of Geta.	212–16 Baths of Caracalla.
	212 Antonine Constitution.	
213–14 Campaigns on the Danube. 215–17 Campaigns in the East.		
	217 Assassination of Caracalla. Macrinus emperor.	219 The Baal of Emesa is received in Rome.
	218 Death of Macrinus. Elagabalus emperor.	220 House-church of Dura-Europus.
	222 Assassination of Elagabalus. Accession of Severus Alexander.	ca. 229–30 Dio Cassius, *Roman History*.
224 Sassanid dynasty in Persia.		
231–2 Campaigns against the Sassanids.		
234–5 Campaigns in Germania.	235 Assassination of Severus Alexander at Mainz. Maximinus proclaimed emperor.	
	235–8 Maximinus Thrax.	
Wars: Alemanni, Dacians, and Sarmatians, Carpi and Goths.	238 Civil war (Africa: Gordian I and Gordian II; Italy: Pupienus and Balbinus).	
	238–44 Gordian III.	
Wars: Carpi and Goths.	244–9 Philip the Arabian. Usurpations: Uranius, Pacatian, Jotapian.	241 Beginning of Mani's preaching.
240 Capture of Nisibis by the Persians.	249–51 Decius. The plague in the Empire.	248 (April 21) Rome's millennium.
		249 Aventine baths.
Wars: Carpi and Goths, Persians, Alemanni.	251–253 Trebonianus Gallus.	250–1 Persecution of Christianity.

Wars: Carpi and Goths.

Wars: Franks and Alemanni, Goths and Persians.

Wars: Goths, Persians, Saxons, Moors, Quadi and Marcomanni, Roxolani and Sarmatians.

253 Franks and Alemanni in Gaul.
258 The Alemanni in north Italy.

259–60 Capture and death of Valerian.

Wars: Franks and Alemanni, Persians and Goths.

Wars: Alemanni, Persians.
270 Victory at Nish over the Goths.

Wars: Franks and Alemanni, Carpi and Goths, Marcomanni, Vandals, Sarmatians.

271 Evacuation of Dacia.
275 Evacuation of the *Agri Decumates*.

Wars: Goths and Franks.

Wars: Burgundii and Vandals, Goths and Getae, Blemmyes.

253–259/60 Valerian. Usurpation: Ingenuus (259–60). Secession of Palmyra (Odaenathus) and Gaul (Postumus).

259/260–8 Gallienus. Vaballathus (son of Zenobia) replaces Odaenathus. Postumus replaced by Laelianus, then Marius. Usurpations by Macrianus, Quietus, Regalianus, and Aureolus.
268/70 Claudius II.
269 Appearance of the Bagaudes. Usurpation by Quintillus. Victorinus replaces Marius in Gaul.
270–5 Aurelian.
273 Palmyra returned to the Empire.
274 Surrender of Tetricus, Victorinus' successor.
274 Monetary reform.
275–6 Tacitus. Hypothetical senatorial restoration. Usurpation: Florian.
276–82 Probus.
282–3 Carus.
283–4 Numerian.
283–5 Carinus.
284–305 Diocletian.
285 Maximian Caesar.
284–6 The Bagaudes in Gaul.

257–8 Persecution of Christianity (death of St Cyprian). Plotinus. Ludovisi sarcophagus.
260 Decree of toleration of Christianity.

274 Primacy of the cult of the Sun.
275 Death of Mani.

MILITARY EVENTS	POLITICAL AND SOCIAL EVENTS	CULTURAL AND RELIGIOUS EVENTS
276–8 Franks and Alemanni in Gaul. Wars: Sarmatians and Persians. Other wars: Franks and Alemanni, Iazyges and Carpi. 298 War against the Moors. Treaty of Nisibis with the Persians.	286 (April 1) Maximian Augustus. 288 Insurrection of Carausius in Britain. 293 (March 1) Galerius and Constantius Chlorus appointed *Caesares*. 294 Monetary reform. 296 Britain reconquered from Allectus, the successor of Carausius. 305 (May 1) Abdication of the two *Augusti*. 306–37 Constantine. 306 Death of Constantius; Constantine is *Augustus*, Maxentius Augustus. 308 Conference of Carnuntum ("Second Tetrarchy"). 310 Usurpation of Domitius Alexander. 311 Monetary reform (gold *solidus*). 312 Defeat of Maxentius in the Battle of the Milvian Bridge. 312–26 Disappearance of the equestrian order. 313 Victory of Licinius over Daia.	ca. 295 Arnobius, *Against the Nations*. 297 Law against the Manicheans. 303 Celebration of the *vicennalia*. 303–4 Persecution of the Christians. ca. 305 Lactantius, *Human and Divine Institutions*. *The Tetrarchs* (now in Venice). Baths in Rome. Arch of Thessalonica. 311 Decree of Galerius (toleration of Christianity). 312 Daia's decree against the Christians. 313 Edict of Milan. 314 Synod of Arles (Donatism).

ca. 319 Church of St John Lateran.

325 Council of Nicaea (Arianism).
328 Athanasius bishop of Alexandria.
330 (May 11) Inauguration of Constantinople.
331 Inventory of temples' possessions, the first confiscations.

340 Death of Eusebius of Caesarea.
341 First ban on pagan sacrifices.

ca. 350 The preaching of Wulfila. The *Chronicler of 354*.

356 Death of St Anthony.

358 Julian, *On Royalty*.
359 Sarcophagus of Junius Bassus.
360 First Council of Constantinople.
361 Re-establishment of paganism; first measures against the Christians.

317 Crispus, Constantine II, and Licinius II appointed *Caesares*.
324 Licinius defeated at Adrianople; Constantius II appointed *Caesar*.
326 Execution of Crispus and Fausta.
333 Constans appointed *Caesar*.
335 Dalmatius appointed *Caesar*.
337 Baptism and death of Constantine. Constantine's sons in power; assassination of Dalmatius.
340 Death of Constantine II.
340–7 Circumcellions in Africa.

350 Usurpation by Magnentius; death of Constans.
351 Battle of Mursa.
353 Death of Magnentius.
354 Death of Gallus Caesar.
355 Julian Caesar.
357 Journey to Rome by Constantius II.

360 Julian acclaimed *Augustus*.
361 Death of Constantius II.
361–3 Julian.
363–4 Jovian.
364–95 Valentinian dynasty; Theodosius.
364–75 Valentinian I.
364–78 Valens.
365 Usurpation by Procopius.

337 Attack by the Persians.
338 Siege of Nisibis.

343 Constantius II in Adiabene.

357 Battle of Strasbourg (Alemanni).

363 War against the Persians.

MILITARY EVENTS	POLITICAL AND SOCIAL EVENTS	CULTURAL AND RELIGIOUS EVENTS
Peace with the Persians.	367–83 Gratian.	366–84 Damasius pope.
Wars of Theodosius the Elder against the Scots and Saxons.	368 Creation of the "defender of the *plebs.*"	372 St Martin bishop of Tours.
364 Troubles in Tripolitania.	372–5 Rebellion of Firmus.	373 Death of Athanasius; St Ambrose bishop of Milan.
366–74 Attacks by the Alemanni.	375–92 Valentinian II.	379 Consulship of Ausonius; St Jerome becomes a priest; death of St Basil.
367–9 Attacks by the Goths.	378–95 Theodosius.	380 Decree against the Arians.
372–3 War against the Persians.		381 Second Council of Constantinople; renewed ban on pagan sacrifices.
374–5 War against the Quadi and Sarmatians.	383–8 Usurpation by Maximus.	382–402 Affair of the altar of Victory (Symmachus).
378 Disaster of Adrianople.		386 Destruction of temples.
380 Treaty with the Goths.		387 Baptism of St Augustine.
	393–4 Usurpation by Eugenius.	390 Libanius, *On Behalf of the Temples*; death of St Gregory of Nazianzus.
	394 Battle of the River Frigidus.	391–2 Ban on pagan worship.
390 Treaty of Constantinople with the Persians.	395–408 Arcadius (East).	394 Death of St Gregory of Nyssa and St Martin.
	395–423 Honorius (West).	394–404 Claudian, propagandist for Stilicho.
	395–8 Gildo's revolt.	396 St Augustine bishop of Hippo.
		397 Death of St Ambrose.
		397–8 St Augustine, *Confessions.*

398 Invasion by the Huns.	408 Execution of Stilicho.	ca. 400 *The Augustan History*.
401 Victory of Aquileia over the Visigoths.	408–50 Theodosius II in the East.	407 Death of St John Chrysostom.
406 Victory of Fiesole over the Ostrogoths.	411–21 Constantius in command of the West (as Constantius III in 421).	410 Death of Commodian.
406 (**December 31**) Vandals, Alani, and Suebi cross the Rhine.		411 Conference of Carthage (end of Donatism).
410 Capture of Rome by Alaric.	425–55 Valentinian III in the West, with the master of the militia Aetius.	413–26 St Augustine, *The City of God*.
		415 Murder of Hypatia.
		417 Rutilius Namatianus, *The Return*.
		420 Death of St Jerome.
		429–38 Theodosian Code.
	450–71 The Alani Aspar in command of the East.	430 Death of St Augustine.
		431 Council of Ephesus (Monophysitism).
		435 Renewed ban on pagan sacrifices.
	457–72 Ricimer master of the militia in the West.	451 Council of Chalcedon (Monophysitism).
	476 Deposition of Romulus Augustulus.	472 Sidonius Apollinaris bishop of Clermont-Ferrand.
	488 Theodoric sent to the West.	
	493 Theodoric in Rome.	
451 Battle of the Campus Mauriacus.		533 *Digest*.
		534 Code of Justinian.

GLOSSARY

Aediles. Patrician (curule) and plebeian magistrates, who superintended the provisioning of Rome, trade, markets (especially weights and measures), public games, roadways, sanitation, and police.

Album senatorium. Roll of senators drawn up by the censors every five years, later by the emperor. The senators were classed in order of seniority according to the offices they had held: first former consuls, next former praetors, aediles, and tribunes, lastly former quaestors.

Annales. Annual account of events concerning Rome and Roman life drawn up by the pontiffs and recorded on whitened boards set up in the Regia. Included records of magistrates and events of cult importance.

Apotheosis. Ceremony whereby a mortal was admitted to the number of the gods (*divus*). It was customary under the Empire, decided by the Senate as the prerogative of "good" emperors. "Bad" emperors (those who had persecuted the Senate) were subjected to the condemnation of their memory (*damnatio memoriae*); their names were struck off inscriptions and their enactments cancelled.

Arianism. The theory of Arius which resulted in one of the first major doctrinal divisions in the early Church. Condemned as a heretic at the Council of Nicaea in AD 325, he asserted that Christ was a man, distinct from and subordinate to God.

Arval Brethren. A college of 12 priests, devoted to the worship of Dea Dia, a corn deity. Their place of worship was a sacred wood (*lucus*), on the road from Rome to Ostia. They were held to have drawn up their *Records* no later than between 30 and 28 BC.

Arx. Rome's citadel, on the Capitol.

Augurs. College of priests skilled in interpreting the flight of birds, and from that determining the will of the gods. They were consulted before any official action and could interrupt any discussion or decision if they had perceived a divine sign: two words were enough: *alio die* ("till another day").

Seviri Augustales (priests of Augustus). Associations of six people, generally freedmen, formed to celebrate imperial worship at municipal level. See **Flamines**.

Auspices. Signs of the divine will, observed by the augurs in a *templum*, a "space marked out" with the help of a curved stick (*lituus*). Most frequent were the flights of birds, but also thunder and lightning, the behavior of the sacred chickens, and threatening omens. Under the Empire only the emperor had the right to take the auspices; all victories were thus won under his auspices.

Calends. The first day of the month; belonged to Janus.

Capitoline Triad. Jupiter, Juno, and Minerva, the triad that replaced the initial triad of Jupiter, Mars, and Quirinus. Worshiped on the Capitol in Rome and all the capitols of the Roman world.

Carmen. An incantatory formula, magical and usually in verse, uttered on a certain note and with a certain rhythm.

Censor. Magistrate charged with the task of conducting a "census" every five years of citizens and their possessions, and of drawing up a list of senators.

Chaldeans. Generic title for magicians, charlatans.

Comitatus. Campaign army, starting with Constantine.

Comitia centuriata. Assembly of the people, gathered for the election of senior magistrates, voting on laws and justice. Voting was by *centuria*, according to classes established on the basis of their wealth at the time of the census.

Comitia curiata. Ancient assembly of the people (voting was by *curia*), which retained only a religious role; it conferred the *imperium* on magistrates.

Comitia tributa. Plebeian assembly charged with the election of aediles, tribunes, and quaestors, and voting on plebiscites. Voting was by tribe.

Consul. Head of state under the Republic; survived under the Empire with reduced powers. The office was annual and collegial: two consuls under the Republic; two ordinary and eponymous consuls plus two substitute consuls under the Empire.

Conventus. A district of a province in which citizens assembled, and where the governor administered justice.

Curia. The customary meeting place of the Senate in the Forum. There was also a curia in Pompey's theater on the Campus Martius. In the colonies and townships in the provinces, the meeting place of the municipal council, generally in the open on the Forum.

Curialis. A member of a *curia*, a municipal notable; the term was used in the fourth century to designate decurions.

Cursus honorum. Ascending order of Roman magistracies. The political career ladder.

Curule (seat). Folding X-shaped seat, reserved for senators.

Decemvirs. Legislators who replaced the consuls in 451 and 450 BC; the compilers of the Law of the Twelve Tables.

Devotio. Ceremony during which a general devoted (offered) himself and his army to the *Manes* (benevolent spirits) and the Earth by reciting a formula, dictated to him by the *pontifex maximus*, to ward off a major peril to the army and obtain victory from the gods on the occasion of a battle.

Dictator. Magistrate appointed legally with full powers, but for a specified period (less than six months) and in order to accomplish a precise task, when grave danger threatened the state.

Dilectus. Regular enrolment of soldiers into the army.

Diocese. Administrative division comprising several provinces, entrusted to the authority of a *vicarius* (vicar).

Epulones. College of seven priests whose duty was to organize the sacred banquets (*epula*); created in 196 BC.

Euergetism. The generosity of a private person who, out of his own money, participated in the embellishment of a town, distributed money to his compatriots, or bore the expenses of banquets and distributions of oil on the occasion of dedications of monuments. It was often connected with election to municipal magistracies.

Evocatio. Religious ceremony intended to compel a divinity to abandon the city he or she protected in order to take up residence in the city that "wanted" to extend a welcome.

Fasces. A bundle of rods bound round an axe. Carried by the lictors accompanying the magistrates *cum imperio* (senior magistrates with civil and military powers).

Fathers (of the Church). Post-classical designation of the many first–sixth-century theologians who developed the doctrine of the Church.

Fetiales. A college of 20 diplomat-priests entrusted with international affairs: declarations of war, making of peace and treaties.

Flamines. College of 15 priests attached to the worship of a divinity: 3 major *flamines* (Jupiter, Mars, and Quirinus) and 12 minor. In Italy and provincial towns, the *flamines* administered the imperial cult.

Galli. Eunuch priests of Cybele, Great Mother of the gods.

Genius. A god's power of creation. Each man also had his protective *genius*, as each woman had her *Juno*.

Gens (pl. gentes). A Roman clan or group of families linked by a common name and by a belief in a common ancestor.

Gentilicius. Name (generally ending -ius) borne by all the members of the same *gens*, family clan composed of descendants of the same ancestor. The word also indicated everything relating to the *gens*: for instance, gentilitial cult.

Haruspices. Of Etruscan origin, college of 60 councilors (later priests) who were specialists in examining the entrails of sacrificial victims, notably the liver and heart. They also interpreted the 11 categories of lightning that could occur.

Ides. Day of the month: the 15th in March, May, July, and October; the 13th in the other months; belonged to Jupiter.

Imperium. Sovereign civil and military power; under the Republic was held by dictators, consuls, and praetors. Under the Empire, only the emperor could hold it; he could delegate it.

Inauguration. When the augurs took the auspices to consecrate the investiture of a magistrate, or the opening of a temple or a public place (= dedication).

Lectio senatus. A reading or calling of the roll of the senators, carried out by the censor, who could strike from the list the names of those he considered unworthy.

Lectisternium. Ceremony of Greek origin during which statues of the gods laid on couches took part in a sacred banquet. The first took place in 339 BC; in 217 BC the first *lectisternium* offered to *all* the chief gods took place.

Loca sanctorum. All the places in which relics of martyrs were honored.

Ludi. Public games.

Lupercus (priests of). Fraternity of 12 (later 24) priests attached to the worship of Faunus. On February 15 (Lupercalia), animals were sacrificed in the Lupercal (the cave where the she-wolf was supposed to have suckled Romulus and Remus); the festival combined fertility and purificatory rituals, and included flagellation.

Lustration. Performance of a purificatory ceremony, e.g. a body of people, a piece of land, a city.

Lustrum. Five-yearly purification performed by the censors after carrying out the census; hence the space of five years (*lustrum*) between two purifications.

Martyrium. Church constructed around a burial of relics.

Nones. Day of the month: the 7th in March, May, July, and October; the 5th in other months.

Numen. A divinity's power of decision; often meant the divinity himself or herself.

Nundinae. A market day. Also used to denote a weekly market.

Optimates. Roman political group, through not an organized party. Aristocratic and conservative, members of the Senate, they opposed the *populares*.

Pagus. The smallest recognized territorial unit, often subordinate to an urban community (*oppidum*, *municipium*).

Pater patratus. Head of the Fetiales.

Patrician. Originally a member of the *de facto* nobility providing senators (*patres*), then a member of the nobility by birth, for whom access to certain priesthoods and the consulate was reserved. The republican patriciate was defined and formed in the fifth century BC.

Patron. Important personage with whom, by a bilateral commitment, individuals (*clientes*) or public collectives (cities, peoples, provinces) were linked. The patron ensured the daily security and legal defense of his clients, who in return owed him respect, help, and their votes. He acted as intermediary between the state and the public collectives to whom he was patron.

Pax deorum. Harmony between men and gods, considered indispensable for the well-being of the state.

Plebs, plebeians. Political grouping, which appeared in 494/493 BC, of all those in Rome, of any class, who opposed the patrician organization of the state. Made up of rich and poor, patrons and clients, native Romans and foreigners (Latins, Sabines, etc.) who had come into the city. At first their sole point in common was their opposition to the privileges of the patricians. Subsequently plebeian *gentes* were formed, in opposition to the patrician *gentes*. At the end of the Republic, the word defined the common people.

Pomoerium. Sacred boundary of Rome. The land that lay inside it could not receive the tombs of the dead, temples to foreign gods, or the army except for triumphs. Magistrates with *imperium* lost it by crossing the boundary.

Pontiffs (pontifices). College of six, later nine and then 16 priests with the duty of administering sacred and family law, religious jurisdiction and keeping the *Annales*. They set the calendar, and their Books were a liturgical manual. At their head was the great pontiff (*pontifex maximus*), who also had authority over all the other priests, whom he appointed and inaugurated. Under the Empire, the emperor was the *pontifex maximus*.

Populares. Roman political group, though not an organized party, who worked through and supposedly on behalf of the people, challenging the *optimates* in the Senate.

Potestas. Civil (executive) powers of a magistrate, inferior to *imperium*.

Praetor. Senior magistrate specially responsible for justice. Performed some of the functions of the consuls in their absence.

Princeps iuventutis. Leader of the equestrian order. Under the emperors, the probable successor to the throne (i.e. the Crown Prince).

Princeps senatus. Leader of the Senate. Inscribed first on the official list drawn up by the censors, and had the privilege of speaking first at meetings of the Senate. Under the Empire, the emperor was *princeps senatus.*

Prodigy. Spontaneous and unusual manifestation of the divine will, for example rain of blood or ashes, lightning in a clear sky, etc. Gave rise to an expiatory ceremony.

Proletarian. Someone whose only belongings were his offspring (*proles*).

Publican. A private individual who "farmed" public services (*publica*); levying taxes, contracting for public works and for equipping armies and the navy. In the late third century BC they formed companies and soon large joint stock companies (*societates*).

Quaestor. Minor magistrate whose special task was finance.

Quindecimviri sacris faciundis. College of two (*duumviri*), later ten (*decemviri*), then 15 (*quindecimviri*) priests charged with custody and interpretation of the Sibylline Books, the worship of Apollo, and overseeing foreign cults established in Rome.

Quirites. Denomination of the Roman people, i.e. members of the civilian body: as opposed to *milites*, which designated citizens under arms.

Regia. Abode of the king on the Forum, near the temple of Vesta, and then frequently the dwelling of the *pontifex maximus.* Religious center of Rome.

Rex sacrorum. First of the Roman priests, successor to the kings, from whom he inherited religious authority. Entrusted with the worship of Janus.

Rostra. A platform from which speakers delivered their addresses, situated near the Curia under the Republic and subsequently moved farther west. Decorated with the prows of boats captured at the Battle of Antium (338 BC), whence its name *rostra* (cutwaters).

Sacer. Sacred, thus reserved for the gods (as opposed to profane), whence taboo, sacrosanct (e.g. the tribunes of the *plebs*).

Sacramentum. Solemn oath taken by the conscript on his enrolment. It bound the soldier to the state and his superiors and rendered "accursed" anyone who broke it.

Salians. Fraternity of 12, later 24 priests of Mars and Quirinus. They opened and closed the war cycle of the year: March–October.

Senate. Assembly of 300 members, then 600 under Sulla, 900 under Caesar, again 600 from Augustus, composed of former magistrates, a list of whom was drawn up every five years by the censors, later by the emperor, who carried out the *lectio senatus* (calling the roll). It was the government of the republican state. Under the Empire it maintained its prestige, but its role diminished to the point where it became Rome's municipal council.

Senatus consultum. Decision of the Senate which, under the Empire, had the force of a law. In the event of major danger, under the Republic, the "senatus consultum ultimum," or ultimate senatorial decree, gave full powers to the consuls.

Sibylline Books. Collection of prophecies attributed to the Sibyl, preserved by the *Quindecimviri sacris faciundis*, who were specialists in the interpretation of these writings. From 38 BC they were kept in the Palatine temple of Apollo.

Sodality. College of priests, generally attached to the worship of archaic divinities: Arvales, Luperci, Salians.

Sportula. Gift in kind distributed by patrons to their clients.

Suovetaurilia. Major sacrifice of a bull (*taurus*), a ram (*ovis*), and a boar (*sus*), principally offered to the Capitoline Triad, Jupiter, Juno, and Minerva.

Supplication. Religious ceremony celebrated in the event of danger or as thanksgiving on escape from a danger.

Taurobolium. Sacrifice of a bull, followed by a "baptism" accomplished by sprinkling the blood in a trench. Practiced in the worship of Cybele.

Tribunes of the plebs. College of ten magistrates whose task was the protection of the *plebs*; they were inviolable (*sacri*) and had the right of intercession (= veto) over decisions of the magistrates, with the exception of dictators. Starting with Augustus, the emperor held the power of the tribunes (*tribunicia potestas*).

Vestals. College of six priestesses whose duty was to watch over the flame, the guarantee of Rome's power, a flame that must never be extinguished, kept in the temple of Vesta on the Forum.

Vexillatio. Military detachment, a unit formed temporarily with soldiers taken from other bodies of troops.

Vicarius. High functionary responsible for a diocese.

Vicus. A village or hamlet; or a district or quarter of a city.

Vow. Promise which religiously committed whoever made it (*votum susceptum*) and which it was imperative that he carry out (*votum solutum*).

GUIDE TO GREEK AND ROMAN WRITERS

The works of classical authors are preserved mainly in manuscripts, which were re-copied by hand, often many times, over the course of the Middle Ages. They were written continuously, and normally without punctuation; their division into "books" (referred to below) and "chapters" is a modern editorial convention meant to facilitate citation.

The two most complete and authoritative collections of Greek and Latin works are the Oxford Classical Texts (Oxford University Press) and the Bibliotheca Teubneriana (B. G. Teubner). Reliable translations of most works can be found in the Loeb Classical Library, and in the Penguin Classics series. A growing number of Internet sites, of varying quality, act as repositories for classical texts and translations; a good place to start is the site entitled "Electronic Resources for Classicists," maintained by the University of California at Irvine.

In what follows, authors like Appian, who lived in the second century AD but wrote about the Republican era, have been grouped according to the period they describe, rather than the one in which they lived.

THE ROMAN REPUBLIC (TO 31 BC)

Appian (ca. AD 95–165). A Greek from Alexandria, Appian spent much of his working life at Rome, as a lawyer and civil servant. His ethnographically arranged *Roman History* is partially preserved. An admirer of Roman imperialism, he is perhaps most important for what he reveals of political and social conditions at Rome in the period from the Gracchi to the end of the Republic, mainly in books 13–17 (covering 133–35 BC), which are often cited separately as *Civil Wars*, books 1–5.

Julius Caesar (100–44 BC). The most important political and military leader of his time, Gaius Julius Caesar wrote primarily for political reasons – to justify his actions and to defend his policies. His *Gallic War*, which describes his conquest of Gaul in the period 58–52 BC, is the earliest surviving account of the culture and customs of the Gauls and Germans. His *Civil War*, in three books, is a transparently partisan account of the events of 49–48 BC.

Cato the Elder (234–149 BC). Marcus Porcius Cato, born at Tusculum, in central Italy, was a vocal proponent of traditional Roman virtues, and spokesperson of a conservative and patriotic ideology. His sole surviving work is *On Agriculture*, a manual on farming and estate management written about 160 BC. It is an important source of information on contemporary social and economic institutions, including agricultural slavery.

Catullus (ca. 84–54 BC). Gaius Valerius Catullus of Verona (in northern Italy) spent much of his short life at Rome, where he moved in fashionable circles. Passionate and immediate, his poems range across a wide variety of styles and subjects, including his tempestuous and sometimes debilitating affair with a woman whom he addresses as "Lesbia," and who was, in real life, Clodia, the sister of Publius Clodius, tribune in 58 BC.

Cicero (106–43 BC). Marcus Tullius Cicero of Arpinum (in central Italy), consul in 63 BC, and self-styled defender of Republican institutions, is probably better known through his own works than any other writer of classical antiquity. Most of his 57 surviving speeches, which belong to the period 81–43 BC, deal with civil and criminal cases, and with the doings of the politically active. An extensive set of his letters, 864 in all (774 written by Cicero, 90 by his correspondents), was published after his death, in four collections: one to friends and members of his household (*Ad familiares*), a second to his friend Atticus, a third, in three books, to his brother Quintus, the fourth to Brutus, Caesar's assassin. He also wrote extensively about political theory, rhetoric, and philosophy.

Diodorus Siculus (ca. 80–after 21 BC). Pedestrian and occasionally inaccurate, Diodorus' *Historical Library*, of which books 1–5 and 11–20 are fully preserved, is a general world history from mythological times to 54 BC, important mainly for what it records about developments at Rome in the period 480–302.

Dionysius of Halicarnassus (ca. 60/55–after 7 BC). A literary critic and teacher of rhetoric, Dionysius lived at Rome from 30 BC. Given to long and unhistorical speeches, his *Roman Antiquities*, a history of Rome from its foundation to 264 BC, is sometimes insightful, more often tedious and antiquarian. The whole of books 1–10 and most of 11 (to 446 BC) are extant; the rest survives in fragments.

Livy (59 BC–AD 17 or 64 BC–AD 12). In many ways the pre-eminent historian of the Republic, Titus Livius was raised at Patavium (mod. Padua) in northern Italy. A skillful story-teller, fond of idealized (and sometimes fictionalized) examples of old-fashioned heroism, he is rarely critical of his sources. Of his *History of Rome*, from its origins to 9 BC (in 142 books), books 1–10 (to 293) and 21–45 (218–167) are preserved more or less intact.

Lucan (AD 39–65). Born at Corduba (mod. Córdoba), Spain, a nephew of the philosopher Seneca the Elder, Marcus Annaeus Lucanus lived at Rome until he was forced to commit suicide for having plotted against the emperor Nero. His only surviving work, *Civil War*, is an unfinished, and staunchly anti-Caesarian, epic poem on the causes and course of the war between Caesar and Pompey.

Lucretius (ca. 94–55 BC). Almost nothing is known of the life of the poet and philosopher Titus Lucretius Carus, whose only work, *On the Nature of Things*, borrows from Epicurus to construct a mechanical and atomic view of the universe, intended to allay fears of the gods' intervention in human affairs, and of the after-life.

Cornelius Nepos (ca. 99–24 BC). A correspondent of Cicero, and acquaintance of Catullus, Cornelius Nepos is important for having authored the earliest surviving

Latin biographies (*On Illustrious Men*), eulogizing and sometimes careless accounts of the lives of writers, kings, and generals.

Plautus (died after 184 BC). Credited in one tradition with having authored 130 plays, of which 21 are extant, Titus Maccius Plautus was born at Sarsina in Umbria, a proverbially backward region of north-central Italy. Set in Greece, and based on Greek models (like Menander), but informed by Roman ideas and practices, his imaginative, and sometimes fantastic, comedies afford a tantalizing glimpse into the social conventions and attitudes of the middle Republic.

Polybius (ca. 200–after 118 BC). A politically active Greek from Megalopolis, Polybius was taken hostage in 167 BC and deported to Rome, where he befriended the Roman general and statesman Publius Cornelius Scipio Aemilianus. Of the 40 books of his *Histories*, a general history of the Mediterranean world written mainly to explain the rise of Rome to his fellow Greeks, only the first five (to 216 BC) survive intact. Unromantic and explicitly un-rhetorical, he is easily our most reliable source for the period from the beginning of the Second Carthaginian War to about the middle of the second century BC.

Sallust (86–ca. 35 BC). A partisan of Julius Caesar from 50 BC, Gaius Sallustius Crispus of Amiternum (in central Italy) retired from political life after Caesar's assassination to write history. Two monographs are preserved: the *Jugurthine War*, which recounts the incompetence and venality of the senatorial generals sent to North Africa to campaign against the renegade Jugurtha in the period 112–107 BC, and the *Catilinarian War*, which accepts, for the most part, Cicero's tendentious account of Catiline's alleged attempt to overthrow the government in 63. We have only fragments of Sallust's *Histories*, which probably described what he considered to be the moral decline of the Republic.

Terence (ca. 190–159 BC). Brought to Rome as a slave from his native North Africa, and subsequently freed, Publius Terentius Afer is known to have written six comedies, all of which were produced in the period 166–160 BC. Heavily dependent on Hellenistic models, especially Menander, his plays are almost entirely Greek in subject and manner.

Varro (116–27 BC). An antiquarian, and uncommonly prolific writer, Marcus Terentius Varro of Reate (in central Italy) was at one time a partisan of Pompey; subsequently restored to favor by Caesar, he was later outlawed by Antony. Of the 74 works attributed to him, only 2 survive: a manual on farm management (*On Agriculture*), published in 37 BC, and a much cited but probably little read treatise *On the Latin Language*, in 25 books, of which 5–10 are partly extant.

THE ROMAN WORLD, 31 BC–AD 235

Apuleius (born ca. AD 123). Born to a wealthy family at Madaurus, North Africa, Apuleius was educated at Carthage, Athens, and Rome. A lawyer, poet, rhetorician, philosopher, and lecturer, his extant works include the only Latin novel to have survived intact, the *Metamorphoses* (or *Golden Ass*), the charming story of a young man named

Lucius, who, having been turned into an ass, endures a series of strange and amusing adventures before being restored to human form by the goddess Isis.

Cassius Dio (AD 164/5–after 229). A native of Nicaea, in Asia Minor, and a senator from the time of Commodus, Cassius Dio Cocceianus is said to have spent 22 years writing his *Roman History*, an annalistic narrative of events from the foundation of Rome to his own day, of which only books 36–54, covering the period 68–10 BC, survive intact. (Others are partially preserved, in the epitomes made by the Byzantine compilers Xiphilinus and Zonaras, or, like 55–60, on the period 9 BC–AD 46, in abbreviated form.) It is valuable chiefly for its account of the age of Augustus, and of Dio's own time.

Celsus (time of Tiberius). Aulus Cornelius Celsus wrote an encyclopedia covering agriculture, medicine, rhetoric, and military science (possibly also philosophy and law), of which only the medical books are preserved. *On Medicine* is important mainly for what it reveals about Hellenistic medical theories.

Columella (mid-first century AD). Lucius Iunius Moderatus Columella, born to a land-owning family at Gades (mod. Cádiz), Spain, became an army officer and the owner of several estates in Italy. *On Agriculture* (written AD 60–5), which draws mainly from his own experience, is easily our most comprehensive source of information about agricultural practices and farm management.

Dio Chrysostom (ca. AD 40–after 112). An orator and popular philosopher, once banished by the emperor Domitian, Dio Cocceianus Chrysostomos is a valuable source of information about society and civic affairs in the Greek cities of his native Asia Minor. The 80 speeches attributed to him cover a wide variety of themes, including popular morality, Stoic (and Cynic) ideals, mythology, and literary criticism.

Florus (time of Hadrian?). All that is known of Lucius Annaeus Florus is that he was born in North Africa. He may be the Florus who is said to have been a poet and friend of the emperor Hadrian. His short, almost exclusively military, history of Rome, from its origins to the time of Augustus (*Epitome bellorum omnium annorum DCC*), is derivative, unimaginative, and often inaccurate.

Fronto (ca. AD 100–66). Marcus Cornelius Fronto of Cirta, North Africa, was the leading orator of his day, and, for a time, tutor of the future emperor Marcus Aurelius. His correspondence (*Epistulae*) is concerned mostly with the study of rhetoric, but also reveals something of the character of the imperial court.

Gaius (mid-second century AD). Nothing at all is known of Gaius, not even his full name. His *Institutes*, written probably about AD 160, is easily our best surviving introduction to Roman civil law. Lucid and economical, it was later used as a kind of textbook for first-year students at law schools in the East, and served as the model for the emperor Justinian's *Institutes*, published in AD 533.

Galen (AD 129–ca. 199). Galen of Pergamum was physician to the imperial court at Rome in the time of Marcus Aurelius. An accomplished anatomist and physiologist, he is also a valuable source of information about earlier theories of pathology, pharmacology, and dietetics.

Aulus Gellius (ca. AD 130–80). An antiquarian about whom little is known, Aulus Gellius wrote *Attic Nights*, in 20 books, to entertain and educate his children. Ranging over a great variety of subjects, including history, law, grammar, and philosophy, it is valuable partly because it quotes extensively from earlier writers whose works have not survived.

Herodian (ca. AD 165–255). A Syrian-born Greek, Herodian worked as a civil servant at Rome. His *History*, a narrative of events AD 180–238, is moralizing and superficial, useful only because it covers a period which is otherwise badly documented.

Horace (65–8 BC). Born at Venusia, in southern Italy, the son of an ex-slave, Quintus Horatius Flaccus became part of the literary circle patronized by Augustus' friend Maecenas. His surviving works include the *Epodes*, 17 poems written in imitation of the Greek poet Archilochus, and the *Satires*, published probably in 30 BC, broadly autobiographical reflections on life, literature, food, family, and friends. The *Odes* (*Carmina*), the first three books of which were published probably about 23 BC, are generally agreed to be his greatest accomplishment. Vivid and sophisticated, technically and stylistically flawless, they tackle a remarkably wide variety of topics, including death, love, and even politics. The *Epistles*, verse letters published probably in 20 BC, are conversational set-pieces warning against greed, and extolling, among other things, the virtues of the "simple life." He also wrote a hymn (*Carmen saeculare*) for Augustus' celebration of the Secular Games in 17 BC, and the disappointingly unimaginative *Art of Poetry*.

Josephus (AD 37/8–ca. 100). A Jewish priest of aristocratic birth, assigned to defend Galilee against the Romans in the Jewish rebellion of AD 66–70, Flavius Josephus was captured in 67, pardoned by the future emperor Titus, and later awarded Roman citizenship. His *Jewish War*, written originally in Aramaic, is a narrative of the revolt that draws mainly on his own knowledge of it. His other surviving works are an *Autobiography*, written to defend his conduct during the rebellion, the *Jewish Antiquities*, a full-scale history of the Jews from creation to AD 65, and *Against Apion*, which defends Judaism against the misrepresentations of anti-Semitic writers.

Juvenal (ca. AD 60–140). Little is known with certainty about the life or career of Decimus Iunius Iuvenalis of Aquinum (in central Italy). Consumed, it seems, by a bitter sense of failure and injustice, he is said to have been banished at one point for lampooning a favorite of the imperial court. His sixteen *Satires*, which ruthlessly ridicule the vices and vulgarities of the wealthy, include (6) a famously savage and unfunny denunciation of women.

Lucian (ca. AD 120–after 180). A native of Samosata (mod. Samsât, Turkey) who made his living first as an advocate in court, and later as a traveling lecturer, Lucian moved eventually (probably when he was about 40) to Athens, where he abandoned rhetoric for philosophy. His 80 or so surviving works, many of which are in dialogue form, satirize a variety of contemporary institutions and manners, including popular religion and philosophical pretensions.

Martial (ca. AD 40–104). A penetratingly keen observer of human nature, Marcus Valerius Martialis of Bilbilis, Spain, lived at Rome from AD 64 until a few years before his death. His verse *Epigrams* (in 12 books) are succinct, and sometimes obscene, portraits of contemporary men and women. They are a rich source of information about private life and social customs in the last decades of the first century AD.

Ovid (43 BC–AD 17). Born at Sulmo, in central Italy, Publius Ovidius Naso was a prominent part of the literary culture of Rome in the time of Augustus. In AD 8, for reasons that are unclear, he was banished by Augustus to Tomis, on the Black Sea, where he spent the rest of his life, complaining (in *Letters from the Black Sea* and *Tristia*) about his isolation. His other surviving works include two collections of love poems, the *Amores* and the *Heroides*, the *Art of Love*, a cleverly subversive guide to seduction and intrigue, its companion-piece, the *Remedies of Love*, the *Metamorphoses*, an epic and original collection of stories about changes of shape, and the *Fasti*, a verse calendar of religious festivals and anniversaries.

Pausanius (mid-second century AD). Nothing is known about the life of Pausanius, a Greek geographer and traveler whose *Description of Greece*, in ten books, was meant to be a kind of tourist's guide to Greece, including its historical and religious artefacts.

Petronius (first century AD). Possibly the Petronius who is said to have been "arbiter of elegance" at the court of the emperor Nero, Petronius wrote both poetry (a small collection of which survives) and a novel, the *Satyricon*, which is only partially preserved. It recounts the adventures of two rather dissolute young men, Encolpius (the narrator) and Giton, including a fantastically extravagant dinner they attend at the home of a wealthy and comically vulgar ex-slave named Trimalchio.

Philo (ca. 30 BC–AD 45). Commonly known as Philo Judaeus, Philon was the head of the Jewish community in his native Alexandria. A theologian and philosopher, he is important mainly for his political writings *Against Flaccus*, which catalogs Jewish complaints about the governor of Egypt, and the *Embassy to Gaius*, his first-hand account of a delegation sent to Rome in AD 39/40 to ask Caligula to exempt the Jews from the duty of worshiping the emperor.

Pliny the Elder (AD 23/4–79). Uncle and adoptive father of Pliny the Younger, Gaius Plinius Secundus was born at Comum, in northern Italy. At one time commander of a cavalry squadron on the Rhine, he later held a series of prominent posts under the emperors Vespasian and Titus, culminating in his appointment as commander of the fleet stationed at Misenum (on the bay of Naples). He died observing the eruption of Mt. Vesuvius in AD 79. His only surviving work is the *Natural History*, an encyclopedic collection of pseudo-scientific lore, wondrous, and sometimes fanciful, stories about natural phenomena, people, animals, plants, metals, and stones.

Pliny the Younger (ca. AD 61–112). Like his uncle, Gaius Plinius Caecilius Secundus was born at Comum. A wealthy and well-connected lawyer, he had a long and distinguished public career, culminating in his appointment as governor of the province of Bithynia-Pontus (in mod. Turkey) in about AD 111/12. His *Letters*, 368 in all, are mostly formal and literary, many of them short essays on contemporary political and social issues. The tenth book, written when he was governor of Bithynia-Pontus, consists of his official correspondence with the emperor Trajan; it is an important source of information about Roman provincial administration. We possess also his *Panegyricus*, a ponderously effusive speech in praise of Trajan that he delivered in the Senate in AD 100.

Plutarch (before AD 50–after 120). Philosopher, priest (at Delphi), and occasional lecturer, Plutarch spent most of his life in his native Chaeronea, in central Greece. Most of his surviving works are contained in the *Moralia*, a collection of more than 60 short essays on a variety of topics, many of them ethical and religious. Extant also is the deservedly famous *Parallel Lives*, 50 biographies of Greek and Roman generals and political leaders, most of them organized in Greek–Roman pairs. They are adulatory, anecdotal, moralizing, vivid, and irresistibly readable.

Propertius (54/47–before 2 BC). Born to a prominent family at Assisi, Sextus Propertius became part of the literary circle at Rome patronized by Maecenas. His self-consciously elegant love poems, addressed to a woman he calls Cynthia (and whose real name is said to have been Hostia), are a window on Augustan thought and society.

Quintilian (ca. AD 30/5–100). A distinguished teacher of oratory, reportedly the first to be paid a salary by the state, Marcus Fabius Quintilianus was born at Calagurris (mod. Calahorra), Spain. His painstakingly detailed (and often lumbering) *Institutes of Oratory*, in 12 books, is easily our most comprehensive source of information about the nature and ideals of Roman education.

Seneca the Elder (ca. 55 BC–AD 37/41). Little is known of the life of Lucius Annaeus Seneca, father of the philosopher Seneca the Younger. Born at Corduba (mod. Córdoba), Spain, he acquired a considerable fortune, perhaps through trade, and probably spent much of his life at Rome. His surviving works on rhetoric, five books of *Controversiae* ("Debates") and one of *Suasoriae* ("Pleadings"), are a valuable source for the literary history of the early Empire.

Seneca the Younger (4 BC/AD 1–AD 65). Born, like his father, at Corduba, Lucius Annaeus Seneca served as tutor and adviser to Nero until AD 65, when he was implicated in a conspiracy against the emperor and forced to commit suicide. His many surviving works, which constitute our fullest guide to Roman Stoicism, include *Dialogues* on various ethical topics (e.g., anger), 124 *Moral Epistles*, 7 technical and tiresome books *On Benefits*, and 2 others, *On Clemency*, that he presented to Nero in AD 56. He also wrote *Natural Questions*, on physics and cosmology, 8 (perhaps 9) uninspired tragedies, and the *Apocolocyntosis* ("Pumpkinization"), a clever and original satire on the deification of the emperor Claudius.

Strabo (64/3 BC–after AD 21). A Greek historian and geographer, Strabo seems to have spent most of his life at his native Amaseia, in the province of Pontus. His *Geography*, which covers (in 17 books) the whole of Europe, western Asia, and North Africa, is an important source of information not only about historical geography, but also about economic and political history.

Suetonius (ca. AD 69–150). Born to a wealthy and politically active Roman family, Gaius Suetonius Tranquillus was a lawyer and, for a time, a secretary to the emperor Hadrian. His surviving works include several biographies of grammarians, rhetoricians, and poets (in the partially preserved *On the Lives of Illustrious Men*), and *The Lives of the Caesars*, biographies of Julius Caesar and of the first 11 emperors (i.e., from Augustus to Domitian). Anecodotal, credulous, and not infrequently gossipy, they present a fascinating and often arresting picture of the imperial court.

Tacitus (ca. AD 56–after 113). Arguably the greatest Roman historian, Cornelius Tacitus was born probably in southern Gaul or in northern Italy. He was consul in AD 97, and later (probably in 112/13) governor of the province of Asia. The earliest of his surviving works is the *Dialogue on Orators*, a pessimistic account of the decline of oratory. The *Agricola*, a biography of his father-in-law, Gnaeus Julius Agricola, governor of Britain, AD 78–84, provides valuable information about the pacification and Romanization of the province. The *Germania*, written about AD 100, is a fascinating account of the ethnography, military and political institutions, religion, and customs of the Germanic tribes. The *Annals*, a full-scale history (in 18 books) of the period AD 14–68, is only partially preserved: we have the whole of books 1–4, the beginning of 5, all of 6, the last part of 11, and all of 12–16 (covering the periods AD 14–29, 31–7, and 47–66). Eloquently incisive, often cynical, too narrowly focused on Rome and on the person of the emperor, it is far and away our most reliable source for the history of the early Empire. Of his *Histories*, which covered the period AD 69–96, only books 1–4 and the beginning of 5 survive (AD 69–70).

Tibullus (55/48–19 BC). Little is known about Tibullus (an anonymous biography makes him out to be something of a dilettante). His surviving love poetry, much of it addressed to a woman he calls Delia, and to a boy, Marathus, is a valuable source for the social and literary climate of Augustan Rome.

Valerius Maximus (time of Tiberius). Nothing at all is known about the life of Valerius Maximus, whose *Memorable Deeds and Sayings*, published probably soon after AD 31, is a collection of moralizing anecdotes for the use of teachers and rhetoricians. Simple and uncritical, it preserves some valuable information about famous people and about Roman institutions.

Velleius Paterculus (ca. 19 BC–after AD 30). An army officer from Campania (in central Italy), Velleius Paterculus wrote a *History of Rome* in two books, of which only the second, covering the period 146 BC–AD 30, is intact. Amateur and adulatory, it is valuable mainly for what it reveals (unintentionally) of the content and character of official propaganda in the time of Augustus and Tiberius.

Virgil (70–19 BC). Publius Vergilius Maro was born at Andes, a village near Mantua, in northern Italy. He studied rhetoric at Rome, where he befriended Horace, and became a prominent part of the literary circle of Maecenas. The *Eclogues*, written probably 45–37 BC, are ten pastoral poems (about shepherds and the like) set in Greece and modeled on Greek originals (especially Theocritus). The *Georgics*, written probably 36–29 BC to praise agriculture and Italy, deal in turn with crops, fruit trees, animals, and bees. It was, however, the *Aeneid*, begun in 26 BC and not quite finished at Vergil's death in 19, which established his reputation as the greatest Latin poet. Modeled on Homer, but infused with a nationalistic Roman patriotism, it recounts, in epic style, the adventures and travails of the legendary Trojan hero Aeneas.

Vitruvius (time of Augustus). An architect and military engineer, about whom little is known, Vitruvius Pollio is the author of *De architectura*, the only surviving Roman work on architecture. Written probably about 25–23 BC, it also discusses town-planning, water supply, and machines.

THE LATER ROMAN EMPIRE

Ammianus Marcellinus (ca. AD 330–95). A career military officer, Ammianus Marcellinus was born to a moderately wealthy family at Antioch, in Syria. Of the 31 books of his *History*, written in Latin (though his native language was Greek), only the last 18 survive, covering the period AD 353–78. A pagan who greatly admired the emperor Julian, he writes tolerantly of Christianity.

The Augustan History (fourth century AD?). Written perhaps in the middle of the fourth century AD, probably by a single author, the *Augustan History* (or *Lives of the Later Caesars*) is a collection of 30 biographies of the emperors (and usurpers) from Hadrian to Carinus and Numerianus (AD 117–284). They are entertaining, anecdotal, uncritical, and generally unreliable.

Aurelius Victor (mid-/late fourth century AD). Governor of the province of Pannonia (Secunda) in AD 361, and prefect of the city of Rome in 389, Sextus Aurelius Victor of North Africa was the author of *The Caesars*, a moralizing and biographically inspired history of the period from Augustus to Constantius (AD 360), which is much concerned with prodigies, and generally not of much value.

Ausonius (died ca. AD 395). Decimus Magnus Ausonius taught grammar and rhetoric at his native Bordeaux for 30 years, before being appointed tutor to the future emperor Gratian; he was later governor of Gaul, and, in AD 379, consul. His surviving works include 25 letters, and many poems, of which the most important, and charming, is the *Mosella*, written in praise of the river (it describes, in some detail, the various kinds of fish that could be found in it).

Claudian (ca. AD 370–404). A Greek-speaking native of Alexandria, Claudius Claudianus moved to Italy sometime before AD 395, where he served as court-poet to the emperor Honorius, and propagandist of Honorius' minister, Stilicho. A number of his poems survive, many of them political in purpose; they are a useful (if tendentious) guide to the history of the period.

Eutropius (late fourth century AD). Little is known of Eutropius, whose *Breviarium ab urbe condita* narrates the whole of Roman history from Romulus to AD 364. Drawn mainly from secondary materials, it is valuable chiefly for filling gaps in other sources.

Julian (AD 332–63). Caesar from AD 355, and emperor 361–3, Flavius Claudius Julianus is probably best known for his attempt to revive paganism. His surviving works include *The Beard-Hater*, a satirical defense of his policies, *The Banquet* (or *The Caesars*), a waggish account of Constantine's reception on Mt. Olympus, 8 speeches, and about 80 *Letters*, many of which are anti-Christian.

Libanius (AD 314–ca. 393). Libanius spent much of his life at his native Antioch (in Syria), where he taught rhetoric. A pagan who admired the emperor Julian, he was not altogether unsympathetic to Christianity. A great many of his works are preserved, including 64 speeches, most of which are concerned with public and municipal affairs, and about 1,600 letters, which constitute a storehouse of information about the social, cultural, and political life of the urban elite of the eastern half of the empire in the fourth century AD.

Macrobius (late fourth/early fifth centuries AD). Little is known about the life of Ambrosius Theodosius Macrobius; he may have been North African. His most important work is the antiquarian *Saturnalia*, a fictitious symposium, in seven books, which deals mainly with philology, history, and literary criticism (especially of Virgil).

Procopius (ca. AD 500–after 562). Born at Caesarea in Palestine, trained in law and rhetoric, Procopius held a series of military and administrative posts under the emperor Justinian, culminating in his appointment as prefect of the city of Constantinople in AD 562. His main works are the generally reliable *History of the Wars of Justinian*, in eight books, and the *Secret History*, written about AD 550, a sustained and scurrilous attack on Justinian and his policies.

Symmachus (ca. AD 340–402). Widely acknowledged to be the greatest orator of his day, Quintus Aurelius Symmachus held a number of prominent positions in the imperial administration, including a consulship in AD 391. A vigorous opponent of Christianity, he wrote numerous letters (many of which survive) and speeches, including two in praise of the emperors Valentinian I and Gratian, which are important sources for the history of the period.

Zosimus (late fifth century AD). Not much is known about the life of Zosimus, who is said to have held several imperial posts. His *New History*, which covers the period from Augustus to AD 410, is valuable mainly for its account of the years after 305, and for its interpretation of the decline of the Empire, which Zosimus attributes to neglect of the pagan gods.

CHRISTIAN WRITERS

Augustine (AD 354–430). Born at Thagaste (mod. Souk Ahras, Algeria), Aurelius Augustinus taught rhetoric at Carthage and in Italy (at Rome and Milan), where he converted to Christianity. From AD 395, he was bishop of Hippo (mod. Bône, Algeria). More than a hundred of his works are preserved, including many letters and sermons, and what are probably his two most important works, the *City of God*, a reply to anti-Christian propaganda (in 22 books), and the *Confessions*, a vivid and highly personal account of his life (to 388), and of his conversion.

Cyprian (ca. AD 200–58). The son of a wealthy and well-connected family, Thascius Caecilius Cyprianus became bishop of Carthage in AD 248. His surviving works include *On the Unity of the Catholic Church* and *On Those Who Have Lapsed*, which deal mainly with the consequences of the persecutions that began under the emperor Decius in 249,

To Donatus, a denunciation of worldliness, and *Letters*, most of which are concerned with the organization and management of the Church.

Eusebius (ca. AD 260–340). Born in Palestine, Eusebius became bishop of Caesarea about AD 314. His most important work is the *Ecclesiastical History*, which describes, in ten books, the development of the church to AD 324. He also wrote an adulatory *Life of Constantine*, and a chronology of universal history, which is preserved in an Armenian version and in a Latin adaptation by Jerome.

Jerome (ca. AD 348–420). A vocal champion of asceticism, Eusebius Hieronymus was widely considered to be the most learned man of his time. Best known for his Latin translation of the Bible (the Vulgate), he also wrote *On the Lives of Illustrious Men*, an introduction to 135 Christian writers, an historical chronology (*Chronicle*), based on Eusebius, and numerous letters.

Lactantius (ca. AD 240–320). Born probably at Carthage, Lucius Caecilius Firmianus, who was known also as Lactantius, taught rhetoric for a time at Nicomedia (near mod. Istanbul); he was later appointed tutor to the emperor Constantine's eldest son, Crispus. His most important surviving works are the *Divine Institutes*, a reply, in seven books, to pagan attacks on Christianity, and *On the Deaths of the Persecutors*, an account of the sufferings of the persecutors, written probably about AD 318.

Minucius Felix (early/mid-third century AD). Nothing is known of the life of Marcus Minucius Felix. His only surviving work is the *Octavius*, a dialogue between a Christian, Octavius, and a pagan, Caecilius Natalis, whose case against Christianity borrows heavily from Fronto.

Origen (ca. AD 185/6–254/5). Origenes Adamantius spent much of his life as a teacher, first at his native Alexandria, later at Caesarea (in Palestine). His writing, which included commentaries on the Bible and an exposition of Christian doctrine (*De principiis*), is preserved only in bits and pieces. The main surviving work is *Against Celsus*, written, probably about AD 249, to counter anti-Christian propaganda.

Orosius (early fifth century AD). A native of Spain, Paulus Orosius was a student of Augustine from AD 414. His *History Against the Pagans* is a history of the world, in seven books, from creation to AD 417. Rhetorical, and not infrequently mistaken, it was written to demonstrate that the calamities of the imperial period were not a consequence of the spread of Christianity.

Prudentius (AD 348–after 405). Aurelius Clemens Prudentius of Spain abandoned a distinguished administrative career to write Christian poetry. His surviving works include hymns, allegories, and *Against Symmachus*, a polemic against paganism.

Tertullian (ca. AD 160–240). Born at (or near) Carthage, Quintus Septimius Florens Tertullianus was trained as a lawyer, but converted to Christianity about AD 195. His more than 30 surviving works include *To the Pagans* and *Apology*, both written (in about 197) to defend Christianity against popular charges of atheism and black magic.

GUIDE TO FURTHER READING

GENERAL

REFERENCE WORKS

Cary, M. *The Geographic Background of Greek and Roman History.* Oxford, 1949.

Crawford, M. H. *Roman Republican Coinage*, 2 vols. Cambridge, 1987.

Dilke, O. A. W. *Greek and Roman Maps.* London, 1985.

Hammond, N. G. L. (ed.). *Atlas of the Greek and Roman World in Antiquity.* Park Ridge, NJ, 1981.

Hammond, N. G. L. and Scullard, H. H. (eds). *The Oxford Classical Dictionary*, 2nd edn. Oxford, 1970.

Keppie, L. *Understanding Roman Inscriptions.* Baltimore, 1991.

Stillwell, R., MacDonald, W. L. and McAllister, M. H. (eds). *The Princeton Encyclopedia of Classical Sites.* Princeton, 1976.

Sutherland, C. H. V. and Carson, R. A. G. (eds). *The Roman Imperial Coinage*, 9 vols. London, 1984.

GENERAL STUDIES

Boardman, J., Griffin, J. and Murray, O. (eds). *The Oxford History of the Roman World.* Oxford, 1991.

Kenney, E. J. (ed.). *Latin Literature.* Vol. 2 of *The Cambridge History of Classical Literature.* Cambridge, 1982.

Wacher, J. (ed.). *The Roman World*, 2 vols. London, 1987.

THE ROMAN REPUBLIC TO 133 BC

GENERAL HISTORIES

Astin, A. E., Walbank, F. W., Fredericksen, M. W. and Ogilvie, R. M. (eds). *Rome and the Mediterranean to 133 B.C.* Vol. 8 of *The Cambridge Ancient History*, 2nd edn. Cambridge, 1989.

Brunt, P. A. *Social Conflicts in the Roman Republic.* New York and London, 1971.

Cornell, T. J. *The Beginnings of Rome: Italy and Rome from the Bronze Age to the Punic Wars (c. 1000–264 BC).* London and New York, 1995.

Heurgon, J. *The Rise of Rome.* Trans. J. Willis. Berkeley, 1973.

Scullard, H. H. *A History of the Roman World, 753–146 B.C.*, 4th edn. London and New York, 1980.

Walbank, F. W., Astin, A. E., Fredericksen, M. W., Ogilvie, R. M. and Drummond, A. (eds). *The Rise of Rome to 220 B.C.* Vol. 7, Part 2 of *The Cambridge Ancient History*, 2nd edn. Cambridge, 1989.

PRE-ROMAN ITALY

Barker, G. *Landscape and Society: Prehistoric Central Italy.* London, 1981.

Boardman, J. *The Greeks Overseas: Their Early Colonies and Trade*, new and enlarged edn. London, 1980.

Bonfante, L. *Etruscan Life and Afterlife: A Handbook of Etruscan Studies.* Detroit, 1986.

Hencken, H. *Tarquinia and Etruscan Origins.* New York and Washington, 1968.

Pallottino, M. *The Etruscans*, revised and enlarged edn. Trans. J. Cremona. Bloomington, 1975.

Pallottino, M. *A History of Earliest Italy.* Trans. M. Ryle and K. Soper. Ann Arbor, 1991.

Ridgway, D. and Ridgway, F. R. (eds). *Italy before the Romans: The Iron Age, Orientalizing and Etruscan Periods.* London, 1979.

Scullard, H. H. *The Etruscan Cities and Rome.* Ithaca, NY, 1967.

PRE-REPUBLICAN ROME

Alföldi, A. *Early Rome and the Latins.* Ann Arbor, 1965.

Bloch, R. *The Origins of Rome.* New York and Washington, 1960.

Bremmer, J. N. and Horsfall, N. M. *Roman Myth and Mythography.* London, 1987.

Ogilvie, R. M. *A Commentary on Livy, Books 1–5.* Oxford, 1965.

POLITICS AND GOVERNMENT

Kunkel, W. *An Introduction to Roman Legal and Constitutional History*, 2nd edn. Trans. J. M. Kelly. Oxford, 1972.

Millar, F. "The Political Character of the Classical Roman Republic, 200–151 B.C." *Journal of Roman Studies*, 74 (1984), 1–19.

Mitchell, R. E. *Patricians and Plebeians: The Origin of the Roman State.* Ithaca, NY, 1990.

Nicolet, C. *The World of the Citizen in Republican Rome*, 2nd edn. Trans. P. S. Falla. Berkeley and Los Angeles, 1980.

Raaflaub, K. A. (ed.). *Social Struggles in Archaic Rome: New Perspectives on the Conflict of the Orders.* Berkeley and Los Angeles, 1986.

Scullard, H. H. *Roman Politics, 220–150 B.C.*, 2nd edn. Oxford, 1973.

Sherwin-White, A. N. *The Roman Citizenship*, 2nd edn. Oxford, 1973.

THE ARMY, WAR, AND IMPERIALISM

Caven, B. *The Punic Wars.* New York, 1980.

Curchin, L. A. *Roman Spain: Conquest and Assimilation.* London, 1991.

David, J.-M. *The Roman Consquest of Italy.* Trans. Antonia Nevill. Oxford, 1996.

Dyson, S. *The Creation of the Roman Frontier.* Princeton, 1985.

Harris, W. V. *Rome in Etruria and Umbria.* Oxford, 1971.

Harris, W. V. *War and Imperialism in Republican Rome, 327–70 B.C.* Oxford, 1979.

Harris, W. V. (ed.). *The Imperialism of Mid-Republican Rome.* Rome, 1984.

Lazenby, J. F. *Hannibal's War: A Military History of the Second Punic War.* Warminster, 1978.

Lazenby, J. F. *The First Punic War: A Military History.* London, 1996.

Richardson, J. S. *Hispaniae: Spain and the Development of Roman Imperialism, 218–82 B.C.* Cambridge, 1986.

Salmon, E. T. *Samnium and the Samnites.* Cambridge, 1967.

Salmon, E. T. *Roman Colonization under the Republic.* Ithaca, NY, 1970.

Salmon, E. T. *The Making of Roman Italy.* Ithaca, NY, 1982.

Toynbee, A. J. *Hannibal's Legacy: The Hannibalic War's Effect on Roman Life*, 2 vols. London, 1965.

FOREIGN POLICY AND EXTERNAL RELATIONS
Badian, E. *Foreign Clientelae (264–70 B.C)*. Oxford, 1958.
Badian, E. "Notes on Roman Policy in Illyria (230–201 B.C.)," in E. Badian, *Studies in Greek and Roman History* (Oxford, 1964), 1–33.
Crawford, M. H. "Rome and the Greek World: Economic Relations," *Economic History Review*, 30 (1977), 42–52.
Eckstein, A. M. *Senate and General: Individual Decision-Making and Roman Foreign Relations, 264–194 B.C.* Berkeley and Los Angeles, 1987.
Gruen, E. S. *The Hellenistic World and the Coming of Rome*, 2 vols. Berkeley and Los Angeles, 1984.

RELIGION
Dumézil, G. *Archaic Roman Religion: With an Appendix on the Religion of the Etruscans.* Trans. P. Krapp, 2 vols. Chicago and London, 1970.
Michels, A. K. *The Calendar of the Roman Republic.* Princeton, 1967.
Scullard, H. H. *Festivals and Ceremonies of the Roman Republic.* Ithaca, NY, 1981.

INTELLECTUAL LIFE
Gruen, E. S. *Studies in Greek Culture and Roman Policy.* Leiden, 1990.
Gruen, E. S. *Culture and National Identity in Republican Rome.* London, 1993.
Momigliano, A. *Alien Wisdom: The Limits of Hellenization.* Cambridge, 1975.
Segal, E. *Roman Laughter: The Comedy of Plautus*, 2nd edn. London, 1987.
Wardman, A. *Rome's Debt to Greece.* London, 1976.

HISTORIANS AND HISTORIOGRAPHY
Badian, E. "The Early Historians," in T. A. Dorey (ed.), *Latin Historians* (London, 1966), 1–38.
Walbank, F. W. *Polybius.* Berkeley and Los Angeles, 1972.
Walsh, P. G. *Livy: His Historical Aims and Methods*, 2nd edn. Bristol, 1989.

LAW
Bauman, R. A. *Lawyers in Roman Republican Politics: A Study of the Roman Jurists in their Political Setting, 316–82 B.C.* Munich, 1983.
Watson, A. *Roman Private Law around 200 B.C.* Princeton, 1971.
Watson, A. *Rome of the Twelve Tables: Persons and Property.* Princeton, 1976.

BIOGRAPHY
Astin, A. E. *Scipio Aemilianus.* Oxford, 1967.
Astin, A. E. *Cato the Censor.* Oxford, 1978.
Scullard, H. H. *Scipio Africanus: Soldier and Politician.* Ithaca, NY, 1970.

THE ROMAN WORLD, 133 BC–AD 235

GENERAL HISTORIES
Beard, M. and Crawford, M. H. *Rome in the Late Republic: Problems and Interpretations.* Ithaca, NY, 1985.

Bowman, A. K., Champlin, E. and Lintott, A. (eds). *The Augustan Empire, 43* B.C.–A.D. *69.* Vol. 10 of *The Cambridge Ancient History,* 2nd edn. Cambridge, 1996.

Crook, J. A., Lintott, A., and Rawson, E. (eds). *The Last Age of the Roman Republic, 146–43* B.C. Vol. 9 of *The Cambridge Ancient History,* 2nd edn. Cambridge, 1994.

Garzetti, A. *From Tiberius to the Antonines: A History of the Roman Empire,* A.D. *14–192.* Trans. J. R. Foster. London, 1976.

Millar, F. et al. *The Roman Empire and its Neighbors,* 2nd edn. New York, 1981.

Scullard, H. H. *From the Gracchi to Nero: A History of Rome from 133* B.C. *to* A.D. *68,* 5th edn. London and New York, 1982.

Wells, C. M. *The Roman Empire,* 2nd edn. London, 1992.

POLITICS AND GOVERNMENT

Badian, E. *Publicans and Sinners: Private Enterprise in the Service of the Roman Republic,* revised edn. Ithaca and London, 1983.

Bowersock, G. W. *Augustus and the Greek World.* Oxford, 1965.

Brunt, P. A. *The Fall of the Roman Republic and Related Essays.* Oxford, 1988.

Brunt, P. A. *Roman Imperial Themes.* Oxford, 1990.

Earl, D. *The Moral and Political Tradition of Rome.* Ithaca, NY, 1967.

Earl, D. *The Age of Augustus.* London, 1968.

Gelzer, M. *The Roman Nobility.* Trans. R. Seager. Oxford, 1969.

Gruen, E. S. *The Last Generation of the Roman Republic.* Berkeley and Los Angeles, 1974.

Hopkins, K. *Death and Renewal: Sociological Studies in Roman History, Vol. 2.* Cambridge, 1983.

MacMullen, R. *Enemies of the Roman Order: Treason, Unrest and Alienation in the Empire.* Cambridge, Mass., 1966.

Millar, F. *The Emperor in the Roman World, 31* B.C.–A.D. *337,* 2nd edn. London, 1992.

Raaflaub, K. and Toher, M. (eds). *Between Republic and Empire: Interpretations of Augustus and his Principate.* Berkeley, 1990.

Seager, R. (ed.). *The Crisis of the Roman Republic: Studies in Political and Social History.* Cambridge, 1969.

Shatzman, I. *Senatorial Wealth and Roman Politics.* Brussels, 1975.

Stockton, D. *The Gracchi.* Oxford, 1979.

Syme, R. *The Roman Revolution.* Oxford, 1939.

Syme, R. *Roman Papers,* 7 vols. New York, 1979–91.

Talbert, R. J. A. *The Senate of Imperial Rome.* Princeton, 1984.

Taylor, L. R. *Party Politics in the Age of Caesar.* Berkeley and Los Angeles, 1949.

Wirszubski, C. *Libertas as a Political Idea at Rome during the Late Republic and Early Principate.* Cambridge, 1950.

Wiseman, T. P. *New Men in the Roman Senate 139* B.C.–A.D. *14.* London, 1971.

Yavetz, Z. *Plebs and Princeps.* Oxford, 1969.

Zanker, P. *The Power of Images in the Age of Augustus.* Trans. A. Shapiro. Ann Arbor, 1988.

THE ARMY AND THE FRONTIERS

Badian, F. *Roman Imperialism in the Late Republic,* 2nd edn. Ithaca, NY, 1968.

Birley, E. *The Roman Army: Papers, 1929–1986.* Amsterdam, 1988.

Breeze, D. J. and Dobson, B. *Roman Officers and Frontiers.* Stuttgart, 1993.

Brunt, P. A. "The Army and the Land in the Roman Revolution," in P. A. Brunt, *The Fall of the Roman Republic and Related Essays* (Oxford, 1988), 240–80.

Brunt, P. A. "Laus Imperii," in P. A. Brunt, *Roman Imperial Themes* (Oxford, 1990), 288–323.

Campbell, J. B. *The Emperor and the Roman Army, 31 B.C.–A.D. 235.* New York, 1984.

Davies, R. W. *Service in the Roman Army,* ed. D. J. Breeze and V. A. Maxfield. New York, 1989.

Dixon, K. R. and Southern, P. *The Roman Cavalry: From the First to the Third Century A.D.* London, 1992.

Gabba, E. *Republican Rome: The Army and the Allies.* Trans. P. J. Cuff. Berkeley and Los Angeles, 1976.

Goldsworthy, A. K. *The Roman Army at War, 100 BC–AD 200.* Oxford, 1996.

Isaac, B. *The Limits of Empire: The Roman Army in the East,* 2nd edn. Oxford, 1992.

Keppie, L. *The Making of the Roman Army: From Republic to Empire.* Totowa, NJ, 1984.

Keppie, L. *Colonization and Veteran Settlement in Italy, 47–14 B.C.* London, 1985.

Luttwak, E. N. *The Grand Strategy of the Roman Empire: From the First Century A.D. to the Third.* Baltimore, 1976.

Mann, J. C. *Legionary Recruitment and Veteran Settlement during the Principate,* ed. M. M. Roxan. London, 1983.

Maxfield, V. A. et al. "The Frontiers," in J. Wacher (ed.), *The Roman World* (London, 1987), vol. 1, 139–325.

Robinson, H. R. *The Armour of Imperial Rome.* New York, 1975.

Saddington, D. B. *The Development of the Roman Auxiliary Forces from Caesar to Vespasian (49 B.C.–A.D. 79).* Harare, 1982.

Smith, R. E. *Service in the Post-Marian Roman Army.* Manchester, 1958.

Watson, G. R. *The Roman Soldier.* London, 1969.

Webster, G. *The Roman Imperial Army of the First and Second Centuries A.D.,* 3rd edn. Totowa, NJ, 1985.

Whittaker, C. R. *Frontiers of the Roman Empire: A Social and Economic Study.* Baltimore, 1994.

REGIONAL HISTORIES

Alföldy, G. *Noricum.* Trans. A. R. Birley. London, 1974.

Blagg, T. and Millett, M. (eds). *The Early Roman Empire in the West.* Oxford, 1990.

Bowersock, G. *Roman Arabia.* Cambridge, Mass., 1983.

Collingwood, R. G. and Richmond, I. A. *The Archaeology of Roman Britain,* rev. edn. London, 1969.

Drinkwater, J. F. *Roman Gaul: The Three Provinces, 58 B.C.–A.D. 260.* Ithaca, NY, 1983.

Frere, S. S. *Britannia: A History of Roman Britain,* 3rd edn. London, 1987.

Goodman, M. *State and Society in Roman Galilee, A.D. 132–212.* Totowa, NJ, 1983.

Keay, S. J. *Roman Spain.* Berkeley, 1988.

Lewis, N. *Life in Egypt under Roman Rule.* New York, 1983.

Magie, D. *Roman Rule in Asia Minor to the End of the Third Century after Christ,* 2 vols. London, 1950.

Millar, F. *The Roman Near East, 31 B.C.–A.D. 337.* Cambridge, Mass. and London, 1993.

Millett, M. *The Romanization of Britain: An Essay in Archaeological Interpretation.* Cambridge, 1990.

Mócsy, A. *Pannonia and Upper Moesia: A History of the Middle Danube Provinces of the Roman Empire.* Trans. S. S. Frere. Boston, 1974.

529

Potter, T. W. *Roman Italy.* Berkeley, 1987.

Raven, S. *Rome in Africa,* 3rd edn. New York, 1993.

Richardson, J. S. *The Romans in Spain.* Oxford, 1996.

Salway, P. *Roman Britain.* Oxford, 1981.

Schürer, E. *The History of the Jewish People in the Age of Jesus Christ* (*175* B.C.–A.D. *135*), rev. edn., 3 vols. Trans. T. A. Burkill et al. Edinburgh, 1973–87.

Sherwin-White, A. N. *Roman Foreign Policy in the East, 168* B.C.–A.D. *1.* Norman and London, 1984.

Sullivan, R. *Near Eastern Royalty and Rome, 100–30* B.C. Toronto, 1990.

Todd, M. (ed.). *Research on Roman Britain, 1960–89.* London, 1989.

Wightman, E. M. *Gallia Belgica.* Berkeley, 1985.

Wilkes, J. J. *Dalmatia.* Cambridge, Mass., 1969.

Wilson, R. J. A. *Sicily under the Roman Empire: The Archaeology of a Roman Province, 36* B.C.–A.D. *535.* Warminster, 1990.

ECONOMY, DEMOGRAPHY, AND MATERIAL CONDITIONS

Bagnall, R. S. and Frier, B. W. *The Demography of Roman Egypt.* Cambridge, 1994.

Barker, G. and Lloyd, J. (eds). *Roman Landscapes: Archaeological Survey in the Mediterranean Region.* London, 1991.

Brunt, P. A. "Free Labour and Public Works," *Journal of Roman Studies,* 70 (1980), 81–100.

Brunt, P. A. *Italian Manpower 225* B.C.–A.D. *14,* reprinted edn. Oxford, 1989.

Crawford, M. H. *Coinage and Money under the Roman Republic: Italy and the Mediterranean Economy.* London, 1985.

D'Arms, J. and Kopff, E. C. (eds). *The Seaborne Commerce of Ancient Rome: Studies in Archaeology and History.* Rome, 1980.

Duncan-Jones, R. P. *The Economy of the Roman Empire: Quantitative Studies,* 2nd edn. Cambridge, 1982.

Duncan-Jones, R. P. *Structure and Scale in the Roman Economy.* Cambridge, 1990.

Duncan-Jones, R. P. *Money and Government in the Roman Empire.* Cambridge, 1994.

Finley, M. I. (ed.). *Studies in Roman Property.* Cambridge, 1976.

Finley, M. I. *The Ancient Economy,* 2nd edn. Berkeley, 1985.

Garnsey, P. *Famine and Food Supply in the Graeco-Roman World: Responses to Risk and Crisis.* Cambridge, 1988.

Garnsey, P., Hopkins, K. and Whittaker, C. R. (eds). *Trade in the Ancient Economy.* Berkeley, 1983.

Garnsey, P. and Saller, R. P. *The Roman Empire: Economy, Society and Culture.* Berkeley, 1987.

Garnsey, P. and Whittaker, C. R. (eds). *Trade and Famine in Classical Antiquity.* Cambridge, 1983.

Greene, K. *The Archaeology of the Roman Economy.* Berkeley, 1986.

Hopkins, K. "Taxes and Trade in the Roman Empire (200 B.C.–A.D. 400)," *Journal of Roman Studies,* 70 (1980), 101–25.

Jongman, W. *The Economy and Society of Pompeii.* Amsterdam, 1988.

Kehoe, D. P. *The Economics of Agriculture on Roman Imperial Estates in North Africa,* Göttingen, 1988.

Parker, A. J. *Ancient Shipwrecks of the Mediterranean and the Roman Provinces.* Oxford, 1992.

Parkin, T. G. *Demography and Roman Society*. Baltimore and London, 1992.

Peacock, D. P. S. and Williams, D. F. *Amphorae and the Roman Economy: An Introductory Guide*. London, 1986.

Raschke, M. G. "New Studies in Roman Commerce with the East," *Aufstieg und Niedergang der römischen Welt*, 9.2 (1978), 604–1378.

Rich, J. and Wallace-Hadrill, A. (eds). *City and Country in the Ancient World*. London, 1991.

Rostovtzeff, M. *The Social and Economic History of the Roman Empire*, 2nd edn, ed. P. M. Fraser, 2 vols. Oxford, 1957.

Spurr, M. S. *Arable Cultivation in Roman Italy, c. 200 B.C.–A.D. 100*. London, 1986.

Veyne, P. *Bread and Circuses: Historical Sociology and Political Pluralism*. Trans. B. Pearce. London, 1990.

White, K. D. *Roman Farming*. Ithaca, NY, 1970.

Whittaker, C. R. (ed.). *Pastoral Economies in Classical Antiquity*. Cambridge, 1988.

Whittaker, C. R. *Land, City and Trade in the Roman Empire*. Brookfield, Vt., 1993.

SOCIETY

Balsdon, J. P. V. D. *Life and Leisure in Ancient Rome*. London, 1974.

Bradley, K. R. *Slavery and Rebellion in the Roman World, 140 B.C.–70 B.C.* Bloomington, 1989.

Bradley, K. R. *Slavery and Society at Rome*. Cambridge, 1994.

Brunt, P. A. "The Roman Mob," in M. I. Finley (ed.), *Studies in Ancient Society* (London and Boston, 1974), 74–102.

D'Arms, J. *Romans on the Bay of Naples: A Social and Cultural Study of the Villas and their Owners from 150 B.C. to A.D. 400*. Cambridge, Mass., 1970.

D'Arms, J. *Commerce and Social Standing in Ancient Rome*. Cambridge, Mass. and London, 1981.

Dyson, S. L. *Community and Society in Roman Italy*. Baltimore, 1992.

Finley, M. I. (ed.). *Classical Slavery*. Totowa, NJ, 1987.

Gardner, J. F. *Being a Roman Citizen*. London and New York, 1993.

Garnsey, P. *Social Status and Legal Privilege in the Roman Empire*. Oxford, 1970.

Hopkins, K. *Conquerors and Slaves: Sociological Studies in Roman History*, vol. I. Cambridge, 1978.

Lintott, A. W. *Violence in Republican Rome*. New York, 1968.

MacMullen, R. *Roman Social Relations, 50 B.C. to A.D. 284*. New Haven, 1974.

MacMullen, R. *Changes in the Roman Empire: Essays in the Ordinary*. Princeton, 1990.

de Ste Croix, G. E. M. *The Class Struggle in the Ancient Greek World from the Archaic Age to the Arab Conquests*. Ithaca, NY, 1981.

Saller, R. P. *Personal Patronage under the Early Empire*. Cambridge, 1982.

Sebesta, J. L. and Bonfante, L. (eds). *The World of Roman Costume*. Madison, Wis., 1994.

Sherwin-White, A. N. *Racial Prejudice in Imperial Rome*. Cambridge, 1970.

Snowden, Jr, F. M. *Before Color Prejudice: The Ancient View of Blacks*. Cambridge, Mass., 1983.

Thompson, L. A. *Romans and Blacks*. Norman, 1989.

Treggiari, S. *Roman Freedmen during the Late Republic*. Oxford, 1969.

Veyne, P. (ed.). *From Pagan Rome to Byzantium*. Vol. 1 of *A History of Private Life*, ed. P. Ariès and G. Duby. Trans. A. Goldhammer. Cambridge, Mass., 1987.

Wallace-Hadrill, A. "Patronage in Roman Society: From Republic to Empire," in A. Wallace-Hadrill (ed.), *Patronage in Ancient Society* (London and New York, 1989), 63–87.

Wallace-Hadrill, A. *Houses and Society in Pompeii and Herculaneum.* Princeton, 1994.

Wiedemann, T. E. J. *Emperors and Gladiators.* London and New York, 1992.

WOMEN AND THE FAMILY

Bradley, K. *Discovering the Roman Family: Studies in Roman Social History.* New York, 1991.

Dixon, S. *The Roman Mother.* Norman and London, 1988.

Dixon, S. *The Roman Family.* Baltimore, 1992.

Evans, J. K. *War, Women and Children in Ancient Rome.* London and New York, 1991.

Fantham, E., Foley, H. P., Kampen, N. B., Pomeroy, S. B. and Shapiro, H. A. *Women in the Classical World: Image and Text.* Oxford, 1994.

Gardner, J. F. *Women in Roman Law and Society.* Bloomington, 1986.

Gardner, J. F. and Wiedemann, T. E. J. *The Roman Household: A Sourcebook.* London and New York, 1991.

Hallett, J. *Fathers and Daughters in Roman Society: Women and the Elite Family.* Princeton, 1984.

Kampen, N. *Image and Status: Roman Working Women in Ostia.* Berlin, 1981.

Pomeroy, S. *Goddesses, Whores, Wives and Slaves: Women in Classical Antiquity.* New York, 1975.

Rawson, B. (ed.). *The Family in Ancient Rome: New Perspectives.* Ithaca, NY, 1986.

Rawson, B. (ed.). *Marriage, Divorce and Children in Ancient Rome.* Oxford and New York, 1992.

Rawson, B. and Weaver, P. (eds). *The Roman Family in Italy: Status, Sentiment, Space.* Canberra and Oxford, 1997.

Saller, R. P. *Patriarchy, Property and Death in the Roman Family.* Cambridge, 1994.

Treggiari, S. *Roman Marriage: Iusti Coniuges from the Time of Cicero to the Time of Ulpian.* Oxford, 1991.

Wiedemann, T. E. J. *Adults and Children in the Roman Empire.* New Haven and London, 1989.

PAGAN RELIGION

Ferguson, J. *The Religions of the Roman Empire.* London, 1970.

Heyob, S. K. *The Cult of Isis among Women in the Graeco-Roman World.* Leiden, 1975.

Hinnells, J. R. (ed.). *Mithraic Studies: Proceedings of the First International Congress of Mithraic Studies,* 2 vols. Totowa, NJ, 1975.

Liebeschuetz, J. H. W. G. *Continuity and Change in Roman Religion.* New York, 1979.

MacMullen, R. *Paganism in the Roman Empire.* New Haven, 1981.

Ogilvie, R. M. *The Romans and their Gods in the Age of Augustus.* London, 1969.

Price, S. R. F. *Rituals and Power: The Roman Imperial Cult in Asia Minor.* Cambridge, 1984.

Turcan, R. *The Cults of the Roman Empire.* Trans. Antonia Nevill. Oxford, 1996.

Vermaseren, M. J. *Cybele and Attis: The Myth and Cult.* Trans. A. M. H. Lemmers. London, 1977.

Wardman, A. *Religion and Statecraft among the Romans.* London, 1982.

Weinstock, S. *Divus Iulius.* Oxford, 1971.

JUDAISM AND CHRISTIANITY

Benko, S. *Pagan Rome and the Early Christians*. Bloomington, 1984.

Chadwick, H. *The Early Church*. Grand Rapids, Mich., 1967.

Frend, W. H. C. *Martyrdom and Persecution in the Early Church: A Study of Conflict from the Maccabees to Donatus*. Oxford, 1965.

Frend, W. H. C. *The Rise of Christianity*. London, 1984.

Lane Fox, R. *Pagans and Christians in the Mediterranean World from the Second Century A.D. to the Conversion of Constantine*. Harmondsworth and New York, 1986.

Leon, H. J. *The Jews of Ancient Rome*. Philadelphia, 1960.

Lieu, J., North, J. A. and Rajak, T. (eds). *The Jews among Pagans and Christians in the Roman Empire*. London, 1992.

MacMullen, R. *Christianizing the Roman Empire* (A.D. *100–400*). New Haven, 1984.

Meeks, W. A. *The First Urban Christians: The Social World of the Apostle Paul*. New Haven, 1983.

Musurillo, H. (ed.). *The Acts of the Christian Martyrs*. Oxford, 1972.

Wilcken, R. L. *The Christians as the Romans Saw Them*. New Haven, 1984.

INTELLECTUAL LIFE
(LITERATURE, PHILOSOPHY, EDUCATION)

Barnes, T. D. *Tertullian: A Historical and Literary Study*. Oxford, 1971.

Beard, M. et al. (eds). *Literacy in the Roman World*. Ann Arbor, 1991.

Bonner, S. F. *Education in Ancient Rome: From the Elder Cato to the Younger Pliny*. Berkeley and Los Angeles, 1977.

Bowersock, G. W. *Greek Sophists in the Roman Empire*. Oxford, 1969.

Bowman, A. K. and Woolf, G. (eds). *Literacy and Power in the Ancient World*. Cambridge, 1994.

Champlin, E. *Fronto and Antonine Rome*. Cambridge, Mass., 1980.

Griffin, J. *Latin Poets and Roman Life*. Chapel Hill, 1986.

Harris, W. V. *Ancient Literacy*. Cambridge, Mass., 1986.

Jones, C. P. *Plutarch and Rome*. Oxford, 1972.

Jones, C. P. *The Roman World of Dio Chrysostom*. Cambridge, Mass., 1978.

Kennedy, G. *The Art of Rhetoric in the Roman World 300 B.C.–A.D. 300*. Vol. 2 of G. Kennedy, *A History of Rhetoric*. Princeton, 1972.

Rawson, E. *Intellectual Life in the Late Roman Republic*. Baltimore, 1985.

Sandbach, F. H. *The Stoics*, 2nd edn. Bristol, 1989.

Sherwin-White, A. N. *The Letters of Pliny: A Historical and Social Commentary*. Oxford, 1985.

Wiseman, T. P. *Roman Studies: Literary and Historical*. Liverpool, 1987.

Woodman, A. J. and West, D. (eds). *Poetry and Politics in the Age of Augustus*. Cambridge, 1984.

ART, ARCHITECTURE, AND ENGINEERING

Andreae, B. *The Art of Rome*. Trans. R. E. Wolf. New York, 1977.

Blake, M. E. *Ancient Roman Construction in Italy from the Prehistoric Period to Augustus*. Washington, 1949.

Blake, M. E. *Roman Construction in Italy from Tiberius through the Flavians*. Washington, 1959.

Blake, M. E. and Bishop, D. T. *Roman Construction in Italy from Nerva through the Antonines*. Philadelphia, 1973.

Boatwright, M. T. *Hadrian and the City of Rome.* Princeton, 1987.

Bruun, C. *The Water Supply of Ancient Rome: A Study of Roman Imperial Administration.* Helsinki, 1991.

Chevallier, R. *Roman Roads,* rev. edn. Trans. N. H. Field. London, 1989.

Clarke, J. R. *The Houses of Roman Italy, 100 B.C.–A.D. 250: Ritual, Space and Decoration.* Berkeley, 1991.

Dunbabin, K. M. D. *The Mosaics of Roman North Africa: Studies in Iconography and Patronage.* New York, 1978.

Henig, M. (ed.). *A Handbook of Roman Art: A Comprehensive Survey of All the Arts of the Roman World.* Ithaca, NY, 1983.

Higgins, R. *Greek and Roman Jewellery,* 2nd edn. Berkeley, 1980.

Hodge, A. T. *Roman Aqueducts.* London, 1992.

Humphrey, J. H. *Roman Circuses: Arenas for Chariot Racing.* Berkeley, 1986.

Kleiner, D. E. E. *Roman Sculpture.* New Haven, 1992.

Ling, R. *Roman Painting.* New York, 1991.

MacDonald, W. L. *The Architecture of the Roman Empire,* 2 vols. New Haven, 1982–86.

Nash, F. *Pictorial Dictionary of Ancient Rome,* rev. edn, 2 vols. London, 1968.

Newby, M. and Painter, K. (eds). *Roman Glass: Two Centuries of Art and Invention.* London, 1991.

O'Connor, C. *Roman Bridges.* Cambridge, 1993.

Peacock, D. P. S. *Pottery in the Roman World: An Ethnoarchaeological Approach.* London, 1982.

Percival, J. *The Roman Villa: An Historical Introduction.* Berkeley, 1976.

Ramage, N. H. and Ramage, A. *Roman Art: Romulus to Constantine.* Englewood Cliffs, NJ, 1991.

Richardson, Jr, L. *A New Topographical Dictionary of Ancient Rome.* Baltimore and London, 1992.

Strong, D. E. *Roman Art,* 2nd edn. New York, 1988.

Strong, D. E. and Brown, D. (eds). *Roman Crafts.* New York, 1976.

Ward-Perkins, J. B. *Cities of Ancient Greece and Italy: Planning in Classical Antiquity.* New York, 1974.

Ward-Perkins, J. B. *Roman Imperial Architecture,* 2nd edn. Harmondsworth, 1981.

Wheeler, M. *Roman Art and Architecture.* London, 1964.

White, K. D. *Greek and Roman Technology.* Ithaca, NY, 1984.

Yegül, F. K. *Baths and Bathing in Classical Antiquity.* Cambridge, Mass., 1992.

HISTORIANS AND HISTORIOGRAPHY

Cameron, A. (ed.). *History as Text: The Writing of Ancient History.* Chapel Hill, 1990.

Earl, D. *The Political Thought of Sallust.* Cambridge, 1961.

Martin, R. *Tacitus.* Berkeley, 1981.

Mellor, R. *Tacitus.* New York and London, 1993.

Millar, F. *A Study of Cassius Dio.* Oxford, 1964.

Rajak, T. *Josephus: The Historian and his Society.* Philadelphia, 1983.

Sacks, K. *Diodorus Siculus and the First Century.* Princeton, 1990.

Syme, R. *Tacitus,* 2 vols. Oxford, 1958.

Syme, R. *Sallust.* Berkeley and Los Angeles, 1964.

Wallace-Hadrill, A. *Suetonius: The Scholar and his Caesars.* New Haven, 1983.

Wiseman, T. P. "Practice and Theory in Roman Historiography," in T. P. Wiseman, *Roman Studies: Literary and Historical* (Liverpool, 1987), 244–62.
Woodman, A. J. *Rhetoric in Classical Historiography: Four Studies.* Portland, 1988.

LAW

Brunt, P. A. "Judiciary Rights in the Republic," in P. A. Brunt, *The Fall of the Roman Republic and Related Essays* (Oxford, 1988), 194–239.
Buckland, W. W. *A Text-Book of Roman Law from Augustus to Justinian*, 3rd edn, ed. P. Stein. Cambridge, 1963.
Champlin, E. *Final Judgments: Duty and Emotion in Roman Wills, 200 B.C.–A.D. 250.* Berkeley, 1991.
Crawford, M. H. (ed.). *Roman Statutes*, 2 vols. London, 1996.
Crook, J. A. *Law and Life of Rome, 90 B.C. to A.D. 212.* Ithaca, NY, 1967.
Crook, J. A. *Legal Advocacy in the Roman World.* London, 1995.
Daube, D. *Forms of Roman Legislation.* Oxford, 1956.
Daube, D. *Roman Law: Linguistic, Social and Philosophical Aspects.* Edinburgh, 1969.
Frier, B. W. *Landlords and Tenants in Imperial Rome.* Princeton, 1980.
Frier, B. W. *The Rise of the Roman Jurists: Studies in Cicero's Pro Caecina.* Princeton, 1985.
Jones, A. H. M. *The Criminal Courts of the Roman Republic and Principate.* Oxford, 1972.
Kelly, J. M. *Roman Litigation.* Oxford, 1966.
Kelly, J. M. *Studies in the Civil Judicature of the Roman Republic.* Oxford, 1976.
Nicholas, B. *An Introduction to Roman Law.* Oxford, 1962.
Sherwin-White, A. N. *Roman Society and Roman Law in the New Testament.* Oxford, 1963.
Watson, A. *The Law of Persons in the Later Roman Republic.* Oxford, 1967.
Watson, A. *The Law of Property in the Later Roman Republic.* Oxford, 1968.
Watson, A. *Law Making in the Later Roman Republic.* Oxford, 1974.
Watson, A. *Roman Slave Law.* Baltimore, 1987.

BIOGRAPHY

Barrett, A. A. *Caligula: The Corruption of Power.* New Haven, 1989.
Birley, A. R. *Marcus Aurelius: A Biography*, rev. edn. New Haven, 1987.
Birley, A. R. *Septimius Severus: The African Emperor*, rev. edn. New Haven, 1989.
Carney, T. F. *A Biography of Marius.* Salisbury, 1962.
Clarke, M. L. *The Noblest Roman.* Ithaca, 1981.
Gelzer, M. *Caesar: Politician and Statesman*, 6th edn. Trans. P. Needham. Cambridge, Mass., 1968.
Greenhalgh, P. *Pompey*, 2 vols. Columbia, 1980–1.
Griffin, M. T. *Seneca: A Philosopher in Politics.* Oxford, 1976.
Griffin, M. T. *Nero: The End of a Dynasty.* New Haven, 1984.
Huzar, E. *Mark Antony: A Biography.* London, 1986.
Jones, B. W. *The Emperor Titus.* New York, 1984.
Jones, B. W. *The Emperor Domitian.* London, 1992.
Keaveney, A. *Sulla: The Last Republican.* London, 1982.
Keaveney, A. *Lucullus: A Life.* London and New York, 1992.
Levick, B. *Tiberius the Politician.* London, 1976.
Levick, B. *Claudius.* New Haven, 1990.

Rawson, E. *Cicero: A Portrait*. Ithaca, 1975.

Seager, R. *Tiberius*. Berkeley, 1972.

Seager, R. *Pompey: A Political Biography*. Berkeley and Los Angeles, 1979.

Shackleton Bailey, D. R. *Cicero*. New York, 1971.

Spann, P. O. *Quintus Sertorius and the Legacy of Sulla*. Fayetteville, 1987.

Stockton, D. *Cicero: A Political Biography*. London, 1971.

Ward, A. M. *Marcus Crassus and the Late Roman Republic*. Columbia and London, 1977.

THE LATER ROMAN EMPIRE

GENERAL STUDIES

Brown, P. *The World of Late Antiquity, A.D. 150–750*. New York, 1971.

Bury, J. B. *History of the Later Roman Empire from the Death of Theodosius I to the Death of Justinian (A.D. 395 to A.D. 565)*, 2 vols. London, 1923.

Cameron, A. *The Later Roman Empire, A.D. 284–430*. Cambridge, Mass., 1993.

Cameron, A. *The Mediterranean World in Late Antiquity*. London, 1993.

Cameron, A. and Garnsey, P. (eds). *The Late Empire, A.D. 337–425*. Vol. 13 of *The Cambridge Ancient History*, 2nd edn. Cambridge, 1998.

Jones, A. H. M. *The Decline of the Ancient World*. London, 1966.

MacMullen, R. *Corruption and the Decline of Rome*. New Haven, 1988.

Walbank, F. W. *The Awful Revolution: The Decline of the Roman Empire in the West*. Liverpool, 1978.

POLITICS AND GOVERNMENT

Barnes, T. D. *Constantine and Eusebius*. Cambridge, Mass., 1981.

Barnes, T. D. *The New Empire of Diocletian and Constantine*. Cambridge, Mass., 1982.

de Blois, L. *The Policy of the Emperor Gallienus*. Leiden, 1976.

MacMullen, R. *Roman Government's Response to Crisis, A.D. 235–337*. New Haven, 1976.

Matthews, J. *Western Aristocracies and Imperial Court, A.D. 364–425*. Oxford, 1975.

O'Flynn, J. M. *Generalissimos of the Western Roman Empire*. Edmonton, 1983.

THE ARMY, WAR, AND FOREIGN RELATIONS

Burns, T. S. *A History of the Ostrogoths*. Bloomington, 1984.

Dodgeon, M. H. and Lieu, S. N. C. (eds). *The Roman Eastern Frontier and the Persian Wars (A.D. 226–363)*. London, 1990.

Elton, H. *Warfare in Roman Europe, A.D. 350–425*. Oxford, 1996.

Ferrill, A. *The Fall of the Roman Empire: The Military Explanation*. London, 1986.

Goffart, W. *Barbarians and Romans, A.D. 418–584*. Princeton, 1980.

Heather, P. *Goths and Romans, 332–489*. New York, 1991.

MacMullen, R. *Soldier and Civilian in the Later Roman Empire*. Cambridge, Mass., 1963.

Maenchen-Helfen, O. *The World of the Huns*. Berkeley and Los Angeles, 1973.

Thompson, E. A. *Romans and Barbarians: The Decline of the Western Empire*. Madison, 1982.

REGIONAL AND LOCAL HISTORIES

Bagnall, R. S. *Egypt in Late Antiquity*. Princeton, 1993.

Brock, S. P. *Syriac Perspectives on Late Antiquity*. London, 1984.

Drinkwater, J. F. *The Gallic Empire: Separatism and Continuity in the North-Western Provinces of the Roman Empire.* Stuttgart, 1987.

Drinkwater, J. F. and Elton, H. (eds). *Fifth-Century Gaul: A Crisis of Identity?* Cambridge, 1992.

Esmonde Cleary, A. S. *The Ending of Roman Britain.* Savage, Md., 1989.

Johnson, S. *Later Roman Britain.* London, 1980.

King, A. and Henig, M. (eds). *The Roman West in the Third Century: Contributions from Archaeology and History.* Oxford, 1981.

Liebeschuetz, J. H. W. G. *Antioch: City and Imperial Administration in the Later Roman Empire.* Oxford, 1972.

Rousseau, P. *Pachomius: The Making of a Community in Fourth-Century Egypt.* Berkeley, 1985.

Van Dam, R. *Leadership and Community in Late Antique Gaul.* Berkeley, 1985.

Warmington, B. H. *The North African Provinces from Diocletian to the Vandal Conquest.* Cambridge, 1954.

ECONOMY AND TRADE

Crawford, M. H. "Finance, Coinage, and Money from the Severans to Constantine," *Aufstieg und Niedergang der römischen Welt,* 2.2 (1975), 560–93.

King, C. E. (ed.). *Imperial Revenues, Expenditure and Monetary Policy in the Fourth Century A.D.* Oxford, 1980.

Stevens, C. E. "Agriculture and Rural Life in the Later Roman Empire," in M. M. Postan (ed.), *The Cambridge Economic History of Europe,* 2nd edn (Cambridge, 1971), vol. 1, 92–124.

Walbank, F. W. "Trade and Industry under the Later Roman Empire in the West," in M. M. Postan and E. Miller (eds), *The Cambridge Economic History of Europe,* 2nd edn (Cambridge, 1987), vol. 2, 71–131.

SOCIETY

Arjava, A. *Women and Law in Late Antiquity.* Oxford, 1996.

Brown, P. *The Making of Late Antiquity.* Cambridge, Mass., 1978.

Brown, P. *Society and the Holy in Late Antiquity.* Berkeley, 1982.

Brown, P. *Power and Persuasion in Late Antiquity: Towards a Christian Empire.* Madison, 1992.

Cameron, A. *Circus Factions.* Oxford. 1976.

Clark, G. *Women in Late Antiquity: Pagan and Christian Life-Styles.* Oxford, 1993.

MacCormack, S. G. *Art and Ceremony in Late Antiquity.* Berkeley, 1981.

Shaw, B. D. "Latin Funerary Epigraphy and Family Life in the Later Roman Empire," *Historia: Zeitschrift für alte Geschichte,* 33 (1984), 457–97.

Shaw, B. D. "The Family in Late Antiquity: The Experience of Augustine," *Past and Present,* 115 (1987), 3–51.

Whittaker, C. R. "Circe's Pigs: From Slavery to Serfdom in the Later Roman World," *Slavery and Abolition,* 8 (1987), 88–123.

RELIGION

Brown, P. *Religion and Society in the Age of Saint Augustine.* London, 1972.

Brown, P. *The Cult of the Saints: Its Rise and Function in Latin Christianity.* Chicago, 1982.

Brown, P. *The Body and Society: Men, Women and Sexual Renunciation in Early Christianity*. New York, 1988.

Cameron, A. *Christianity and the Rhetoric of Empire*. Berkeley and Los Angeles, 1991.

Chuvin, P. *A Chronicle of the Last Pagans*. Cambridge, Mass., 1990.

Clark, G. *Ascetic Piety and Women's Faith*. Lewiston, NY, 1986.

Croke, B. and Harries, J. (eds). *Religious Conflict in Fourth Century Rome*. Sydney, 1982.

Dodds, E. R. *Pagan and Christian in an Age of Anxiety*. Cambridge, 1965.

Frend, W. H. C. *The Donatist Church: A Movement of Protest in Roman North Africa*. Oxford, 1952.

Hunt, E. D. *Holy Land Pilgrimage in the Later Roman Empire*. Oxford, 1982.

Momigliano, A. (ed.). *The Conflict between Paganism and Christianity in the Fourth Century*. Oxford, 1963.

Williams, R. L. *Arius, Heresy and Tradition*. London, 1987.

INTELLECTUAL LIFE (LITERATURE AND PHILOSOPHY)

Binns, J. W. (ed.). *Latin Literature of the Fourth Century*. London, 1974.

Bowersock, G. W. *Hellenism in Late Antiquity*. Ann Arbor, 1990.

Cameron, A. *Claudian: Poetry and Propaganda at the Court of Honorius*. Oxford, 1970.

Cox, P. *Biography in Late Antiquity: A Quest for the Holy Man*. Berkeley, 1983.

Kaster, R. A. *Guardians of Language: The Grammarian and Society in Late Antiquity*. Berkeley, 1988.

Palmer, A.-M. *Prudentius on the Martyrs*. New York, 1989.

Rist, J. M. *Plotinus: The Road to Reality*. Cambridge, 1967.

ART AND ARCHITECTURE

Bandinelli, R. B. *Rome, The Late Empire: Roman Art, A.D. 200–400*. Trans. P. Green. New York, 1971.

Dorigo, W. *Late Roman Painting*. Trans. J. Cleugh and J. Warrington. New York, 1970.

Milburn, R. *Early Christian Art and Architecture*. Berkeley, 1988.

HISTORIANS AND HISTORIOGRAPHY

Barnes, T. D. *The Sources of the Historia Augusta*. Brussels, 1978.

Bird, H. W. *Sextus Aurelius Victor: A Historiographical Study*. Liverpool, 1984.

Blockley, R. C. *Ammianus Marcellinus: A Study of his Historiography and Political Thought*. Brussels, 1975.

den Boer, W. *Some Minor Roman Historians*. Leiden, 1972.

Croke, B. and Emmett, A. M. (eds). *History and Historians in Late Antiquity*. Sydney, 1983.

Matthews, J. *The Roman Empire of Ammianus*. Baltimore, 1989.

Syme, R. *Ammianus and the Historia Augusta*. Oxford, 1968.

Syme, R. *Emperors and Biography: Studies in the Historia Augusta*. Oxford, 1971.

Syme, R. *Historia Augusta Papers*. New York, 1983.

BIOGRAPHY

Athanassiadi, P. *Julian: An Intellectual Biography*, rev. edn. London, 1992.

Bowersock, G. W. *Julian the Apostate*. Cambridge, Mass., 1978.

Bregman, J. *Synesius of Cyrene: Philosopher-Bishop*. Berkeley, 1982.

Brown, P. *Augustine of Hippo*. London, 1967.

Clark, G. *The Life of Melania the Younger*, Lewiston, NY, 1984.
MacMullen, R. *Constantine*. New York, 1969.
Rousseau, P. *Basil of Caesarea*. Berkeley, 1994.
Williams, S. *Diocletian and the Roman Recovery*. New York, 1985.

INDEX